This book is a

Gift

From

....

To

....

Date

....

May God bless you through this book

40 PRAYER GIANTS

(COMPLETE VERSION)

40 PRAYER GIANTS

(COMPLETE VERSION)

PRAYER M. MADUEKE

PRAYER PUBLICATIONS
1 Babatunde close, Off Olaitan Street,
Surulere, Lagos, Nigeria
+234 803 353 0599

40 PRAYER GIANTS (COMPLETE VERSION)

PRAYER M. MADUEKE

ISBN: 9781500294298

Prayer Publications

Unless otherwise indicated, all Scripture quotations are taken from the King James Version of the Bible, and used by permission. All emphasis within quotations is the author's additions.

First Edition, 2014

For further information of permission

1 Babatunde close, off Olaitan Street,
Surulere, Lagos, Nigeria
+234 803 353 0599
Email: pastor@prayermadueke.com,
Website: www.prayermadueke.com

TABLE OF CONTENTS

DEDICATION

This book is dedicated to individuals and families, who are sincerely trusting God to experience His blessings and joy in their lives and marriage according to His will.

"[8] *And God* is *able to make all grace abound toward you; that ye, always having all sufficiency in all things, may abound to every good work*" (2 Corinthians 9:8).

Prayer M. Madueke

"And thy seed shall be as the dust of the earth, and thou shalt spread abroad to the west, and to the east, and to the north, and to the south: and in thee and in thy seed shall all the families of the earth be blessed" (Genesis 28:14).

1

Chapter

PRAYERS TO MARRY WITHOUT DELAY

CHAPTER OVERVIEW

- *Seeking for a right partner*
- *The purpose of marriage*
- *Power that hinders marriages*
- *Idolatry and forsaking god*
- *Prayers to marry without delay*

SEEKING FOR A RIGHT PARTNER

Marriage is a legally recognized relationship, established by a civil or religious ceremony, between two people who intend to live together as sexual and domestic partners. In a marriage institution, a man and woman are legally joined together to start a new family.

The best place to start when planning to get married is to understand that marriage is for matured adults. That is why you must be matured physically, emotionally, socially and spiritually before you think of getting married. Likewise, marriage of convenience is not always the best type of marriage. It would be wrong to enter into any marriage relationship because of economic advantages, while disregarding the role of mutual affection and conviction. Marriages contracted on conveniences or solely for pragmatic reasons do not fulfill the spiritual purpose of marriage. Even an ant prepares itself for summer.

> *"Go to the ant, thou sluggard; consider her ways, and be wise: Which having no guide, overseer, or ruler, Provideth her meat in the summer, and gathereth her food in the harvest"* (Proverbs 6:6-8).

The choice of who to marry is never a decision to be done in haste. A lazy person that is looking for someone to marry because he or she wants to live comfortably would likely not fulfill God's purpose for marriage.

> *"Love not sleep, lest thou come to poverty; open thine eyes, and thou shalt be satisfied with bread"* (Proverbs 20:13).

Entering into marriage without needful knowledge and due preparation can be destructive. It is possible to accomplish an immediate need of comfort and satisfaction, but the problem is that you would have entered into a life of misery. Be mindful also, that marriage can provide momentary solutions to present problems, change of environment and temporal joy but also presents new set of challenges you have never imagined. Nevertheless, when you have the proper knowledge you needed, the new challenges will not overwhelm you.

Many people experience unfounded pleasures at the wake of their marriages instead of genuine intimacy and inner strength that sustain marriage. A temporal pleasure may not be very useful, especially when it is void of true and genuine love. Marriage should not be done in a rush. You need to develop some level of physical, temperamental, emotional, social and spiritual maturity in advance. Cultivate life of discipline, temperance, self-denial and selflessness, as these may be highly treasured by your spouse.

> "[8]*And the LORD God planted a garden eastward in Eden; and there he put the man whom he had formed.* [15]*And the LORD God took the man, and put him into the Garden of Eden to dress it and to keep it.* [18]*And the LORD God said, It is not good that the man should be alone; I will make him a help meet for him*" (Genesis 2:8, 15, 18).

Notice that Adam was in-charge of the garden before God made wife for him. He had a job already. He was the custodian of the garden. He knew God, and had intimate relationship with Him. God saw that it was not good for him to remain alone and made wife for him. Then, a big question arises - why do we need to marry?

THE PURPOSE OF MARRIAGE

God had a plan for establishing marriage union. That is why anyone who wants to marry must have idea of God's purpose in focus before deciding whom to marry. Unfortunately, many people have not bothered to find out God's purpose for marriage before entering into it.

> *"And the LORD God said, it is not good that the man should be alone; I will make him a help meet for him. And the rib, which the LORD God had taken from man, made he a woman, and brought her unto the man. Therefore shall a man leave his father and his mother, and shall cleave unto his wife: and they shall be one flesh"* (Genesis 2:18, 22, 24).

God concluded that it was not good that the man He made remained alone. In order to balance the equation, God created the woman. He used the rib, which He took from the man to make a woman. From the beginning, marriage has been part of God's plan, purpose and provision. God initiated this plan when man was at his original nature of purity.

> *"27 So God created man in his own image, in the image of God created he him; male and female created he them. 28 And God blessed them, and God said unto them, Be fruitful, and multiply, and replenish the earth, and subdue it: and have dominion over the fish of the sea, and over the fowl of the air, and over every living thing that moveth upon the earth"* (Genesis 1:27, 28).

Therefore, even at the height of our spirituality, we need to get married. God's blessings are complete upon a man when he is married, even though marriage is only necessary to earthly life, and has no part in eternal existence in heaven. Another important thing to observe is that God did not create many women for one man. He made one man and one woman. That is why men leave fathers and mothers and cleave to their wives to become one flesh.

> *"And he answered and said unto them, Have ye not read, that he which made them at the beginning made them male and female, And said, For this cause shall a man leave father and mother, and shall cleave to his wife: and they twain shall be one flesh? Wherefore they are no more twain, but one flesh. What therefore God hath joined together, let not man put asunder"* (Matthew 19:4-6).

> *"For the man is not of the woman; but the woman of the man. Neither was the man created for the woman; but the woman for the man. For this cause ought the woman to have power on her head because of the angels. Nevertheless neither is the man without the woman, neither the woman without the man, in the Lord. For as the woman is of*

the man, even so is the man also by the woman; but all things of God" (1 Corinthians 11:8-12).

God created the woman for the man and made them one. Therefore, the failure of the woman is the failure of the man, and the failure of the man is that of the woman. Lack of knowledge makes husband and wife to fight each other. Instead, husband and wife should succeed together. It is also foolishness for a woman to ruin the husband. God's plan is for both to make it together. Man needs a woman to succeed on earth because they were created as social beings to complement each other in marriage relationship.

"God setteth the solitary in families: he bringeth out those which are bound with chains: but the rebellious dwell in a dry land" (Psalms 68:6).

"Lo, children are a heritage of the LORD: and the fruit of the womb is his reward" (Psalms 127:3).

God's ultimate purpose for instituting marriage is for a man and a woman to start a family, live as a family and succeed together as one family. Husband and wife are destined according to God's plan to bear children, rear and nurture them until they are matured enough to start their own families. Husband and wife are to put their faith together and fight barrenness.

"[5]And Moses commanded the children of Israel according to the word of the LORD, saying, The tribe of the sons of Joseph hath said well. [6]This is the thing which the LORD doth command concerning the daughters of Zelophehad, saying, Let them marry to whom they think best; only to the family of the tribe of their father shall they marry. [7]So shall not the inheritance of the children of Israel remove from tribe to tribe: for every one of the children of Israel shall keep himself to the inheritance of the tribe of his fathers. [8]And every daughter, that possesseth an inheritance in any tribe of the children of Israel, shall be wife unto one of the family of the tribe of her father, that the children of Israel may enjoy every man the inheritance of his fathers. [9]Neither shall the inheritance remove from one tribe to another tribe; but every one of the tribes of the children of Israel shall keep himself to his own inheritance. [13]These are the commandments and the judgments, which the LORD commanded by the hand of Moses unto the children of Israel in the plains of Moab by Jordan near Jericho" (Numbers 36:5-9, 13).

Any power that attacks people's marriages is not from God. Individuals, families and the body of Christ must confront the scourge of late marriage or the powers that prevent matured adults from getting married. The presence of unmarried adults in the family is often very precarious. It has caused many problems especially in the developing world.

The spirit that causes adults not to be married must be confronted vigorously. All believers, including churches, must rise to fight this menace. Moses advised the tribes of the sons of Joseph to let the daughters of Zelophehad get married to whom they thought best. When one is due for marriage but is not married, there is an inclination that such person would be unhappy and this would affect people around him or her. In this way, such people become a burden to the family and community.

> *"And hath made of one blood all nations of men for to dwell on all the face of the earth, and hath determined the times before appointed, and the bounds of their habitation"* (Acts 17:26).

Marriages must take place, in a right way and purpose, for people to live in peace in families, communities and nations. Marriage is fundamental to the stability and continuation of societies. When adults do not marry, there would be lack of peace in many families. In addition, when people refuse to leave and cleave, they eventually block the way for others to progress. However, unseen forces hold back many people's destinies. Even when such victims determine to marry, they cannot break loose from those forces holding them back. Others even go ahead to marry wrong people, who would later force them into unimaginable misery. Marriage is a necessity but requires wisdom and prayers.

> *"And the LORD God said, It is not good that the man should be alone; I will make him a help meet for him"* (Genesis 2:18).

It is tragic to marry someone who cannot complement your destiny and work. People who find themselves in such cases often live in their families like strangers. A breakdown of marriage results in breakdown of families, communities and nations. This is the primary reason for never-ending divorce and separation cases, which bedevil nations of the world today. Ironically, many victims of divorce and separation would run back to their parents' homes to bother them. They fail to realize that after marriage, partners' top priority is each other and not parents.

> *"Two are better than one; because they have a good reward for their labor. For if they fall, the one will lift up his fellow: but woe to him that is alone when he falleth; for he hath not another to help him up. Again, if two lie together, then they have heat: but how can one be warm alone? And if one prevails against him, two shall withstand him; and a threefold cord is not quickly broken. Better is a poor and a wise child than an old and foolish king, who will no more be admonished. For out of prison he cometh to reign; whereas also he that is born in his kingdom becometh poor"* (Ecclesiastes 4:9-14).

"And did not he make one? Yet had he the residue of the spirit. And wherefore one? That he might seek a godly seed. Therefore take heed to your spirit, and let none deal treacherously against the wife of his youth" (Malachi 2:15).

Regrettably, many people are convinced already that they were better off when they were not married than after marriage. Experiencing a few challenges in marriage forces weak men and women to conclude that marriage is a burden and evil. Probably, because of wrong choices here and there, they set their hearts on escaping from their marriages.

However, not allowing God to lead you to a right partner can result in regrets after getting married. The Scriptures equally made it clear that two is better than one because they have a good reward for their labor. Moreover, if one falls, the other will lift up his fellow. However, in many families today, there verse is the case. Because of irreconcilable differences, when both the man and his wife fall, none can lift up the other. This is also one of the reasons we have more widows on earth today. Couples defile the institution of marriage on daily basis. That is why one of the most effective witchcraft operations on earth today is the witchcraft of connecting two incompatible partners in marriage.

"Let not a widow be taken into the number under threescore years old, having been the wife of one man, Well reported of for good works; if she have brought up children, if she have lodged strangers, if she have washed the saints' feet, if she have relieved the afflicted, if she have diligently followed every good work. But the younger widows refuse: for when they have begun to wax wanton against Christ, they will marry; Having damnation, because they have cast off their first faith. And withal they learn to be idle, wandering about from house to house; and not only idle, but tattlers also and busybodies, speaking things, which they ought not. I will therefore that the younger women marry, bear children, guide the house, give none occasion to the adversary to speak reproachfully" (1 Timothy 5:9-14).

Many people have married more than twice and separated. Others were married, divorced and re-married. While some separated couples marry their right partners finally, others end up marrying their enemies. God's perfect will for marriage is one man, one wife. We have many matured single women who are not married. They move from one man to another, causing problems in families, communities and nations. Most of them are young, beautiful and more seductive than Delilah was.

They break homes, break hearts and cause a lot of hardship. When they break homes apart, the families enter into trouble and it affects the whole society. Many of these young ladies are idle, wandering from house to house, causing problems capable of tearing families and nations apart. They promote sexual sins and spread diseases on earth.

> *"Nevertheless, to avoid fornication, let every man have his own wife, and let every woman have her own husband. Let the husband render unto the wife due benevolence: and likewise the wife unto the husband. The wife hath not power of her own body, but the husband: and likewise also the husband hath not power of his own body, but the wife. Defraud ye not one the other, except it be with consent for a time, that ye may give yourselves to fasting and prayer; and come together again, that Satan tempt you not for your incontinency"* (1 Corinthians 7:2-5).

Some of these men and women possess strange fires of immorality from the marine realms of the spirit. Once you have sex with them, the love and sexual affections you have for your legally married partner transfers to them, and problems set in.

> *"For this cause shall a man leave his father and mother, and shall be joined unto his wife, and they two shall be one flesh. This is a great mystery: but I speak concerning Christ and the church. Nevertheless let every one of you in particular so love his wife even as himself; and the wife see that she reverence her husband"* (Ephesians 5:31-33).

EVIL INHERITANCE: There are people that are marked before their birth to marry a demon-possessed personality. For such persons to get married to someone else other than the demon-possessed individual designated for them would be very difficult. They have to contend with wicked force of evil inheritance until they get their deliverance. However, you have to be born-again before you can prayerfully separate yourself from such evil captivity.

"The word of the LORD came also unto me, saying, Thou shalt not take thee a wife, neither shalt thou have sons or daughters in this place" (Jeremiah 16:1-2).

Jeremiah sent the Word of God to a particular people to avoid marrying people from a particular place. He warned the people not to take wives from that community or have children with them. The all-seeing eyes of God had traced an evil mark upon the people from that particular place. This also means that one can be a true child of God, and yet lacks spiritual eyes to foresee evil. When a man or woman of God does not depend on God to make a choice for him or her in marriage, he or she is bound to make a costly mistake. However, this shall not be your portion, in the name of Jesus.

"O LORD, I know that the way of man is not in himself: it is not in man that walketh to direct his steps" (Jeremiah 10:23).

"And it came to pass, when they were come, that he looked on Eliab, and said, Surely the LORD'S anointed is before him. But the LORD said unto Samuel, Look not on his countenance, or on the height of his stature; because I have refused him: for the LORD seeth not as man seeth; for man looketh on the outward appearance, but the LORD looketh on the heart" (1 Samuel 16:6-7).

Man cannot direct his course on earth regardless of how righteous he is, and so needs to depend on God for direction. Many true children of God have made heart-breaking and painful mistakes in the area of marriage. While some thought that they have become matured adults and do not need God's direction, others believed the only problem they have is money. Once they get enough money to finance their marriage, they rush into a regrettable marriage. Jeremiah, with all his gifts, acknowledged that it is not in man's capacity to author his steps. If you do, you may actually marry someone that has evil inheritance and be doomed.

"For thus saith the LORD concerning the sons and concerning the daughters that are born in this place, and concerning their mothers that bare them, and concerning their fathers that begat them in this land; They shall die of grievous deaths; they shall not be lamented; neither shall they be buried; but they shall be as dung upon the face of the

earth: and they shall be consumed by the sword, and by famine; and their carcasses shall be meat for the fowls of heaven, and for the beasts of the earth" (Jeremiah 16:3-4).

Accursed inheritance brings death verdicts upon some people even before they are born. It takes only God's grace and Word to erase such curses. If God directs you to marry in such place, He is also able to give you grace to deal with any inherited bondage. Let no man therefore do this unless under God's leadership. Today, many families are battling with diverse problems because they neglected God's leadership and went ahead to confront evil verdicts.

Many people go through unimaginable sufferings as a result. Such people suffer loss of things that makes one truly happy before finally losing their lives. They live in this world without any true helper. Though they are alive, they are not be better than dead people are. People avoid them as if they are dung on the face of the earth. Others reject and hate them without reasons. They suffer famine of every good thing that makes one happy. They are easy preys to witches and wizards and all manner of problems. These things sound like fairy tales but people go through them indeed.

Such people fail where others are succeeding. No matter how much faith you have, if God is not leading you, you must be careful when marrying, especially to people going through these unimaginable sufferings. For this reason also, any marriage of convenience would like backfire. However, the best assistance you can offer to such victims is to introduce them to Christ and probably teach them how to face spiritual battles of life regardless of how beautiful, handsome, rich or influential the person is. This is important because goodies, which are used to entice women, often disappear after marriage. Hence, the real battle of life starts immediately after marriage. This is not to scare you, but you must allow God be the stronghold of your marriage so you would not worry about challenges afterwards.

Appearance can be deceptive. Even Samuel, in all his gifts and relationship with God, made an error of judgment. He wanted to anoint Eliab because of his outward appearance. He preferred Eliab because of his excellent appearance, but God preferred David, a man after His heart. Do not allow beauty, certificates, money, wealth, good jobs and good things of life to hoodwink you in your choice of a partner. Depend on God and trust Him entirely.

"16 And I will bring the blind by a way that they knew not; I will lead them in paths that they have not known: I will make darkness light before them, and crooked things straight. These things will I do unto them, and not forsake them. 19 Who is blind, but my servant? Or deaf, as my messenger that I sent? Who is blind as he that is perfect, and blind as the LORD'S servant? 20 Seeing many things, but thou observest not; opening the ears, but he heareth not" (Isaiah 42:16, 19-20).

God regards us, His children, as blind even in all our righteousness. God promised in His Word to lead us in the paths that we have not known. He said that He would bring light in our darkness and make crooked things straight. Whatever decisions you take in marriage, make sure God is leading you. As a man, you can only see the beginning of a road but not the end. No matter how experienced you are, God is more experienced. No matter how old you are, God is older and wiser; He is the ancient of days, the beginning and the end. He is the Alpha and He is the Omega.

More so, you could have made so many mistakes in the past, but God cannot make any mistake. Trust God who knows how to lead you. Many people may appear good for marriage, but not all that appear excellent outwardly are worthy as your partner. Therefore, it would be heartbreaking and sad to marry someone who turns out to be incompatible.

Many people are in covenant with unseen powers. If you marry such people, you are doomed. In this book, I have provided suitable prayers to break you loose from marital bondage. You can also read one of my books titled "*Reality of Spirits of Marriage*." That book will inform you about characteristics of men and women that you cannot afford to marry.

IDOLATRY AND FORSAKING GOD

Idolatry means worshipping or walking after other gods, speaking in their names and setting them up in your heart. Other times, idolatry relates to covetousness, sensuality and sexuality. An idol is anything you put before God. Examples of idolatry include material possession, love of money, self or people above God.

> *"Mortify therefore your members which are upon the earth; fornication, uncleanness, inordinate affection, evil concupiscence, and covetousness, which is idolatry"* (Colossians 3:5).

> *"And he said unto them, Take heed, and beware of covetousness: for a man's life consisteth not in the abundance of the things which he possesseth. And he spake a parable unto them, saying, The ground of a certain rich man brought forth plentifully: And he thought within himself, saying, What shall I do, because I have no room where to bestow my fruits? And he said, This will I do: I will pull down my barns, and build greater; and there will I bestow all my fruits and my goods. And I will say to my soul, Soul, thou hast much goods laid up for many years; take thine ease, eat, drink, and be merry. But God said unto him, Thou fool, this night thy soul shall be required of thee: then whose shall those things be, which thou hast provided? So is he that layeth up treasure for himself, and is not rich toward God"* (Luke 12:15-21).

God gave man a freedom of choice; you either choose to bow to God or to idols. Many spend their time, energy, and resources on gathering possessions at the expense of loving God and worshipping Him. While many people have not been married because of traces of idolatry in their foundation, others continue to practice it. Many others, who are married, are still going through unimaginable problems because of their link to evil worship.

> *"Of righteousness, because I go to my Father, and ye see me no more; Of judgment, because the prince of this world is judged. I have yet many things to say unto you, but ye cannot bear them now"* (John 16:10-12).

Observing a tradition that contradicts God's Word in your marriage is an open invitation to demons to come into your marriage.

> *"Beware lest any man spoil you through philosophy and vain deceit, after the tradition of men, after the rudiments of the world, and not after Christ"* (Colossians 2:8).

God removes His protection upon your marriage when you engage in idolatry and forsake God. Satan has released many sexual demons to attack families. The only way to marry and remain happy is through total repentance and warfare. No one can marry and enjoy God's presence without breaking covenant with evil spirits and their agents, and then enter into covenant with God.

> *"And Samuel spake unto all the house of Israel, saying, If ye do return unto the LORD with all your hearts, then put away the strange gods and Ashtaroth from among you, and prepare your hearts unto the LORD, and serve him only: and he will deliver you out of the hand of the Philistines. Then the children of Israel did put away Baalim and Ashtaroth, and served the LORD only"* (1 Samuel 7:3-4).

You must return to God in repentance; forsake your sins and cleave to God. You must prepare your heart and serve God only. You must hate sin in its entirety and love God, His Word and His children. After this, you have to go into prayers of warfare to resist the devil.

> *"Submit yourselves therefore to God. Resist the devil, and he will flee from you"* (James 4:7).

Prayers in this book will provide a good starting point for you to get to a level that will be too hot for your enemy to handle. By the grace and mercy of God, you will surely recover all your loss and marry to the glory of God.

The kind of prayers you are expected to pray -

1. Prayers against evil spirits that hinder marriages.
2. Prayers to cast out demons that resist your marriage.
3. Prayers to frustrate powers warring against your marriage.
4. Prayers to invoke the power of God to appear in the battlefield for your sake.
5. Prayers to destroy evil yoke of captivity and inheritance.
6. Prayers to command evil marks in your body to disappear.
7. Prayers to break inherited covenant and curses.
8. Prayers to command curses in your life to expire.
9. Prayers to ask for God's mercy upon you.
10. Prayers to silence evil voices crying against your marriage.
11. Prayers to command your spouse to appear by force.
12. Prayers to strengthen your faith in God and confess positively.

PRAYERS TO MARRY WITHOUT DELAY

"And the LORD God said, It is not good that the man should be alone; I will make him a help meet for him" (Genesis 2:18).

"Marriage is honorable in all, and the bed undefiled: but whoremongers and adulterers God will judge" (Hebrews 13:4).

Begin with praise and worship

1. Any power that stands against my marriage, be frustrated, in the name of Jesus.
2. Let maturity I needed to demonstrate before marriage manifest by force, in the name of Jesus.
3. Let every property of devil in my life that is preventing my marriage catch fire, in the name of Jesus.
4. Every satanic embargo that was placed upon my marriage, be lifted, in the name of Jesus.
5. Father Lord, help me to get everything I needed to get before I marry, in the name of Jesus.
6. Every weapon against my marriage, catch fire, in the name of Jesus.
7. Any problem that is designed to make me miserable, I reject you, in the name of Jesus.
8. I break and loose myself from any marriage devil is planning for me, in the name of Jesus.
9. Any satanic offer that is enticing me to marry a wrong person, I reject you, in the name of Jesus.
10. Father Lord, empower me to be fit in every area of my life before I marry, in the name of Jesus.
11. Blood of Jesus, speak my right partner into existence, in the name of Jesus.
12. Every enemy of God's will for my marriage, be disgraced, in the name of Jesus.
13. O Lord, give me a better job that will sustain my marriage, in the name of Jesus.

14. Let the perfect will of God for my marriage manifest, in the name of Jesus.
15. Let everything aspect of my life embrace Jesus before my marriage, in the name of Jesus.
16. O Lord, make my partner and I compatible, in the name of Jesus.
17. O Lord, give me Your own perfect choice that will make my life complete, in the name of Jesus.
18. Let my marriage usher the blessings of God into my life, in the name of Jesus.
19. I refuse to marry my enemy, in the name of Jesus.

2
Chapter

PRAYERS FOR MARRIAGES IN DISTRESS

CHAPTER OVERVIEW

- *Reality of hostilities in marriage*
- *There is no more wine*
- *List of things that can cause your marriage's wine to finish*
- *What happens when marriage's wine finishes?*
- *Deliverance for families in distress*

REALITY OF HOSTILITIES IN MARRIAGE

It is arguable that majority of problems the world face today link to distresses experienced at homes. This is because many marriages have fallen into hands of destroyers and manipulators. Evil forces have invaded people's homes, which explain why societies are constantly dealing with conflicts and hostilities emanating from distressed homes and marriages.

> *"Therefore I say unto you, Take no thought for your life, what ye shall eat, or what ye shall drink; nor yet for your body, what ye shall put on. Is not the life more than meat, and the body than raiment? Behold the fowls of the air: for they sow not, neither do they reap, nor gather into barns; yet your heavenly Father feedeth them. Are ye not much better than they? Which of you by taking thought can add one cubit unto his stature? And why take ye thought for raiment? Consider the lilies of the field, how they grow; they toil not, neither do they spin"* (Matthew 6:25-28).

The core problem is that man has abandoned his creator and established his own way. Anxiety and greed have taken over the hearts of men. Majority of people on earth do not care any longer for a personal experience with their creator. They take thoughts for their lives and carry on with agendas that satisfy their objectives. Nevertheless, it is rather absurd that people come into the world, ignore their creator and pursue what pleased their hearts without putting God's Word, His thought and plans towards them into consideration. Instead, what motivates this kind of people, often in their billions, is what they would eat, drink and put on. That is when you realize that most people do not care to find out their mission or purpose on earth.

> *"[30]Wherefore, if God so clothe the grass of the field, which today is, and tomorrow is cast into the oven, shall he not much more clothe you, O ye of little faith? [31]Therefore take no thought, saying, what shall we eat? Or, what shall we drink? Or, Wherewithal shall we be clothed? [33]But seek ye first the kingdom of God, and his righteousness; and all these things shall be added unto you"* (Matthew 6:30-31, 33).

When you determine to know God and keep His commandments, He will surely bless you. Our primary duty on earth should not be to struggle for earthly possessions, which we need or do not need, but to seek God, His Kingdom and righteousness first.

> *"For we are but of yesterday, and know nothing, because our days upon earth are a shadow"* (Job 8:9).

"For man also knoweth not his time: as the fishes that are taken in an evil net, and as the birds that are caught in the snare; so are the sons of men snared in an evil time, when it falleth suddenly upon them" (Ecclesiastes 9:12).

Oftentimes, man is ignorant of his primary need on earth. So many people believe all they needed is pleasure, money and other things they can imagine. However, we know that God revealed man's primary need in the Bible. Our days on earth are like shadow. Therefore, we must not pursue other things without putting God first. God is the only One who knows how best we ought to spend our lives on earth. That is why when you seek other things first ignoring God's purpose for your life, you cannot experience peace or fulfillment, even when you have acquired all your heart desired.

When you abandon God to pursue other things, it becomes easy for the devil to lure and capture you for his own program. Devil knows how to change maps of people's lives and lead them into error.

"The fear of the LORD is the beginning of knowledge: but fools despise wisdom and instruction" (Proverbs 1:7).

"The way of peace they know not; and there is no judgment in their goings: they have made them crooked paths: whosoever goeth therein shall not know peace" (Isaiah 59:8)

"Therefore I said, Surely these are poor; they are foolish: for they know not the way of the LORD, nor the judgment of their God" (Jeremiah 5:4).

God's presence covers the whole universe. Equally, Satan labors to establish his own presence. What this means is that when you ignore God, it becomes easy for devil to deceive you and become your master by default. People, who chose the things of this world or entered into marriages without seeking God's consent, have found themselves in trouble as a result. Their lives bear a resemblance to fishes caught in evil nets or birds in hunter's snare. Moreover, when such people face difficult challenges in their marriages, they become extremely confused.

Let us therefore trust God in whatever we want to do, commit our ways into His hands and wait for His divine intervention. We do not know the ways of the Spirit or how bones form in the womb. Likewise, we cannot tell how God works except He shows us. Jesus came to show us the way to God. That is why we must follow Him.

"Come unto me, all ye that labor and are heavy laden, and I will give you rest. Take my yoke upon you, and learn of me; for I am meek and lowly in heart: and ye shall find rest unto your souls. For my yoke is easy, and my burden is light" (Matthew 11:28-30).

Jesus Christ is the only way of peace. He came to lead us back to God of peace. He wants to restore peace in our lives and marriages. No matter how much the devil has taken away from you and your marriage, Jesus can restore all your loss.

> *"He was in the world, and the world was made by him, and the world knew him not"* (John 1:10).
>
> *"Jesus answered and said unto her, If thou knewest the gift of God, and who it is that saith to thee, Give me to drink; thou wouldest have asked of him, and he would have given thee living water"* (John 4:10).
>
> *"Jesus said unto them, If ye were blind, ye should have no sin: but now ye say, We see; therefore your sin remaineth"* (John 9:41).
>
> *"Because thou sayest, I am rich, and increased with goods, and have need of nothing; and knowest not that thou art wretched, and miserable, and poor, and blind, and naked"* (Revelation 3:17).

Jesus was in the world before the creation of the universe. He made the world. Nothing succeeds without Him (*See* John 15:5). The truth that we have all erred and need Jesus Christ for reconciliation with God cannot be over emphasized. Therefore, when you humble yourself and surrender to the Lord's leadership, He forgives your sins and reconciles you to God. Christ is the gift of God to humanity, for without Him no one would be reconciled to God. You cannot have peace in your marriage when you continue to reject Jesus Christ. He is our peace and rest. Accept Him and receive peace and rest in your marriage today.

THERE IS NO MORE WINE

So many people refused to welcome Christ into their marriages because of how they lived their lives. However, what most people do not know is that when you break the spiritual principle of marriage according to the law of God, the wine of your marriage finishes.

> *"And he answered and said unto them, Have ye not read, that he which made them at the beginning made them male and female, And said, For this cause shall a man leave father and mother, and shall cleave to his wife: and they twain shall be one flesh? Wherefore they are no more twain, but one flesh. What therefore God hath joined together, let not man put asunder"* (Matthew 19:4-6).

If you are married and you are as well planning to get a second wife, while your first legal wife still lives, Jesus cannot endorse that wedding. Your second marriage remains illegal because God made marriage to be one man and one wife. Even when you have enough wealth to attract uncountable dignitaries from around the world to your wedding feast, your second marriage remains illegal. You can even gratify the world with gifts and get people intoxicated but eventually, the wine of your marriage would finish. Your marriage would lack the ingredients that keep marriages integral. When you nullify God's instruction, then your marriage cannot succeed.

> *"Marriage is honorable in all, and the bed undefiled: but whoremongers and adulterers God will judge"* (Hebrew 13:4).

God's ultimate plan for marriage was to make it honorable and complete. If you are a married person that sleeps around with other people outside your marriage, you are defiling your marital bed and God promised to judge whoremongers and all adulterers including you. God has a way of judging people eventually. Likewise, when you enter into the house of God and begin to commit immorality, you are drinking your marriage wine in sin. When a woman gets pregnant or a man impregnates a woman outside marriage, they have humiliated God's name. Similarly, when you sleep with someone's daughter without first marrying her, you are drinking the wine of marriage without permission. It is sinful and brings a curse because you have blasphemed the name of God and broken a holy tradition. Marrying without your parents' consent also amounts to breaking God's law. There is no peace for lawbreakers.

> *"Thou shalt not remove thy neighbor's landmark, which they of old time have set in thine inheritance, which thou shalt inherit in the land that the LORD thy God giveth thee to possess it"* (Deuteronomy 19:14).

"Cursed be he that removeth his neighbor's landmark. And all the people shall say, Amen" (Deuteronomy 27:17).

Marriage is an ancient landmark. Therefore, you cannot relegate God to the background in the issue of marriage. If you remove your neighbors' landmark, you get a curse. Churches have their tradition of conducting marriages. Likewise, different communities and tribes have their own ways of conducting marriages. You must observe all these in accordance to God's Word. It is not wrong for you to observe traditions, except that which is contrary to your faith and pure conscience. Where God's authority is lifted up, traditions or church customs bow and cease. No church or family custom should require anything that contradicts God's Word in the course of your marriage.

"But Peter and John answered and said unto them, Whether it be right in the sight of God to hearken unto you more than unto God, judge ye" (Acts 4:19).

"Then Peter and the other apostles answered and said, We ought to obey God rather than men" (Acts 5:29).

With the consent of your parents and the church, God accepts your marriage. Anything that is worth doing is worth doing well. There are many reasons why marriage's wine finishes in many families. Marrying someone who you are not compatible with, both in faith and in other areas of life, can cause your marriage's wine to run out before time.

"Neither shalt thou make marriages with them; thy daughter thou shalt not give unto his son, nor his daughter shalt thou take unto thy son" (Deuteronomy 7:3).

"Be ye not unequally yoked together with unbelievers: for what fellowship hath righteousness with unrighteousness? And what communion hath light with darkness?" (2 Corinthians 6:14).

It is often detrimental to marry outside your faith without God's leading. You need God's leading to marry the person God wants you to marry. Someone who is suitable for another person may not necessarily be suitable for you as well. God knows how to make the best choice for you. However, when you hurriedly make a choice for yourself without God's direction, your marriage's wine may finish eventually.

It is very dangerous to marry someone who is an unbeliever. This is because two cannot walk together if they do not agree. This issue is very critical because there is no room for divorce in God's New Testament book. Sex outside marriage or living as a husband and wife before a legal marriage is having a fellowship with the unfruitful works of darkness. All these things can cause the wine in marriages to drain.

"And have no fellowship with the unfruitful works of darkness, but rather reprove them. For it is a shame even to speak of those things which are done of them in secret" (Ephesians 5:11-12).

"For he that biddeth him God speed is partaker of his evil deeds" (2 John 11).

These lifestyles bring shame to families and cause marriages to collapse. Any marriage that starts with sin and disobedience to God's Word will definitely suffer terrible attacks.

LIST OF THINGS THAT CAN CAUSE YOUR MARRIAGE'S WINE TO FINISH

- Eating the forbidden fruit before legal marriage
- Going to beg for bread in Egypt in time of famines and problems, or seeking help outside God when problems come in the family.
- Being impatient for God's visitation in the event of satanic attacks or delay (*See* Genesis 16:1-21).
- Being or acting wickedly to other people.
- Despising your birthright, cheating in your marriage and adultery.
- Complaining in times of difficulties instead of praying and waiting for God's time.
- Marrying a wrong person and trying to resolve the impasse on your own without consulting God for possible solution.
- Sleeping with different women or men outside marriage (*See* 1 King 11:1-19).
- Picking up issues with people who tell you the truth (*See* Matthew 14:1-13, Mark 6:17-28).
- Bewitching others or practicing witchcraft (*See* Acts 8:9-13, 18-24).
- Shedding of innocent blood (*See* Acts 12:1-9, 20-25, 2 Samuel 21:1-9).

WHAT HAPPENS WHEN MARRIAGE'S WINE FINISHES?

- When the wine of any marriage finishes, Satan intrudes into that home and attacks it.
- The presence of forces that attack homes increases.
- Strange men and women like Jezebel and Delilah invade the marriage.
- Evil interference of in-laws and unfriendly friends multiply.
- The presence of conflicts and hostilities become visible and unbearable.
- It becomes easy for devil to alter God's original plan for the marriage.
- Hatred overwhelms couples and forces them into bondage of hatred and anger. Incidences of communication gaps, foolishness and irrational compromises begin to unveil.
- Partial separation, incomplete leaving and incomplete cleaving become imminent.
- Sin of adultery, partial submission, rudeness and selfishness become the norm.
- Unconscious link to ancient covenants and renewal of inherited curses become imminent. This is because some couples would return to their parents' houses in search of solution, and in so doing return to former family evil altars or patterns.
- The family becomes demonized. Familiar spirits return through sexual encounters in dreams, sin, etc.
- The whole family begins to suffer. Father, mother (and children) suffers terribly.
- Bitterness, rejection, depression, fears, worry, etc. multiply.
- Unforgiving spirits, compromise, confusion and premature deaths set in.

DELIVERANCE FOR FAMILIES IN DISTRESS

Many people take different directions when their marriages get into trouble. Most people separate, divorce or marry other wives. The all-knowing God knew that many people would exhaust their marriages' wine through willful mistakes, wrong choices and sin. That is why He made a way of escape from trouble. Obviously, separation, divorce or remarrying cannot be the way of escape God established. That is why it is very important that when you discover the wine of your marriage is running out, you must invite Christ into your marriage as a matter of urgency.

> *"And the third day there was a marriage in Cana of Galilee; and the mother of Jesus was there"* (John 2:1).

It may be a perfect time to acknowledge any particular sin, repent of it and forsake them. Christ is willing to restore your family from trouble. When a Pharisee invited Jesus into his house, He went in and ate with him. No matter how sinful or bad the trouble in your family is, Jesus is willing to honor your invitation. Mary Magdalene was a terrible sinner in her time, yet Jesus delivered her. When you repent truthfully, Jesus will bring His wine into your marriage and your whole story would change.

> *"And when they wanted wine, the mother of Jesus saith unto him, They have no wine. Jesus saith unto her, Woman, what have I to do with thee? Mine hour is not yet come. His mother saith unto the servants, Whatsoever he saith unto you, do it. And there were set there six water pots of stone, after the manner of the purifying of the Jews, containing two or three firkins apiece. Jesus saith unto them, Fill the water pots with water. And they filled them up to the brim. And he saith unto them, Draw out now, and bear unto the governor of the feast. And they bare it. When the ruler of the feast had tasted the water that was made wine, and knew not whence it was: (but the servants which drew the water knew;) the governor of the feast called the bridegroom, And saith unto him, Every man at the beginning doth set forth good wine; and when men have well drunk, then that which is worse: but thou hast kept the good wine until now"* (John 2:3-10).

Jesus is ready to perform a miracle in your marriage in an instant. He wants to bring peace, joy and happiness that you need and everyone would see it and testify to the glory of God. In a home where Christ is, the wife is spiritual, meek, quiet, humble, obedient, and submissive in everything that does not oppose God's Word. She is loving, diligent, hospitable and prayerful; a true mother and dependable wife. The husband in such family works hard and provides for the whole family. He teaches, guides, leads, prays and provides for the whole family. As the head, he stays with the body.

"[28]So ought men to love their wives as their own bodies. He that loveth his wife loveth himself. [29]For no man ever yet hated his own flesh; but nourisheth and cherisheth it, even as the Lord the church... [31]For this cause shall a man leave his father and mother, and shall be joined unto his wife, and they two shall be one flesh... [33]Nevertheless let every one of you in particular so love his wife even as himself; and the wife see *that she reverence* her *husband"* (Ephesians 5:28-29, 31, 33).

He loves his wife not because of what he gets from her but because God commanded him to do so.

Jesus intervention in godly homes

Even though there are difficulties and problems in families that host Jesus into their homes, but such problems do not last. Jesus answers their prayers when they pray and delivers them from all their troubles according to His Word and promise.

Examples of God's intervention

God visited Adam and Eve the day the serpent deceived them. If Adam and Eve had repented of their disobedience and asked for forgiveness, God was able to provide immediate deliverance. Instead, they blamed each another.

When you notice any evil visitor in your home, cry out to God for deliverance. The purpose of this book is to encourage you to cry out to God. When you pray, believe that He is able to deliver you. He is able to restore His wine to your marriage. No one has ever cried to God sincerely and He failed to respond. Let us consider some key people who cried to God for help:

- Abel cried to God and He answered him.
- Noah obeyed God and cried for salvation, God provided an ark and saved his family from the flood disaster.
- Abraham cried for Sodom and Gomorrah and God delivered his nephew, Lot.
- Ishmael cried and God delivered him and provided for him (*See* Genesis 21:1-21).
- Jacob cried and God showed him the way to heaven. He cried again, and God changed his name and blessed him.
- Leah cried and God opened her womb (*See* Genesis 29:35-30).
- Rachael cried and God opened her womb (*See* Genesis 30:22-24).
- Abraham cried to God, his wife conceived at an old age and gave birth to a baby boy.

- The children of Israel cried out in their bondage, and God chose Moses to go and speak to Pharaoh for their deliverance.
- Moses cried to God and He provided food for His people. He received a law to guide the children of Israel.
- Joshua cried to God and received power to stop the moon and the sun for a whole day.
- Gideon cried to God and He empowered him to deliver his people.
- Samson cried to God and he enabled him to destroy the Philistines.
- Hannah cried to God and she received a godly child that served his generation faithfully.
- David cried unto God and he recovered his lost family (1 Samuel 30:1-32).
- Elijah cried and God used him to restore rain to Israel.
- Elisha cried to God and received a double portion
- Hezekiah cried to God and He delivered him from premature death.
- Jabez cried and God enlarged his coast.
- Daniel cried to God and He delivered him from lions' den.
- Esther and Mordecai cried to God and He reversed evil decrees made against the Jews.

In the same manner, when you cry to God, He is able to answer and bless your family with wine from heaven. He is your peace and He is willing to restore peace to your family. You will enjoy your marriage again because God removed every trouble. What you need is to repent and forsake your sins and it is well with you.

When you repent, ask God to come and dine with your family. Forgive all those that offended you, especially those of your household - your wife, your husband, child, brother, sister, cousin, etc. Ask God to enable you to forgive. Prayers in this book would help you in your earnest prayers.

- Ask God to drive away the serpent in the garden of your family.
- Invite Christ into your home and ask Him to reign and rule in your family forever.
- Ask Him to remove every trouble in your home, and uproot the pillar of witchcraft in your family that attacks your family incessantly.

- Use God's anointing to destroy every deep-rooted problem in your family, and all the works of devil operating in your family.
- Ask God to deliver you and every member of your family
- Cease from observing any evil tradition in your family.
- Rebuild bridges of love, peace and happiness that have been broken in your family.
- Frustrate the works of witchcraft in your family through consistent prayers to God.
- Chase away every stranger in your home.

In these ways, you would trouble the enemies that are attacking your home and gain victory over them all in the name of Jesus, Amen.

PRAYERS FOR MARRIAGES IN DISTRESS

"And the man said, the woman whom thou gavest to be with me, she gave me of the tree, and I did eat"

Bible references: Genesis 3:12; Ephesians 5:25-33)

Begin with praise and worship

1. Any witch or wizard that is expanding problems in my marriage, be disgraced, in the name of Jesus.
2. I divert the rain of affliction that was channeled into my marriage, in the name of Jesus.
3. Any evil eye that is observing my marriage, become blind, in the name of Jesus.
4. Any evil personality that has hijacked love and peace in my marriage, die, in the name of Jesus.
5. Blood of Jesus, destroy witchcraft handwritings upon my marriage, in the name of Jesus.
6. I break the backbone of marriage destroyers for the sake of my marriage, in the name of Jesus.
7. Every satanic arrow that was fired at my marriage, I fire you back, in the name of Jesus.
8. Any demonic spy that is spying on my marriage, die, in the name of Jesus.
9. Let the fire of God burn evil deposits in my marriage to ashes, in the name of Jesus.
10. I break evil covenants that are working against my marriage, in the name of Jesus.
11. Father Lord, deliver my marriage from spirit of death and hell, in the name of Jesus.
12. I command the spirit of tragedy to be cast out of my marriage, in the name of Jesus.
13. Let curses placed that were upon my marriage expire, in the name of Jesus.
14. Let any spirit of coffin that is attacking my marriage be disgraced, in the name of Jesus.

15. Every messenger of poverty and lack in my marriage, die with your message, in the name of Jesus.

16. Every agent that is on an assignment to destroy my marriage, die, in the name of Jesus.

17. Any evil mouth that has opened to swallow my marriage, close forever, in the name of Jesus.

18. Any satanic minister that is ministering against my marriage, be disgraced, in the name of Jesus.

19. Let death swallow any power that is resisting the progress of my marriage, in the name of Jesus.

20. Let the blood of Jesus remove every evil mark placed upon my marriage, in the name of Jesus.

21. Let evil reports about my marriage die off, in the name of Jesus.

22. Any evil agent that is contending with the glory of God in my marriage, be frustrated, in the name of Jesus.

23. I cut off every architect of conflict and hostility in my marriage, in the name of Jesus.

24. Every home wrecker that was assigned to wreck my marriage, be disgraced, in the name of Jesus.

25. Let evil experts that break marriages receive confusion, in the name of Jesus.

26. I command any power that is chasing my partner away from me to die, in the name of Jesus.

27. Any intelligent woman or man that is on a mission to seduce my partner or myself, fail woefully, in the name of Jesus.

28. Let all Jezebel and Delilah in my marriage receive shocks in their brain, in the name of Jesus.

29. Any evil association that was designed to destroy my marriage, scatter and die, in the name of Jesus.

30. Let shame or disgrace in my marriage die, in the name of Jesus.

31. Every cause of trouble in my marriage, be exposed and be destroyed, in the name of Jesus.

32. I dissolve every spiritual marriage in place of my marriage by force, in the name of Jesus.

33. I destroy the spirit of polygamy and infertility that defeated my parents, in the name of Jesus.

34. Any problem that has vowed to destroy my marriage, fail woefully, in the name of Jesus.

35. O Lord, arise and do something that will cause my marriage to succeed, in the name of Jesus.

36. Any evil leg that has walked into my marriage, spiritually or physically, walk out, in the name of Jesus.

37. Father Lord, restore the original map You have for my marriage from the beginning, in the name of Jesus.

38. Any power that is manipulating my marriage in the dream, die forever, in the name of Jesus.

39. Let oppressors of my marriage be oppressed to death, in the name of Jesus.

40. Let distributors of shame in my marriage die with your shame, in the name of Jesus.

41. Owners of evil loads in my marriage, carry your loads, in the name of Jesus.

42. Every evil sacrifice or satanic prayers that was said against my marriage, backfire, in the name of Jesus.

43. Holy Ghost fire, burn every problem in my marriage to ashes, in the name of Jesus.

3 Chapter

PRAYERS TO PREVENT SEPARATION OF COUPLES

CHAPTER OVERVIEW

- *Separation is not God's perfect will*
- *The enemy in the garden of your marriage*
- *How to handle complications in marriage*
- *Reasons why most couples separate*

SEPARATION IS NOT GOD'S PERFECT WILL

Separation is a state or period of time when legally married couples stay apart from each other, often due to irreconcilable differences. Today, numerous marriages are experiencing serious problems. Many husbands and their wives live under the same roof without talking to each other for extend period. Couples that lived in the same home separate spiritually, while those who could no longer tolerate the sight of each other and lived differently separate both spiritually and physically.

However, we know that the only time a man and a woman have rights to remain separate is at the period of courtship before consummation of marriage. At this period, a man and woman are not allow to join themselves together in any sexual relationship, not until their marriage is sealed.

> *"[31]It hath been said , Whosoever shall put away his wife, let him give her a writing of divorcement: [32]But I say unto you, That whosoever shall put away his wife, saving for the cause of fornication, causeth her to commit adultery: and whosoever shall marry her that is divorced committeth adultery"* (Matthew 5:31, 32).

> *And I say unto you, Whosoever shall put away his wife, except it be for fornication, and shall marry another, committeth adultery: and whoso marrieth her which is put away doth commit adultery"* (Matthew 19:9).

Moreover, when you marry officially, the issue of fornication expires because married people do not commit fornication. The undeviating teaching of the scripture is that marriage is a lifetime union and relationship.

> *"And said, for this cause shall a man leave father and mother, and shall cleave to his wife: and they twain shall be one flesh? Wherefore they are no more twain, but one flesh. What therefore God hath joined together, let not man put asunder"* (Matthew 19:5-6).

From the beginning, God instituted marriage as a union between one man and one woman. Hence the decree, 'What God has joined, no man should put asunder'. Separation is not part of God's perfect will.

> *"Now the birth of Jesus Christ was on this wise: When as his mother Mary was espoused to Joseph, before they came together, she was found with child of the Holy Ghost. Then Joseph her husband, being a just man, and not willing to make her a public example, was minded to put her away privily. But while he thought on these things, behold, the angel of the Lord appeared unto him in a dream, saying, Joseph,*

thou son of David, fear not to take unto thee Mary thy wife: for that which is conceived in her is of the Holy Ghost. And she shall bring forth a son, and thou shalt call his name JESUS: for he shall save his people from their sins. Now all this was done, that it might be fulfilled which was spoken of the Lord by the prophet, saying, Behold, a virgin shall be with child, and shall bring forth a son, and they shall call his name Emmanuel, which being interpreted is, God with us. Then Joseph being raised from sleep did as the angel of the Lord had bidden him, and took unto him his wife" (Matthew 1:18-24).

God did not permit Joseph to put Mary away when he found out that Mary was pregnant. It was obvious it was not Joseph's responsibility. Otherwise, Joseph was determined to put Mary away secretly and marry another woman. Thanks to God, that Joseph obeyed God's instruction. That is why when you would have faith and patience with God, He is able to correct every negative thing you notice in your partner's behavior or conduct. It is better to hearken to God's instruction and leading that your own thoughts.

When Joseph saw that Mary was with a child, He harkened to God's instruction. Joseph's obedience made him to remain with the most virtuous woman on earth the rest of his life, and ironically became a father to his creator. He listened to an angel that came to him from God and obeyed God's instruction.

Similarly, separation may not necessarily be the best solution to the serious conflict you are facing in your marriage right now. Like Joseph, seek for God's guidance and direction on what to do. God is able to instruct you on a way to follow that would lead to His goodness and His mercy. Pray for Spirit of wisdom. You need wisdom because there are people, who have lost their lives trying to live together, when their partner wished they separated. For safety reasons, some people have separated instead of risking death or being killed by their partners.

"For the woman which hath a husband is bound by the law to her husband so long as he liveth; but if the husband be dead, she is loosed from the law of her husband. So then if, while her husband liveth, she be married to another man, she shall be called an adulteress: but if her husband be dead, she is free from that law; so that she is no adulteress, though she be married to another man" (Romans 7:2-3).

Oftentimes, the problem is not always the conflict itself but lack of knowledge on how to handle conflicts when they present themselves. Whatever kind of conflict you are experiencing right now, God knows about them even before they came into being, and He is able to provide the perfect solution you need. No one has ever solved his or her problems by running away from them. Rather, you will find all the answers and solutions to family problems in the Word of God.

THE ENEMY IN THE GARDEN OF YOUR MARRIAGE

Let us focus more on driving the serpent out from the garden of our marriages when resolving problems in our families. Some characters are peculiar to the serpent, the devil. That is why a husband and his wife must insist on resolving their problems through godly means. However, when you go outside the boundary of God's Word, you end up increasing and worsening your problems. Believers should have no other alternative than God and His Word. No problem is too big that God cannot provide solution. God, who instituted marriage, is able also to provide solutions to challenges that arise in marriages.

> *"And I will wait upon the LORD, that hideth his face from the house of Jacob, and I will look for him"* (Isaiah 8:17).

> *"And when Saul enquired of the LORD, the LORD answered him not, neither by dreams, nor by Urim, nor by prophets. Then said Saul unto his servants, Seek me a woman that hath a familiar spirit that I may go to her, and enquire of her. And his servants said to him, Behold, there is a woman that hath a familiar spirit at Endor. And Saul disguised himself, and put on other raiment, and he went, and two men with him, and they came to the woman by night: and he said, I pray thee, divine unto me by the familiar spirit, and bring me him up, whom I shall name unto thee"* (1 Samuel 28:6-8).

When you remain faithful to God and His Word, He helps you to overcome your problem. Nevertheless, those that attempt to solve their problems without God never found any solution. They end up incurring more problems.

> *"Because thou obeyedst not the voice of the LORD, nor executedst his fierce wrath upon Amalek, therefore hath the LORD done this thing unto thee this day. Moreover, the LORD will also deliver Israel with thee into the hand of the Philistines: and tomorrow shalt thou and thy sons be with me: the LORD also shall deliver the host of Israel into the hand of the Philistines. Then Saul fell straightway all along on the earth, and was sore afraid, because of the words of Samuel: and there was no strength in him; for he had eaten no bread all the day, nor all the night"* (1 Samuel 28:18-20).

For some people, when they encounter problems in their marriages, the first option usually is running away or dissolving their marriages. Morally and ethically, it is wrong to avoid a battle that you must fight. Some people encounter problems in their marriages just at the beginning of their union. Others, at the middle of it, while others at old age.

Problems are inevitable in marriage. Therefore, a wise person prepares for them. Do not run away from problems. With God's Word, you can confront and conquer the serpent in the garden of your marriage victoriously.

> *"Man that is born of a woman is of few days, and full of trouble"* (Job 14:1).

Multitudes of believers manifest great faith in various areas of life but they fail in their marriages. They did not fail because they do not possess weapons to defeat the enemy. They were not prepared for battles and the enemy took them unawares. Many young people succeed as singles, but as soon as they marry, they fail woefully. It is usually a problem of preparation.

When you underestimate the strength of your enemies to destroy your marriage, you put your marriage at risk. In marriage, the forces of good and forces of evil are always involved. God is ready to help you succeed in your marriage. You cannot afford to fail to prepare yourself for future challenges. Martial life is not a honeymoon fiesta. But with God, you can be sure of nothing but success.

> *"Finally, my brethren, be strong in the Lord, and in the power of his might. Put on the whole armor of God that ye may be able to stand against the wiles of the devil. For we wrestle not against flesh and blood, but against principalities, against powers, against the rulers of the darkness of this world, against spiritual wickedness in high places. Wherefore take unto you the whole armor of God that ye may be able to withstand in the evil day, and having done all, to stand. Stand therefore, having your loins girt about with truth, and having on the breastplate of righteousness; And your feet shod with the preparation of the gospel of peace; Above all, taking the shield of faith, wherewith ye shall be able to quench all the fiery darts of the wicked. And take the helmet of salvation, and the sword of the Spirit, which is the word of God: Praying always with all prayer and supplication in the Spirit, and watching thereunto with all perseverance and supplication for all saints"* (Ephesians 6:10-18).

God's power and grace remains unprofitable to those that do not seek God's face. That is why such people fight each other in their marriages instead of confronting devil, who is the architect of their problems. As Christians, God has called us to resist the devil, put on divinely provided armor of God and refrain from fighting carnally. Notice that devil also offers the option of separation. It is so sad that most people settle for Satan's offer.

> *"Fight the good fight of faith, lay hold on eternal life, where unto thou art also called, and hast professed a good profession before many witnesses"* (1 Timothy 6:12).

"And every man that striveth for the mastery is temperate in all things. Now they do it to obtain a corruptible crown; but we an incorruptible. I therefore so run, not as uncertainly; so fight I, not as one that beateth the air: But I keep under my body, and bring it into subjection: lest that by any means, when I have preached to others, I myself should be a castaway" (1 Corinthians 9:25-27).

Great marriages face great challenges. Devil does not spare any person who plans to set up a family. Devil does not wish to see any family fruitfully blessed or multiplies in order to replenish the earth. Once you start thinking about marriage, devil begins to confront you with difficult situations, with the purpose of keeping you from God's plans and blessing. Whenever devil noticed God's great plan to bless and prosper you, he looks for ways to destroy you or your home so that you would not benefit in God's blessing. One of the strategic areas he attacks successfully is people's marriage. May your marriage never fall because of Satan's attacks, in the name of Jesus.

"[28]And God blessed them, and God said unto them, Be fruitful, and multiply, and replenish the earth, and subdue it: and have dominion over the fish of the sea, and over the fowl of the air, and over every living thing that moveth upon the earth. [31]And God saw everything that he had made, and, behold, it was very good. And the evening and the morning were the sixth day" (Genesis 1:28, 31).

People who have not realized that the world is a battleground fail easily, even where they are supposed to succeed. That is why Christian life is likened to wrestling, fighting or warfare.

"For though we walk in the flesh, we do not war after the flesh: (For the weapons of our warfare are not carnal, but mighty through God to the pulling down of strong holds;) Casting down imaginations, and every high thing that exalteth itself against the knowledge of God, and bringing into captivity every thought to the obedience of Christ" (2 Corinthians 10:3-5).

"And why stand we in jeopardy every hour? I protest by your rejoicing, which I have in Christ Jesus our Lord, I die daily. If after the manner of men I have fought with beasts at Ephesus, what advantageth it me, if the dead rise not? Let us eat and drink; for tomorrow we die" (1 Corinthians 15:30-32).

HOW TO HANDLE COMPLICATIONS IN MARRIAGE

Handling complications in marriage require wisdom. However, one thing you must know is that marriages face one challenge or the other and there are not exceptions. Your family's problem may be different from that of the other marriage. However, that does not mean that the other marriage is immune from problems. Therefore, when you experience problems, understand that you are not the first person to face problems, and would not be the last to experience problems. More so, God has provided perfect solutions to every problem on earth.

> *"[21]And Moses was content to dwell with the man: and he gave Moses Zipporah his daughter. [22]And she bare him a son, and he called his name Gershom: for he said, I have been a stranger in a strange land"* (Exodus 2:21, 22).

Even Moses had many problems. He decided to marry Zipporah without seeking God's consent, and he later discovered that his wife had different conviction that was different from his faith. He was not knowledgeable about marriage before taking Zipporah as his wife. He ran away from Egypt empty handed. He left the comfort of a palace to live in the wilderness. He needed an accommodation badly that he married because of convenience. He married the daughter of a priest of Midian, who was pagan.

> *"Now the priest of Midian had seven daughters: and they came and drew water, and filled the troughs to water their father's flock. And the shepherds came and drove them away: but Moses stood up and helped them, and watered their flock. And when they came to Reuel their father, he said, How is it that ye are come so soon to day? And they said, An Egyptian delivered us out of the hand of the shepherds, and also drew water enough for us, and watered the flock. And he said unto his daughters, And where is he? Why is it that ye have left the man? Call him, that he may eat bread"* (Exodus 2:16-20).

He knew little or nothing about his wife, the god she was dedicated to and her convictions before he accepted to marry her. He married in the dark, without any instruction, counsel or guidance from God. He entered into marriage in a hurry and later it caused him many sorrows. Moses' marriage did not only put him in trouble, it also put others into trouble.

> *"[5]And the LORD came down in the pillar of the cloud, and stood in the door of the tabernacle, and called Aaron and Miriam: and they both came forth. [6]And he said, Hear now my words: If there be a prophet among you, I the LORD will make myself known unto him in a vision, and will speak unto him in a dream. [7]My servant Moses is not so, who is faithful in all mine house. [8]With him will I speak mouth to mouth, even apparently, and not in dark speeches; and the similitude of the LORD*

shall he behold: wherefore then were ye not afraid to speak against my servant Moses? [9]And the anger of the LORD was kindled against them; and he departed. [10]And the cloud departed from off the tabernacle; and, behold, Miriam became leprous, white as snow: and Aaron looked upon Miriam, and, behold, she was leprous. [11]And Aaron said unto Moses, Alas, my lord, I beseech thee, lay not the sin upon us, wherein we have done foolishly, and wherein we have sinned" (Numbers 12:11, 5-10).

It is very dangerous to marry a wrong person. It can cause many troubles in future. Nevertheless, when you trust God, He is able to intervene and bring perfect solutions that you need. Bad marriage results to conflicts, hostilities and incessant problems.

"And it came to pass by the way in the inn, that the LORD met him, and sought to kill him. Then Zipporah took a sharp stone, and cut off the foreskin of her son, and cast it at his feet, and said, Surely a bloody husband art thou to me. So he let him go: then she said, A bloody husband thou art, because of the circumcision" (Exodus 4:24-26).

Notice that Moses' wife would later trouble him, disagree with him in doctrines and opposed his calling. She even separated from him, but his father in-law, Jethro, later intervened.

"When Jethro, the priest of Midian, Moses' father in-law, heard of all that God had done for Moses, and for Israel his people, and that the LORD had brought Israel out of Egypt; Then Jethro, Moses' father in law, took Zipporah, Moses' wife, after he had sent her back" (Exodus 18:1-2).

While Moses had encounters with Pharaoh and the children of Israel, his wife and children were not with him. They probably did not have the opportunity to know the law of God very well from their father. Instead, they grew up with their mother, Zipporah. That was enough trouble for Moses, but thanks to God, he later recovered his wife by the intervention of God.

Manoah, Samson's father, was plagued with childlessness. He had no child until old age. His wife was barren until her old age. That was enough reason for most couples to divorce or separate, but they stayed together and waited upon their God, who did not disappoint them.

"[1]And the children of Israel did evil again in the sight of the LORD; and the LORD delivered them into the hand of the Philistines forty years. [2]And there was a certain man of Zorah, of the family of the Danites, whose name was Manoah; and his wife was barren, and bare not. [3]And the angel of the LORD appeared unto the woman, and said unto her, Behold now, thou art barren, and bearest not: but thou shalt

conceive, and bear a son. [24]*And the woman bare a son, and called his name Samson: and the child grew, and the LORD blessed him.* [25]*And the Spirit of the LORD began to move him at times in the camp of Dan between Zorah and Eshtaol"* (Judges 13:1-3, 24, 25).

Regardless of what your problems are, when you trust God for perfect solution, he is able to visit you, bless your marriage and make you to shine like a light for others to see. Many people must have given Manoah wrong counsel. The thought of separation and divorce must have tormented him as well. However, he believed God and waited on God's timing.

A similar fate befell Hannah. She had serious trouble in her marriage. Her adversaries provoked her sorely. They made her fret because she was barren. She bore the shame, reproach, and disgrace for many years. Yet, Hannah did not divorce her husband or separate from him.

"[5]*But unto Hannah he gave a worthy portion; for he loved Hannah: but the LORD had shut up her womb.* [6]*And her adversary also provoked her sore, for to make her fret, because the LORD had shut up her womb.* [7]*And as he did so year by year, when she went up to the house of the LORD, so she provoked her; therefore she wept, and did not eat.* [10]*And she was in bitterness of soul, and prayed unto the LORD, and wept sore.* [11]*And she vowed a vow, and said, O LORD of hosts, if thou wilt indeed look on the affliction of thine handmaid, and remember me, and not forget thine handmaid, but wilt give unto thine handmaid a man child, then I will give him unto the LORD all the days of his life, and there shall no razor come upon his head.* [20]*Wherefore it came to pass, when the time was come about after Hannah had conceived, that she bare a son, and called his name Samuel, saying, Because I have asked him of the LORD"* (1 Samuel 1:5- 7, 10-11, 20).

Hannah refused to separate from her husband. Rather, she fought the serpent in the garden of her marriage until she drove the serpent away. You can do the same today. Hannah refused to bow to pressures from her adversaries. She never fought with her husband or her adversaries. When Hannah got tired of receiving temporal comfort from her husband that could not solve her problem, she went into the house of God for deliverance.

Notice how Hannah did not waste her time weeping before men pathetically. She went before God to ask for deliverance. She wept and refused eat. The priest mistook her to be drunk. Of course, her determination to let God undo her burden paid off. Through Christ, you can do the same. Instead of considering separating from your spouse, let God undo your burden. Would it not be wise to ask God to deal with your troubles instead? Even when your case is different from Hannah's, nothing is impossible with God. Hannah prayed to the Lord in the bitterness of her soul and wept sorely. She decided to drive her problems out of her home and was successful. Just like Hannah did, do not allow your problem to drive you away. Drive you problems away by letting God deal with them.

REASONS WHY MOST COUPLES SEPARATE

One of the major reasons many marriages crash is inability to obey God's Word. Disobedience to God's Word is a big disservice. It brings unhappiness, lack of love and peace in the family. However, how can a couple obey God's Word when they have no knowledge of His Word? Lack of knowledge and understanding cause many crashes in marriage as well. A husband and wife that do not determine to build their marriage upon God's commandment find it hard not to separate at any slightest frustration.

> *"So ought men to love their wives as their own bodies. He that loveth his wife loveth himself. For no man ever yet hated his own flesh; but nourisheth and cherisheth it, even as the Lord the church: For we are members of his body, of his flesh, and of his bones. For this cause shall a man leave his father and mother, and shall be joined unto his wife, and they two shall be one flesh"* (Ephesians 5: 28-31).

God commanded the man to leave his father and mother and be joined to his wife that two of them become one. If husbands would obey this simple piece of instruction in the scripture, and then love their wives as their own bodies, no man would ever imagine separating from his wife. The Scripture held that it is not possible for any man to hate his flesh. No matter how bad your eyes, nose or any part of your body looked, you still cared for them.

However, we know that evil forces induce men to hate their wives and even attack them. This is absolutely wrong and unlawful. The big challenge is, what do we do? Do we keep quiet and let these evil forces continue to rule our lives? Do we keep silent so that sin would abound much more? No, we cannot keep quiet. You have to resist evil spirits behind hatred. It is such a beautiful thing to love your wife or husband.

To leave parents and cleave to each other demands determination to resist any power that attempts to separate you from your partner.

> *"But from the beginning of the creation, God made them male and female. For this cause, shall a man leave his father and mother, and cleave to his wife; and they twain shall be one flesh: so then, they are no more twain, but one flesh. What therefore God hath joined, let not man put asunder"* (Mark 10:6-9).

> *"Therefore shall a man leave his father and his mother, and shall cleave unto his wife: and they shall be one flesh"* (Genesis 2:24).

Repeatedly, the old and New Testaments held that husbands and wives should stay together for a lifetime. Anything or person that opposes this verdict not only opposes the institution of marriages but God also. Use all spiritual weapons available to you to resist the urge and scourge of separation because it is the wish of your enemy. Therefore, understand the spiritual implication of leaving parents in order to cleave to each other. Then, do not give the devil a place.

> *"Therefore to him that knoweth to do good, and doeth it not, to him it is sin"* (James 4:17).

> *"Casting all your care upon him; for he careth for you. Be sober, be vigilant; because your adversary the devil, as a roaring lion, walketh about, seeking whom he may devour: Whom resist steadfast in the faith, knowing that the same afflictions are accomplished in your brethren that are in the world"* (1 Peter 5:7-9).

> *"Submit yourselves therefore to God. Resist the devil, and he will flee from you"* (James 4:7).

Devil does not seek for a place in our homes only but in our personal lives also. Therefore, you cannot afford to give devil an inch in your life. He can be very destructive.

> *"Wives, submit yourselves unto your own husbands, as unto the Lord. For the husband is the head of the wife, even as Christ is the head of the church: and he is the savior of the body. Therefore as the church is subject unto Christ, so let the wives be to their own husbands in everything"* (Ephesians 5:22-24).

Likewise, a wife that refuses to submit to her husband's authority gives the devil a place in her family. By the time the devil takes that place, he knows how to cause separation in the shortest period. God expects the love, tenderness and gentleness of wives to their husbands to be perfect.

A good wife submits to her husband as unto the Lord and does not think that she is doing her husband any favor. Anytime she disagreed with her husband, she does so with mildness and gentleness until her husband considered her opinion. A good wife states her reasons humbly, and then prayerfully commits every other thing to God. After doing this, she does not fight. Instead, she endeavors to make everyone at home happy.

> *"She stretcheth out her hand to the poor; yea, she reacheth forth her hands to the needy. She is not afraid of the snow for her household: for all her household are clothed with scarlet. She maketh herself coverings of tapestry; her clothing is silk and purple. Her husband is known in the gates, when he sitteth among the elders of the land. She maketh fine linen, and selleth it; and delivereth girdles unto the merchant. Strength and honor are her clothing; and she shall rejoice in time to come. She*

openeth her mouth with wisdom; and in her tongue is the law of kindness. She looketh well to the ways of her household, and eateth not the bread of idleness. Her children arise up, and call her blessed; her husband also, and he praiseth her. Many daughters have done virtuously, but thou excellest them all. Favor is deceitful, and beauty is vain: but a woman that feareth the LORD, she shall be praised. Give her of the fruit of her hands; and let her own works praise her in the gates" (Proverbs 31:20-31).

Submission does not make any woman a slave. Rather, it is a demonstration of your love for Christ and His Word. A man who beats his wife is ignorant and fights his own body. A wife who refuses to submit to her husband is equally ignorant and attacks her own head. If the husband and wife follow these scriptural injunctions as commanded, God is honored, and the Spirit of God would dwell in our homes and the world will know peace. Sarah did it and peace reigned in her home.

"But let it be the hidden man of the heart, in that which is not corruptible, even the ornament of a meek and quiet spirit, which is in the sight of God of great price. For after this manner in the old time the holy women also, who trusted in God, adorned themselves, being in subjection unto their own husbands: Even as Sara obeyed Abraham, calling him lord: whose daughters ye are, as long as ye do well, and are not afraid with any amazement" (1 Peter 3:4-6).

Sarah was meek and quiet at her home, before her husband and other members of the family. She paid the price for a peaceful home and her husband, Abraham, enjoyed an atmosphere of prosperity. She trusted in her God and submitted to her husband. She never called Abraham bad names. She addressed him as lord or master.

"[7]And he brought up Hadassah, that is, Esther, his uncle's daughter: for she had neither father nor mother, and the maid was fair and beautiful; whom Mordecai, when her father and mother were dead, took for his own daughter. [8]So it came to pass, when the king's commandment and his decree was heard, and when many maidens were gathered together unto Shushan the palace, to the custody of Hegai, that Esther was brought also unto the king's house, to the custody of Hegai, keeper of the women. [9]And the maiden pleased him, and she obtained kindness of him; and he speedily gave her her things for purification, with such things as belonged to her, and seven maidens, which were meet to be given her, out of the king's house: and he preferred her and her maids unto the best place of the house of the women. [10]Esther had not shewed her people nor her kindred: for Mordecai had charged her that she should not shew it. [17]And the king loved Esther above all the women, and she obtained grace and favor in his sight more than all the virgins; so that he set the royal crown upon her head, and made her queen instead of Vashti" (Esther 2:7-10, 17).

Good husbands are always ready to do everything necessary to protect their families and make their wives happy. A good husband would be ready to die for the safety of his family. They love their wives, as not only Adam, Abraham, etc., did. They love their wives as Christ loves His church. Good husbands are selfless and dependable. It is a good thing to be a good husband.

> *"Husbands, love your wives, even as Christ also loved the church, and gave himself for it; That he might sanctify and cleanse it with the washing of water by the word, That he might present it to himself a glorious church, not having spot, or wrinkle, or any such thing; but that it should be holy and without blemish. So ought men to love their wives as their own bodies. He that loveth his wife loveth himself. For no man ever yet hated his own flesh; but nourisheth and cherisheth it, even as the Lord the church: For we are members of his body, of his flesh, and of his bones. For this cause shall a man leave his father and mother, and shall be joined unto his wife, and they two shall be one flesh. This is a great mystery: but I speak concerning Christ and the church. Nevertheless let every one of you in particular so love his wife even as himself; and the wife see that she reverence her husband"* (Ephesians 5:25-33).

In families where love exists, there are no animosity, fighting, struggle, etc. Instead, there is fullness of joy, love, care, perfection, unity and concern for each other to the glory of God. Love is a mystery. The greatest secret of conjugal happiness is mutual love, tenderness, kindness and lowliness of character at home. A good husband loves, cares and shows concern for his wife. In return, a good wife honors and obeys her husband as unto the lord.

The Holy Spirit fills and leads such couple. That is why they walk and work in the fear of God. They speak the truth, exhort each other, edify, encourage and thank God for keeping them together in love. The father in-law of Moses was against the principle of separation, which was why he took her daughter back to Moses. He reunited a separated family. Today God is reuniting your family, in the name of Jesus.

To make things easy, you do not need to wait for your parents to come before your start doing something. Trust God for a revelation and work on yourself first. You need to take some practical actions as well, as you pray.

SOME IMPORTANT STEPS YOU CAN TAKE

- Reexamine yourself, your relationship with God and man.
- Identify your personal faults and weaknesses in your marriage.
- Repent of your mistakes, confess and forsake them.
- If you come from a family where separation is common, repent on behalf of your ancestors and ask for God's forgiveness.
- Take the initiative to reconcile with your partner. Pay the price of love and unity.
- Swallow your pride, say sorry where you need to do so.
- Pray against evil inheritance and captivity, and separate yourself from any common evil practice in your family.
- Pray for your partner earnestly.
- Share a copy of this book with your partner. Pray seriously on it and give it to him or her secretly unless God permits you to do so openly.
- Enter into prayers for restoration of your home
- Use the Word to nullify evil sacrifices and satanic interests on your marriage.
- Break satanic strongholds that stand against your marriage.
- Pray for God's wisdom and understanding for your partner and yourself.

PRAYERS TO PREVENT SEPARATION OF COUPLES

Begin with praise and worship

1. Father Lord, empower me to keep my marriage at all cost, in the name of Jesus.
2. Angels of the living God, disconnect any evil relationship that exists in my marriage, in the name of Jesus.
3. I break and loose my marriage from the hands of evil designers, in the name of Jesus.
4. Blood of Jesus, flow into my life and command peace into my marriage, in the name of Jesus.
5. O Lord, create a wall of fire around my marriage, in the name of Jesus.
6. I cast out every enemy of divine love in my marriage, in the name of Jesus.
7. Let any strange man or woman that is attacking my marriage die by fire, in the name of Jesus.
8. I cast out every demon of immorality that is working against my marriage, in the name of Jesus.
9. Let every Jezebel or Delilah that was assigned to destroy my marriage be disgraced, in the name of Jesus.
10. Any strongman that is militating against my marriage, be frustrated, in the name of Jesus.
11. I stand against every messenger of polygamy, in the name of Jesus.
12. Every property of devil that exists in my marriage, catch fire and burn to ashes, in the name of Jesus.
13. Every arrow of separation that was fired at my marriage, backfire, in the name of Jesus.
14. O Lord, empower my marriage for marital breakthroughs, in the name of Jesus.
15. I draw a line between my partner and any strange woman or man, in the name of Jesus.
16. Anything that is attacking my marriage from within me, come out and die, in the name of Jesus.

17. Every arrow of confusion that was fired at my marriage, backfire, in the name of Jesus.

18. Let any evil character that is being used to cause separation of my marriage be destroyed, in the name of Jesus.

19. Father Lord, cause Your love to dwell in my marriage, in the name of Jesus.

20. O Lord, make my relationship with my life partner better, in the name of Jesus.

21. I reverse any evil judgment that was passed against my marriage, in the name of Jesus.

22. I recover every respect that I lost in my marriage, in the name of Jesus.

23. Father Lord, empower my marriage to recover its glory, in the name of Jesus.

24. Let any evil marriage that is attacking my marriage break by fire, in the name of Jesus.

25. Lion of Judah, destroy every fake lion in my life, in the name of Jesus.

26. Blood of Jesus, speak my family out of every trouble, in the name of Jesus.

27. Any demonic serpent that attached itself to my marriage, I cut you into pieces, in the name of Jesus.

28. I terminate every demonic activity that is going on in my marriage, in the name of Jesus.

29. Let every trap that was set for my marriage catch its owner, in the name of Jesus.

30. Every injury my marriage has suffered, receive healing now, in the name of Jesus.

31. Father Lord, keep my marriage in peace, in the name of Jesus.

32. Let the habitation of problems in my marriage become desolate, in the name of Jesus.

33. Let every household wickedness that exists in my marriage be destroyed, in the name of Jesus.

34. I deliver my marriage from the captivity of evil associations, in the name of Jesus.

35. Any parental curse that stands against my marriage, die, in the name of Jesus.

36. Every problem that has vowed to bring separation to my marriage, be destroyed, in the name of Jesus.

37. I release my marriage from marriage breakers, in the name of Jesus.

38. You my marriage, reject the pressure of separation, in the name of Jesus.
39. I terminate any bewitchment that stands in my marriage, in the name of Jesus.
40. Let blood of Jesus deliver my marriage from evil, in the name of Jesus.

4
Chapter

PRAYERS FOR RESTORATION OF PEACE IN MARRIAGE

CHAPTER OVERVIEW

- *God's standard for marriage*
- *Problems and solution*
- *Decision and deliverance*
- *Dealing with devil's arrows*
- *How to restore peace to your marriage*

GOD'S STANDARD FOR MARRIAGE

"[31]It hath been said, Whosoever shall put away his wife, let him give her a writing of divorcement: [32]But I say unto you, That whosoever shall put away his wife, saving for the cause of fornication, causeth her to commit adultery: and whosoever shall marry her that is divorced committeth adultery" (Matthew 5:31, 32).

In his teaching on marriage, Jesus Christ referred to the Law of Moses concerning separation and divorce. In the Law of Moses, divorce was allowed conditionally. Nevertheless, Christ preached against divorce. Married people are not allowed to separate because marriage is a lifetime union. Jesus taught that whoever divorces and remarries commits adultery. Moreover, anyone who marries a divorced person commits adultery.

"Who knowing the judgment of God, that they which commit such things are worthy of death, not only do the same, but have pleasure in them that do them" (Romans 1:32).

In the above reference, we are not only advised to shun divorce and adultery, but we are mandated to discourage its practice. In His teaching on marriage, Jesus clearly defined God's perfect will for marriage, as seen when God created man and woman. He also explained why Moses permitted divorce.

"They say unto him, Why did Moses then command to give a writing of divorcement, and to put her away? He saith unto them, Moses because of the hardness of your hearts suffered you to put away your wives: but from the beginning it was not so. And I say unto you, Whosoever shall put away his wife, except it be for fornication, and shall marry another, committeth adultery: and whoso marrieth her which is put away doth commit adultery" (Matthew 19:7-9).

Moses' ruling on marriage and divorce was not perfect because he was human. Moses bowed to pressures because of the hardness of their hearts. They complained and pressurized Moses until he gave in to their yearnings and permitted them to divorce. Even in the days of Moses, divorce was not the perfect plan of God, though Moses permitted it. Again, Jesus Christ faced the same pressure during His days on earth. However, He insisted on the perfect will of God, which did not permit divorce.

"And the Pharisees came to him, and asked him, Is it lawful for a man to put away his wife? tempting him. And he answered and said unto them, What did Moses command you? And they said, Moses suffered to write a bill of divorcement, and to

put her away. And Jesus answered and said unto them, For the hardness of your heart he wrote you this precept. But from the beginning of the creation God made them male and female. For this cause shall a man leave his father and mother, and cleave to his wife; And they twain shall be one flesh: so then they are no more twain, but one flesh. What therefore God hath joined together, let not man put asunder. And in the house his disciples asked him again of the same matter. And he saith unto them, Whosoever shall put away his wife, and marry another, committeth adultery against her. And if a woman shall put away her husband, and be married to another, she committeth adultery" (Mark 10:2-12).

"[2]For the woman which hath an husband is bound by the law to her husband so long as he liveth; but if the husband be dead, she is loosed from the law of her husband. [3]So then if, while her husband liveth, she be married to another man, she shall be called an adulteress: but if her husband be dead, she is free from that law; so that she is no adulteress, though she be married to another man" (Roman 7:2, 3).

Separation causes more damage than its causes. The problem with so many people today is that they prefer running away from their problems rather than facing them courageously. Unfortunately, most people have entered into more severe problems while running away from challenges. Nevertheless, when you face your challenges courageously, God provides divine solutions.

Separation cannot be the perfect will of God because it sets you up for more severe problems. God, in His infinite mercies, has provided solutions for all sorts of challenges through His Word.

PROBLEMS AND SOLUTION

When God created Adam, He gave him charge over every other creature. God commanded Adam to be fruitful, multiply, replenish, subdue the earth and have dominion over all creatures. Afterwards, God added a wife to him in the garden. However, the first problem on earth occurred when Eve paid attention to the lies of Satan. Willfully, she looked at the forbidden fruit, and doubted God's instruction. Finally, she desired what God forbade.

> *"And when the woman saw that the tree was good for food, and that it was pleasant to the eyes, and a tree to be desired to make one wise, she took of the fruit thereof, and did eat, and gave also unto her husband with her; and he did eat"* (Genesis 3:6).

> *"Love not the world, neither the things that are in the world. If any man love the world, the love of the Father is not in him"* (1 John 2:15).

Eve became the first human to commit sin and lured her husband to do the same. Thus, sin separated them from God. This is the first separation that occurred between God and man. However, instead of repenting of their sins, they thought of escaping from the presence of God. Even when it becomes clear that you have married a wrong partner, yet separation cannot be the best option.

> *"And they heard the voice of the LORD God walking in the garden in the cool of the day: and Adam and his wife hid themselves from the presence of the LORD God amongst the trees of the garden. And the LORD God called unto Adam, and said unto him, Where art thou? And he said, I heard thy voice in the garden, and I was afraid, because I was naked; and I hid myself. And he said, Who told thee that thou wast naked? Hast thou eaten of the tree, whereof I commanded thee that thou shouldest not eat? And the man said, The woman whom thou gavest to be with me, she gave me of the tree, and I did eat. And the LORD God said unto the woman, What is this that thou hast done? And the woman said, The serpent beguiled me, and I did eat. And the LORD God said unto the serpent, Because thou hast done this, thou art cursed above all cattle, and above every beast of the field; upon thy belly shalt thou go, and dust shalt thou eat all the days of thy life: And I will put enmity between thee and the woman, and between thy seed and her seed; it shall bruise thy head, and thou shalt bruise his heel. Unto the woman he said, I will greatly multiply thy sorrow and thy conception; in sorrow thou shalt bring forth children; and thy desire shall be to thy husband, and he shall rule over thee. And unto Adam he said, Because thou hast hearkened unto the voice of thy wife, and hast eaten of the tree, of which I commanded thee, saying, Thou shalt not eat of it: cursed is the ground for thy sake; in sorrow shalt thou eat of it all the days of thy life"* (Genesis 3:8-17).

In times of trouble or sin, which separates one from God, running away from God would be counterproductive. Adam blamed God and his wife. He said, *"It was the woman that You gave to be with me..."* In turn, the woman blamed the serpent and justified herself instead of showing remorse and repenting.

Most couples today still follow the model of Adam and Eve shifting blames. When the enemy comes into their homes, instead of acknowledging their faults and looking up to God for peaceful solution, they pride themselves and shift blames. Adam and Eve had problems because they refused to acknowledge their sin and repent. Thus, all men inherited original sin of Adam and became guilty before God.

> *"Dearly beloved, avenge not yourselves, but* rather *give place unto wrath: for it is written, Vengeance* is *mine; I will repay, saith the Lord"* (Romans 12:19).

> *"Now we know that what things soever the law saith, it saith to them who are under the law: that every mouth may be stopped, and all the world may become guilty before God"* (Romans 3:19).

The Pharisees had so much troubles separating from their wives and remarrying. Their conviction was that Moses permitted such practices. They did not understand that when you put away your wife or separate from her, you fall into the dangers of adultery. However, Jesus confronted them with truth.

I want to believe that when you humble yourself and go to God, He is able and willing to supply peaceful solutions for your marital problems.

DECISION AND DELIVERANCE

When you take any decision according to the will of God, your deliverance appears. Nevertheless, when you take any decision that contradicts God's Word, just as Adam and Eve did, it attracts curses that would lead you, and if possible your offspring, into severe bondage. The truth is that if you are going through any challenge in your marriage now, you are not the first or only person that is going through challenges in marriage. The best you can do is to take all your troubles to God through prayers and then trust Him for peaceful solutions.

> *"And Enoch lived sixty and five years, and begat Methuselah. And Enoch walked with God after he begat Methuselah three hundred years, and begat sons and daughters: And all the days of Enoch were three hundred sixty and five years: And Enoch walked with God: and he was not; for God took him"* (Genesis 5:21-24).

There was once a man called Enoch, who lived without committing sin in his generation. Iniquities and sin were so popular during his time, yet he did not yield. After sixty-five years, he took an enormous decision and walked with God. He avoided sin. He lived life of righteousness. On daily basis, while others were dining with devil, he walked with God. For three hundred years, he maintained good relationship with God.

However, many people today are in the business of marrying and separating from their wives. The foundation of marriage in our generation is under enormous attack from the devil. Many people, who have not divorced or separated, live on the edge. What separated Enoch was his decision to walk according to the Word of God.

> *"Remove not the ancient landmark, which thy fathers have set"* (Proverbs 22:28).

> *"Thou shalt not remove thy neighbor's landmark, which they of old time have set in thine inheritance, which thou shalt inherit in the land that the LORD thy God giveth thee to possess it"* (Deuteronomy 19:14).

> *"Cursed be he that removeth his neighbor's landmark. And all the people shall say, Amen"* (Deuteronomy 27:17).

God instituted marriage institution. It was one of the first ancient landmarks, which God set from the beginning. We are therefore warned not to remove this ancient landmark. God blesses those that obey the scriptures. We are also warned not to remove our neighbor's landmark. Nobody has the right or power to dissolve an ordained marriage. Mothers, fathers, brothers, sisters, friends etc., must not remove this ancient landmark. Marriage started from God, and our ancestors were involved in it. Breaking marriage vows through separation bring curses.

"Yet ye say, Wherefore? Because the LORD hath been witness between thee and the wife of thy youth, against whom thou hast dealt treacherously: yet is she thy companion, and the wife of thy covenant. And did not he make one? Yet had he the residue of the spirit. And wherefore one? That he might seek a godly seed. Therefore take heed to your spirit, and let none deal treacherously against the wife of his youth" (Malachi 2:14-15).

Most problems on earth today are associated with dysfunctional families. Once God witnessed your marriage, it can no longer be separated. Husbands are to love their wives as Christ loved the Church and gave His life for it. Instead, many husbands today are not ready to pay any price for their families. Yet from the beginning, it was not so.

"Husbands, love your wives, even as Christ also loved the church, and gave himself for it; That he might sanctify and cleanse it with the washing of water by the word, [27] That he might present it to himself a glorious church, not having spot, or wrinkle, or any such thing; but that it should be holy and without blemish. So ought men to love their wives as their own bodies. He that loveth his wife loveth himself. For no man ever yet hated his own flesh; but nourisheth and cherisheth it, even as the Lord the church" (Ephesians 5:25-29).

Whatever the problem was, husbands should encourage their wives to perform their duties well. Assuming you have a bad eye, would you not do all that you can to make that eye better? Would you not wash the eye, clean it and use it again? Obviously, you would not blind your eye, pluck it out or hate it. Likewise, men should love their wives as their own bodies. When you love your wife, you love yourself also. It is therefore strange and contrary to God's Word to claim that you love your wife, and yet you beat her or separate from her.

Ironically, many husbands care for their cars, houses and businesses more than they care for their wives. Others hunt for inept excuses to separate from their wives. The scriptures did supported anyone to do away with his wife, except on issue of fornication, which is not always the case because once married, the issue of fornication ceases to exist. Therefore, whether your wife knows how to dress or cook well, or does not, marriage remains a lifetime union.

"And the LORD God said, It is not good that the man should be alone; I will make him an help meet for him. And out of the ground the LORD God formed every beast of the field, and every fowl of the air; and brought them unto Adam to see what he would call them: and whatsoever Adam called every living creature, that was the name thereof. And Adam gave names to all cattle, and to the fowl of the air, and to every beast of the field; but for Adam there was not found a helpmeet for him. And the LORD God caused a deep sleep to fall upon Adam, and he slept: and he took one of

his ribs, and closed up the flesh instead thereof; And the rib, which the LORD God had taken from man, made he a woman, and brought her unto the man. And Adam said, This is now bone of my bones, and flesh of my flesh: she shall be called Woman, because she was taken out of Man. Therefore shall a man leave his father and his mother, and shall cleave unto his wife: and they shall be one flesh. And they were both naked, the man and his wife, and were not ashamed" (Genesis 2:18-25).

From the beginning, God constituted and blessed the union of one-man one-woman. Therefore, regardless of societal pressures that are forcing more people to separate or divorce, we cannot accept any other thing different from God's original plan. Whatever is right is right and whatever is wrong is wrong equally. Regardless of who was involved in divorce, they are wrong and cannot be right. You must insist on the Word of God, regardless the pressures.

"Wives, submit yourselves unto your own husbands, as unto the Lord. For the husband is the head of the wife, even as Christ is the head of the church: and he is the savior of the body. Therefore as the church is subject unto Christ, so let the wives be to their own husbands in everything" (Ephesians 5:22-24).

The Scriptures mandated the women to submit to their husbands as if they are submitting to Christ. Even when you are the one working while your husband remained out of job, yet you must submit to him. In addition, when your husband failed to love you as the bible commanded, yet you still need to submit to him. Your submission should not be because of what your husband provides for you. Rather, you understand that you submit to Christ when you submit to your husband.

Likewise, your refusal to submit to your husband would tantamount to disobeying Christ. Many women think they do their husbands favor when they submit to them. This is wrong. When you submit to your husband, you are submitting to Christ, and it attracts blessing. These simple decisions and actions are capable of bringing great peace into your home and remove conflicts and hostilities. Disobedience to God's commandments concerning marriage drives away God's presence in the home. At that point, devil fires his arrows freely.

DEALING WITH DEVIL'S ARROWS

Let us talk about arrows the devil fires at marriages. As I mentioned earlier, one of the most effective arrows that gets at marriages is disobedience to God's Word. When your character counters God's Word, you clear the way for devil's arrows to hit your marriage. Moreover, when they hit your marriage and last for a while, different problems infest your marriage. That is when you begin to witness strange conflicts at home, sicknesses and all manner of problems. When you fail to address these problems properly and prayerfully, these problems eventually result in separation or divorce. Often, these problems take a good number of people to hell fire.

> *"So ought men to love their wives as their own bodies. He that loveth his wife loveth himself. For no man ever yet hated his own flesh; but nourisheth and cherisheth it, even as the Lord the church: For we are members of his body, of his flesh, and of his bones. For this cause shall a man leave his father and mother, and shall be joined unto his wife, and they two shall be one flesh"* (Ephesians 5:28-31).

> *"Therefore shall a man leave his father and his mother, and shall cleave unto his wife: and they shall be one flesh"* (Genesis 2:24).

When God commanded that you "Leave your father, mother (*not necessarily abandoning them*), and be joined to your husband or wife, so that two of you become one," He expects you to obey. The problem with most couples is that some husbands and wives return to their parents' houses, especially when there is conflict, instead of running to God.

Increasingly, the failure to leave parents and cleave to each other aids the separation of marriages all over the world. When God commanded you to love your wife as your own body, but you choose to share greater part of that love with your cars, office, work, profession above your wife, there will be massive problems. Likewise, when you love other women and hate your wife, you break God's law concerning marriage.

In addition, when you take good care of your body and neglect your wife's body, you break God's law. When you dress and eat well away from your house while your wife goes naked and hungry at home, you break God's law concerning marriage. Whatever that is contrary to God's commandments concerning your marriage takes away your peace and joy, and causes the wine of your marriage to expend before time.

> *"And the third day there was a marriage in Cana of Galilee; and the mother of Jesus was there: And both Jesus was called, and his disciples, to the marriage. And when they wanted wine, the mother of Jesus saith unto him, They have no wine"* (John 2:1-3).

Similarly, God expects a wife to submit to her husband as if she is doing it unto Christ. It is not a favor to her husband but obedience to God's Word. Anything less is disobedience and is capable of causing problems in the family. That was why God addressed the wives first. A good and virtuous wife puts submission above her husband's responsibility towards her, whether he meets them or not.

> *"That they may teach the young women to be sober, to love their husbands, to love their children, To be discreet, chaste, keepers at home, good, obedient to their own husbands, that the word of God be not blasphemed"* (Titus 2:4-5).

Many wives have let their husbands down because they found themselves with good jobs and supply the needs of the family. Nevertheless, a virtuous woman understands and takes pleasure in helping her husband meet the needs of their family. She does everything possible to help her husband. She does not impose other family duties upon him. She does not force him to become the assistant mother or part-time nurse, house cleaner, house cleaner or a babysitter. She does not lord over her husband.

When the need arises that she was constrained to differ from her husband, she does so with respect and gentleness. A good wife knows how to present her reasons humbly with right manner of approach, full of respect and honor for her husband. Even after making her points known and her husband insisted, she knows how to commit such matters to God through prayers and patience.

Notwithstanding her husband's nonchalance, she plays her own part very well, trying to be a better wife and doing everything possible to maintain peace in her family. Unless her husband demands anything contrary to faith and pure conscience, she submits to her husband completely. She knows how to say no with humility and takes her stand faithfully when the authority of the husband contradicts the scriptures.

> *"But Peter and John answered and said unto them, Whether it be right in the sight of God to hearken unto you more than unto God, judge ye"* (Acts 4:19).

> *"Then Peter and the other apostles answered and said, We ought to obey God rather than men"* (Acts 5:29).

HOW TO RESTORE PEACE TO YOUR MARRIAGE

The roles of husband and wife in restoration of peace to a troubled marriage are numerous. They include -

1. The first thing God expects from the man and his wife is humility. They have to examine themselves. Discover areas they made mistakes and seek for forgiveness.

2. They have to pay the price seeking reconciliation and restoration of their marriage.

3. The husband does not desire another wife except his only wife (Proverbs 5:18-19).

4. They allow God to direct the affairs of their marriage through His Words (Proverbs 5:21).

5. The husband remains industrious, making sure that he retains his rightful position in the family as stated in God's Word (Ephesians 5:28-30, 1 Corinthians 13:4-7, Colossians 3:19).

6. Husband and his wife are always ready to receive divine counsel, take correction and listen to reasons (Proverbs 20:5).

7. They are faithful, walk in integrity and train their children in God's ways (Proverbs 70:6-8, 22, 27:5).

8. Husband and wife live righteously and transparently before each other, other people and God. They are always happy, make others happy, especially their household, and work mates (Proverbs 29:6-8).

9. The husband is peaceful, just, humble and a visionary.

10. He knows how to distance himself from sinners, depends on God's solely and trusts his wife (Proverbs 29:27, 31:3, 10-11).

11. The wife knows how to repent thoroughly and sincerely when she was wrong (1 Samuel 7:3-4).

12. She goes to any extent to restore peace in her home.

13. She submits to her husband in humbly and meekness, and she works hard (1 Peter 3:1-4, 1 Timothy 2:9, Titus 2:5).

14. A virtuous wife keeps herself pure, holy, and remains a loving wife (Titus 2:4-5, 1 Peter 3:5, 1 Timothy 2:15).

15. She is diligent, hospitable and prayerful (Psalms 128:3, Songs of Solomon 8:6-7, Psalms 144:11-12, Proverbs 31:20, 2 King 4:8-10, Matthew 15:22-28).

16. She studies the life of other virtuous women and emulates them.

Such virtuous women include -

- Esther - (Esther 2:7-10, 17 5:1-4, 7:1-6).
- Elizabeth - (Luke 1:5-7, 23-25, 57-64).
- Sarah - (1 Peter 3:4-6).
- Mary - (Luke 2:19, Matthew 2:13-14, 19-22, Luke 2:41-48).

It is not wrong to emulate people with good virtues. God instituted marriage in a way that was pleasing to Him. Therefore, you must not depart from godly way of conducting a marriage. When you play your role well, following God's pattern, God honors your marriage and you would experience peace. Finally, sex must not be used as a weapon against the weaker vessel. Let us therefore learn to live together in love, peace and harmony.

PRAYERS FOR RESTORATION OF PEACE IN MARRIAGE

Bible reference: Matthew 18:3-9

Begin with praise and worship

1. I break and lose my marriage from spiritual and physical separation, in the name of Jesus.
2. Every serpent in the garden of my marriage, I cut you to pieces, in the name of Jesus.
3. O Lord, deliver my marriage from any problem that is pushing it into separation, in the name of Jesus.
4. O Lord, bring solution to every disagreement in my home, in the name of Jesus.
5. Father Lord, deliver my marriage from costly errors, in the name of Jesus.
6. Any satanic tradition or custom that was observed in my marriage, die with your demons, in the name of Jesus.
7. I close every door that I have opened to the spirit of separation, in the name of Jesus.
8. Any evil personality that is standing between my partner and I, be removed, in the name of Jesus.
9. O Lord, help us to leave our parents and cleave to one another, in the name of Jesus.
10. Let unfriendly friends in my marriage be exposed and disgraced, in the name of Jesus.
11. Any ungodly in-law that is causing problems in my marriage, be frustrated, in the name of Jesus.
12. I withdraw every invitation that I have given to the devil, in the name of Jesus.
13. Any evil personality that is sharing my love for my partner, be disgraced, in the name of Jesus.
14. I withdraw any place that was given to the devil and his agents in my marriage, in the name of Jesus.

15. I cast out every spirit of worldliness and extravagance that is tearing my home apart, in the name of Jesus.

16. I bind and cast out the spirit of criticism from my home, in the name of Jesus.

17. I break and lose my marriage from the grip of unforgiving spirit and hatred, in the name of Jesus.

18. Father Lord, restore Your true love of marriage to my home, in the name of Jesus.

19. Let all lost affections in my marriage be restored, in the name of Jesus.

20. I cast out the spirit of impatience, strife and malice out of my home, in the name of Jesus.

21. Father Lord, deliver my marriage from evil misplacement, in the name of Jesus.

22. Let my family members be positioned according to God's will in my home, in the name of Jesus.

23. Let the spirit of nagging, bitterness and fighting leave my home now, in the name of Jesus.

24. I command the spirit of pride, wickedness and prayerlessness to quit my home, in the name of Jesus.

25. O Lord, fulfill Your purpose of marriage in my home, in the name of Jesus.

26. Let the power of procreation fall upon my marriage, in the name of Jesus.

27. Any seed of polygamy in marriage, die, in the name of Jesus.

28. Any Delilah or Jezebel that has hijacked my marriage, be disgraced, in the name of Jesus.

29. I command any oppression that is going on against my marriage to stop, in the name of Jesus.

30. Let any witch or wizard that has swallowed my marriage vomit it now, in the name of Jesus.

31. Let arrows of separation that was fired at my marriage backfire, in the name of Jesus.

32. Any evil personality that has stolen my love for my partner, release it now, in the name of Jesus.

33. Father Lord, bring my partner and I together again, in the name of Jesus.

34. Any curse, spell or evil seed that is working against my marriage, expire, in the name of Jesus.

35. Blood of Jesus, deliver my marriage from separation, in the name of Jesus.

36. Any evil force that has vowed to separate my marriage, scatter, in the name of Jesus.

37. Every arrow of death and hell that was fired at my marriage, backfire, in the name of Jesus.

38. Any evil priest that is ministering against my marriage, be disgraced, in the name of Jesus.

39. Any evil leg that has walked into my marriage, walk out, in the name of Jesus.

40. Let any evil arrest of my marriage be terminated, in the name of Jesus.

5
Chapter

PRAYERS TO TRIUMPH OVER DIVORCE

CHAPTER OVERVIEW

- *Divorce is forbidden*
- *Christ's teaching on marriage*
- *The pressure is on*
- *Killing the seed of divorce*

DIVORCE IS FORBIDDEN

Divorce has often been the topic of debates across the world. However, we know that the Scripture was clear in its position on divorce. The Scriptures clearly revealed that divorce is not the perfect will of God, therefore, God forbid divorce. This generation needs the intervention of God to save countless marriages from divorce and its devastating effects.

In His sermon on the mount, Jesus preached against divorce.

> *"It hath been said, Whosoever shall put away his wife, let him give her a writing of divorcement: But I say unto you, That whosoever shall put away his wife, saving for the cause of fornication, causeth her to commit adultery: and whosoever shall marry her that is divorced committeth adultery"* (Matthew 5:31-32).

> *"And I say unto you, Whosoever shall put away his wife, except it be for fornication, and shall marry another, committeth adultery: and whoso marrieth her which is put away doth commit adultery"* (Matthew 19:9).

Jesus spoke with authority as one who came to correct misconceptions about the Law of Moses. In those days in Israel, young women were bound by law to remain virgins until marriage, otherwise, they are stoned to death.

> *"They say unto him, Master, this woman was taken in adultery, in the very act. Now Moses in the law commanded us, that such should be stoned: but what sayest thou?"* (John 8:4-5).

> *"And the man that committeth adultery with another man's wife, even he that committeth adultery with his neighbor's wife, the adulterer and the adulteress shall surely be put to death"* (Leviticus 20:10).

> *"If a man be found lying with a woman married to an husband, then they shall both of them die, both the man that lay with the woman, and the woman: so shalt thou put away evil from Israel"* (Deuteronomy 22:22).

Traditionally, after wedding ceremony, young virgins usually accompanied the bride to her husband's house. The man and his bride would go to bed with a piece of cloth received from the father of the bride. If the man finds his bride a virgin, he cleans her blood with the white cloth and hands it to young virgins who waited upon them.

With joy, these virgins would sing and dance until they return to the bride's father and give him the stained cloth as a token of her daughter's virginity. In so doing, the man cannot divorce his wife forever. However, if he divorces her, the father would take the stained cloth to court as evidence. She would remain under the care of the man all her life and he cannot divorce or maltreat her because she is a daughter of Zion.

"When a man hath taken a wife, and married her, and it come to pass that she find no favors in his eyes, because he hath found some uncleanness in her: then let him write her a bill of divorcement, and give it in her hand, and send her out of his house" (Deuteronomy 24:1).

"And if a man entice a maid that is not betrothed, and lie with her, he shall surely endow her to be his wife. If her father utterly refuse to give her unto him, he shall pay money according to the dowry of virgins" (Exodus 22:16, 17).

When a man finds out that his bride is not a virgin, he surrenders her to be stoned to death. However, if he loves the bride that was deflowered, he can retain her as his wife. Nevertheless, he could still divorce her anytime because she committed fornication. That was the case with Mary and Joseph before the angel visited Joseph.

"Now the birth of Jesus Christ was on this wise: When as his mother Mary was espoused to Joseph, before they came together, she was found with child of the Holy Ghost. Then Joseph her husband, being a just man, and not willing to make her a public example, was minded to put her away privily. But while he thought on these things, behold, the angel of the Lord appeared unto him in a dream, saying, Joseph, thou son of David, fear not to take unto thee Mary thy wife: for that which is conceived in her is of the Holy Ghost. And she shall bring forth a son, and thou shalt call his name JESUS: for he shall save his people from their sins. Now all this was done, that it might be fulfilled which was spoken of the Lord by the prophet, saying, Behold, a virgin shall be with child, and shall bring forth a son, and they shall call his name Emmanuel, which being interpreted is, God with us. Then Joseph being raised from sleep did as the angel of the Lord had bidden him, and took unto him his wife" (Matthew 1:18-24).

"For the woman which hath a husband is bound by the law to her husband so long as he liveth; but if the husband be dead, she is loosed from the law of her husband. So then if, while her husband liveth, she be married to another man, she shall be called an adulteress: but if her husband be dead, she is free from that law; so that she is no adulteress, though she be married to another man" (Romans 7:2-3).

Joseph found out that Mary, who was engaged to him, was pregnant. However, Joseph was a just man and was not willing to make the matter public. When he decided to put

Mary away privately, an angel of God intervened. The angel informed Joseph that Mary's conception has nothing to do with sin of fornication.

Until Jesus Christ came to the world, marriage, separation and divorce were highly contested and controversial issues. However, Christ brought clarity to these issues.

CHRIST'S TEACHING ON MARRIAGE

Nicodemus, who was one of the notable Pharisees and highly respected ruler of the Jews, went to meet Jesus at night. He revealed to Jesus what the Pharisees had concluded about Him. He confirmed that the Pharisees knew that Jesus was a teacher that came from God, after seeing all the miracles Jesus did. Therefore, both the friends of Jesus and His enemies believed that He came from God. They also believed that His Words are God's perfect Word for humanity.

> *"There was a man of the Pharisees, named Nicodemus, a ruler of the Jews: The same came to Jesus by night, and said unto him, Rabbi, we know that thou art a teacher come from God: for no man can do these miracles that thou doest, except God be with him"* (John 3:1- 2).

The topic of marriage and divorce was one of the most confusing topics to the Pharisees for hundreds of years. That was why they had to confront Jesus with these important questions on marriage.

> *"But Jesus beheld them, and said unto them, With men this is impossible; but with God all things are possible"* (Matthew 19:26).

Jesus in answering their tempting questions referred them to the beginning when God first instituted marriage. They had referred Jesus to the Laws of Moses concerning marriage and divorce. However, Jesus declared the final answer.

> *"They say unto him, Why did Moses then command to give a writing of divorcement, and to put her away? He saith unto them, Moses because of the hardness of your hearts suffered you to put away your wives: but from the beginning it was not so. And I say unto you, Whosoever shall put away his wife, except it be for fornication, and shall marry another, committeth adultery: and whoso marrieth her which is put away doth commit adultery"* (Matthew 19:7-9).

The way the heart of this generation is hardened is the same way hearts of men were hardened in those days. It is very unfortunate that great ministers of God are altering the true teachings of Christ for selfish gains and interests. That is why many people have come under curses in this age, because they have changed the ancient landmark. The original design for marriage is one man, one wife. Modernists are continuously seeking to remove ancient landmarks and are substitute truth with tolerance and humanism.

> *"And Solomon made all the vessels that pertained unto the house of the LORD: the altar of gold, and the table of gold, whereupon the shewbread was, And the candlesticks of pure gold, five on the right side, and five on the left, before the oracle,*

with the flowers, and the lamps, and the tongs of gold, And the bowls, and the snuffers, and the basons, and the spoons, and the censers of pure gold; and the hinges of gold, both for the doors of the inner house, the most holy place, and for the doors of the house, to wit, of the temple" (1 Kings 7:48-50).

When Solomon built the temple for the LORD, he made vessels and put them in the house of God. He dedicated pure gold, five on the right side and five on the other side before the candlestick. However, when king Shishak of Egypt conquered Jerusalem, he took away all the treasures that Solomon put in the house of God. This prompted the king of Israel, Rehoboam, to make other vessels of his choice and place them at the altar. The only problem was that Rehoboam's vessels were not the original vessels.

"And it came to pass in the fifth year of king Rehoboam, that Shishak king of Egypt came up against Jerusalem: And he took away the treasures of the house of the LORD, and the treasures of the king's house; he even took away all: and he took away all the shields of gold which Solomon had made. And king Rehoboam made in their stead brasen shields, and committed them unto the hands of the chief of the guard, which kept the door of the king's house. And it was so, when the king went into the house of the LORD, that the guard bare them, and brought them back into the guard chamber" (1 Kings 14:25-28).

"Now the Spirit speaketh expressly, that in the latter times some shall depart from the faith, giving heed to seducing spirits, and doctrines of devils" (1 Timothy 4:1).

Likewise, most marriages today are not original as God ordained them to be. In most cases, many people have changed and modernized their marriages to their satisfaction, while disregarding God.

"Remove not the ancient landmark, which thy fathers have set" (Proverbs 22:28).

"Why, seeing times are not hidden from the Almighty, do they that know him not see his days? Some remove the landmarks; they violently take away flocks, and feed thereof" (Job 24:1-2).

God the Father, the Son and the Holy Ghost cannot change or lower His standards on marriage in order to suit the 'modern' men. He is still the same, yesterday, today and forever.

"I marvel that ye are so soon removed from him that called you into the grace of Christ unto another gospel: Which is not another; but there be some that trouble you, and would pervert the gospel of Christ. But though we, or an angel from heaven, preach any other gospel unto you than that, which we have preached unto you, let him be accursed. As we said before, so say I now again, If any man preach any other gospel unto you than that ye have received, let him be accursed" (Galatians 1:6-9).

Christians are encouraged to pursue God's perfect will as revealed through His Word, and not to compromise or lower the standards, regardless of pressures. Let us therefore consider some recorded events or incidences where pressure played a major role.

- In Egypt, the children of Israel complained bitterly concerning their bondage and cried for deliverance. Moses came under pressure that he took an action that changed his life. Moses committed murder while trying to save his fellow Hebrew brother, and this offense drove him into the wilderness for 40 years.

"And it came to pass in those days, when Moses was grown, that he went out unto his brethren, and looked on their burdens: and he spied an Egyptian smiting an Hebrew, one of his brethren. And he looked this way and that way, and when he saw that there was no man, he slew the Egyptian, and hid him in the sand. And when he went out the second day, behold, two men of the Hebrews strove together: and he said to him that did the wrong, Wherefore smitest thou thy fellow? And he said, Who made thee a prince and a judge over us? Intendest thou to kill me, as thou killedst the Egyptian? And Moses feared, and said, Surely this thing is known" (Exodus 2:11-14).

- Moses' wife, Zipporah, prevented Moses from circumcising his son, Geshom, according to God's commandments. This incident nearly cost the life of their son, and Zipporah cursed Moses.

"Then Zipporah took a sharp stone, and cut off the foreskin of her son, and cast it at his feet, and said, Surely a bloody husband art thou to me. So he let him go: then she said, A bloody husband thou art, because of the circumcision" (Exodus 4:25-26).

Because of pressures from the family of Moses, he could not do that which God commanded.

- When Moses went to the mountain to receive the Ten Commandments from God, the children of Israel pressurized Aaron to make a god for them. Surprisingly, Aaron yielded to their demands.

"And when the people saw that Moses delayed to come down out of the mount, the people gathered themselves together unto Aaron, and said unto him, Up, make us gods, which shall go before us; for as for this Moses, the man that brought us up out of the land of Egypt, we wot not what is become of him. And Aaron said unto them, Break off the golden earrings, which are in the ears of your wives, of your sons, and of your daughters, and bring them unto me. And all the people brake off the golden earrings, which were in their ears, and brought them unto Aaron. And he received them at their hand, and fashioned it with a graving tool, after he had made it a molten calf: and they said, These be thy gods, O Israel, which brought thee up out of the land of Egypt. And when Aaron saw it, he built an altar before it; and Aaron made proclamation, and said, Tomorrow is a feast to the LORD. And they rose up early on the morrow, and offered burnt offerings, and brought peace offerings; and the people sat down to eat and to drink, and rose up to play" (Exodus 32:1-6).

- Because of the hardness of their hearts, the children of Israel complained until they displeased God (*See* Numbers 11:1-3). Even when the fire of God burned among them, they cried to Moses instead of crying to God. At other times, they all fell and wept before Moses saying, *"Who shall give us flesh to eat."*

- On one occasion, Miriam and Aaron confronted Moses concerning his marriage (*See* Numbers 12:1-15). They despised his anointing and belittled God in him. Moses came under pressure from people close to him. This incident delayed their journey for seven days.

- Ten spies who went to spy the land of Promise brought back an evil report to the people (*See* Numbers 13:2, 26-33). Their evil report discouraged the people from going ahead to possess the land. In haste, they forgot all the great things God had done for them. The people compared themselves as grasshoppers in the sights of their enemies.

"And Joshua the son of Nun, and Caleb the son of Jephunneh, which were of them that searched the land, rent their clothes: And they spake unto all the company of the children of Israel, saying, The land, which we passed through to search it, is an exceeding good land. If the LORD delight in us, then he will bring us into this land, and give it us; a land which floweth with milk and honey. Only rebel not ye against the LORD, neither fear ye the people of the land; for they are bread for us: their defence is departed from them, and the LORD is with us: fear them not. But all the congregation bade stone them with stones. And the glory of the LORD appeared in the tabernacle of the congregation before all the children of Israel" (Numbers 14:4, 6-10).

In their hardened hearts, they desired to return to Egypt. They murmured against Moses. However, brave Joshua and Caleb sought to restore confidence and encouragement among the people that God would deliver their enemies into their hands. This infuriated all the people that they sought to stone them. Even when the people repented, they were still reluctant and majority of them perished as a result.

> *"And they rose up early in the morning, and gat them up into the top of the mountain, saying, Lo, we be here, and will go up unto the place which the LORD hath promised: for we have sinned. And Moses said, Wherefore now do ye transgress the commandment of the LORD? But it shall not prosper. Go not up, for the LORD is not among you; that ye be not smitten before your enemies. For the Amalekites and the Canaanites are there before you, and ye shall fall by the sword: because ye are turned away from the LORD, therefore the LORD will not be with you. But they presumed to go up unto the hilltop: nevertheless the ark of the covenant of the LORD, and Moses, departed not out of the camp. Then the Amalekites came down, and the Canaanites which dwelt in that hill, and smote them, and discomfited them, even unto Hormah"* (Numbers 14:40-45).

- Moses came under another pressure during the rebellion of Korah, Dathan and Abiram, who envied Moses and sought to wrestle control from him. They accused Moses of being a murderer. Later, the people strove without the Lord, complained for water and influenced Moses to smite the rock instead of speaking to it.

> *"And it came to pass, as he had made an end of speaking all these words, that the ground clave asunder that was under them: And the earth opened her mouth, and swallowed them up, and their houses, and all the men that appertained unto Korah, and all their goods. They, and all that appertained to them, went down alive into the pit, and the earth closed upon them: and they perished from among the congregation. And all Israel that were round about them fled at the cry of them: for they said, Lest the earth swallow us up also. And there came out a fire from the LORD, and consumed the two hundred and fifty men that offered incense"* (Numbers 16:31-35).

The Pharisees inherited their forefathers' hardened and uncircumcised hearts. They confronted Jesus on the issue of marriage and divorce.

> *"The Pharisees also came unto him, tempting him, and saying unto him, Is it lawful for a man to put away his wife for every cause? And he answered and said unto them, Have ye not read, that he which made them at the beginning made them male and female, And said, For this cause shall a man leave father and mother, and shall cleave to his wife: and they twain shall be one flesh? Wherefore they are no more twain, but one flesh. What therefore God hath joined together, let not man put asunder. They say unto him, Why did Moses then command to give a writing of divorcement, and to put her away? He saith unto them, Moses because of the hardness of your hearts suffered you to put away your wives: but from the beginning it was not so. And I say unto you, Whosoever shall put away his wife, except it be for fornication, and shall*

marry another, committeth adultery: and whoso marrieth her which is put away doth commit adultery" (Matthew 19:3-9).

The all-knowing Jesus courageously took the Pharisees back to where marriage began for them to see if they complied with God's law concerning marriage. Christ was not someone they could easily influence with their hardened hearts. He depended on God's Word. He is God. Yet, He entered Mary's womb to be born like every other man. He however started His ministry at the age of thirty. Jesus came at the right time to deliver humanity from hell.

He healed all manner of sicknesses and diseases, and preached the gospel of the kingdom. He healed lepers, cast out demons, opened eyes of blind folks, restored withered hands and fed the hungry. Jesus did nothing that contradicted the Word of God. He did not break any commandment. He attended marriage ceremonies but He did join any man with a second wife. He did not support anyone to marry without the parents' consent. He turned water into wine but His wine was a different type of wine, because after taking His wine, none was reported drunk.

In the wedding Jesus attended, the atmosphere manifested the glory of God. That is how marriages ought to be. Jesus cannot attend any second marriage when the first wife is still alive. However, you can convince your pastor to wed you and your second wife, but you will not receive blessing from Jesus Christ for that marriage.

With hardness of heart, you can also influence your pastor to search for fake power to heal you, but Jesus cannot truly heal you. Famine could drive Abraham out of his place but it would not drive Jesus. Lot chose by sight, but Jesus does not choose by sight. Sarah became impatient and influenced her husband to sleep with her maid, but Jesus cannot make mistakes. Worldly things forced the wife of Lot to look behind, but Jesus cannot look behind. Esau sold his birthright, but Jesus cannot. Onan was not faithful to redeem his brother's name, but Jesus remains faithful.

"And Judah said unto Onan, Go in unto thy brother's wife, and marry her, and raise up seed to thy brother. And Onan knew that the seed should not be his; and it came to pass, when he went in unto his brother's wife, that he spilled it on the ground, lest that he should give seed to his brother" (Genesis 38:8-9).

Samson, Solomon and David made mistakes and women influenced them negatively, but no woman can influence Jesus in a negative way. Do not follow the crowd to break God's commandment. Do not remove the ancient landmarks that God laid and it shall be well with you.

It is unimaginable how much pressure most pastors face. However, pastors and elders of the church should never compromise their faith or lower their standards. Even in a time of flood, when most homes are flooded and yours stands the danger of being flooded, you must take stand. If you do not take any decision now to pray and trust God, evil messengers of divorce may knock at your door.

> *"There were present at that season some that told him of the Galilæans, whose blood Pilate had mingled with their sacrifices. And Jesus answering said unto them, Suppose ye that these Galilæans were sinners above all the Galilæans, because they suffered such things? I tell you, Nay: but, except ye repent, ye shall all likewise perish. Or those eighteen, upon whom the tower in Siloam fell, and slew them, think ye that they were sinners above all men that dwelt in Jerusalem? I tell you, Nay: but, except ye repent, ye shall all likewise perish"* (Luke 13:1-5).

> *"Watch and pray, that ye enter not into temptation: the spirit indeed is willing, but the flesh is weak"* (Matthew 26:41).

Now is the time to be vigilant because the enemy of our souls roams about searching whom to devour. You must watch and pray because the rate of divorce among true believers is quite alarming.

KILLING THE SEED OF DIVORCE

It is the duty of every Christian to uproot the seed of divorce whenever it manifests. Devil sows this seed in people's homes and uses his agents to do the same. He gains foothold into people's marriages by planting diverse evil seeds, which includes divorce.

> *"Submit yourselves therefore to God. Resist the devil, and he will flee from you"* (James 4:7).

> *"Be ye angry, and sin not: let not the sun go down upon your wrath: Neither give place to the devil"* (Ephesians 4:26-27).

That is why the Scriptures admonished us to resist the devil even in our marriage. Usually, what happens when you fail to resist the devil is that he gains a place in your marriage. You cannot underestimate what devil could do with a little foothold in your marriage. A little pride or anger can give the devil a place.

> *"Casting all your care upon him; for he careth for you. Be sober, be vigilant; because your adversary the devil, as a roaring lion, walketh about, seeking whom he may devour: Whom resist steadfast in the faith, knowing that the same afflictions are accomplished in your brethren that are in the world"* (1 Peter 5:7-9).

Without fruits of the Spirit, none would live any peaceful life with his wife or husband. This is because little manifestation of the works of flesh is capable of selling your home to devil.

> *"Now the works of the flesh are manifest, which are these; Adultery, fornication, uncleanness, lasciviousness, Idolatry, witchcraft, hatred, variance, emulations, wrath, strife, seditions, heresies, Envyings, murders, drunkenness, revellings, and such like: of the which I tell you before, as I have also told you in time past, that they which do such things shall not inherit the kingdom of God"* (Galatians 5:19-21).

When you are not born again truthfully, you would likely manifest the works of the flesh.

> *"Now the serpent was more subtil than any beast of the field which the LORD God had made. And he said unto the woman, Yea, hath God said, Ye shall not eat of every tree of the garden? And the woman said unto the serpent, We may eat of the fruit of the trees of the garden: But of the fruit of the tree which is in the midst of the garden, God hath said, Ye shall not eat of it, neither shall ye touch it, lest ye die. And the serpent said unto the woman, Ye shall not surely die: For God doth know that in the day ye eat thereof, then your eyes shall be opened, and ye shall be as gods, knowing*

good and evil. And when the woman saw that the tree was good for food, and that it was pleasant to the eyes, and a tree to be desired to make one wise, she took of the fruit thereof, and did eat, and gave also unto her husband with her; and he did eat" (Genesis 3:1-6).

Eve gave the devil a place in her life and it ruined human race. The same devil still roams about today, seeking whom to devour. He has devoured many families already by engineering divorce, polygamy and many other wicked lifestyles. He uses house helps, relatives, gossip, suspicion, false prophecies and prayerlessness to destroy marriages.

"And he spake a parable unto them to this end, that men ought always to pray, and not to faint; Saying, There was in a city a judge, which feared not God, neither regarded man: And there was a widow in that city; and she came unto him, saying, Avenge me of mine adversary. And he would not for a while: but afterward he said within himself, Though I fear not God, nor regard man; Yet because this widow troubleth me, I will avenge her, lest by her continual coming she weary me. And the Lord said, Hear what the unjust judge saith. And shall not God avenge his own elect, which cry day and night unto him, though he bears long with them? I tell you that he will avenge them speedily. Nevertheless when the Son of man cometh, shall he find faith on the earth?" (Luke 18:1-8).

So many husbands and wives cannot sit together to plan for the future of their families. They do not discuss their challenges, share their burdens or pray over them. A state of prayerlessness can ruin any family and cause an end of any marriage. Many families have needs but they do not tell God about their needs.

Similarly, so many husbands and wives do not fellowship together or present their marriages to God in prayers. The devil uses such avenues to enter into such families and bring divorce. A great challenge lies before every family and when families do not pray together, it becomes impossible to fulfill the purpose of marriage. An unforgiving spirit is another seed of divorce.

"Moreover if thy brother shall trespass against thee, go and tell him his fault between thee and him alone: if he shall hear thee, thou hast gained thy brother. But if he will not hear thee, then take with thee one or two more, that in the mouth of two or three witnesses every word may be established. And if he shall neglect to hear them, tell it unto the church: but if he neglects to hear the church, let him be unto thee as an heathen man and a publican. Verily I say unto you, Whatsoever ye shall bind on earth shall be bound in heaven: and whatsoever ye shall loose on earth shall be loosed in heaven. Again I say unto you, That if two of you shall agree on earth as touching anything that they shall ask, it shall be done for them of my Father, which is in heaven. For where two or three are gathered together in my name, there am I in the

midst of them. Then came Peter to him, and said, Lord, how oft shall my brother sin against me, and I forgive him? Till seven times? Jesus saith unto him, I say not unto thee, Until seven times: but, Until seventy times seven. Therefore is the kingdom of heaven likened unto a certain king, which would take account of his servants. And when he had begun to reckon, one was brought unto him, which owed him ten thousand talents. But forasmuch as he had not to pay, his lord commanded him to be sold, and his wife, and children, and all that he had, and payment to be made. The servant therefore fell down, and worshipped him, saying, Lord, have patience with me, and I will pay thee all. Then the lord of that servant was moved with compassion, and loosed him, and forgave him the debt. But the same servant went out, and found one of his fellow servants, which owed him an hundred pence: and he laid hands on him, and took him by the throat, saying, Pay me that thou owest. And his fellow servant fell down at his feet, and besought him, saying, Have patience with me, and I will pay thee all. And he would not: but went and cast him into prison, till he should pay the debt. So, when his fellow servants saw what was done, they were very sorry, and came and told unto their lord all that was done. Then his lord, after that he had called him, said unto him, O thou wicked servant, I forgave thee all that debt, because thou desiredst me: Shouldest not thou also have had compassion on thy fellow servant, even as I had pity on thee? And his lord was wroth, and delivered him to the tormentors, till he should pay all that was due unto him. So likewise shall my heavenly Father do also unto you, if ye from your hearts forgive not everyone his brother their trespasses" (Matthew 18:15-35).

It is not possible for two persons to live together without one offending the other at one point or another. That is why God made a provision for forgiveness. When your partner offends you, tell your partner his or her fault. Even when he or she refuses to ask for forgiveness, forgive your partner. Recall that Jesus forgave His enemies when they did not ask for forgiveness.

"Then said Jesus, Father, forgive them; for they know not what they do. And they parted his raiment, and cast lots" (Luke 23:34).

Stephen forgave his persecutors.

"When they heard these things, they were cut to the heart, and they gnashed on him with their teeth. But he, being full of the Holy Ghost, looked up steadfastly into heaven, and saw the glory of God, and Jesus standing on the right hand of God, And said, Behold, I see the heavens opened, and the Son of man standing on the right hand of God. Then they cried out with a loud voice, and stopped their ears, and ran upon him with one accord, And cast him out of the city, and stoned him: and the witnesses laid down their clothes at a young man's feet, whose name was Saul. And they stoned Stephen, calling upon God, and saying, Lord Jesus, receive my spirit. And he kneeled

down, and cried with a loud voice, Lord, lay not this sin to their charge. And when he had said this, he fell asleep" (Acts 7:54-60).

David forgave Saul.

"Moreover, my father, see, yea, see the skirt of thy robe in my hand: for in that I cut off the skirt of thy robe, and killed thee not, know thou and see that there is neither evil nor transgression in mine hand, and I have not sinned against thee; yet thou huntest my soul to take it. The LORD judge between me and thee, and the LORD avenge me of thee: but mine hand shall not be upon thee. As saith the proverb of the ancients, Wickedness proceedeth from the wicked: but mine hand shall not be upon thee. After whom is the king of Israel come out? After whom dost thou pursue? After a dead dog, after a flea. The LORD therefore be judge, and judge between me and thee, and see, and plead my cause, and deliver me out of thine hand. And it came to pass, when David had made an end of speaking these words unto Saul, that Saul said, Is this thy voice, my son David? And Saul lifted up his voice, and wept. And he said to David, Thou art more righteous than I: for thou hast rewarded me good, whereas I have rewarded thee evil. And thou hast shewed this day how that thou hast dealt well with me: forasmuch as when the LORD had delivered me into thine hand, thou killedst me not. For if a man find his enemy, will he let him go well away? Wherefore the LORD reward thee good for that thou hast done unto me this day. And now, behold, I know well that thou shalt surely be king, and that the kingdom of Israel shall be established in thine hand. Swear now therefore unto me by the LORD, that thou wilt not cut off my seed after me, and that thou wilt not destroy my name out of my father's house. And David sware unto Saul. And Saul went home; but David and his men gat them up unto the hold" (1 Samuel 24:11-22).

"And David said, Is there yet any that is left of the house of Saul, that I may shew him kindness for Jonathan's sake? And there was of the house of Saul a servant whose name was Ziba. And when they had called him unto David, the king said unto him, Art thou Ziba? And he said, Thy servant is he. And the king said, Is there not yet any of the house of Saul, that I may shew the kindness of God unto him? And Ziba said unto the king, Jonathan hath yet a son, which is lame on his feet. And the king said unto him, Where is he? And Ziba said unto the king, Behold, he is in the house of Machir, the son of Ammiel, in Lo-debar. Then king David sent, and fetched him out of the house of Machir, the son of Ammiel, from Lo-debar. Now when Mephibosheth, the son of Jonathan, the son of Saul, was come unto David, he fell on his face, and did reverence. And David said, Mephibosheth. And he answered, Behold thy servant! And David said unto him, Fear not: for I will surely shew thee kindness for Jonathan thy father's sake, and will restore thee all the land of Saul thy father; and thou shalt eat bread at my table continually. And he bowed himself, and said, What is thy servant, that thou shouldest look upon such a dead dog as I am? Then the king

called to Ziba, Saul's servant, and said unto him, I have given unto thy master's son all that pertained to Saul and to all his house. Thou therefore, and thy sons, and thy servants, shall till the land for him, and thou shalt bring in the fruits, that thy master's son may have food to eat: but Mephibosheth thy master's son shall eat bread always at my table. Now Ziba had fifteen sons and twenty servants. Then said Ziba unto the king, According to all that my lord the king hath commanded his servant, so shall thy servant do. As for Mephibosheth, said the king, he shall eat at my table, as one of the king's sons. And Mephibosheth had a young son, whose name was Micha. And all that dwelt in the house of Ziba were servants unto Mephibosheth. So Mephibosheth dwelt in Jerusalem: for he did eat continually at the king's table; and was lame on both his feet" (2 Samuel 9:1-13).

Joseph forgave his brethren and took care of them.

"Now therefore be not grieved, nor angry with yourselves, that ye sold me hither: for God did send me before you to preserve life. For these two years hath the famine been in the land: and yet there are five years, in the which there shall neither be earring nor harvest. And God sent me before you to preserve you a posterity in the earth, and to save your lives by a great deliverance. So now it was not you that sent me hither, but God: and he hath made me a father to Pharaoh, and lord of all his house, and a ruler throughout all the land of Egypt. Haste ye, and go up to my father, and say unto him, Thus saith thy son Joseph, God hath made me lord of all Egypt: come down unto me, tarry not: And thou shalt dwell in the land of Goshen, and thou shalt be near unto me, thou, and thy children, and thy children's children, and thy flocks, and thy herds, and all that thou hast: And there will I nourish thee; for yet there are five years of famine; lest thou, and thy household, and all that thou hast, come to poverty. And, behold, your eyes see, and the eyes of my brother Benjamin, that it is my mouth that speaketh unto you. And ye shall tell my father of all my glory in Egypt, and of all that ye have seen; and ye shall haste and bring down my father hither. And he fell upon his brother Benjamin's neck, and wept; and Benjamin wept upon his neck. Moreover he kissed all his brethren, and wept upon them: and after that his brethren talked with him" (Genesis 45:5-15).

"And Joseph said unto them, Fear not: for am I in the place of God? But as for you, ye thought evil against me; but God meant it unto good, to bring to pass, as it is this day, to save much people alive. Now therefore fear ye not: I will nourish you, and your little ones. And he comforted them, and spake kindly unto them" (Genesis 50:19-21).

Moses forgave the children of Israel and interceded for them for many times.

"And the LORD said unto Moses, Go, get thee down; for thy people, which thou broughtest out of the land of Egypt, have corrupted themselves: They have turned

aside quickly out of the way which I commanded them: they have made them a molten calf, and have worshipped it, and have sacrificed thereunto, and said, These be thy gods, O Israel, which have brought thee up out of the land of Egypt. And the LORD said unto Moses, I have seen this people, and, behold, it is a stiffnecked people: Now therefore let me alone, that my wrath may wax hot against them, and that I may consume them: and I will make of thee a great nation. And Moses besought the LORD his God, and said, LORD, why doth thy wrath wax hot against thy people, which thou hast brought forth out of the land of Egypt with great power, and with a mighty hand? Wherefore should the Egyptians speak, and say, For mischief did he bring them out, to slay them in the mountains, and to consume them from the face of the earth? Turn from thy fierce wrath, and repent of this evil against thy people. Remember Abraham, Isaac, and Israel, thy servants, to whom thou swarest by thine own self, and saidst unto them, I will multiply your seed as the stars of heaven, and all this land that I have spoken of will I give unto your seed, and they shall inherit it for ever. And the LORD repented of the evil which he thought to do unto his people...
[31]And Moses returned unto the LORD, and said, Oh, this people have sinned a great sin, and have made them gods of gold. [32]Yet now, if thou wilt forgive their sin—; and if not, blot me, I pray thee, out of thy book which thou hast written. [33]And the LORD said unto Moses, Whosoever hath sinned against me, him will I blot out of my book" (Exodus 32:7-14, 31-33).

Having seen these evidences, therefore you have no reason why you should never forgive your wife or husband of any offence. Forgiveness is part of God's commandments in the bible. Refusing to forgive is disobeying God's commandment.

"And when ye stand praying, forgive, if ye have ought against any: that your Father also which is in heaven may forgive you your trespasses. But if ye do not forgive, neither will your Father which is in heaven forgive your trespasses" (Mark 11:25-26).

"But love ye your enemies, and do good, and lend, hoping for nothing again; and your reward shall be great, and ye shall be the children of the Highest: for he is kind unto the unthankful and to the evil. Be ye therefore merciful, as your Father also is merciful. Judge not, and ye shall not be judged: condemn not, and ye shall not be condemned: forgive, and ye shall be forgiven" (Luke 6:35-37).

Unforgiving spirit is a potential evil seed that can cause divorce. When you fail to forgive your partner, you create a gap that another man or woman would readily be willing to fill. When such thing happens, there is lost of affection and love for your family. At that point, any strange man or woman would easily take over your partner, and the result is divorce.

PRAYERS TO TRIUMPH OVER DIVORCE

Bible Reference: Matthew 19:5-6; Romans 2:3; Ephesians 5:28-33

Begin with praise and worship

1. Every seed of divorce in my marriage, I reject you perfectly, in the name of Jesus.
2. I paralyze spiritual and physical enemies that have gathered against my marriage, in the name of Jesus.
3. Any negative movement that is going on against my marriage, be demobilized in shame, in the name of Jesus.
4. Let every enchantment made in order to bring divorce in my marriage be exposed and disgraced, in the name of Jesus.
5. Any evil personality that is behind the idea of divorce in my marriage, loose you brain, in the name of Jesus.
6. Let any evil utterance that is militating against my marriage be silenced forever, in the name of Jesus.
7. Any spirit of death that was programmed into my marriage, I cast you out by force, in the name of Jesus.
8. Let agents of divorce in my marriage be exposed and disgraced, in the name of Jesus.
9. Any power that is frustrating my marriage, die, in the name of Jesus.
10. Every spirit of hatred that is attacking my marriage, I cast you out now, in the name of Jesus.
11. Any power that has displaced the divine love that existed in marriage, restore it and die, in the name of Jesus.
12. Any strange personality that is sitting upon my marriage, I unseat by force, in the name of Jesus.
13. Any evil pressure that has come to destroy my marriage, stop and die, in the name of Jesus.

14. Any door that was opened to the spirit of divorce in my marriage, close forever, in the name of Jesus.

15. Let any damage that has been done in my marriage be repaired by force, in the name of Jesus.

16. I recover double all the grounds that I lost to the spirit of divorce in my marriage, in the name of Jesus.

17. O Lord, expose all evil forces that are gathering against my marriage, in the name of Jesus.

18. Lord Jesus, terminate evil activities that are going on to promote divorce in my marriage, in the name of Jesus.

19. Blood of Jesus, speak death to the voice of divorce in my marriage, in the name of Jesus.

20. I rejected every inherited spirit of divorce in my marriage, in the name of Jesus.

21. Any witch or wizard that has vowed to bring divorce in my marriage, be disgraced, in the name of Jesus.

22. Any evil covenant that is promoting divorce in my marriage, break, in the name of Jesus.

23. Any battle that is going on to bring divorce in my marriage, end to my favor, in the name of Jesus.

24. Let the opponents of my marriage begin to destroy themselves, in the name of Jesus.

25. Every weapon of divorce that is being used against my marriage, become impotent, in the name of Jesus.

26. I convert the mourning that divorce is about to bring into my marriage to dancing and joy, in the name of Jesus.

27. I bind and paralyze the spirit in charge of divorce in my marriage, in the name of Jesus.

28. Let all evil attacks that are going on against my life become impotent sevenfold, in the name of Jesus.

29. Every satanic decree that is standing against my marriage, be revoked immediately, in the name of Jesus.

30. O Lord, block any evil path that my enemies are clearing to bring divorce into my marriage, in the name of Jesus.

31. I receive the mandate to put to flight every enemy of my marriage, in the name of Jesus.

32. Any weakness that exists in the body of my partner or my body, die, in the name of Jesus.

33. Let the strongman of divorce for my marriage die immediately, in the name of Jesus.

34. Any evil seed of divorce that was planted for the sake of my marriage, catch fire and die, in the name of Jesus.

35. O Lord, arise and take my marriage away from the grip of divorce plans, in the name of Jesus.

36. I dismiss and disband thoughts of divorce from my heart and that of my partner, in the name of Jesus.

37. Let the angel of God roll away the stones of divorce from my marriage, in the name of Jesus.

38. Any impossible problem that is influencing divorce in my marriage, die, in the name of Jesus.

39. Blood of Jesus, speak death over the weapon and agents of divorce in my marriage, in the name of Jesus.

40. Lord Jesus, arise and intimidate divorce out of my marriage, in the name of Jesus.

41. Every arrow of hatred, rejection and confusion in my marriage, backfire, in the name of Jesus.

42. Every weapon of criticism, unreasonable behavior, pride, etc., in my marriage, die, in the name of Jesus.

43. O Lord, remove dishonesty, lying, anger and all works of the flesh from my marriage, in the name of Jesus.

44. Every inherited curse of divorce in my marriage, I reject you, die, in the name of Jesus.

45. Every demonic determination to kill my marriage, fail woefully, in the name of Jesus.

46. Let evil boasters that are confronting my marriage be disgraced forever, in the name of Jesus.

47. I withdraw my marriage from the hands of wicked manipulators, in the name of Jesus.

48. Any power that has vowed to chase away my marriage from divine presence, die, in the name of Jesus.

49. O Lord, bring Your perfect peace and love back in my marriage, in the name of Jesus.

50. O Lord, increase Your presence in my marriage by fire, in the name of Jesus.

51. I refuse to cooperate with agents of divorce for my marriage, in the name of Jesus.

52. Let the anointing for marital breakthroughs possess my marriage now, in the name of Jesus.

53. Let any evil sacrifice that was offered for the sake of my marriage expire, in the name of Jesus.

54. You, my marriage, reject divorce plans forever, in the name of Jesus.

55. O Lord, speak Your Word of togetherness and love in my marriage today, in the name of Jesus.

6

Chapter

PRAYERS TO HEAL BROKEN RELATIONSHIP

CHAPTER OVERVIEW

- *The crying of blood*
- *Blood cries against unborn generation*
- *The bloody family*
- *What makes a family bloody?*
- *What is idolatry?*
- *What is a covenant?*
- *Why did God design covenant?*
- *What happens when blood cries out?*

THE CRYING OF BLOOD

In a general sense, relationship is the way in which two or more people or organizations regard and behave toward each other. Whether it is human or organizational relationship, same principles abound. There are things that destroy relationships fast. One of such is the cry of blood in the foundation of a person or an organization.

When there is blood crying out against any person or organization, it is difficult to achieve anything useful in relationship. Crying of blood can empower witches and wizards to fight against people with ease.

> *And Cain talked with Abel his brother: and it came to pass, when they were in the field, that Cain rose up against Abel his brother, and slew him. And the LORD said unto Cain, Where is Abel thy brother? And he said, I know not: Am I my brother's keeper? And he said, What hast thou done? The voice of thy brother's blood crieth unto me from the ground. And now art thou cursed from the earth, which hath opened her mouth to receive thy brother's blood from thy hand; When thou tillest the ground, it shall not henceforth yield unto thee her strength; a fugitive and a vagabond shalt thou be in the earth. And Cain said unto the LORD, My punishment is greater than I can bear. Behold, thou hast driven me out this day from the face of the earth; and from thy face shall I be hid; and I shall be a fugitive and a vagabond in the earth; and it shall come to pass, that every one that findeth me shall slay me"* (Genesis 4:8-14).

When Cain shed the blood of his younger brother, Abel, God cursed his life on earth and he became a fugitive and vagabond. Therefore, his presence scared people away. People got irritated at the sight of Cain. God's presence departed from him. In such case, Cain could do nothing that would make people relate with him any longer because his brother's blood cried against him. The kind of demon that follows a person who shed blood is a chief demon and even legion of demons. People close to murderers do not always know what they pass through because when they shed blood, demons celebrated. That was the case with Cain and Lamech and they complained bitterly.

> *"Behold, thou hast driven me out this day from the face of the earth; and from thy face shall I be hid; and I shall be a fugitive and a vagabond in the earth; and it shall come to pass, that every one that findeth me shall slay me. And Lamech said unto his wives, Adah and Zillah, Hear my voice; ye wives of Lamech, hearken unto my speech: for I have slain a man to my wounding, and a young man to my hurt. If Cain shall be avenged sevenfold, truly Lamech seventy and sevenfold"* (Genesis 4:14, 23-24).

God hates bloodshed and when blood is shed, His presence departs. At other times, demons that influenced murder overwhelm murderers so fast. Whenever blood is shed, it goes to God to lodge complaint against the person that shed it.

> *"And he said, What hast thou done? The voice of thy brother's blood crieth unto me from the ground. And now art thou cursed from the earth, which hath opened her mouth to receive thy brother's blood from thy hand"* (Genesis 4:10-11).

The cry of innocent blood has no limit of space or time. It can cry against a generation forever and ever.

> *"And it came to pass, when Ahab heard that Naboth was dead, that Ahab rose up to go down to the vineyard of Naboth the Jezreelite, to take possession of it. And the word of the LORD came to Elijah the Tishbite, saying, Arise, go down to meet Ahab king of Israel, which is in Samaria: behold, he is in the vineyard of Naboth, whither he is gone down to possess it. And thou shalt speak unto him, saying, Thus saith the LORD, Hast thou killed, and also taken possession? And thou shalt speak unto him, saying, Thus saith the LORD, In the place where dogs licked the blood of Naboth shall dogs lick thy blood, even thine. And Ahab said to Elijah, Hast thou found me, O mine enemy? And he answered, I have found thee: because thou hast sold thyself to work evil in the sight of the LORD. Behold, I will bring evil upon thee, and will take away thy posterity, and will cut off from Ahab him that pisseth against the wall, and him that is shut up and left in Israel, And will make thine house like the house of Jeroboam the son of Nebat, and like the house of Baasha the son of Ahijah, for the provocation wherewith thou hast provoked me to anger, and made Israel to sin. And of Jezebel also spake the LORD, saying, The dogs shall eat Jezebel by the wall of Jezreel. Him that dieth of Ahab in the city the dogs shall eat; and him that dieth in the field shall the fowls of the air eat"* (1 Kings 21:16-24).

When the family of Ahab shed the blood of Naboth, it was as if nothing happened. Jezebel informed her husband, Ahab, to go and take possession of Naboth's vineyard. However, as he entered the land, he met prophet Elijah, who confronted him saying, *'Hast thou killed, and also taken possession? In the place where dogs licked the blood of Naboth, shall dogs lick thy blood.'*

It was an open confrontation and release of multiple curses on Ahab and his household. These curses put Ahab's entire household into generational bondage. The blood of Naboth cried against the family of Ahab until God avenged. We know that Ahab later regretted the murder of Naboth and humbled himself before God.

> *"But there was none like unto Ahab, which did sell himself to work wickedness in the sight of the LORD, whom Jezebel his wife stirred up. And he did very abominably in following idols, according to all things as did the Amorites, whom the LORD cast out before the children of Israel. And it came to pass, when Ahab heard those words, that he rent his clothes, and put sackcloth upon his flesh, and fasted, and lay in sackcloth, and went softly. And the word of the LORD came to Elijah the Tishbite, saying, Seest thou how Ahab humbleth himself before me? Because he humbleth himself before me,*

I will not bring the evil in his days: but in his son's days will I bring the evil upon his house" (1 Kings 21:25-29).

Because of Ahab's prayers, the family enjoyed peace for a few more years. The point is that God heard Ahab's prayer. Therefore, if you are coming from a family that shed innocent blood, you can repent as Ahab did and separate yourself from your family's bondage. Otherwise, you suffer the consequence of your family's evil deed.

"And they continued three years without war between Syria and Israel" (1 Kings 22:1).

"And when Jehu was come to Jezreel, Jezebel heard of it; *and she painted her face, and tired her head, and looked out at a window. And as Jehu entered in at the gate, she said,* Had *Zimri peace, who slew his master? And he lifted up his face to the window, and said, Who is on my side? Who? And there looked out to him two* or *three eunuchs. And he said, Throw her down. So they threw her down: and* some *of her blood was sprinkled on the wall, and on the horses: and he trode her under foot. And when he was come in, he did eat and drink, and said, Go, see now this cursed* woman, *and bury her: for she* is *a king's daughter. And they went to bury her: but they found no more of her than the skull, and the feet, and the palms of* her *hands. Wherefore they came again, and told him. And he said, This* is *the word of the LORD, which he spake by his servant Elijah the Tishbite, saying, In the portion of Jezreel shall dogs eat the flesh of Jezebel: And the carcass of Jezebel shall be as dung upon the face of the field in the portion of Jezreel;* so that *they shall not say, This* is *Jezebel"* (2 Kings 9:30-37).

"And it came to pass, when the letter came to them, that they took the king's sons, and slew seventy persons, and put their heads in baskets, and sent him them to Jezreel" (2 Kings 10:7).

It is very difficult to be successful in relating with other people when blood is crying against you or your family. You will not prevail in any business or work. If you do not handle the issue of blood crying against you, you will continue to suffer. Even true believers whose families shed innocent blood need to do something to be free.

"Then there was a famine in the days of David three years, year after year; and David enquired of the LORD. And the LORD answered, It is for Saul, and for his bloody house, because he slew the Gibeonites. And the king called the Gibeonites, and said unto them; (now the Gibeonites were not of the children of Israel, but of the remnant of the Amorites; and the children of Israel had sworn unto them: and Saul sought to slay them in his zeal to the children of Israel and Judah.) Wherefore David said unto the Gibeonites, What shall I do for you? And wherewith shall I make the atonement, that ye may bless the inheritance of the LORD?" (2 Samuel 21:1-3).

In the days of David, the entire nation of Israel, including David, suffered for three years because blood cried against them. Though David was not guilty of the crime, however, as soon as he ascended the throne, Israel experienced severe famine for three years. He could not trace the cause of their suffering until after three years.

For three solid years, the whole nation of Israel experienced dire suffering and hardship. It was at the third year that David went into serious prayers of enquiry. Then the Lord revealed the cause of the famine. Had David prayed earlier, the famine would have not lasted for three years. If he did not pray at all, the famine would have continued for more years.

The lesson here is that blood can also cry against good Christians. There may be things you need to do to free yourself to enjoy successful relationship. Without allowing God to reveal such things to you, you may remain miserable and unable to marry even when you have the assurance of heaven and salvation.

This same thing happened to David and the nation of Israel. If the blood of an uncircumcised Gideonite could hold a whole nation to ransom, then your family, city, etc., could not be better or more precious than the nation of Israel. If God could not spare David and the children of Israel, then God will surely hold you or your family accountable for any shed blood. However, the good news was that immediately David prayed, God answered and revealed the cause of the famine to him.

One may wonder why David did not pray until after three years. Actually, David prayed but he did not pray the right prayers. In your own case, could it be that you have been praying wrong prayers? However, when David prayed the right prayers, God heard him. Likewise, when you pray the right prayers God will hear you.

THE BLOODY FAMILY

Saul and his family killed the Gibeonites and the whole nation of Israel would later suffer the consequence for three years, including David and his family. Who were the Gibeonites? The Gibeonites deceitfully made a covenant of peace with Israel. However, when the children of Israel discovered their deceit, it was too late.

> *"And Joshua made peace with them, and made a league with them, to let them live: and the princes of the congregation sware unto them. And Joshua called for them, and he spake unto them, saying, Wherefore have ye beguiled us, saying, We are very far from you; when ye dwell among us? Now therefore ye are cursed, and there shall none of you be freed from being bondmen, and hewers of wood and drawers of water for the house of my God. And Joshua made them that day hewers of wood and drawers of water for the congregation, and for the altar of the LORD, even unto this day, in the place which he should choose"* (Joshua 9:15, 22, 23, 27).

The Gibeonites tricked Joshua to enter into covenant of peace with them. He made the princes of the congregation to swear to the Gibeonites. Later, when Joshua found out the truth, he cursed the Gibeonites because of their unfaithfulness.

Many years later, Saul broke that covenant by destroying the Gibeonites and it affected the whole nation of Israel. It could be possible that you are not the cause of your present suffering and repeated failures in relationships. Nevertheless, it is your responsibility to pray and inquire of the Lord for the sake of your deliverance.

> *"Our fathers have sinned, and are not; and we have borne their iniquities. Servants have ruled over us: there is none that doth deliver us out of their hand. We gat our bread with the peril of our lives because of the sword of the wilderness. Our skin was black like an oven because of the terrible famine. They ravished the women in Zion, and the maids in the cities of Judah. Princes are hanged up by their hand: the faces of elders were not honored. They took the young men to grind, and the children fell under the wood. The elders have ceased from the gate, the young men from their music. The joy of our heart is ceased; our dance is turned into mourning. The crown is fallen from our head: woe unto us that we have sinned! For this our heart is faint; for these things our eyes are dim"* (Lamentation 5:7-17).

Proverbs 26:2 reveals that *"The curse causeless shall not come."* Therefore, there must be a reason for whatever that is going on in your life. If your family were bloody, then you would suffer failures in relationships.

WHAT MAKES A FAMILY BLOODY?

- When a member of the family sheds blood, the family becomes bloody
- When a member of the family commits abortion, the family becomes bloody
- When a member of the family performs blood or animal sacrifice, the family becomes bloody
- When a member of the family offers blood sacrifice to any idol, the family becomes bloody

> *"And God spake all these words, saying, [2]I am the LORD thy God, which have brought thee out of the land of Egypt, out of the house of bondage. Thou shalt have no other gods before me. Thou shalt not make unto thee any graven image, or any likeness of any thing that is in heaven above, or that is in the earth beneath, or that is in the water under the earth: Thou shalt not bow down thyself to them, nor serve them: for I the LORD thy God am a jealous God, visiting the iniquity of the fathers upon the children unto the third and fourth generation of them that hate me"*(Exodus 20:1-5).

Idolatry separates man from God. It destroys relationships quickly. Family's ancestors can severe relationship between their unborn children and God through idolatry.

WHAT IS IDOLATRY?

- Idolatry is bowing down to images
- It is sacrificing to other gods
- It is fearing other gods
- It is worshipping other gods
- It is trying to worship God through an image
- It is sacrificing to images
- It is swearing by other gods
- It is walking after other gods
- It is looking up to other gods
- It is serving other gods with your resources
- It is worshipping angels
- It is worshipping the hosts of heaven
- It is worshipping devil
- It is setting up of idols in your heart
- It is worshipping of dead people
- It is covetousness and sensuality
- It is worshipping symbols instead of God

> *"Therefore the people came to Moses, and said, We have sinned, for we have spoken against the LORD, and against thee; pray unto the LORD, that he take away the serpents from us. And Moses prayed for the people. And the LORD said unto Moses, Make thee a fiery serpent, and set it upon a pole: and it shall come to pass, that every one that is bitten, when he looketh upon it, shall live. And Moses made a serpent of brass, and put it upon a pole, and it came to pass, that if a serpent had bitten any man, when he beheld the serpent of brass, he lived"* (Numbers 21:7-9).

While most Africans and Asians worship idols in the above-mentioned ways, westerners worship idols through the following ways:

1. Possession -Matthew 6:19-21, 24-33
2. Plenty -Luke 12:15-21, Colossians 3:5
3. Pride -Acts 12:30-23, 2 Timothy 3:1-2
4. People -Matthew 10:37, John 9:18-23, 5:44

5. Pleasure - 2 Timothy 3:1-2, 1 John 2:15-17

If you are serious about restoring lost relationships, then deal with issues of idolatry and blood crying in your bloodline. These two things bring curses upon people. These curses ruin people's chances to enjoy successful relationships. They also keep people out of God's presence and from the reach of their divine helpers. If you fail to overcome these two things, you could remain a victim, even as a true Christian.

WHAT IS A COVENANT?

- A covenant is a mutual understanding between two or more parties, each binding itself to fulfill specific obligations.
- It is also a legal contract.
- It is a binding agreement to do or not to do specified things.

WHY DID GOD DESIGN COVENANT?

- God designed covenant to establish friendship (*See* 1 Samuel 18:3).
- To establish basis for mutual protection and benefit (*See* Genesis 26:28-29).
- To guarantee alliance or assistance in time of war (*See* 1 Kings 15:18).

A fact about covenant is that as soon as it is confirmed, it becomes unutterable or irrevocable.

> *"And I will put enmity between thee and the woman, and between thy seed and her seed; it shall bruise thy head, and thou shalt bruise his heel"* (Genesis 3:15).

In a covenant, legal representative represents self, the people and the children (born and unborn) from generation to generation. Unless you break such covenants publicly or with the other party, you remain bound and suffer consequences, even when you are a true Christian.

Christian life qualifies you to resist devil through the help of Jesus Christ. That is why James admonished that we must resist the devil for him to flee. Likewise, Paul likened Christian life to fighting a warfare and wrestling.

> *"For we wrestle not against flesh and blood, but against principalities, against powers, against the rulers of the darkness of this world, against spiritual wickedness in high places"* (Ephesians 6:12).

> *"Fight the good fight of faith, lay hold on eternal life, where unto thou art also called, and hast professed a good profession before many witnesses"* (1 Timothy 6:12).

> *"For though we walk in the flesh, we do not war after the flesh:(For the weapons of our warfare are not carnal, but mighty through God to the pulling down of strong holds;) Casting down imaginations, and every high thing that exalteth itself against*

the knowledge of God, and bringing into captivity every thought to the obedience of Christ" (2 Corinthians 10:3-5).

If you refuse to fight or wrestle, some old things would not leave on their own. Covenant is an irrevocable commitment that you must confront and break. That was what David did when the blood of Abner was approached his throne to cause a personal and national disaster.

"And afterward when David heard it, he said, I and my kingdom are guiltless before the LORD for ever from the blood of Abner the son of Ner: Let it rest on the head of Joab, and on all his father's house; and let there not fail from the house of Joab one that hath an issue, or that is a leper, or that leaneth on a staff, or that falleth on the sword, or that lacketh bread" (2 Samuel 3:28- 29).

The most effective type of covenant is blood covenant. For instance, a person that broke a lady's virginity entered into blood covenant with the lady, which she must break at all cost. Also abortion is a blood covenant whether legalized or not by the state. The blood shed through abortions could cry against nations and destroy nation's relationship with other nations. It can cry against an individual, family or entire nation. Evil covenants or curses can cause various misfortunes. Idolatry and bloodshed are very disastrous.

- When blood cries, relationships cannot last or yield lasting fruits.
- Hatred and rejection appear in the middle of relationships to abort such relationships.
- Victims are rejected easily, hated and abandoned without convincing reasons.
- Relationships are manipulated or bewitched by satanic agents.
- The character of victims changes for worse and they behave abnormally, even to their own surprise and hurt.
- Hard work cannot yield good result.
- Good relationships cannot last.
- People engage and disengage quickly.
- Marriages suffer divorces and separation.
- Enemies manipulate and control people's relationships.
- Peace disappears and strife abounds.
- Divine helpers disappear and evil helpers dictate extreme conditions to render help.
- People suffer premature deaths.
- People achieve nothing in their lifetimes.
- More people marry late, and others marry wrong person.
- More people end their lives depressed and consider suicide.

THE BEST WAY OUT

- Repent truly and fervently.
- Determine to fight your battle and ask the Holy Spirit to assist you.
- Break all evil covenants and curses from their roots.
- Silence the crying of blood in your foundation.
- Appropriate and invoke the blood of Jesus.

- Withdraw yourself from any bondage.
- Have faith in God.
- Live a holy life
- Endeavour to be baptized with the Holy Spirit with the evidence of speaking in tongues.

PRAYERS TO HEAL BROKEN RELATIONSHIP

Bible References: Matthew 1:18-25, John 15:1-2

Begin with praise and worship

1. Father Lord, deliver me from the woes of evil relationships, in the name of Jesus.
2. Any evil personality that is standing between my creator and I, be frustrated, in the name of Jesus.
3. Any power that wants to take the place of Christ in my life, I disengage you, in the name of Jesus.
4. I destroy any evil design to keep me out of good relationships, in the name of Jesus.
5. Let envy and rivalries that exist in my relationships be exposed and disgraced, in the name of Jesus.
6. I break and lose myself from evil dedication that is frustrating my relationships, in the name of Jesus.
7. O Lord, arise and empower me to keep good relationships, in the name of Jesus.
8. Any evil covenant that is frustrating my relationships, break, in the name of Jesus.
9. Father Lord, deliver me from parental curses that are affecting my relationships, in the name of Jesus.
10. I destroy family idols that are waging war against my relationships, in the name of Jesus.
11. I cast out demons that are militating against my relationship, in the name of Jesus.
12. I terminate any fellowship with evil spirits, in the name of Jesus.
13. I deliver myself from inherited bondage of evil relationship, in the name of Jesus.
14. Blood of Jesus, flow into my foundation and deliver me from troubles, in the name of Jesus.
15. Blood of Jesus, flush out evil characters in my life, in the name of Jesus.
16. I destroy evil traits that are scaring good people away from me, in the name of Jesus.

17. Let problems that transferred into my life to destroyed my chances to enjoy good relationships catch fire, in the name of Jesus.

18. Blood of Jesus, cleanse my life from failures of my parents, in the name of Jesus.

19. I cast out spirit of death that is ruining my chances of good relationship with people, in the name of Jesus.

20. I discard any false information that is designed to destroy my relationship, in the name of Jesus.

21. Every satanic monitoring gadget that is fashioned to destroy my relationship, catch fire, in the name of Jesus.

22. Any evil utterance that was spoken over my relationships, expire, in the name of Jesus.

23. Let resurrection power of Jesus quicken my relationships, in the name of Jesus.

24. I recover every good thing that I have lost in my relationship, in the name of Jesus.

25. I expose strangers that are attacking my successes in relationship, in the name of Jesus.

26. I uproot evil imaginations that are targeting my relationships, in the name of Jesus.

27. Let every destructive plans of my enemies to keep me out of relationships expire, in the name of Jesus.

28. I erase and disband evil information from the heart of my helpers, in the name of Jesus.

29. I cast out the spirit of fear, doubt, and discouragement in my heart, in the name of Jesus.

30. I cancel all ungodly and false information that was gathered against me, in the name of Jesus.

31. Let angels of God restore good relationships that I have lost, in the name of Jesus.

32. I refuse to break my relationship with my divine helpers, in the name of Jesus.

33. O Lord, heal broken relationships that you have designed to help me, in the name of Jesus.

34. Any evil record that was designed to terminate my relationships, catch fire, in the name of Jesus.

35. Any strongman that is standing against my success in relationships, die, in the name of Jesus.

36. I bind and cast out demons that are promoting disagreements in my life, in the name of Jesus.

37. I close every doorway of the enemy into my relationships, in the name of Jesus.

38. I vomit spiritual parasites that are eating deep into my relationship, vomit it now, in the name of Jesus.

39. I break demonic padlocks that were used to lock up my relationship, in the name of Jesus.

40. Let demonic eyes that are monitoring my relationship go blind, in the name of Jesus.

41. Any evil leg that has walked into my relationship, walk out now, in the name of Jesus.

42. O Lord, reactivate my lost relationship opportunities, in the name of Jesus.

43. Let any evil plantation that is growing in my relationship die by fire, in the name of Jesus.

44. Lord Jesus, grant my success in relationships, in the name of Jesus.

45. Any devourer that is eating up my success in relationships, die, in the name of Jesus.

46. Any blood sacrifice that is crying against my relationships, expire, in the name of Jesus.

47. I silence evil voices that are speaking against my relationships, in the name of Jesus.

48. Let any strange personality that has vowed to stand on my way die, in the name of Jesus.

49. I destroy strange behaviors and curses in my relationships, in the name of Jesus.

50. O Lord, arise and heal every wound my relationship has suffered, in the name of Jesus.

7

Chapter

PRAYERS TO PRAY DURING COURTSHIP

CHAPTER OVERVIEW

- *Time for courtship*
- *Put God first in your courtship*
- *Unprofitable courtship*
- *Profitable courtship*
- *Correcting mistakes during courtship*

TIME FOR COURTSHIP

Courtship is a period during which couples develop a romantic relationship, especially with a view to marriage. In order words, courtship is a process leads a man and woman to marriage. During this time, intending couples come together to know each other well. They find out if they are compatible, and as well find out God's plan for them. It is a time to check if the love they claim to have would stand the test of time without offending God or breaking His Word. If they involve and honor God truly, He would sustain their love for each other.

> *"A friend loveth at all times, and a brother is born for adversity"* (Proverbs 17:17).

> *"Two are better than one; because they have a good reward for their labor. For if they fall, the one will lift up his fellow: but woe to him that is alone when he falleth; for he hath not another to help him up"* (Ecclesiastes 4:9-10).

> *"And Hiram king of Tyre sent his servants unto Solomon; for he had heard that they had anointed him king in the room of his father: for Hiram was ever a lover of David"* (1 Kings 5:1).

> *"I had no rest in my spirit, because I found not Titus my brother: but taking my leave of them, I went from thence into Macedonia"* (2 Corinthians 2:13).

> *"Henceforth I call you not servants; for the servant knoweth not what his lord doeth: but I have called you friends; for all things that I have heard of my Father I have made known unto you"* (John 15:15).

During courtship, problems and disagreements may arise, but people that make God their bedrock will surely overcome. Godly people disagree in order to agree again. They cannot be weak at the same time. With supernatural strength, they can surmount every challenge. No matter what happens between godly people who are in courtship, they is always solution. This is because God is the source of their love for each other. Because they put God first in everything they do, they will surely stand the test of time.

PUT GOD FIRST IN YOUR COURTSHIP

In every Christian courtship, the love for God supersedes every other love including the love the man has for the woman and vice versa. However, when the love the man has for the woman or vice versa surpasses the love they have for God, devil takes advantage and enthrones himself in their relationship while pushing God aside. That is why it is important that Christians in courtship engage in discussions, plans and other things that are pure and of good conscience.

> *"Now the end of the commandment is charity out of a pure heart, and of a good conscience, and of faith unfeigned... Now unto the King eternal, immortal, invisible, the only wise God, be honor and glory forever and ever. Amen. This charge I commit unto thee, son Timothy, according to the prophecies which went before on thee, that thou by them mightest war a good warfare; Holding faith, and a good conscience; which some having put away concerning faith have made shipwreck"* (1 Timothy 1:5, 17-19).

Christians in courtship must realize their need to uphold and honor their relationship with God in their quest to get married. They must not put away their faith in Christ in order to satisfy their carnal desires.

> *"But thou, O man of God, flee these things; and follow after righteousness, godliness, faith, love, patience, meekness. Fight the good fight of faith, lay hold on eternal life, where unto thou art also called, and hast professed a good profession before many witnesses. I give thee charge in the sight of God, who quickeneth all things, and before Christ Jesus, who before Pontius Pilate witnessed a good confession; That thou keep this commandment without spot, unrebukeable, until the appearing of our Lord Jesus Christ... O Timothy, keep that which is committed to thy trust, avoiding profane and vain babblings, and oppositions of science falsely so called: Which some professing have erred concerning the faith. Grace be with thee. Amen. The first to Timothy was written from Laodicea, which is the chiefest city of Phrygia Pacatiana"* (1 Timothy 6:11-14, 20-21).

Courtship is not a time to satisfy your carnal lusts. Rather, it is a time to flee from anything that displeased God in order to pursue righteousness, faith, godliness, etc. Therefore, when you lose your faith during courtship, the devil earns a place in the real marriage. However, when you maintain a genuine love for God during your courtship, God would be glorified in your marriage. If you have true love, you would fear God that you would not want to break His law during courtship.

> *"Love worketh no ill to his neighbor: therefore love is the fulfilling of the law"* (Romans 13:10).

"Whether therefore ye eat, or drink, or whatsoever ye do, do all to the glory of God" (1 Corinthians 10:31).

"He that is soon angry dealeth foolishly: and a man of wicked devices is hated" (Proverbs 14:17).

During courtship, most people determine in their hearts to have carnal relationship with their partner at all cost. Unwise people in courtship put pressures on themselves to have sex. Usually, turning down such pressure gets such unwise people angry. Nevertheless, it is better for you to break such relationship at that point than to compromise and live the rest of your life in regrets.

So many problems in most families today are results of selling their birthrights to devil in the name of love. Having sex during courtship gives birth to innumerable problems in marriages. Divine love of God that is enjoyed in marriages disappears whenever people in courtship have sex before their marriage. It is necessary to get together and plan, or even travel together during courtship. However, whatever you do so, do them to the glory of God.

It would be foolish to do something that could only give you satisfaction for a short period during courtship and then keep you in sorrow for the rest of your life. The devil knows how to encourage you to fall out of grace, but you have to resist him. You must consider God in every action you take during your courtship. Courtship is the foundation or pillar that holds every marriage. Therefore, if the foundation is weak, the marriage itself would have problems. Nevertheless, many people fail during the courtship stage.

"For other foundation can no man lay than that is laid, which is Jesus Christ. Now if any man build upon this foundation gold, silver, precious stones, wood, hay, stubble; Every man's work shall be made manifest: for the day shall declare it, because it shall be revealed by fire; and the fire shall try every man's work of what sort it is. If any man's work abide which he hath built thereupon, he shall receive a reward. If any man's work shall be burned, he shall suffer loss: but he himself shall be saved; yet so as by fire" (1 Corinthians 3:11-15).

Some actions you take during courtship are capable of introducing serpent, strange fires and other evil forces into the foundation of your marriage. When you give devil a place in your courtship, he comes in with all manner of problems. In most cases, devil makes a woman to hate the husband and love other men outside her home. At other times, he causes the love the man had for his wife to expire just at the point of their real marriage. For some people, their love may last for a while before it finally expires. That is why many families are suffering today.

Most couples live together physically but spiritually they are divorced. Devil could get at such couples through criticism, lack of affection, failure to leave and cleave, abdication of duties, childlessness and other problems, which lead most people into polygamy or separation. Many married people who claimed to be Christians are having many problems today because they refused to deal with their past.

Strange wives and husbands torment others in their dreams. Others have separated, remarried and yet there is no peace in sight. Some have succeeded in their careers but remained empty in their marital lives. Others face divorce threats, terrible marriage instabilities, frustrations, rebellious children and waste of health. They experience difficulties, lusts for other men or women. The list is endless.

Victims of troubled marriages experience denial of sex from their partners, feigned love from their partners, barrenness and mysterious miscarriages, or consistent complications during delivery. I want to tell you this truth today; sins you committed during courtship could be the reason for reoccurring failures and problems you face in your marriage. In addition, inadequate repentance has made it impossible for many to receive deliverance from God. Therefore, today is another day of grace. Repent and be saved.

> *"And Samuel spake unto all the house of Israel, saying, If ye do return unto the LORD with all your hearts, then put away the strange gods and Ashtaroth from among you, and prepare your hearts unto the LORD, and serve him only: and he will deliver you out of the hand of the Philistines. Then the children of Israel did put away Baalim and Ashtaroth, and served the LORD only"* (1 Samuel 7:3-4).

If people could repent truthfully and faithfully, deliverance would be easy. Instead of blaming God, blame yourself. It is not possible for God to make mistakes. Examine your past and amend your ways. Do not allow your past to destroy your present and future.

UNPROFITABLE COURTSHIP

When you ignore God and reject His counsels during your courtship, He cannot attend your wedding no matter the amount or quality of crowd you are able to attract on your wedding day.

> *"Because I have called, and ye refused; I have stretched out my hand, and no man regarded; But ye have set at nought all my counsel, and would none of my reproof: I also will laugh at your calamity; I will mock when your fear cometh; When your fear cometh as desolation, and your destruction cometh as a whirlwind; when distress and anguish cometh upon you. Then shall they call upon me, but I will not answer; they shall seek me early, but they shall not find me: For that they hated knowledge, and did not choose the fear of the LORD: They would none of my counsel: they despised all my reproof. Therefore shall they eat of the fruit of their own way, and be filled with their own devices. For the turning away of the simple shall slay them, and the prosperity of fools shall destroy them"* (Proverbs 1:24-32).

The most important time to bring God into your marriage is during your courtship. Once you allow God to lay the foundation of your marriage, you have achieved a lot already. When God builds the foundation of your marriage during your courtship, no power can overcome your marriage.

> *"Therefore whosoever heareth these sayings of mine, and doeth them, I will liken him unto a wise man, which built his house upon a rock: And the rain descended, and the floods came, and the winds blew, and beat upon that house; and it fell not: for it was founded upon a rock. And every one that heareth these sayings of mine, and doeth them not, shall be likened unto a foolish man, which built his house upon the sand: And the rain descended, and the floods came, and the winds blew, and beat upon that house; and it fell: and great was the fall of it"* (Matthew 7: 24-27).

A wise builder takes time to build. He builds with good materials and at the right place. A good builder builds upon the rock.

> *"And it came to pass afterward, that he loved a woman in the valley of Sorek, whose name was Delilah. And the lords of the Philistines came up unto her, and said unto her, Entice him, and see wherein his great strength lieth, and by what means we may prevail against him, that we may bind him to afflict him: and we will give thee every one of us eleven hundred pieces of silver.... And she made him sleep upon her knees; and she called for a man, and she caused him to shave off the seven locks of his head; and she began to afflict him, and his strength went from him. And she said, The Philistines be upon thee, Samson. And he awoke out of his sleep, and said, I will go*

out as at other times before, and shake myself. And he wist not that the LORD was departed from him" (Judges 16:4-5, 19-20).

"For she hath cast down many wounded: yea, many strong men have been slain by her. Her house is the way to hell, going down to the chambers of death" (Proverbs 7:26- 27).

When you give God His rightful place from the beginning of the relationship, He determines the right path for the marriage to His glory. The reason many Christians fail in marriage today is that they do not learn enough about marriage before going into it. Thus, inevitable challenges that take place in marriage take them unawares.

"Now the priest of Midian had seven daughters: and they came and drew water, and filled the troughs to water their father's flock. And the shepherds came and drove them away: but Moses stood up and helped them, and watered their flock. And when they came to Reuel their father, he said, How is it that ye are come so soon to day? And they said, An Egyptian delivered us out of the hand of the shepherds, and also drew water enough for us, and watered the flock. And he said unto his daughters, And where is he? Why is it that ye have left the man? Call him, that he may eat bread. And Moses was content to dwell with the man: and he gave Moses Zipporah his daughter" (Exodus 2:16-21).

"And it came to pass by the way in the inn, that the LORD met him, and sought to kill him. Then Zipporah took a sharp stone, and cut off the foreskin of her son, and cast it at his feet, and said, Surely a bloody husband art thou to me. So he let him go: then she said, A bloody husband thou art, because of the circumcision" (Exodus 4: 24-26).

Unpreparedness and God's absence are able to kill the joy, peace and rest of any marriage. People who think they are very experienced and knowledgeable are often ignorant about marriage and how it works. In the case of Solomon, women messed him up with all his wisdom through his ludicrous marriages.

"But king Solomon loved many strange women, together with the daughter of Pharaoh, women of the Moabites, Ammonites, Edomites, Zidonians, and Hittites; Of the nations concerning which the LORD said unto the children of Israel, Ye shall not go in to them, neither shall they come in unto you: for surely they will turn away your heart after their gods: Solomon clave unto these in love. And he had seven hundred wives, princesses, and three hundred concubines: and his wives turned away his heart" (1 Kings 11:1-3).

"Moreover the Nethinims dwelt in Ophel, unto the place over against the water gate toward the east, and the tower that lieth out" (Nehemiah 3:26).

The truth is, if Solomon, with all his wisdom, could fail in marriage, then we all need God in our relationships. You must ensure that you invite God in your courtship. Most problems in the world today have their roots in failed marriages and families. The absence of God in our courtships, marriages and families reflect in our nations.

> *"For which of you, intending to build a tower, sitteth not down first, and counteth the cost, whether he have sufficient to finish it? Lest haply, after he hath laid the foundation, and is not able to finish it, all that behold it begin to mock him, Saying, This man began to build, and was not able to finish"* (Luke 14:28-30).

Marriage is not something one must rush into. It is not an opportunity to satisfy the flesh and despise God's Word. People who are intending to marry must sit down to think and plan how to lay the foundation of their marriage. It is good to know your partner very well. It is wrong to disobey God's Word because you want to please your partner. While it is good to start a relationship, enter into courtship and plan for your marriage, if God is not involved in your plans, you would not receive His blessing.

The foundation of so many marriages today is unclean. That is why devil is mocking these marriages. The reason we hear of so much troubles in many families today is that unwise couples despise the presence of God in their families. Therefore, strive to live a matured Christian life in your courtship. You need to discipline yourself. Nurture good temperament. Cultivate the spirit of self-denial and selflessness. If you want to enjoy a good Christian marriage, it has to be on God's terms.

> *"Thus saith the LORD, Stand ye in the ways, and see, and ask for the old paths, where is the good way, and walk therein, and ye shall find rest for your souls. But they said, We will not walk therein"* (Jeremiah 6:16).

As a Christian, you must conduct your marriage in a Christian way.

> *"Know ye not that they which run in a race run all, but one receiveth the prize? So run, that ye may obtain.... And every man that striveth for the mastery is temperate in all things. Now they do it to obtain a corruptible crown; but we an incorruptible. I therefore so run, not as uncertainly; so fight I, not as one that beateth the air: But I keep under my body, and bring it into subjection: lest that by any means, when I have preached to others, I myself should be a castaway"* (1 Corinthians 9:24-27).

One of the reasons many people are not enjoying their marriages now is because of what they did during courtship. You must let God into your courtship in order to have a fruitful marriage. With purity of heart, you must wait patiently until the right time. Through prayers, trust God faithfully until the marriage celebration.

PROFITABLE COURTSHIP

As a true Christian, insist on getting married in a right way and with the right person. You must remain prayerful and watchful during courtship. Do not enter into marriage because you want to solve a present problem or because you want to change your present environment and escape a perceived bondage. If those were your basic reasons for getting married, then eventually, you would discover new set of problems, which may be worse than the ones you were avoiding.

Also, do not marry because of pressures from yourself or from others. Sex and intimate physical pleasures or gratification should not also be the purpose you want to marry. You need to encounter God's love bestowed on your heart and the heart of your partner. Do not marry because of temporary need or attraction. These things are limited.

> *"Set me as a seal upon thine heart, as a seal upon thine arm: for love is strong as death; jealousy is cruel as the grave: the coals thereof are coals of fire, which hath a most vehement flame. Many waters cannot quench love, neither can the floods drown it: if a man would give all the substance of his house for love, it would utterly be contemned"* (Song of Solomon 8:6-7).

> *"I am come into my garden, my sister, my spouse: I have gathered my myrrh with my spice; I have eaten my honeycomb with my honey; I have drunk my wine with my milk: eat, O friends; drink, yea, drink abundantly, O beloved"* (Song of Solomon 5:1).

> *"Who is this that cometh out of the wilderness like pillars of smoke, perfumed with myrrh and frankincense, with all powders of the merchant? Behold his bed, which is Solomon's; threescore valiant men are about it, of the valiant of Israel"* (Song of Solomon 3:6-7).

Allow the Spirit of God to lead you. Determine to honor God's purpose in your life with eternity in view. Your right partner will go to any length to marry you when you show your determination to do God's will, which He revealed to you.

> *"Not with eye service, as men pleasers; but as the servants of Christ, doing the will of God from the heart; With good will doing service, as to the Lord, and not to men: Knowing that whatsoever good thing any man doeth, the same shall he receive of the Lord, whether he be bond or free"* (Ephesians 6:6-8).

Your right partner may disagree with you or abandon you for a while but God has a way of bringing him or her back to you when He sees your sincerity in doing His will and determination to fulfill His purpose for your life. When you trust God in faith, God would answer your prayers.

> *"Shadrach, Meshach, and Abed–nego, answered and said to the king, O Nebuchadnezzar, we are not careful to answer thee in this matter. If it be so, our God whom we serve is able to deliver us from the burning fiery furnace, and he will deliver us out of thine hand, O king. But if not, be it known unto thee, O king, that we will not serve thy gods, nor worship the golden image which thou hast set up"* (Daniel 3:16-18).

You must be determined to abandon popular worldviews of getting married and look through the eyes of the Spirit. The Spirit is able to provide the leadership that you need.

> *"Can two walk together, except they be agreed?"* (Amos 3:3).

> *"Thou shalt not plow with an ox and an ass together"* (Deuteronomy 22:10).

Let your decision be based on your findings as led by the Holy Spirit. You may listen to a prophecy or an elder's counsel, but you have to prove and test them.

> *"I have not sent these prophets, yet they ran: I have not spoken to them, yet they prophesied. But if they had stood in my counsel, and had caused my people to hear my words, then they should have turned them from their evil way, and from the evil of their doings. Am I a God at hand, saith the LORD, and not a God afar off? Can any hide himself in secret places that I shall not see him? Saith the LORD. Do not I fill heaven and earth? Saith the LORD. I have heard what the prophets said, that prophesy lies in my name, saying, I have dreamed, I have dreamed. How long shall this be in the heart of the prophets that prophesy lies? Yea, they are prophets of the deceit of their own heart; Which think to cause my people to forget my name by their dreams which they tell every man to his neighbor, as their fathers have forgotten my name for Baal. The prophet that hath a dream, let him tell a dream; and he that hath my word, let him speak my word faithfully. What is the chaff to the wheat? Saith the LORD. Is not my word like as a fire? Saith the LORD; and like a hammer that breaketh the rock in pieces? Therefore, behold, I am against the prophets, saith the LORD, that steal my words every one from his neighbor. Behold, I am against the prophets, saith the LORD, that use their tongues, and say, He saith. Behold, I am against them that prophesy false dreams, saith the LORD, and do tell them, and cause my people to err by their lies, and by their lightness; yet I sent them not, nor commanded them: therefore they shall not profit this people at all, saith the LORD"* (Jeremiah 23:21-32).

"For he that speaketh in an unknown tongue speaketh not unto men, but unto God: for no man understandeth him; howbeit in the spirit he speaketh mysteries" (1 Corinthians 14:2).

"Beloved, believe not every spirit, but try the spirits whether they are of God: because many false prophets are gone out into the world. Hereby know ye the Spirit of God: Every spirit that confesseth that Jesus Christ is come in the flesh is of God: And every spirit that confesseth not that Jesus Christ is come in the flesh is not of God: and this is that spirit of antichrist, whereof ye have heard that it should come; and even now already is it in the world. Ye are of God, little children, and have overcome them: because greater is he that is in you, than he that is in the world. They are of the world: therefore speak they of the world, and the world heareth them. We are of God: he that knoweth God heareth us; he that is not of God heareth not us. Hereby know we the spirit of truth, and the spirit of error" (1 John 4:1-6).

Be mindful that many false prophets have deceived many people with their wrong teachings concerning marriage. Scrutinize every prophecy by the Spirit of God that is in you so that you do not fail prey to false prophesy. Your decision is the one that matters. Make sure that you and your partner are spiritually compatible. Intellectual and physical compatibility are not enough. You need spiritual compatibility also. Utilize the time of your courtship wisely. It is the only time to study and know each other. It is a time of preparation and discussions about the future. It is a time to share your goals in life and things that would affect your family.

"Let us therefore follow after the things which make for peace, and things wherewith one may edify another. For meat destroy not the work of God. All things indeed are pure; but it is evil for that man who eateth with offence. It is good neither to eat flesh, nor to drink wine, nor any thing whereby thy brother stumbleth, or is offended, or is made weak. Hast thou faith? Have it to thyself before God. Happy is he that condemneth not himself in that thing which he alloweth. And he that doubteth is damned if he eat, because he eateth not of faith: for whatsoever is not of faith is sin" (Romans 14:19-23).

From the time of courtship to the wedding day, do everything to the glory of God and to the edification of all believers.

CORRECTING MISTAKES DURING COURTSHIP

The problem with many people in courtship is pride and stubbornness. People know how to pretend to be holy when they are not. God cannot praise anyone for committing sin. When you delay your repentance and continue in your sins, you receive punishment. When you fail to resist the devil, he comes with guilt and condemnation to make you suffer.

> *"Submit yourselves therefore to God. Resist the devil, and he will flee from you"* (James 4: 7).

> *"If we say that we have no sin, we deceive ourselves, and the truth is not in us. If we confess our sins, he is faithful and just to forgive us our sins, and to cleanse us from all unrighteousness. If we say that we have not sinned, we make him a liar, and his word is not in us"* (1 John 1:8-10).

When you commit sin with your partner during your courtship, there is need for both of you to confess your sins and repent of them before going into marriage.

> *"Examine yourselves, whether ye be in the faith; prove your own selves. Know ye not your own selves, how that Jesus Christ is in you, except ye be reprobates?"* (2 Corinthians 13:5).

> *"And Joshua said unto Achan, My son, give, I pray thee, glory to the LORD God of Israel, and make confession unto him; and tell me now what thou hast done; hide it not from me. And Achan answered Joshua, and said, Indeed I have sinned against the LORD God of Israel, and thus and thus have I done: When I saw among the spoils a goodly Babylonish garment, and two hundred shekels of silver, and a wedge of gold of fifty shekels weight, then I coveted them, and took them; and, behold, they are hid in the earth in the midst of my tent, and the silver under it. And Joshua said, Why hast thou troubled us? The LORD shall trouble thee this day. And all Israel stoned him with stones, and burned them with fire, after they had stoned them with stones"* (Joshua 7:19-21, 25).

Do not postpone your repentance until troubles start. Confess your sins at the right time to avoid destruction. Your deliverance cannot be complete without true repentance. True repentance is the turning away from all sins after confession. You must have a change of mind, purpose and character. Godly sorrow helps you to abhor sin with perfect hatred and to reject sin with all your heart.

> *"The men of Nineveh shall rise in judgment with this generation, and shall condemn it: because they repented at the preaching of Jonas; and, behold, a greater than Jonas is here"* (Matthew 12:41).

"But let man and beast be covered with sackcloth, and cry mightily unto God: yea, let them turn every one from his evil way, and from the violence that is in their hands. Who can tell if God will turn and repent, and turn away from his fierce anger that we perish not? And God saw their works, that they turned from their evil way; and God repented of the evil, that he had said that he would do unto them; and he did it not" (Jonah 3:8-10).

"Therefore I will judge you, O house of Israel, every one according to his ways, saith the Lord GOD. Repent, and turn yourselves from all your transgressions; so iniquity shall not be your ruin" (Ezekiel 18:30).

It is a dangerous thing to transfer sins of your courtship into your marriage. If you have done so already, you can still repent with all your heart. I also want to tell you that repentance has levels. It must be deep before true deliverance can come. No one can mock God.

"Be not deceived; God is not mocked: for whatsoever a man soweth, that shall he also reap. For he that soweth to his flesh shall of the flesh reap corruption; but he that soweth to the Spirit shall of the Spirit reap life everlasting" (Galatians 6:7-8).

True repentance and restitution bring complete and deep deliverance.

"And there was a man of mount Ephraim, whose name was Micah. And he said unto his mother, The eleven hundred shekels of silver that were taken from thee, about which thou cursedst, and spakest of also in mine ears, behold, the silver is with me; I took it. And his mother said, Blessed be thou of the LORD, my son" (Judges 17:1-2).

Restitution is restoring anything that was lost to its rightful owner. Restitution makes a person pay back debts and restore stolen items. Before your marriage, do not pretend to be holy when you are not.

PRAYERS DURING COURTSHIP

Bible Reference: Matthew 1:18-25

Begin with praise and worship

1. Let every enemy of my courtship be exposed and disgraced, in the name of Jesus.
2. Any evil power that is standing between my life partner and I, die, in the name of Jesus.
3. Father Lord, reveal to me all that I need to know during this courtship, in the name of Jesus.
4. Let darkness in my courtship be exposed by divine light, in the name of Jesus.
5. I disgrace any power that wants me to offend my God during this courtship, in the name of Jesus.
6. I refuse to fall victim to any painful and heart-breaking mistake that was prepared to destroy my courtship, in the name of Jesus.
7. I receive power to honor God during my courtship, in the name of Jesus.
8. O Lord, empower me for a godly marriage, in the name of Jesus.
9. Any evil plantation that exists in my courtship, die, in the name of Jesus.
10. Let the fire of God burn every problem that has risen in my courtship, in the name of Jesus.
11. Every disagreement that was designed to destroy God's presence in my courtship, be frustrated, in the name of Jesus.
12. O Lord, arise and take charge over my courtship, in the name of Jesus.
13. Every arrow of immorality and sinful characters that was planted in my courtship, backfire, in the name of Jesus.
14. O Lord, help my partner and I to understand ourselves to Your glory, in the name of Jesus.
15. Let the presence of God characterize the period of my courtship, in the name of Jesus.

16. Every enemy of godliness in my courtship, be disgraced by fire, in the name of Jesus.

17. Any evil seed that was planted to destroy my courtship, die, in the name of Jesus.

18. Every serpent of darkness in the garden of my courtship, die, in the name of Jesus.

19. I destroy witches or wizards that were empowered to destroy my courtship, in the name of Jesus.

20. O Lord, help me to please You in my courtship, in the name of Jesus.

21. O Lord, if this relationship is not from You, terminate it peacefully, in the name of Jesus.

22. Every demonic impossibility that is standing against this courtship, be removed, in the name of Jesus.

23. O Lord, help me to avoid evil actions during this courtship, in the name of Jesus.

24. Any invitation that I have given to devil in this courtship, I withdraw you, in the name of Jesus.

25. Any problem that wants to enter into my marriage from this courtship, die, in the name of Jesus.

26. O Lord, expand our love from this courtship to our marriage, in the name of Jesus.

27. O Lord, let Your affection increase during this courtship to Your glory, in the name of Jesus.

28. Every enemy of peace in this courtship, be disgraced by fire, in the name of Jesus.

29. Let every hidden problem in this courtship be exposed and disgraced, in the name of Jesus.

30. Any power that has vowed to remove God in this courtship, die, in the name of Jesus.

31. Let the power that terminates joy, love and peace during courtships die for my sake, in the name of Jesus.

32. Every arrow of inherited problem that was fired into my courtship, I fire you back, in the name of Jesus.

33. I Waste any power that wants to stop my marriage through this courtship, in the name of Jesus.

34. Blood of Jesus, speak Your peace into my courtship, in the name of Jesus.

35. Any power that wants to make my courtship unprofitable, die in shame, in the name of Jesus.

36. I refuse to ignore God and His Word in my courtship, in the name of Jesus.

37. Father Lord, give me Your counsel that will make my courtship profitable, in the name of Jesus.

38. O Lord, arise and build my marriage during this courtship, in the name of Jesus.

39. Every good thing that will make my courtship profitable, appear, in the name of Jesus.

40. Let failure that was prepared against my marriage during courtship collapse, in the name of Jesus.

41. Let any power that has vowed to ruin my joy during my courtship be wasted, in the name of Jesus.

42. I refuse to enter into proper marriage without God's approval, in the name of Jesus.

43. Father Lord, lead me from the beginning until the end of this courtship, in the name of Jesus.

44. Any power that has vowed to divert me to unprofitable courtship, die, in the name of Jesus.

45. O Lord, forgive me from every sin I committed before and during this courtship, in the name of Jesus.

46. Any evil that wants to live in my courtship, you are a liar, die, in the name of Jesus.

47. Blood of Jesus, speak me out of problems during this courtship, in the name of Jesus.

48. O Lord, if You are not involved fully in this relationship, stop it now, in the name of Jesus.

49. I refuse to postpone my repentance and confession in this relationship, in the name of Jesus.

50. I cut off every problem that wants to see the light on my weeding day, in the name of Jesus.

51. Let the angels of the living God oppose every enemy of my marriage, in the name of Jesus.

52. Let the earth open to swallow every enemy of my courtship and wedding, in the name of Jesus.

53. Father Lord, perfect this courtship and deliver us from errors, in the name of Jesus.

8

Chapter

PRAYERS FOR YOUR WEDDING

CHAPTER OVERVIEW

- *The foundation of Christian wedding*
- *Dangers of making wrong choices*
- *Wedding after courtship*
- *Tough questions and frightening answers*

THE FOUNDATION OF CHRISTIAN WEDDING

The best time to lay good and proper foundation for adulthood is from childhood. How your physical, emotional, temperamental, social and spiritual aspects of your life develop would largely affect your adulthood and determine how mature or immature you become. Before you think of getting married, endeavor to nurture a matured life of discipline, temperance and selflessness.

> *"For three things the earth is disquieted, and for four which it cannot bear: For a servant when he reigneth; and a fool when he is filled with meat; For an odious woman when she is married; and an handmaid that is heir to her mistress"* (Proverbs 30:21-23).

> *And the LORD God planted a garden eastward in Eden; and there he put the man whom he had formed. And the LORD God took the man, and put him into the garden of Eden to dress it and to keep it. And the LORD God said, It is not good that the man should be alone; I will make him an help meet for him"* (Genesis 2:8, 15, 18).

Without proper development in the above areas of life, in addition with experience, one is bound to remain immature in lifestyle and outlook. An inexperienced servant who suddenly gets promoted to the throne would be carried away easily and the kingdom remains at risk. When a woman that is not stable in temperament and character marries, there is bound to be trouble.

> *"And he went in unto Hagar, and she conceived: and when she saw that she had conceived, her mistress was despised in her eyes. And Sarai said unto Abram, My wrong be upon thee: I have given my maid into thy bosom; and when she saw that she had conceived, I was despised in her eyes: the LORD judge between me and thee. And the angel of the LORD said unto her, Return to thy mistress, and submit thyself under her hands"* (Genesis 16:4-5, 9).

A man that wants to marry must at least have a job, a home and kitchen utensils. He must have a plate, spoon, pots and a bed to sleep on. Recall that God planted a garden in Eden for Adam to keep, before giving him a wife. Sadly, many ladies that are saying all manner of prayers to get married do not know how to dress a bed. They cannot cook a simple meal and do not know how to serve others with respect. They have no education, trade or any job. Yet, they are too lazy to wash clothes. Such ladies are used to living with servants and housemaids at their parents' houses. So they get so lazy that they do not know how to do anything.

Others are too lazy because their parents have pampered them. Boyfriends have pampered some and they do not want to change even after they became born-again. Others need deliverance from demons of pride, laziness, extravagance and selfishness. Some ladies are only used to their parents that they find it so difficult to relate well with mother or father in-laws, etc. Others were demonized socially with wasteful lifestyles and freedom to do anything without control or advice.

> *"He that tilleth his land shall be satisfied with bread: but he that followeth vain persons is void of understanding"* (Proverbs 12:11)

These categories of people are weak minded, poor in understanding, lazy and spiritually blinded to the realities of life. They despise close and intimate relationship with Christ. Many beautiful ladies in churches today are not born-again though they belong to the choir and prayer groups. Churches are also filled with assorted professional men, who are well behaved, religious and dutifully but they are not born-again.

It is rather absurd that many Christians claim to be very prayerful but cannot truly repent or determine to forsake their sins. They attend churches in order to date desperate men or rich young ladies. These categories of people cannot give their lives to Christ and are not capable of showing genuine love. Yet, they account for the most religious group, which are very dutiful in service.

> *"Be ye not unequally yoked together with unbelievers: for what fellowship hath righteousness with unrighteousness? And what communion hath light with darkness?"* (2 Corinthians 6:14).

> *"Marriage is honorable in all, and the bed undefiled: but whoremongers and adulterers God will judge"* (Hebrews 13:4).

When you identify any of these inglorious character or threat, it is enough warning to you because marriage is honorable. Rather, you can commit more time in prayers about these things before you start thinking of your wedding. This is the purpose of courtship. Before going to the altar with any man or lady, make sure you know your man or woman very well.

You must avoid pressures from others and from yourself. Do not rush into marriage without God leading you through His Holy Spirit. Do not accept to marry someone because you want to appease your parents. Equally, do not give your consent based on someone's dream, vision or prophecy when you do not have the leading of the Holy Spirit. If you are not convinced enough, it would be wise to request for more time to pray. Check spiritual, physical and financial compatibility.

"Thou shalt not plow with an ox and an ass together" (Deuteronomy 22:10).

"Can two walk together, except they be agreed?" (Amos 3:3).

Before going to the altar, make sure God is directly leading you. You must tell yourselves the truth.

"And Samuel spake unto all the house of Israel, saying, If ye do return unto the LORD with all your hearts, then put away the strange gods and Ashtaroth from among you, and prepare your hearts unto the LORD, and serve him only: and he will deliver you out of the hand of the Philistines. Then the children of Israel did put away Baalim and Ashtaroth, and served the LORD only" (1 Samuel 7:3- 4).

"But a certain man named Ananias, with Sapphira his wife, sold a possession, And kept back part of the price, his wife also being privy to it, and brought a certain part, and laid it at the apostles' feet. But Peter said, Ananias, why hath Satan filled thine heart to lie to the Holy Ghost, and to keep back part of the price of the land? Whiles it remained, was it not thine own? And after it was sold, was it not in thine own power? Why hast thou conceived this thing in thine heart? Thou hast not lied unto men, but unto God. And Ananias hearing these words fell down, and gave up the ghost: and great fear came on all them that heard these things. And the young men arose, wound him up, and carried him out, and buried him. And it was about the space of three hours after, when his wife, not knowing what was done, came in. And Peter answered unto her, Tell me whether ye sold the land for so much? And she said, Yea, for so much. Then Peter said unto her, How is it that ye have agreed together to tempt the Spirit of the Lord? Behold, the feet of them which have buried thy husband are at the door, and shall carry thee out. Then fell she down straightway at his feet, and yielded up the ghost: and the young men came in, and found her dead, and, carrying her forth, buried her by her husband" (Acts 5:1-10).

DANGERS OF MAKING WRONG CHOICES

Countless children of God have continued to make serious and heartbreaking mistakes in their choices of marriage partners. One of the major reasons for this is that most of these people did not seek for God's consent before making their choices. They chose their partners with God's guidance. Time has shown that regardless of how experienced and knowledgeable you are in other areas of life, you need God's leading to choose a right partner.

The major reason you need God is that God is omniscient while you are limited. Your perfection is not enough and it can be influenced by emotional strain and stress. God is eternal and cannot be deceived because He knows all things even before they exist. God knows everyone's hearts and can tell in detail what shall happen from start to finish.

God knows someone who suits you in marriage and also knows people who do not. Whomever He forbids you to marry, He has a reason to do so. He does not consider physical appearances or prosperity. That means that even a well-behaved, religious, dutiful churchgoer may not be suitable for you.

Someone may appear physically satisfactory and very intelligent but lacks the discipline, temperance and selflessness that would make two of you to live in peace. He or she may have the wealth and industry, yet lacks the character of Christ.

> *"Neither shalt thou make marriages with them; thy daughter thou shalt not give unto his son, nor his daughter shalt thou take unto thy son. For they will turn away thy son from following me, that they may serve other gods: so will the anger of the LORD be kindled against you, and destroy thee suddenly"* (Deuteronomy 7:3-4).

> *"Else if ye do in any wise go back, and cleave unto the remnant of these nations, even these that remain among you, and shall make marriages with them, and go in unto them, and they to you: Know for a certainty that the LORD your God will no more drive out any of these nations from before you; but they shall be snares and traps unto you, and scourges in your sides, and thorns in your eyes, until ye perish from off this good land which the LORD your God hath given you"* (Joshua 23:12-13).

For a born-again Christian to marry an unconverted person is a disaster no matter how much tongue that person speaks. It is risky to think that you would lead your partner to Christ after marriage. Instead, it is wiser to lead your partner to Christ before your marriage. The danger is that your partner may turn you away from following God, or influence you to serve other gods. Believers who made such mistakes have either lost their ministries or died prematurely.

It is dangerous to marry someone who would become a snare or scourge to you. To marry such people is synonymous to exposing yourself to an early grave. Many beautiful people out there are devil incarnates. Scores of people are going through unimaginable hardships they cannot tell others because of making wrong choices in marriage.

> *"Now therefore give not your daughters unto their sons, neither take their daughters unto your sons, nor seek their peace or their wealth for ever: that ye may be strong, and eat the good of the land, and leave it for an inheritance to your children for ever. And after all that is come upon us for our evil deeds, and for our great trespass, seeing that thou our God hast punished us less than our iniquities deserve, and hast given us such deliverance as this"* (Ezra 9:12-13).

> *"But there was none like unto Ahab, which did sell himself to work wickedness in the sight of the LORD, whom Jezebel his wife stirred up. And he did very abominably in following idols, according to all things as did the Amorites, whom the LORD cast out before the children of Israel. And it came to pass, when Ahab heard those words, that he rent his clothes, and put sackcloth upon his flesh, and fasted, and lay in sackcloth, and went softly"* (1 Kings 21:25-27).

You should be courageous enough to reject a proposal from a wealthy and good-looking person when you are certain that God would not support such marriage. Do not be enticed by fake peace or wealth presented before you in other to sway you. These things should not be the basis for you to accept marrying any person because they are capable of weakening your strength with time. They will surely cause you to offend God, weaken your spiritual life or make you a candidate of hell.

An evil partner is capable of making a strong person to become weak and a weak person weaker. They can turn a righteous to unrighteousness and help the wicked to commit horrible things in the sight of God. Jezebel made her husband, Ahab, to become a wicked king. She stirred up evil on Ahab's heart and he did abominable things as a king.

An evil partner will facilitate your journey to hell and closes every good door against you. It is a high risk to marry an unbeliever, who has no desire to fear or love God.

> *"And I contended with them, and cursed them, and smote certain of them, and plucked off their hair, and made them swear by God, saying, Ye shall not give your daughters unto their sons, nor take their daughters unto your sons, or for yourselves. Did not Solomon king of Israel sin by these things? yet among many nations was there no king like him, who was beloved of his God, and God made him king over all Israel: nevertheless even him did outlandish women cause to sin. Shall we then*

hearken unto you to do all this great evil, to transgress against our God in marrying strange wives?" (Nehemiah 13:25-27).

Nehemiah's treaty with the Jews who presented reasons for marrying unbelievers was that unless they could overthrow Solomon with all his wisdom, no one should try it. Nehemiah contended with them, and even cursed some of them. He plucked off their hairs and made them to swear by God.

Solomon ruined his love for God when he went into ridiculous marriages with unbelievers. Therefore, it is difficult to marry an unbeliever or someone who is not compatible with you. Such union is capable of diverting your focus in life and reducing you to nothing. Women, who do not believe in God, are usually characterized with strange and wicked characters, flattering lips and they have no regard for covenant with God.

"On the seventh day, when the heart of the king was merry with wine, he commanded Mehuman, Biztha, Harbona, Bigtha, and Abagtha, Zethar, and Carcas, the seven chamberlains that served in the presence of Ahasuerus the king, To bring Vashti the queen before the king with the crown royal, to shew the people and the princes her beauty: for she was fair to look on. But the queen Vashti refused to come at the king's commandment by his chamberlains: therefore was the king very wroth, and his anger burned in him. [19]If it please the king, let there go a royal commandment from him, and let it be written among the laws of the Persians and the Medes, that it be not altered, That Vashti come no more before king Ahasuerus; and let the king give her royal estate unto another that is better than she. [21]And the saying pleased the king and the princes; and the king did according to the word of Memucan" (Esther 1:10-12, 19, 21).

Demons guide women that do not fear God. Such women can insult their husbands and disobey every authority regardless of whatever consequence. They obey the commands of evil spirits more than their partners' instruction or God's. At the command of or under the influence of evil spirits, they humiliate their partners without mercy.

People that are possessed by demons do not bow to any standing rules and their desires are strange and must be met at all cost. They hate God, His servants and all His children. Human life means nothing to them. Demons have destroyed many lives and have continued to do so.

"For John had said unto Herod, It is not lawful for thee to have thy brother's wife. Therefore Herodias had a quarrel against him, and would have killed him; but she could not: For Herod feared John, knowing that he was a just man and an holy, and observed him; and when he heard him, he did many things, and heard him gladly. And when a convenient day was come, that Herod on his birthday made a supper to his

lords, high captains, and chief estates of Galilee; And when the daughter of the said Herodias came in, and danced, and pleased Herod and them that sat with him, the king said unto the damsel, Ask of me whatsoever thou wilt, and I will give it thee. And he sware unto her, Whatsoever thou shalt ask of me, I will give it thee, unto the half of my kingdom. And she went forth, and said unto her mother, What shall I ask? And she said, The head of John the Baptist. And she came in straightway with haste unto the king, and asked, saying, I will that thou give me by and by in a charger the head of John the Baptist. And the king was exceeding sorry; yet for his oath's sake, and for their sakes which sat with him, he would not reject her. And immediately the king sent an executioner, and commanded his head to be brought: and he went and beheaded him in the prison, And brought his head in a charger, and gave it to the damsel: and the damsel gave it to her mother" (Mark 6:18-28).

Demons detest righteousness. They influence people to become unreliable and change like chameleon in character. They shed innocent blood and indulge in all kinds of wicked thoughts. They defile hearts and bodies and commit evil with mastery and dexterity.

An evil partner bears false witness and tells lies. Such partner is capable of sowing discord among brethren and entangles people in their words. They wrestle for ability to control people.

"And she said unto him, How canst thou say, I love thee, when thine heart is not with me? thou hast mocked me these three times, and hast not told me wherein thy great strength lieth. And it came to pass, when she pressed him daily with her words, and urged him, so that his soul was vexed unto death; That he told her all his heart, and said unto her, There hath not come a razor upon mine head; for I have been a Nazarite unto God from my mother's womb: if I be shaven, then my strength will go from me, and I shall become weak, and be like any other man. And when Delilah saw that he had told her all his heart, she sent and called for the lords of the Philistines, saying, Come up this once, for he hath shewed me all his heart. Then the lords of the Philistines came up unto her, and brought money in their hand. And she made him sleep upon her knees; and she called for a man, and she caused him to shave off the seven locks of his head; and she began to afflict him, and his strength went from him. And she said, The Philistines be upon thee, Samson. And he awoke out of his sleep, and said, I will go out as at other times before, and shake myself. And he wist not that the LORD was departed from him. But the Philistines took him, and put out his eyes, and brought him down to Gaza, and bound him with fetters of brass; and he did grind in the prison house" (Judges 16:15-21).

As a believer, you do not have any reason to marry an unbeliever, who does not have a heart to repent. In so doing, you expose yourself to high risks. You cannot afford to have confidence in an unbeliever because they are like wind that you cannot control. The question you should always ask yourself is, if unbelievers dealt with Solomon, David and Samson, then who am I that I cannot be dealt with? More so, who are you to ignore warnings?

> *"Did not Solomon king of Israel sin by these things? Yet among many nations was there no king like him, who was beloved of his God, and God made him king over all Israel: nevertheless even him did outlandish women cause to sin"* (Nehemiah 13:26).

To marry a man, who is an unbeliever that does not have a heart to repent, is very dangerous. Unbelieving men in their greed seek for worldly things. A wise sister would prayerfully disconnect herself from such men and run away from their alluring wealth. It is very risky to marry a greedy man, who does not fear God because such men hate the path of righteousness. You may not notice it immediately, but if you were prayerful during your courtship, it would definitely manifest with time. Evil men thrive in the dark and engage in dark businesses. They rejoice in doing evil and they are violent, wicked and incorrigible.

Sisters that are not carried away by deceptive appearances easily notice evil personalities during courtship. Evil men love multiple women at a time, make haste to be rich, flatters and do not consider the poor. They are usually very rude and thirsty for blood. They exhibit anger easily. They are proud, unjust and rejoice in injustices. Christian sisters that are seeking for husbands must avoid rich and evil men at all cost.

Courtship is very important because most marriages that were contracted in haste failed. Courtship is a period when intending couples discuss their future plans, expectations, family structure, life goals, money managements, etc. During courtship, you are expected to prayerfully depend on God to confirm your proposed partner. In order to achieve this, you must be alert spiritually. You must maintain purity and mutual respect for your partner. Courtship is not a time for carnal pleasure or carelessness.

> *"Whether therefore ye eat, or drink, or whatsoever ye do, do all to the glory of God. Give none offence, neither to the Jews, nor to the Gentiles, nor to the church of God"* (1 Corinthians 10: 31- 32).

> *"Submit yourselves to every ordinance of man for the Lord's sake: whether it be to the king, as supreme; Or unto governors, as unto them that are sent by him for the punishment of evildoers, and for the praise of them that do well. For so is the will of God, that with well doing ye may put to silence the ignorance of foolish men: As free, and not using your liberty for a cloke of maliciousness, but as the servants of God. Honor all men. Love the brotherhood. Fear God. Honor the king"* (1 Peter 2:13-17).

You must carry on with your courtship with eternity in view. Realize that Christ could come at anytime, even before your wedding day. Determine to maintain a closer relationship with God and man. Labor to please God and endeavor to live in peace with others. When you discover that God is not involved in your relationship, it is better to pull out than to yoke yourself with an incompatible person.

> *"Be ye not unequally yoked together with unbelievers: for what fellowship hath righteousness with unrighteousness? And what communion hath light with darkness? And what concord hath Christ with Belial? Or what part hath he that believeth with an infidel? And what agreement hath the temple of God with idols? for ye are the temple of the living God; as God hath said, I will dwell in them, and walk in them; and I will be their God, and they shall be my people. Wherefore come out from among them, and be ye separate, saith the Lord, and touch not the unclean thing; and I will receive you, And will be a Father unto you, and ye shall be my sons and daughters, saith the Lord Almighty"* (2 Corinthians 6:14-18).

Broken relationship is said to be better than hasty marriage. After marriage, remember, there is no room for divorce, separation or re-marriage. It is for better or worse. So, be warned!!!

WEDDING AFTER COURTSHIP

If Christ should come on your wedding day, will you be sorrowful or joyful? Are you more concern about your wedding gown or your robe of righteousness? Are you willing to keep God's commandments before your wedding day or break them? Are you going to get your guests drunk and insane or is your wedding going to glorify God? Will the prince of peace, Jesus Christ, going to be comfortable with your wedding or will the events compel Him to leave earlier? Think on these things.

> *"Let us therefore follow after the things which make for peace, and things wherewith one may edify another. For meat destroy not the work of God. All things indeed are pure; but it is evil for that man who eateth with offence. It is good neither to eat flesh, nor to drink wine, nor any thing whereby thy brother stumbleth, or is offended, or is made weak. Hast thou faith? Have it to thyself before God. Happy is he that condemneth not himself in that thing which he alloweth. And he that doubteth is damned if he eat, because he eateth not of faith: for whatsoever is not of faith is sin"* (Romans 14:19-23).

Wedding is the closest bond that exists between humans. When a man and a woman decide to be united in marriage, it becomes a sacred event. When two believers say it is God's will to get married, they come together before God, a minister and before witnesses to answer some questions before they are joined together.

At a wedding ceremony, miracle takes place because two hearts and lives join as long as they shall live. God unites them and they become as one in the sight of God. Many people have the opinion that marriage is simply a legal contract, which is also true. But while it is a legal contract, it is also a spiritual contract. A miracle takes place once two people are joined together in marriage.

> *"The Pharisees also came unto him, tempting him, and saying unto him, Is it lawful for a man to put away his wife for every cause? And he answered and said unto them, Have ye not read, that he which made them at the beginning made them male and female, And said, For this cause shall a man leave father and mother, and shall cleave to his wife: and they twain shall be one flesh? Wherefore they are no more twain, but one flesh. What therefore God hath joined together, let not man put asunder. They say unto him, Why did Moses then command to give a writing of divorcement, and to put her away? He saith unto them, Moses because of the hardness of your hearts suffered you to put away your wives: but from the beginning it was not so. And I say unto you, Whosoever shall put away his wife, except it be for fornication, and shall marry another, committeth adultery: and whoso marrieth her which is put away doth commit adultery"* (Matthew 19:3-9).

Marriage becomes a binding covenant before God and man as long as they live. It is irrevocable. As soon as they are pronounced husband and wife, it is therefore confirmed and cannot be altered.

> *"Brethren, I speak after the manner of men; Though it will be but a man's covenant, yet if it be confirmed, no man disannulled, or addeth thereto"* (Galatians 3:15).

TOUGH QUESTIONS AND FRIGHTENING ANSWERS

It is good for two people that are going to be united in marriage to go through these questions in private before doing so in public. Any involuntary answer to any question can attract a curse. You are encouraged to take time to understand your roles and responsibilities to each other before taking your vows.

> *"Wives, submit yourselves unto your own husbands, as unto the Lord. For the husband is the head of the wife, even as Christ is the head of the church: and he is the savior of the body. Therefore as the church is subject unto Christ, so let the wives be to their own husbands in every thing. Husbands, love your wives, even as Christ also loved the church, and gave himself for it; That he might sanctify and cleanse it with the washing of water by the word, That he might present it to himself a glorious church, not having spot, or wrinkle, or any such thing; but that it should be holy and without blemish. So ought men to love their wives as their own bodies. He that loveth his wife loveth himself. For no man ever yet hated his own flesh; but nourisheth and cherisheth it, even as the Lord the church"* (Ephesians 5:22-29)

The first question goes to the father of the bride:

1. Who gives this woman to marry this man? The father of the bride or representative responds: I do.

   After this confirmation, the father of the bride returns to his seat.

2. To the groom: (*groom's name*) Have you been born-again and made a new creature by faith in the atoning blood of Jesus Christ?

   The groom responds – I have.

3. To the bride: (*bride's name*) Have you been born-again and made a new creature by faith in the atoning blood of Jesus Christ?

   The bride responds – I have.

   The minister then places the right hand of the bride in the right hand of the groom, and turns to the bridegroom and say:

4. To the groom: (*groom's name*) Do you take (*bride's name*) whose right hand you now hold to be your lawful wedded wife and solemnly promise, God helping you, that you will be a true and devoted husband to her; that you will love her even as Christ loved the church, and honor her, cherish, protect and care for her for the rest of your lives and that you will give yourself to her and to her alone until God, by death shall separate you?

The groom responds – I do.

The minister the will ask the brother to make a profession of his faith: I, (*groom's name*) according to the Word of God, leave my father and my mother and join myself to you, to be a husband to you. From this moment forward, we shall be one.

5. To the bride: (*bride's name*) Do you take (*groom's name*) whose right hand you now hold to be your lawful wedded husband and solemnly promise, God helping you, that you will be a true and devoted wife to him; that you will love him even as Christ loves the church, and honor him, cherish, protect and care for him for the rest of your lives and that you will give yourself to him and to him alone until God, by death shall separate you?

   The bride responds– I do.

To witnesses:

Jesus said in the 18th chapter of Matthew's Gospel, "Again, I say unto you, that if two of you shall agree on earth as touching anything that they shall ask, it shall be done for them by my Father which is in heaven." You are not here just because of tradition. You are here to bear witness forever of the "mystery" of the union that takes place, this day, and to add your agreement before God to that which takes place.

TO GROOM AND THE BRIDE:

Join right hands please. A miracle took place when you made Jesus Christ your Lord and Savior. The power of God that raised Jesus from the dead joined you to Jesus. I want you to understand that this day, you are joined together and have become one. The same power that joined you with Jesus when you made him your Lord and Savior has this day joined you together. Do not ever tamper with this union. Do not ever tamper with this miracle. You are one never to be separated or divorced.

As a representative of Jesus Christ before Almighty God and in the name of the father, the Son, Jesus, and by the power of the Holy Spirit of God, I now pronounce you as one together. You are now husband and wife.

From today, when you agree on things, they will happen. You have an awesome power at your disposal. You are going to notice from now on a new realm beginning in your life because of a spiritual law that says one can put a thousand to fight and two ten thousand to fight. From now on, your everyday life will be ten times more powerful spiritually than ever before. Remember, do not ever tamper with the agreement of today. From this day forward, whatever may happen, you are in agreement with this union. Do not ever attempt in any way to cause it to be anything other than a happy union.

TO THE CONGREGATION:

In as much as (*groom's name*) and (*bride's name*) have both signified that they believed with all their hearts that it is the perfect will of God for them to be joined together in the holy bond of matrimony, and have become witness of this marriage before God and this company, and have pledged their fidelity and love each to the other, I, by virtue of the authority rested in me as a minister of the gospel of Jesus Christ and by the laws of our country now pronounce them husband and wife, in the name of the Father, and of the Son, and of the Holy Ghost. "What therefore God hath joined together, let no man put asunder".

The entire congregation remains quiet in the attitude of worship as marriage register is signed.

* **The blessing of the union:**

The minister reads Galatians 3:13-14; 1 Peter 3, where it says that a man and his wife are heirs together of the grace of life. According to Deuteronomy 28:1-13 and as the minister reads, the congregation will be saying Amen.

* **The minister turns to the congregation:**

Ladies and gentlemen, I present to you Mr. and Mrs. (*the groom's name and the bride's name*).

PRAYERS FOR YOUR WEDDING

Bible References: Matthew 19:6; Romans 19:7-9; Philippians 4:4-5, 1 Corinthians 10:31-32, Romans 2:18-22, 14:12-21; James 1:9

Begin with praise and worship

1. Every enemy of my wedding, be exposed and be disgraced forever, in the name of Jesus.
2. Father Lord, prepare me adequately for my wedding, in the name of Jesus.
3. Lord Jesus, make me matured in every area, in the name of Jesus.
4. Blood of Jesus, speak peace upon my wedding, in the name of Jesus.
5. O Lord, provide everything I need for my wedding, in the name of Jesus.
6. I receive the anointing to leave and cleave with my partner by fire, in the name of Jesus.
7. O Lord, help me to meet up with my responsibilities in this marriage, in the name of Jesus.
8. Let the spirit of humility and servant hood possess me before my wedding, in the name of Jesus.
9. Power to plan for my own family and succeed with my partner, possess me, in the name of Jesus.
10. Let the nine fruits of the Holy Spirit possess me by fire, in the name of Jesus.
11. O Lord, assure me that You are the one backing my wedding, in the name of Jesus.
12. Father Lord, if this wedding is not from You, stop it miraculously, in the name of Jesus.
13. Every weapon of darkness that was prepared against my wedding, catch fire, in the name of Jesus.
14. If I am under evil influence to wed, O Lord, deliver me now, in the name of Jesus.
15. If this marriage will destroy my soul in hell, I reject it now, in the name of Jesus.

16. Let the power of God release me if I have entered any bondage, in the name of Jesus.
17. Any covenant that was prepared to waste my life through this wedding, break, in the name of Jesus.
18. If God is behind this wedding, let it prosper by fire, in the name of Jesus.
19. Any problem that wants to destroy my wedding plans, die, in the name of Jesus.
20. I cast out evil spirits that my wedding has attracted, in the name of Jesus.
21. Every evil force that has risen against this wedding, be arrested to death, in the name of Jesus.
22. Blood of Jesus flow into the foundation of this wedding, in the name of Jesus.
23. I repent of every sin I committed before and during my courtship, in the name of Jesus.
24. Let evil forces that have vowed to destroy my wedding be destroyed, in the name of Jesus.
25. O Lord, lead me through this wedding by fire, in the name of Jesus.
26. Blessed Holy Trinity, join me as You are joined in heaven, in the name of Jesus.
27. Let this wedding become fruitful to the glory of God, in the name of Jesus.
28. As I enter into this agreement, let heaven open to bless me forever, in the name of Jesus.
29. I revoke any evil decree that stands against my wedding, in the name of Jesus.
30. Any spot or wrinkle in my life, be washed by the blood of Jesus, in the name of Jesus.
31. Father Lord, help me to confess and forsake my sins before I wed, in the name of Jesus.
32. My wedding, I command you to bring me closer to God, in the name of Jesus.
33. Let my wedding become too hot to be touched by devil, in the name of Jesus.
34. I give my hand in marriage to the right person, in the name of Jesus.
35. Any evil plan to destroy my wedding, fail woefully, in the name of Jesus.
36. Let God arise and bless the day of my wedding, in the name of Jesus.

37. You, my wedding day, prosper and bless my marriage forever, in the name of Jesus.

38. Any curse that was prepared for me, backfire, in the name of Jesus.

39. Let my enemies turn around and bless me on my wedding day, in the name of Jesus.

40. Let the heavens open and release mighty blessings on my wedding day, in the name of Jesus.

41. I cut off evil visitors on the day of my wedding, in the name of Jesus.

42. Any invitation that was given to devil for my wedding, I withdraw you, in the name of Jesus.

43. I break evil legs that plan to walk into my marriage, in the name of Jesus.

44. Every evil gang-up for my wedding day, scatter in shame, in the name of Jesus.

45. Power of positive agreement, possess my partner and me on our wedding day, in the name of Jesus.

46. Father Lord, convert my mistakes to blessings, in the name of Jesus.

47. Lord Jesus, convert every mistake of my partner to blessings, in the name of Jesus.

48. Every failure that was prepared for my marriage, I convert it to success, in the name of Jesus.

49. Any satanic mockery over my wedding, I convert you to sorrow, in the name of Jesus.

50. Every hindrance on my wedding day, melt by fire, in the name of Jesus.

51. Let agents of devil on my wedding day be disgraced forever, in the name of Jesus.

52. Every evil arrow that is prepared against me, backfire, in the name of Jesus.

53. I silence every evil word that was spoken over my wedding, in the name of Jesus.

54. Blood of Jesus, defeat my difficulties on my wedding day, in the name of Jesus.

55. Every satanic instruction against my wedding day, be rejected, in the name of Jesus.

56. Any evil messenger on my wedding day, return your message to your sender, in the name of Jesus.

9
Chapter

PRAYERS TO PRAY DURING HONEYMOON

CHAPTER OVERVIEW

- *The meaning of honeymoon*
- *Honeymoon is a time to study*
- *The pre-eminence of the bible*
- *Study about marriage*
- *Why do we marry?*
- *Things to study during honeymoon*
- *Qualities of a virtuous wife*

THE MEANING OF HONEYMOON

Honeymoon originally denotes the period following a wedding. It is a vacation spent together by a newly married couple. Most couples view honeymoon as a period of harmony immediately after marriage. People believe that the first month of marriage is the sweetest. It is a period of unusual harmony following the establishment of a new relationship. The newly married couples often take a trip or vacation to enjoy their honeymoon.

> *"And what man is there that hath betrothed a wife, and hath not taken her? Let him go and return unto his house, lest he die in the battle, and another man take her"* (Deuteronomy 20:7).

> *"When a man hath taken a new wife, he shall not go out to war, neither shall he be charged with any business: but he shall be free at home one year, and shall cheer up his wife which he hath taken"* (Deuteronomy 24:5).

> *"Let thy fountain be blessed: and rejoice with the wife of thy youth"* (Proverb 5:18).

In the scriptures, newly married men are permitted to take some time to stay with their wives. Moses exempted them from going to war for a period. In the Law of Moses, they are to be freed from every work. They are expected to be at home for one year in order to cheer up their wives. They are to stay back and rejoice with their wives.

However, in modern times, most people observe their honeymoon for a full month. Honeymoon should be a time to be committed to God, His Word and to each other. It is a time to reexamine yourselves to see whether both of you are in faith.

> *"Examine yourselves, whether ye be in the faith; prove your own selves. Know ye not your own selves, how that Jesus Christ is in you, except ye be reprobates?"* (2 Corinthians 13:5).

It is a time to review your past lives and tell yourselves the truth. It is a time to review all your activities from the beginning of the relationship until the wedding. It is also a time to reconcile how much money that was spent and how much that is available. This is the only way to know if you have incurred debts during your wedding. You also need to discuss with your partner how much both of you have in bank accounts. Honeymoon is the best time to discuss the future of your new family.

You can discuss domestic matters like styles or living standards and mode of expenditures.

You can also discuss family life like the direction the new family would take, education, employment, and size of the family. Discuss how to relate with extended family members as well and how to manage what both of you have.

HONEYMOON IS A TIME TO STUDY

It could not have been easy to study the bible alone. However, you have a companion now. Honeymoon is a time to evaluate each other's convictions about God's Word and your commitment to the Word of God.

As Christians, you should treat the bible as an authentic written Word of God. The Scriptures is to be preferred over your thoughts, dream, tradition, philosophy and doctrines. You must reject things that contradict God's Word.

> *"Making the Word of God of none effect through your tradition, which ye have delivered: and many such like things do ye"* (Mark 7:13).

> *"For in that he died, he died unto sin once: but in that he liveth, he liveth unto God. But God be thanked, that ye were the servants of sin, but ye have obeyed from the heart that form of doctrine which was delivered you"* (Romans 6:10, 17).

> *"But he answered and said, It is written, Man shall not live by bread alone, but by every word that proceedeth out of the mouth of God"* (Matthew 4:4).

Jesus died on the cross that He might pay the price of our sins. He resurrected and lives forever. Those who accept Him cannot be servants to sin any longer. You can use the period of your honeymoon to study God's Word, and practically deal with any sin in your lives. You must always live according to God's Word. His Word cannot fail.

> *"Seek ye out of the book of the LORD, and read: no one of these shall fail, none shall want her mate: for my mouth it hath commanded, and his spirit it hath gathered them"* (Isaiah 34:16).

> *"For the word of God is quick, and powerful, and sharper than any two-edged sword, piercing even to the dividing asunder of soul and spirit, and of the joints and marrow, and is a discerner of the thoughts and intents of the heart"* (Hebrew 4:12).

> *"Let the word of Christ dwell in you richly in all wisdom; teaching and admonishing one another in psalms and hymns and spiritual songs, singing with grace in your hearts to the Lord"* (Colossians 3:16).

You have to believe God's Word and more importantly put them into practice. The air, water and other fast moving creatures may be quick and powerful, but the Word of God is quicker, more powerful, and sharper. It can enter the soul, spirit, joints and marrow. It heals, delivers, saves, sanctifies and empowers more than anything else empowers.

The Word of God is able to guide a husband and his wife to live in peace and harmony. It is rich in wisdom, and good for teaching or admonishing members of the family. There is no other book in which God revealed His mind other than His written Word. Intelligence, exposure and education would not be enough without the knowledge of the bible.

THE PRE-EMINENCE OF THE BIBLE

The bible is a book for every Christian family. Other books on earth can disappoint but not the bible. While emotional strains and stress could influence authors of other books, it could not influence the author of the bible. The author of the bible, the Almighty God, is omniscient and perfect. He cannot make mistake.

> *"For verily I say unto you, Till heaven and earth pass, one jot or one tittle shall in no wise pass from the law, till all be fulfilled"* (Matthew 5:18).

> *"Forever, O LORD, thy word is settled in heaven"* (Psalms 119:89)

> *"The grass withereth, the flower fadeth: but the word of our God shall stand for ever"* (Isaiah 40:8)

Stress does not affect God. He is eternal. He is the same yesterday, today and forever. Any form of disguise by men and women cannot deceive our God, the author of the bible.

> *"At that time Abijah the son of Jeroboam fell sick. And Jeroboam said to his wife, Arise, I pray thee, and disguise thyself, that thou be not known to be the wife of Jeroboam; and get thee to Shiloh: behold, there is Ahijah the prophet, which told me that I should be king over this people. And take with thee ten loaves, and cracknels, and a cruse of honey, and go to him: he shall tell thee what shall become of the child. And Jeroboam's wife did so, and arose, and went to Shiloh, and came to the house of Ahijah. But Ahijah could not see; for his eyes were set by reason of his age. And the LORD said unto Ahijah, Behold, the wife of Jeroboam cometh to ask a thing of thee for her son; for he is sick: thus and thus shalt thou say unto her: for it shall be, when she cometh in, that she shall feign herself to be another woman. And it was so, when Ahijah heard the sound of her feet, as she came in at the door, that he said, Come in, thou wife of Jeroboam; why feignest thou thyself to be another? For I am sent to thee with heavy tidings"* (1 Kings 14:1-6).

God knows the content of the human heart and other creatures that have hearts. He knows the beginning and the ending of everything in the universe.

> *"Now when he was in Jerusalem at the Passover, in the feast day, many believed in his name, when they saw the miracles which he did. But Jesus did not commit himself unto them, because he knew all men, And needed not that any should testify of man: for he knew what was in man"* (John 2:23-25).

Since man cannot tell the future, we need God and His Word to guide us through our journey in marriage.

"Because to every purpose there is time and judgment, therefore the misery of man is great upon him. For he knoweth not that which shall be: for who can tell him when it shall be?" (Ecclesiastes 8:6-7).

"Remember the former things of old: for I am God, and there is none else; I am God, and there is none like me, Declaring the end from the beginning, and from ancient times the things that are not yet done, saying, My counsel shall stand, and I will do all my pleasure" (Isaiah 46:9-10).

One of the most beautiful things a newly wedded couple could do during their honeymoon is to pray, study God's Word and seek His blueprint for their marriage. It is only God's counsel that would stand. Therefore, you need His counsel. His Word reveals His counsel.

Men write books that reveal their thoughts, which is finite. However, the Scriptures are God's revelation of God's mind and will to humanity. The Word of God has solution to every problem in the universe.

"Heaven and earth shall pass away, but my words shall not pass away" (Matthew 24:35).

"But the word of the Lord endureth for ever. And this is the word which by the gospel is preached unto you" (1 Peter 1:25)

Likewise, you cannot compare heaven and earth with the Word of God. They will pass away but the Word of God will endure forever. God's original copy of the bible is in heaven and one jot or title shall in no way pass from the law, until all be fulfilled. In family and other matters, the Word of God is good for doctrine, reproof, correction, and instruction in righteousness. Husbands and wives, who wish to succeed in their marriages, must obey God's Word.

"Persecutions, afflictions, which came unto me at Antioch, at Iconium, at Lystra; what persecutions I endured: but out of them all the Lord delivered me. [17]That the man of God may be perfect, throughly furnished unto all good works" (2 Timothy 3:11, 17)

"For the prophecy came not in old time by the will of man: but holy men of God spake as they were moved by the Holy Ghost" (2 Peter 1:21).

With the help of His Spirit, God inspired over forty different writers to write the 66 books of the bible during a period of over 1,800 years. The bible is versatile and can meet the needs of every race, nation, language and culture.

"But he answered and said, It is written, Man shall not live by bread alone, but by every word that proceedeth out of the mouth of God" (Matthew 4:4).

STUDY ABOUT MARRIAGE

When you have a rich father who died and left a will for you, you would wish to read your father's will to know his thoughts towards you. However, when you have no knowledge of your father's will, you may die without benefiting from your father's blessing.

A will is a legal declaration of a person's wishes regarding the disposal of his or her property or estate after death.

> *"And this is the confidence that we have in him, that, if we ask any thing according to his will, he heareth us: And if we know that he hear us, whatsoever we ask, we know that we have the petitions that we desired of him"* (1 John 5: 14-15)

If you do not know God's will for your marriage, how would you know what His thoughts towards your marriage are? If you do not know that your father left one billion dollars for you in a particular bank, you will not bother to demand from such bank your inheritance. It is also possible you could live, suffer and die because of poverty when you have one billion dollars kept for you in the bank. Ignorance is a deadly disease.

> *"How God anointed Jesus of Nazareth with the Holy Ghost and with power: who went about doing good, and healing all that were oppressed of the devil; for God was with him"* (Acts 10:38).

> *"When he was come down from the mountain, great multitudes followed him. And, behold, there came a leper and worshipped him, saying, Lord, if thou wilt, thou canst make me clean. And Jesus put forth his hand, and touched him, saying, I will; be thou clean. And immediately his leprosy was cleansed"* (Matthew 8:1-3).

A father's will grant you much power and right to get what the testator wrote concerning you. A will is a written document that backs you as God backed Jesus Christ when He started doing good and healing all that were possessed of the devil. Jesus Christ knew that God anointed Him with power. Therefore, He did not stop at knowledge alone. He went about enforcing His Father's will.

Well, you may argue that Jesus is God and He knows everything. Nevertheless, the truth is that you have the right to know God's will concerning your marriage also. They are written in the bible, therefore search for them. The leper who did not know God's will for his healing took a step of faith and asked if he had rights to receive healing and Jesus told him it was his right. Jesus cleansed him. However, other lepers, who did not make attempts in faith, died even though it was God's will to heal them.

"And the LORD will take away from thee all sickness, and will put none of the evil diseases of Egypt, which thou knowest, upon thee; but will lay them upon all them that hate thee" (Deuteronomy 7:15).

"Beloved, I wish above all things that thou mayest prosper and be in health, even as thy soul prospereth" (3 John 2)

"Thy kingdom come. Thy will be done in earth, as it is in heaven" (Matthew 6:10).

It is not the will of God that sickness attacks you during your honeymoon. It is not God's will that you start your married life with disease. If you do not ask, you may not receive. God's written will for you is to be blessed and for your marriage to prosper. God's will for you is true prosperity, sound body, soul, and spirit. It is God's will for you to bring God's kingdom into your home. You can live in peace, prosperity and in abundance just as it is in your spirit. These should form basis of your prayer requests during your honeymoon.

"And the inhabitant shall not say, I am sick: the people that dwell therein shall be forgiven their iniquity" (Isaiah 33:24)

"The thief cometh not, but for to steal, to kill, and to destroy: I am come that they might have life, and that they might have it more abundantly" (John 10:10).

People who do not know God's will for their marriage think that honeymoon is the best time to enjoy sex. Of course, sex is a big part of it, but over 21 percent of the time should be devoted to finding out what God wants you to know about each other; that is His will for both of you to end your honeymoon without traces of problems or iniquity.

He wants to forgive both of you all your sins. These include sins against God, against your fellow human beings, yourself and against each other. If you have to, tell yourselves what each other need to know. It is God's will to give you life in abundance, therefore do not end your honeymoon without exhausting every important discussion. God has made provisions in His Word concerning your new family. Therefore, do not miss it.

"For where a testament is, there must also of necessity be the death of the testator. For a testament is of force after men are dead: otherwise it is of no strength at all while the testator liveth" (Hebrews 9:16-17).

If you are born-again and a true child of God, then you have the power to enforce God's will as you wish, when it pleases you or suits your new family. Always remember that the written will of God for your marriage is in His Word. You have to be conversant with His commandments, promises and provisions, and claim them for your marriage.

WHY DO WE MARRY?

This is the first question every intending couple needs to be acquainted with. You and your partner must understand the purpose of marriage. This is important because any family that negates the teachings of God or modifies it for its convenience would have much trouble and curses.

> *"Great peace has they, which love thy law: and nothing shall offend them"* (Psalms 119:165).

> *"[18]And the LORD God said, It is not good that the man should be alone; I will make him an help meet for him. [20]And Adam gave names to all cattle, and to the fowl of the air, and to every beast of the field; but for Adam there was not found a helpmeet for him. [22]And the rib, which the LORD God had taken from man, made he a woman, and brought her unto the man. [24]Therefore shall a man leave his father and his mother, and shall cleave unto his wife: and they shall be one flesh"* (Genesis 2:18, 20, 22, 24).

God declared that it was not good for you to be alone. Hence, regardless of any form of weakness that you would discover in your partner as your marriage progressed, you have to still agree with God that it is not good that you should be alone. You are not perfect, so is your partner. Therefore, the best you could do is to pray that God helps both of you to overlook whatever weaknesses you would come across in your marriage.

Adam gave names to all other creatures and they did not argue. Likewise, you can begin to give names to all your problems and send them to where they belong, not in your family. God's purpose for marriage is for you not to feel lonely.

> *"And he answered and said unto them, Have ye not read, that he which made them at the beginning made them male and female, And said, For this cause shall a man leave father and mother, and shall cleave to his wife: and they twain shall be one flesh?"* (Matthew 19:4-5).

> *"But fornication, and all uncleanness, or covetousness, let it not be once named among you, as becometh saints"* (Ephesians 5:3).

Your honeymoon should be between your partner and you. Therefore, pray that no strange woman, man or any creature interferes. Pray that you would remain one flesh. This is God's plan, purpose and provision from the beginning.

> *"For the husband is the head of the wife, even as Christ is the head of the church: and he is the savior of the body"* (Ephesians 5:23).

God's plan for marriage is to give a woman a head. A man without a wife is like a head without a body. God's purpose is to make a husband and a wife one indivisible entity. You need your wife and your wife needs you.

> *"Nevertheless, to avoid fornication, let every man have his own wife, and let every woman have her own husband. [9]But if they cannot contain, let them marry: for it is better to marry than to burn. [10]And unto the married I command, yet not I, but the Lord, Let not the wife depart from her husband: [11]But and if she depart, let her remain unmarried, or be reconciled to her husband: and let not the husband put away his wife"* (1 Corinthians 7:2, 9-11).

> *"His disciples say unto him, If the case of the man be so with his wife, it is not good to marry. But he said unto them, All men cannot receive this saying, save they to whom it is given"* (Matthew 19:10-11).

One of the reasons God instituted marriage was to preserve purity at home, community and the nation. It is not His will for people to commit sexual sins at will. That is the reason God made two of you to get married. He does not want you to go after other women or men in order to satisfy your sexual urge.

Your wife or husband is the only legal person permitted to have sex with you. This is because God wants to preserve purity and holiness in the church and communities. Never you have sex with any other person except your rightful partner. When you disobey this rule, you defy, pollute and contaminate not only your body, but also the church and the nation. God has not made any provision for sex outside marriage. Pray now that it will never happen in your family in Jesus name.

> *"For the husband is the head of the wife, even as Christ is the head of the church: and he is the savior of the body. [29]For no man ever yet hated his own flesh; but nourisheth and cherisheth it, even as the Lord the church: [30]For we are members of his body, of his flesh, and of his bones. [31]For this cause shall a man leave his father and mother, and shall be joined unto his wife, and they two shall be one flesh"* (Ephesians 5:23, 29-31)

> *"Two are better than one; because they have a good reward for their labor. For if they fall, the one will lift up his fellow: but woe to him that is alone when he falleth; for he hath not another to help him up. Again, if two lie together, then they have heat: but how can one be warm alone?"* (Ecclesiastes 4:9-11).

It is your duties to protect each other so that none would have any reason to search for pleasure or satisfaction elsewhere. Pray against the spirit of hatred, fighting, quarrelling, conflicts and hostility. Pray against intruders also. The purpose of marriage is to find completeness and fulfillment of living. You may not see the whole picture at once, but you and your partner would complement each other. God will use what is in your wife that is not in you to fill the vacuum, likewise you. If you give God a chance in your marriage, He would prove to you that He is a perfect matchmaker.

> *"So God created man in his own image, in the image of God created he him; male and female created he them. And God blessed them, and God said unto them, Be fruitful, and multiply, and replenish the earth, and subdue it: and have dominion over the fish of the sea, and over the fowl of the air, and over every living thing that moveth upon the earth"* (Genesis 1:27-28).

> *"And God blessed Noah and his sons, and said unto them, Be fruitful, and multiply, and replenish the earth"* (Genesis 9:1).

> *"Thy wife shall be as a fruitful vine by the sides of thine house: thy children like olive plants round about thy table"* (Psalms 128:3).

Moreover, God instituted marriage for procreation. The institution of marriage is the primary place to rear children before they integrate into local communities. Procreation is fundamental to the stability and continuation of societies. That is why the main objective of any marriage relationship is to grow together in unity sharing your intellect, emotion, personality and spirituality.

THINGS TO STUDY DURING HONEYMOON

1. HUSBAND'S RESPONSIBILITY

It will be admirable to get a paper and pen before reading the following Scriptures. Doing so would give you the opportunity of writing your roles down as a husband and reminding yourself what you ought to do always in order to please God.

(*See* Ephesians 5:23-33, 1 Corinthians 11:3, 1 Timothy 3:4-5, Colossians 3:17-18, 14,1 Peter 3:4-7, John 13:1, 15:13, 11:36, 1 John 3:14-18, 1 Corinthians 13:4-7, Malachi 2:14-16, 3:16, Romans 7:2, Matthew 19:3-6).

Though the man is the head and has right to direct the affairs of his family, yet, he has no right to require of his wife or any member of his household anything that contradicts the will and Word of God.

> *"But Peter and John answered and said unto them, Whether it be right in the sight of God to hearken unto you more than unto God, judge ye"* (Acts 4:19).

> *"And kept back part of the price, his wife also being privy to it, and brought a certain part, and laid it at the apostles' feet. But Peter said, Ananias, why hath Satan filled thine heart to lie to the Holy Ghost, and to keep back part of the price of the land? Whiles it remained, was it not thine own? And after it was sold, was it not in thine own power? Why hast thou conceived this thing in thine heart? Thou hast not lied unto men, but unto God. And Ananias hearing these words fell down, and gave up the ghost: and great fear came on all them that heard these things. And the young men arose, wound him up, and carried him out, and buried him. And it was about the space of three hours after, when his wife, not knowing what was done, came in. And Peter answered unto her, Tell me whether ye sold the land for so much? And she said, Yea, for so much. Then Peter said unto her, How is it that ye have agreed together to tempt the Spirit of the Lord? Behold, the feet of them which have buried thy husband are at the door, and shall carry thee out"* (Acts 5:2-9)

Wherever God's authority is made of no effect, the husband's authority ceases. He has no right to require his wife to disobey God. A replica of Christ's love for His church is what God demands from husbands.

> *"Husbands, love your wives, even as Christ also loved the church, and gave himself for it; That he might sanctify and cleanse it with the washing of water by the word, That he might present it to himself a glorious church, not having spot, or wrinkle, or any such thing; but that it should be holy and without blemish. So ought men to love their*

wives as their own bodies. He that loveth his wife loveth himself. For no man ever yet hated his own flesh; but nourisheth and cherisheth it, even as the Lord the church: For we are members of his body, of his flesh, and of his bones. For this cause shall a man leave his father and mother, and shall be joined unto his wife, and they two shall be one flesh" (Ephesians 5:25-31).

A husband is in no danger of loving his wife too much as long as he does not love her in greater quality than He loves God. Christ loved His church and died for her. If the need arises, the husband must be willing to deny himself, toil and bear trials in order to provide and care for his wife and defend her. Husbands must have the same care he has for himself for his wife. He should provide her needs, clothes and all her necessities. The greatest secrets of conjugal happiness are mutual love, kindness, loveliness and tenderness of character at home.

God expects a wife to respect and obey her husband, while the husband loves and cares for his wife. A true child of God would never beat or insult his wife no matter the situation. The husband remains the head of the wife until death, and the body cannot decide to be independent of the head and yet stay alive.

What a husband gets from his wife cannot motivate his love for her. Rather, it is God's command that a husband must love his wife. Christ displayed publicly His love for His church when he went to the cross and sacrificed himself. Husband's love for his wife is not complete until he is sacrifice like as Christ was.

"But God commendeth his love toward us, in that, while we were yet sinners, Christ died for us" (Romans 5:8).

Loving your wife must be a sacrificial, unmerited and not conditional.

2. WIFE'S RESPONSIBILITY

It will be admirable to get a paper and pen before reading the following Scriptures. Doing so would give you the opportunity of writing your roles down as a wife and reminding yourself what you ought to do always in order to please God.

(*See* Ephesians 5:22-33, 1 Corinthians 14:34, Colossians 3:18, Titus 2:4-5, 1 Peter 3:1-6, Proverbs 31:10-31).

A wife's submission is not a favor to the husband. It is God's command. Therefore, she should submit in love, not as a slave. She should do it without grudge in her heart. She should love her husband with respect and treat him with honor and dignity. Sometimes, your husband may fail to meet up with his duties towards you. Nevertheless, that does not empower you to fail in your own duty towards him. Spiritually, a wife submits not unto the husband per se, but unto the Lord.

> *"But let it be the hidden man of the heart, in that which is not corruptible, even the ornament of a meek and quiet spirit, which is in the sight of God of great price. For after this manner in the old time the holy women also, who trusted in God, adorned themselves, being in subjection unto their own husbands: Even as Sara obeyed Abraham, calling him lord: whose daughters ye are, as long as ye do well, and are not afraid with any amazement"* (1 Peter 3:4-6).

In the ancient times, great and holy women of God also submitted to their husbands. They believed that if they trusted God's Word and submitted, God would touch their husbands. They did it and it worked for them. God has not changed. If you submit to your husband as unto the Lord, you cannot regret doing so. Sarah did not obey Abraham because Abraham was good but because it was God's' commandment for wives to do so.

> *"And he brought up Hadassah, that is, Esther, his uncle's daughter: for she had neither father nor mother, and the maid was fair and beautiful; whom Mordecai, when her father and mother were dead, took for his own daughter. So it came to pass, when the king's commandment and his decree was heard, and when many maidens were gathered together unto Shushan the palace, to the custody of Hegai, that Esther was brought also unto the king's house, to the custody of Hegai, keeper of the women. And the maiden pleased him, and she obtained kindness of him; and he speedily gave her her things for purification, with such things as belonged to her, and seven maidens, which were meet to be given her, out of the king's house: and he preferred her and her maids unto the best place of the house of the women. Esther had not shewed her people nor her kindred: for Mordecai had charged her that she should not shew it. [17]And the king loved Esther above all the women, and she obtained grace and favor in his sight*

more than all the virgins; so that he set the royal crown upon her head, and made her queen instead of Vashti" (Esther 2:7-10, 17).

"Now it came to pass on the third day, that Esther put on her royal apparel, and stood in the inner court of the king's house, over against the king's house: and the king sat upon his royal throne in the royal house, over against the gate of the house. And it was so, when the king saw Esther the queen standing in the court, that she obtained favor in his sight: and the king held out to Esther the golden sceptre that was in his hand. So, Esther drew near, and touched the top of the sceptre. Then said the king unto her, What wilt thou, queen Esther? And what is thy request? It shall be even given thee to the half of the kingdom. And Esther answered, If it seem good unto the king, let the king and Haman come this day unto the banquet that I have prepared for him" (Esther 5:1-4).

When you honor God's Word by fulfilling your part towards your husband, God's favor, grace and mercy would be your portion. When you have God's favor, He answers your prayers. God cannot turn you down in times of trouble. Your husband could be very wicked but with time as you perform your part on his behalf, God can touch his heart. When God does so, you would enjoy your honeymoon.

Esther's humility, meekness and good character made her to obtain favor from a heathen king. Her character announced her and made her to be preferred above others (*See* Esther 7:1-6, 2 Kings 4:8-10, Luke 2:19, Matthew 2:13-14).

Esther was a woman of honor and very great. Her greatness was based on how she loved God, his prophets and her husband. She studied her husband and knew how and when to approach him. She was more spiritual and greater than her husband was but she respected him.

A good wife should emulate Esther. Even when she provides for her family, she would never publicize it. She takes care of her husband, her household and the people of God around her. She cannot do anything without her husband's permission.

A good wife is very industrious, spiritual and strong. She would not make a decision without obtaining her husband's permission respectfully. Mary, the mother of Jesus was never a talkative. She never boasted to her husband or disrespected him. An angel of God empowered her and the Holy Spirit overshadowed her to conceive the Savior of the whole world.

Nevertheless, these things did not make her proud. She submitted to her husband and kept these things in her heart. Other women would have made great noise, but not Mary.

When her husband planned to divorce her, she did not fight or argued with him. She did not go to court. She simply went to God and prayed as she pondered in her heart. That night, God sent an angel to talk to Joseph.

So many wives know how to prove things right before their husbands and talk in the court but they cannot talk to God. They can talk and get court judgments delivered in their favor. However, you cannot enjoy a man as a friend and a husband.

Mary was prayerful to the extent that angel of God made prayers on her behalf. If you emulate Mary's character, no matter how wicked your husband is, you can win him over. The reason is that God is able to send an angel to handle your husband.

> *"But when Herod was dead, behold, an angel of the Lord appeareth in a dream to Joseph in Egypt, Saying, Arise, and take the young child and his mother, and go into the land of Israel: for they are dead which sought the young child's life. And he arose, and took the young child and his mother, and came into the land of Israel. But when he heard that Archelaus did reign in Judaea in the room of his father Herod, he was afraid to go thither: notwithstanding, being warned of God in a dream, he turned aside into the parts of Galilee"* (Matthew 2:19-22).

> *"Now his parents went to Jerusalem every year at the feast of the Passover. And when he was twelve years old, they went up to Jerusalem after the custom of the feast. And when they had fulfilled the days, as they returned, the child Jesus tarried behind in Jerusalem; and Joseph and his mother knew not of it. But they, supposing him to have been in the company, went a day's journey; and they sought him among their kinsfolk and acquaintance. And when they found him not, they turned back again to Jerusalem, seeking him. And it came to pass, that after three days they found him in the temple, sitting in the midst of the doctors, both hearing them, and asking them questions. And all that heard him were astonished at his understanding and answers. And when they saw him, they were amazed: and his mother said unto him, Son, why hast thou thus dealt with us? Behold, thy father and I have sought thee sorrowing"* (Luke 2:41-48).

If you are prayerful, Herod may seek to kill your children, but he would die while your children live. Your prayers will always bring down an angel to guide you through all your troubles.

> *"There was in the days of Herod, the king of Judæa, a certain priest named Zacharias, of the course of Abia: and his wife was of the daughters of Aaron, and her name was Elisabeth. And they were both righteous before God, walking in all the commandments and ordinances of the Lord blameless. And they had no child, because that Elisabeth was barren, and they both were now well stricken in years. [23]And it came to pass, that, as soon as the days of his ministration were accomplished, he departed to his own*

house. [24]And after those days his wife Elisabeth conceived, and hid herself five months, saying, [25]Thus hath the Lord dealt with me in the days wherein he looked on me, to take away my reproach among men. [57]Now Elisabeth's full time came that she should be delivered; and she brought forth a son. [58]And her neighbors and her cousins heard how the Lord had shewed great mercy upon her; and they rejoiced with her. [59]And it came to pass, that on the eighth day they came to circumcise the child; and they called him Zacharias, after the name of his father. [60]And his mother answered and said, Not so; but he shall be called John. [61]And they said unto her, There is none of thy kindred that is called by this name. [62]And they made signs to his father, how he would have him called. [63]And he asked for a writing table, and wrote, saying, His name is John. And they marveled all. [64]And his mouth was opened immediately, and his tongue loosed, and he spake, and praised God" (Luke 1:5-7, 23-25, 57-64).

If you are prayerful and remain righteous, no problem can break your marriage. Not even barrenness, lack, shame or reproach. Women who submit to their husbands as unto the Lord never bow because of problems. No matter how long challenges last, they remain candidates of miracles. The marriage of husband and wife, who obey God's command, will flourish until the end of their lives on earth.

- She is submissive (*See* 1 Timothy 2:11-14, 1 Peter 3:1, Colossians 3:18).
- She is humble (*See* 1 Peter 3:3-4, 1 Timothy 2:9).
- She is reverent (*See* Ephesians 5:33,1 Peter 2:18-33, 3:5).
- She is obedience (*See* 1 Peter 3:1, Titus 2:5).
- She is hospitable (*See* Proverbs 31:20, 2 Kings 4:8-10, Hebrew 13:2; Acts 9:36, 16:14-15).
- She is meek (*See* 1 Peter 3:4, Esther 1:10-12).
- She is diligent (*See* Psalms 144:11-12, Proverbs 12:4, 1 Samuel 25:14-37, Proverbs 31:10-31).
- She is holy and loving (*See* Titus 2:4-5, Song of Solomon 8:6-7).
- She is a mother (Psalms 128:3, Deuteronomy 6:6-9, Proverbs 6:20-25).
- She is prayerful (*See* Esther 4:7-16, 2 Kings 4:18-37).

Luther once said of his wife, "*The greatest gift of God is a pious, amiable spouse, who fears God, loves her house, with which one can live in perfect confidence.*"

The founder of the Salvation Army, General Booth, also had a submissive wife. When he was still in the Wesleyan ministry, crises arose. He believed that God has called him to do the work of an evangelist. However, the Wesleyan conference voted against allowing him to devote fulltime to this work. It was indeed a huge crisis for William Booth. If refused to accept the ministry's decision, then he would leave the Wesleyan ministry. That means that he and his family would lose their source of livelihood, their home and fortune. However, in the midst of the crises, just at the point when Mr. Booth decided to yield to the decision of Wesleyan board, he heard a woman's voice in the gallery shouting, "*William, never!*" Behold, it was Mrs. Booth. She summoned much courage and urged William not to give in.

Instead of being very anxious and fearful of the consequences of resigning, she supported her husband. Her encouragement would later become the bedrock of Salvation Army.

At her funeral, her husband described her as "*A tree that had shadowed him from the burning sun, whose flowers had been the adornment and beauty of his life. A tree, whose fruits had been the stay of his existence and a counselor who had ever advised him and seldom advised him wrongly. A friend who had understood his very nature; a wife who for forty years had never given him real cause for grief, who had been the strongest when the battle was strongest. She was the delight of his eyes and the inspiration of his soul. She was a spiritual warrior."*

One may say that a true Christian wife is to her husband and family what Shakespeare said sleep is to the body.

What testimony will your husband give if you pass away? Aristotle, the prince of Greek philosophy, said, *"If women be good, the half of the commonwealth may be happy where they are."*

I read about a woman whose husband did not hang up his clothes, as he should. This trait was sorely aggravating to the wife, who was neat and tidy, and she nagged him constantly in regard to it until she lost sight of the fact that her husband was a good provider, ambitious, gentle and kind at home, deeply spiritual, and an earnest worker in the God's service.

The scriptures did not say that we would go to hell fire if you do not hang up our clothes or if we do not know how to cook very well. However, all these are very important and can be learnt when you give your partner a chance. I also read of a man who nagged so much about his wife's inability to cook well that he became blind to see that his wife was a wonderful mother, an efficient home keeper, of sweet personality, a true and devoted mate.

J.R Miller said, *"The only thing that follows him around and refuses to be buried is the character of a man."* This is true.

PRAYERS DURING HONEYMOON

Bible references: Ephesians 5:31-33, Genesis 2:24; Malachi 2:14-16, 3:16; Romans 7:2, Matthew 19:3-6

Begin with praise and worship

1. Father Lord, lead us and perfect Your will in our lives in our honeymoon, in the name of Jesus.
2. Every enemy of our honeymoon, die, in the name of Jesus.
3. Blood of Jesus, flow into our life and speak to us during our honeymoon, in the name of Jesus.
4. Father Lord, direct Your angels to guide us in our honeymoon, in the name of Jesus.
5. We dedicate our marriage fully to You, O Lord, through our honeymoon, in the name of Jesus.
6. I cast out every unclean spirit that has joined us to this place, in the name of Jesus.
7. Let every ghost of our past be frustrated, in the name of Jesus.
8. Let any curse that was issued against us by any living or dead person expire, in the name of Jesus.
9. Let the activities of our enemies be frustrated, in the name of Jesus.
10. We break inherited bondages from our parents, in the name of Jesus.
11. O Lord, arise and move this marriage forward, in the name of Jesus.
12. Father Lord, give us Your divine program for this marriage, in the name of Jesus.
13. O Lord, destroy anything that is contrary to Your will in this marriage, in the name of Jesus.
14. Every plan of God for this marriage, begin to manifest, in the name of Jesus.
15. Any power that was assigned to modify God's will for this marriage, die by fire, in the name of Jesus.
16. Any evil personality that was assigned to frustrate this marriage, be disgraced, in the name of Jesus.

17. O Lord, fulfill Your purpose and plans for our marriage forever, in the name of Jesus.

18. Any evil sacrifice that was made over our marriage, expire by force, in the name of Jesus.

19. Let every agent of separation, divorce and witchcraft in this marriage die, in the name of Jesus.

20. Let evil spirits that resists progress, joy and peace in marriages be disgraced, in the name of Jesus.

21. I frustrate any evil personality that is attacking the love of God in my marriage, in the name of Jesus.

22. Owners of evil loads in my marriage, appear and carry your loads, in the name of Jesus.

23. O Lord, frustrate every Jezebel, Delilah and home breakers, in the name of Jesus.

24. Any strongman that was assigned to destroy my marriage, fall down and die, in the name of Jesus.

25. Let marital problems that are frustrating my marriage die, in the name of Jesus.

26. Any power that was assigned to delay God's miracles in my marriage, die, in the name of Jesus.

27. Let inherited covenant over this marriage break and expire, in the name of Jesus.

28. Power of darkness that attacks marriages in dreams, my marriage is not your candidate, in the name of Jesus.

29. I remove evil limitations that were placed over my marriage, in the name of Jesus.

30. Let every evil program for this marriage be terminated forever, in the name of Jesus.

31. I command covenants with spirit beings to break, in the name of Jesus.

32. Let every garment of shame and reproach in this marriage burn to ashes, in the name of Jesus.

33. Every invitation that was given to evil spirit and satanic agents to my marriage, die, in the name of Jesus.

34. I destroy every architect of conflict and hostility in my marriage, in the name of Jesus.

35. Any evil personality that wants to redesign God's map for my marriage, die, in the name of Jesus.

36. I cast out spirit of hatred that was planted in my marriage by home wreckers, in the name of Jesus.

37. Let marriage breakers that are working against my marriage be exposed and disgraced, in the name of Jesus.

38. Let evil imaginations, thoughts, plans, desires, decisions and expectations in my marriage die in the name of Jesus.

39. Every weapon of barrenness, miscarriage and hardship that was formed against my marriage, catch fire, in the name of Jesus.

40. O Lord, help me to occupy my rightful position in my marriage, in the name of Jesus.

41. Let every problem that would arise in my marriage receive immediate solution, in the name of Jesus.

42. Any evil counsel that was designed to overthrow my marriage, be rejected, in the name of Jesus.

43. I frustrate interferences from demonic in-laws, in the name of Jesus.

44. Let every work of devil before, during and after my marriage expire by force, in the name of Jesus.

45. Let every evil wish against my marriage be converted to blessings, in the name of Jesus.

46. Any evil cage that was designed to cage this marriage, catch fire and burn to ashes, in the name of Jesus.

47. Let the blessings of God capture every area of my marriage by fire, in the name of Jesus.

48. Let any manipulator that was assigned to manipulate my marriage be manipulated, in the name of Jesus.

49. O Lord, arise, destroy any spirit of sin, adultery, selfishness, lack of submission, and love in my marriage, in the name of Jesus.

50. I withdraw my marriage from the list of marriage failures, in the name of Jesus.

51. Let prosperity that will move my marriage forward appear by force, in the name of Jesus.

52. Lord Jesus, reign as the prince of peace in my marriage, in the name of Jesus.

53. Every good thing that would keep my marriage in peace, manifest, in the name of Jesus.

54. Any property of devil that is bringing demons into my home, catch fire, in the name of Jesus.

55. Let Jesus reign as the prince of peace in my marriage forever, in the name of Jesus.

56. Any spirit wife, husband, children and evil relations in this marriage, die, in the name of Jesus.

10

Chapter

PRAYERS FOR NEWLY MARRIED COUPLE

CHAPTER OVERVIEW

- *Understanding God's plan for marriage*
- *Divine expectations in a marriage*
- *Dealing with ghosts of the past*
- *True relationship outside marriage*
- *God's purpose for marriage*
- *Enemies of marriage*

UNDERSTANDING GOD'S PLAN FOR MARRIAGE

Without knowing God's plan and purpose for marriage, it is difficult to know the right prayers to say when preparing for marriage.

> *"And the LORD God said, It is not good that the man should be alone; I will make him an help meet for him. And Adam gave names to all cattle, and to the fowl of the air, and to every beast of the field; but for Adam there was not found a helpmeet for him. And the rib, which the LORD God had taken from man, made he a woman, and brought her unto the man. And Adam said, This is now bone of my bones, and flesh of my flesh: she shall be called Woman, because she was taken out of Man. Therefore shall a man leave his father and his mother, and shall cleave unto his wife: and they shall be one flesh"* (Genesis 2:18, 20, 22-24).

When God saw that man needed a helpmeet, He made provisions for Adam's helpmeet. God used Adam's rib to create the woman and they became one flesh. God is the same yesterday, today and forever. Whatever He pronounced to be good is good. Except for the few who are eunuchs, all others cannot survive alone and fulfill their destiny on earth except they get married.

> *"The Pharisees also came unto him, tempting him, and saying unto him, Is it lawful for a man to put away his wife for every cause? And he answered and said unto them, Have ye not read, that he which made them at the beginning made them male and female, And said, For this cause shall a man leave father and mother, and shall cleave to his wife: and they twain shall be one flesh? For there are some eunuchs, which were so born from their mother's womb: and there are some eunuchs, which were made eunuchs of men: and there be eunuchs, which have made themselves eunuchs for the kingdom of heaven's sake. He that is able to receive it, let him receive it"* (Matthew 19:3-5,12).

Another problem is that many people jump into marriages without due preparations. The same people eventually quit halfway when challenges come.

DIVINE EXPECTATIONS IN A MARRIAGE

For any marriage to work and meet its divine expectations, there must be total leaving and cleaving. The Scriptures was clear on this.

> *"So ought men to love their wives as their own bodies. He that loveth his wife loveth himself. For no man ever yet hated his own flesh; but nourisheth and cherisheth it, even as the Lord the church: For we are members of his body, of his flesh, and of his bones. For this cause shall a man leave his father and mother, and shall be joined unto his wife, and they two shall be one flesh"* (Ephesians 5:28-31).

Marriage detaches a man and woman from their parents and brings them together to become one. Before being married, you sought counsel from parents, friends and people close to you. However, as soon as you get married, you then have limit to which you can relate with your family and friends, though you are not to abandon them completely. You are expected to devote your time and resources to your partner.

After marriage, you are expected to leave your parents and friends to cleave to your partner. You cannot insist on doing things the way you used to do in the past. You have the responsibility to put your partner into consideration in whatever you do. Your parents and friends may expect you to do some things the way you used to, but doing so can potentially bring problems into your marriage.

It is common for parents and friends to demand for more details about your spouse. However, you need to be wise not to make your family vulnerable. Some friends and family members can go as far as accusing you of withdrawing from them or your partner controlling your movements. You do not need to apologize to anyone for cleaving to your partner. Take your stand and do what is right before God as if your happiness depends on it.

Marriage is for people who have matured mind. Discipline, good temperance, self-control, self-denial and selflessness are key elements that are needful in marriage. You must be independent to some extent with a life of industry and ability to provide for yourself. It is very risky to depend on someone to provide for you and your family. Such dependence is catastrophic.

> *"But from the beginning of the creation God made them male and female. For this cause shall a man leave his father and mother, and cleave to his wife; And they twain shall be one flesh: so then they are no more twain, but one flesh. What therefore God hath joined together, let not man put asunder"* (Mark 10:6-9).

It is your duty to do everything possible to protect your marriage because as long as your partner is alive, you have no other alternative. Usually, the first assignment for newly married couple is to leave and cleave. If they fail in this area, the purpose of marriage stands a chance of failing. God can only fulfill His purpose in a marriage that leaving and cleaving was honored. Therefore, if you are married and you know there are still loopholes, correct them. When you do so, God blesses your marriage.

DEALING WITH GHOSTS OF THE PAST

Believers who failed to maintain godly relationship during courtship by getting into lust and immorality before getting married require genuine repentance. You must do everything possible to deal with the sins of your past and determine not to return to them. Otherwise, they ruin your marriage. You must abandon relationships outside your marriage that do not propagate purity. Nevertheless, if you choose to commit adultery, you will suffer the consequence of your soul being entangled.

TRUE RELATIONSHIP OUTSIDE MARRIAGE

After getting married, you can still maintain healthy and profitable relationships with other people through work and family. Such relationships must have nothing to do with lust and sexual sins.

> *"A friend loveth at all times, and a brother is born for adversity"* (Proverbs 17:17).

> *"Now the end of the commandment is charity out of a pure heart, and of a good conscience, and of faith unfeigned: Holding faith, and a good conscience; which some having put away concerning faith have made shipwreck"* (1 Timothy 1:5, 19).

You must also abandon any relationship that does not promote chastity out of pure heart. Without pure and good conscience that promotes faith in Christ, no relationship can be fruitful. Returning to your old sinful lifestyle after marriage breaks God's heart and attracts demons to attack families. That is why it is necessary to leave completely in order to cleave. Many men and women have given their partners their bodies but not their hearts and Spirits. While their bodies are with their partners, their minds think of old affairs with their old lovers.

> *"Rebuke not an elder, but entreat him as a father; and the younger men as brethren; The elder women as mothers; the younger as sisters, with all purity... Lay hands suddenly on no man, neither be partaker of other men's sins: keep thyself pure"* (1 Timothy 5:1-2, 22).

> *"Flee also youthful lusts: but follow righteousness, faith, charity, peace, with them that call on the Lord out of a pure heart. But foolish and unlearned questions avoid, knowing that they do gender strifes"* (2 Timothy 2:22-23).

While you are expected to respect people, you must insist on honoring your relationship with God more. God commanded us to flee from lusts, foolishness and sins. Regardless of how pleasant your past sinful relationship with your former lover was before you married, you must repent and cut off any link that exists, which links you to your old vomit. When you fail to do this, you cannot see God's purpose and plan being fulfilled in your marriage. No matter how poor you are, avoid gifts from old lovers in order to avoid evil traps.

> *"For the love of money is the root of all evil: which while some coveted after, they have erred from the faith, and pierced themselves through with many sorrows. But thou, O man of God, flee these things; and follow after righteousness, godliness, faith, love, patience, meekness. Fight the good fight of faith, lay hold on eternal life, where unto thou art also called, and hast professed a good profession before many witnesses. I give thee charge in the sight of God, who quickeneth all things, and before Christ Jesus, who before Pontius Pilate witnessed a good confession; That thou keep this commandment without spot, unrebukeable, until the appearing of our Lord Jesus Christ: O Timothy, keep that which is committed to thy trust, avoiding profane and vain babblings, and oppositions of science falsely so called: Which some professing have erred concerning the faith. Grace be with thee. Amen. The first to Timothy was written from Laodicea, which is the chiefest city of Phrygia Pacatiana"* (1 Timothy 6:10-14, 20-21).

> *"He that leadeth into captivity shall go into captivity: he that killeth with the sword must be killed with the sword. Here is the patience and the faith of the saints"* (Revelation 13:10).

Learn how to hold on to your faith at home, office or wherever you find yourself regardless of the consequence. Always keep eternal life in view. I have discovered that the area where devil takes greatest advantage is in the failure of most married people to leave former lives completely and cleave to official partners. Any human or thing that comes in-between your marriage and you is evil. Do not allow love of money to tear your marriage apart. At the initial stages of marriage, you are bound to encounter problems. Nevertheless, when couples determine truthfully to leave former things behind in order to cleave to each other, overcoming challenges becomes very easy.

> *"Go from the presence of a foolish man, when thou perceivest not in him the lips of knowledge"* (Proverbs 14:7).

> *"Cease, my son, to hear the instruction that causeth to err from the words of knowledge"* (Proverbs 19:27).

> *"Dearly beloved, I beseech you as strangers and pilgrims, abstain from fleshly lusts, which war against the soul; Having your conversation honest among the Gentiles: that, whereas they speak against you as evildoers, they may by your good works, which they shall behold, glorify God in the day of visitation"* (1 Peter 2:11-12).

Avoid any person or thing that is capable of breaking the covenant of marriage. It is better to suffer loss of an old friend than to disobey God. He will surely reward all obedience to His Word and will. In addition, it is catastrophic to disobey God no matter what you gain immediately or afterwards. True relationships outside of marriage are those that propagate purity and faith in Christ Jesus.

GOD'S PURPOSE FOR MARRIAGE

God has a reason behind the 'why' He established the institution of marriage. Besides procreation, there are other relevant reasons, which I want to discuss.

1. TO PRESERVE PURITY

There is no place in the Scriptures where God permitted youths, adults or teenagers to practice a little bit of immorality. It is unacceptable. All immoralities attract severe punishment from God.

> *"We lie down in our shame, and our confusion covereth us: for we have sinned against the LORD our God, we and our fathers, from our youth even unto this day, and have not obeyed the voice of the LORD our God"* (Jeremiah 3:25).

> *"And Samson went down to Timnath, and saw a woman in Timnath of the daughters of the Philistines. And he came up, and told his father and his mother, and said, I have seen a woman in Timnath of the daughters of the Philistines: now therefore get her for me to wife. Then his father and his mother said unto him, Is there never a woman among the daughters of thy brethren, or among all my people, that thou goest to take a wife of the uncircumcised Philistines? And Samson said unto his father, Get her for me; for she pleaseth me well"* (Judges 14:1-3).

God forbids immorality and it causes shame and confusion. Samson tried got involved in immorality and it brought calamity upon him. The elders in Israel practiced immorality and twenty-three thousands men died. King David, who was close to God, succumbed to immorality and God chastised him.

> *"A foolish woman is clamorous: she is simple, and knoweth nothing. For she sitteth at the door of her house, on a seat in the high places of the city, To call passengers who go right on their ways: Whoso is simple, let him turn in hither: and as for him that wanteth understanding, she saith to him, Stolen waters are sweet, and bread eaten in secret is pleasant. But he knoweth not that the dead are there; and that her guests are in the depths of hell"* (Proverbs 9:13-18).

Even licensed prostitutes are not free the wrath of God. It is a foolish thing to engage in immorality. Unrepentant prostitutes will eventually end up in hell fire with all their lusts.

"For a whore is a deep ditch; and a strange woman is a narrow pit. She also lieth in wait as for a prey, and increaseth the transgressors among men" (Proverbs 23:27-28).

"Whoso loveth wisdom rejoiceth his father: but he that keepeth company with harlots spendeth his substance" (Proverbs 29:3).

"Do not prostitute thy daughter, to cause her to be a whore; lest the land fall to whoredom, and the land become full of wickedness" (Leviticus 19:29).

The Scripture described a whore as deep ditch and narrow pit. Those who practice immorality multiply their sorrows. Rewards for immorality include woes, sorrow, contention and incurable diseases. Immorality promotes poverty and leads to hell fire. Where immorality abounds, wickedness and all manner of evil abound much more.

"Will ye steal, murder, and commit adultery, and swear falsely, and burn incense unto Baal, and walk after other gods whom ye know not; And come and stand before me in this house, which is called by my name, and say, We are delivered to do all these abominations?" (Jeremiah 7:9-10).

"Notwithstanding I have a few things against thee, because thou sufferest that woman Jezebel, which calleth herself a prophetess, to teach and to seduce my servants to commit fornication, and to eat things sacrificed unto idols. And I gave her space to repent of her fornication; and she repented not. Behold, I will cast her into a bed, and them that commit adultery with her into great tribulation, except they repent of their deeds" (Revelation 2:20-22).

"There shall be no whore of the daughters of Israel, nor a sodomite of the sons of Israel" (Deuteronomy 23:17).

However, immoralities that Christians practice in churches are worse. They grieve God's heart and bring immediate judgment on earth. People that practice immorality in churches are very wicked. It is like raping a woman before her husband. Therefore, God's purpose for marriage is to preserve purity, holiness in the church and the nations at large.

"Nevertheless, to avoid fornication, let every man have his own wife, and let every woman have her own husband. But if they cannot contain, let them marry: for it is better to marry than to burn. And unto the married I command, yet not I, but the Lord, Let not the wife depart from her husband: But and if she depart, let her remain unmarried, or be reconciled to her husband: and let not the husband put away his wife" (1 Corinthians 7:2, 9-11).

"Let not a widow be taken into the number under threescore years old, having been the wife of one man, Well reported of for good works; if she have brought up children, if she have lodged strangers, if she have washed the saints' feet, if she have relieved the afflicted, if she have diligently followed every good work. But the younger widows refuse: for when they have begun to wax wanton against Christ, they will marry; Having damnation, because they have cast off their first faith. And withal they learn to be idle, wandering about from house to house; and not only idle, but tattlers also and busybodies, speaking things, which they ought not. I will therefore that the younger women marry, bear children, guide the house, give none occasion to the adversary to speak reproachfully. For some are already turned aside after Satan" (1 Timothy 5:9-15).

It is good to get married instead of prostituting. Immorality or sex outside marriage defiles the land and attracts divine judgment. God instituted marriage to keep people away from immorality. Lust, secret love and fleshly desires have no support in Scriptures. They attract curses. Any relationship that propagates immorality provokes God and brings His wrath upon the parties involved.

2. TO MAKE COMPLETE AND BRING FULFILLMENT

God ordained that men should marry in order to become complete or fulfilled. After creating Adam, God took a part of Adam and created Eve. This means that Eve made Adam complete.

"And he answered and said unto them, Have ye not read, that he which made them at the beginning made them male and female, And said, For this cause shall a man leave father and mother, and shall cleave to his wife: and they twain shall be one flesh? Wherefore they are no more twain, but one flesh. What therefore God hath joined together, let not man put asunder. They say unto him, Why did Moses then command to give a writing of divorcement, and to put her away? He saith unto them, Moses because of the hardness of your hearts suffered you to put away your wives: but from the beginning it was not so. And I say unto you, Whosoever shall put away his wife, except it be for fornication, and shall marry another, committeth adultery: and whoso marrieth her which is put away doth commit adultery. His disciples say unto him, If the case of the man be so with his wife, it is not good to marry. But he said unto them, All men cannot receive this saying, save they to whom it is given. For there are some eunuchs, which were so born from their mother's womb: and there are some eunuchs, which were made eunuchs of men: and there be eunuchs, which have made themselves eunuchs for the kingdom of heaven's sake. He that is able to receive it, let him receive it" (Matthew 19:4-12).

Marriage provides companionship, comfort, love, fellowship, and partnership. It is difficult to enjoy these things except in a divine marriage.

"Two are better than one; because they have a good reward for their labor. For if they fall, the one will lift up his fellow: but woe to him that is alone when he falleth; for he hath not another to help him up. Again, if two lie together, then they have heat: but how can one be warm alone?" (Ecclesiastes 4:9-11).

Marriages initiated by God as His perfect will receive perfect joy. He knows what you do not have and knows a perfect partner who has it. Through marriage, God is able to satisfy your need through your partner. Things you cannot do could be your partner's area of expertise. That is why your strength and differences should complement or balance each other in marriage.

When God helps you to marry a perfect partner, your life improves greatly. Such improvement enhances productivity, which eventually makes one to have good rewards for labor. In any area you lack, your partner gladly fills it, and in any area your partner lacks, you gladly do the same.

When you are weak and likely to fail, your partner remains strong to encourage you. These things may appear minor sometimes, but your success in life would greatly depend on it. Humble yourself and ask God to give you the wisdom you need to know the areas of your weakness and strength, and that of your partner. That is why you need to start appreciating your partner more so that God would bless you and increase your love for your partner.

"For the husband is the head of the wife, even as Christ is the head of the church: and he is the savior of the body. For no man ever yet hated his own flesh; but nourisheth and cherisheth it, even as the Lord the church: For we are members of his body, of his flesh, and of his bones. For this cause shall a man leave his father and mother, and shall be joined unto his wife, and they two shall be one flesh" (Ephesians 5:23, 29-31).

A woman without a husband is like a headless person without direction. You may not really appreciate the headship of your husband until you lose him. For a woman to have true direction, she needs a husband. However, when you have a husband and you do not appreciate him, you may not succeed or be happy. Likewise, when you prefer other men to your husband for whatever reason, you will never enjoy your marriage. A genuine acceptance of your husband or wife and your willingness to always provide encouragement is capable of changing your situation forever.

"Wives, submit yourselves unto your own husbands, as unto the Lord. For the husband is the head of the wife, even as Christ is the head of the church: and he is the

savior of the body. Therefore as the church is subject unto Christ, so let the wives be to their own husbands in every thing" (Ephesians 5:22-24).

As a wife, when you refuse to submit to your head, you will remain confused. You cannot achieve your purpose on earth and be happy when you are confused. A woman needs to be patient and pray to God when her husband does not show her love. By so doing, she wins back his love and enjoys the purpose of her marriage in full.

Husbands who search for love and satisfaction outside their marriage will never find one. There can be no genuine satisfaction outside marriage. When you fail to love your wife, whatever love you show to other women is lust and it leads to death eventually. The best and the only option is for you to fear and obey God, who commanded all men to love their wives as Christ loves the church.

In situations where your wife refuses to submit to you as Scriptures commanded, you do not need to hate or fight her. Whatever you can do to love your wife as your own body, do so. If it causes you to pray more, fast or take insults, go ahead and do so. When your obedience is complete, the Lord would intervene on your behalf.

True fellowship, companionship, partnership and comfort start when you determine to do all that Scriptures demand of you. Couples that quarrel and fight cannot enjoy peace in marriage until they repent and determine to obey God's Word. If it stresses you to obey God's commands in marriage, it is worth it. Therefore, if you must choose to stay single, let it not be because of childlessness, faithlessness, confusion and religious compulsion.

"This is a true saying, If a man desire the office of a bishop, he desireth a good work. A bishop then must be blameless, the husband of one wife, vigilant, sober, of good behavior, given to hospitality, apt to teach; Not given to wine, no striker, not greedy of filthy lucre; but patient, not a brawler, not covetous; One that ruleth well his own house, having his children in subjection with all gravity; (For if a man know not how to rule his own house, how shall he take care of the church of God?)" (1 Timothy 3:1-5).

Apart from being a eunuch, all should marry to become complete and fulfilled.

3. FOR PROCREATION

Another important reason for marriage is for procreation.

"So God created man in his own image, in the image of God created he him; male and female created he them. And God blessed them, and God said unto them, Be fruitful,

and multiply, and replenish the earth, and subdue it: and have dominion over the fish of the sea, and over the fowl of the air, and over every living thing that moveth upon the earth" (Genesis 1:27-28).

"And God blessed Noah and his sons, and said unto them, Be fruitful, and multiply, and replenish the earth" (Genesis 9:1).

God wants couples to be fruitful, multiply and replenish the earth. Man is created as a social being to enjoy a marriage relationship and live in families.

"The earth shook, the heavens also dropped at the presence of God: even Sinai itself was moved at the presence of God, the God of Israel" (Psalms 68:8).

"Lo, children area heritage of the LORD: and the fruit of the womb is his reward" (Psalms 127:3).

God wants married couples to have children that will take after them. It is not the will of God to be childless. Children are God's heritage. Any power that opposes childbirth is a deadly enemy.

"And hath made of one blood all nations of men for to dwell on all the face of the earth, and hath determined the times before appointed, and the bounds of their habitation" (Acts 17:26).

Children that are born in families increase to make a nation from different communities. That is why marriage is important for the continuation of the society. When marriages begin to fail or break down, societies begin to suffer.

ENEMIES OF MARRIAGE

Every marriage has enemies that attack it. Some of these enemies have succeeded in ruining countless families. Money is a major enemy that has paralyzed many marriages by instigating incessant conflicts and hostilities because of lack of money.

> *"For the love of money is the root of all evil: which while some coveted after, they have erred from the faith, and pierced themselves through with many sorrows"* (1 Timothy 6:10).

Many families do not know how to budget for their needs according to their income. They go on spending all that they have and even borrow money to satisfy their wants. This is a sure way to enter into bondage. A family that cannot sit down and plan how to spend money according to its income is bound to enter into debt and bondage. By the time such family enters into bondage, other problems arise.

> *"Husbands, love your wives, even as Christ also loved the church, and gave himself for it; That he might sanctify and cleanse it with the washing of water by the word, That he might present it to himself a glorious church, not having spot, or wrinkle, or any such thing; but that it should be holy and without blemish. So ought men to love their wives as their own bodies. He that loveth his wife loveth himself"* (Ephesians 5:25-28).

Lack of love and affection is another great enemy of marriage. When the love of a husband for the wife ceases to exist, there is bound to be trouble. There are evil spirits that exchange or transfer people's love for their partners to their agents. Once they succeed in doing this, the affection of husbands towards their wives or vice versa transfer to strange women or men. When devil truncates love in marriage, fierce trouble starts. Strife, impatience, malice, bitterness, nagging and fighting would characterize that marriage. This is because joy, peace and happiness that belong to that marriage have been truncated.

> *"Judge not, that ye be not judged. For with what judgment ye judge, ye shall be judged: and with what measure ye mete, it shall be measured to you again. And why beholdest thou the mote that is in thy brother's eye, but considerest not the beam that is in thine own eye? Or how wilt thou say to thy brother, Let me pull out the mote out of thine eye; and, behold, a beam is in thine own eye? Thou hypocrite, first cast out the beam out of thine own eye; and then shalt thou see clearly to cast out the mote out of thy brother's eye. Give not that which is holy unto the dogs, neither cast ye your pearls before swine, lest they trample them under their feet, and turn again and rend you. Ask, and it shall be given you; seek, and ye shall find; knock, and it shall be*

opened unto you it shall be given you; seek, and ye shall find; knock, and it shall be opened unto you" (Matthew 7:1-7).

Couples that quarrel all the time cannot discuss or plan for the future of their family. Rather they spend their time looking for faults and failures. Criticism is also common between them. Unforgivingness and hostilities are characteristics of such couple. That is when the man or the woman starts searching for love outside marriage citing hostility in the family.

"Neither give place to the devil" (Ephesians 4:27).

"Casting all your care upon him; for he careth for you. Be sober, be vigilant; because your adversary the devil, as a roaring lion, walketh about, seeking whom he may devour: Whom resist steadfast in the faith, knowing that the same afflictions are accomplished in your brethren that are in the world" (1 Peter 5:7-9).

Devil knows how to take control of such marriages and dictate the affairs of the family. The result of hostility in marriages is usually hatred, pride and spiritual apathy. When the headship of a man in the family is threatened, he may begin to search elsewhere for love. He begins to come home late at nights. He begins to neglect his responsibilities. Likewise, when the woman is not loved, she may begin to search for love elsewhere. She begins to withdraw her love for her husband. All these cause spiritual or physical separation and divorce. If they have children, the children suffer at the end.

"And Laban gave to Rachel his daughter Bilhah his handmaid to be her maid. And he went in also unto Rachel, and he loved also Rachel more than Leah, and served with him yet seven other years. And when the LORD saw that Leah was hated, he opened her womb: but Rachel was barren. And Leah conceived, and bare a son, and she called his name Reuben: for she said, Surely the LORD hath looked upon my affliction; now therefore my husband will love me" (Genesis 29:29-32).

"And when Rachel saw that she bare Jacob no children, Rachel envied her sister; and said unto Jacob, Give me children, or else I die. And Jacob's anger was kindled against Rachel: and he said, Am I in God's stead, who hath withheld from thee the fruit of the womb?" (Genesis 30:1-2).

The final stage could be a polygamous war, and eternal consequences of life in hell. These things are not your portions in the name of Jesus Amen.

PRAYERS FOR NEWLY MARRIED COUPLE

Bible References: Genesis 2:18-24; Matthew 19:4-5, 10-11; Ephesians 5:31

Begin with praise and worship

1. Every enemy of my marriage, you are finished, die by force, in the name of Jesus.
2. Any problem that has entered into my marriage, come out and die, in the name of Jesus.
3. Any serpent in the garden of my marriage, die, in the name of Jesus.
4. I command every problem that entered my marriage from my foundation to die, in the name of Jesus.
5. Every inherited bondage in my marriage, break, in the name of Jesus.
6. I disgrace any power that is challenging God's plan for my marriage, in the name of Jesus.
7. O Lord, help my partner and I to meet each other's needs, in the name of Jesus.
8. O Lord, help me to leave and cleave forever to my life partner, in the name of Jesus.
9. Let any evil attachment in my marriage catch fire and burn to ashes, in the name of Jesus.
10. Any evil personality that is controlling my marriage, be exposed and disgraced, in the name of Jesus.
11. Any evil carry-over from my past into my marriage, I reject you, in the name of Jesus.
12. Every problem that attacked my parents and that is now attacking me, die, in the name of Jesus.
13. Blood of Jesus, wash my marriage and deliver it from evil past, in the name of Jesus.
14. O Lord, give my partner and I understanding that will promote our marriage, in the name of Jesus.
15. I destroy any devilish wisdom that exists in my marriage, in the name of Jesus.

16. Any power that is attacking my marriage in my dreams, attack yourself and die, in the name of Jesus.

17. Let every good thing that has departed from my marriage come back by force, in the name of Jesus.

18. Every demon of immorality that is assigned to torment my marriage, die, in the name of Jesus.

19. I reject any relationship outside my marriage, in the name of Jesus.

20. Blood of Jesus, speak my marriage out of evil captivity, in the name of Jesus.

21. I discard any evil friend that is interfering in my marriage, in the name of Jesus.

22. Any spirit husband or wife that is attacking my marriage, die, in the name of Jesus.

23. I separate my marriage from demonic interference, in the name of Jesus.

24. Any satanic poison that was injected into my marriage, dry up by fire, in the name of Jesus.

25. I reject every parental curse that was placed upon my marriage, in the name of Jesus.

26. Any family idol that is controlling my marriage, lose your hold by force, in the name of Jesus.

27. I command every evil utterance that was made over my marriage to expire, in the name of Jesus.

28. Let every evil covenant and curse over my marriage be frustrated, in the name of Jesus.

29. I disgrace any witch or wizard that is manipulating my marriage, in the name of Jesus.

30. Let all hidden and open curses over my marriage expire forever, in the name of Jesus.

31. I terminate every periodical problem that is tormenting my marriage, in the name of Jesus.

32. Let divination, enchantments and bewitchment that was made over my marriage backfire, in the name of Jesus.

33. I release every organ of my body that agents of devil captured, in the name of Jesus.

34. I terminate demonic harassments in my dreams over my marriage, in the name of Jesus.

35. Let arrows of marital disgrace and infirmity that was fired at my marriage backfire, in the name of Jesus.

36. I uproot every strange growth, evil plantations and deposits in my marriage, in the name of Jesus.

37. Let strife and controversies cease from existing in my marriage, in the name of Jesus.

38. Let ungodly family pressures, foolish advices and all manner of evil interference in my marriage stop, in the name of Jesus.

39. O Lord, use my marriage to preserve my purity, completeness and fulfillments, in the name of Jesus.

40. Every enemy of divine procreation in my marriage, die, in the name of Jesus.

41. I terminate every attack made on my marriage in the dreams, in the name of Jesus.

42. Let demonic criticism, evil accusation, pride, intimidation and anger over my marriage cease forever, in the name of Jesus.

43. I command the spirit of fighting, quarrelling, lying and dishonesty in my marriage to die, in the name of Jesus.

44. O Lord, deliver my marriage from hatred, violence and lust of the flesh, in the name of Jesus.

45. O Lord, deliver my family from prayerlessness and weakness, in the name of Jesus.

46. Blood of Jesus, remove every satanic communication gap in my marriage, in the name of Jesus.

47. Every evil counselor that was assigned to ruin my marriage, be disgraced, in the name of Jesus.

48. Any power that has soured my relationship with suspicion, die, in the name of Jesus.

49. Let the spirit of murmuring, sexual weakness, and negative medical reports in my marriage die, in the name of Jesus.

50. I uses the blood of Jesus against every demonic delay in my marriage, in the name of Jesus.

51. I use the blood of Jesus against defeats and works of devil, in the name of Jesus.

52. Father Lord, deliver my marriage from consequences of ancestral sins, in the name of Jesus.

53. Any wicked personality that is promoting problem in my family, die with your problems, in the name of Jesus.

54. Let the backbone of problems in my marriage be broken now, in the name of Jesus.

55. Lord Jesus, uproot every evil thing that stands against my advancement, in the name of Jesus.

11

Chapter

PRAYERS TO EXPERIENCE LOVE IN YOUR MARRIAGE

CHAPTER OVERVIEW

- *Where is the love of God?*
- *God expects us to love one another*
- *Christ demonstrated divine love*
- *Service, care and showing concern*
- *Manifestations of true love in a Christian home*
- *Considering one another*
- *Comforting one another*
- *Bearing each other's burden*

WHERE IS THE LOVE OF GOD?

Can you testify that the love of God prevails in your family today? This is a critical area where many Christian families need prayers and deliverance. Love of God no longer existed in their homes, and as a result, devil and all his agents are celebrating in these homes as they continue to cause more damages on daily basis.

This should not be so. In fact, families that do not love do not know God, for God is love (*See* 1 John 4:8). That is why you must do everything possible to host God in your family. When God dwells in a family, there is love, peace, joy, happiness, forgiveness, and a whole lot more.

Therefore, before you go any further, take time to reevaluate the kind of love, which exists in your family.

> *"Ye have heard that it hath been said, Thou shalt love thy neighbor, and hate thine enemy. But I say unto you, Love your enemies, bless them that curse you, do good to them that hate you, and pray for them which despitefully use you, and persecute you; That ye may be the children of your Father which is in heaven: for he maketh his sun to rise on the evil and on the good, and sendeth rain on the just and on the unjust. For if ye love them which love you, what reward have ye? Do not even the publicans the same? And if ye salute your brethren only, what do ye more than others? Do not even the publicans so? Be ye therefore perfect, even as your Father which is in heaven is perfect"* (Matthew 5:43-48).

If you love only those who love you, then you have the least kind of love. If you do not do something about it, your partner would eventually become a victim of your kind of love because you cannot give what you do not have. You need a perfect love of God to succeed in your marriage in order to make heaven.

Families make up communities, villages and nations. Therefore, what happens in a family is important. The family is where spiritual experiences, love, endurance, tolerance, knowledge and obedience take place among family members, especially between a husband and wife. If the husband and his wife do not have the love of Christ in them, then the failure extends to the nation at large.

> *"And you hath he quickened, who were dead in trespasses and sins; Wherein in time past ye walked according to the course of this world, according to the prince of the power of the air, the spirit that now worketh in the children of disobedience: Among whom also we all had our conversation in times past in the lusts of our flesh, fulfilling*

the desires of the flesh and of the mind; and were by nature the children of wrath, even as others" (Ephesians 2:1-3).

"For the wages of sin is death; but the gift of God is eternal life through Jesus Christ our Lord" (Romans 6:23).

"For to be carnally minded is death; but to be spiritually minded is life and peace" (Romans 8:6)

A natural man is spiritually dead and misses God's perfect mark or standard. Such person is a child of disobedience and cannot be a child of God regardless of any church title or accomplishment.

"Wherein in time past ye walked according to the course of this world, according to the prince of the power of the air, the spirit that now worketh in the children of disobedience" (Ephesians 2:2).

"For as many as are led by the Spirit of God, they are the sons of God. For ye have not received the spirit of bondage again to fear; but ye have received the Spirit of adoption, whereby we cry, Abba, Father. The Spirit itself beareth witness with our spirit, that we are the children of God" (Romans 8:14-16).

Such person always fulfills the desires of the flesh and follows whatever the mind determines because the person is a child of wrath and not a follower of Christ. You need to be born-again before you can manifest God's love in your marriage. You need salvation that would deliver you from your sinful nature and it comes through Christ alone.

"But God, who is rich in mercy, for his great love wherewith he loved us, Even when we were dead in sins, hath quickened us together with Christ, (by grace ye are saved;) And hath raised us up together, and made us sit together in heavenly places in Christ Jesus: That in the ages to come he might shew the exceeding riches of his grace in his kindness toward us through Christ Jesus" (Ephesians 2:4-7).

"These things were done in Bethabara beyond Jordan, where John was baptizing" (John 1:28).

"And ye know that he was manifested to take away our sins; and in him is no sin" (1 John 3:5).

When you receive salvation through Christ, you can bring God's presence into your family. The love of God, which is God's divine nature, is the only love that works perfect and mighty things in families.

"Though I speak with the tongues of men and of angels, and have not charity, I am become as sounding brass, or a tinkling cymbal. And though I have the gift of prophecy, and understand all mysteries, and all knowledge; and though I have all faith, so that I could remove mountains, and have not charity, I am nothing. And though I bestow all my goods to feed the poor, and though I give my body to be burned, and have not charity, it profiteth me nothing. Charity suffereth long, and is kind; charity envieth not; charity vaunteth not itself, is not puffed up, Doth not behave itself unseemly, seeketh not her own, is not easily provoked, thinketh no evil; Rejoiceth not in iniquity, but rejoiceth in the truth; Beareth all things, believeth all things, hopeth all things, endureth all things. Charity never faileth: but whether there be prophecies, they shall fail; whether there be tongues, they shall cease; whether there be knowledge, it shall vanish away" (1 Corinthians 13:1-8).

However, experiencing the love of God does not exempt your family from temptation, trials, afflictions and problems. In fact, Paul, Job, Jeremiah and even Christ endured temptation. Nevertheless, the love of God would always see your family through.

"Ye know that ye were Gentiles, carried away unto these dumb idols, even as ye were led. [8]For to one is given by the Spirit the word of wisdom; to another the word of knowledge by the same Spirit" (1 Corinthians 12:2, 8).

"And the LORD said unto Satan, Hast thou considered my servant Job, that there is none like him in the earth, a perfect and an upright man, one that feareth God, and escheweth evil?" (Job 1:8).

"So went Satan forth from the presence of the LORD, and smote Job with sore boils from the sole of his foot unto his crown" (Job 2:7).

"For we have not an high priest which cannot be touched with the feeling of our infirmities; but was in all points tempted like as we are, yet without sin" (Hebrews 4:15).

The Spirit of God motivates your heart with the love of God, which controls your thoughts, words and actions. Our daily walk with God must reflect His nature. That is the only way we can inspire people, who desire to enjoy their marriage on earth and see God in the end to live with Him eternally.

Without the love of God in your heart, pride, selfishness, murmuring, disrupting, party spirit, division, envy, jealousy and other similar vices would ruin your marriage easily.

However, when your heart is pure and filled with God's love, the Holy Spirit dwells in you and your family enjoys boundless peace.

> *"Let this mind be in you, which was also in Christ Jesus: Who, being in the form of God, thought it not robbery to be equal with God: But made himself of no reputation, and took upon him the form of a servant, and was made in the likeness of men: And being found in fashion as a man, he humbled himself, and became obedient unto death, even the death of the cross"* (Philippians 2: 5-8).

> *"Who shall ascend into the hill of the LORD? Or who shall stand in his holy place? He that hath clean hands, and a pure heart; who hath not lifted up his soul unto vanity, nor sworn deceitfully"* (Psalms 24:3-4).

The mind of Christ produces perfect love of God. Christ reigns in a home where love of God is the bedrock of its numerous achievements and reputation. The Spirit of God makes people to obey the Word of God. Also, the Spirit of God energizes couples to obey and fear God in their marriage.

The love of God empowers a husband and his wife to live in peace as it is in heaven. This kind of love aids them to overcome difficult situations. Whatever the enemy brings in their way, the love of God keeps them going. Though the devil may mobilize humiliation, gossip, opposition, etc., it would not make this kind of husband and wife angry or force them to join issues with God.

A tree is known by its fruits. A husband and wife guided by the love of God are holy, regardless of their circumstances. They are dead to sin. They are not worldly, but are humble, lowly and meek.

> *"There remaineth therefore a rest to the people of God. For he that is entered into his rest, he also hath ceased from his own works, as God did from his"* (Hebrew 4:9-10).

> *"Then said Jesus unto his disciples, If any man will come after me, let him deny himself, and take up his cross, and follow me. For whosoever will save his life shall lose it: and whosoever will lose his life for my sake shall find it"* (Matthew 16:24-25).

> *"I beseech you therefore, brethren, by the mercies of God, that ye present your bodies a living sacrifice, holy, acceptable unto God, which is your reasonable service. And be not conformed to this world: but be ye transformed by the renewing of your mind, that ye may prove what is that good, and acceptable, and perfect, will of God"* (Romans 12:1-2).

A husband and wife guided by the love of God know how to wait upon God. They can endure affliction with hope. They consider each other always. They are not belligerent, undisciplined or rude. This is because they allow the Spirit of God to guide them.

God has enabled His children to bear His character. Therefore, desire to bear God's character so that your family would enjoy in it. Equally, any family that lives in the love of God cannot be rude, proud, boastful and envious. They would live by the fruits of the Holy Spirit.

> *"But the fruit of the Spirit is love, joy, peace, longsuffering, gentleness, goodness, faith, Meekness, temperance: against such there is no law"* (Galatians 5:22-23)

The fruits of the spirit manifest in such family beautifully. This is what makes all intentions, motives and thoughts pure. God's love in a man's heart helps him to endure reproaches and overcome every misunderstanding. He is not easily irritated and does not worry.

> *"Wives, submit yourselves unto your own husbands, as unto the Lord. For the husband is the head of the wife, even as Christ is the head of the church: and he is the savior of the body. Therefore as the church is subject unto Christ, so let the wives be to their own husbands in everything. Husbands, love your wives, even as Christ also loved the church, and gave himself for it; That he might sanctify and cleanse it with the washing of water by the word, That he might present it to himself a glorious church, not having spot, or wrinkle, or any such thing; but that it should be holy and without blemish. So ought men to love their wives as their own bodies. He that loveth his wife loveth himself. For no man ever yet hated his own flesh; but nourisheth and cherisheth it, even as the Lord the church: For we are members of his body, of his flesh, and of his bones. For this cause shall a man leave his father and mother, and shall be joined unto his wife, and they two shall be one flesh. This is a great mystery: but I speak concerning Christ and the church. Nevertheless let every one of you in particular so love his wife even as himself; and the wife see that she reverence her husband"* (Ephesians 5:22-33).

You need to pray that the love of God thrives in your family. There is nothing like it. How can we obtain this perfect nature of God?

It is simple - confess your sins and forsake them truthfully. Pray for divine impartation of God's nature in your life. You cannot obtain God's love through religious seclusion or exercises, or through human effort. You must receive this experience from God through His Spirit. When God fills your heart with His love, you can work for Him and do exploits with ease.

> *"Wherefore Jesus also, that he might sanctify the people with his own blood, suffered without the gate"* (Hebrew 13:12).

> *"And the very God of peace sanctify you wholly; and I pray God your whole spirit and soul and body be preserved blameless unto the coming of our Lord Jesus Christ. Faithful is he that calleth you, who also will do it"* (1 Thessalonians 5:23-24).

Christ suffered and died for the purpose of love. His death benefits all humanity. Salvation is for those that sin held captive. It is also for those who want to see God, hear and experience His presence in their personal lives and families.

Follow these three steps and activate the presence of God in your family –

- Realize that you and your family need the love of God to be evident at your home.
- Devote your life wholeheartedly to loving God through His Word, holding nothing back.
- Offer prayers of faith and claim God's promises.

> *"God is the LORD, which hath shewed us light: bind the sacrifice with cords, even unto the horns of the altar"* (Psalms 118:27).
>
> *"And all things, whatsoever ye shall ask in prayer, believing, ye shall receive"* (Matthew 21:22).
>
> *"Blessed be the God and Father of our Lord Jesus Christ, which according to his abundant mercy hath begotten us again unto a lively hope by the resurrection of Jesus Christ from the dead, To an inheritance incorruptible, and undefiled, and that fadeth not away, reserved in heaven for you"* (1 Peter 1:3-4)

Jesus has paid the price for the salvation of the world. Therefore, all you need is to ask in faith. As you pray, believe with all your heart and God shall answer all your prayers.

GOD EXPECTS US TO LOVE ONE ANOTHER

God expects us to love one another the way He loved us, and sent His Son to die for our sins. He expects nothing less. God's love passes all understanding and remains above all reproaches. God expects His children to model His character and love.

"Be ye therefore followers of God, as dear children" (Ephesians 5:1).

"As obedient children, not fashioning yourselves according to the former lusts in your ignorance: But as he which hath called you is holy, so be ye holy in all manner of conversation; Because it is written, Be ye holy; for I am holy. And if ye call on the Father, who without respect of persons judgeth according to every man's work, pass the time of your sojourning here in fear: Forasmuch as ye know that ye were not redeemed with corruptible things, as silver and gold, from your vain conversation received by tradition from your fathers; But with the precious blood of Christ, as of a lamb without blemish and without spot" (1 Peter 1:14-19).

As soon as we become Christians, we become God's dear children. He invites us to share in His love, which we should not limit to only those we love, but to all humanity. God's love must be evident in our homes and places of work. As God's dear children, we must be obedient to Him in order to show examples with our lives. We cannot return to our former lifestyles, but remain holy even in our conversations.

"But I say unto you, Love your enemies, bless them that curse you, do good to them that hate you, and pray for them which despitefully use you, and persecute you; That ye may be the children of your Father which is in heaven: for he maketh his sun to rise on the evil and on the good, and sendeth rain on the just and on the unjust. For if ye love them which love you, what reward have ye? Do not even the publicans the same? And if ye salute your brethren only, what do ye more than others? Do not even the publicans so? Be ye therefore perfect, even as your Father which is in heaven is perfect" (Matthew 5:44-48).

Our main duty as God's dear children is to reproduce the love of our Father in heaven on earth. When we love one another, the world will know that we are the children of our Father in heaven.

CHRIST DEMONSTRATED DIVINE LOVE

Jesus demonstrated His love for us when He died on the cross of Calvary. This love was not abstract, but concrete. We saw Him die on the cross in order to save us. Therefore, the love that exists in your family must be concrete, not abstract. Christ's love for us is tangible. A husband and his wife that claim to love each other must demonstrate practical for each other.

> *"And walk in love, as Christ also hath loved us, and hath given himself for us an offering and a sacrifice to God for a sweet-smelling savor"* (Ephesians 5:2).

> *"And whosoever doth not bear his cross, and come after me, cannot be my disciple"* (Luke 14:27).

> *"He that saith he abideth in him ought himself also so to walk, even as he walked"* (1 John 2:6)

> *"Take my yoke upon you, and learn of me; for I am meek and lowly in heart: and ye shall find rest unto your souls"* (Matthew 11:29).

Christ loved us, and gave up Himself for an offering and a sacrifice to God for the sake of our sins. He carried our cross. Likewise, there is always a cross to carry in marriage, which varies from family to family. Do not leave your marriage because of weightiness of the cross that you bear. When you do that, you are no longer a disciple of Christ.

The love for us compelled Jesus to carry a cross for us to Calvary. He also sacrificed His life for us because of love. Similarly, you would sacrifice anything to keep your marriage for the sake of love.

If anyone claims to be a Christian, such one must walk as Christ walked. We must model the kind of love Christ had for us in order to transform our marriages. Loving God with all your heart will enable you to love your wife practically, regardless of her shortcoming. The love of Christ inspires you to serve rather than desiring to be served. Jesus served with love and compassion.

> *"Even as the Son of man came not to be ministered unto, but to minister, and to give his life a ransom for many"* (Matthew 20:28).

> *"For whether is greater, he that sitteth at meat, or he that serveth? Is not he that sitteth at meat? But I am among you as he that serveth"* (Luke 22:27).

> *"He riseth from supper, and laid aside his garments; and took a towel, and girded himself. After that he poureth water into a bason, and began to wash the disciples' feet, and to wipe them with the towel wherewith he was girded"* (John 13:4-5).

SERVICE, CARE AND SHOWING CONCERN

Wise Christians pray for the kind of love Jesus has for His church to prevail in their marriages. This love compelled Jesus to take the position of servant, though He was God, great master and Savior of the world. Whatever your title, position and background are, as a believer, it is better to have a mind of a servant. You must be ready and willing to serve, care and show concern to your wife or husband for the love of God to reign in your marriage.

> *"How God anointed Jesus of Nazareth with the Holy Ghost and with power: who went about doing good, and healing all that were oppressed of the devil; for God was with him"* (Acts 10:38).

> *"When he was come down from the mountain, great multitudes followed him. And, behold, there came a leper and worshipped him, saying, Lord, if thou wilt, thou canst make me clean. And Jesus put forth his hand, and touched him, saying, I will; be thou clean. And immediately his leprosy was cleansed. And Jesus saith unto him, See thou tell no man; but go thy way, shew thyself to the priest, and offer the gift that Moses commanded, for a testimony unto them"* (Matthew 8:1-4).

Jesus healed all manner of sickness and diseases in His service to humanity. He delivered people that were possessed by demons of lunacy and paltry.

> *"And Jesus went about all Galilee, teaching in their synagogues, and preaching the gospel of the kingdom, and healing all manner of sickness and all manner of disease among the people. And his fame went throughout all Syria: and they brought unto him all sick people that were taken with divers diseases and torments, and those which were possessed with devils, and those which were lunatick, and those that had the palsy; and he healed them. And there followed him great multitudes of people from Galilee, and from Decapolis, and from Jerusalem, and from Judaea, and from beyond Jordan"* (Matthew 4:23-25).

- In His ministration and compassion, Jesus related with lepers, lunatic, blind and hungry people (*See* Matthew 8:1-4, 9:27-31, 14:15-21).
- Jesus healed the lame, dumb, maimed and epileptic people. He healed all manner of sickness and diseases (*See* Matthew 15:21-28, 17:14-18, 19:2).
- He paid tax, casted out unclean spirits, healed plagues, broke evil chains and raised the dead (*See* Matthew 17:24-27, Mark 1:23-29, 3:10-11, 4:37-41, 5:22-24, 35-42).

- Jesus healed a woman with an issue of blood for twelve years, empowered disabled people and rebuked demons that possessed people He delivered (*See* Mark 5:25-34, 6:53-56).

- Jesus destroyed barrenness, great fever and infirmities and casted out evil spirits (*See* Luke 1:5-24, 57-63, 4:38-39, 7:18-23, 13:11-13).

- He restored hope to people without hope, supplied people's needs, sponsored a wedding, healed impotent persons and raised the dead (*See* Luke 5:1-11, John 2:1-11, 5:1-9, 11:1-6, 11-45).

If you are not satisfied with the measure of love you presently give to your partner, ask Jesus to reveal His measure of love to you today and He will hear your prayers. It is better to marry and love your partner with the measure of love Jesus has for His church than to offend God through immoralities and wickedness. Against such God will judge.

> *"But fornication, and all uncleanness, or covetousness, let it not be once named among you, as becometh saints; Neither filthiness, nor foolish talking, nor jesting, which are not convenient: but rather giving of thanks"* (Ephesians 5:3-4).

There are things that people who love and fear God do not do because God commanded His children not to do them. These include -

1. FORNICATION

Fornication is sexual sin between two people who are not married. The sin of fornication is a sin against God and the body.

> *"For it seemed good to the Holy Ghost, and to us, to lay upon you no greater burden than these necessary things; That ye abstain from meats offered to idols, and from blood, and from things strangled, and from fornication: from which if ye keep yourselves, ye shall do well. Fare ye well"* (Acts 15:28-29).

> *"Mortify therefore your members which are upon the earth; fornication, uncleanness, inordinate affection, evil concupiscence, and covetousness, which is idolatry"* (Colossians 3:5).

God forbids fornication. It should not be mentioned among born-again Christians. Someone who loves God does not commit fornication because the sin of fornication ruins the love of God.

> *"But fornication, and all uncleanness, or covetousness, let it not be once named among you, as becometh saints"* (Ephesians 5:3).

> *"And changed the glory of the incorruptible God into an image made like to corruptible man, and to birds, and four-footed beasts, and creeping things. Wherefore God also gave them up to uncleanness through the lusts of their own hearts, to dishonor their own bodies between themselves"* (Romans 1:23-24).

> *"What fruit had ye then in those things whereof ye are now ashamed? For the end of those things is death"* (Romans 6:21).

> *"For God hath not called us unto uncleanness, but unto holiness"* (1 Thessalonians 4:7)

Those who break God's commandment by committing fornication cannot claim to love God.

2. UNCLEANNESS

Uncleanness is being impure in the light of the Word of God. Homosexuality and lesbianism is very unclean and none that loves God would engage in such debasing evil character. A believer that loves God would hate all forms of uncleanness.

3. COVETOUSNESS

"But fornication, and all uncleanness, or covetousness, let it not be once named among you, as becometh saints" (Ephesians 5:3).

"Mortify therefore your members which are upon the earth; fornication, uncleanness, inordinate affection, evil concupiscence, and covetousness, which is idolatry" (Colossians 3:5).

"Thou shalt not covet thy neighbor's house, thou shalt not covet thy neighbor's wife, nor his manservant, nor his maidservant, nor his ox, nor his ass, nor any thing that is thy neighbor's" (Exodus 20:17).

"Again the word of the LORD came unto me, saying" (Ezekiel 33:1).

To covert is to have strong desire for what does not belong to you. Covetousness is idolatry and those that fear God do not engage in idolatry. Idolatry is letting anything else take the place of God. In modern times, idolatry takes the form of extreme possession, pride and pleasure.

"Lay not up for yourselves treasures upon earth, where moth and rust doth corrupt, and where thieves break through and steal: But lay up for yourselves treasures in heaven, where neither moth nor rust doth corrupt, and where thieves do not break through nor steal: For where your treasure is, there will your heart be also" (Matthew 6:19-21).

"And he said unto them, Take heed, and beware of covetousness: for a man's life consisteth not in the abundance of the things which he possesseth. And he spake a parable unto them, saying, The ground of a certain rich man brought forth plentifully: And he thought within himself, saying, What shall I do, because I have no room where to bestow my fruits? And he said, This will I do: I will pull down my barns, and build greater; and there will I bestow all my fruits and my goods. And I will say to my soul, Soul, thou hast much goods laid up for many years; take thine ease, eat, drink, and be merry. But God said unto him, Thou fool, this night thy soul shall be required of thee: then whose shall those things be, which thou hast provided? So is he that layeth up treasure for himself, and is not rich toward God" (Luke 12:15-21).

"He that loveth father or mother more than me is not worthy of me: and he that loveth son or daughter more than me is not worthy of me" (Matthew 10:37).

When you trust any possession more than you trusted God, it becomes evident that you do not love God. Inordinate love of pleasure and possession can destroy your marriage. Do not let things of this world draw away your heart. Other enemies of God's love in families include:

- *Lying* - (*See* Ephesians 4:25, Micah 6:12, Romans 3:13, Revelation 21:8).
- *Malice* – (*See* Ephesians 4:3, Colossians 3:8, 1 Peter 2:1).
- *Anger and Glamour* – (*See* Ephesians 4:31, Psalms 37:8, Proverbs 6:32, Matthew 5:22).
- *Stealing* – (*See* Ephesians 4:29, Psalms 12:3).
- *Bitterness* – *See* Ephesians 4:31, Hebrew 12:15-17).
- *Evil speaking* – (*See* Ephesians 4:28, Leviticus 19:11, 13, Isaiah 61:8, John 10:1, 2 Samuel 15:1-6).
- *Filthiness* – (*See* Ephesians 4:4, James 1:21).

MANIFESTATIONS OF TRUE LOVE IN A CHRISTIAN HOME

Many Christian families lack fundamentals of true relationship at homes. While wise Christians are worried about this deficiency, others do not bother. No matter your reasons to be disgruntled, you still have to love your partner as long as you live.

What does it really take to cultivate true love of God in a Christian home? Let us therefore consider few manifestations of true love in a typical Christian home.

GREETING ONE ANOTHER

You may have authentic reasons but you would risk the danger of hell fire when you refuse to greet your partner, members of your family or your neighbors. It is also foolishness for someone to greet you and you refuse to respond because of a grudge. It is the responsibility of every Christian to greet others.

> *"Greet ye one another with a kiss of charity. Peace be with you all that are in Christ Jesus. Amen"* (1 Peter 5:14).

> *"Salute one another with a holy kiss. The churches of Christ salute you"* (Romans 16:16).

Greeting is an outward expression of kindness. It is something you do cheerfully. It is like a debt, which you pay on daily basis especially to people you meet daily. A common adage says that charity begins at home. You must greet people and accept their greetings in return. This is important as it depicts brotherliness and cooperation.

Greeting is a way of showing regard to someone you meet. Peter, the apostle, mandated believers to greet each other with love. Married couples that fail to greet themselves are setting up evil altars at their homes. An evil altar is a spiritual dining table where demons gather.

A husband that quarreled with his wife and both stopped talking or doing things together as a result has handed his family over to the devil. You cannot allow a conflict at home to stop you from doing what is right when you desire the love of God to reign in your family. Moreover, it is said that anything that is worth doing is worth doing well.

> *"Follow peace with all men, and holiness, without which no man shall see the Lord"* (Hebrew 12:14).

"Neither give place to the devil" (Ephesians 4:27).

"Casting all your care upon him; for he careth for you. Be sober, be vigilant; because your adversary the devil, as a roaring lion, walketh about, seeking whom he may devour: Whom resist steadfast in the faith, knowing that the same afflictions are accomplished in your brethren that are in the world" (1 Peter 5:7-9).

A wise person understands that there is no justification for quarrelling no matter the offense. A wise person also studies his or her partner very well in order to avoid trouble and quarrel. God's love reigns in a family where the husband and his wife nurture peace and love. It is wise to make peace with your partner no matter how he or she behaves or opposes you. In so doing, you would not give the devil a chance in your family.

CONSIDERING ONE ANOTHER

The best thing a good husband or wife does is to consider the partner first before taking any action or decision. Do not be selfish. In fact, when you consider your partner before making decisions, there would be no room for criticism, faultfinding or opposition. This common mistake often caused criticism and opposition. State your points or opinion clearly and humbly before your partner, especially when considering any important decision.

> *"And let us consider one another to provoke unto love and to good works"* (Hebrews 10:24).

Being modest and considerate would not permit you to use personal pronouns like I, me, mine all the time. The love of God compels you to consider your partner, especially members of your family. When you are considerate, modest and sincere, it becomes very easy to relate with your partner and every other person.

> *"Then answered all the wicked men and men of Belial, of those that went with David, and said, Because they went not with us, we will not give them ought of the spoil that we have recovered, save to every man his wife and his children, that they may lead them away, and depart. Then said David, Ye shall not do so, my brethren, with that which the LORD hath given us, who hath preserved us, and delivered the company that came against us into our hand. For who will hearken unto you in this matter? But as his part is that goeth down to the battle, so shall his part be that tarrieth by the stuff: they shall part alike. And it was so from that day forward, that he made it a statute and an ordinance for Israel unto this day. And when David came to Ziklag, he sent of the spoil unto the elders of Judah, even to his friends, saying, Behold a present for you of the spoil of the enemies of the LORD; To them which were in Beth–el, and to them which were in south Ramoth, and to them which were in Jattir, And to them which were in Aroer, and to them which were in Siphmoth, and to them which were in Eshtemoa, And to them which were in Rachal, and to them which were in the cities of the Jerahmeelites, and to them which were in the cities of the Kenites, And to them which were in Hormah, and to them which were in Chor–ashan, and to them which were in Athach, And to them which were in Hebron, and to all the places where David himself and his men were wont to haunt"* (1 Samuel 30:22-31).

When you develop this lovely character of putting other people first, you would save yourself many troubles. Inconsideration is one of the major problems in most families, offices and nations. Husbands and wives must consider themselves for God's love and peace to reign in families. For where there is consideration, there is growth and development.

COMFORTING ONE ANOTHER

Another element that many Christian families lack is comfort. Some husbands and wives find it very difficult to comfort themselves. God's true love in the family does not come through prayers alone. It also comes from comforting each other with words of prayer and faith. This is very important.

"Wherefore comfort one another with these words" (1 Thessalonians 4:18).

Many couples have either separated or divorced because they ignored to provide comfort to one another. The best comfort one can give is comfort through the Word of God. None desires to live with someone who does not give him or her comfort through the Word.

Failure to provide comfort is capable of causing a family or nation to collapse. Husbands and wives that do not comfort themselves cannot stay together for long. No soldier or army can win a battle where there is no support or comfort. It is very hard to succeed in life without support or comfort.

Comfort is like a pillar that holds a building. It is like a foundation. Once it fails, the building collapses. A football team that lacks tactical support and comfort from coaching crew cannot win any match no matter how good and talented the team is. When you comfort your partner and your children, they bring out the best in them.

No human is useless, unproductive and valueless, as most people would have us believe. What helps people to develop is the amount of encouragement or discouragement they encounter on daily basis.

> *"And the angel of the LORD appeared unto him, and said unto him, The LORD is with thee, thou mighty man of valor. And Gideon said unto him, Oh my Lord, if the LORD be with us, why then is all this befallen us? And where be all his miracles, which our fathers told us of, saying, Did not the LORD bring us up from Egypt? But now the LORD hath forsaken us, and delivered us into the hands of the Midianites. And the LORD looked upon him, and said, Go in this thy might, and thou shalt save Israel from the hand of the Midianites: have not I sent thee? And he said unto him, Oh my Lord, wherewith shall I save Israel? Behold, my family is poor in Manasseh, and I am the least in my father's house. And the LORD said unto him, Surely I will be with thee, and thou shalt smite the Midianites as one man"* (Judges 6:12-16).

Gideon was born just like every other Jewish boy. He dreaded the strength of the Midianites and did not imagine he could be very instrumental in the deliverance of his people. His tribe, Manasseh, was the poorest in Israel. Though he was from the poorest family in Manasseh, yet he became a mighty man of valor.

The people around him, including circumstances that prevailed in his time, convinced him that he was an ordinary slave who cannot be useful. He accepted that verdict and lived averagely until God sent an angel to reveal his real identity to him. After an encounter with an angel, Gideon became encouraged and the rest was history.

Comforting someone rebirths hope and strength. It also cheers the person that is being comforted and eases grief and trouble. It consoles the heart in times of worry or trouble. That is why your wife or husband needs your comfort now and again. God commanded it. Therefore, comfort yourselves with affirming words.

BEARING EACH OTHER'S BURDEN

One of the main reasons for marriage is to share and bear each other's burden. No single person would make it alone. It is a sin to watch your partner die of a particular burden without helping him or her. It is even worse when you become a burden to your life partner. If your partner dies from carrying burden, then you have a terrible case before God. You are in danger of hell fire. It is foolishness to be a part of your family's problem.

> *"Two are better than one; because they have a good reward for their labor. For if they fall, the one will lift up his fellow: but woe to him that is alone when he falleth; for he hath not another to help him up"* (Ecclesiastes 4:9-10).

> *"And the LORD God said, It is not good that the man should be alone; I will make him a help meet for him. And out of the ground the LORD God formed every beast of the field, and every fowl of the air; and brought them unto Adam to see what he would call them: and whatsoever Adam called every living creature, that was the name thereof"* (Genesis 2:18-19).

God instituted marriage for a husband and his wife to be complete. Two people who agree together are better than one million people who are in disagreement. Husband and wife who agree can solve any problem. They would complement each other's weakness. When one loses his job, the other will bear the burden until he gets another job. Marriage is a divine ordination, in which a man cannot do without a woman, and vice versa.

> *"Nevertheless neither is the man without the woman, neither the woman without the man, in the Lord"* (1 Corinthians 11:11).

> *"And he answered and said unto them, Have ye not read, that he which made them at the beginning made them male and female, And said, For this cause shall a man leave father and mother, and shall cleave to his wife: and they twain shall be one flesh?"* (Matthew 19:4-5).

That is why when you have sexual need in a marriage relationship, your partner meets your sexual need, which helps you to preserve your purity.

> *"Nevertheless, to avoid fornication, let every man have his own wife, and let every woman have her own husband. But if they cannot contain, let them marry: for it is better to marry than to burn. And unto the married I command, yet not I, but the Lord, Let not the wife depart from her husband: But and if she depart, let her remain unmarried, or be reconciled to her husband: and let not the husband put away his wife"* (1 Corinthians 7:2, 9-11).

"Let not a widow be taken into the number under threescore years old, having been the wife of one man, Well reported of for good works; if she have brought up children, if she have lodged strangers, if she have washed the saints' feet, if she have relieved the afflicted, if she have diligently followed every good work. But the younger widows refuse: for when they have begun to wax wanton against Christ, they will marry; Having damnation, because they have cast off their first faith. And withal they learn to be idle, wandering about from house to house; and not only idle, but tattlers also and busybodies, speaking things, which they ought not. I will therefore that the younger women marry, bear children, guide the house, give none occasion to the adversary to speak reproachfully. For some are already turned aside after Satan" (1 Timothy 5:9-15).

It is a mandate that when your partner carries a sexual burden, you relieve the burden no matter your reason. If you hesitate to relieve your partner's burden, you stand the chance of polluting the church and the community if he or she commits adultery. Wives and husbands must come together to relieve their sexual burdens. There is no other provision that God made to relieve your partner of sexual burden. Therefore, when you deny your partner his or her conjugal right, you put yourself in danger of hell fire.

"Bear ye one another's burdens, and so fulfill the law of Christ" (Galatians 6:2).

When Christians bear one another's burden, they fulfill the law of Christ. When you empower another man or woman to relieve your partner of sexual burden outside your marriage, then you are guilty of defiling your marriage.

Shechem raped Dinah and all the males of the land died as a result.

"And Dinah the daughter of Leah, which she bare unto Jacob, went out to see the daughters of the land. And when Shechem the son of Hamor the Hivite, prince of the country, saw her, he took her, and lay with her, and defiled her. And his soul clave unto Dinah the daughter of Jacob, and he loved the damsel, and spake kindly unto the damsel. And Shechem spake unto his father Hamor, saying, Get me this damsel to wife. And Jacob heard that he had defiled Dinah his daughter: now his sons were with his cattle in the field: and Jacob held his peace until they were come" (Genesis 34:1-5).

Reuben did it and lost his birthright and blessing. He sold his entire lineage into bondage

"And it came to pass, when Israel dwelt in that land, that Reuben went and lay with Bilhah his father's concubine: and Israel heard it. Now the sons of Jacob were twelve" (Genesis 35:22).

"And Jacob called unto his sons, and said, Gather yourselves together, that I may tell you that which shall befall you in the last days. Gather yourselves together, and hear, ye sons of Jacob; and hearken unto Israel your father. Reuben, thou art my firstborn, my might, and the beginning of my strength, the excellency of dignity, and the excellency of power" (Genesis 49:1-3).

Samson did it with a wrong woman and he lost his two eyes and life.

"Then went Samson to Gaza, and saw there a harlot, and went in unto her. And it was told the Gazites, saying, Samson is come hither. And they compassed him in, and laid wait for him all night in the gate of the city, and were quiet all the night, saying, In the morning, when it is day, we shall kill him. And Samson lay till midnight, and arose at midnight, and took the doors of the gate of the city, and the two posts, and went away with them, bar and all, and put them upon his shoulders, and carried them up to the top of an hill that is before Hebron. And it came to pass afterward, that he loved a woman in the valley of Sorek, whose name was Delilah. And the lords of the Philistines came up unto her, and said unto her, Entice him, and see wherein his great strength lieth, and by what means we may prevail against him, that we may bind him to afflict him: and we will give thee every one of us eleven hundred pieces of silver. And Delilah said to Samson, Tell me, I pray thee, wherein thy great strength lieth, and wherewith thou mightest be bound to afflict thee. And Samson said unto her, If they bind me with seven green withs that were never dried, then shall I be weak, and be as another man" (Judges 16:1-7).

The sons of Eli did the same and received a curse. They later died in the battlefield. David tried it and the sword never departed from his household, together with the curse of immorality. When Solomon continued in it, his enemies increased, and he lost all respect.

"But king Solomon loved many strange women, together with the daughter of Pharaoh, women of the Moabites, Ammonites, Edomites, Zidonians, and Hittites; Of the nations concerning which the LORD said unto the children of Israel, Ye shall not go in to them, neither shall they come in unto you: for surely they will turn away your heart after their gods: Solomon clave unto these in love. And he had seven hundred wives, princesses, and three hundred concubines: and his wives turned away his sheart. For it came to pass, when Solomon was old, that his wives turned away his heart after other gods: and his heart was not perfect with the LORD his God, as was the heart of David his father. For Solomon went after Ashtoreth the goddess of the Zidonians, and after Milcom the abomination of the Ammonites. And Solomon did evil in the sight of the LORD, and went not fully after the LORD, as did David his father. Then did Solomon build an high place for Chemosh, the abomination of Moab, in the hill that is before Jerusalem, and for Molech, the abomination of the children of

Ammon. And likewise did he for all his strange wives, which burnt incense and sacrificed unto their gods. And the LORD was angry with Solomon, because his heart was turned from the LORD God of Israel, which had appeared unto him twice, And had commanded him concerning this thing, that he should not go after other gods: but he kept not that which the LORD commanded. Wherefore the LORD said unto Solomon, Forasmuch as this is done of thee, and thou hast not kept my covenant and my statutes, which I have commanded thee, I will surely rend the kingdom from thee, and will give it to thy servant. And it came to pass at that time when Jeroboam went out of Jerusalem, that the prophet Ahijah the Shilonite found him in the way; and he had clad himself with a new garment; and they two were alone in the field: And Ahijah caught the new garment that was on him, and rent it in twelve pieces: And he said to Jeroboam, Take thee ten pieces: for thus saith the LORD, the God of Israel, Behold, I will rend the kingdom out of the hand of Solomon, and will give ten tribes to thee: (But he shall have one tribe for my servant David's sake, and for Jerusalem's sake, the city which I have chosen out of all the tribes of Israel:)Because that they have forsaken me, and have worshipped Ashtoreth the goddess of the Zidonians, Chemosh the god of the Moabites, and Milcom the god of the children of Ammon, and have not walked in my ways, to do that which is right in mine eyes, and to keep my statutes and my judgments, as did David his father" (1 Kings 11:1-11, 29-33).

I do not know what really happened but David unburdened his burden outside his marriage and he entered into trouble, collective captivities with his family.

PRAYERS TO EXPERIENCE LOVE IN YOUR MARRIAGE

Bible references: Ephesians 5:25-33, 1 Corinthians 13:1-7, Ephesians 4:32, Colossians 3:19

Begin with praise and worship

1. I command every fake love in my marriage to die forever, in the name of Jesus.
2. Father Lord, impart Your love on my marriage today, in the name of Jesus.
3. I disgrace every enemy of divine love in my marriage, in the name of Jesus.
4. Blood of Jesus, speak divine and true love unto my marriage, in the name of Jesus.
5. Let the love of God in my marriage increase, in the name of Jesus.
6. Let the tree of divine love in my marriage begin to bear fruits, in the name of Jesus.
7. I command the presence of lusts of the flesh in my marriage to die, in the name of Jesus.
8. Let any evil arrow that was fired at my marriage from evil altars backfire, in the name of Jesus.
9. I unseat evil personalities that are hindering God's love in my marriage, in the name of Jesus.
10. Blessed Holy Ghost, increase the love of God in my marriage today, in the name of Jesus.
11. I disgrace satanic agents that were hired to steal God's love in my marriage, in the name of Jesus.
12. Let any curse that was placed upon my marriage expire, in the name of Jesus.
13. I deliver my marriage from the hands of enemies of love, in the name of Jesus.
14. Every seed of hatred that was planted in my marriage, catch fire and burn to ashes, in the name of Jesus.
15. Every negative word that was spoken over my marriage, be nullified, in the name of Jesus.
16. I uproot any sin that was planted to destroy God's love in my marriage, in the name of Jesus.

17. I break the backbone of enemies of divine love in my marriage, in the name of Jesus.
18. I break and loose my marriage from spiritual forces of the waters, in the name of Jesus.
19. You, my marriage, receive double grace to manifest God's love forever, in the name of Jesus.
20. Let the rivers of divine love begin to flow into my marriage, in the name of Jesus.
21. I disengage every enemy of divine love that was assigned to my marriage, in the name of Jesus.
22. I release divine expectation of true love into my marriage, in the name of Jesus.
23. Let my marriage imitate true love of God forever, in the name of Jesus.
24. Let the pattern of love from above begin to manifest in my marriage, in the name of Jesus.
25. I receive power to love my partner more than before, in the name of Jesus.
26. Let there be evidence of divine love in my family, in the name of Jesus.
27. Every enemy of divine love in my marriage, be disgraced, in the name of Jesus.
28. O Lord, perform a miracle of love in my marriage today, in the name of Jesus.
29. I disgrace any power that is polluting God's love in my marriage, in the name of Jesus.
30. I disengage every agent of hatred and rejection in my marriage, in the name of Jesus.
31. Any negative character that is attacking divine love in my marriage, die, in the name of Jesus.
32. Let every demonic storm that is attacking God's love in my marriage cease, in the name of Jesus.
33. Anointing of divine love, fall upon my marriage, in the name of Jesus.
34. I terminate every evil word that is frustrating God's love in my marriage, in the name of Jesus.
35. Fire of God, burn every instrument of devil in my marriage, in the name of Jesus.
36. Let the resurrection power quicken every dead area of love in my marriage, in the name of Jesus.

37. Father Lord, command Your divine love to manifest in my marriage forever, in the name of Jesus.
38. Any womb that has swallowed divine love in my marriage, vomit it now, in the name of Jesus.
39. I release the love of God upon my marriage, in the name of Jesus.
40. I reclaim divine love that belongs to my marriage, in the name of Jesus.

12
Chapter

PRAYERS FOR FERTILITY IN YOUR MARRIAGE

CHAPTER OVERVIEW

- *Believers and the ability to bear fruits*
- *Benefits of salvation*
- *Dangers of a curse prevailing in a person's life or circumstance*
- *Evil inheritance and satanic attacks*
- *The covenant of healing*

BELIEVERS AND THE ABILITY TO BEAR FRUITS

God destined all His true children, through His Word, to be fruitful and to reproduce. Therefore, infertility is not part of the inheritance for God's children. As a true believer, you are to bear fruit in everything you do in life. Also, God gave all females, through His Word, the capability to conceive, grow or develop egg, even at an old age. That is why you cannot afford to accept anything other than fruitfulness in your marriage.

> *"And all these blessings shall come on thee, and overtake thee, if thou shalt hearken unto the voice of the LORD thy God. [4]Blessed shall be the fruit of thy body, and the fruit of thy ground, and the fruit of thy cattle, the increase of thy kine, and the flocks of thy sheep"* (Deuteronomy 28:2, 4).

Therefore, great resourcefulness to give birth to plenty of children characterizes the nature of a woman. Believers have the power to bear whatever numbers of children they wanted.

> *"And he is the propitiation for our sins: and not for ours only, but also for* the sins of *the whole world"* (1 John 2:2).

ATTACKS ON ORGANS OF THE BODY

When God created man in His image, there was no error or malfunctioning. In addition, God gave man dominion over all that He created. He commanded man to be fruitful and reproduce his kind.

> *"So God created man in his* own *image, in the image of God created he him; male and female created he them. And God blessed them, and God said unto them, Be fruitful, and multiply, and replenish the earth, and subdue it: and have dominion over the fish of the sea, and over the fowl of the air, and over every living thing that moveth upon the earth. [31]And God saw everything that he had made, and, behold,* it was *very good. And the evening and the morning were the sixth day"* (Genesis 1:27-28, 31).

Originally, man walked in innocence, holiness and purity until he voluntarily disobeyed God. Adam and Eve transgressed the law of God and fell into sin and death. Adam's fall corrupted human race. Man became a polluted being, sharpened in iniquity and utterly lost the righteousness God, which the Word of God required from him. Sin opens the door of our lives to problems and disease. That was how man became a traitor and an outcast, and all creatures turned against him.

Adam incurred the wrath of God and God rejected him. He lost his spiritual position before God, which made it easy for Satan to attack him incessantly. Sin exposed him to evil. Satan terrorized humanity with sickness, shame, incurable diseases and death. Adam's fall is the source of all evil attacks on people's organs.

> *"So went Satan forth from the presence of the LORD, and smote Job with sore boils from the sole of his foot unto his crown"* (Job 2:7).

> *"Ye are of* your *father the devil, and the lusts of your father ye will do. He was a murderer from the beginning, and abode not in the truth, because there is no truth in him. When he speaketh a lie, he speaketh of his own: for he is a liar, and the father of it"* (John 8:44).

> *"Afterward Jesus findeth him in the temple, and said unto him, Behold, thou art made whole: sin no more, lest a worse thing come unto thee"* (John 5:14).

God is not the author of infertility. It is the work of the devil. However, God loves you and wants you to enjoy His promise of fruitfulness. He wants to deliver you from captivity of barrenness. He wants to heal and restore the organs of your body and make you fertile. However, are you willing to receive God's blessing?

> *"For God so loved the world, that he gave his only begotten Son, that whosoever believeth in him should not perish, but have everlasting life"* (John 3:16).

> *"The thief cometh not, but for to steal, and to kill, and to destroy: I am come that they might have life, and that they might have* it *more abundantly"* (John 10:10).

God's love for humanity compelled Him to offer His only begotten Son as an acceptable sacrifice for the remission of the sins of the world. Jesus Christ took our place and suffered for us so that we would no longer suffer. God sent Him to this world so that whosoever believes in Him would not perish, but have everlasting life. It is simple. If you believe in Christ, you will no longer suffer from failures of organs of your body. Christ will heal your infertility.

> *"And Jesus went about all Galilee, teaching in their synagogues, and preaching the gospel of the kingdom, and healing all manner of sickness and all manner of disease among the people. And his fame went throughout all Syria: and they brought unto him all sick people that were taken with divers diseases and torments, and those, which were possessed with devils, and those, which were lunatic, and those that had the palsy; and he healed them. And there followed him great multitudes of people from*

Galilee, and from *Decapolis, and from Jerusalem, and* from *Judaea, and* from *beyond Jordan"* (Matthew 4:23-25).

When Christ entered into the city of Galilee, He taught and preached the gospel of the kingdom and healed people as well. As I am teaching you now, so it was in those days. Some of the people, who listened to Jesus, suffered from diverse sicknesses and diseases. Devil possessed some in many parts of their bodies. Some were lunatics, while others were paralyzed in the womb, eyes, ears, etc.

However, as soon as they heard Jesus and believed Him, they received their deliverance and healing. Jesus solved all their problems. He traversed many cities teaching people to believe in God, and in Him, whom God had sent.

> *"How God anointed Jesus of Nazareth with the Holy Ghost and with power: who went about doing good, and healing all that were oppressed of the devil; for God was with him"* (Acts 10:38).

> *"When the even was come, they brought unto him many that were possessed with devils: and he cast out the spirits with* his *word, and healed all that were sick: That it might be fulfilled which was spoken by Esaias the prophet, saying, Himself took our infirmities, and bare* our *sicknesses"* (Matthew 8:16-17).

Today, Jesus has come to your city because of your faith. He wants to do you good, heal you and deliver you from oppression. He cleansed lepers, healed diseases, delivered the oppressed, restored sights, healed the lame, loosed the dumb, fed the hungry, cast out unclean spirits, destroyed plagues, calmed storms and raised the dead. If Jesus did all these things, then He has the power to energize your barren womb and make you mother of many children. Jesus wants to take aware your burden. Will you give Him a chance?

> *"Forasmuch as ye know that ye were not redeemed with corruptible things,* as *silver and gold, from your vain conversation* received *by tradition from your fathers; But with the precious blood of Christ, as of a lamb without blemish and without spot: Who verily was foreordained before the foundation of the world, but was manifest in these last times for you, Who by him do believe in God, that raised him up from the dead, and gave him glory; that your faith and hope might be in God"* (1 Peter 1:18-21).

> *"Neither is there salvation in any other: for there is none other name under heaven given among men, whereby we must be saved"* (Acts 4:12).

There is no other source of salvation or deliverance other than the blood of Jesus. Christ was the perfect sacrifice, which pleased God. He died, yet He rose again. He lives and mediates between God and man. The application of the blood of Jesus transforms the most evil and sinful person into a spotless child of the living God. If you repent now and accept Jesus as your only Savior, a miracle would take place.

> *"Who his own self bare our sins in his own body on the tree, that we, being dead to sins, should live unto righteousness: by whose stripes ye were healed"* (1 Peter 2:24).

> *"And I heard a loud voice saying in heaven, Now is come salvation, and strength, and the kingdom of our God, and the power of his Christ: for the accuser of our brethren is cast down, which accused them before our God day and night. And they overcame him by the blood of the Lamb, and by the word of their testimony; and they loved not their lives unto the death"* (Revelation 12:10-11).

The sacrifice of Jesus was the only death that was necessary and acceptable to satisfy the demands of divine justice.

> *"Look unto me, and be ye saved, all the ends of the earth: for I* am *God, and* there is *none else"* (Isaiah 45:22).

> *"The next day John seeth Jesus coming unto him, and saith, Behold the Lamb of God, which taketh away the sin of the world"* (John 1:29).

> *"And the Spirit and the bride say, Come. And let him that heareth say, Come. And let him that is athirst come. And whosoever will, let him take the water of life freely"* (Revelation 22:17).

God invites all humanity to repent and accept the sacrifice of Jesus at Calvary, so that He would deliver, heal and save all men from sin and death.

> *"For God so loved the world that he gave his only begotten Son, that whosoever believeth in him should not perish, but have everlasting life. For God sent not his Son into the world to condemn the world; but that the world through him might be saved"* (John 3:16-17).

All sinners who refused to repent of their sins and accept Christ will be condemned eternally for rejecting the salvation, which Jesus offers. True repentance demands total abandonment of sin and turning oneself in to God. Someone who is in God abhors sin and turns away from them.

When you repent and confess that Jesus is Lord through faith, Jesus saves you. You may not comprehend how it happened. It is by grace that we are saved, not by works or personal effort. Naturally, the sin of Adam corrupts all men to be blind and deaf. Nevertheless, through the grace of God, we obtain a spiritual nature that helps us to live righteously for God.

BENEFITS OF SALVATION

There are tremendous benefits of salvation. When Jesus saves a sinner, the same sinner obtains complete deliverance from God. He is no longer slave to sin and consequences of sinful past. The salvation that Jesus gives means that we are no longer under the powers of our enemies, slavery, physical pain, suffering, infirmities and death.

The gospel of repentance and salvation was the pillar of the gospel Jesus and the apostles preached. If you have not received salvation, then you have nothing. Moreover, if you have fallen from faith, you need to return to God. It is dangerous to backslide because it is capable of taking you back to satanic bondage, sorrow, affliction and attacks of all manner of sicknesses.

> *"Again, when I say unto the wicked, Thou shalt surely die; if he turns from his sin, and do that which is lawful and right;* If *the wicked restore the pledge, give again that he had robbed, walk in the statutes of life, without committing iniquity; he shall surely live, he shall not die. None of his sins that he hath committed shall be mentioned unto him: he hath done that which is lawful and right; he shall surely live"* (Ezekiel 33:14-16).

The surest way for sinners and backsliders to come home is through genuine repentance of sin and confessing that Jesus is Lord. The best illustration of this is the story of the prodigal son. It was not until he realized how deeply he had fallen and how wretched he had become that he desired to return to his father's house, where, at least, he could eat a decent meal.

There was once a man called Robert Robinson, who wrote the Hymn '*Come, thou fount of every blessings*'. Sometime in his life, he backslid and wandered into the path of iniquity. Eventually, he became frustrated and deeply troubled in his spirit. Hoping to relieve his mind, he decided to embark on a journey to a faraway country where no one knew him.

However, in the course of his journey, he became acquainted with a young woman who asked him what he thought of a hymn she had been reading. To his surprise, he found out it was none other than his own composition. He struggled to evade her question, but she continued to press him for an answer. In a moment of time, he began to cry. With tears streaming down his cheeks, he said, *"I am the man who wrote that hymn many years ago. I would give anything to experience again the joy I knew then"*.

The woman was greatly surprised, and she reassured him that the "streams of mercy" detailed in his song still flowed. Robinson was deeply touched. Running home with a wounded heart, like the prodigal son, the Lord welcomed him with opened arms and restored him to full relationship and fellowship with Him. You too can return to God, no matter how far you have wandered away.

> *"And when he came to himself, he said, How many hired servants of my father's have bread enough and to spare, and I perish with hunger! I will arise and go to my father, and will say unto him, Father, I have sinned against heaven, and before thee, And am no more worthy to be called thy son: make me as one of thy hired servants. And he arose, and came to his father. But when he was yet a great way off, his father saw him, and had compassion, and ran, and fell on his neck, and kissed him"* (Luke 15:17-20).

When the prodigal son remembered the love and care of his father, he arose and returned home to the enduring love of his caring father. You need the joy and fellowship of Christ to flourish in your life. If the Holy Spirit is convicting you through these words, cry unto God for His mercy, forgiveness and grace to live right again. In addition, determine to return home today. It is better at home that in that wilderness.

I encourage you to do away with cheap and false commendations of men and seek true fellowship with God through fervent prayers instead. You must make practical decisions against sin, wherever it exists in your life. Guard your salvation fervently with fear and trembling.

> *"And Ehud came unto him; and he was sitting in a summer parlor, which he had for himself alone. And Ehud said, I have a message from God unto thee. And he arose out of* his *seat. And Ehud put forth his left hand, and took the dagger from his right thigh, and thrust it into his belly: And the haft also went in after the blade; and the fat closed upon the blade, so that he could not draw the dagger out of his belly; and the dirt came out. Then Ehud went forth through the porch, and shut the doors of the parlor upon him, and locked them"* (Judges 3:20-23).

> *"I have fought a good fight, I have finished* my *course, I have kept the faith: Henceforth there is laid up for me a crown of righteousness, which the Lord, the righteous judge, shall give me at that day: and not to me only, but unto all them also that love his appearing"* (2 Timothy 4:7-8).

Your faith in Christ is a priceless treasure, which you must hold fast. Do not exchange it with anything else. You must persevere to the end and never allow the threat of the devil in form of infertility to sweep away your faith in Christ Jesus. In the darkest hour when it seemed all hope is lost, trust in God as Abraham, Zachariah and Hannah did.

DANGERS OF A CURSE PREVAILING IN A PERSON'S LIFE OR CIRCUMSTANCE

Before we discuss the issue of curses, let us consider how demons possess people or attack body organs without mercy.

> *"If I shut up heaven that there be no rain, or if I command the locusts to devour the land, or if I send pestilence among my people; If my people, which are called by my name, shall humble themselves, and pray, and seek my face, and turn from their wicked ways; then will I hear from heaven, and will forgive their sin, and will heal their land"* (2 Chronicles 7:13-14).

Sin is the main thing that creates a surest path for problems and satanic attacks. Devil has every right to attack you when you sin and make yourself vulnerable. He knows how to infest your life with so much evil when you consult with familiar spirits, palm readers, fortunetellers and magicians. A wise Christian would never dine with satanic agents.

> *"Afterward Jesus findeth him in the temple, and said unto him, Behold, thou art made whole: sin no more, lest a worse thing come unto thee"* (John 5:14).

> *"Neither give place to the devil"* (Ephesians 4:27).

> *"But the Spirit of the LORD departed from Saul, and an evil spirit from the LORD troubled him. And Saul's servants said unto him, Behold now, an evil spirit from God troubleth thee"* (1 Samuel 16:14-15).

When Jesus Christ healed the lame man, he advised him to go and sin no more, least a worst thing comes upon him. If the man ignored Jesus and went back to sin, devil would have put him a worse condition. When Saul, the first king of Israel, sinned against God, the Spirit of God departed from him, and an evil spirit entered into him and tormented him.

> *"When the men of Israel saw that they were in a strait, (for the people were distressed,) then the people did hide themselves in caves, and in thickets, and in rocks, and in high places, and in pits. And* some *of the Hebrews went over Jordan to the land of Gad and Gilead. As for Saul, he* was *yet in Gilgal, and all the people followed him trembling. And he tarried seven days, according to the set time that Samuel had appointed: but Samuel came not to Gilgal; and the people were scattered from him. And Saul said, Bring hither a burnt offering to me, and peace offerings. And he offered the burnt offering. And it came to pass, that as soon as he had made an end of offering the burnt offering, behold, Samuel came; and Saul went out to meet him, that he might salute him. And Samuel said, What hast thou done? And Saul said, Because I saw*

that the people were scattered from me, and that *thou camest not within the days appointed,* and that *the Philistines gathered themselves together at Michmash; Therefore said I, The Philistines will come down now upon me to Gilgal, and I have not made supplication unto the LORD: I forced myself therefore, and offered a burnt offering. And Samuel said to Saul, Thou hast done foolishly: thou hast not kept the commandment of the LORD thy God, which he commanded thee: for now would the LORD have established thy kingdom upon Israel forever. But now thy kingdom shall not continue: the LORD hath sought him a man after his own heart, and the LORD hath commanded him* to be *captain over his people, because thou hast not kept* that *which the LORD commanded thee"* (1 Samuel 13:6-14).

Another thing that empowers devil to attack some people is their failure to resist the devil. You cannot fail to resist the devil and at the same time enjoy the covenant of healing.

When Adam ate the forbidden fruit, he ran away from God instead of repenting. God laid a curse on him and drove him out from the garden. When Cain killed his brother, God cursed him and he became a vagabond and fugitive upon the earth. When Ham looked at his father's nakedness, he cursed him to remain servants to his brothers. What role does curse play to prevent Christians from the covenant of healing?

"Our fathers have sinned, and are *not; and we have borne their iniquities. Servants have ruled over us: there* is *none that doth deliver* us *out of their hand. The crown is fallen* from *our head: woe unto us that we have sinned"* (Lamentations 5:7-8, 16).

We know that a curse plays a significant role in preventing people from enjoying the covenant of healing and blessing. Nevertheless, a curse that has no cause shall not stand. What then is a curse?

- Curse is the direct opposite of blessing.
- Curse is an evil utterance that is said over a person, in order to cause harm or destruction.
- It refers to evil words put together to torment a person physically.
- A curse is an invisible spiritual barrier that forms to oppose a person's progress or destiny.
- It is like a heap of problems moving from one area of a person's life to another.
- It is a spell cast upon a person to control his or her life contrary to God's plans.

The most important thing to understand at this point is that it is not the will of God that curse prevails in any one's life. God's will is that all men should come to His salvation and blessing, which He provided through Jesus Christ.

However, most people have chosen to remain in spiritual darkness, where devil has continued to torment them. Such people remain at high risk because everything they do fail to yield good results. Life's efforts amount to nothing useful when curse prevails in a person's life. The devil knows how to abort or thwart efforts of a cursed person. Some things that happen to a cursed person would defy any natural explanation. There have been cases of sudden disappearance of riches and incessant trials.

> "[15]*And Joshua made peace with them, and made a league with them, to let them live: and the princes of the congregation sware unto them.* [22]*And Joshua called for them, and he spake unto them, saying, Wherefore have ye beguiled us, saying, We* are *very far from you; when ye dwell among us?* [23]*Now therefore ye* are *cursed, and there shall none of you be freed from being bondmen, and hewers of wood and drawers of water for the house of my God.* [27]*And Joshua made them that day hewers of wood and drawers of water for the congregation, and for the altar of the LORD, even unto this day, in the place which he should choose"* (Joshua 9:15, 22, 23, 27).

Cursed people face limitation and satanic attacks always. They suffer premature death, hatred and rejection. Some of them suffer from infertility, barrenness, prolonged pregnancies or miscarriage. Believers who are under inherited curses cannot enjoy their lives on earth. Some of them marry but cannot enjoy their marriages. In some cases, medical science would fail to explain reasons for their barrenness, miscarriage at advanced stages and prolonged pregnancies. Sin brings a curse and if you do not cease from sin, worst things could still come upon you.

> "[35]*The LORD shall smite thee in the knees, and in the legs, with a sore botch that cannot be healed, from the sole of thy foot unto the top of thy head.* [66]*And thy life shall hang in doubt before thee; and thou shalt fear day and night, and shalt have none assurance of thy life:* [67]*In the morning thou shalt say, Would God it were even! And at even thou shalt say, Would God it were morning! For the fear of thine heart wherewith thou shalt fear, and for the sight of thine eyes which thou shalt see"* (Deuteronomy 28:35, 66-67).

EVIL INHERITANCE AND SATANIC ATTACKS

In the fourth chapter of 2nd Kings, we read the story of the wife of one of the sons of the prophet. Though she was innocent, she came under attack because of her late husband's debt. The creditors also threatened to seize her two sons for an offence they did not commit. Debt cannot be good inheritance.

> *"Now there cried a certain woman of the wives of the sons of the prophets unto Elisha, saying, Thy servant my husband is dead; and thou knowest that thy servant did fear the LORD: and the creditor is come to take unto him my two sons to be bondmen"* (2 Kings 4:1).

> *"The leprosy therefore of Naaman shall cleave unto thee, and unto thy seed for ever. And he went out from his presence a leper* as white *as snow"* (2 Kings 5:27).

Gehazi inherited Naaman's leprosy because of his greed and lies. The curse did not stop with Gehazi who sinned but went down to his seed forever. Such inheritance also cannot be good inheritance.

> *"Then there was a famine in the days of David three years, year after year; and David enquired of the LORD. And the LORD answered, It is for Saul, and for his bloody house, because he slew the Gibeonites"* (2 Samuel 21:1).

> *"And when the child was grown, it fell on a day, that he went out to his father to the reapers. And he said unto his father, My head, my head. And he said to a lad, Carry him to his mother. And when he had taken him, and brought him to his mother, he sat on her knees till noon, and* then *died"* (2 Kings 4:18-20).

The sin of slaughtering the Gibeonites, which Saul committed, brought famine upon David and all Israelites for three years. The famine also affected children, who were not born when Saul committed the sin. Nevertheless, thank God for David's wisdom to inquire of the Lord for the source of the problem. This was another case of evil inheritance.

Then there was a case of satanic attack on the son of the woman of Shunem. Devil attacked him when he was to be useful to his parents. Notice that devil attacks people with curses when they are about to move into destiny. Devil fired arrows of premature death at his head without announcement and he died.

Likewise, devil has continued to fire arrows of infertility at many wombs because of the reality of evil inheritance or inability to resist the devil. However, we know that Jesus has given us the power to resist the devil:

"Submit yourselves therefore to God. Resist the devil, and he will flee from you" (James 4:7).

It is only possible for devil to shut your womb when you backslide or remain to sin. Sins of dead ancestors can make someone impotent, barren, or even cause death. Problems can still attack your womb or organ of your body even when you are a true child of God like Job. The good news is that you can resist the devil successfully. Therefore, learn how to resist the devil and enter into the covenant of healing today.

THE COVENANT OF HEALING

Covenant is a legal contract into which two or more people enter and by which they bind their course of action. In the case of God and His children, God made a covenant of healing with His children through His Word. It is very important therefore that every Christian understands and partakes in God's covenant of healing. The psalmist wrote of God:

> *"Who forgiveth all thine iniquities; who healeth all thy diseases"* (Psalms 103:3).

When the children of Israel entered the wilderness, the Lord brought them into the covenant of healing with Him. They enjoyed sound health until they began to murmur. Instead of praying, they complained against God and Moses and it became a sin to them.

> *"So Moses brought Israel from the Red sea, and they went out into the wilderness of Shur; and they went three days in the wilderness, and found no water. And when they came to Marah, they could not drink of the waters of Marah, for they* were *bitter: therefore, the name of it was called Marah. And the people murmured against Moses, saying, What shall we drink? And he cried unto the LORD; and the LORD shewed him a tree,* which *when he had cast into the waters, the waters were made sweet: there he made for them a statute and an ordinance, and there he proved them, And said, If thou wilt diligently hearken to the voice of the LORD thy God, and wilt do that which is right in his sight, and wilt give ear to his commandments, and keep all his statutes, I will put none of these diseases upon thee, which I have brought upon the Egyptians: for I* am *the LORD that healeth thee"* (Exodus 15:22-26).

Because of their murmur and grumble, they usually encountered troubles on a large scale. However, when Moses began to pray, God brought them into a covenant of healing. That is why you need to enter into this covenant of healing today so that simple prayers of faith would eliminate your problems easily. God promised to forgive all your iniquities and heal all your diseases today. Cue into this covenant and receive your healing.

> *"And ye shall serve the LORD your God, and he shall bless thy bread, and thy water; and I will take sickness away from the midst of thee. There shall nothing cast their young, nor be barren, in thy land: the number of thy days I will fulfill. I will send my fear before thee, and will destroy all the people to whom thou shalt come, and I will make all thine enemies turn their backs unto thee. And I will send hornets before thee, which shall drive out the Hivite, the Canaanite, and the Hittite, from before thee. I will not drive them out from before thee in one year; lest the land become desolate and the beast of the field multiply against thee. By little and little I will drive them out from*

before thee, until thou be increased, and inherit the land. And I will set thy bounds from the Red sea even unto the sea of the Philistines, and from the desert unto the river: for I will deliver the inhabitants of the land into your hand; and thou shalt drive them out before thee" (Exodus 23:25-31).

"Wherefore it shall come to pass, if ye hearken to these judgments, and keep, and do them, that the LORD thy God shall keep unto thee the covenant and the mercy which he swore unto thy fathers: And he will love thee, and bless thee, and multiply thee: he will also bless the fruit of thy womb, and the fruit of thy land, thy corn, and thy wine, and thine oil, the increase of thy kine, and the flocks of thy sheep, in the land which he swore unto thy fathers to give thee. Thou shalt be blessed above all people: there shall not be male or female barren among you, or among your cattle. And the LORD will take away from thee all sickness, and will put none of the evil diseases of Egypt, which thou knowest, upon thee; but will lay them upon all them *that hate thee"* (Deuteronomy 7:12-15).

When you repent today and begin to serve the Lord in your own little way and at every given opportunity, God would bless your bread and water. That bread and water with God's blessing on them are able to bring healing to all your sicknesses. No matter how powerful your problems are, they cannot withstand the power of God. Let there be no more miscarriages, barrenness or premature deaths in everything you do, in the name of Jesus.

"Blessed shall be *the fruit of thy body, and the fruit of thy ground, and the fruit of thy cattle, the increase of thy kine, and the flocks of thy sheep"* (Deuteronomy 28:4).

"Thou shalt be blessed above all people: there shall not be male or female barren among you, or among your cattle. And the LORD will take away from thee all sickness, and will put none of the evil diseases of Egypt, which thou knowest, upon thee; but will lay them upon all them *that hate thee"* (Deuteronomy 7:14-15).

Barrenness, infertility and miscarriage would surrender to you when you enter into covenant of healing with God. You are among the people of God's covenant, a holy people and a peculiar treasure. Start enjoying the benefit and blessing of being in the covenant of healing with God.

Sickness, demonic attack, pestilence, plague, heart failure, fever, cancer, fibroid, boil, swelling, itching, inflammation, barrenness, etc., cannot overcome you anymore because you are now in a covenant of healing with God. God will make your womb fertile again because you have entered into His covenant of healing.

Do not be in doubt because God clearly said:

"If I shut up heaven that there be no rain, or if I command the locusts to devour the land, or if I send pestilence among my people; If my people, which are called by my name, shall humble themselves, and pray, and seek my face, and turn from their wicked ways; then will I hear from heaven, and will forgive their sin, and will heal their land" (2 Chronicles 7:13-14).

Now, it is up to you to trust God and repent of your sins or not. Tell God whatever you want through prayers and He shall answer your.

PRAYERS FOR FERTILITY IN YOUR MARRIAGE

Bible References Exodus 23:25-26, Deuteronomy 28: 1-14

Begin with praise and worship

1. You, wicked infertility that is prevailing in my life, die, in the name of Jesus.
2. You, my body, receive power of Jesus and be fertile now, in the name of Jesus.
3. Blood of Jesus, flow into my life and empower the organs of my body, in the name of Jesus.
4. Holy Ghost fire, burn enemies of my fertility to ashes, in the name of Jesus.
5. Any problem that entered into my body through dream, come out and die, in the name of Jesus.
6. You my body, begin to bear fruits by fire, in the name of Jesus.
7. Every undeveloped area of my life, begin to develop now, in the name of Jesus.
8. O Lord, arise and perfect Your work of creation in my life, in the name of Jesus.
9. Any strange fire that is burning in my body, quench immediately, in the name of Jesus.
10. I receive power to bear godly children without stress, in the name of Jesus.
11. Let evil pollution in my body catch fire and burn to ashes, in the name of Jesus.
12. Any satanic terrorist in my reproductive organ, die immediately, in the name of Jesus.
13. Any power that is eating up my fertility eggs, die, in the name of Jesus.
14. O Lord, arise and remove Your wrath from my life, in the name of Jesus.
15. Every disease, germ and sickness in my body, die from your root, in the name of Jesus.
16. I withdraw my body from the captivity of evil altars, in the name of Jesus.
17. I expose and disgrace witches and wizards that are frustrating my fertility, in the name of Jesus.

18. I refuse to give my body organs for evil burials, in the name of Jesus.
19. Let dead areas of my body receive resurrection power of God, in the name of Jesus.
20. Every weapon of death in my body, die and die forever, in the name of Jesus.
21. Any spirit of death that is living in my body, die, in the name of Jesus.
22. I recover my stolen reproductive organs from graveyard, in the name of Jesus.
23. Father Lord, deliver me from the consequences of my past sins, in the name of Jesus.
24. I terminate evil arrest of my reproductive organs, in the name of Jesus.
25. Any evil covenant and curse that is keeping me in bondage, expire, in the name of Jesus.
26. Blood of Jesus, cleanse me and make me spotless, in the name of Jesus.
27. I arrest enemies of my deliverance, in the name of Jesus.
28. I uproot evil plantations that thrive in my body, in the name of Jesus.
29. Any evil attack on my body, be frustrated, in the name of Jesus.
30. O Lord, send Your healing power into my system today, in the name of Jesus.
31. Any satanic arrow that was fired at my body, I fire you back, in the name of Jesus.
32. Any evil power that is feeding me in dreams, die, in the name of Jesus.
33. I vomit evil foods I have ever eaten in my dreams, in the name of Jesus.
34. I lift all satanic embargoes that were placed upon my marriage, in the name of Jesus.
35. I break and loose myself from the bondage of spiritual marriage, in the name of Jesus.
36. O Lord, bless and empower my bread and water today, in the name of Jesus.
37. Let the benefits of healing covenant begin to manifest in my life, in the name of Jesus.
38. Let the power of the Holy Ghost energize my body today, in the name of Jesus.
39. Any evil utterance that is prospering in my life, expire, in the name of Jesus.
40. Let evil yokes in my life break by fire, in the name of Jesus.

41. Every good door that was closed to my marriage, open by force, in the name of Jesus.

42. Lord Jesus, intervene in my situation today, in the name of Jesus.

43. Let the angel of God visit the camp of my enemies today, in the name of Jesus.

44. I command unrepentant enemies of my life to bow and give up the ghost, in the name of Jesus.

13

Chapter

PRAYERS TO CONCEIVE AND BEAR CHILDREN

CHAPTER OVERVIEW

- *God has a purpose for marriage*
- *Stand on the Word of God and decree your conception*
- *The faithful God*

GOD HAS A PURPOSE FOR MARRIAGE

God created everything on the universe with purpose, including marriage. He put everything in order and commanded ordinances that all creatures must follow. In the light of this, you know why, how, who and when to get married, and you do everything to the glory of God, it is impossible for any power to withstand your conception. Clearly, this was reveal in the Word:

> *"Great peace have they which love thy law: and nothing shall offend them"* (Psalms 119:165).

Barrenness cannot prevail over people, who love God and His Word, and labor to keep His commandments for too long. God cannot accept that. His thoughts towards us are of good and not evil. This goodness of God radiated in His will to make a suitable helpmeet for Adam.

> *"18 And the LORD God said,* It is *not good that the man should be alone; I will make him an help meet for him. 20 And Adam gave names to all cattle and to the fowl of the air, and to every beast of the field; but for Adam there was not found a helpmeet for him. 22 And the rib, which the LORD God had taken from man, made he a woman, and brought her unto the man. 24 Therefore shall a man leave his father and his mother, and shall cleave unto his wife: and they shall be one flesh"* (Genesis 2:18, 20, 22, 24).

God determined that it was not good that man should be alone. Adam could not find a suitable helpmeet among other creatures until God gave him a wife. That was how God instituted the institution of marriage. Thus, man and woman have been together as husband and wife from the beginning. That is why your marriage should be a place of blessing and not curse. Barrenness is not your portion in the name of Jesus. Was it not remarkable that Jesus pointed to this ancient landmark?

> *"And he answered and said unto them, Have ye not read, that he which made* them *at the beginning made them male and female, And said, For this cause shall a man leave father and mother, and shall cleave to his wife: and they twain shall be one flesh"* (Matthew 19:4-5).

> *"For this cause shall a man leave his father and mother, and shall be joined unto his wife, and they two shall be one flesh"* (Ephesians 5: 31).

Instead of God's goodness prevailing in marriages, Satan and his forces have brought sorrow, and caused many marriages to separate or divorce. God wants your marriage to succeed. He does not intend your marriage to end in separation or divorce. That is why God would not allow barrenness to drive your marriage towards separation. Otherwise, it would defeat His purpose and plan for marriage.

> *"God setteth the solitary in families: he bringeth out those which are bound with chains: but the rebellious dwell in a dry land"* (Psalms 68:6).

When barrenness leads a couple to separation, it cuts off the head that holds the woman and the man, who is the head, remains a head without a body. Head cannot function without the body, likewise the body without the head. Marriage is a lifelong institution, where a husband and his wife mutually depend on each other. That is why the bible refers to the man as:

> *"For the husband is the head of the wife, even as Christ is the head of the church: and he is the savior of the body"* (Ephesians 5:23).

> *"For as the body is one, and hath many members, and all the members of that one body, being many, are one body: so also* is *Christ"* (1 Corinthians 12:12).

> *"*[2]*Nevertheless,* to avoid *fornication, let every man have his own wife, and let every woman have her own husband.* [9]*But if they cannot contain, let them marry: for it is better to marry than to burn.* [10]*And unto the married I command,* yet *not I, but the Lord, Let not the wife depart from* her *husband:* [11]*But and if she depart, let her remain unmarried, or be reconciled to* her *husband: and let not the husband put away* his *wife"* (1 Corinthians 7:2, 9-11).

> *"His disciples say unto him, If the case of the man be so with* his *wife, it is not good to marry. But he said unto them, All* men *cannot receive this saying, save* they *to whom it is given"* (Matthew 19:10-11).

Any family that permits the issue of barrenness to bring conflict, hostility and separation would fall prey to immorality. This is because the separated couple is likely to enter into another sexual relationship. That is why many couples that have separated or divorced continue to live in danger of hell fire. Putting away their legal partners to enter into evil relationships or remarry, they commit adultery without guilt or shame. The bible was clear on this issue:

> *"Let not a widow be taken into the number under threescore years old, having been the wife of one man, Well reported of for good works; if she have brought up children, if she have lodged strangers, if she have washed the saints' feet, if she have relieved the afflicted, if she have diligently followed every good work. But the younger widows refuse: for when they have begun to wax wanton against Christ, they will marry; Having damnation, because they have cast off their first faith. And withal they learn*

to be *idle, wandering about from house to house; and not only idle, but tattlers also and busybodies, speaking things which they ought not. I will therefore that the younger women marry, bear children, guide the house, give none occasion to the adversary to speak reproachfully. For some are already turned aside after Satan"* (1 Timothy 5:9-15).

Many have denounced their first faith and are now blaspheming the name of the Lord. They have given occasions to the adversary and turned to the devil. They are now agents of pollution and immorality, both in the church and in the community. Most of them argue that they need to move on with their lives. However, *"What shall it profit a man, if he shall gain the whole world, and lose his own soul?"* (Mark 8:36).

Only a handful few have the grace and courage to live on without another marriage. Apart from these few, others are supposed to marry. Many people have fallen into sexual sins because they ignored the issue of marriage and tried to live independently. This often failed because a man and a woman need each other to survive because God created us as social beings in order to enjoy marriage relationship and live in families.

"Two are *better than one; because they have a good reward for their labor.* [10]*For if they fall, the one will lift up his fellow: but woe to him* that is *alone when he falleth; for* he hath *not another to help him up.* [11]*Again, if two lie together, then they have heat: but how can one be warm* alone? [12]*And if one prevail against him, two shall withstand him; and a threefold cord is not quickly broken"* (Ecclesiastes 4:9-12).

"[5]*And Moses commanded the children of Israel according to the word of the LORD, saying, The tribe of the sons of Joseph hath said well.* [6]*This is the thing which the LORD doth command concerning the daughters of Zelophehad, saying, Let them marry to whom they think best; only to the family of the tribe of their father shall they marry.* [7]*So shall not the inheritance of the children of Israel remove from tribe to tribe: for every one of the children of Israel shall keep himself to the inheritance of the tribe of his fathers.* [8]*And every daughter, that possesseth an inheritance in any tribe of the children of Israel, shall be wife unto one of the family of the tribe of her father, that the children of Israel may enjoy every man the inheritance of his fathers.* [9]*Neither shall the inheritance remove from* one *tribe to another tribe; but every one of the tribes of the children of Israel shall keep himself to his own inheritance.* [13]*These* are *the commandments and the judgments, which the LORD commanded by the hand of Moses unto the children of Israel in the plains of Moab by Jordan* near *Jericho"* (Numbers 36:5-9, 13).

The importance of marriage cannot be over emphasized. The only permissible way to bring children into this world, rear them, integrate them into local community and nation is through marriage. The scripture established that children are the LORD's heritage:

"Lo, children are *a heritage of the LORD: and the fruit of the womb* is *his reward"* (Psalms 127:3).

"And hath made of one blood all nations of men for to dwell on all the face of the earth, and hath determined the times before appointed, and the bounds of their habitation" (Acts 17:26).

Man is incomplete without a woman because she helps him to fulfill his destiny on earth. Both need each other. When a man and woman bring together their intellect, emotions, personalities and spirituality, they complement each other. That is when a marriage functions maximally. God could decide to fill up a gap of one person's need through marriage relationship.

I know the story of one man who was not financially established, though he was very spiritual. He met and married a woman who was not spiritual but academically and financially established. Both of them knew their needs and were willing to fill each other's gap.

However, when God brought them together, their lives changed for good and they escaped the verdict of the devil, to keep them away from their destiny. Now, God has blessed them richly and they live as if they are in heaven.

The beauty of their relationship was that they understood that their marriage was not to duplicate what they have already, but to fill their gaps by meeting the needs of each other. They knew what each had, valued them and guarded them jealously. Previously, they had failed to fill their need until they got married. They had relations and colleagues who could not help them until they found each other. Marriage provides delightful fellowship, comfort, companionship and partnership. The man is the head and the woman the body.

"[23]For the husband is the head of the wife, even as Christ is the head of the church: and he is the savior of the body. [29]For no man ever yet hated his own flesh; but nourisheth and cherisheth it, even as the Lord the church: [30]For we are members of his body, of his flesh, and of his bones. [31]For this cause shall a man leave his father and mother, and shall be joined unto his wife, and they two shall be one flesh" (Ephesians 5:23, 29-31).

"His disciples say unto him, If the case of the man be so with his *wife, it is not good to marry. But he said unto them, All* men *cannot receive this saying, save* they *to whom it is given. For there are some eunuchs, which were so born from* their *mother's womb: and there are some eunuchs, which were made eunuchs of men: and there be eunuchs, which have made themselves eunuchs for the kingdom of heaven's sake. He that is able to receive* it, *let him receive* it" (Matthew 19:10-12).

Most importantly, marriage is necessary to promote procreation. God had this purpose in mind when He commanded man to bear fruit:

> *"So God created man in his* own *image, in the image of God created he him; male and female created he them. And God blessed them, and God said unto them, Be fruitful, and multiply, and replenish the earth, and subdue it: and have dominion over the fish of the sea, and over the fowl of the air, and over every living thing that moveth upon the earth"* (Genesis 1:27-28).

> *"And God blessed Noah and his sons, and said unto them, Be fruitful, and multiply, and replenish the earth"* (Genesis 9:1).

> *"And did not he make one? Yet had he the residue of the spirit. And wherefore one? That he might seek a godly seed. Therefore take heed to your spirit, and let none deal treacherously against the wife of his youth"* (Malachi 2:15)

God forbids infertility. His will is that we should be fruitful, multiply and replenish the earth. God mandated us to subdue the earth and have dominion over the creatures. Therefore, it is an affront to God for infertility to have dominion over the children of God.

God also blessed Noah and commanded him to be fruitful, to multiply and replenish the earth. A wife in every family ought to be as a fruitful vine planted by the side of the stream. The children are to be like olive plants around the table. There is no place for infertility in the midst of God's children. Every woman must be fertile and fruitful. Nevertheless, God did not only bless us to have children; He blessed us to have godly children.

This book highlights the need to confront the enemies of your marriage and childbearing. You must confront evil forces that repel your conception without mercy. Any power that has vowed that conception cannot take place in your marriage must fail so that the Word of God would prevail. Let us therefore believe God and confront enemies that oppose conception in our families.

STAND ON THE WORD OF GOD AND DECREE YOUR CONCEPTION

Having seen how God intended that you should conceive and be fruitful through His Word, the next thing is for you to stand on the written Word of God and decree that your conception obeys the Word of God and appear. For *"Thou shalt also decree a thing, and it shall be established unto thee: and the light shall shine upon thy ways"* (Job 22:28). Your prayer of faith shall avail much to you.

Let the will of God in His Word be your confidence and assurance. Understand that a will is a legal declaration by which a person disposes his estate or property to his children. God's will for your life is revealed through His written Word:

> *"For by one offering he hath perfected for ever them that are sanctified.* Whereof *the Holy Ghost also is a witness to us: for after that he had said before, This* is *the covenant that I will make with them after those days, saith the Lord, I will put my laws into their hearts, and in their minds will I write them; And their sins and iniquities will I remember no more"* (Hebrews 10:14-17).

God willed in His Word to bless the fruit of your womb. He commanded that there should not be any male or female barren among His children. Therefore, fibroid and evil plantations do not have any place in your womb. If they existed, God promised to take them away. Impotence, low sperm count and old age do not have the power to usurp God's written Word.

> *"And he will love thee, and bless thee, and multiply thee: he will also bless the fruit of thy womb, and the fruit of thy land, thy corn, and thy wine, and thine oil, the increase of thy kine, and the flocks of thy sheep, in the land which he swore unto thy fathers to give thee. Thou shalt be blessed above all people: there shall not be male or female barren among you, or among your cattle. And the LORD will take away from thee all sickness, and will put none of the evil diseases of Egypt, which thou knowest, upon thee; but will lay them upon all* them *that hate thee"* (Deuteronomy 7:13-15).

God promised to take away every sickness, disease and infertility and to destroy them. He is not a man and cannot lie. No power can deter His promises in His will. All the provisions of God are in His will. Therefore, it is useless to search for God's will outside of His Word.

> *"And this is the confidence that we have in him, that, if we ask any thing according to his will, he heareth us: And if we know that he hear us, whatsoever we ask, we know that we have the petitions that we desired of him"* (1 John 5:14-15).

"I can of mine own self do nothing: as I hear, I judge: and my judgment is just; because I seek not mine own will, but the will of the Father which hath sent me" (John 5:30).

A believer's confidence should be in God and His Word. This is believers' confidence, that when we pray against barrenness and infertility according to His will, we receive answers to our prayers. Jesus came into the world to enforce God's will, as was recorded:

"How God anointed Jesus of Nazareth with the Holy Ghost and with power: who went about doing good, and healing all that were oppressed of the devil; for God was with him" (Acts 10:38).

"When he was come down from the mountain, great multitudes followed him. And, behold, there came a leper and worshipped him, saying, Lord, if thou wilt, thou canst make me clean. And Jesus put forth his *hand, and touched him, saying, I will; be thou clean. And immediately his leprosy was cleansed"* (Matthew 8:1-3).

Jesus demonstrated God's will wherever He went. He healed all the sick and delivered people devil oppressed. In so doing, Jesus demonstrated that God wanted His people to be free from satanic oppression, bondage and sickness. He also cleansed a leper who did not know God's will when he approached Him with faith. Realize today that barrenness is not the will of God concerning you, and then pray against it.

God's will is for you to prosper, above all things, as declared in God's Word. As God's dear children, we are to prosper above barrenness, poverty, fear, deaf and dumbness.

"Beloved, I wish above all things that thou mayest prosper and be in health, even as thy soul prospereth" (3 John 2).

"Thy kingdom come. Thy will be done in earth, as it is in heaven" (Matthew 6:10).

"And the inhabitant shall not say, I am sick: the people that dwell therein shall be forgiven their *iniquity"* (Isaiah 33:24).

When your earthly father's attorney informs you of your father's will for you, you cannot blame your father when you fail to take control of your inheritance. If your father willed seventy-five percent of all he has to you, would you not possess your inheritance? If he willed a house to you, would you rather abandon it? When you see another person taking possession, would you request the person to allow you to stay in a room for only one night? Would you expect your late father to come back to life in order to force the illegal occupier out on your behalf? Likewise, diseases and evil plantations that occupy your womb are illegal occupants. Stand on the Word of God and declare an immediate vacate order to all illegal occupants in your body.

"And take the helmet of salvation, and the sword of the Spirit, which is the word of God" (Ephesians 6:17).

The power and weapons you need to eject problems out of your life are at your disposal. You cannot wait until your pastor comes to eject them out for you when you could. You should start commanding problems to go away in the name of Jesus. You have all the resources and power to fight all illegal occupants. You cannot afford to condone infertility, impotence, cold and fruitless life when God has blessed you to be fruitful and productive. The power of God is always available for your use. You have the belt of truth.

"Let your loins be girded about, and your *lights burning"* (Luke 12:35).

"Wherefore gird up the loins of your mind, be sober, and hope to the end for the grace that is to be brought unto you at the revelation of Jesus Christ" (1 Peter 1:13).

The bible, which contains all the promises and covenant of God for your fruitfulness, is a powerful legal document. Present the written Word of God wherever you go, and you continue to record more victories.

When infertility shows its ugly face, stand on the truth and promises of God. Present your case to God. Invite Jesus, who is your senior advocate. Gird the lions of your mind. Be sober, and expect the grace of God. You will surely recover all your loss.

Insist on biblical truth and do not shiver. Trust in God with all your heart and in His written Word, and pray. I declare to you that you are destined for fruitfulness, even at an old age.

"As obedient children, not fashioning yourselves according to the former lusts in your ignorance: But as he which hath called you is holy, so be ye holy in all manner of conversation; Because it is written, Be ye holy; for I am holy." (1 Peter 1:14-16).

"For I am not ashamed of the gospel of Christ: for it is the power of God unto salvation to everyone that believeth; to the Jew first, and also to the Greek. For therein is the righteousness of God revealed from faith to faith: as it is written, The just shall live by faith" (Romans 1:16-17).

Remain obedient to the Word of God and do not return to the fashion of this world. Do not follow the people of this world to seek for children in places God would not want you to. Do not defile yourself or desire their ways but remain holy and blameless, as you trust God for children. Do not doubt God. Stand on the truth and God will remember you at the right time.

"And what shall I more say? For the time would fail me to tell of Gedeon, and of Barak, and of Samson, and of Jephthae; of David also, and Samuel, and of the prophets: Who through faith subdued kingdoms, wrought righteousness, obtained promises, stopped the mouths of lions, Quenched the violence of fire, escaped the edge of the sword, out of weakness were made strong, waxed valiant in fight, turned to flight the armies of the aliens" (Hebrew 11:32-34).

"Whom resist steadfast in the faith, knowing that the same afflictions are accomplished in your brethren that are in the world" (1 Peter 5:9).

"For whatsoever is born of God overcometh the world: and this is the victory that overcometh the world, even *our faith"* (1 John 5:4).

With the grace of God that is available to you, withstand arrows of shame, reproach and disgrace, which devil fires to get at you. Do not depart from truth and righteousness, as revealed in the Word of God. Surely, there is reward for them that remain steadfast.

Do not be ashamed of being a Christian. Insist on getting pregnant in godly way. Do not help yourself to get pregnant outside the will of God. Put on the shield of faith, which would help you to quench and extinguish all the fiery darts of the enemy.

Even when devil and his agents mock you and your bible, do not be moved. When they fire arrows of impurity, selfishness, doubts, fear, vanity and discouragement to uproot your faith from the written will of God, remain steadfast. When they instigate a negative medical report against you, do not fear. When they remind you that your age has exceeded the bounds of God's blessing and grace, do not doubt God's promises concerning you in His Word. It is well with you in the name of Jesus.

"And I will wait upon the LORD, that hideth his face from the house of Jacob, and I will look for him" (Isaiah 8:17).

"Hast thou not known? Hast thou not heard, that the everlasting God, the LORD, the Creator of the ends of the earth, fainteth not, neither is weary? There is no searching of his understanding. He giveth power to the faint; and to them that have no might he increaseth strength. Even the youths shall faint and be weary, and the young men shall utterly fall: But they that wait upon the LORD shall renew their strength; they shall mount up with wings as eagles; they shall run, and not be weary; and they shall walk, and not faint" (Isaiah 40:28-31).

When they attack you through witchcraft and seduction, take your stand and resist the devil. When opposition increases, pressurizing you to seek for solution outside the provisions of God, stand firm. Employ your defensive weapon, which is the shield of faith. Always remember how Jesus also endured hardship:

> *"Then was Jesus led up of the Spirit into the wilderness to be tempted of the devil. And when he had fasted forty days and forty nights, he was afterward an hungered. And when the tempter came to him, he said, If thou be the Son of God, command that these stones be made bread. But he answered and said, It is written, Man shall not live by bread alone, but by every word that proceeded out of the mouth of God. Then the devil taketh him up into the holy city, and setteth him on a pinnacle of the temple, And saith unto him, If thou be the Son of God, cast thyself down: for it is written, He shall give his angels charge concerning thee: and in* their *hands they shall bear thee up, lest at any time thou dash thy foot against a stone. Jesus said unto him, It is written again, Thou shalt not tempt the Lord thy God. Again, the devil taketh him up into an exceeding high mountain, and sheweth him all the kingdoms of the world, and the glory of them; And saith unto him, All these things will I give thee, if thou wilt fall down and worship me. Then saith Jesus unto him, Get thee hence, Satan: for it is written, Thou shalt worship the Lord thy God, and him only shalt thou serve. Then the devil leaveth him, and, behold, angels came and ministered unto him"* (Matthew 4:1-11).

Your only defenses are these weapons, which you can employ through prayers of faith. They include -

- Belt of truth
- Breastplate of righteousness
- Shoes of the gospel of peace
- Shield of faith
- Helmet of salvation
- Sword of the spirit

> *"Finally, my brethren, be strong in the Lord, and in the power of his might. Put on the whole armor of God, that ye may be able to stand against the wiles of the devil. For we wrestle not against flesh and blood, but against principalities, against powers, against the rulers of the darkness of this world, against spiritual wickedness in high* places. *Wherefore take unto you the whole armor of God that ye may be able to withstand in the evil day, and having done all, to stand. Stand therefore, having your loins girt about with truth, and having on the breastplate of righteousness; And your feet shod with the preparation of the gospel of peace; Above all, taking the shield of faith, wherewith ye shall be able to quench all the fiery darts of the wicked. And take the helmet of salvation, and the sword of the Spirit, which is the word of God: Praying always with all prayer and supplication in the Spirit, and watching thereunto with all perseverance and supplication for all saints"* (Ephesians 6:10-18).

A wise and victorious Christian is one who protects himself with these defensive weapons and confronts the enemy with the offensive weapons. Jesus Christ had victory over Satan because He used the sword of the Spirit (which is the Word of God) to fight Satan. You cannot lose any battle when you fight with the Word of God.

> *"Thy word have I hid in mine heart, that I might not sin against thee"* (Psalms 119:11).

> *"For the word of God* is *quick, and powerful, and sharper than any two-edged sword, piercing even to the dividing asunder of soul and spirit, and of the joints and marrow, and* is *a discerner of the thoughts and intents of the heart"* (Hebrew 4:12).

> *"But sanctify the Lord God in your hearts: and* be *ready always to* give *an answer to every man that asketh you a reason of the hope that is in you with meekness and fear"* (1 Peter 3:15).

For instance, a Roman soldier cannot go to war without protecting his head with a helmet. Their helmet was designed to protect their head from arrows and the broadsword.

You must learn how to quote the Word of God to the devil. The sword of the spirit refers to Rhema, a specific Word of God laced with power. Every problem and demon has a specific sword in the Word that would slaughter it. It is therefore your duty to find specific swords in the Word for targeted problems and demons.

> *"And the inhabitant shall not say, I am sick: the people that dwell therein* shall be *forgiven* their *iniquity"* (Isaiah 33:24).

> *"[10]The thief cometh not, but for to steal, and to kill, and to destroy: I am come that they might have life, and that they might have* it *more abundantly"* (John 10:10).

It is foolishness to accept barrenness as God's will for your life because it is not your portion. The devil would try to keep you sick, but insist that your destiny does not accept sickness. Tell the devil that you are not destined to be barren and declare your destiny of fruitfulness to his hearing.

THE FAITHFUL GOD

Our God is a covenant keeping God who has never broken any covenant. He is faithful in keeping all his promises, even when we fail in our obligations. Despite the unimaginable number of years the children of Israel spent in captivity, God still remembered His covenant with Abraham, Isaac and Jacob.

> *"He brought them forth also with silver and gold: and* there was *not one feeble* person *among their tribes"* (Psalms 105:37).

> *"And they journeyed from mount Hor by the way of the Red sea, to compass the land of Edom: and the soul of the people was much discouraged because of the way. And the people spake against God, and against Moses, Wherefore have ye brought us up out of Egypt to die in the wilderness? For* there is *no bread, neither* is there any *water; and our soul loatheth this light bread. And the LORD sent fiery serpents among the people, and they bit the people; and much people of Israel died. Therefore, the people came to Moses, and said, We have sinned, for we have spoken against the LORD, and against thee; pray unto the LORD, that he take away the serpents from us. And Moses prayed for the people. And the LORD said unto Moses, Make thee a fiery serpent, and set it upon a pole: and it shall come to pass, that every one that is bitten, when he looketh upon it, shall live. And Moses made a serpent of brass, and put it upon a pole, and it came to pass, that if a serpent had bitten any man, when he beheld the serpent of brass, he lived"* (Numbers 21:4-9).

He promised Moses that He would take Israel, His people, out of Egypt, from the bondage of Pharaoh and He kept it. He brought them forth with silver and gold. There was not one feeble person among their tribes. He provided water and food for them in the desert. Even when serpents bit the people because of their stubbornness, He healed them.

> *"For a multitude of the people,* even *many of Ephraim, and Manasseh, Issachar, and Zebulun, had not cleansed themselves, yet did they eat the Passover otherwise than it was written. But Hezekiah prayed for them, saying, The good LORD pardon every one* That *prepareth his heart to seek God, the LORD God of his fathers, though* he be *not* cleansed *according to the purification of the sanctuary. And the LORD hearkened to Hezekiah, and healed the people"* (2 Chronicles 30:18-20).

> *"Bless the LORD, O my soul: and all that is within me,* bless *his holy name. Bless the LORD, O my soul, and forget not all his benefits: Who forgiveth all thine iniquities; who healeth all thy diseases; Who redeemeth thy life from destruction; who crowneth thee with lovingkindness and tender mercies; Who satisfieth thy mouth with good* things; so that *thy youth is renewed like the eagle's"* (Psalms 103:1-5).

When you humble yourself and acknowledge your sins, and repent of them, God is able to pardon you as He promised. He can heal every disease at a moment's notice. He can forgive iniquities and heal our land. He can redeem the lives of the children of His covenant from destruction and crown them with love and mercy. He satisfies the children of His covenant with good things and they cannot lack.

> *"Fools because of their transgression, and because of their iniquities, are afflicted. Their soul abhorreth all manner of meat; and they draw near unto the gates of death. Then they cry unto the LORD in their trouble,* and *he saveth them out of their distresses. He sent his word, and healed them, and delivered* them *from their destructions"* (Psalms 107:17-20).

God would send His Word of healing to you when you pray, regardless of your affliction, suffering and pain. If He could heal people who lived in iniquity, then He would also heal the children of His covenant. As a child of God, if you would cry to God for deliverance, He would deliver you. If you have not been born again (in the spirit), God can still save and deliver you out of all your troubles and distress. However, there is one requirement to meet as a sinner: repent of your sins and pray.

As a believer, you also have a requirement to meet; pray in faith and your freedom would manifest. God is able to send His Word to heal you, and deliver you from destruction.

Are you under the attack of sickness, pestilence, swelling, disease or sore sickness? God's Word can heal all diseases. Learn how to take authority in the written Word of God. Jesus went about declaring the Word of God, which healed all manner of sicknesses.

> *"And Jesus went about all Galilee, teaching in their synagogues, and preaching the gospel of the kingdom, and healing all manner of sickness and all manner of disease among the people. And his fame went throughout all Syria: and they brought unto him all sick people that were taken with divers diseases and torments, and those, which were possessed with devils, and those which were lunatic, and those that had the palsy; and he healed them. And there followed him great multitudes of people from Galilee, and* from *Decapolis, and* from *Jerusalem, and* from *Judaea, and* from *beyond Jordan"* (Matthew 4:23-25).

It was amazing that His teaching and preaching brought the healing. At the mentioning of the name of Christ, demons that possessed people for so many years were cast out. Use the name of Jesus to set yourself free from barrenness and infertility as Jesus did.

> *"When the even was come, they brought unto him many that were possessed with devils: and he cast out the spirits with* his *word, and healed all that were sick: That it*

might be fulfilled which was spoken by Esaias the prophet, saying, Himself took our infirmities, and bare our *sicknesses"* (Matthew 8:16-17).

When they brought many people who were possessed by the devil to Him, He did not use physical weapons against them. He simply cast the spirits out with His words and healed all that were sick. Some of those demons were dangerous demons that attacked people from tombs.

"And when he was come to the other side into the country of the Gergesenes, there met him two possessed with devils, coming out of the tombs, exceeding fierce, so that no man might pass by that way. And, behold, they cried out, saying, What have we to do with thee, Jesus, thou Son of God? Art thou come hither to torment us before the time? And there was a good way off from them a herd of many swine feeding. So the devils besought him, saying, If thou cast us out, suffer us to go away into the herd of swine. And he said unto them, Go. And when they were come out, they went into the herd of swine: and, behold, the whole herd of swine ran violently down a steep place into the sea, and perished in the waters" (Matthew 8:28-32).

There was an incident in the bible when demons in their numbers came out of the tomb and possessed a man. The possessed man became exceedingly fierce that no man could pass by the same path he was. Nevertheless, Jesus passed by and confronted the evil spirits. He did not use gun or any weapon. He used the sword of the Spirit, which is the Word of God.

When Jesus spoke, the evil spirits came out and went into swine. Jesus did not condone demons, how much less barrenness and infertility. He dealt with demons that destroyed people's eyes, ears, hands, legs, etc.

Jesus casted out evil spirits of fever, epilepsy, lunacy and hunger, and they all obeyed him. He expelled unclean spirits and plagues, and commanded marine powers in the waters to be still and that was the end.

"And there arose a great storm of wind, and the waves beat into the ship, so that it was now full. And he was in the hinder part of the ship, asleep on a pillow: and they awake him, and say unto him, Master, carest thou not that we perish? And he arose, and rebuked the wind, and said unto the sea, Peace, be still. And the wind ceased, and there was a great calm. And he said unto them, Why are ye so fearful? How is it that ye have no faith? And they feared exceedingly, and said one to another, What manner of man is this, that even the wind and the sea obey him?" (Mark 4:37-41).

He met a destructive demon of death and frustrated its plan. He told a deceased damsel not to worry, "THAL-THA-CU-MI".

When Jesus met some people who were about to bury a dead boy, He had compassion on the mother of the dead boy. He simply said to her, *"Weep not"*, and to the dead young man he said, *"I say unto thee, Arise!"* The young boy jumped up immediately at the hearing of the voice of Jesus.

> *"And it came to pass the day after, that he went into a city called Nain; and many of his disciples went with him, and much people. Now when he came nigh to the gate of the city, behold, there was a dead man carried out, the only son of his mother, and she was a widow: and much people of the city was with her. And when the Lord saw her, he had compassion on her, and said unto her, Weep no. And he came and touched the bier: and they that bare* him *stood still. And he said, Young man, I say unto thee, Arise. And he that was dead sat up, and began to speak. And he delivered him to his mother. And there came a fear on all: and they glorified God, saying, That a great prophet is risen up among us; and, That God hath visited his people. And this rumor of him went forth throughout all Judæa, and throughout all the region round about"* (Luke 7:11-17).

All powers belong to Jesus. The power to stop evil movements in your reproductive organs belongs to Jesus. The power to destroy tumor, fibroid, cancer, ulcer, itching, HIV, AIDS, heart failure and all manner of sicknesses belong to Jesus. If you repent of your sins today, and ask Jesus to heal you, He will surely heal you.

> *"If I shut up heaven that there be no rain, or if I command the locusts to devour the land, or if I send pestilence among my people; If my people, which are called by my name, shall humble themselves, and pray, and seek my face, and turn from their wicked ways; then will I hear from heaven, and will forgive their sin, and will heal their land"* (2 Chronicles 7:13-14).

Men's words and negative medical reports generate fear, doubt and distrust. However, God's Word builds faith in the heart. Therefore, embrace God's Word today and your story would change forever.

PRAYERS TO CONCEIVE AND BEAR CHILDREN

Bible references: Exodus 23:25-26, Deuteronomy 28:1-14

Begin with praise and worship

1. I frustrate every enemy of my conception to death, in the name of Jesus.
2. Every enemy of God's purpose for my life, die, in the name of Jesus.
3. I repair damages that sexual immorality did to my life, in the name of Jesus.
4. Let the resurrection power possess every organ of my body now, in the name of Jesus.
5. Blood of Jesus, speak life into my body today, in the name of Jesus.
6. O Lord, arise and deliver me from infertility, in the name of Jesus.
7. I command the backbone of low sperm count in my body to break to pieces, in the name of Jesus.
8. I disgrace evil powers that are fighting God's will for my marriage, in the name of Jesus.
9. O Lord, arise and bless the fruit of my womb, in the name of Jesus.
10. Every seed of barrenness in my life, die in the name of Jesus.
11. I uproot evil plantations of fibroid in my womb, in the name of Jesus.
12. O Lord, take away evil deposits in my life forever, in the name of Jesus.
13. I uproot the root of impotence in my life by fire, in the name of Jesus.
14. I disgrace any power that is manipulating my conception, in the name of Jesus.
15. Let every promise of God for my conception manifest immediately, in the name of Jesus.
16. Let every sickness or disease in my life die, in the name of Jesus.
17. Let evil forces against conception in my life be destroyed forever, in the name of Jesus.

18. Any power that is eating up my children before I conceive, die, in the name of Jesus.
19. I oppose every opposition of my pregnancy with fire, in the name of Jesus.
20. Holy Ghost fire, burn enemies of my reproductive organs, in the name of Jesus.
21. I receive the anointing to conceive and deliver in this season, in the name of Jesus.
22. I put strange fires that are burning inside my body off forever, in the name of Jesus.
23. Any evil chain that is holding my conception, break to pieces, in the name of Jesus.
24. I command the goodness of Jesus to manifest in my marriage today, in the name of Jesus.
25. O Lord, command Your presence to appear in my home now and forever, in the name of Jesus.
26. Let the fire of God enter my womb and cause immediate conception, in the name of Jesus.
27. Let satanic poison that is sucking my conception dry up by fire, in the name of Jesus.
28. Let every strongman that is resisting my conception die, in the name of Jesus.
29. I remove satanic blockages over my conception by force, in the name of Jesus.
30. I reject every evil thing that has entered my life through my dreams, in the name of Jesus.
31. I break and lose my conception from attacks of spiritual partners, in the name of Jesus.
32. I reject satanic contamination, abortion and sex in dreams, in the name of Jesus.
33. I deliver my womb, fallopian tube and ovary from evil powers, in the name of Jesus.
34. Any devourer that was assigned to resist my conception, die, in the name of Jesus.
35. I silence evil voices that are speaking against my conception forever, in the name of Jesus.
36. Let evil eyes that are monitoring my conception go blind completely, in the name of Jesus.
37. Father Lord, correct every disorder in my reproductive system, in the name of Jesus.
38. I command every disease or germ in my body to die immediately, in the name of Jesus.

39. Let every curse that stands against my conception waste, in the name of Jesus.

40. Let agents of death that target my conception die immediately, in the name of Jesus.

41. O Lord, arise and empower me for immediate conception, in the name of Jesus.

42. I release my body, soul and spirit from captivity, in the name of Jesus.

14

Chapter

PRAYERS TO PRESERVE YOUR MARRIAGE

CHAPTER OVERVIEW

- *Marriage is a life contract*
- *What is a covenant?*
- *Dealing with family problems*
- *Marital challenges you must confront*
- *Solutions to marital challenges*

MARRIAGE IS A LIFE CONTRACT

The Christian vow in a marriage ceremony defines marriage as a lifetime union. The Scripture upholds the same definition:

> *"Wives, submit yourselves unto your own husbands, as unto the Lord. For the husband is the head of the wife, even as Christ is the head of the church: and he is the savior of the body. Therefore as the church is subject unto Christ, so* let *the wives* be *to their own husbands in everything"* (Ephesians 5:22-24).

Wives are commanded to submit to their husbands as unto the Lord. It is a lifetime commitment as long as they both live. Every woman needs prayers to do it so that she will receive blessings in her marriage. The body that does not cooperate with the head would be in trouble. The neck that troubles the head and refuses to carry the head will live without the head. The head will save the body in times of trouble.

Wives that rebel against God's Word do not have peace in their marriages. Separation and divorce do not help matters because the scriptures say that it is not good for man to be alone.

> *"Husbands, love your wives, even as Christ also loved the church, and gave himself for it; That he might sanctify and cleanse it with the washing of water by the word, That he might present it to himself a glorious church, not having spot, or wrinkle, or any such thing; but that it should be holy and without blemish. So ought men to love their wives as their own bodies. He that loveth his wife loveth himself. For no man ever yet hated his own flesh; but nourisheth and cherisheth it, even as the Lord the church: For we are members of his body, of his flesh, and of his bones. For this cause shall a man leave his father and mother, and shall be joined unto his wife, and they two shall be one flesh. This is a great mystery: but I speak concerning Christ and the church. Nevertheless let every one of you in particular so love his wife even as himself; and the wife* see *that she reverence* her *husband"* (Ephesians 5:25-33).

If it is good to be alone, God would have allowed man to be without a wife from the beginning. Rather, God said it is not good. Therefore, God's Word is still the same today and forever. There are husbands who find it difficult to love their wives. As a result, they think the only solution is to find a lover outside the home. However, husbands are commanded to love their wives as their own bodies. It must be as Christ loves the church and offered Himself for her.

Failing to love your wife is the same thing as hating your own body. God cannot tell lies. You may not really realize that you hate yourself or your own body by not loving your wife, but it is true because God's Word has said so. More so, many people have realized that it is true. Remember that you promised God that you would love your wife before the officiating minister and the entire crowd during your wedding. In most Christian weddings, the second question to a man by officiating minister is a lifetime commitment. The first question normally goes like this.

(Brother's name) Do you take (sister's name) whose right hand you now hold to be your lawful wedded wife and solemnly promise, God helping you, that you will be a true and devoted husband to her; that you will love her even as Christ love the church, and honor, cherish, protect and care for her for the rest of your lives and that you will keep yourself to her and to her alone until God, by death, shall separate you? If you answered I DO, then you have entered into a lifetime covenant.

The words that were used on your wedding day may not be exactly the same with the above, but the implications are the same. The vow bounds you for life as long as both of you live.

> *"And he answered and said unto them, Have ye not read, that he which made* them *at the beginning made them male and female, And said, For this cause shall a man leave father and mother, and shall cleave to his wife: and they twain shall be one flesh? Wherefore they are no more twain, but one flesh. What therefore God hath joined together, let not man put asunder"* (Matthew 19:4-6).

> *"But from the beginning of the creation God made them male and female. For this cause shall a man leave his father and mother, and cleave to his wife; And they twain shall be one flesh: so then they are no more twain, but one flesh. What therefore God hath joined together, let not man put asunder"* (Mark 10:6-9).

After you responded, 'I DO,' the minister will ask you to turn to her and make this profession of your faith:

I, (brother's name) according to the Word of God, leave my father and my mother and join myself to you, to be a husband to you. From this moment forward, we shall be one.

The minister then turns to the bride and asks:

(Sister's name) do you take (Brother's name) whose right hand you now hold to be your lawfully wedded husband and solemnly promise, God helping you, that you will be a true and devoted wife to him; that you will submit yourself to him as unto the Lord showing reverence to him as the head of this union, that you will love, honor, cherish and that you will keep yourself to him and to him alone until God, by death, shall separate you? If your response is, I DO, you have made an irrevocable vow for your lifetime.

Meanwhile, for centuries, men have sought for ways to satisfy their desires of putting away their wives. It was not surprising the Pharisees put this question on Jesus:

> *"The Pharisees also came unto him, tempting him, and saying unto him, Is it lawful for a man to put away his wife for every cause? And he answered and said unto them, Have ye not read, that he which made* them *at the beginning made them male and female, And said, For this cause shall a man leave father and mother, and shall cleave to his wife: and they twain shall be one flesh? Wherefore they are no more twain, but one flesh. What therefore God hath joined together, let not man put asunder"* (Matthew 19:3-6).

The minister will address the witnesses as follows: Jesus said in the 18th chapter of Matthew's gospel, *"Again, I say unto you that whatever two of you shall agree on earth as touching anything that they shall ask, it shall be done for them of my Father which is in heaven"*. You are not here just because of tradition. You are here for a serious purpose to bear witness forever of the "mystery" of the union that takes place this day, and to add your agreement before God to that which takes place.

SOLEMN PRONOUNCEMENT

(To the groom and bride) Join your hands please. A miracle took place when you made Jesus Christ, your Lord and Savior. The power of God that raised Jesus from the dead joined you to Jesus. I want you to understand that this day you are joined together and have become one. The same power that joined you with Jesus when you made Him your Lord and Savior has this day joined you together. Do not ever tamper with this union. Do not ever tamper with this miracle. You are one never to be separated or divorced. As a representative of Jesus Christ before Almighty God and in the name of the father, in the name of the son Jesus and by the power of the Holy Spirit of God, I now pronounce you as one together. You are now husband and wife.

From today, when you agree on things, they will come to pass. You have an awesome power at your disposal. You are going to notice from now a new realm beginning in your life because of a spiritual law that says one can put a thousand to flight and two ten thousand to flight. From now on, your everyday life will be ten times more powerful spiritually than ever before.

Remember; do not ever tamper with the agreement of today. From this day forward, whatever may happen, you are in agreement with this union. Do not ever attempt in any way to cause it to be anything other than a happy union.

TO THE CONGREGATION

In as much as (brother's name) and (sister's name) have both signified that they believed with all their hearts that it is the perfect will of God for them to be joined together in the holy bond of matrimony, have borne witness of this before God and this company and have pledged their fidelity and love each to the other, I, by virtue of the authority vested in me as a minister of the Gospel of Jesus Christ and by the laws of our country now pronounce them as husband and wife, in the name of the Father, and of the Son, and of the Holy Ghost. "What therefore God hath joined together, let no man put asunder".

SIGNING OF MARRIAGE REGISTERS

All the members of the congregation remain quiet in an attitude of worship as marriage register is signed.

BLESSING OF THE UNION

> *"Christ hath redeemed us from the curse of the law, being made a curse for us: for it is written, Cursed* is *every one that hangeth on a tree: That the blessing of Abraham might come on the Gentiles through Jesus Christ; that we might receive the promise of the Spirit through faith"*(Galatians 3:13-14).
>
> *"And all these blessings shall come on thee, and overtake thee, if thou shalt hearken unto the voice of the LORD thy God. Blessed* shalt *thou* be *in the city, and blessed* shalt *thou* be *in the field. Blessed* shall be *the fruit of thy body, and the fruit of thy ground, and the fruit of thy cattle, the increase of thy kine, and the flocks of thy sheep. Blessed* shall be *thy basket and thy store. Blessed* shalt *thou* be *when thou comest in, and blessed* shalt *thou* be *when thou goest out. The LORD shall cause thine enemies that rise up against thee to be smitten before thy face: they shall come out against thee one way, and flee before thee seven ways. The LORD shall command the blessing upon thee in thy storehouses, and in all that thou settest thine hand unto; and he shall bless thee in the land which the LORD thy God giveth thee. The LORD shall establish thee a holy people unto himself, as he hath sworn unto thee, if thou shalt keep the commandments of the LORD thy God, and walk in his ways. And all people of the earth shall see that thou art called by the name of the LORD; and they shall be afraid of thee. And the LORD shall make thee plenteous in goods, in the fruit of thy body, and in the fruit of thy cattle, and in the fruit of thy ground, in the land which the LORD sware unto thy fathers to give thee. The LORD shall open unto thee his good*

treasure, the heaven to give the rain unto thy land in his season, and to bless all the work of thine hand: and thou shalt lend unto many nations, and thou shalt not borrow. And the LORD shall make thee the head, and not the tail; and thou shalt be above only, and thou shalt not be beneath; if that thou hearken unto the commandments of the LORD thy God, which I command thee this day, to observe and to do them" (Deuteronomy 28:2-13).

PRESENTATION TO THE CONGREGATION

Ladies and gentlemen, I present to you, brother and sister (their names). This is what is called marriage, vow or covenant. Yours might not be the exact words, but they all lead to the same end, whether it is done in a church, court or according to tradition. Marriage is for life and a lifetime contract.

WHAT IS A COVENANT?

Most people do not know that a vow or covenant is a very serious thing. It is even more serious when it is a marriage vow. A marriage vow is more binding than ordinary vows. A covenant is a mutual understanding between two or more parties, each binding himself to fulfill specific obligations. It is a legal agreement to do or not to do certain things.

Marriage covenant empowers people to live in families, rear children and live in local community or nation. The Word of God captured this essence:

> *"God setteth the solitary in families: he bringeth out those which are bound with chains: but the rebellious dwell in a dry land"* (Psalms 68:6).

> *"Lo, children* are *a heritage of the LORD:* and *the fruit of the womb* is his *reward"* (Psalms 127:3).

> *"[5]And Moses commanded the children of Israel according to the word of the LORD, saying, The tribe of the sons of Joseph hath said well. [6]This is the thing which the LORD doth command concerning the daughters of Zelophehad, saying, Let them marry to whom they think best; only to the family of the tribe of their father shall they marry. [7]So shall not the inheritance of the children of Israel remove from tribe to tribe: for every one of the children of Israel shall keep himself to the inheritance of the tribe of his fathers. [8]And every daughter, that possesseth an inheritance in any tribe of the children of Israel, shall be wife unto one of the family of the tribe of her father, that the children of Israel may enjoy every man the inheritance of his fathers. [9]Neither shall the inheritance remove from* one *tribe to another tribe; but every one of the tribes of the children of Israel shall keep himself to his own inheritance. [13]These* are *the commandments and the judgments, which the LORD commanded by the hand of Moses unto the children of Israel in the plains of Moab by Jordan* near *Jericho"* (Numbers 36:5-9, 13).

Marriage is also designed for preservation of purity and holiness in the church and community.

> *"[2]Nevertheless,* to avoid *fornication, let every man have his own wife, and let every woman have her own husband. [9]But if they cannot contain, let them marry: for it is better to marry than to burn. [10]And unto the married I command,* yet *not I, but the Lord, Let not the wife depart from* her *husband: [11]But and if she depart, let her remain unmarried, or be reconciled to* her *husband: and let not the husband put away* his *wife"* (1 Corinthians 7:2, 9-11).

Marriage is one of God's methods to keep men and women free from immorality. God did not make any provision in His Word for people to have sexual relationships except through marriage. Any open or secret love among people can bring curse, but marriage brings completeness and fulfillment of true living in life.

> *"And it shall come to pass, if they will not believe also these two signs, neither hearken unto thy voice, that thou shalt take of the water of the river, and pour* it *upon the dry* land*: and the water which thou takest out of the river shall become blood upon the dry* land. *And Moses said unto the LORD, O my Lord, I* am *not eloquent, neither heretofore, nor since thou hast spoken unto thy servant: but I* am *slow of speech, and of a slow tongue. And the LORD said unto him, Who hath made man's mouth? Or who maketh the dumb, or deaf, or the seeing, or the blind? Have not I the LORD?"* (Exodus 4:9–11).

Marriage provides true fellowship, comfort, companionship and fellowship. Our likenesses and differences complement one another in a marriage relationship.

> *"And God blessed Noah and his sons, and said unto them, Be fruitful, and multiply, and replenish the earth"* (Genesis 9:1).

Marriage also is to complement God's work of procreation. Generally, covenant is designed to establish friendship, procure assistance in wars and guarantee mutual protection.

> *"Then Jonathan and David made a covenant, because he loved him as his own soul"* (1 Samuel 18:3).

> *"And the LORD sent thee on a journey, and said, Go and utterly destroy the sinners the Amalekites, and fight against them until they be consumed. Wherefore then didst thou not obey the voice of the LORD, but didst fly upon the spoil, and didst evil in the sight of the LORD?"* (1 Samuel 15:18-19).

> *"And they said, We saw certainly that the LORD was with thee: and we said, Let there be now an oath betwixt us,* even *betwixt us and thee, and let us make a covenant with thee; That thou wilt do us no hurt, as we have not touched thee, and as we have done unto thee nothing but good, and have sent thee away in peace: thou* art *now the blessed of the LORD"* (Genesis 26:28-29)

As soon as marriage vows are completed and confirmed, it cannot be altered.

> *"Brethren, I speak after the manner of men; Though* it be *but a man's covenant, yet* if it be *confirmed, no man disannulleth, or addeth thereto"* (Galatians 3:15).

Marriage is an irrevocable commitment. It comes into effect by answering marriage vows. Holding of hands and signing the marriage register. It is sealed with a kiss, a hug and sexual relationship. Marriage covenant is the most powerful covenant on earth and cannot be toyed with.

> *"Yet ye say, Wherefore? Because the LORD hath been witness between thee and the wife of thy youth, against whom thou hast dealt treacherously: yet is she thy companion, and the wife of thy covenant. And did not he make one? Yet had he the residue of the spirit. And wherefore one? That he might seek a godly seed. Therefore take heed to your spirit, and let none deal treacherously against the wife of his youth"* (Malachi 2:14-15).

DEALING WITH FAMILY PROBLEMS

Devil has deployed abundant marital challenges to shake families of the earth. While majority of people attempt to solve their family problems by running away from them, few that are wise run to God to deliver them from troubles. Others ironically opt for easy way outs which devil provides to them. This option would eventually put them into greater bondage. Learn how to endure because the bible put it this way:

> *"Man that is born of a woman is of few days, and full of trouble"* (Job 14:1).

> *"Jesus saith unto him, I am the way, the truth, and the life: no man cometh unto the Father, but by me"* (John 14:6).

The scripture revealed that troubles must come, and the only way out is through Lord Jesus, who has provided the right way. Any other way leads to greater bondage and damnation. Great struggle awaits all married couples. Good things are equally devil's targets.

At times, problems emerge as soon as a couple gets married. Other times, it comes at the middle of their marriage. Some other times, it may come at the tail end of their marriage. Whichever time, we are encouraged to wrestle and fight war against the devil and not to surrender to him.

> *"For we wrestle not against flesh and blood, but against principalities, against powers, against the rulers of the darkness of this world, against spiritual wickedness in high* places" (Ephesians 6:12).

> *"Fight the good fight of faith, lay hold on eternal life, whereunto thou art also called, and hast professed a good profession before many witnesses"* (1 Timothy 6:12).

> *"And why stand we in jeopardy every hour? I protest by your rejoicing, which I have in Christ Jesus our Lord, I die daily. If after the manner of men I have fought with beasts at Ephesus, what advantageth it me, if the dead rise not? Let us eat and drink; for tomorrow we die"* (1 Corinthians 15: 30-32).

As Christian families, we must depend on God and use right weapons to fight the devil. Christians who do not expect or realize how strong the enemy is would likely fail on the day of battle. God's power to win has been made available to all God's children and they did not use it.

> *"Blessed* be *the God and Father of our Lord Jesus Christ, which according to his abundant mercy hath begotten us again unto a lively hope by the resurrection of Jesus*

Christ from the dead, To an inheritance incorruptible, and undefiled, and that fadeth not away, reserved in heaven for you, Who are kept by the power of God through faith unto salvation ready to be revealed in the last time. Wherein ye greatly rejoice, though now for a season, if need be, ye are in heaviness through manifold temptations: That the trial of your faith, being much more precious than of gold that perisheth, though it be tried with fire, might be found unto praise and honor and glory at the appearing of Jesus Christ: Whom having not seen, ye love; in whom, though now ye see him *not, yet believing, ye rejoice with joy unspeakable and full of glory: Receiving the end of your faith,* even *the salvation of* your *souls"* (1 Peter 1:3-9).

"Wherefore the rather, brethren, give diligence to make your calling and election sure: for if ye do these things, ye shall never fall: For so an entrance shall be ministered unto you abundantly into the everlasting kingdom of our Lord and Savior Jesus Christ" (2 Peter 1:10-11).

"Submit yourselves therefore to God. Resist the devil, and he will flee from you" (James 4:7).

When you discover God's will for your marriage, insist on its manifestation. You must reject other things that oppose God's purpose for your marriage. You have the divine power, authority to confront any power that would seek to redraw the map of your marriage. You must resist things that are against godliness and the promises of God concerning your marriage.

Problems and temptations in marriage should bring you and your wife together in order to help you to know God and prove Him the more. Bearing fruits of the spirit, which is God's nature, makes you more fruitful than barren. Lack of it brings blindness and leads people astray. You must resist the devil and chase him out of your marriage.

It is not possible to mention all family problems in this book. However, the most important thing is for you to know, define and insist on God's plan, purpose and provisions for your marriage.

> "[18]*And the LORD God said,* It is *not good that the man should be alone; I will make him a help meet for him.* [22]*And the rib, which the LORD God had taken from man, made he a woman, and brought her unto the man.* [24]*Therefore shall a man leave his father and his mother, and shall cleave unto his wife: and they shall be one flesh"* (Genesis 2:18, 22, 24).

> *"And he answered and said unto them, Have ye not read, that he which made* them *at the beginning made them male and female, And said, For this cause shall a man leave father and mother, and shall cleave to his wife: and they twain shall be one flesh?"* (Matthew 19:4-5).

> *"For this cause shall a man leave his father and mother, and shall be joined unto his wife, and they two shall be one flesh"* (Ephesians 5:31).

When you know God's plan, purpose and provision for your marriage, you would be able to discern when devil is establishing his own plan. You should know that no matter the gravity of problem, conflict or hostility in your marriage, divorce and separation is not God's perfect will for you. God who instituted your marriage has already planned and adequately provided for solutions to all marital problems even before they rise.

Whatever your family needs is available until you to claim them. You only need to approach problems the right way. The Lord commanded that you leave and cleave to your partner. Therefore, whatever that opposes your obedience to that Word is an enemy. You must resist that power now. Obedience to God's Word brings joy, happiness and peace.

> *"So ought men to love their wives as their own bodies. He that loveth his wife loveth himself. For no man ever yet hated his own flesh; but nourisheth and cherisheth it, even as the Lord the church: For we are members of his body, of his flesh, and of his bones. For this cause shall a man leave his father and mother, and shall be joined unto his wife, and they two shall be one flesh"* (Ephesians 5:28-31).

> *"But from the beginning of the creation God made them male and female. For this cause shall a man leave his father and mother, and cleave to his wife; And they twain shall be one flesh: so then they are no more twain, but one flesh. What therefore God hath joined together, let not man put asunder"* (Mark 10:6-9).

Whoever or whatever that comes between you and your legally married partner is an enemy. Obey the Word of God first. Failure to leave and cleave has caused so many problems in families. It is still a problem in many families today. The problem is that most Christians give devil a place in their marriages when God commanded us not to do so:

> *"Neither give place to the devil"* (Ephesians 4:27)

> *"Casting all your care upon him; for he careth for you. Be sober, be vigilant; because your adversary the devil, as a roaring lion, walketh about, seeking whom he may devour: Whom resist steadfast in the faith, knowing that the same afflictions are accomplished in your brethren that are in the world"* (1 Peter 5:7-9).

Giving the devil a place is a massive problem in many Christian families today. There are husbands and wives who stop greeting themselves because of minor issues. What a pity!

> *"Greet ye one another with a kiss of charity. Peace* be *with you all that are in Christ Jesus. Amen"* (1 Peter 5:14).

> *"Salute one another with a holy kiss. The churches of Christ salute you"* (Romans 16:16).

No matter what your partner causes you or how many indignities your partner brings, you must endeavor to great your partner. Kiss one another with a kiss of love. Husbands and wives must salute themselves with a holy kiss. You give devil a huge place in your marriage when you fail to do so. In fact, it is a dangerous thing to do. You must prefer one another; bear each other's burden so that you do not give the devil a place.

> "Be *kindly affectioned one to another with brotherly love; in honor preferring one another"* (Romans 12:10).

> "Bear *ye one another's burdens, and so fulfill the law of Christ"* (Galatians 6:2).

You must have a kind affection and prefer one another. Do not wait for your partner to do it first. Let it be a family competition. Always try to do good first. Bearing one another's burden is fulfilling the law of Christ and it comes with blessings. If you do not practice these things, you allow the devil to take down your family through gossips, suspicion, false prophecy and other things. When you give devil a place in the family, he can bring your marriage to a halt. As the Scripture puts it:

> *"For where two or three are gathered together in my name, there am I in the midst of them. Then came Peter to him, and said, Lord, how oft shall my brother sin against*

me, and I forgive him? Till seven times? Jesus saith unto him, I say not unto thee, Until seven times: but, Until seventy times seven. Therefore is the kingdom of heaven likened unto a certain king, which would take account of his servants. And when he had begun to reckon, one was brought unto him, which owed him ten thousand talents. But forasmuch as he had not to pay, his lord commanded him to be sold, and his wife, and children, and all that he had, and payment to be made. The servant therefore fell down, and worshipped him, saying, Lord, have patience with me, and I will pay thee all. Then the lord of that servant was moved with compassion, and loosed him, and forgave him the debt. But the same servant went out, and found one of his fellow servants, which owed him an hundred pence: and he laid hands on him, and took him by the throat, saying, Pay me that thou owest. And his fellow servant fell down at his feet, and besought him, saying, Have patience with me, and I will pay thee all. And he would not: but went and cast him into prison, until he should pay the debt. So when his fellow servants saw what was done, they were very sorry, and came and told unto their lord all that was done. Then his lord, after that he had called him, said unto him, O thou wicked servant, I forgave thee all that debt, because thou desiredst me: Shouldest not thou also have had compassion on thy fellow servant, even as I had pity on thee? And his lord was wroth, and delivered him to the tormentors, until he should pay all that was due unto him. So likewise shall my heavenly Father do also unto you, if ye from your hearts forgive not everyone his brother their trespasses" (Matthew 18:20-35).

It is possible that your partner would definitely offend you no matter how holy your partner may be. Nevertheless, God commanded us to forgive one another and continue in love for each other. Even when your partner backslides, becomes careless and offends you, forgive. In order to live in peace and remain a child of God, you must forgive and forget.

"This is my commandment, That ye love one another, as I have loved you. Greater love hath no man than this that a man lay down his life for his friends. Ye are my friends, if ye do whatsoever I command you" (John 15:12-14).

Lack of forgiveness brings barriers between husbands and wives. Once any barrier exists, devil occupies every available space and kills the affection between the two of you. At that point, carnal lusts for outsiders would begin to develop. Different problems would start to bud because of a little space. Here, the Scripture revealed the works of the flesh:

"Now the works of the flesh are manifest, which are these; *Adultery, fornication, uncleanness, lasciviousness, Idolatry, witchcraft, hatred, variance, emulations, wrath, strife, seditions, heresies, Envyings, murders, drunkenness, revellings, and such like:*

of the which I tell you before, as I have also told you *in time past, that they which do such things shall not inherit the kingdom of God"* (Galatians 5:19-21).

Manifestation of impatience, strife, malice, nagging, bitterness and fighting becomes the norm. The next thing may be pride and failure to pray together. The real agreement in the marriage covenant is affected at this point.

"Verily I say unto you, Whatsoever ye shall bind on earth shall be bound in heaven: and whatsoever ye shall loose on earth shall be loosed in heaven. Again I say unto you, That if two of you shall agree on earth as touching anything that they shall ask, it shall be done for them of my Father which is in heaven" (Matthew 18:18-19).

At this time, couples start looking for solace outside their marriages. The real purpose for marriage is affected. Strange men, women, house helps and evil people get opportunities to take control over the management of the family. The devil and his evil agents get the opportunity to cause more damage.

In similar cases, a man begins keeping late at nights. The devil destroys family fellowship and provides an evil alternative with himself and his agents. He removes divine marriage comfort and replaces it with demonic comfort. The fulfillment of true living, which is the original plan of God, ceases to exist.

"For the husband is the head of the wife, even as Christ is the head of the church: and he is the savior of the body. For no man ever yet hated his own flesh; but nourisheth and cherisheth it, even as the Lord the church: For we are members of his body, of his flesh, and of his bones. For this cause shall a man leave his father and mother, and shall be joined unto his wife, and they two shall be one flesh" (Ephesians 5:23, 29-31).

"Two are *better than one; because they have a good reward for their labor. For if they fall, the one will lift up his fellow: but woe to him* that is *alone when he falleth; for* he hath *not another to help him up. Again, if two lie together, then they have heat: but how can one be warm* alone*?"* (Ecclesiastes 4:9-11).

The devil would seek to remove the marriage companionship and partnership. If they have children, the children would begin to suffer. Some of them begin to misbehave and become wayward, rebellious and belligerent. The devil would harvest their destinies. Sickness, diseases, poverty, suffering and premature death to life and properties begin to manifest. To worsen the matter, such couple may end up in separation, divorce or polygamy.

"And Laban gave to Rachel his daughter Bilhah his handmaid to be her maid. And he went in also unto Rachel, and he loved also Rachel more than Leah, and served with

him yet seven other years. And when the LORD saw that Leah was hated, he opened her womb: but Rachel was barren. And Leah conceived, and bare a son, and she called his name Reuben: for she said, Surely the LORD hath looked upon my affliction; now therefore my husband will love me" (Genesis 29:29-32).

"And when Rachel saw that she bare Jacob no children, Rachel envied her sister; and said unto Jacob, Give me children, or else I die. And Jacob's anger was kindled against Rachel: and he said, Am *I in God's stead, who hath withheld from thee the fruit of the womb?"* (Genesis 30:1-2).

Polygamy has destroyed so many families and sent them to early graves and hell fire.

SOLUTIONS TO MARITAL CHALLENGES

Consider these few solutions, as you trust God to help you overcome challenges in your marriage. Understand that everyone has a cross to bear in the family. However, if you carry your cross to the Calvary, to Jesus, He will make all things light. Nevertheless, when you drop your cross at Satan's feet in your search for cheap solutions, you will carry a worse cross through eternity.

Jesus said, *"Come unto me, all ye that labor and are heavy laden, and I will give you rest. Take my yoke upon you, and learn of me; for I am meek and lowly in heart: and ye shall find rest unto your souls. For my yoke is easy, and my burden is light"* (Matthew 11: 28-30).

Do not allow the devil to be your guide. No matter what the problem is, we must comfort, exhort and admonish one another.

> *"Wherefore comfort one another with these words"* (1 Thessalonians 4:18).
>
> *"But exhort one another daily, while it is called Today; lest any of you be hardened through the deceitfulness of sin"* (Hebrews 3:13).
>
> *"Not forsaking the assembling of ourselves together, as the manner of some is; but exhorting* one another*: and so much the more, as ye see the day approaching"* (Hebrews 10:25).
>
> *"And I myself also am persuaded of you, my brethren, that ye also are full of goodness, filled with all knowledge, able also to admonish one another"* (Romans 15:14).
>
> *"Let the word of Christ dwell in you richly in all wisdom; teaching and admonishing one another in psalms and hymns and spiritual songs, singing with grace in your hearts to the Lord"* (Colossians 3:16).

Our comfort comes from God and that provides our comfort for each other. You must learn to reject any other comfort or comforter that is not from God. Comfort one another based on the Word of God. Do not forsake the Assembly of God's children because of problems. Do not take anyone to consult any other power except the power of God. Do not accept any solution that is not of God. Always insist on God's way with God's people.

In your trials, fill your thought with the goodness and your knowledge of God, and refuse to be discouraged. Fill your thoughts with the Word of God. When you succeed in preserving your marriage without compromise, you would fulfill the purpose of marriage and make it to heaven. Perhaps, your marriage is messed up already. You can still make amends. Jesus is never too late or too early. Delay is not denial.

"And when he came to himself, he said, How many hired servants of my father's have bread enough and to spare, and I perish with hunger! I will arise and go to my father, and will say unto him, Father, I have sinned against heaven, and before thee, And am no more worthy to be called thy son: make me as one of thy hired servants. And he arose, and came to his father. But when he was yet a great way off, his father saw him, and had compassion, and ran, and fell on his neck, and kissed him (Luke 15:17-20).

God is ready to accept you back. God expects you to make your ways right before Him and come out of sin. The consistent teaching of God's Word is that marriage is a lifetime contract.

If you preserve your marriage, despite all odds, the Lord will answer your prayers and make you happy to enjoy your marriage in an old age.

PRAYERS TO PRESERVE YOUR MARRIAGE

Bible references: Exodus 23:25-26; Deuteronomy 28:1-14

Begin with praise and worship

1. I break and loose my partner and me from every unprofitable association, in the name of Jesus.
2. I disgrace the power of darkness that has vowed to scatter my marriage, in the name of Jesus.
3. Every demonic authority that is working against my marriage, be frustrated, in the name of Jesus.
4. I terminate evil control over my marriage, in the name of Jesus.
5. Let the bewitchment and manipulation of my marriage expire, in the name of Jesus.
6. Fire of God, burn every enemy of my marriage, in the name of Jesus.
7. Any evil relationship designed to break my marriage, break, in the name of Jesus.
8. Let strangers in my marriage be disgraced, in the name of Jesus.
9. Any evil soul-tie that is attacking my marriage, break by force, in the name of Jesus.
10. I terminate ungodly relationships that are creating problems in my marriage, in the name of Jesus.
11. Any evil society that is causing trouble in my marriage, be frustrated, in the name of Jesus.
12. I expose and disgrace hidden problems that are attacking my marriage, in the name of Jesus.
13. Any evil counsel that is affecting my marriage, I reject you, in the name of Jesus.
14. I break and loose my marriage from undue interference of our parents, in the name of Jesus.
15. Any demonic in-law that has vowed to destroy my marriage, be destroyed, in the name of Jesus.

16. Let every curse that is placed upon my marriage expire immediately, in the name of Jesus.

17. I cast out forever demons that are attacking my marriage, in the name of Jesus.

18. I disengage my marriage from any marriage in the spiritual realm, in the name of Jesus.

19. Let every covenant and curse that is attacking my marriage be broken, in the name of Jesus.

20. I command my partner to be delivered from bewitchments and evil traps, in the name of Jesus.

21. Let every fake love that exists in my marriage expire and die, in the name of Jesus.

22. Every evil yoke that is placed upon my marriage, break to pieces, in the name of Jesus.

23. Let the fire of God burn every evil spirit that is fighting my marriage, in the name of Jesus.

24. I cast out every spirit of misunderstanding in my marriage, in the name of Jesus.

25. Let every demon that has followed me since my wedding day die, in the name of Jesus.

26. I receive deliverance from the mistakes I have ever made in this marriage, in the name of Jesus.

27. Blood of Jesus, flow into my foundation and deliver my marriage, in the name of Jesus.

28. Any strongman that is militating against my marriage, die, in the name of Jesus.

29. Any evil arrow that was fired at my marriage, backfire, in the name of Jesus.

30. Every sin that has followed us into our marriage, receive pardon, in the name of Jesus.

31. Let the spirit of anger, pride, domineering character and other works of the flesh cease in my marriage, in the name of Jesus.

32. Any evil utterance ever spoken against my marriage, expire, in the name of Jesus.

33. I silence evil voices that are tormenting my marriage, in the name of Jesus.

34. Lord Jesus, arise and take over my marriage forever, in the name of Jesus.

35. O Lord, help me to keep the vows of my marriage, in the name of Jesus.

36. I disgrace agents of separation and divorce in my marriage, in the name of Jesus.

37. Let every problem that is attacking my marriage die, in the name of Jesus.

38. Blood of Jesus, speak everlasting peace into my marriage, in the name of Jesus.

15

Chapter

PRAYERS FOR PREGNANT WOMEN

CHAPTER OVERVIEW

- *The weaker vessel*
- *Qualities of a virtuous wife*
- *Husband's care during pregnancy*
- *What a husband and wife must do*

THE WEAKER VESSEL

A woman's softness and tenderness depicts her as the weaker vessel. A woman is not tough like a man is. Therefore, she requires prayers and encouragement, especially during pregnancy. You must not be negative and rigid against your wife during her pregnancy. However, these weak attributes should not influence a woman's relationship with God or character negatively. If a pregnant woman dies in her pregnancy as a sinner, she would definitely go to hell fire. Therefore, as a pregnant woman, you should maintain your relationship with God, with your husband and others.

> *"Who can find a virtuous woman? For her price* is *far above rubies. The heart of her husband doth safely trust in her, so that he shall have no need of spoil. She will do him good and not evil all the days of her life. She seeketh wool, and flax, and worketh willingly with her hands. She is like the merchants' ships; she bringeth her food from afar"* (Proverbs 31:10-14).

Virtue is one word for the excellent qualities, the desirable personality traits and the endearing comportment in character, which every man longs for in his wife. A virtuous woman's price is far above rubies and she is the joy of her husband. In times of pregnancy, the weakness of the woman should not affect her character and relationship with others.

QUALITIES OF A VIRTUOUS WIFE

A virtuous wife does everything possible to preserve her respect and trust for her husband at all times. Even during her pregnancy, she endeavors to be good to her husband and her household. A virtuous woman can go the extra mile to retain her honor and build her house. She is stable in character. A virtuous woman possesses enviable qualities and lives an industrious life. She is resourceful, liberal and submissive. She inspires confidence in her husband's life. The bible honored virtuous women severally.

> *"A gracious woman retaineth honor: and strong* men *retain riches"* (Proverbs 11:16).

> *"A virtuous woman* is *a crown to her husband: but she that maketh ashamed* is *as rottenness in his bones"* (Proverbs 12:4).

"Every wise woman buildeth her house: but the foolish plucketh it down with her hands" (Proverbs 14:1).

No matter how weak her body is, she remains strong in character and never loses her respect no matter what.

"[15]She riseth also while it is yet night, and giveth meat to her household, and a portion to her maidens. [16]She considereth a field, and buyeth it: with the fruit of her hands, she planteth a vineyard. [17]She girdeth her loins with strength, and strengtheneth her arms. [18]She perceiveth that her merchandise is *good: her candle goeth not out by night. [19]She layeth her hands to the spindle, and her hands hold the distaff. [22]She maketh herself coverings of tapestry; her clothing* is *silk and purple"* (Proverbs 31:15-19, 22).

Even during her pregnancy, she maintains her life of industry and kindness. She may not participate fully during pregnancy, but she plans her timetable and gives instructions with respect and wisdom.

SHE MAINTAINS HER DISCRETION

Discretion is very important to every virtuous woman. They want to maintain good judgment at all times at their homes. She cares for all persons under her control and supervision. She is a good planner, a sustainer of good behavior and knows how to approach matters carefully. She knows the cost of foolishness.

> *"As a jewel of gold in a swine's snout, so is a fair woman which is without discretion"* (Proverbs 11:22).

> *"And Nabal answered David's servants, and said, Who* is *David? And who* is *the son of Jesse? There be many servants now a days that break away every man from his master. Shall I then take my bread, and my water, and my flesh that I have killed for my shearers, and give* it *unto men, whom I know not whence they* be? *So David's young men turned their way, and went again, and came and told him all those sayings. And David said unto his men, Gird ye on every man his sword. And they girded on every man his sword; and David also girded on his sword: and there went up after David about four hundred men; and two hundred abode by the stuff"* (1 Samuel 25:10-13).

Her wisdom moves her into action at the right time. A virtuous woman is determined to obey her husband, submit to him and play her own part well. No matter how wicked her husband may be, she tries to satisfy him in order to obey God's Word.

> "18 *Then Abigail made haste, and took two hundred loaves, and two bottles of wine, and five sheep ready dressed, and five measures of parched* corn, *and an hundred clusters of raisins, and two hundred cakes of figs, and laid* them *on asses.* 19 *And she said unto her servants, Go on before me; behold, I come after you. But she told not her husband Nabal.* 20 *And it was* so, *as she rode on the ass, that she came down by the covert of the hill, and, behold, David and his men came down against her; and she met them.* 23 *And when Abigail saw David, she hasted, and lighted off the ass, and fell before David on her face, and bowed herself to the ground,* 24 *And fell at his feet, and said, Upon me, my lord,* upon *me* let this *iniquity* be: *and let thine handmaid, I pray thee, speak in thine audience, and hear the words of thine handmaid.* 25 *Let not my lord, I pray thee, regard this man of Belial,* even *Nabal: for as his name* is, *so* is *he; Nabal* is *his name, and folly* is *with him: but I thine handmaid saw not the young men of my lord, whom thou didst send.* 26 *Now therefore, my lord, as the LORD liveth, and* as *thy soul liveth, seeing the LORD hath withholden thee from coming* to shed *blood, and from avenging thyself with thine own hand, now let thine enemies, and they that seek evil to my lord, be as Nabal.* 27 *And now this blessing which thine handmaid hath brought unto my lord, let it even be given unto the young men that follow my lord.* 35 *So David received of her hand* that *which she had brought him, and said unto*

her, Go up in peace to thine house; see, I have hearkened to thy voice, and have accepted thy person" (1 Samuel 25:18-20, 23-27, 35).

Her godly character and behavior can challenge the worst man on earth to change his mind to do well instead of evil. Discretion has to do with wisdom in conduct and the tactful handling of difficult situations. A virtuous woman knows that her chief calling is to take care of her home.

"And she said, Truth, Lord: yet the dogs eat of the crumbs which fall from their masters' table. Then Jesus answered and said unto her, O woman, great is *thy faith: be it unto thee even as thou wilt. And her daughter was made whole from that very hour"* (Matthew 15:27-28).

A virtuous wife knows how to cry to God or prays extensively in order to save every soul under her care. The woman of Canaan came out of the coast all the way to cry unto Jesus. She prayed until Jesus had mercy on her daughter. Virtuous women concentrate their energy working hard to make everyone at their homes happy.

They are excellent in home management. They are not wasteful, quarrelsome or rude in character. They are prayerful and careful in making choices.

"That they may teach the young women to be sober, to love their husbands, to love their children, To be *discreet, chaste, keepers at home, good, obedient to their own husbands, that the word of God be not blasphemed"* (Titus 2:4-5).

Her positive lifestyle influences everyone in her house to behave well, be sober and respectful.

SHE IS DILIGENT

A virtuous wife helps the less privileged people and gives gifts to the needy at every given opportunity. She is known for her kindness. She can take risks to see that the people around her are happy. Like Jesus, she has a deep love for compassion and seeing people set free from bondage. A virtuous woman is ready to do anything to help people get well and serve God. She understands that time is too short and that eternity is endless. That is why she is always willing to see people liberated from sin, sickness and death. No trouble is so great for her to handle.

> *"[20]She stretcheth out her hand to the poor; yea, she reacheth forth her hands to the needy. [24]She maketh fine linen, and selleth* it; *and delivereth girdles unto the merchant. [27]She looketh well to the ways of her household, and eateth not the bread of idleness"* (Proverbs 31:20, 24, 27).

There is no humiliation to deep, no labor to hard, and no love too strong in her efforts to save souls from trouble. A virtuous woman is a great overseer with wisdom in administration at the home front. At home, she is involved. She does not enjoy relaxing and issuing orders. Instead, she engages in the daily assignments at her home and offices where she is in-charge.

> *"Whatsoever thy hand findeth to do, do* it *with thy might; for* there is *no work, nor device, nor knowledge, nor wisdom, in the grave, whither thou goest"* (Ecclesiastes 9:10).

> *"Now there was at Joppa a certain disciple named Tabitha, which by interpretation is called Dorcas: this woman was full of good works and alms deeds which she did. Then Peter arose and went with them. When he was come, they brought him into the upper chamber: and all the widows stood by him weeping, and shewing the coats and garments which Dorcas made, while she was with them"* (Acts 9:36, 39).

A virtuous woman is not lazy or wicked. She works with all her might, a willing heart and divine wisdom. She is full of good works and deeds. She wins many souls for God. Her distinctions cannot be hidden.

> *"Strength and honor* are *her clothing; and she shall rejoice in time to come. She openeth her mouth with wisdom; and in her tongue* is *the law of kindness. [28]Her children arise up, and call her blessed; her husband* also, *and he praiseth her. Many daughters have done virtuously, but thou excellest them all. Favor* is *deceitful, and beauty* is *vain:* but *a woman* that *feareth the LORD, she shall be praised. Give her of the fruit of her hands; and let her own works praise her in the gates"* (Proverbs 31:25-26, 28-31).

Virtuous women work with eternity in view and do not procrastinate. They are always with honor and are usually very kind. They are very spiritual and they control their tongues very well. They are the perfect models to follow because they fear God. They are filled with honest reports.

> *"And in the sixth month the angel Gabriel was sent from God unto a city of Galilee, named Nazareth, To a virgin espoused to a man whose name was Joseph, of the house of David; and the virgin's name* was *Mary. And the angel came in unto her, and said, Hail,* thou that art *highly favored, the Lord* is *with thee: blessed* art *thou among women"* (Luke 1:26-28).

> *"In like manner also, that women adorn themselves in modest apparel, with shamefacedness and sobriety; not with broided hair, or gold, or pearls, or costly array; But (which becometh women professing godliness) with good works"* (1 Timothy 2:9-10).

The beauty of a virtuous wife resonates in her character. Her children, husband and family members respect and praise her. Her works are rooted in God and she is special among women.

> *"Likewise, ye wives,* be *in subjection to your own husbands; that, if any obey not the word, they also may without the word be won by the conversation of the wives; While they behold your chaste conversation* coupled *with fear. Whose adorning let it not be that outward* adorning *of plaiting the hair, and of wearing of gold, or of putting on of apparel; But* let it be *the hidden man of the heart, in that which is not corruptible,* even the ornament *of a meek and quiet spirit, which is in the sight of God of great price. For after this manner in the old time the holy women also, who trusted in God, adorned themselves, being in subjection unto their own husbands"* (1 Peter 3:1-5).

She is submissive, obedient and a specialists in approaching matters prudently. She tries to excel in every good thing in life. She is always distinguishable, outshining and first rated above others. Virtuous women try their best to be outstanding, exceptional, superior and best of the best.

SHE SUBMITS TO HER HUSBAND

One of the qualities of a virtuous woman is submission to the authority of her husband even during pregnancy. A virtuous woman recognizes and accepts God's ordained headship of her husband. This she does, not because her husband is fulfilling his own part in the marriage but because she wants to obey God's Word as a Christian. The Word of God guides her:

> *"Likewise, ye wives, be in subjection to your own husbands; that, if any obey not the word, they also may without the word be won by the conversation of the wives"* (1 Peter 3:1).

> *"Wives, submit yourselves unto your own husbands, as it is fit in the Lord"* (Colossians 3:18).

A Christian wife has nothing to lose in submitting to the headship of her husband. By doing so, she receives the blessing of obeying God's Word.

> *"Wives, submit yourselves unto your own husbands, as unto the Lord.* [24]*Therefore as the church is subject unto Christ, so* let *the wives* be *to their own husbands in everything"* (Ephesians 5:22, 24).

Submitting as "unto the Lord" means that the wife is to submit in love, not as slaves who fearfully obey. Virtuous women manifest the quality of being meek and quiet to the glory of God.

> *"On the seventh day, when the heart of the king was merry with wine, he commanded Mehuman, Biztha, Harbona, Bigtha, and Abagtha, Zethar, and Carcas, the seven chamberlains that served in the presence of Ahasuerus the king, To bring Vashti the queen before the king with the crown royal, to shew the people and the princes her beauty: for she* was *fair to look on. But the queen Vashti refused to come at the king's commandment by* his *chamberlains: therefore was the king very wroth, and his anger burned in him"* (Esther 1: 10-12).

Consider Esther, who was so quiet, meek and gentle. She was also hospitable, loving and humble.

> *"And it fell on a day, that Elisha passed to Shunem, where* was *a great woman; and she constrained him to eat bread. And* so *it was,* that *as oft as he passed by, he turned in thither to eat bread. And she said unto her husband, Behold now, I perceive that this* is *a holy man of God, which passeth by us continually. Let us make a little chamber, I pray thee, on the wall; and let us set for him there a bed, and a table, and a stool, and a candlestick: and it shall be, when he cometh to us that he shall turn in thither. And it fell on a day, that he came thither, and he turned into the chamber, and lay there. And*

he said to Gehazi his servant, Call this Shunammite. And when he had called her, she stood before him. And he said unto him, Say now unto her, Behold, thou hast been careful for us with all this care; what is to be done for thee? Wouldest thou be spoken for to the king, or to the captain of the host? And she answered, I dwell among mine own people. And he said, What then is to be done for her? And Gehazi answered, Verily she hath no child, and her husband is old" (2 King 4:8-14).

A virtuous woman is very conscious and heavenly bound. She is loving and prayerful.

"And, behold, a woman of Canaan came out of the same coasts, and cried unto him, saying, Have mercy on me, O Lord, thou *Son of David; my daughter is grievously vexed with a devil. But he answered her not a word. And his disciples came and besought him, saying, Send her away; for she crieth after us. But he answered and said, I am not sent but unto the lost sheep of the house of Israel. Then came she and worshipped him, saying, Lord, help me. But he answered and said, It is not meet to take the children's bread, and to cast* it *to dogs. And she said, Truth, Lord: yet the dogs eat of the crumbs, which fall from their masters' table. Then Jesus answered and said unto her, O woman, great* is *thy faith: be it unto thee even as thou wilt. And her daughter was made whole from that very hour"* (Matthew 15: 22-28).

They are also humble in character. She makes her home a paradise, conducive for her husband, children and the servants.

HUSBAND'S CARE DURING PREGNANCY

Every husband has so much to do during the wife's pregnancy. It is the responsibility of a husband to bring out the best in his wife. No matter how much progress a woman has made before marriage, if her husband plays his role very well, the woman will rise to greater positions of excellence.

> *"For the husband is the head of the wife, even as Christ is the head of the church: and he is the savior of the body"* (Ephesians 5:23).

> *"But I would have you know, that the head of every man is Christ; and the head of the woman* is *the man; and the head of Christ* is *God"* (1 Corinthian 11:3).

> *"One that ruleth well his own house, having his children in subjection with all gravity; (For if a man know not how to rule his own house, how shall he take care of the church of God?)"* (1 Timothy 3:4-5).

The husband is the head of the wife and the head of the man is Christ, while the head of Christ is God. The harmony between God and Christ dislodged the devil. Jesus was able to do all that He did because He was one with God.

> *"At that time Jesus answered and said, I thank thee, O Father, Lord of heaven and earth, because thou hast hid these things from the wise and prudent, and hast revealed them unto babes"* (Matthew 11:25).

> *"And when Jesus had cried with a loud voice, he said, Father, into thy hands I commend my spirit: and having said thus, he gave up the ghost"* (Luke 23:46).

> *"I can of mine own self do nothing: as I hear, I judge: and my judgment is just; because I seek not mine own will, but the will of the Father which hath sent me"* (John 5:30).

A husband and his wife must stay together in order to achieve their aim and purpose of their marriage. Jesus never wanted to be independent of His Father. He was always grateful to His Father. At the cross, He commended His Spirit unto God, His Father and head. He knows that a body without head can do nothing. He depended on His Father to do all things He did on earth. This is how a husband and his wife must depend on each other.

A good husband who understands what a head is to the body cannot plan alone. He must stay with the wife, plan with her spiritually and provide all her earthly needs. As the head, he must plan for the welfare of the whole family including the baby in the womb. This is a God's given responsibility. In order to be a responsible man and a good head, he must plan, teach, guide, direct, lead and control the family according to God's Word. He prays together with his wife and provides for the entire family. The head stays with the body until death.

> "[28]*So ought men to love their wives as their own bodies. He that loveth his wife loveth himself.* [29]*For no man ever yet hated his own flesh; but nourisheth and cherisheth it, even as the Lord the church:* [31]*For this cause shall a man leave his father and mother, and shall be joined unto his wife, and they two shall be one flesh*"(Ephesians 5:28- 29, 31).

Christ was fully involved with His disciples until the end. Even when they scattered and denied Him, he loved them. He showed His love and died to save the church. Even after death, He rose, gathered them again and empowered them to continue the work of the gospel.

> "*Afterward he appeared unto the eleven as they sat at meat, and upbraided them with their unbelief and hardness of heart, because they believed not them which had seen him after he was risen. And he said unto them, Go ye into all the world, and preach the gospel to every creature. He that believeth and is baptized shall be saved; but he that believeth not shall be damned. And these signs shall follow them that believe; In my name shall they cast out devils; they shall speak with new tongues; They shall take up serpents; and if they drink any deadly thing, it shall not hurt them; they shall lay hands on the sick, and they shall recover. So then after the Lord had spoken unto them, he was received up into heaven, and sat on the right hand of God. And they went forth, and preached everywhere, the Lord working with* them, *and confirming the word with signs following. Amen*" (Mark 16:14-20).

Christ did not only die for the church, he resurrected and empowered the church. Up until today, he is with the church, working with the church and confirming the Word they speak with signs following. Christ was not just a head to the church, but a good head and not a figurehead. He is still involved in life and functions of the church until this day.

INCREASE OF MAN'S RESPONSIBILITY

Jesus love, care and concern for His bride, the church, increase at our weakest moments. Christ came to save us when it was necessary that His perfect nature of godhead and sinless blood would remove guilt, shame and death from us. His grace appeared at our hopeless and helpless moment. As the scriptures put it:

"Your lamb shall be without blemish, a male of the first year: ye shall take it *out from the sheep, or from the goats"* (Exodus 12:5).

"And whosoever offereth a sacrifice of peace offerings unto the LORD to accomplish his vow, or a freewill offering in beeves or sheep, it shall be perfect to be accepted; there shall be no blemish therein" (Leviticus 22:21).

"Giving thanks unto the Father, which hath made us meet to be partakers of the inheritance of the saints in light: Who hath delivered us from the power of darkness, and hath translated us *into the kingdom of his dear Son: In whom we have redemption through his blood,* even *the forgiveness of sins"* (Colossians 1:12-14).

We received the grace of Jesus when we were blind, deaf and dead. If Christ did not come to save us, we would be in hell by now. A husband is expected to discharge his God-given role and responsibility over his wife during the time of pregnancy. This is because women are usually weak at this period and needs more help and love.

"Husbands, love your wives, even as Christ also loved the church, and gave himself for it; That he might sanctify and cleanse it with the washing of water by the word, That he might present it to himself a glorious church, not having spot, or wrinkle, or any such thing; but that it should be holy and without blemish. So ought men to love their wives as their own bodies. He that loveth his wife loveth himself. For no man ever yet hated his own flesh; but nourisheth and cherisheth it, even as the Lord the church: For we are members of his body, of his flesh, and of his bones. For this cause shall a man leave his father and mother, and shall be joined unto his wife, and they two shall be one flesh. This is a great mystery: but I speak concerning Christ and the church. Nevertheless let every one of you in particular so love his wife even as himself; and the wife see *that she reverence* her *husband"* (Ephesians 5:25-33).

Husbands are expected to take care of their wives just as they do to their own bodies. Every man naturally feeds, protects, washes, cleans and cares for his body. Nobody wishes to cut off his leg because it was dirty, or force his hands to sleep under the rain because they were dirty.

Unfortunately, some unreasonable husbands insist that their wives sweep, wash, cook and do all the works alone even at their ninth month of pregnancy. They cannot allow their wives to rest even when it is clear they are weak and need to rest. Even at their wives' sick beds, they expect them to get up to wash the plates and clean the room.

Such men knew how to sympathize with everybody else except their wives. They know how to take good care of their bodies, rest when they are sick or tired but insist that their wives do not. They grant their bodies rest well but force their wives to wake up early. They cannot tell when their wives are in pain. They increase their wives' sorrows, pains and cause them to get weaker. Ironically, they also claim to be born-again, but beat their wives, abuse them and forbid them from complaining to others. Do you love your wife as Christ loves the church and gave His life for her?

> *"For when we were yet without strength, in due time Christ died for the ungodly. For scarcely for a righteous man will one die: yet peradventure for a good man some would even dare to die. But God commendeth his love toward us, in that, while we were yet sinners, Christ died for us. Much more then, being now justified by his blood, we shall be saved from wrath through him. For if, when we were enemies, we were reconciled to God by the death of his Son, much more, being reconciled, we shall be saved by his life"* (Romans 5:6-10).

> *"And as they went to tell his disciples, behold, Jesus met them, saying, All hail. And they came and held him by the feet, and worshipped him. Then said Jesus unto them, Be not afraid: go tell my brethren that they go into Galilee, and there shall they see me"* (Matthew 28:9-10).

Imagine how Christ washed the feet of His disciples when they all had the strength to do so. What Christ demonstrated was a remarkable service to one another. He demonstrated the ministry of love, which places the interest of *self* behind and below that of others.

> *"So after He had washed their feet, and had taken his garments, and was set down again, he said unto them, Know ye what I have done to you? Ye call me Master and Lord: and ye say well; for so I am. If I then,* your *Lord and Master, have washed your feet; ye also ought to wash one another's feet. For I have given you an example that ye should do as I have done to you. Verily, verily, I say unto you, The servant is not greater than his lord; neither he that is sent greater than he that sent him"* (John 13: 12-16).

> *"For, brethren, ye have been called unto liberty; only use not liberty for an occasion to the flesh, but by love serve one another"* (Galatians 5:13).

> *"Bear ye one another's burdens, and so fulfill the law of Christ. As we have therefore opportunity, let us do good unto all* men, *especially unto them who are of the household of faith"* (Galatians 6:2, 10).

The washing of feet was an oriental custom of great antiquity as a mark of hospitality. The Scriptures pointed out the significance of the washing of feet:

> *"Let a little water, I pray you, be fetched, and wash your feet, and rest yourselves under the tree"* (Genesis 18: 4).

"And he said, Behold now, my lords, turn in, I pray you, into your servant's house, and tarry all night, and wash your feet, and ye shall rise up early, and go on your ways. And they said, Nay; but we will abide in the street all night" (Genesis 19:2).

If you could care for others, Christ demanded that you care more for your wife. Christ did it for us when we could not. For when we were yet without strength, Christ died for the ungodly and unworthy. Loving, caring and cherishing your wife is a commandment, which you must do whether she deserves it or not. It is a command that you must obey and there is blessing in obeying God's Word.

As God showered us with His love without minding that we are not worthy, so shall we do to our wives without minding their failures.

"Now before the feast of the Passover, when Jesus knew that his hour was come that he should depart out of this world unto the Father, having loved his own which were in the world, he loved them unto the end" (John 13:1).

"Greater love hath no man than this, that a man lay down his life for his friends" (John 15:13).

Do not love only when you are sure of what you can get from your wife. You must establish your love on the written Word of God, which commands you to love. Christ's love for us was sacrificial. Therefore, your love for your wife must be sacrificial before God accepts it.

"56 But all this was done, that the scriptures of the prophets might be fulfilled. Then all the disciples forsook him, and fled. 66 What think ye? They answered and said, He is guilty of death. 67 Then did they spit in his face, and buffeted him; and others smote him with the palms of their hands, 68 Saying, Prophesy unto us, thou Christ, Who is he that smote thee? 69 Now Peter sat without in the palace: and a damsel came unto him, saying, Thou also wast with Jesus of Galilee. 70 But he denied before them *all, saying, I know not what thou sayest. 71 And when he was gone out into the porch, another maid saw him, and said unto them that were there, This* fellow *was also with Jesus of Nazareth. 72 And again he denied with an oath, I do not know the man. 73 And after a while came unto* him *they that stood by, and said to Peter, Surely thou also art* one *of them; for thy speech bewrayeth thee. 74 Then began he to curse and to swear,* saying, *I know not the man. And immediately the cock crew. 75 And Peter remembered the word of Jesus, which said unto him, Before the cock crow, thou shalt deny me thrice. And he went out, and wept bitterly"* (Matthew 26: 56, 66-75)

Imagine the disciples of Jesus fleeing at the time Jesus needed them most. They arrested Jesus, spit on his face and smote him. Yet, He went ahead and died for our sins. What has your wife or husband done to you that you cannot forgive for Christ's sake?

WHAT A HUSBAND AND WIFE MUST DO

The place of love in a Christian home cannot be over emphasized. No husband and wife can fulfill God's purpose in their marriage without practicing the true love. At the presence of true love, a husband and his wife can move mountains. Christ our perfect example demonstrated true love by loving God, His followers and His enemies at all times in a sacrificial manner. What does the Scripture demand from us in reciprocation?

> *"Hereby perceive we the love* of *God, because he laid down his life for us: and we ought to lay down* our *lives for the brethren"* (1 John 3:16).

> *"[1]Now before the feast of the Passover, when Jesus knew that his hour was come that he should depart out of this world unto the Father, having loved his own which were in the world, he loved them unto the end. [13]Ye call me Master and Lord: and ye say well; for* so *I am. [14]If I then,* your *Lord and Master, have washed your feet; ye also ought to wash one another's feet. [15]For I have given you an example that ye should do as I have done to you"* (John 13:1, 13-15).

Love demands and should be demonstrated in deed as Christ did. True love when demonstrated gives contentment to live and stay in fellowship.

> *"And when he was come into the ship, he that had been possessed with the devil prayed him that he might be with him"* (Mark 5:18).

A husband who must love his wife as God demanded must die to self and where this kind of love exists, there is no animosity, struggle, fighting, but a perfect and glorious harmony. The great secret of joy, happiness and peace in marriage is mutual love, tenderness, loveliness and kindness of character at home. God demands that the wife should respect, honor and obey the husband, while the husband should love and care for the wife and direct the affairs of the house.

> *"Forbearing one another, and forgiving one another, if any man have a quarrel against any: even as Christ forgave you, so also* do *ye"* (Colossians 3:13).

> *"And be ye kind one to another, tenderhearted, forgiving one another, even as God for Christ's sake hath forgiven you"* (Ephesians 4:32).

Husbands and wives must forgive each other no matter the offence. If they quarrel, they must take decision in advanced to forgive each other. They must not allow bitterness, anger, wrath, clamor, evil speaking or gossip to come between them. They must be kind, and of tender heart to one another. They are commanded by God's Word to prefer one to another, minister to one another and consider one another.

"Be kindly affectioned one to another with brotherly love; in honor preferring one another" (Romans 12:10).

"And let us consider one another to provoke unto love and to good works" (Hebrew 10:24).

You must be kindly affected with love to one another, preferring one another in love. You are also commanded to consider one another, provoke one another unto love. The husband should consider his wife by taking over most of her job during her pregnancy. Things like finding faults, hatred, quarrelling, malice, criticism, revenge, bitterness, selfishness, backbiting and unforgiving attitude should not be mentioned or found in your home, especially during your wife's pregnancy.

PRAYERS FOR PREGNANT WOMEN

Bible references: Exodus 23:25-26; Proverbs 31:10-31

Begin with praise and worship

1. Father Lord, arise and protect me from defilement, in the name of Jesus.
2. I receive power to function without satanic attacks, in the name of Jesus.
3. Every weakness that is designed to destroy my divine character, die by fire, in the name of Jesus.
4. O Lord, arise and deliver me from strange weaknesses, in the name of Jesus.
5. Any power that wants to use my pregnancy to ruin my Christian life, die, in the name of Jesus.
6. Let the arrow of death that was fired at me backfire by force, in the name of Jesus.
7. Blood of Jesus, speak life unto my baby in the womb, in the name of Jesus.
8. Every weapon of witchcraft against my pregnancy, catch fire, in the name of Jesus.
9. Holy Ghost fire, saturate my womb and protect my pregnancy, in the name of Jesus.
10. Let my relationship with God and man be preserved within and outside this pregnancy, in the name of Jesus.
11. Any power that wants to attack my virtue during my pregnancy, die, in the name of Jesus.
12. Any satanic door that was opened to this pregnancy, close by force, in the name of Jesus.
13. I reject evil weakness that was designed to abort my pregnancy, in the name of Jesus.
14. O Lord, empower me to respect my husband throughout my pregnancy period, in the name of Jesus.
15. Let the plans of devil to destroy me with the works of the flesh die, in the name of Jesus.

16. O Lord, empower me to maintain peace and joy during my pregnancy, in the name of Jesus.

17. Let every good thing inside me be sustained during this pregnancy, in the name of Jesus.

18. I refuse to take any negative action during this pregnancy, in the name of Jesus.

19. I frustrate demons of miscarriage in my life, in the name of Jesus.

20. Holy Ghost fire, cover my womb and protect my baby to Your own glory, in the name of Jesus.

21. O Lord, increase my strength during this pregnancy, in the name of Jesus.

22. Let star hijackers of pregnancies be disgraced for my sake, in the name of Jesus.

23. Let evil eyes that are monitoring my pregnancy go blind, in the name of Jesus.

24. I frustrate every manipulation of my pregnancy, in the name of Jesus.

25. Killers of babies in the womb, my pregnancy is not available, in the name of Jesus.

26. Every arrow of death that was fired at my pregnancy, I fire you back, in the name of Jesus.

27. Any evil altar that is attacking my pregnancy, scatter by fire, in the name of Jesus.

28. Blood of Jesus, cleanse every evil mark that is made on my pregnancy, in the name of Jesus.

29. Any curse that was placed upon my pregnancy, expire by fire, in the name of Jesus.

30. Every unclean spirit that is contending with my pregnancy, I cast you out, in the name of Jesus.

31. I command the destroying fire of God to destroy every enemy of my pregnancy, in the name of Jesus.

32. Every satanic rage against my pregnancy, be calmed, in the name of Jesus.

33. Any power that is oppressing my pregnancy, I oppress you, in the name of Jesus.

34. Any evil brain that is planning to destabilize my pregnancy, scatter, in the name of Jesus.

35. Wherever they mention my pregnancy for evil, blood of Jesus, answer, in the name of Jesus.

36. Let every enemy of my pregnancy receive double destruction, in the name of Jesus.

37. Any poison that is prepared against my pregnancy, dry up and die, in the name of Jesus.

38. Father Lord, protect my pregnancy forever, in the name of Jesus.

39. Every arrow that was fired at my pregnancy, backfire, in the name of Jesus.

40. You my pregnancy, refuse to be aborted, in the name of Jesus.

16

Chapter

PRAYERS TO RETAIN YOUR PREGNANCY

CHAPTER OVERVIEW

- *Guard your pregnancy*
- *Put on the whole armor of God*
- *Powers that terminate pregnancies*

GUARD YOUR PREGNANCY

In this world of increasing complexities, even in the midst of breakthrough scientific and medical inventions, many pregnant women continue to struggle to retain their pregnancies. In this book, I will reveal to you how Satan labors to destroy many pregnancies, in order to equip you with the Word of God on how to guard your pregnancy.

The scripture revealed that the world is a battleground. The war is between good and evil; between God's children and Satan's agents.

> *"For we wrestle not against flesh and blood, but against principalities, against powers, against the rulers of the darkness of this world, against spiritual wickedness in high* places" (Ephesians 6:12).

> *"Fight the good fight of faith, lay hold on eternal life, where unto thou art also called, and hast professed a good profession before many witnesses"* (1 Timothy 6:12).

> *"For though we walk in the flesh, we do not war after the flesh: (For the weapons of our warfare* are *not carnal, but mighty through God to the pulling down of strong holds;) Casting down imaginations, and every high thing that exalteth itself against the knowledge of God, and bringing into captivity every thought to the obedience of Christ"* (2 Corinthians 10:3-5).

Every human alive is involved in spiritual warfare and only true believers know how to achieve real victory in the Word of God. Being ignorant of these spiritual conflicts would prove very costly. The first defeat all humans suffer on earth is the curse of the sin of Adam, which puts all humanity into slavery.

> *"Now we know that what things soever the law saith, it saith to them who are under the law: that every mouth may be stopped, and all the world may become guilty before God"* (Romans 3:19).

> *"[18]He that believeth on him is not condemned: but he that believeth not is condemned already, because he hath not believed in the name of the only begotten Son of God. [36] He that believeth on the Son hath everlasting life: and he that believeth not the Son shall not see life; but the wrath of God abideth on him"* (John 3:18, 36).

> *"Behold, I was shapen in iniquity; and in sin did my mother conceive me"* (Psalms 51:5).

Many people live under the power of sin without knowing how to escape. They were born into sin, they lived and died in sin without receiving deliverance and salvation. They lived under the oppression of the devil and never reigned over any circumstance in their lives.

> *"For the Son of man is come to seek and to save that which was lost"* (Luke 19:10).

> *"And saying, The time is fulfilled, and the kingdom of God is at hand: repent ye, and believe the gospel"* (Mark 1:15).

> *"For by grace are ye saved through faith; and that not of yourselves:* it is *the gift of God: Not of works, lest any man should boast"* (Ephesians 2:8-9).

On the cross of Calvary, Jesus Christ paid the full price for our freedom. Christ's death brought deliverance for us and destined us to overcome sin, Satan, evil spirits and all problems in life. The devil is the cause of all sicknesses, afflictions and problems. He uses sin to bring people into problems and bondage. Problems enter into people's lives through sins they commit or inherit. However, if you repent, confess your sins and forsake them, you can resist the devil and he will flee. Christians have power over the devil and all his works. Praise God!

> *"And he said unto them, I beheld Satan as lightning fall from heaven. Behold, I give unto you power to tread on serpents and scorpions, and over all the power of the enemy: and nothing shall by any means hurt you. Notwithstanding in this rejoice not, that the spirits are subject unto you; but rather rejoice, because your names are written in heaven"* (Luke 10: 18-20)

> *"Then he called his twelve disciples together, and gave them power and authority over all devils, and to cure diseases"* (Luke 9:1).

> *"He that committeth sin is of the devil; for the devil sinneth from the beginning. For this purpose the Son of God was manifested, that he might destroy the works of the devil"* (1 John 3:8).

However, if you desire for true deliverance, then do away with sin. Even after overcoming sin, if you do not resist the devil, he will come back to oppress you. Jesus has to heal the sick and deliver the oppressed by rebuking the devil and casting out the evil spirit that caused the sickness.

> *"As they went out, behold, they brought to him a dumb man possessed with a devil. And when the devil was cast out, the dumb spake: and the multitudes marvelled, saying, It was never so seen in Israel"* (Matthew 9:32-33).

"And when they were come to the multitude, there came to him a certain *man, kneeling down to him, and saying, Lord, have mercy on my son: for he is lunatic, and sore vexed: for ofttimes he falleth into the fire, and oft into the water. And I brought him to thy disciples, and they could not cure him. Then Jesus answered and said, O faithless and perverse generation, how long shall I be with you? How long shall I suffer you? Bring him hither to me. And Jesus rebuked the devil; and he departed out of him: and the child was cured from that very hour. Then came the disciples to Jesus apart, and said, Why could not we cast him out? And Jesus said unto them, Because of your unbelief: for verily I say unto you, If ye have faith as a grain of mustard seed, ye shall say unto this mountain, Remove hence to yonder place; and it shall remove; and nothing shall be impossible unto you. Howbeit this kind goeth not out but by prayer and fasting"* (Matthew 17:14-21).

"Was returning, and sitting in his chariot read Esaias the prophet. Then the Spirit said unto Philip, Go near, and join thyself to this chariot. And Philip ran thither to him, *and heard him read the prophet Esaias, and said, Understandest thou what thou readest? And he said, How can I, except some man should guide me? And he desired Philip that he would come up and sit with him. The place of the scripture which he read was this, He was led as a sheep to the slaughter; and like a lamb dumb before his shearer, so opened he not his mouth: In his humiliation his judgment was taken away: and who shall declare his generation? For his life is taken from the earth. And the eunuch answered Philip, and said, I pray thee, of whom speaketh the prophet this? Of himself, or of some other man?"* (Acts 8:28-34).

Jesus casted them out by the Spirit of God and the same Spirit of God lives in us. We can cast out the devil and conduct deliverance like the one Jesus did. The Scripture confirmed this:

"And these signs shall follow them that believe; In my name shall they cast out devils; they shall speak with new tongues; They shall take up serpents; and if they drink any deadly thing, it shall not hurt them; they shall lay hands on the sick, and they shall recover" (Mark 16:17-18).

Salvation or being born-again cannot remove all stubborn demons from us. We need to confront them as we work out our salvation with fear and trembling (*See* Philippians 2:12).

"But I see another law in my members, warring against the law of my mind, and bringing me into captivity to the law of sin which is in my members" (Romans 7:23).

"And after those days his wife Elisabeth conceived, and hid herself five months, saying, Thus hath the Lord dealt with me in the days wherein he looked on me, *to take*

away my reproach among men. And in the sixth month the angel Gabriel was sent from God unto a city of Galilee, named Nazareth" (Luke 1:24-26).

"Submit yourselves therefore to God. Resist the devil, and he will flee from you" (James 4:7).

The battle will rage on until Jesus returns, and only those who received Christ and lean on the written Word of God wholeheartedly will receive perfect deliverance. You may need to deal with your religious doctrines and barriers, family limitations and abandon your Sodom before your deliverance can be affected.

Many people dine with Satan. Some live with Delilah, while others pitch their tents near Sodom and Gomorrah. There are people who swim in their affluence and spend their time in far countries. If you want true and lasting deliverance, do not give yourself access to sin, the flesh or things that oppose holiness.

Do not forget that you are in a warfare situation. You have to be in the camp of Jesus to win the battle. This is because where you are in times of warfare determines your end. You have to position yourself rightly in Christ before you can use God's resources and power to overcome the devil.

"Then he answered and spake unto me, saying, This is *the word of the LORD unto Zerubbabel, saying, Not by might, nor by power, but by my spirit, saith the LORD of hosts"* (Zechariah 4:6).

"Hast thou not known? Hast thou not heard, that the everlasting God, the LORD, the Creator of the ends of the earth, fainteth not, neither is weary? There is no searching of his understanding. He giveth power to the faint; and to them that have no might he increaseth strength. Even the youths shall faint and be weary, and the young men shall utterly fall: But they that wait upon the LORD shall renew their strength; they shall mount up with wings as eagles; they shall run, and not be weary; and they shall walk, and not faint" (Isaiah 40:28-31).

If you are going to overcome the devil, his evil spirits and agents, then you have to be spiritually strong through Jesus Christ. You may need to add fasting to your prayers. If you are already pregnant, you may pray alone in faith. Ask for divine strength so that you do not faint or be weary.

You cannot fight spiritual battles carnally or with human techniques. God has made His power available to all His children to appropriate by being obedient and putting on the whole armor of God. There are Christians who were destined for victory, but they fell on the day of battle.

"Be sober, be vigilant; because your adversary the devil, as a roaring lion, walketh about, seeking whom he may devour: Whom resist steadfast in the faith, knowing that the same afflictions are accomplished in your brethren that are in the world" (1 Peter 5: 8-9).

"And he said unto me, My grace is sufficient for thee: for my strength is made perfect in weakness. Most gladly therefore will I rather glory in my infirmities, that the power of Christ may rest upon me" (2 Corinthians 12:9).

Without God's grace and power of the Holy Spirit, it will be impossible for you to make it to the end. Those who are confident in themselves always fail in ordinary battles and minor temptations because they rely upon their own strength. You must vacate Satan's territory. Otherwise, he would capture you eventually. Whatever your spiritual experiences and gifting are, you must arise and reposition yourself in order to resist the devil.

"And the LORD God prepared a gourd, and made it *to come up over Jonah, that it might be a shadow over his head, to deliver him from his grief. So, Jonah was exceeding glad of the gourd. But God prepared a worm when the morning rose the next day, and it smote the gourd that it withered"* (Jonah 4:6-7).

"For though we walk in the flesh, we do not war after the flesh: (For the weapons of our warfare are *not carnal, but mighty through God to the pulling down of strong holds;) Casting down imaginations, and every high thing that exalteth itself against the knowledge of God, and bringing into captivity every thought to the obedience of Christ"* (2 Corinthians 10:3-5).

You can overcome all your enemies with spiritual weapons, which is the whole armor of God. You must be sober and vigilant, and fight as if your eternal destiny depends on your victory. Whatever you do, pray wisely. If you have to wait on the Lord a bit longer, fast and keep praying all night. Do not be mindful of your flesh, and do not take it easy on your enemy. Let your greatest concern be how to win the enemy and break the backbone of all the powers behind your problems.

"Thou therefore endure hardness, as a good soldier of Jesus Christ. No man that warreth entangleth himself with the affairs of this *life; that he may please him who hath chosen him to be a soldier"* (2 Timothy 2:3-4).

"For the love of money is the root of all evil: which while some coveted after, they have erred from the faith, and pierced themselves through with many sorrows. But thou, O man of God, flee these things; and follow after righteousness, godliness, faith, love, patience, meekness. Fight the good fight of faith, lay hold on eternal life, where unto

thou art also called, and hast professed a good profession before many witnesses" (1 Timothy 6:10-12).

Separate yourself from every distraction and other issues. Apportion enough time to fight against problems that bother your life. Two armies cannot fight and win decisively at the same time. Satan has to lose and God has to win.

Jacob separated himself from the affairs of this world in order to settle with Esau finally. Free yourself from temporary enjoyment, youthful lusts and vehemently strive to set yourself free from bondage.

"Wherefore seeing we also are compassed about with so great a cloud of witnesses, let us lay aside every weight, and the sin which doth so easily beset us, *and let us run with patience the race that is set before us, Looking unto Jesus the author and finisher of* our *faith; who for the joy that was set before him endured the cross, despising the shame, and is set down at the right hand of the throne of God. For consider him that endured such contradiction of sinners against himself, lest ye be wearied and faint in your minds. Ye have not yet resisted unto blood, striving against sin"* (Hebrews 12:1-4).

"But I say unto you, That whosoever looketh on a woman to lust after her hath committed adultery with her already in his heart. And if thy right eye offend thee, pluck it out, and cast it *from thee: for it is profitable for thee that one of thy members should perish, and not* that *thy whole body should be cast into hell. And if thy right hand offend thee, cut it off, and cast* it *from thee: for it is profitable for thee that one of thy members should perish, and not* that *thy whole body should be cast into hell"* (Matthew 5:28-30).

"Dearly beloved, I beseech you *as strangers and pilgrims, abstain from fleshly lusts, which war against the soul"* (1 Peter 2:11).

What you stand to gain if you win the battle is much more. Stand and fight for your right strongly and your enemies would surrender. Cut off every source of distraction, temptation and as much as it lays in your power, resist the devil.

Persistence, faith and resistance are common to all winners no matter their experiences. Our life on earth is short and the challenge before us is for us to face the enemy now. You have a life to live and if you must, it has to be to the glory of God who has created you for His glory. Do not die at the mercy of the devil. If you were able to get married, then you will also be able to have children. God is able.

"And not only they, *but ourselves also, which have the first fruits of the Spirit, even we ourselves groan within ourselves, waiting for the adoption,* to wit, *the redemption of our body"* (Romans 8:23).

PUT ON THE WHOLE ARMOR OF GOD

God, the Father of all blessings, made His power to get victory over Satan and the world available to all His children. He knew that there is a spiritual battle going on. That was why God did not want us to be vulnerable to the attacks of the devil. This is the reason why wise and victorious Christians put on the whole armor of God always. Otherwise, the devil would pull you down by any means. This is a wakeup call for you to rise up and put on the whole armor of God as the Scripture advised us to do in order to resist the devil successfully.

> *"Finally, my brethren, be strong in the Lord, and in the power of his might. Put on the whole armor of God, that ye may be able to stand against the wiles of the devil. For we wrestle not against flesh and blood, but against principalities, against powers, against the rulers of the darkness of this world, against spiritual wickedness in high* places. *Wherefore take unto you the whole armor of God that ye may be able to withstand in the evil day, and having done all, to stand. Stand therefore, having your loins girt about with truth, and having on the breastplate of righteousness; And your feet shod with the preparation of the gospel of peace; Above all, taking the shield of faith, wherewith ye shall be able to quench all the fiery darts of the wicked. And take the helmet of salvation, and the sword of the Spirit, which is the word of God"* (Ephesians 6:10-17).

All things are possible with God. Therefore, be strong in Him. If you would stand out as one of the victors in this generation, you must to wrestle against principalities, powers and rulers of darkness of this world and against spiritual wickedness on high places successfully. You need God's amour in these evil days. I want you to note carefully the importance of each of the parts of the armor of God.

THE BELT OF TRUTH

Having the belt of truth is standing on what you know is right and insisting on doing things the right way. You must pattern your life according to all truth as revealed in the written Word of God.

> *"Wherefore gird up the loins of your mind, be sober, and hope to the end for the grace that is to be brought unto you at the revelation of Jesus Christ"* (1 Peter 1:13).

Do not allow problems to sway your mind from the truth. It is always easy to drift off. Always look at the bigger picture of life, where all things are working out for good to them that love God. Hold on to the truth with hope and you will overcome.

THE BREAST PLATE OF RIGHTEOUSNESS

Usually during desert or storm experiences, Satan knows how to open many doors of escape. Even when such doors appear certain to offer solace, shun those doors and keep in the way of righteousness. Maintain your relationship with Christ and He will not abandon you.

> *"As obedient children, not fashioning yourselves according to the former lusts in your ignorance: But as he which hath called you is holy, so be ye holy in all manner of conversation; Because it is written, Be ye holy; for I am holy"* (1 Peter 1:14-16).

Remain in your obedience to the Word of God and refuse to look back or compromise your faith in Christ. Holiness must be your goal strictly in order to win the enemy at the end. Devil will send many evil messengers to get you off track, but take a stand and remain on the path of righteousness.

> *"And your feet shod with the preparation of the gospel of peace"* (Ephesians 6:15).

THE SHOES OF THE GOSPEL OF PEACE

Establish your feet on the Word of God. Do not accept anything that contradicts the gospel of peace. The devil has a way offering deliverance that can bring temporary peace. However, insist on the gospel of peace that is rooted on God's Word as Paul did.

> *"For I am not ashamed of the gospel of Christ: for it is the power of God unto salvation to everyone that believeth; to the Jew first, and also to the Greek. For therein is the righteousness of God revealed from faith to faith: as it is written, The just shall live by faith"* (Romans 1:16-17).

Barrenness, miscarriage and reproach may stir you in your face, yet, do not let any of them sway your faith and trust in the gospel of Jesus. Clothe yourself with the gospel of peace. The devil has deceived many people with fake blessings that brought them sorrow, pains and eternal damnation. Therefore, do not allow temporary shame, reproach or disgrace to force you into accepting the devil's solution.

Trust in the power of God that can bring true blessings without sorrow. That is why the gospel of Christ said that the just shall live by faith.

THE SHIELD OF FAITH

Faith is the key that unlocks the doors of heavenly resources and prayer without faith is useless. The Scriptures reckoned that great men subdued kingdoms through faith:

> *"And what shall I more say? For the time would fail me to tell of Gedeon, and* of *Barak, and* of *Samson, and* of *Jephthae; of David also, and Samuel, and of the prophets: Who through faith subdued kingdoms, wrought righteousness, obtained promises, stopped the mouths of lions, Quenched the violence of fire, escaped the edge of the sword, out of weakness were made strong, waxed valiant in fight, turned to flight the armies of the aliens"* (Hebrews 11:32-34)

> *"Whom resist steadfast in the faith, knowing that the same afflictions are accomplished in your brethren that are in the world"* (1 Peter 5:9).

> *"For whatsoever is born of God overcometh the world: and this is the victory that overcometh the world,* even *our faith"* (1 John 5:4).

If you have been praying, have faith. Trust in God's Word that He may answer your prayers. You can subdue kingdoms through faith. Evil forces that resist your conception, or cause you to suffer barrenness, miscarriage and abortion could be the kingdoms that are standing before you. If mighty men could subdue their kingdoms through faith, then you can also subdue yours through faith.

God is not partial, so believe Him and see your own kingdom subdued. The powers that resist your prayers now have done the same to others in the past. Therefore, do not allow any particular problem to shift your faith from Christ.

The shield of faith quenches or extinguishes the fieriest darts of the enemy. The devil fire arrows of impurity, selfishness, doubt, fear, discouragement, unbelief and many evil thoughts to dislodge your faith and focus on Christ. Use the shield of faith to defend yourself.

THE HELMET OF SALVATION

Salvation is deliverance and preservation from evil, sin and the consequence of the fall of man. It is the foundation pillar of the gospel. Without salvation, everything else is useless and worst than nothing. It is a priceless treasure that devil is willing to offer anything on earth in exchange of it. Devil can promise you a child, prosperity or even the whole world in exchange of your salvation. However, remember that nothing on earth is worth the price of your salvation.

> *"And take the helmet of salvation, and the sword of the Spirit, which is the word of God"* (Ephesians 6:17).

> *"But let us, who are of the day, be sober, putting on the breastplate of faith and love; and for a helmet, the hope of salvation"* (1 Thessalonians 5:8).

A Roman soldier would never go into battle without putting his helmet on. The helmet protects the head from arrows and broadsword. You must resist anything that draws you back to sin. This is because evil arrows are capable of wasting your destiny and commit your soul to hell. The battle will soon be over, so do not allow unbelief from the devil and his agents to abort your salvation.

THE SWORD OF THE SPIRIT

> *"And the LORD spake unto Moses and unto Aaron, saying, Take the sum of the sons of Kohath from among the sons of Levi, after their families, by the house of their fathers, From thirty years old and upward even until fifty years old, all that enter into the host, to do the work in the tabernacle of the congregation. This* shall be *the service of the sons of Kohath in the tabernacle of the congregation,* about *the most holy things: And when the camp setteth forward, Aaron shall come, and his sons, and they shall take down the covering vail, and cover the ark of testimony with it: And shall put thereon the covering of badgers' skins, and shall spread over* it *a cloth wholly of blue, and shall put in the staves thereof. And upon the table of showbread they shall spread a cloth of blue, and put thereon the dishes, and the spoons, and the bowls, and covers to cover withal: and the continual bread shall be thereon: And they shall spread upon them a cloth of scarlet, and cover the same with a covering of badgers' skins, and shall put in the staves thereof. And they shall take a cloth of blue, and cover the candlestick of the light, and his lamps, and his tongs, and his snuff dishes, and all the oil vessels thereof, wherewith they minister unto it: And they shall put it and all the vessels thereof within a covering of badgers' skins, and shall put* it *upon a bar. And upon the golden altar they shall spread a cloth of blue, and cover it with a covering of badgers' skins, and shall put to the staves thereof"* (Numbers 4:1-11).

"Thy word have I hid in mine heart, that I might not sin against thee" (Psalms 119:11)

God's Word makes us wiser than the cleverest tempter. If the devil could surrender when Jesus quoted God's Word, then he would also surrender as you keep quoting the Word of God. Obedience to God's Word at all times will go a long way to prepare you for victory.

"For the word of God is *quick, and powerful, and sharper than any two-edged sword, piercing even to the dividing asunder of soul and spirit, and of the joints and marrow, and* is *a discerner of the thoughts and intents of the heart"* (Hebrews 4:12).

"But sanctify the Lord God in your hearts: and be *ready always to* give *an answer to every man that asketh you a reason of the hope that is in you with meekness and fear"* (1 Peter 3:15).

The devil may tempt you through the corruption of your heart, or entice you through your eyes or through your carelessness. Temptation can come through what you love most. It could be an idol in your mind. You must fight your battle with the sword of the spirit (Rhema), which is specific utterance of God. There is always a specific Word of God for every temptation. God's armor is powerful enough to help you overcome every problem and keep your pregnancy. Therefore, trust in His Word.

POWERS THAT TERMINATE PREGNANCIES

The bible revealed that devil's (your enemy) mission is to steal, kill and destroy. Therefore, is it hard for you to understand that there are evil powers that seek to terminate pregnancies? Devil's chief work is to oppose God, His works and children, and to counterfeit everything that God created.

> *"[10]And Moses and Aaron went in unto Pharaoh, and they did so as the LORD had commanded: and Aaron cast down his rod before Pharaoh, and before his servants, and it became a serpent. [11]Then Pharaoh also called the wise men and the sorcerers: now the magicians of Egypt, they also did in like manner with their enchantments. [12]For they cast down every man his rod, and they became serpents: but Aaron's rod swallowed up their rods. [13]And he hardened Pharaoh's heart that he hearkened not unto them; as the LORD had said. [20]And Moses and Aaron did so, as the LORD commanded; and he lifted up the rod, and smote the waters that* were *in the river, in the sight of Pharaoh, and in the sight of his servants; and all the waters that* were *in the river were turned to blood. [21]And the fish that* was *in the river died; and the river stank, and the Egyptians could not drink of the water of the river; and there was blood throughout all the land of Egypt. [22]And the magicians of Egypt did so with their enchantments: and Pharaoh's heart was hardened, neither did he hearken unto them; as the LORD had said"* (Exodus 7:10-13, 20-22).

The devil knows how to counterfeit God's work. He creates counterfeit of every genuine thing God created, in order to confuse men and deceive those who desire to serve God. People who consult agents of devil in order to get pregnant are taking a dangerous risk. Many false prophets are parading themselves as solution providers and ignorant people are going to ask for their prophecies, prayers and blessings to get children. If you want godly children, stay in the Word of God. Often, some prophecies come true. However, you should run away when prophets and ministers of the gospel start demanding that you do anything that contradicts the Word of God.

> *"And it came to pass on the morrow, that the evil spirit from God came upon Saul, and he prophesied in the midst of the house: and David played with his hand, as at other times: and* there was *a javelin in Saul's hand. And Saul cast the javelin; for he said, I will smite David even to the wall* with it. *And David avoided out of his presence twice"* (1 Samuel 18:10-11).

> *"He cried also in mine ears with a loud voice, saying, Cause them that have charge over the city to draw near, even every man* with *his destroying weapon in his hand. And, behold, six men came from the way of the higher gate, which lieth toward the north, and every man a slaughter weapon in his hand; and one man among them* was *clothed with linen, with a writer's inkhorn by his side: and they went in, and stood*

beside the brasen altar. And the glory of the God of Israel was gone up from the cherub, whereupon he was, to the threshold of the house. And he called to the man clothed with linen, which had *the writer's inkhorn by his side; And the LORD said unto him, Go through the midst of the city, through the midst of Jerusalem, and set a mark upon the foreheads of the men that sigh and that cry for all the abominations that be done in the midst thereof"* (Ezekiel 9:1-4).

Many miracle workers today are disguised agents of Satan. They perform wonders but they do not have the likeness of God in their lives. They prophesy to people, but secretly hate God's children and plan for their deaths. They claim to be prophets and holy men and women of God while the works of the flesh rule their lives.

"Now the works of the flesh are manifest, which are these; *Adultery, fornication, uncleanness, lasciviousness, Idolatry, witchcraft, hatred, variance, emulations, wrath, strife, seditions, heresies, Envyings, murders, drunkenness, revellings, and such like: of the which I tell you before, as I have also told* you *in time past, that they which do such things shall not inherit the kingdom of God"* (Galatians 5:19-21).

They cannot control their fleshly desires. They commit adultery, fornication and worship idols. They envy and murder innocent people, yet they perform deceptive wonders. The devil is at work through these false apostles and deceivers, who transformed themselves into apostles of Christ.

"For such are *false apostles, deceitful workers, transforming themselves into the apostles of Christ. And no marvel; for Satan himself is transformed into an angel of light. Therefore* it is *no great thing if his ministers also be transformed as the ministers of righteousness; whose end shall be according to their works"* (2 Corinthians 11:13-15).

Many of these prophets are like Samson who did not know that the Spirit of God has departed from him. Whenever you notice any sign of greed, pride, unforgiving spirit, immorality, jealousy, anger, covetousness, unfaithfulness in the family, financial irresponsibility, etc., in any of these so-called miracle workers, know that the devil is in-charge.

When sin sits on the throne of a man's life, all, which is left, is fake and unprofitable. These groups of people are Satan's agents. They want to destroy your pregnancy. They want to shut your womb. Devil can insert an arrow of death in a womb to remain permanently barren. Satanic agents can influence children in the womb to convert them to strange children. They can target an organ of the body, injure unborn babies or place evil marks upon people. Do not visit places where satanic agents present themselves as ministers of solutions. Nevertheless, if you have done so, you need some prayers of deliverance.

"Another parable put he forth unto them, saying, The kingdom of heaven is likened unto a man which sowed good seed in his field: But while men slept, his enemy came and sowed tares among the wheat, and went his way" (Matthew 13:24-25).

Another deadly enemy of women during pregnancy is evil dream. This is when devil begins to attack women through their dreams. When he feeds a pregnant woman in the dream or shows her red things, miscarriage would take place, if she does not pray effective prayers. But such shall not be your portion in the name of Jesus.

"Send thine hand from above; rid me, and deliver me out of great waters, from the hand of strange children" (Psalms 144:7).

"And when he came to him, behold, he stood by his burnt offering, and the princes of Moab with him. And Balak said unto him, What hath the LORD spoken?" (Numbers 23:17).

There was a case where evil agents summoned a womb and placed it at their altar to control the pregnancy. They can raise spirit husband or wife from their altars or invoke a spirit from your place of birth to marry you spiritually.

"6 And the angels which kept not their first estate, but left their own habitation, he hath reserved in everlasting chains under darkness unto the judgment of the great day. 8 Likewise also these filthy *dreamers defile the flesh, despise dominion, and speak evil of dignities"* (Jude 1:6, 8)

Do not take food and sex you have in the dreams lightly because they are not ordinary. Evil dreams, eating, drinking, sex and other demonic activities in the dream have negative consequences. Evil things that could happen through dreams include:

- Inflicting a woman with a strange sickness that affects pregnancies.
- The killing, stealing or destroying of the destiny of the baby in the womb (Acts 16:16, 18-19).
- Depression, weakness and strange tiredness that discourage people to pray more.
- Sudden disaster or miscarriage.
- Abnormal bleeding, plantation of fibroid and evil growth.
- Induced hatred, rejection, marital problems and divorce.
- Premature or prolonged labor and birth.
- Incision of evil marks, curse or spell.

- Strange problems and events.

As a wise woman, you must pray seriously during your pregnancies. Your prayers can keep your baby safe, break evil padlocks, chains, and deliver your unborn baby from witchcraft attacks.

PRAYERS TO RETAIN YOUR PREGNANCY

Bible references: Exodus 23:25; Deuteronomy 28:1-14

Begin with praise and worship

1. Every agent of miscarriage in my life, die, in the name of Jesus.
2. Every messenger of abortion in my life, carry your message to your sender, in the name of Jesus.
3. Agent of premature death to my pregnancy, be frustrated, in the name of Jesus.
4. Let every weak part of my womb receive power, in the name of Jesus.
5. I command the eaters of the flesh and the drinkers of blood to die, in the name of Jesus.
6. I command every agent of affliction against my pregnancy to be terminated, in the name of Jesus.
7. Any evil priest that has vowed to terminate my pregnancy, be disgraced, in the name of Jesus.
8. Every arrow of death that is fired at my pregnancy, backfire, in the name of Jesus.
9. Blood of Jesus deliver my pregnancy from the reach of evil spies, in the name of Jesus.
10. Any power that is manipulating my pregnancy, die, in the name of Jesus.
11. I command every power that has arrested my pregnancy to release it by force, in the name of Jesus.
12. Any evil altar that is attacking my pregnancy, scatter by fire, in the name of Jesus.
13. I paralyze any satanic minister that was assigned to minister to my pregnancy, in the name of Jesus.
14. Let the power of the grave that has buried my pregnancy break to pieces, in the name of Jesus.
15. I reject evil summons that was issued to my pregnancy, in the name of Jesus.
16. Every evil observer that is monitoring my pregnancy, die, in the name of Jesus.

17. I cleanse all witchcraft handwritings over my pregnancy with the blood of Jesus, in the name of Jesus.

18. I reverse satanic arrows that were fired at my pregnancy, in the name of Jesus.

19. I command every satanic bullet that entered my pregnancy to come out by force, in the name of Jesus.

20. I cast out every spirit of tragedy that was programmed to my pregnancy, in the name of Jesus.

21. Any evil covenant that is working against my pregnancy, break to pieces, in the name of Jesus.

22. Any curse that is prevailing over my pregnancy, expire by force, in the name of Jesus.

23. I wipe out all evil marks on my pregnancy, in the name of Jesus.

24. I destroy any power that was assigned to amputate my pregnancy, in the name of Jesus.

25. Any evil personality that is contending with my pregnancy, die, in the name of Jesus.

26. Every dark agent that is promoting abortion in my life, be disgraced, in the name of Jesus.

27. Any evil voice that is announcing my pregnancy, I silence you forever, in the name of Jesus.

28. Let the killers of pregnancies be arrested and destroyed by fire, in the name of Jesus.

29. I terminate any evil advertisement that is advertising my pregnancy, in the name of Jesus.

30. I command any evil program that is going on for my pregnancy to stop, in the name of Jesus.

31. Any attack on my pregnancy through my dreams, be frustrated, in the name of Jesus.

32. I demobilize any evil movement that is going on against my pregnancy, in the name of Jesus.

33. Let evil prophecies fail on the account of my pregnancy, in the name of Jesus.

34. Any evil conversion over my pregnancy, fail woefully, in the name of Jesus.

35. Every evil deposit that is made over pregnancy, I uproot you by fire, in the name of Jesus.

36. I destroy every pregnancy killer on a mission to terminate my pregnancy, in the name of Jesus.

37. Every unprofitable load that sits upon my pregnancy, drop by force, in the name of Jesus.

38. Let evil reinforcements to attack my pregnancy scatter in shame, in the name of Jesus.

17

Chapter

PRAYERS TO OVERCOME MISCARRIAGE

CHAPTER OVERVIEW

- *The reality of miscarriage*
- *Grievous deaths*
- *Evil diversion*
- *How to triumph over miscarriage*
- *Victory over miscarriage*
- *The battle for godly child*

THE REALITY OF MISCARRIAGE

Miscarriage is premature expulsion of fetus: an involuntary ending of a pregnancy through the discharge of the fetus from the womb at too early a stage in its development for it to survive. Technically, it is the mishandling or failure of something such as a plan or project.

While this definition clearly explains the meaning of miscarriage, I will seek to unravel the spiritual cause of miscarriages in this book.

EATERS OF FLESH AND DRINKERS OF BLOOD

Powers of darkness and their human agents like to feed on human flesh and blood. I hope this is not surprising to you. These wicked powers and their agents hunt human beings from their conception to the grave seeking to harvest their destinies. They monitor lives of babies in the womb to abort the lives of innocent babies.

These agents offer sacrifices to the devil to obtain information. They raise altars to know when their enemies are pregnant in order to induce abortion. They obtain powers from the devil to cause deaths. In so doing, they make the cities bloody.

> *"Woe to the bloody city! It is all full of lies* and *robbery; the prey departeth not; The horseman lifteth up both the bright sword and the glittering spear: and* there is *a multitude of slain, and a great number of carcasses; and* there is *none end of* their *corpses; they stumble upon their corpses: Because of the multitude of the whoredoms of the well-favored harlot, the mistress of witchcrafts, that selleth nations through her whoredoms, and families through her witchcrafts"* (Nahum 3:1, 3-4).

These agents of the devil increase lies and carry out spiritual and physical robberies to thrive. They plant the spirit of death in people's wombs to kill and abort their babies. They use witchcraft powers to bewitch pregnant women. They summon people's pregnancies in their evil altars to induce bleeding, premature births and mysterious miscarriages.

The story of Balak and Balaam captured this reality:

> *"13 And Balak said unto him, Come, I pray thee, with me unto another place, from whence thou mayest see them: thou shalt see but the utmost part of them, and shalt not see them all: and curse me them from thence. 14 And he brought him into the field of*

Zophim, to the top of Pisgah, and built seven altars, and offered a bullock and a ram on every *altar.* [27]*And Balak said unto Balaam, Come, I pray thee, I will bring thee unto another place; peradventure it will please God that thou mayest curse me them from thence.* [28]*And Balak brought Balaam unto the top of Peor that looketh toward Jeshimon.* [29]*And Balaam said unto Balak, Build me here seven altars, and prepare me here seven bullocks and seven rams.* [30]*And Balak did as Balaam had said, and offered a bullock and a ram on* every *altar"* (Numbers 23:13-14, 27-30).

Agents of the devil erect different altars to monitor their victims and know when conception has taken place. Whatever you allow them to accomplish in your life in their altars would manifest physically eventually. Their altars are their spiritual dining tables where they feast on human flesh and drink their blood. It is a place they fellowship with the devil to obtain power and information concerning people's destinies.

"And when he came to him, behold, he stood by his burnt offering, and the princes of Moab with him. And Balak said unto him, What hath the LORD spoken?" (Numbers 23:17).

They are willing to spend time and more money in order to obtain more information about your destiny and how best to destroy it. They have discovered and wasted many great destinies already. They put evil marks on many people in order to identify and manipulate them easily. That is why occult people program demons into people's lives so they can control their destinies as long as they are alive.

I remember a story of a young girl in the bible that illustrated this reality:

"[16]*And it came to pass, as we went to prayer, a certain damsel possessed with a spirit of divination met us, which brought her masters much gain by soothsaying:* [19]*And when her masters saw that the hope of their gains was gone, they caught Paul and Silas, and drew* them *into the marketplace unto the rulers"* (Acts 16:16, 19).

Occult people seek to arrest people's stars when they are young. A victim of these eaters of flesh and drinkers of blood can be influenced to make an unimaginable and heartbreaking mistake. They attack destinies, capture people's progresses and divert them. They can cause their victims to labor and suffer while they siphon their rewards spiritually. They arrest people when they are yet babies in the womb, control their actions on earth when they are of age and bury their promising greatness and opportunities finally. This is wickedness at its peak.

They can permit you to conceive a child, or an idea, or start a promising program, but they cannot allow a peaceful conclusion. They would seek to abort them half way to delivery and fruition. These evil personalities abort destinies, hijack stars, waste progresses and are graveyards of great projects. They place curses on people, bewitch their brains, limit people and cause them to struggle in vain through their lives and make people to become depressed and commit suicide.

> *"[15]And Moses was very wroth, and said unto the LORD, Respect not thou their offering: I have not taken one ass from them, neither have I hurt one of them. [35]And there came out a fire from the LORD, and consumed the two hundred and fifty men that offered incense"* (Numbers 16:15, 35).

Unless you refuse to permit them to prosper in your life without vigorous confrontation, they would never choose to allow you to fulfill your destiny and be happy in life. That is why they trade on human souls, eat flesh and drink blood. Become wise today and wake up spiritually, and it shall be well with you in the name of Jesus.

> *"The nakedness of thy father's wife's daughter, begotten of thy father, she* is *thy sister, thou shalt not uncover her nakedness. Thou shalt not uncover the nakedness of thy father's sister: she* is *thy father's near kinswoman. Thou shalt not uncover the nakedness of thy mother's sister: for she* is *thy mother's near kinswoman"* (Leviticus 18:11-13).

The activities of spiritual wicked entities cannot be over emphasized. While other merchants on earth deal on gold, silver and other jewels, these wicked personalities reduce people to slaves and perpetual bondservants. Many doctors have examined most women and have given them numerous medications to conceive to no avail. This is the reason why some women are beautiful physically and medically okay, yet they experience miscarriages.

There is a power that specializes in causing miscarriages. These powers strive from your conception until the ninth month to devour your babies through miscarriage or induced abortion. It is possible that while your womb cannot produce or carry a baby physically, it is doing so at evil altars. It is bizarre that your womb that cannot give you children is giving birth elsewhere.

However, the truth is that God does create useless wombs. Though it seems you cannot carry a child, but when you trust God in His Word, you will carry your own child eventually in the name of Jesus.

> *"And it came to pass, as we went to prayer, a certain damsel possessed with a spirit of divination met us, which brought her masters much gain by soothsaying: The same followed Paul and us, and cried, saying, These men are the servants of the most high God, which shew unto us the way of salvation. And this did she many days. But Paul, being grieved, turned and said to the spirit, I command thee in the name of Jesus Christ to come out of her. And he came out the same hour. And when her masters saw*

that the hope of their gains was gone, they caught Paul and Silas, and drew them *into the marketplace unto the rulers"* (Acts 16:16-19).

Consider the reality of these spirits that induce miscarriage and abortion. If they live inside any womb, or were assigned to monitor any pregnancy, that womb will not deliver babies successfully. The only way to deal with this reality is to confront these spirits through prayers of faith.

Evil spirits are in different categories. While some specialize in causing barrenness, others induce unexplainable miscarriages, prolonged pregnancies and abortion close to the week of delivery. Others allow people to deliver prematurely or they kill the woman as soon as she delivers in the labor room.

In the book of Revelation, there was an instance where Satan, the dragon, waited upon a woman that was at the point of delivery, in order to devour her baby:

> *"And there appeared a great wonder in heaven; a woman clothed with the sun, and the moon under her feet, and upon her head a crown of twelve stars: And she being with child cried, travailing in birth, and pained to be delivered. And there appeared another wonder in heaven; and behold a great red dragon, having seven heads and ten horns, and seven crowns upon his heads. And his tail drew the third part of the stars of heaven, and did cast them to the earth: and the dragon stood before the woman which was ready to be delivered, for to devour her child as soon as it was born"* (Revelation 12:1-4).

Devil can cause prolonged labor or consistent child delivery via caesarean. The truth is that if you do resist devil and his agents, they will deal with you.

MISCARRIAGE IN ADVANCED STAGE

The principal cause of miscarriage is sin, whether conscious or unconscious. Miscarriage can be inherited or it comes in form of an attack. In the Scriptures, a word came to Jeremiah concerning a curse that prevailed in a certain place:

> *"The Word of the LORD came also unto me, saying, Thou shalt not take thee a wife, neither shalt thou have sons or daughters in this place. For thus saith the LORD concerning the sons and concerning the daughters that are born in this place, and concerning their mothers that bare them, and concerning their fathers that begat them in this land; They shall die of grievous deaths; they shall not be lamented; neither shall they be buried;* but *they shall be as dung upon the face of the earth: and they shall be consumed by the sword, and by famine; and their carcasses shall be meat for the fowls of heaven, and for the beasts of the earth"* (Jeremiah 16:1-4).

This passage of the bible provided great insights to unsolvable problems that have bedeviled so many families. There are places you go or things you do that puts you into spiritual bondage without your knowledge. As a result, children inherit the curse of bondage. Such bondages work in diverse ways.

It is highly advisable that you inquire from God first before relating with such people or places. Even when God is leading you, you have to make sure that you do everything to the glory of God, according to God's guidance. If you must marry someone from an area like that, you must make sure that you involve God deeply.

GRIEVOUS DEATHS

> *"They shall die of grievous deaths; they shall not be lamented; neither shall they be buried; but they shall be as dung upon the face of the earth: and they shall be consumed by the sword, and by famine; and their carcasses shall be meat for the fowls of heaven, and for the beasts of the earth. For thus saith the LORD, Enter not into the house of mourning, neither go to lament nor bemoan them: for I have taken away my peace from this people, saith the LORD, even loving-kindness and mercies"* (Jeremiah 16:4-5).

A grievous death is such a cruel way to die. The word *grievous* connotes severity, and requires urgent solution. It speaks of unimaginable type of malady, which occurs to abort everything good in a place or a person.

Such things can occur in some people's lives after their birth. Such persons would be allowed to live while everything that will make such persons happy are aborted prematurely.

Miscarriage in advanced stages can allow you to be born, but will not allow you to start any good thing and finish it peacefully. Any true helper that comes your way with determination to help you becomes a subject of spiritual attack. Your relationship with your divine helpers would vanish sooner than expected.

As you lose valuable things, marvelous open doors and opportunities, no true sympathizers would come your way. Any program or project such a person embarks on dies halfway and efforts or labor invested goes without rewards. Whenever they expect peace, they receive troubles and sorrow.

If you marry a victim of grievous death without God leading you, you may not experience peace, love and true joy in your marriage, which might eventually end in separation or divorce. Even at the point of death, relatives, true helpers and friends cannot render any help. They are attacked each time they want to help. Some determined helpers would experience great loses or big problems that would force them to look for help also.

> *"Both the great and the small shall die in this land: they shall not be buried, neither shall* men *lament for them, nor cut themselves, nor make themselves bald for them: Neither shall* men *tear* themselves *for them in mourning, to comfort them for the dead; neither shall* men *give them the cup of consolation to drink for their father or for their mother. Thou shalt not also go into the house of feasting, to sit with them to eat and to drink. For thus saith the LORD of hosts, the God of Israel; Behold, I will cause to cease out of this place in your eyes, and in your days, the voice of mirth, and the*

voice of gladness, the voice of the bridegroom, and the voice of the bride" (Jeremiah 16:6-9).

People with great destinies can be targeted at the prime of their successes. They may die in accidents, or from an incurable disease or in a mysterious way. Grievous death attack people when they are to be celebrated or elevated to envious positions. Some people would die in a place where their dead bodies cannot be recovered for burial.

While people under the curse of grievous death live on earth, without achieving any purpose, people would avoid them, hate them and reject them anywhere they go. They die grievous deaths, not to be lamented, buried, and while alive, they face all manner of shameful, disgraceful and reproachful problems.

Anyone who does business with them is attacked also. If they do not repent, their condition would be worse. However, it is better for someone under the curse of grievous death to repent, and fight legion of demons in his or her foundation. The only help to offer to such people is to introduce them to Christ, who alone can set captives free.

> *"Jesus saith unto him, I am the way, the truth, and the life: no man cometh unto the Father, but by me"* (John 14:6).

> *"Come unto me, all* ye *that labor and are heavy laden, and I will give you rest. Take my yoke upon you, and learn of me; for I am meek and lowly in heart: and ye shall find rest unto your souls. For my yoke* is *easy, and my burden is light"* (Matthew 11:28-30).

If such victims refuse to repent and be born-again, their curse will continue to increase and their lives will be vexed, rebuked, until they perish on earth. Different kinds of pestilence, evil consumption, inflammation, strange fires, evil pursuit and destruction will harvest their efforts on earth.

> *"And it shall come to pass, when thou shalt shew this people all these words, and they shall say unto thee, Wherefore hath the LORD pronounced all this great evil against us? Or what is our iniquity? Or what is our sin that we have committed against the LORD our God? Then shalt thou say unto them, Because your fathers have forsaken me, saith the LORD, and have walked after other gods, and have served them, and have worshipped them, and have forsaken me, and have not kept my law; And ye have done worse than your fathers; for, behold, ye walk every one after the imagination of his evil heart, that they may not hearken unto me"* (Jeremiah 16:10-12).

Grievous deaths have ruined many people's lives and wasted their investments. That is why you need to be careful when making important decisions. When you insist on marrying a person under the yoke of grievous death without divine direction, you may make a costly mistake that would ruin your life.

Many people insist that you observe strange marital traditions or customs that contradict God's Word. By observing such traditions, you enter into covenant with them and their evil powers. In this way, people enter into covenants that put them in captivity. You may be a child to godly parents, but if you marry wrongly without God's permission, you will suffer for the rest of your life.

EVIL DIVERSION

All men are born with great destinies on earth. Many people that were born to rule and reign in their lives fail because of evil diversion. Devil diverted their destinies through making wrong choices they make. They forsook God's ways and followed their own way. You cannot follow your own way and still be successful in this life.

> *"And Enoch walked with God after he begat Methuselah three hundred years, and begat sons and daughters: And all the days of Enoch were three hundred sixty and five years: And Enoch walked with God: and he* was *not; for God took him. And Methuselah lived an hundred eighty and seven years, and begat Lamech: And Methuselah lived after he begat Lamech seven hundred eighty and two years, and begat sons and daughters: And all the days of Methuselah were nine hundred sixty and nine years: and he died"* (Genesis 5:22-27).

Methuselah was the son of Enoch. He was born by a godly father who walked with God for three hundred years after he beget Methuselah. However, after he left the earth, his son Methuselah was distracted and diverted. Possibly, he could have arrogantly married a wrong woman against the will of God. He could have compromised in his marriage. Maybe he was compelled to observe an ungodly tradition that moved him from God's presence. Whatever was the case, he was distracted, and diverted from his destiny.

However, the bible likened all men's relationship to God and His Word to seeds that a sower sowed in his field.

> *"But other fell into good ground, and brought forth fruit, some a hundredfold, some sixtyfold, some thirtyfold"* (Matthew 13:8).

> *"Beware lest any man spoil you through philosophy and vain deceit, after the tradition of men, after the rudiments of the world, and not after Christ"* (Colossians 2:8).

Methuselah's philosophy on life was different from that of God. He did not live majority of his life in God's presence. He was the oldest man to live on earth but he had no remarkable relationship with God. He spent 969 years on earth giving birth to children who had no reference for God. He led his generation away from the true God. He could have been deceived by ungodly tradition of men. He could have observed rules that contradicted God's Word.

When you allow traditions and philosophies of men to divert your destiny from God, you may live for a long time on earth but in great pain. Death creeps around the homes of many people, especially people that have abandoned God. You can easily notice death hanging around their marriages, over their lives and their children. It is possible to be under the torment of death without dying physically. This is a grievous death.

Such death will not allow you to experience joy, peace or rest in your life. When you lack help or true supporters, you will live a difficult and hard life. If people reject you while you still live or hate you for no tangible reason, you are in trouble. No matter how long you stay on earth or how old you are, when you suffer grievous death, only God can save you.

You need to be born-again by repenting and confessing your sins, and accepting Christ as your Lord and Savior. Otherwise, there is no hope for you. Furthermore, when you notice that good things do not last with you, it may be a sign that you are under the power of miscarriage. Things might be going well with you now, but if you are not born- again, you may soon lose all. You may have so many children, but if you are not born-again, you may lose them.

Do you know that you could lose your children while they remain alive? David almost lost all his children while they were alive. That is why you need to ask God to deliver you from the hands of strange children.

> *"Send thine hand from above; rid me, and deliver me out of great waters, from the hand of strange children"* (Psalms 144:7).

Had David failed to pray, he would have lost all his children to evil powers of the waters. Marine kingdom almost finished him using his children against him.

> *"And the king said, What have I to do with you, ye sons of Zeruiah? So let him curse, because the LORD hath said unto him, Curse David. Who shall then say, Wherefore hast thou done so? And David said to Abishai, and to all his servants, Behold, my son, which came forth of my bowels, seeketh my life: how much more now* may this *Benjamite* do it? *Let him alone, and let him curse; for the LORD hath bidden him. It may be that the LORD will look on mine affliction, and that the LORD will requite me good for his cursing this day. And as David and his men went by the way, Shimei went along on the hill's side over against him, and cursed as he went, and threw stones at him, and cast dust. And the king, and all the people that* were *with him, came weary, and refreshed themselves there"* (2 Samuel 16:10-14).

David witnessed his investments on some of his children collapse before his eyes. Children can be miscarried even after they become adults. Children can miscarry while they remain alive. This is what we call *advanced miscarriage* during deliverance sessions.

Furthermore, events can also cause your children to be miscarried. Like in the case of Zedekiah, he witnessed the slaughter of all his children.

> *"And the city was broken up, and all the men of war* fled *by night by the way of the gate between two walls, which* is *by the king's garden: (now the Chaldees* were *against the city round about:) and the king went the way toward the plain. And the army of the Chaldees pursued after the king, and overtook him in the plains of Jericho: and all his army were scattered from him. So they took the king, and brought him up to the king of Babylon to Riblah; and they gave judgment upon him. And they slew the sons of Zedekiah before his eyes, and put out the eyes of Zedekiah, and bound him with fetters of brass, and carried him to Babylon"* (2 Kings 25:4-7).

The enemy broke into his city and he ran away. Later, they arrested him and judged him. Before they plucked out his eyes, he watched all his children killed before he they bound him with chains.

Miscarriage can come at young age or middle age. However, the worst is the one that comes at an old age. Whichever time it comes, it is painful and you need to deal with it.

HOW TO TRIUMPH OVER MISCARRIAGE

There was a woman in the bible referred to as the great woman of Shunammite. This woman had no child until her husband became too old to have children. In my own understanding, this woman must have suffered from so many miscarriages. The spirit of miscarriage was determined to harvest her destiny and keep her childless for the rest of her life.

> *"And he said to Gehazi his servant, Call this Shunammite. And when he had called her, she stood before him. And he said unto him, Say now unto her, Behold, thou hast been careful for us with all this care; what* is *to be done for thee? Wouldest thou be spoken for to the king, or to the captain of the host? And she answered, I dwell among mine own people. And he said, What then* is *to be done for her? And Gehazi answered, Verily she hath no child, and her husband is old. And he said, Call her. And when he had called her, she stood in the door"* (2 Kings 4:12-15).

The demon that imposed miscarriage upon her was on a suicide mission. Eventually, Elisha sent for her and told her that she was going to have a son by that time next year. Because of what she passed through in life, it was difficult for her to believe it.

> *"And he said, About this season, according to the time of life, thou shalt embrace a son. And she said, Nay, my lord,* thou *man of God, do not lie unto thine handmaid. And the woman conceived, and bare a son at that season that Elisha had said unto her, according to the time of life"* (2 Kings 4:16-17).

Though she did not believe, she conceived and bore a son at that season that Elisha prophesied. Nevertheless, that was not the end of the battle. The battle advanced to another level. The demon that troubled her did not leave her family. He monitored the child everywhere he went.

The Shunammite woman and her husband spent a lot training their child. When the child came of age, the demon of advanced miscarriage fired an arrow of death at him. That is why it is possible that demons of miscarriage could postpone a battle in order to attack your children when they have grown up.

They have used the arrows of premature death to waste great destinies. They can strike when a person has grown fully. They can also strike when enough investment has been made and the person is about to be celebrated or announced to the world. They bring sorrows to parents and harvest their joy at their old age. The evil power in-charge of advanced miscarriage is very wicked.

> *"And when the child was grown, it fell on a day, that he went out to his father to the reapers. And he said unto his father, My head, my head. And he said to a lad, Carry*

him to his mother. And when he had taken him, and brought him to his mother, he sat on her knees till noon, and then *died"* (2 Kings 4:18-20).

VICTORY OVER MISCARRIAGE

Arrows of premature deaths come from satanic department of miscarriage. They terminate great-destined lives at their primes. They can allow you to invest but will not allow you to harvest. They can kill a victim when he needs his life most. There are people who are barren or suffer incessant miscarriages. After so many years, they tried to help themselves in their own way against God's Word. Such people always had problems.

> *"Now Sarai Abram's wife bare him no children: and she had a handmaid, an Egyptian, whose name* was *Hagar. And Sarai said unto Abram, Behold now, the LORD hath restrained me from bearing: I pray thee, go in unto my maid; it may be that I may obtain children by her. And Abram hearkened to the voice of Sarai. And Sarai Abram's wife took Hagar her maid the Egyptian, after Abram had dwelt ten years in the land of Canaan, and gave her to her husband Abram to be his wife. And he went in unto Hagar, and she conceived: and when she saw that she had conceived, her mistress was despised in her eyes"* (Genesis 16:1-4).

When Sarah became impatient, she took a step to modify God's plan to get a child. She exchanged her matrimonial bed with her maidservant. This would have caused her marriage if not that Abraham was a righteous man. She sold her birthright to a handmaid. Some men would have divorced her and she would have died childless. But thank God that her husband was a righteous man.

However, Ishmael, the son of the bondwoman later became a great burden to her and her son, Isaac. There are people who have left God to consult the devil in times of trouble. They felt that God is too slow in answering their prayers. There are such people in the Scriptures also:

> *"And when Saul enquired of the LORD, the LORD answered him not, neither by dreams, nor by Urim, nor by prophets. Then said Saul unto his servants, Seek me a woman that hath a familiar spirit that I may go to her, and enquire of her. And his servants said to him, Behold,* there is *a woman that hath a familiar spirit at Endor. And Saul disguised himself, and put on other raiment, and he went, and two men with him, and they came to the woman by night: and he said, I pray thee, divine unto me by the familiar spirit, and bring me* him *up, whom I shall name unto thee"* (1 Samuel 28:6-8).

Saul abandoned God in the time of his troubles and inquired of familiar spirit. He wanted a quick or an immediate solution. Sometimes, you may need to wait for God a little longer to get a true miracle from him. Saul went to a witch, a person that had a familiar spirit for a solution. Many Christians have gone to seek for children from the devil. Like Sarah, who drifted off in God's plan, many Christians have missed God's visitation while they were on consultation with the devil for solutions.

> *"And it came to pass after these things that God did tempt Abraham, and said unto him, Abraham: and he said, Behold,* here *I* am. *And he said, Take now thy son, thine only* son *Isaac, whom thou lovest, and get thee into the land of Moriah; and offer him there for a burnt offering upon one of the mountains which I will tell thee of And Abraham rose up early in the morning, and saddled his ass, and took two of his young men with him, and Isaac his son, and clave the wood for the burnt offering, and rose up, and went unto the place of which God had told him"* (Genesis 22:1-3).

God eventually visited Sarah because of Abraham. However, Ishmael was conceived already. The battle of polygamy ensued. Most children that were born with the help of the devil give their parents so much trouble. If they eventually live longer, their parents would not enjoy any benefit for having them. Some parents get afflictions from the birth of such children until they die. They are normally tormented and troubled for life.

These children hate their parents, hate God and God's people. They cause a lot of trouble in the cities. Most of them die grievous deaths. Evil spirits of miscarriage follow them everywhere they go. Unless they repent, they always suffer under the evil influence of spirits of miscarriage. The only way to avoid and overcome them is to stay with God, no matter how bad. It is better to remain childless than to get a child in a wrong way. Those who tried it lived to regret their actions afterwards.

Such children send their parents to early graves. Some infest their parents with so much trouble and abandon their parents to die at their old age without help. The devil would possess them all through their lives. Until you deliver them from the hands of the devil, there is no hope for such children.

It is better to die in a battle with miscarriage than to compromise and submit your life to demons behind miscarriage. If you persist in your prayers to God for a godly child, God will give you a child someday. When God blesses you with a child, no evil power can take him away from you. When you are sure you got your child from God, you must not allow the devil to take that child from you. Even when it appears the child has been snatched by the devil, you will not give up on God.

> *"[20]And when he had taken him, and brought him to his mother, he sat on her knees till noon, and* then *died.* [21]*And she went up, and laid him on the bed of the man of God, and shut* the door *upon him, and went out.* [22]*And she called unto her husband, and said, Send me, I pray thee, one of the young men, and one of the asses, that I may run to the man of God, and come again.* [23]*And he said, Wherefore wilt thou go to him today?* It is *neither new moon, nor Sabbath. And she said,* It shall be *well.* [24]*Then she saddled an ass, and said to her servant, Drive, and go forward; slack not* thy *riding for me, except I bid thee.* [25]*So she went and came unto the man of God to Mount Carmel. And it came to pass, when the man of God saw her afar off, that he said to Gehazi his servant, Behold,* yonder is *that Shunammite:* [30] *And the mother of the child said,* As *the LORD liveth, and* as *thy soul liveth, I will not leave thee. And he arose, and followed her.* [32]*And when Elisha was come into the house, behold, the child was dead,* and *laid upon his bed.* [33]*He went in therefore, and shut the door upon them twain, and prayed unto the LORD.* [34]*And he went up, and lay upon the child, and put his mouth upon his mouth, and his eyes upon his eyes, and his hands upon his hands: and he stretched himself upon the child; and the flesh of the child waxed warm.* [35]*Then he returned, and walked in the house to and fro; and went up, and stretched himself upon him: and the child sneezed seven times, and the child opened his eyes.* [36]*And he called Gehazi, and said, Call this Shunammite. So he called her. And when she was come in unto him, he said, Take up thy son.* [37]*Then she went in, and fell at his feet, and bowed herself to the ground, and took up her son, and went out"* (2 Kings 4:20-25, 30, 32-37).

When you know your right and remain faithful to God, you will disgrace miscarriage, barrenness and all manner of infertility in your marriage. No matter where you meet miscarriage, you will overcome it in the name of Jesus.

> *"No weapon that is formed against thee shall prosper; and every tongue* that *shall rise against thee in judgment thou shalt condemn. This* is *the heritage of the servants of the LORD, and their righteousness* is *of me, saith the LORD"* (Isaiah 54:17).

Abraham and Sarah overcame their barrenness and Abraham became a father of many nations. Isaac gave birth to Esau and Jacob. God opened the womb of Leah and she had her own child.

> *"And when the LORD saw that Leah* was *hated, he opened her womb: but Rachel* was *barren. And Leah conceived, and bare a son, and she called his name Reuben: for she said, Surely the LORD hath looked upon my affliction; now therefore my husband will love me. And she conceived again, and bare a son; and said, Because the LORD hath heard that I* was *hated, he hath therefore given me this* son *also: and she called his name Simeon. And she conceived again, and bare a son; and said, Now this time will my husband be joined unto me, because I have born him three sons: therefore was his name called Levi. And she conceived again, and bare a son: and she said, Now will I praise the LORD: therefore she called his name Judah; and left bearing"* (Genesis 29:31-35).

The Lord will open your womb and chase away the demons of barrenness and miscarriages for your sake. Leah's womb that was medically defined as barren was opened and she had so many children. When Rachael was attacked by these demons of barrenness, she was also delivered.

When you wait on God prayerfully, and believe that God is able to open your womb, you will conceive and give birth repeatedly.

> *"And God remembered Rachel, and God hearkened to her, and opened her womb. And she conceived, and bare a son; and said, God hath taken away my reproach: And she called his name Joseph; and said, The LORD shall add to me another son"* (Genesis 30:22-24).

God who remembered Rachael will remember you today in the name of Jesus. Rachael was the mother of Joseph and many other children. You will bear children who are greater than Joseph in the name of Jesus. Do you know that Manoah's wife was barren for many years? One day, an angel came to his wife and said, *"Thou art barren and bearest not, but thou shalt conceive and bare a son."* What happened later? She conceived and bore a son and called his name Samson.

> *"[1]And the children of Israel did evil again in the sight of the LORD; and the LORD delivered them into the hand of the Philistines forty years. [2]And there was a certain man of Zorah, of the family of the Danites, whose name* was *Manoah; and his wife* was *barren, and bare not. [3]And the angel of the LORD appeared unto the woman, and said unto her, Behold now, thou* art *barren, and bearest not: but thou shalt conceive, and bear a son. [24]And the woman bare a son, and called his name Samson: and the child grew, and the LORD blessed him. [25]And the Spirit of the LORD began*

to move him at times in the camp of Dan between Zorah and Eshtao" (Judges 13:1-3, 24-25)

You do not need to worry, you will have as many children as you desire when you believe. The devil knew that you are destined to give birth to a special child. That is why he is attacking you with barrenness and miscarriage. Stay with God, for you must surely have your own child in the name of Jesus.

Have you heard the story of a woman called Hannah?

"[2]And he had two wives; the name of the one was *Hannah, and the name of the other Peninnah: and Peninnah had children, but Hannah had no children. [6]And her adversary also provoked her sore, for to make her fret, because the LORD had shut up her womb. [19]And they rose up in the morning early, and worshipped before the LORD, and returned, and came to their house to Ramah: and Elkanah knew Hannah his wife; and the LORD remembered her. [20]Wherefore it came to pass, when the time was come about after Hannah had conceived, that she bare a son, and called his name Samuel,* saying, *Because I have asked him of the LORD"* (1 Samuel 1:2, 6, 19, 20).

Who said that God would not remember you? You will have your own godly *Samuel* and many other children in the name of Jesus.

PRAYERS TO OVERCOME MISCARRIAGE

Bible references: Exodus 23:25-26; Deuteronomy 7:14, 28:4

Begin with praise and worship

1. Every unclean spirit that is living inside me, come out by force and die, in the name of Jesus.
2. Every enemy of abundant life that is living in my body, I force you out, in the name of Jesus.
3. Any sickness and disease that is occupying my reproductive organs, die at your root, in the name of Jesus.
4. Any satanic serpent that is living inside me, die, in the name of Jesus.
5. Let Holy Ghost fire burn satanic agents that oppose my pregnancy, in the name of Jesus.
6. Every seed of miscarriage that is planted in my life, dry up and die, in the name of Jesus.
7. Every yoke of abortion in my life, break, in the name of Jesus.
8. I disappoint witches and wizards that are attacking me with miscarriage, in the name of Jesus.
9. Any evil spirit that is eating my babies before they are born, I cast you out to die, in the name of Jesus.
10. I terminate evil programs that are going on against my childbearing, in the name of Jesus.
11. You drinkers of my baby's blood in the womb, drink your own blood, in the name of Jesus.
12. Let all eaters of my baby's flesh eat their own flesh and die, in the name of Jesus.
13. Any evil eye that is monitoring my pregnancy, go blind completely, in the name of Jesus.
14. Any evil sacrifice that was offered to abort my baby, backfire, in the name of Jesus.

15. Wherever they summon my pregnancy in this world, Lord Jesus answer, in the name of Jesus.

16. Any spiritual coffin that exists in my womb, catch fire, in the name of Jesus.

17. You, spirit of death that is killing babies in my womb, be frustrated, in the name of Jesus.

18. I waste every weapon of death that is fashioned against my pregnancies, in the name of Jesus.

19. I destroy evil priests that are ministering over my pregnancies, in the name of Jesus.

20. Any evil summon to my pregnancy, backfire, in the name of Jesus.

21. I command my pregnancy to mature and I will deliver without any problem, in the name of Jesus.

22. My womb and children shall not be bewitched by fire, in the name of Jesus.

23. Every satanic effort to kill the baby in my womb, fail woefully, in the name of Jesus.

24. O Lord, arise and disgrace the spirit of miscarriage and abortion in my life, in the name of Jesus.

25. Any occult attack on my pregnancy, backfire by fire, in the name of Jesus.

26. Let the power of God correct everything that is wrong with my reproductive organs, in the name of Jesus.

27. I uproot anything that has occupied the place of my babies in the womb, in the name of Jesus.

28. I remove satanic properties in my reproductive organs, in the name of Jesus.

29. Any evil dream that attempts to abort my babies, be terminated, in the name of Jesus.

30. I reject sex, food and drinks from satanic tables, in the name of Jesus.

31. O Lord, arise and empower me to overcome the power of miscarriage, in the name of Jesus.

32. Any plan to defile the baby in my womb, I reject you by force, in the name of Jesus.

33. Let arrows of miscarriage and death that was fired into my womb backfire, in the name of Jesus.

34. I break and loose myself from the powers of the water spirits, in the name of Jesus.

35. Every determined enemy of my pregnancy, be exposed and disgraced, in the name of Jesus.

36. Any battle that is going on against my pregnancy, end to my favor, in the name of Jesus.

37. I receive the anointing to keep my pregnancy and give birth to a godly baby, in the name of Jesus.

38. O Lord, empower me to conceive and give birth to many babies, in the name of Jesus.

39. I refuse to die without bearing godly children, in the name of Jesus.

40. Let the glory of God appear and bring forth godly children, in the name of Jesus.

18
Chapter

PRAYERS TO END A PROLONGED PREGNANCY

CHAPTER OVERVIEW

- *The reality of prolonged pregnancy*
- *God's verdict over witchcraft*
- *What is witchcraft?*
- *The foolishness of practicing witchcraft*

THE REALITY OF PROLONGED PREGNANCY

The normal time for a woman to carry a baby in her womb is nine months. Any other length of time above nine months is not normal. It is abnormal for a woman to carry a child for ten months and beyond because God has not made it so.

However, as we approach the end of this age, devil will continue to unfold many terrible things through his agents on earth. There are bound to be witchcraft revivals and evil demonstrations on earth. Unless believers rise up to wage a worthy warfare against evil, humanity shall loose many lives. Witches and wizards are increasing their manipulative attacks against humanity. These attacks have been there at the inception of Christianity:

> *"But there was a certain man, called Simon, which beforetime in the same city used sorcery, and bewitched the people of Samaria, giving out that himself was some great one"* (Acts 8:9).

Many people, cities and nations have been bewitched already. So many destinies and marriages are under heavy witchcraft attacks. Many wombs have been bewitched through false prophecies, eating of food under the influence of witches and wizards. It is not surprising that many pregnant women are under the arrest of witchcraft powers.

Few years ago, when I was a pastor in one village that devil bewitched. When I saw how the village was given into idolatry and witchcrafts wholly, my spirit was stirred up. I declared for prayers and fasting against the throne of darkness in that village. My wife was pregnant at that time. In one of her outings, one terrible and a fearless wizard, who was also the native doctor, encountered her. The man threatened her and said, *"Let me know if you would deliver your baby successfully or you would vomit it."*

At that time, I was not informed well about witchcraft powers and their activities, as I am today. However, as we continued in our prayer and fasting program, my wife fell down on one of the village market days. That was how her problem started. So many mysterious things began to happen in her pregnancy. I did not see them as spiritual problems then and I did not even prayed against them.

Then on the ninth month of her pregnancy, there was no sign of labor. The babies in her womb came under heavy witchcraft attacks. However, we continued praying and most of our prayers were in tongues. I knew that the most important person we needed was the Spirit of God. As the Scripture puts it:

"Likewise the Spirit also helpeth our infirmities: for we know not what we should pray for as we ought: but the Spirit itself maketh intercession for us with groanings which cannot be uttered. And he that searcheth the hearts knoweth what is the mind of the Spirit, because he maketh intercession for the saints according to the will of *God"* (Romans 8:26-27).

The scriptures revealed that when we have prayed all that we are supposed to pray in the language we know, the spirit of God takes over through the speaking of unknown tongues. In our helpless situations, God's Spirit prays for us according to the will of God. The Holy Ghost dismantles entire obstacles put in place by evil powers when we speak in tongues.

Then, at the end of the tenth month, my wife delivered twin baby boys to the shame of the devil. For the intervention of Holy Spirit through our prayers of faith and trust, may all glory be to God Amen. My wife's delivery confirmed that we put the witch doctor to spiritual death through our prayers.

"A man also or woman that hath a familiar spirit, or that is a wizard, shall surely be put to death: they shall stone them with stones: their blood shall be *upon them"* (Leviticus 20:27).

"There shall not be found among you any one *that maketh his son or his daughter to pass through the fire,* or *that useth divination,* or *an observer of times, or an enchanter, or a witch, Or a charmer, or a consulter with familiar spirits, or a wizard, or a necromancer. For all that do these things* are *an abomination unto the LORD: and because of these abominations the LORD thy God doth drive them out from before thee"* (Deuteronomy 18: 10-12).

I can assure you that the best way to stone a witch or wizard is by using stones of prayers. In the midst of our prayer and fasting program, all the witch and wizard native doctors conspired and killed their big boss. Then the villagers gathered and killed that small native doctor, who confronted my wife. This is what God can do. This is what I call spiritual sanitation.

Witches and wizards are the brains behind evil manipulation of pregnancies. That is why when you fail to challenge their powers through prayers, they would continue to harvest your destiny and wipe away your family members. When you give a witch a place, she would waste the blood of a whole city, and fill the city with lies, robberies and whoredom.

Witchcraft powers can attack people at the point of their breakthrough. They can cause you trouble and restlessness. Witchcraft powers are responsible for mysterious failures of marriages. They are responsible for barrenness, miscarriage, loss of advanced pregnancies and consistent child delivery via caesareans, incurable diseases, prolonged labor and pregnancies. If you allow witchcraft to prosper in your life, witches would capture everything about you, including your brain and harvest your soul in hell fire. I pray that this would not be your portion in the name of Jesus.

GOD'S VERDICT OVER WITCHCRAFT

God commanded His children not to use enchantment, nor observe times. God's children are not to regard people that have familiar spirits, or seek after wizards. The reason is that people with familiar spirits have the ability to defile people's lives.

> "[26]*Ye shall not eat* anything *with the blood: neither shall ye use enchantment, nor observe times.* [31]*Regard not them that have familiar spirits, neither seek after wizards, to be defiled by them: I am the LORD your God"* (Leviticus 19:26, 31).

> *"And when they shall say unto you, Seek unto them that have familiar spirits, and unto wizards that peep, and that mutter: should not a people seek unto their God? For the living to the dead?"* (Isaiah 8:19).

It is surprising that many people today seek for evil powers, healing and deliverance from people that have familiar spirits. God gave us the opportunity to seek Him in times of trouble. Why do men then seek for evil powers in times of trouble?

> *"And he brought me to the door of the court; and when I looked, behold a hole in the wall. Then said he unto me, Son of man, dig now in the wall: and when I had digged in the wall, behold a door. And he said unto me, Go in, and behold the wicked abominations that they do here. So I went in and saw; and behold every form of creeping things, and abominable beasts, and all the idols of the house of Israel, pourtrayed upon the wall round about. And there stood before them seventy men of the ancients of the house of Israel, and in the midst of them stood Jaazaniah the son of Shaphan, with every man his censer in his hand; and a thick cloud of incense went up. Then said he unto me, Son of man, hast thou seen what the ancients of the house of Israel do in the dark, every man in the chambers of his imagery? For they say, The LORD seeth us not; the LORD hath forsaken the earth"* (Ezekiel 8:7-12).

The practice of witchcraft is an ancient practice. Saul, the first king of Israel, was judged for seeking after a woman that had a familiar spirit.

> *"Then said Saul unto his servants, Seek me a woman that hath a familiar spirit that I may go to her, and enquire of her. And his servants said to him, Behold,* there is *a woman that hath a familiar spirit at Endor"* (1 Samuel 28:7).

Nobody has used witchcraft powers and failed to receive God's wrath. Jezebel tried it and died a shameful death.

"And it came to pass, when Joram saw Jehu, that he said, Is it *peace, Jehu? And he answered, What peace, so long as the whoredoms of thy mother Jezebel and her witchcrafts* are so *many?"* (2 Kings 9:22).

God would place a judgment of death upon anyone that practices witchcraft. During the time of Moses, such people were stoned to death. They are not allowed to live because they are abomination unto God.

Anyone that uses enchantment, witchcraft or deals with familiar spirits is an enemy of God because that person has provoked God to anger. Witchcraft powers can manipulate and control God's children. That is why you need to be very careful as a Christian. Witchcraft manipulation is one of the main causes of confusion in many families, marriages and businesses. Ironically, most of these people do not even know that they are under the influence and manipulation of witches and wizards.

Many talented people today are going through mysterious witchcraft attacks without knowing it. Witches and wizards are using many without knowing. Others are sick and still suffering from the attacks of witchcrafts without knowing. The few that have realized they are under witchcrafts attacks do not know what to do about it. This is so sad.

"And it came to pass, as we went to prayer, a certain damsel possessed with a spirit of divination met us, which brought her masters much gain by soothsaying: The same followed Paul and us, and cried, saying, These men are the servants of the most high God, which shew unto us the way of salvation. And this did she many days. But Paul, being grieved, turned and said to the spirit, I command thee in the name of Jesus Christ to come out of her. And he came out the same hour. And when her masters saw that the hope of their gains was gone, they caught Paul and Silas, and drew them *into the marketplace unto the rulers"* (Acts 16:16-19).

Witchcraft is so wicked that they can be using you without your knowledge. But if the children of God would rise up to confront witchcraft powers in the nations, they will surely bow to the name of Jesus.

WHAT IS WITCHCRAFT?

Two kingdoms exist in the spirit realm in this universe. The first kingdom is the kingdom of God, which is built on righteousness, while the other is the kingdom of Satan and darkness that is based on lies. Devil controls the powers of witchcraft.

> *"How art thou fallen from heaven, O Lucifer, son of the morning!* How *art thou cut down to the ground, which didst weaken the nations! For thou hast said in thine heart, I will ascend into heaven, I will exalt my throne above the stars of God: I will sit also upon the mount of the congregation, in the sides of the north: I will ascend above the heights of the clouds; I will be like the most High"* (Isaiah 14:12-14).

> *"[6]And the angels which kept not their first estate, but left their own habitation, he hath reserved in everlasting chains under darkness unto the judgment of the great day. [8]Likewise also these* filthy *dreamers defile the flesh, despise dominion, and speak evil of dignities"* (Jude 1: 6, 8).

Lucifer who is also called Satan, the devil, etc., was pushed out of heaven when he rebelled against God and His kingdom. He was once an angel but he lost his position because of sin. He was pushed out of his original estate and habitation. Since he lost his position, Lucifer has been furious with men on earth.

That is why he organizes attacks on people through filthy dreams and eating, drinking, having sex and other events in dreams. Witchcraft kingdom is under the control of Lucifer, who uses filthy dreams to defile the body and bewitch babies in the womb through miscarriages or prolong pregnancies. However, the truth is that when you are in God's kingdom, you are bound to overcome the devil and dismantle the witchcraft powers that are working against you. The kingdom of darkness cannot subdue the kingdom of God.

> *"But he, knowing their thoughts, said unto them, Every kingdom divided against itself is brought to desolation; and a house* divided *against a house falleth. If Satan also be divided against himself, how shall his kingdom stand? Because ye say that I cast out devils through Beelzebub"* (Luke 11:17-18).

> *"And if a kingdom be divided against itself, that kingdom cannot stand. And if a house be divided against itself, that house cannot stand. And if Satan rise up against himself, and be divided, he cannot stand, but hath an end"* (Mark 3:24-26).

A good study of the bible and events that are happening all over the world will prove to you that Satan's kingdom is already divided. I can assure you that the queen of heaven and the leviathan have divided Satan's kingdom.

"So he carried me away in the spirit into the wilderness: and I saw a woman sit upon a scarlet colored beast, full of names of blasphemy, having seven heads and ten horns. And the woman was arrayed in purple and scarlet color, and decked with gold and precious stones and pearls, having a golden cup in her hand full of abominations and filthiness of her fornication: And upon her forehead was *a name written, MYSTERY, BABYLON THE GREAT, THE MOTHER OF HARLOTS AND ABOMINATIONS OF THE EARTH"* (Revelation 17:3-5).

Already, the queen of heaven who was favored by the devil is sitting upon leviathan, the beast. Leviathan's refusal to bow to the queen of heaven has caused a split in the kingdom of darkness. Satan, the devil, is in a very serious trouble because his kingdom is not united.

You need to read my books titled ***Leviathan the Beast*** and ***The Queen of Heaven*** to understanding these divisions in depth. If you peep into the realm of the spirit, you will discover that Satan's kingdom is desolate. Satan's divided kingdom is collapsing. The confusion has created many rebellious kingdoms under the devil that have risen against each other. They may appear organized, but Satan's kingdom is not organized, so they are bound to fall and end.

If you look at his kingdom, which his agents are trying to bring into the church and world governments, you will discover that devil is really in trouble. They use their evil powers to fight each other always. The truth is that the devil first deceived, confused and destroyed himself before doing the same to his followers. That is what we call witchcraft.

For this same reason, no people that serve Satan have peace, rest or hope. The devil is a hopeless deceiver, who is full of lies and wickedness.

Here are some tips about witchcraft -

- Witchcraft thrives on dislodging destinies.
- It employs magical and mysterious powers to manifest wickedness.
- It promotes doing evil in a skillful manner.
- It manipulates people to do evil.
- Witchcraft prospers in the absence of God in thoughts, desires, decisions and actions.
- It forbids having natural affections and likes to contradict God's Word.
- It is determined to do evil at any cost.

- It strives to cause righteous people to feel guilty.
- It seduces people to live unfaithful, pretentious, unforgiving and revengeful lives.
- Witchcraft makes straight ways crooked and forces people to believe and do the same.
- It seeks to move in the realm of the spirit without God.
- It is having a meeting with the devil to carry out actions against God and his children on earth.
- It is summoning evil powers to carry out evil assignments.
- It is being involved in satanic programs
- It is having an intercourse with evil spirits in order to carry out wicked operations.
- Witchcraft is attempts to access wicked powers from the earth and from the heavenlies.
- It is the use of evil powers to undo or subdue others.
- It is the practice of magic, sorcery and wizardry.
- It is the use of evil powers to destroy things and human beings.
- It seeks to dominate, manipulate and control people through spirits.
- It is the use of supernatural powers by possessed persons in league with the devil or evil spirits.
- It causes troubles to torment and oppress people.

THE FOOLISHNESS OF PRACTICING WITCHCRAFT

Any relationship with the devil over God and his Word is witchcraft. It is therefore foolishness to be involved in witchcraft. From the beginning, witchcraft has not done anyone any good. God has put a curse on witchcraft and people that practiced it.

> *"And I will put enmity between thee and the woman, and between thy seed and her seed; it shall bruise thy head, and thou shalt bruise his heel"* (Genesis 3:15).

God's Word declared that there is an enmity between man and the devil. In the history of humanity, no one has successfully befriended the devil without serious consequences. Adam and Eve tried it in the Garden of Eden and they received curses from God. Cain tried it and received a curse to become the first vagabond and fugitive on earth. Ham the son of Noah co-operated with the devil and was cursed to serve his brothers. The family of Noah compromised with the devil and was confounded. God scattered them upon the face of the earth.

The men of Sodom and Gomorrah became wicked and some of them were blinded. All of them were later destroyed with brimstone and fire from heaven (*See* Genesis 18:16, 11, 20, 24; 19:5-9). Lot's wife tried it and before she realized her mistake, she was converted to a useless pillar of salt (*See* Genesis 19:26). Esau despised his birthright and missed his blessing forever.

> *"And Jacob sod pottage: and Esau came from the field, and he* was *faint: And Esau said to Jacob, Feed me, I pray thee, with that same red* pottage; *for I* am *faint: therefore was his name called Edom. And Jacob said, Sell me this day thy birthright. And Esau said, Behold, I am at the point to die: and what profit shall this birthright do to me? And Jacob said, Swear to me this day; and he sware unto him: and he sold his birthright unto Jacob. Then Jacob gave Esau bread and pottage of lentiles; and he did eat and drink, and rose up, and went his way: thus Esau despised* his *birthright"* (Genesis 25:29-34).

Any act that contradicts God's Word is witchcraft. Laban cheated Jacob and his blessings went to Jacob (*See* Genesis 31:1-7, 38-42). Reuben, the first son of Jacob, tried it and his father cursed him.

> *"And it came to pass, when Israel dwelt in that land, that Reuben went and lay with Bilhah his father's concubine: and Israel heard* it. *Now the sons of Jacob were twelve"* (Genesis 35:22).

> *"Reuben, thou art my firstborn, my might, and the beginning of my strength, the excellency of dignity, and the excellency of power: Unstable as water, thou shalt not*

excel; because thou wentest up to thy father's bed; then defiledst thou it: he went up to my couch" (Genesis 49:3-4).

Onan practiced witchcraft and God Himself killed him without mercy. The magicians of Egypt tried it and they all lost their first born and later died shameful deaths. Dathan, Korah and Abiriam practiced witchcraft and the earth could not bear with them. The earth opened and swallowed them together with their families. Achan practiced it and lost his life and every member of his family. Eli's sons practiced witchcrafts and suffered defeats to death. Saul, the first king of Israel, practiced witchcraft and God ended his kingdom. He later died by committing suicide. Absalom practiced witchcraft and heaven and earth rejected him before he died.

"And the LORD was gracious unto them, and had compassion on them, and had respect unto them, because of his covenant with Abraham, Isaac, and Jacob, and would not destroy them, neither cast he them from his presence as yet. So Hazael king of Syria died; and Ben–hadad his son reigned in his stead. And Jehoash the son of Jehoahaz took again out of the hand of Ben–hadad the son of Hazael the cities, which he had taken out of the hand of Jehoahaz his father by war. Three times did Joash beat him, and recovered the cities of Israel" (2 Kings 13:23-25).

Ahithophel practiced witchcraft and killed himself. All the false prophets of Baal that got involved in it were shamefully disgraced and died in shame. Jezebel, who so much got involved in witchcraft, died a shameful death and dogs licked her blood and ate her flesh.

"And when Jehu was come to Jezreel, Jezebel heard of it; *and she painted her face, and tired her head, and looked out at a window. And as Jehu entered in at the gate, she said,* Had *Zimri peace, who slew his master? And he lifted up his face to the window, and said, Who* is *on my side? Who? And there looked out to him two* or *three eunuchs. And he said, Throw her down. So they threw her down: and* some *of her blood was sprinkled on the wall, and on the horses: and he trode her under foot. And when he was come in, he did eat and drink, and said, Go, see now this cursed* woman, *and bury her: for she is a king's daughter. And they went to bury her: but they found no more of her than the skull, and the feet, and the palms of* her *hands. Wherefore they came again, and told him. And he said, This* is *the word of the LORD, which he spake by his servant Elijah the Tishbite, saying, In the portion of Jezreel shall dogs eat the flesh of Jezebel: And the carcass of Jezebel shall be as dung upon the face of the field in the portion of Jezreel;* so *that they shall not say, This* is *Jezebel"* (2 Kings 9:30-37).

She lost all her properties, the kingdom and her sons in a mysterious way. Individuals who practiced it never lived to tell their stories. Gehazi tried it and became a leper for life and after his death, he transferred it to his generation, born and unborn. If you join occult people to practice divination, charms, enchantment, you will regret the rest of your life. Do you not know that some of these people in the bible that practiced witchcraft were forced to kill their own children?

> *"[1]And when Athaliah the mother of Ahaziah saw that her son was dead, she arose and destroyed all the seed royal. [2]But Jehosheba, the daughter of king Joram, sister of Ahaziah, took Joash the son of Ahaziah, and stole him from among the king's sons* which were *slain; and they hid him,* even *him and his nurse, in the bedchamber from Athaliah, so that he was not slain. [3]And he was with her hid in the house of the LORD six years. And Athaliah did reign over the land. [13]And when Athaliah heard the noise of the guard* and *of the people, she came to the people into the temple of the LORD. [14]And when she looked, behold, the king stood by a pillar, as the manner* was, *and the princes and the trumpeters by the king, and all the people of the land rejoiced, and blew with trumpets: and Athaliah rent her clothes, and cried, Treason, Treason. [20]And all the people of the land rejoiced, and the city was in quiet: and they slew Athaliah with the sword* beside *the king's house. "* (2 Kings 11:1-3, 13-14, 20).

After being used to destroy their own children, they were shamefully disgraced out of this world. Why would you get involved in a thing that will waste your lifetime investment, kill all your children and die later under the same power? It is very foolish to get involved with the occult or evil group because you will pay dearly with your Life.

> *"Manasseh* was *twelve years old when he began to reign, and he reigned fifty and five years in Jerusalem: But did* that which was *evil in the sight of the LORD, like unto the abominations of the heathen, whom the LORD had cast out before the children of Israel. For he built again the high places which Hezekiah his father had broken down, and he reared up altars for Baalim, and made groves, and worshipped all the host of heaven, and served them. Also he built altars in the house of the LORD, whereof the LORD had said, In Jerusalem shall my name be forever. And he built altars for all the host of heaven in the two courts of the house of the LORD. And he caused his children to pass through the fire in the valley of the son of Hinnom: also he observed times, and used enchantments, and used witchcraft, and dealt with a familiar spirit, and with wizards: he wrought much evil in the sight of the LORD, to provoke him to anger"* (2 Chronicles 33:1-6).

At the beginning of practicing witchcraft, it may be sweet, but your end would be very painful and destructive. Witchcraft powers are very wicked. They use people to destroy others, their own investment including their unborn children. Judas tried it and lost everything he ever earned on earth.

> *"Now this man purchased a field with the reward of iniquity; and falling headlong, he burst asunder in the midst, and all his bowels gushed out. And it was known unto*

all the dwellers at Jerusalem; insomuch as that field is called in their proper tongue, Aceldama, that is to say, The field of blood. For it is written in the book of Psalms, Let his habitation be desolate, and let no man dwell therein: and his bishoprick let another take" (Acts 1:18-20).

"For before these days rose up Theudas, boasting himself to be somebody; to whom a number of men, about four hundred, joined themselves: who was slain; and all, as many as obeyed him, were scattered, and brought to nought. After this man rose up Judas of Galilee in the days of the taxing, and drew away much people after him: he also perished; and all, even *as many as obeyed him, were dispersed"* (Acts 5:36-37).

Witchcraft powers can help you to purchase your destruction on credit. They can allow you to enjoy for a little while but you will surely pay with your life in eternity after you have lost all. It is also foolish to follow a witch or wizard. If you believe in them, you are doomed. Those who joined witchcraft groups were destroyed and brought to nothing. Others perished or dispersed.

When you consult a familiar spirit for palm reading, magic, witchcraft, fortunetelling, charms, etc., you have entered into wicked relationship with devil and his agents, and you have become a witch or wizard in the making. You need to repent and believe in Jesus Christ now before it is too late.

If you have put yourself in a relationship with Satan through any of the actions above, you need to run away from Satan and run to Jesus. Only Jesus can save you and deliver you completely.

"Afterward Jesus findeth him in the temple, and said unto him, Behold, thou art made whole: sin no more, lest a worse thing come unto thee" (John 5:14).

"Submit yourselves therefore to God. Resist the devil, and he will flee from you" (James 4:7).

When you open your heart to any occult or demonic practice, they quickly take such advantage to pull you in. You become one body with them. The Spirit of God would depart in such event.

"But the Spirit of the LORD departed from Saul, and an evil spirit from the LORD troubled him. And Saul's servants said unto him, Behold now, an evil spirit from God troubleth thee" (1 Samuel 16:14-15).

"Be sober, be vigilant; because your adversary the devil, as a roaring lion, walketh about, seeking whom he may devour: Whom resist steadfast in the faith, knowing that the same afflictions are accomplished in your brethren that are in the world" (1 Peter 5:8-9).

"Neither give place to the devil" (Ephesians 4:27).

"Then he saith, I will return into my house from whence I came out; and when he is come, he findeth it *empty, swept, and garnished. Then goeth he, and taketh with himself seven other spirits more wicked than himself, and they enter in and dwell there: and the last* state *of that man is worse than the first. Even so shall it be also unto this wicked generation"* (Matthew 12:44-45).

The other category of people that remain under the influence and attack of witchcraft is ignorant people. Witchcraft people can attack you easily if you are ignorant of the Word of God. They have put so many people in bondage because of their ignorance. They can occupy your stomach, womb, eyes or any organ of your body when you fail to resist them.

At your weakest moments, witches and wizards can attack you. They can weigh if the Spirit of God lives in your body. If they find the absence of the Spirit of God, they will enter into your business, marriage, ministry or any organ of your body through pride and postponement to confess your sins to accept Jesus. If you harbor sin or have unforgiving spirit, they can also enter into your life to attack you, especially when you have refused to repent and resist the devil.

If you are not sober, vigilant, they can walk into your marriage, womb and devour your baby. They can postpone the day of your delivery. If you do not do what you are supposed to do, your pregnancy may last for years. Satan and his agents can convert your womb to a coffin, a burial ground or a place where they eat and drink human flesh and blood.

More so, when you keep any property in your house that belongs to the devil, he will surely come around to guard his properties. A wise person would not keep any evil property in his or her house. Break every link you have with the devil. Otherwise, he will visit you from time to time. If you are still keeping their charms, amulets, occult books, etc., you remain one of their members.

If you are truly seeking for deliverance, repent, confess, reject and burn evil properties and forsake all their ways. Witchcraft powers are behind barrenness, late marriages, miscarriages, and prolonged pregnancies.

They are responsible for evil pregnancies, the disappearances and reappearances of babies in the womb. They kill people's joy and attack pregnancies with all manner of problems. They are in-charge of eating, drinking, having sex and spiritual marriages in the dream. You need urgent New Testament deliverance now.

PRAYERS TO END A PROLONGED PREGNANCY

Bible references: Nahum 3:4; Isaiah 34:3-5

Begin with praise and worship

1. Any power that wants my pregnancy to over stay, die immediately, in the name of Jesus.
2. Every satanic instrument that is tying my pregnancy, catch fire and burn to ashes, in the name of Jesus.
3. Any evil hand that is holding my babies in the womb, dry up and break to pieces, in the name of Jesus.
4. Any evil utterance that is said over the birth of my babies, expire by force, in the name of Jesus.
5. I nullify evil agreements over the birth of my babies by the blood of Jesus, in the name of Jesus.
6. Any satanic embargo that was placed on the birth of my baby, I lift you by force, in the name of Jesus.
7. Any evil sacrifice that was offered to delay the birth of my baby, backfire, in the name of Jesus.
8. Any evil altar that is holding down the baby in my womb, catch fire, in the name of Jesus.
9. Any satanic minister that is keeping my baby in bondage in the womb, release him and die, in the name of Jesus.
10. Every agent of prolonged pregnancy in my life, die, in the name of Jesus.
11. Let every messenger of death carry their messages to their senders, in the name of Jesus.
12. Blood of Jesus, speak my babies out of the womb by Your power, in the name of Jesus.
13. Any evil force that is keeping my baby from delivery, scatter and die, in the name of Jesus.

14. Let any witch or wizard that is using the sun, the moon or any creature to keep my baby in the womb die, in the name of Jesus.

15. I command my womb to discharge my baby alive at a divine time, in the name of Jesus.

16. Holy Ghost fire, burn every curd that is holding my baby from being born, in the name of Jesus.

17. Any evil seed that is planted to keep my baby in my womb, die by fire, in the name of Jesus.

18. Let evil programs that were organized at the rights for the sake of my delivery fail woefully, in the name of Jesus.

19. I destroy every agent of pollution over my delivery, in the name of Jesus.

20. I destroy any dream that was organized to prolong my delivery date, in the name of Jesus.

21. Any evil sacrifice that has sized my delivery, expire by fire, in the name of Jesus.

22. Satan, I remove you from the event of my delivery, in the name of Jesus.

23. Every agent of birth delay, die without mercy, in the name of Jesus.

24. I remove every agent of devil from my presence in the day of my delivery, in the name of Jesus.

25. Any evil power that is contending with my divine date of birth, I cut off your head, in the name of Jesus.

26. Let the backbone of enemies against my delivery break to pieces, in the name of Jesus.

27. I remove powers that are blocking me from giving birth in peace, in the name of Jesus.

28. I command the powers of darkness against my deliver to scatter in shame, in the name of Jesus.

29. I command my labor to start on time and let my deliver take place without pain, in the name of Jesus.

30. Let every evil presence during my delivery disappear forever, in the name of Jesus.

31. Any power that is prolonging my day of delivery, die, in the name of Jesus.

32. Let manipulators of my delivery collapse and die, in the name of Jesus.

33. Any power that has arrested my baby in the womb, release him and die, in the name of Jesus.

34. Any evil cage that is holding my baby in the womb, open and release him now, in the name of Jesus.

35. Any curse that was placed upon my delivery, expire, in the name of Jesus.

36. Let any evil mark of late delivery disappear from my life now, in the name of Jesus.

37. Every negative medical report on my delivery, I reject you, in the name of Jesus.

38. O Lord, arise and assist me to deliver in peace, in the name of Jesus.

39. I receive the anointing to deliver normally, in the name of Jesus.

40. Any evil roadblock that is mounted for my safe delivery, I dismantle you, in the name of Jesus.

41. Any evil personality that has vowed to keep my baby in the womb, fail woefully, in the name of Jesus.

42. You my baby in the womb, come out miraculously, in the name of Jesus.

19

Chapter

PRAYERS TO DELIVER YOUR CHILD SAFELY

CHAPTER OVERVIEW

- *Removal of curses for safe delivery*
- *The birth of Jesus Christ*
- *Jesus is the answer*
- *The marvelous works of Jesus*
- *How devil moved the creature*
- *Benefits of the blood of Jesus*

REMOVAL OF CURSES FOR SAFE DELIVERY

A prayer to deliver your child safely is very important because of Satan's interest in newborn babies. The devil is all out to fight God's children. When God created man, He blessed him and mandated man to be fruitful, to multiply, to replenish and subdue the earth. That was how God empowered man to have dominion over all creatures.

> *"And God blessed them, and God said unto them, Be fruitful, and multiply, and replenish the earth, and subdue it: and have dominion over the fish of the sea, and over the fowl of the air, and over every living thing that moveth upon the earth"* (Genesis 1:28).

> *"Unto the woman he said, I will greatly multiply thy sorrow and thy conception; in sorrow thou shalt bring forth children; and thy desire shall be to thy husband, and he shall rule over thee"* (Genesis 3:16).

However, through Adam's disobedience, the devil brought curse upon man. A curse was placed upon Eve also. Eve's curse causes women to experience barrenness and complications during delivery. Devil has gone ahead to prevent vulnerable women from conceiving and bearing a child. The good news is that God planned for the redemption of man when he fell from his original state.

> *"And whosoever offereth a sacrifice of peace offerings unto the LORD to accomplish his vow, or a freewill offering in beeves or sheep, it shall be perfect to be accepted; there shall be no blemish therein"* (Leviticus 22:21).

> *"(For the life was manifested, and we have seen it, and bear witness, and shew unto you that eternal life, which was with the Father, and was manifested unto us;) That which we have seen and heard declare we unto you, that ye also may have fellowship with us: and truly our fellowship* is *with the Father, and with his Son Jesus Christ. And these things write we unto you, that your joy may be full. This then is the message, which we have heard of him, and declare unto you, that God is light, and in him is no darkness at all. If we say that we have fellowship with him, and walk in darkness, we lie, and do not the truth: But if we walk in the light, as he is in the light, we have fellowship one with another, and the blood of Jesus Christ his Son cleanseth us from all sin. If we say that we have no sin, we deceive ourselves, and the truth is*

not in us. If we confess our sins, he is faithful and just to forgive us our *sins, and to cleanse us from all unrighteousness"* (1 John 1:2-9).

"We know that we have passed from death unto life, because we love the brethren. He that loveth not his *brother abideth in death. Whosoever hateth his brother is a murderer: and ye know that no murderer hath eternal life abiding in him"* (1 John 3:14-15).

Christ was without blemish, and the perfect lamb for sacrifice that could pay the price to set man free from the curse of Adam and Eve. However, the devil did not know that God could offer His only Son to save humanity. God did and Jesus Christ accepted to die in the place of man to set us free from curse and eternal death that was upon us.

Jesus became a substitute for our sins and a mediator who intercedes for us before His Father in heaven.

"And I saw in the right hand of him that sat on the throne a book written within and on the backside, sealed with seven seals. And I saw a strong angel proclaiming with a loud voice, Who is worthy to open the book, and to loose the seals thereof? And no man in heaven, nor in earth, neither under the earth, was able to open the book, neither to look thereon. And I wept much, because no man was found worthy to open and to read the book, neither to look thereon" (Revelation 5:1-4).

No human was qualified enough, perfect, spotless and sinless to die, live again and intercede for humanity. None in heaven, on earth and under the earth was found worthy of opening the book of life. Christ took the challenge because of His love for humanity. That was the worst thing that happened to the devil since his fall, when God decided to offer His only begotten Son as a perfect sacrifice. Devil did not know that God loves man so much that He had to give Christ up for us. This is the reason why devil hates humanity with great passion.

"And one of the elders saith unto me, Weep not: behold, the Lion of the tribe of Judah, the Root of David, hath prevailed to open the book, and to loose the seven seals thereof. And I beheld, and, lo, in the midst of the throne and of the four beasts, and in the midst of the elders, stood a Lamb as it had been slain, having seven horns and seven eyes, which are the seven Spirits of God sent forth into all the earth. And he came and took the book out of the right hand of him that sat upon the throne. And when he had taken the book, the four beasts and four and *twenty elders fell down before the Lamb, having every one of them harps, and golden vials full of odors, which are the prayers of saints. And they sung a new song, saying, Thou art worthy to take the book, and to open the seals thereof: for thou wast slain, and hast redeemed us to God by thy blood out of every kindred, and tongue, and people, and nation; And hast made us unto our God kings and priests: and we shall reign on the earth. And I beheld, and I heard the*

voice of many angels round about the throne and the beasts and the elders: and the number of them was ten thousand times ten thousand, and thousands of thousands; Saying with a loud voice, Worthy is the Lamb that was slain to receive power, and riches, and wisdom, and strength, and honor, and glory, and blessing. And every creature which is in heaven, and on the earth, and under the earth, and such as are in the sea, and all that are in them, heard I saying, Blessing, and honor, and glory, and power, be *unto him that sitteth upon the throne, and unto the Lamb forever and ever. And the four beasts said, Amen. And the four* and *twenty elders fell down and worshipped him that liveth forever and ever"* (Revelation 5:5-14).

It is foolishness to cooperate with devil and reject Jesus. Man who was under the sentence of death and could not pay his own death penalty now lives and enjoys freedom from sin, in order to carry out the divine purpose for which he was created.

"And I will put enmity between thee and the woman, and between thy seed and her seed; it shall bruise thy head, and thou shalt bruise his heel" (Genesis 3:15).

Jesus Christ fulfilled all the requirements that were required for the salvation of the world. How could you then neglect such a sacrifice that Christ offered for you to be guiltless? This is tragic!

"For if we sin wilfully after that we have received the knowledge of the truth, there remaineth no more sacrifice for sins, But a certain fearful looking for of judgment and fiery indignation, which shall devour the adversaries. He that despised Moses' law died without mercy under two or three witnesses: Of how much sorer punishment, suppose ye, shall he be thought worthy, who hath trodden underfoot the Son of God, and hath counted the blood of the covenant, where with he was sanctified, an unholy thing, and hath done despite unto the Spirit of grace? For we know him that hath said, Vengeance belongeth *unto me, I will recompense, saith the Lord. And again, The Lord shall judge his people"* (Hebrews 10:26-30).

The worst thing that anyone would do in this life is not sins he or she committed, but despising the price that Christ paid for the freedom and salvation of the world. It is a straight ticket to hell.

"Look unto me, and be ye saved, all the ends of the earth: for I am *God, and* there is *none else"* (Isaiah 45:22).

"Come unto me, all ye *that labor and are heavy laden, and I will give you rest. Take my yoke upon you, and learn of me; for I am meek and lowly in heart: and ye shall find rest unto your souls. For my yoke* is easy, *and my burden is light"* (Matthew 11:28-30).

God is offering all humanity the opportunity to repent and believe in Jesus Christ, who He sacrificed for our sake. Sinners are doomed when they fail to receive pardon through Christ blood. Christ is the only solution for the removal of every curse.

THE BIRTH OF JESUS CHRIST

The birth of the Messiah was prophesied long before He came. His birth was one of the greatest mysteries in the history of humanity. Jesus Christ, who was also God, was born of a virgin in the likeness of man, in order to save humanity from eternal damnation.

> *"Now the birth of Jesus Christ was on this wise: When as his mother Mary was espoused to Joseph, before they came together, she was found with child of the Holy Ghost. Then Joseph her husband, being a just* man, *and not willing to make her a publick example, was minded to put her away privily. But while he thought on these things, behold, the angel of the Lord appeared unto him in a dream, saying, Joseph, thou son of David, fear not to take unto thee Mary thy wife: for that which is conceived in her is of the Holy Ghost. And she shall bring forth a son, and thou shalt call his name JESUS: for he shall save his people from their sins. Now all this was done, that it might be fulfilled which was spoken of the Lord by the prophet, saying, Behold, a virgin shall be with child, and shall bring forth a son, and they shall call his name Emmanuel, which being interpreted is, God with us. Then Joseph being raised from sleep did as the angel of the Lord had bidden him, and took unto him his wife: And knew her not till she had brought forth her firstborn son: and he called his name JESUS"* (Matthew 1:18-25).

However, the event that followed after Mary conceived of the Holy Spirit was usual. The devil wanted to influence Joseph to abort his engagement to Mary. When devil failed, he entered into King Herod and influenced him to kill the child. The star of Jesus troubled the kingdom of darkness and Satan moved Herod to order the death of innocent babies.

> *"8 And he sent them to Bethlehem, and said, Go and search diligently for the young child; and when ye have found* him, *bring me word again, that I may come and worship him also. 9 When they had heard the king, they departed; and, lo, the star, which they saw in the east, went before them, until it came and stood over where the young child was. 13 And when they were departed, behold, the angel of the Lord appeareth to Joseph in a dream, saying, Arise, and take the young child and his mother, and flee into Egypt, and be thou there until I bring thee word: for Herod will seek the young child to destroy him. 14 When he arose, he took the young child and his mother by night, and departed into Egypt: 16 Then Herod, when he saw that he was mocked of the wise men, was exceeding wroth, and sent forth, and slew all the children that were in Bethlehem, and in all the coasts thereof, from two years old and under, according to the time which he had diligently enquired of the wise men"* (Matthew 2:8-9, 13-14, 16).

In his attempt to kill Jesus, Herod slew all the children that were in Bethlehem and in all the coasts thereof, from two years old and under, according to the time which he had diligently inquired of the wise men. The devil hated the wise men because they did not inform Herod where the child, Jesus, was. They were indeed wise because they took a different route on their way back.

The devil hates conception, pregnancy and child delivery. He always prowls in darkness looking for ways to destroy children of great destinies. God will not allow him to succeed over your pregnancy in the name of Jesus.

In many occasions, devil has attacked pregnant women to possess the babies in their womb. While some babies died in the womb, some were marked for death and are controlled remotely after birth. Devil is behind the reason why many babies are born with deformities. Some babies are born without important organs. That is why we must pray for divine protection of mothers and their unborn babies. The devil would have succeeded in attacking Jesus physically if Joseph was not sensitive in the spirit. Thank God, Joseph was sensitive in the Spirit that an angel of the Lord appeared to him in a dream.

> *"13And when they were departed, behold, the angel of the Lord appeareth to Joseph in a dream, saying, Arise, and take the young child and his mother, and flee into Egypt, and be thou there until I bring thee word: for Herod will seek the young child to destroy him. 14When he arose, he took the young child and his mother by night, and departed into Egypt: 15And was there until the death of Herod: that it might be fulfilled which was spoken of the Lord by the prophet, saying, Out of Egypt have I called my son. 19But when Herod was dead, behold, an angel of the Lord appeareth in a dream to Joseph in Egypt, 20Saying, Arise, and take the young child and his mother, and go into the land of Israel: for they are dead which sought the young child's life. 21And he arose, and took the young child and his mother, and came into the land of Israel. 22But when he heard that Archelaus did reign in Judaea in the room of his father Herod, he was afraid to go thither: notwithstanding, being warned of God in a dream, he turned aside into the parts of Galilee"* (Matthew 2:13-15, 19-22).

There are special prayers you need to pray before conception, on conception, the period of pregnancy, during and after delivery of your baby. Pregnant women and their babies need divine protection. Otherwise, many newborns would be born without God's character in them. Devil would have possessed them while in the womb or after birth.

> *"Then Herod, when he saw that he was mocked of the wise men, was exceeding wroth, and sent forth, and slew all the children that were in Bethlehem, and in all the coasts thereof, from two years old and under, according to the time which he had diligently enquired of the wise men"* (Matthew 2:16).

"[28]And even as they did not like to retain God in their *knowledge, God gave them over to a reprobate mind, to do those things which are not convenient; [31]Without understanding, covenant breakers, without natural affection, implacable, unmerciful"* (Romans 1:28, 31).

It is no longer news that many women have been fed in their dreams to pollute their babies and defile their destinies. These are the works of the devil and his agents.

"[6]And the angels which kept not their first estate, but left their own habitation, he hath reserved in everlasting chains under darkness unto the judgment of the great day. [8]Likewise also these filthy *dreamers defile the flesh, despise dominion, and speak evil of dignities"* (Jude 1:6, 8).

Devil has established many ways to help desperate women conceive. While some women consult idols in order to conceive, others follow evil prescriptions to invite demons into their wombs. Some women engage in diverse sexual relationships to conceive. This practice pollutes their babies from conception and opens the door for devil to possess their babies. Also, traditions and customs of some people put their newborn babies at risk even before their birth.

"And the king of Egypt spake to the Hebrew midwives, of which the name of the one was *Shiphrah, and the name of the other Puah: And he said, When ye do the office of a midwife to the Hebrew women, and see* them *upon the stools; if it* be *a son, then ye shall kill him: but if it* be *a daughter, then she shall live"* (Exodus 1:15-16).

Many greatly destined children have died through abortion, witchcraft attacks and ritual sacrifices to the devil. Some of these children would be great people. Some would have been greater than Moses was. Moses was born when birth of male children was forbidden in Egypt. Apart from Jesus, Moses was the greatest deliverance minister that the world ever knew. His birth and preservation were remarkable.

"And there went a man of the house of Levi, and took to wife a daughter of Levi. And the woman conceived, and bare a son: and when she saw him that he was a goodly child, she hid him three months. And when she could not longer hide him, she took for him an ark of bulrushes, and daubed it with slime and with pitch, and put the child therein; and she laid it in the flags by the river's brink. And his sister stood afar off, to wit what would be done to him. And the daughter of Pharaoh came down to wash herself at the river; and her maidens walked along by the river's side; and when she saw the ark among the flags, she sent her maid to fetch it. And when she had opened it, she saw the child: and, behold, the babe wept. And she had compassion on him, and said, This is one of the Hebrews' children. Then said his sister to Pharaoh's daughter, Shall I go and call to thee a nurse of the Hebrew women, that she may nurse the child for thee? And Pharaoh's daughter said to her, Go. And the maid went and called the

child's mother. And Pharaoh's daughter said unto her, Take this child away, and nurse it for me, and I will give thee thy wages. And the woman took the child, and nursed it. And the child grew, and she brought him unto Pharaoh's daughter, and he became her son. And she called his name Moses: and she said, Because I drew him out of the water" (Exodus 2:1-10).

The story of Moses was unique. There was no other means to save any male child except to avoid getting pregnant. Moses parents must have prayed very well before his conception. Probably, that was why they had enough courage and wisdom to keep him alive and make plans for his upbringing.

Likewise, many laws exist today to terminate children's lives at conception. Abortion drugs, spiritual forces, human rituals, etc, are all part of this conspiracy. Unless the church stands up to pray and have faith like the parents of Moses, Pharaoh, Herod and other invisible spiritual forces would wipe out a whole lot of greatly destined children.

Hannah fought for Samuels's destiny before conception. Abraham prayed for many years before Sarah conceived Isaac. Rachael and her sister Leah prayed for their children. Jacob cried for Joseph even after he was sold. Samson's parent followed God's guideline for his birth to preserve his greatness.

"[2]And there was a certain man of Zorah, of the family of the Danites, whose name was *Manoah; and his wife* was *barren, and bare not. [3]And the angel of the LORD appeared unto the woman, and said unto her, Behold now, thou* art *barren, and bearest not: but thou shalt conceive, and bear a son. [4]Now therefore beware, I pray thee, and drink not wine nor strong drink, and eat not any unclean* thing: *[5]For, lo, thou shalt conceive, and bear a son; and no razor shall come on his head: for the child shall be a Nazarite unto God from the womb: and he shall begin to deliver Israel out of the hand of the Philistines. [24]And the woman bare a son, and called his name Samson: and the child grew, and the LORD blessed him. [25]And the Spirit of the LORD began to move him at times in the camp of Dan between Zorah and Eshtaol"* (Judges 13:2-5, 24-25).

There are things a pregnant woman must do to preserve the destiny of her unborn child. She must listen to the voice of the Holy Ghost. Zachariah and Elizabeth never allowed their delay in childbirth to lure them to the devil's option for conception. They were both righteous.

"[6]And they were both righteous before God, walking in all the commandments and ordinances of the Lord blameless. [7]And they had no child, because that Elisabeth was barren, and they both were now *well stricken in years. [8]And it came to pass, that while he executed the priest's office before God in the order of his course, [13]But the angel said unto him, Fear not, Zacharias: for thy prayer is heard; and thy wife*

Elisabeth shall bear thee a son, and thou shalt call his name John. [15]*For he shall be great in the sight of the Lord, and shall drink neither wine nor strong drink; and he shall be filled with the Holy Ghost, even from his mother's womb"*(Luke 1:6-8, 13, 15).

We need the intervention of the Holy Spirit to give birth to godly children. Many parents have sold their children to the devil even before conception. Parents should not allow the devil to have a share of their children's destiny. They must remain with God, no matter how difficult or obscure the situation was. God has not changed and can still give you a child at an old age as He did to Zachariah and Elizabeth.

JESUS IS THE ANSWER

Jesus lived a perfect life on earth without sin. He came to bring answers to all the needs of men. He came to destroy all the works of darkness and set men free from the debt of sin and death. Therefore, Jesus is the answer to your prayers to conceive and rear godly children. As the Scriptures put it:

> *"Now is the judgment of this world: now shall the prince of this world be cast out"* (John 12:31).

Jesus is the divine provision and our sin bearer. He dealt with our shame and guilt. That is why you need to know your right in Jesus. In Christ, you have a right to conceive your baby and deliver safely without any evil interference. God wants you to be happy and experience the blessing of fruitfulness.

> *"7 And Isaac spake unto Abraham his father, and said, My father: and he said, Here* am *I, my son. And he said, Behold the fire and the wood: but where* is *the lamb for a burnt offering? 8 And Abraham said, My son, God will provide himself a lamb for a burnt offering: so they went both of them together. 14 And Abraham called the name of that place Jehovah–jireh: as it is said* to *this day, In the mount of the LORD it shall be seen"* (Genesis 22:7-8, 14).

When it was obvious that Isaac had to die, God intervened to save his life. God provided Himself a lamb for a burnt offering. When all first-born males were to die in Egypt, God provided the blemish lamb to save the first-born males of the children of Israel (*See* Exodus 12:1-13).

Every household had a lamb to save the first born of the house. They rubbed the blood on the two side posts and upper doorpost of their houses. When the Lord passed through Egypt that night, the blood of the lamb provided protection to all Israelite first-born males.

> *"And whosoever offereth a sacrifice of peace offerings unto the LORD to accomplish his vow, or a freewill offering in beeves or sheep, it shall be perfect to be accepted; there shall be no blemish therein"* (Leviticus 22:21).

> *"Surely he hath borne our griefs, and carried our sorrows: yet we did esteem him stricken, smitten of God, and afflicted. But he* was *wounded for our transgressions,* he was *bruised for our iniquities: the chastisement of our peace* was *upon him; and with his stripes we are healed. All we like sheep have gone astray; we have turned everyone to his own way; and the LORD hath laid on him the iniquity of us all. He was oppressed, and he was afflicted, yet he opened not his mouth: he is brought as a lamb to the slaughter, and as a sheep before her shearers is dumb, so he openeth not his mouth.*

He was taken from prison and from judgment: and who shall declare his generation? For he was cut off out of the land of the living: for the transgression of my people was he stricken" (Isaiah 53:4-8).

The covering the blood of those blemish lambs provided temporary in the past is what the blood of Jesus will do forever to all that will benefit from His death at the cross of Calvary.

"For if the blood of bulls and of goats, and the ashes of an heifer sprinkling the unclean, sanctifieth to the purifying of the flesh: How much more shall the blood of Christ, who through the eternal Spirit offered himself without spot to God, purge your conscience from dead works to serve the living God? And for this cause he is the mediator of the new testament, that by means of death, for the redemption of the transgressions that were *under the first testament, they which are called might receive the promise of eternal inheritance"* (Hebrews 9:13-15).

THE MARVELOUS WORKS OF JESUS

Jesus Christ served humanity with His life and all His strength to. He used His anointing with the Holy Ghost and His power to heal all that were oppressed of the devil. He was not idle and He did not reserve His power or anointing to Himself. He did not sell them either. Jesus went about doing good.

> *"How God anointed Jesus of Nazareth with the Holy Ghost and with power: who went about doing good, and healing all that were oppressed of the devil; for God was with him"* (Acts 10:38).

Jesus did not relent in saving people from bondage at some point. He healed and delivered people all the way. The day He went to Jericho, there was a certain man who was blind. This man was sitting by the roadside. The devil closed his eyes and limited his life by turning him into a beggar. However, when this blind man heard an unusual noise and multitudes of people passing by the roadside, he asked people what was happening. They told him that Jesus of Nazareth was passing by. He lifted up his voice and cried for mercy.

> *"And it came to pass, that as he was come nigh unto Jericho, a certain blind man sat by the way side begging: And hearing the multitude pass by, he asked what it meant. And they told him, that Jesus of Nazareth passeth by. And he cried, saying, Jesus,* thou *Son of David, have mercy on me. And they which went before rebuked him, that he should hold his peace: but he cried so much the more,* Thou *Son of David, have mercy on me. And Jesus stood, and commanded him to be brought unto him: and when he was come near, he asked him, Saying, What wilt thou that I shall do unto thee? And he said, Lord, that I may receive my sight. And Jesus said unto him, Receive thy sight: thy faith hath saved thee. And immediately he received his sight, and followed him, glorifying God: and all the people, when they saw* it, *gave praise unto God"* (Luke 18:35-43).

His cry of faith attracted Jesus and He opened his eyes. The next set of people he met was ten lepers. The ten lepers called to Him from afar and when Jesus heard their cry for mercy, He gave them a simple instruction, "*Go show yourselves unto the priests*". As they went in obedience, they were healed. What an amazing miracle.

> *"And it came to pass, as he went to Jerusalem that he passed through the midst of Samaria and Galilee. And as he entered into a certain village, there met him ten men that were lepers, which stood afar off: And they lifted up* their *voices, and said, Jesus, Master, have mercy on us. And when he saw* them, *he said unto them, Go shew yourselves unto the priests. And it came to pass, that, as they went, they were cleansed. And one of them, when he saw that he was healed, turned back, and with a*

loud voice glorified God, And fell down on his *face at his feet, giving him thanks: and he was a Samaritan. And Jesus answering said, Were there not ten cleansed? But where* are *the nine? There are not found that returned to give glory to God, save this stranger. And he said unto him, Arise, go thy way: thy faith hath made thee whole"* (Luke 17:11-19).

When you lift up your voice and cry to Jesus for mercy, you will receive mercy. If you will obey Christ's instruction by keeping His Word, then all your problems will end.

"And it came to pass, as he went into the house of one of the chief Pharisees to eat bread on the Sabbath day, that they watched him. And, behold, there was a certain man before him which had the dropsy. And Jesus answering spake unto the lawyers and Pharisees, saying, Is it lawful to heal on the Sabbath day? And they held their peace. And he took him, *and healed him, and let him go"* (Luke 14:1-4).

Jesus Christ does not discriminate. He did not have favorites. He went to the house of the chief of the Pharisees and ate. There, He met a man with dropsy who did not even know his right to receive healing. Though this man was ignorant, Jesus took him and healed him. Jesus Christ ministered to the rich, the poor and the beggars. He is ready to help you if you cry unto Him. He healed a man with an unclean spirit. When the demons inside the man wanted to negotiate, Christ rebuked them and commanded them to hold their peace and come out and they did.

"And in the synagogue there was a man, which had a spirit of an unclean devil, and cried out with a loud voice, Saying, Let us *alone; what have we to do with thee,* thou *Jesus of Nazareth? Art thou come to destroy us? I know thee who thou art; the Holy One of God. And Jesus rebuked him, saying, Hold thy peace, and come out of him. And when the devil had thrown him in the midst, he came out of him, and hurt him not. And they were all amazed, and spake among themselves, saying, What a word* is *this! For with authority and power he commandeth the unclean spirits, and they come out. And the fame of him went out into every place of the country round about"* (Luke 4:33-37).

The man ran into the synagogue, but the unclean spirits followed him to torment him right before the ministers of the gospel, the priests. When the demons saw Jesus, they cried out to be left alone but Christ cast them out. Jesus Christ really dealt with the devil. He rebuked and destroyed the spirit of fever, laid hands on many people and healed them. He cast out the spirit of fear, forgave many of their sins, made many that were lame to walk, healed diseases, fed the hungry, and loosed many that were bound for many years.

"And, behold, there was a woman which had a spirit of infirmity eighteen years, and was bowed together, and could in no wise lift up herself. *And when Jesus saw her, he*

called her to him, *and said unto her, Woman, thou art loosed from thine infirmity. And he laid* his *hands on her: and immediately she was made straight, and glorified God"* (Luke 13:11-13).

He delivered possessed people, restored withered hands, cast out evil spirits that grieved people, healed the deaf and dumb and delivered a lunatic from wicked legions. He paid tax for Himself and his followers. He destroyed many plagues, calmed raging storms, loosed people from evil chains, delivered those who were at the point of death and healed a woman with an issue of blood.

"And a certain woman, which had an issue of blood twelve years, And had suffered many things of many physicians, and had spent all that she had, and was nothing bettered, but rather grew worse, When she had heard of Jesus, came in the press behind, and touched his garment. For she said, If I may touch but his clothes, I shall be whole. And straightway the fountain of her blood was dried up; and she felt in her body that she was healed of that plague. And Jesus, immediately knowing in himself that virtue had gone out of him, turned him about in the press, and said, Who touched my clothes? And his disciples said unto him, Thou seest the multitude thronging thee, and sayest thou, Who touched me? And he looked round about to see her that had done this thing. But the woman fearing and trembling, knowing what was done in her, came and fell down before him, and told him all the truth. And he said unto her, Daughter, thy faith hath made thee whole; go in peace, and be whole of thy plague" (Mark 5:25-34).

In addition, Jesus delivered those who were disabled by demons. He opened ears that were deaf, terminated demons that attacked people with impediment of speeches, and delivered those that were afflicted with epilepsy. Jesus Christ also empowered His disciples to deal with the devil and to destroy his works.

"1 After these things the Lord appointed other seventy also, and sent them two and two before his face into every city and place, whither he himself would come. 17 And the seventy returned again with joy, saying, Lord, even the devils are subject unto us through thy name. 18 And he said unto them, I beheld Satan as lightning fall from heaven. 19 Behold, I give unto you power to tread on serpents and scorpions, and over all the power of the enemy: and nothing shall by any means hurt you" (Luke 10:1, 17-19).

There was a time Jesus visited a city called Nain with His disciples. As they entered the city, behold, there was a group of people leaving the city with a dead man's body with mourners following behind together with a widow. The dead man was the only son of the widow. The situation became a direct encounter with the prince of life and the prince of death at the gate of the city. Unfortunately, for the devil, Jesus saw the woman and had compassion on her, and told her not to weep. Just in a moment, the battle started and Jesus said to the dead young man, "Young man I say unto thee, arise." And he that was dead woke up, and began to speak.

> *"And it came to pass the day after, that he went into a city called Nain; and many of his disciples went with him, and much people. Now when he came nigh to the gate of the city, behold, there was a dead man carried out, the only son of his mother, and she was a widow: and much people of the city was with her. And when the Lord saw her, he had compassion on her, and said unto her, Weep not. And he came and touched the bier: and they that bare* him *stood still. And he said, Young man, I say unto thee, Arise. And he that was dead sat up, and began to speak. And he delivered him to his mother. And there came a fear on all: and they glorified God, saying, That a great prophet is risen up among us; and, That God hath visited his people. And this rumor of him went forth throughout all Judæa, and throughout all the region round about"* (Luke 7:11-17).

The devil cannot force your destiny to the grave when you invite Christ into your life. There are people devil has buried their destinies already. Those people have lost their peace, marriages, businesses, children, etc., to the devil. Many others are living under the affliction, oppression, and influence of evil powers.

Devil has captured people's progress, stars, greatness and prosperities. That is why many people are sick, tormented and live at the mercy of the devil. Already, their real selves have been caged, paralyzed, damaged, cast down, locked up, arrested, defeated and doomed for destruction. Some people are under the judgment of premature deaths, poverty, hatred, rejection, late marriage, barrenness and marital failure. May none of these become your portion in the name of Jesus.

However, the truth is that Jesus Christ can open the grave and restore your life even when Satan has killed and buried your destiny in the grave. Jesus demonstrated this authority when He called Lazarus out from the grave.

> *"[1]Now a certain* man *was sick,* named *Lazarus, of Bethany, the town of Mary and her sister Martha. [2](It was* that *Mary which anointed the Lord with ointment, and wiped his feet with her hair, whose brother Lazarus was sick.) [3]Therefore his sisters sent unto him, saying, Lord, behold, he whom thou lovest is sick. [38]Jesus therefore again groaning in himself cometh to the grave. It was a cave, and a stone lay upon it. [39]Jesus said, Take ye away the stone. Martha, the sister of him that was dead, saith unto him, Lord, by this time he stinketh: for he hath been* dead *four days. [40]Jesus saith unto her, Said I not unto thee, that, if thou wouldest believe, thou shouldest see the glory of God? [41]Then they took away the stone* from the place *where the dead was laid. And Jesus lifted up* his *eyes, and said, Father, I thank thee that thou hast heard me. [42]And I knew that thou hearest me always: but because of the people which standby I said* it, *that they may believe that thou hast sent me. [43]And when he thus*

had spoken, he cried with a loud voice, Lazarus, come forth. [44]*And he that was dead came forth, bound hand and foot with grave clothes: and his face was bound about with a napkin. Jesus saith unto them, Loose him, and let him go"* (John 11:1-3; 38-44).

Your *Lazarus* can move from the grave to its rightful place. Who is your *Lazarus*? Your *Lazarus* is what matters to you most in your life. It could be your marriage, joy or a job that keeps you happy. Christ can recover whatever you have lost. Jesus is never with any blemish and full of good works. However, the devil insisted that good works were not enough to deliver humanity from the penalty of sin. The devil demanded for the death of Jesus. Yet, he did not know that the death of Jesus Christ on the cross would be the remission of sin and death.

"And almost all things are by the law purged with blood; and without shedding of blood is no remission" (Hebrews 9:22).

"Surely he hath borne our griefs, and carried our sorrows: yet we did esteem him stricken, smitten of God, and afflicted. But he was *wounded for our transgressions,* he was *bruised for our iniquities: the chastisement of our peace* was *upon him; and with his stripes we are healed. All we like sheep have gone astray; we have turned everyone to his own way; and the LORD hath laid on him the iniquity of us all. He was oppressed, and he was afflicted, yet he opened not his mouth: he is brought as a lamb to the slaughter, and as a sheep before her shearers is dumb, so he openeth not his mouth. He was taken from prison and from judgment: and who shall declare his generation? For he was cut off out of the land of the living: for the transgression of my people was he stricken"* (Isaiah 53:4-8).

The devil recognized Christ's spotless life, His virtue, character and sinless status. That was why he insisted that Christ had to die and go away. His perfect life and wonderful teachings and making mockery of the devil and his works did not save men completely. Only His blood would bring complete salvation and deliverance from the consequence and curse of Adam's sin.

"And the blood shall be to you for a token upon the houses where ye are: and when I see the blood, I will pass over you, and the plague shall not be upon you to destroy you, when I smite the land of Egypt" (Exodus 12:13).

We have complete removal of guilt and shame through the lamb that was slain. His blood redeemed us from the curse of the law. He purchased us back for His Father.

HOW DEVIL MOVED THE CREATURE

The first battle the devil declared against Christ was at His birth. When he failed to kill Jesus through the wicked king, Herold, he resorted to negotiating with Jesus to compromise His deity in the wilderness. Jesus Christ used the Word of God to defeat and dislodge devil (*See* Matthew 4:1-11). Again, the devil did not give up. He inspired people to laugh Jesus to scorn when Jesus wanted to raise a damsel from a sleep of death.

> *"He said unto them, Give place: for the maid is not dead, but sleepeth. And they laughed him to scorn"* (Matthew 9:24).

Devil used the Pharisees to accuse Jesus of casting out his demons using the power of Beelzebub, the prince of the devil. Later, he used the Pharisees again to tempt Christ to entangle Him. More so, devil used the Sadducees to contradict Christ's teachings on resurrection (*See* Matthew 22:15-33). He went in among the disciples of Jesus and captured Judas Iscariot, who conspired with the chief priests to betray Christ for thirty pieces of silver.

At the garden, the devil gave one of the disciples of Jesus a sword to fight carnally (*See* Matthew 26:14-16, 20-21, 23, 25, 47-50; 27:3-5; 26:51-56). He made Peter to deny Christ three times. He conspired with the chief priests, elders and the people and they took counsel together to put Jesus to death. They arrested Jesus, bound Him, took Him to Pilate, the governor who washed his hand and yet scourged Christ.

> *"11 And Jesus stood before the governor: and the governor asked him, saying, Art thou the King of the Jews? And Jesus said unto him, Thou sayest. 18 For he knew that for envy they had delivered him. 19 When he was set down on the judgment seat, his wife sent unto him, saying, Have thou nothing to do with that just man: for I have suffered many things this day in a dream because of him. 20 But the chief priests and elders persuaded the multitude that they should ask Barabbas, and destroy Jesus. 23 And the governor said, Why, what evil hath he done? But they cried out the more, saying, Let him be crucified. 25 Then answered all the people, and said, His blood* be *on us, and on our children. 26 Then released he Barabbas unto them: and when he had scourged Jesus, he delivered* him *to be crucified. 27 Then the soldiers of the governor took Jesus into the common hall, and gathered unto him the whole band* of soldiers" (Matthew 27:11, 18-20, 23, 25-27).

The devil handed Christ to the wicked and merciless Roman soldiers, who assaulted Him beyond measure. They took Jesus to the common hall, striped off His garments, and used scorpion whips to tear all His body. They put on Him a scarlet robe and platted crown of thorns on His head. They gave Him vinegar to drink. The devil used everything that Christ created to assault Him, hoping that Jesus will change His mind from going to the cross.

Devil thought that if Christ died on the cross His kingdom would end forever. So he inspired the worst armed robber on earth to humiliate Christ on the cross thinking that all those would make Christ to give up, but all was in vain.

"[38]Then were there two thieves crucified with him, one on the right hand, and another on the left. [39]And they that passed by reviled him, wagging their heads, [40]And saying, Thou that destroyest the temple, and buildest it *in three days, save thyself. If thou be the Son of God, come down from the cross. [41]Likewise also the chief priests mocking* him, *with the scribes and elders, said, [42]He saved others; himself he cannot save. If he be the King of Israel, let him now come down from the cross, and we will believe him. [43]He trusted in God; let him deliver him now, if he will have him: for he said, I am the Son of God. [44]The thieves also, which were crucified with him, cast the same in his teeth. [63]Saying, Sir, we remember that that deceiver said, while he was yet alive, After three days I will rise again"* (Matthew 27:38-44, 63).

Unknown to the devil, Christ had already agreed with His Father in heaven to die for the liberation of humanity even a death at the cross. Christ knew that all happened according to God's will and to God's glory.

"Him, being delivered by the determinate counsel and foreknowledge of God, ye have taken, and by wicked hands have crucified and slain" (Acts 2:23).

"The Son of man goeth as it is written of him: but woe unto that man by whom the Son of man is betrayed! It had been good for that man if he had not been born" (Matthew 26:24).

"And truly the Son of man goeth, as it was determined: but woe unto that man by whom he is betrayed!" (Luke 22:22).

"But those things, which God before had shewed by the mouth of all his prophets, that Christ should suffer, he hath so fulfilled" (Acts 3:18).

"And there appeared an angel unto him from heaven, strengthening him. And being in an agony he prayed more earnestly: and his sweat was as it were great drops of blood falling down to the ground. And when he rose up from prayer, and was come to his disciples, he found them sleeping for sorrow, And said unto them, Why sleep ye? Rise and pray, lest ye enter into temptation. And while he yet spake, behold a multitude, and he that was called Judas, one of the twelve, went before them, and drew near unto Jesus to kiss him" (Luke 22:43-47).

Jesus had the power to command legions of angels to fight for His freedom. However, He knew also that His death was necessary for the salvation and deliverance of humanity. God initiated the redemption work, which Christ executed at the cross of Calvary.

> *"Then said Jesus unto him, Put up again thy sword into his place: for all they that take the sword shall perish with the sword. Thinkest thou that I cannot now pray to my Father, and he shall presently give me more than twelve legions of angels? But how then shall the scriptures be fulfilled, that thus it must be?"* (Matthew 26:52-54).

BENEFITS OF THE BLOOD OF JESUS

Our sins and curse were laid upon Christ on the cross and He died to take them out of the way. His death reconciled man to God. Christ gave His life as a ransom for as many as would believe in Him. His blood is the blood of the New Testament, which He shed for the remission of our sins.

> *"All we like sheep have gone astray; we have turned everyone to his own way; and the LORD hath laid on him the iniquity of us all"* (Isaiah 53:6).

> *"Even as the Son of man came not to be ministered unto, but to minister, and to give his life a ransom for many"* (Matthew 20:28).

> *"For this is my blood of the new testament, which is shed for many for the remission of sins"* (Matthew 26:28).

As you lift Christ up in your life, you will no longer perish but enjoy eternal life. Jesus has purchased us with His blood. He paid the price for our deliverance with His blood. He died so that we would live eternally and not die eternally. We are freely justified by God's grace through the redemption that is in Christ Jesus. Praise the LORD!

> *"And as Moses lifted up the serpent in the wilderness, even so must the Son of man be lifted up: [15]That whosoever believeth in him should not perish, but have eternal life"* (John 3:14-15).

> *"Take heed therefore unto yourselves, and to all the flock, over the which the Holy Ghost hath made you overseers, to feed the church of God, which he hath purchased with his own blood"* (Acts 20:28).

> *"Being justified freely by his grace through the redemption that is in Christ Jesus: Whom God hath set forth* to be *a propitiation through faith in his blood, to declare his righteousness for the remission of sins that are past, through the forbearance of God; To declare,* I say, *at this time his righteousness: that he might be just, and the justifier of him which believeth in Jesus"* (Romans 3:24-26).

The only way you can benefit from His death is when you repent and confess you sins, and forsake them. When you do so and accept His righteousness as yours, He justifies and saves you. When you begin to plead the blood of Jesus by faith, your whole life would be transformed. The blood of Jesus has the power to cleanse the vilest and most sinful person in the universe and that person becomes a sin-free child of God.

> *"[6]For when we were yet without strength, in due time Christ died for the ungodly. [7]For scarcely for a righteous man will one die: yet peradventure for a good man some*

would even dare to die. [8]But God commendeth his love toward us, in that, while we were yet sinners, Christ died for us. [9]Much more then, being now justified by his blood, we shall be saved from wrath through him. [10]For if, when we were enemies, we were reconciled to God by the death of his Son, much more, being reconciled, we shall be saved by his life. [11]And not only so, but we also joy in God through our Lord Jesus Christ, by whom we have now received the atonement. [18]Therefore as by the offence of one judgment came *upon all men to condemnation; even so by the righteousness of one* the free gift came *upon all men unto justification of life. [19] For as by one man's disobedience many were made sinners, so by the obedience of one shall many be made righteous"* (Romans 5:6-11, 18-19).

The death of our Lord Jesus Christ can empower the weakest person to live by God's grace without condemnation. When you plead the blood of Jesus, the devil would have no option than to bow and flee from every area of your life that he occupied, both spiritually and physically.

The death of our Lord Jesus delivered us from the wrath of God. His death reconciled us with God and took away the enmity that was between God and us. Through His death, we received atonement for our sins and became the sons of God. The condemnation that came upon all men through the sin of Adam was removed out of the way. Christ's obedience to the cross nullified the effects of man's disobedience and made us righteous before God. The curse of Adam and Eve ceased to exist. This is one of the greatest gifts to every expectant mother. Jesus paid for the sorrow, pain and evil that was associated with child delivery.

"Unto the woman he said, I will greatly multiply thy sorrow and thy conception; in sorrow thou shalt bring forth children; and thy desire shall be to thy husband, and he shall rule over thee" (Genesis 3:16).

"Purge out therefore the old leaven, that ye may be a new lump, as ye are unleavened. For even Christ our Passover is sacrificed for us" (1 Corinthians 5:7).

When you repent of all your sins and receive the redeeming grace of God, the benefits of Christ's death takes effect in your life. Every blessing in life comes because of the atonement of Jesus Christ. Healing, salvation, sanctification, deliverance during child delivery, victory and every answer to prayers come from God because Jesus shed His blood on the cross of Calvary.

"Who his own self bare our sins in his own body on the tree that we, being dead to sins, should live unto righteousness: by whose stripes ye were healed" (I Peter 2:24).

"By the which will we are sanctified through the offering of the body of Jesus Christ once for all*"* (Hebrews 10:10).

"And I heard a loud voice saying in heaven, Now is come salvation, and strength, and the kingdom of our God, and the power of his Christ: for the accuser of our brethren is cast down, which accused them before our God day and night. And they overcame him by the blood of the Lamb, and by the word of their testimony; and they loved not their lives unto the death" (Revelation 12:10-11).

Resources that Christians need to dislodge the devil and possess his possession are readily available and God has provided everything we need for our total freedom. What you need is to believe in the saving power that is in the blood of Jesus. You must obey the Word of God and disobey any contrary power that is opposing God's will for your life.

PRAYERS TO DELIVER YOUR CHILD SAFELY

Bible references: Exodus 23:25-26; Nahum 3:4; Isaiah 37:3-4

Begin with praise and worship

1. I destroy every manipulation to disrupt the delivery of my child, in the name of Jesus.
2. I frustrate deceptive family control mechanisms that affect my delivery, in the name of Jesus.
3. Every satanic judgment that was passed over my delivery, I reverse you, in the name of Jesus.
4. Any curse that was placed on my delivery, I nullify you, in the name of Jesus.
5. Every arrow of impossibility that was shot at my delivery, backfire, in the name of Jesus.
6. I reject every weakness that was programmed to my delivery, in the name of Jesus.
7. O Lord, arise and empower me on the day of my delivery, in the name of Jesus.
8. Every evil conspiracy that is targeting my delivery, be frustrated, in the name of Jesus.
9. Every witchcraft decision that was taken against my delivery, fail woefully, in the name of Jesus.
10. I reject evil utterances uttered against my delivery, in the name of Jesus.
11. Any evil mind that is thinking evil against my delivery, scatter in confusion, in the name of Jesus.
12. I cut off the head of the strongman that is manipulating my delivery, in the name of Jesus.
13. Let the thunder of God destroy every enemy of my delivery, in the name of Jesus.
14. Any evil personality that has vowed to kill my baby or me, die for our sakes, in the name of Jesus.
15. O Lord, arise and deliver me from evil agenda by fire, in the name of Jesus.

16. Any power planning to destroy my baby before delivery, I destroy you, in the name of Jesus.
17. I chase away agents of the devil on the day of my delivery, in the name of Jesus.
18. O Lord, grant me favor on the day of my delivery, in the name of Jesus.
19. I destroy any evil personality that was assigned to destroy me in the labor room, in the name of Jesus.
20. Holy Ghost fire, protect my baby and me on the day of my delivery, in the name of Jesus.
21. I break and loose myself from the consequences of my past mistakes, in the name of Jesus.
22. Let the presence of the Almighty saturate the clinic my people will take me to deliver, in the name of Jesus.
23. Blood of Jesus, speak death to the enemy of my delivery, in the name of Jesus.
24. My day of delivery will not be bewitched, in the name of Jesus.
25. Let the angels of God be present at the venue of my delivery, in the name of Jesus.
26. Every fake helper on the day of my delivery, be exposed and disgraced, in the name of Jesus.
27. I disgrace any evil personality that is ministering to my delivery, in the name of Jesus.
28. That evil river that would flow on the day I will deliver my baby, dry up, in the name of Jesus.
29. Any evil hand that was anointed to touch me on the day of my delivery, dry up and break, in the name of Jesus.
30. Holy Ghost fire, consume every enemy of my delivery, in the name of Jesus.
31. Any evil thing that was prepared for me on the day of my delivery, backfire, in the name of Jesus.
32. I receive enough grace to deliver in the presence of God, in the name of Jesus.
33. Any spiritual vulture and unclean animal that moves around on the day of my delivery, die, in the name of Jesus.
34. Any evil movement on the day of my delivery, be demobilized, in the name of Jesus.
35. Any evil agreement over me on the day of my delivery, scatter, in the name of Jesus.

36. I fire back evil arrows that were fired at me for the sake of my delivery, in the name of Jesus.

37. I break and loose myself from every yoke of the devil, in the name of Jesus.

38. I refuse to respond to any evil command on the day of my delivery, in the name of Jesus.

39. Any power that wants to prolong my labor, be disgraced to death, in the name of Jesus.

40. I cut off the existence of any spirit spouse on the day of my delivery, in the name of Jesus.

41. Let the prince of peace take over my life on the day of my delivery, in the name of Jesus.

42. Let angels of the living God pursue evil spirits on the day of my delivery, in the name of Jesus.

43. Let frustration and disappointment take over the brain of my enemies, in the name of Jesus.

44. Any evil brain that is thinking evil against my delivery, receive confusion and die, in the name of Jesus.

45. I refuse to believe evil reports on the day of my delivery, in the name of Jesus.

46. O Lord, arise and help me to deliver in peace, in the name of Jesus.

20

Chapter

PRAYERS TO RAISE GODLY CHILDREN

CHAPTER OVERVIEW

- *God's command to train children*
- *A parent's commitment to the children*
- *God's Word: A guide for making good decisions*
- *The joy of training a child*
- *Consequence of not training your child*

GOD'S COMMAND TO TRAIN CHILDREN

God takes the issue of raising and training of Children very seriously. Before Abraham gave birth to his only son, Isaac, God knew he was going to train him well.

> *"And the men rose up from thence, and looked toward Sodom: and Abraham went with them to bring them on the way. And the LORD said, Shall I hide from Abraham that thing which I do; Seeing that Abraham shall surely become a great and mighty nation, and all the nations of the earth shall be blessed in him? For I know him, that he will command his children and his household after him, and they shall keep the way of the LORD, to do justice and judgment; that the LORD may bring upon Abraham that which he hath spoken of him"* (Genesis 18:16-19).

God does not hide His secret from those who plan for the continued existence of future generations in accordance to His will and covenant. Failure to guide and train your children in godly ways is total failure, even when you are successful in every other areas of life. Parents who take the issue of training their children lightly are destroying the continued existence of the future generations.

> *"Children, obey your parents in the Lord: for this is right. Honor thy father and mother; (which is the first commandment with promise;) That it may be well with thee, and thou mayest live long on the earth. And, ye fathers, provoke not your children to wrath: but bring them up in the nurture and admonition of the Lord"* (Ephesians 6:1-4).

The first persons a child meets, after birth, are parents. Therefore, parents have lots of work to do as regards training children in godly ways. Training a child in the way of the Lord is nurturing a mighty and godly nation. Parents that lose any child to the devil have lost a mighty nation and have denied a generation of their blessings.

Parents are to know the Lord before they are able to bring their children to God. Any child who fails to follow God's way has been misled. God is looking for godly parents, who are determined to do everything possible to teach their children and their entire household how to keep the commandments of God, do justice and judgment.

The first assignment for children towards their parents is to obey their parents in the Lord, and honor their father and mother. This is the first responsibility of godly children towards their parents. Children who fail to do this assignment would obviously fail in every other assignment in their lives. Such failure can cause a child to die prematurely.

Many children experience premature deaths of joy, peace, happiness, etc., in their lives while they still lived. They also witness God's promises being fulfilled in the lives of obedient children, while they experience horrendous things in their own lives. When a child is not under direct care and government of his parents, the child is then expected to obey the people that are taking care of him or her.

Children cannot know what God has commanded them to do until someone tells them. They cannot discern the Scriptures easily as adults. That is why they need qualified persons to teach and guide them. Parents are responsible for teaching and guiding their children rightly. Any child that comes under your care automatically becomes part of your responsibility. Thus, it is your duty to train that child in the way of the Lord for you will give account of that child before God.

> *"My son, keep thy father's commandment, and forsake not the law of thy mother: Bind them continually upon thine heart, and tie them about thy neck. When thou goest, it shall lead thee; when thou sleepest, it shall keep thee; and when thou awakest, it shall talk with thee. For the commandment is a lamp; and the law is light; and reproofs of instruction are the way of life"* (Proverbs 6:20-23).

> *"But if any widow have children or nephews, let them learn first to shew piety at home, and to requite their parents: for that is good and acceptable before God"* (1 Timothy 5:4).

Parents who train their children well depend on God always and shun iniquities. They accept Christ as their Lord and Savior, and always followed His footsteps in order to lead their children in ways that please God. They master God's Word and pledge obedience to it.

When a child misses the training on the knowledge of God and His Word at a very tender age, that child has missed the vital part of his or her life. Children retain over 80% of what they see, hear and do. That is why it is easier to build up a child than to repair damages done on such child. Parents that failed to train their children at the tender stage of life does great disservice to those children.

> *"Speak, I pray you, in the ears of all the men of Shechem, Whether is better for you, either that all the sons of Jerubbaal,* which are *threescore and ten persons, reign over you, or that one reign over you? Remember also that I* am *your bone and your flesh. And his mother's brethren spake of him in the ears of all the men of Shechem all these words: and their hearts inclined to follow Abimelech; for they said, He* is *our brother. And they gave him threescore and ten* pieces *of silver out of the house of*

Baal–berith, wherewith Abimelech hired vain and light persons, which followed him. And he went unto his father's house at Ophrah, and slew his brethren the sons of Jerubbaal, being *threescore and ten persons, upon one stone: notwithstanding yet Jotham the youngest son of Jerubbaal was left; for he hid himself. And all the men of Shechem gathered together, and all the house of Millo, and went, and made Abimelech king, by the plain of the pillar that* was *in Shechem. And when they told* it *to Jotham, he went and stood in the top of mount Gerizim, and lifted up his voice, and cried, and said unto them, Hearken unto me, ye men of Shechem, that God may hearken unto you. The trees went forth* on a time *to anoint a king over them; and they said unto the olive tree, Reign thou over us. But the olive tree said unto them, Should I leave my fatness, wherewith by me they honor God and man, and go to be promoted over the trees? And the trees said to the fig tree, Come thou,* and *reign over us"* (Judges 9:2-10).

It is the responsibility of parents to teach their children about God's promises and commandments. It is easier for children to forsake God when they do not understand the consequences of doing so. God cannot spare parents who allow or aid their children to die in their sins. Children are futuristic leaders and thus must be nurtured in truth and justice.

"Children, obey your parents in the Lord: for this is right" (Ephesians 6:1).

"He that loveth father or mother more than me is not worthy of me: and he that loveth son or daughter more than me is not worthy of me" (Matthew 10:37).

Children should be taught to fear God, and not man. In fact, the fear of God should form the dominant part of their lives without reserving any for the devil or his angels. Children should be taught to obey God's Word more than man's words. They must understand that thoughts, desires or feelings that contradict God's Word must be abandoned. No parents have rights to require a child to steal, lie or cheat. No parents or governments have rights to forbid a child to worship God.

"But Peter and John answered and said unto them, Whether it be right in the sight of God to hearken unto you more than unto God, judge ye. [20]For we cannot but speak the things which we have seen and heard" (Acts 4:19-20).

A parent's instructions must not contradict the Word of God. Christian children must obey God's Word and abandon the sinful practices of parents.

"Children, obey your parents in the Lord: for this is right. Honor thy father and mother; (which is the first commandment with promise" (Ephesians 6:1-2).

"When my father and my mother forsake me, then the LORD will take me up" (Psalms 27:10).

God multiplies blessings for children that obey His Word. Your parents might turn against you and deny your rights sometimes. Nevertheless, if it is because of your obedience to God's Word, He would surely reward your loyalty to His Word.

"Now, lo, if *he beget a son, that seeth all his father's sins which he hath done, and considereth, and doeth not such like,* That *hath not eaten upon the mountains, neither hath lifted up his eyes to the idols of the house of Israel, hath not defiled his neighbor's wife, Neither hath oppressed any, hath not withholden the pledge, neither hath spoiled by violence,* but *hath given his bread to the hungry, and hath covered the naked with a garment,* That *hath taken off his hand from the poor,* that *hath not received usury nor increase, hath executed my judgments, hath walked in my statutes; he shall not die for the iniquity of his father, he shall surely live.* As for *his father, because he cruelly oppressed, spoiled his brother by violence, and did* that *which* is *not good among his people, lo, even he shall die in his iniquity"* (Ezekiel 18:14-18).

Susan Wesley took time to imbibe the fear of God into her children through prayers and studying the bible. At last, John Wesley became one of the fruits of her labor and dedication. She was an ideal mother, who kept the following rules and principles:

1. Children were always put into regular method of living, in such things, as they were capable of from their birth as in dressing and undressing. They must be taught to fear the rod and to cry softly. The family usually lived in as much quietness as if there had not been a child among them.

2. As soon as they were grown strong, they were confined to three meals a day. Whatever food they had, they were never permitted at those meals to eat of more than one thing and of that sparingly enough. They were not allowed to make choices of their meals but to eat such things as were provided for the entire family.

To form the mind of a child, you have to conquer the will of that child and bring it to subject to God's Word and will. No intentional sin should be forgiven without chastisement. If you do not help your child to grow up rightly, you become a failure with time, regardless of how great your successes are in other areas of life. When you fail your children, you fail their future as well.

Success in your family cannot be measured by the amount of money you have in banks, but how well your children behaved. Your success and glory in this world would not reflect only on your investments but in the character of your children also and the quality of their relationship with God.

I read of one Virginia's psychologists, who conducted a two-year research and study on children aged four to six, asking them the question, "Which do you like better - Television or Daddy? As reported by United Press International, 44% of the total children questioned chose television over their daddies. Only 20% chose their mother over television.

A father's absence in the lives of his children is very unhealthy. A boy needs his father around him to develop healthy images of what it means to be a man. A daughter needs her father around her to strengthen her sense of feminism and learn what to expect from the opposite sex. Children that received enough encouragement from their parents do better than children who did not. Lack of parental encouragement and appreciation force children to develop traits of sadness and anger.

Children, who are properly guided and mobilized, are capable of doing exploits in their lifetime. Otherwise, they would abandon their treasured talents too soon.

Jonathan Edwards was converted at the age of eight and later he became a great preacher. Likewise, Miss Phoebe Bestleth was converted at the age of eleven. Jonathan and Phoebe later became great authors of Bible commentaries.

"And, ye fathers, provoke not your children to wrath: but bring them up in the nurture and admonition of the Lord" (Ephesians 6:4).

"This book of the law shall not depart out of thy mouth; but thou shalt meditate therein day and night, that thou mayest observe to do according to all that is written therein: for then thou shalt make thy way prosperous, and then thou shalt have good success" (Joshua 1:8).

Fathers are not to provoke their children to wrath, but rather nurture and admonish them in the ways of God. The Word of God is the best manual suitable for training children. When a child learns and observes God's Word from tender age, he or she prospers greatly in life. When you teach your child how to meditate on God's Word, day and night, it becomes easier for children to dislodge evil thoughts and wicked desires on their own from time to time.

In the book of Joshua, God revealed to Joshua that good success and prosperity are rooted in observing God's Word. Parents should remind their children repeatedly of how God expects children to live their lives. Many children cannot tell what they need and what to expect from the Lord. That is why the Word of God remains the greatest investment in the life of a child.

"For I know him, that he will command his children and his household after him, and they shall keep the way of the LORD, to do justice and judgment; that the LORD may bring upon Abraham that which he hath spoken of him" (Genesis 18:19).

"And that thou mayest tell in the ears of thy son, and of thy son's son, what things I have wrought in Egypt, and my signs which I have done among them; that ye may know how that I am *the LORD"* (Exodus 10:2).

"Only take heed to thyself, and keep thy soul diligently, lest thou forget the things which thine eyes have seen, and lest they depart from thy heart all the days of thy life: but teach them thy sons, and thy sons' sons; Specially *the day that thou stoodest before the LORD thy God in Horeb, when the LORD said unto me, Gather me the people together, and I will make them hear my words, that they may learn to fear me all the days that they shall live upon the earth, and* that *they may teach their children"* (Deuteronomy 4:9-10).

Word of God is like food to the human soul. Therefore, when a human is not fed well with the Word of God from infancy, the person starves spiritually. Parents are to teach their children constantly about the Word of God in order to keep their souls from corruption. Repeatedly, God reminded the children of Israel to teach their children His Word that they may not depart from it all their lives.

> *"Therefore shall ye lay up these my words in your heart and in your soul, and bind them for a sign upon your hand, that they may be as frontlets between your eyes. And ye shall teach them your children, speaking of them when thou sittest in thine house, and when thou walkest by the way, when thou liest down, and when thou risest up. And thou shalt write them upon the door posts of thine house, and upon thy gates: That your days may be multiplied, and the days of your children, in the land which the LORD sware unto your fathers to give them, as the days of heaven upon the earth"* (Deuteronomy 11:18-21).

GOD'S WORD: A GUIDE FOR MAKING GOOD DECISIONS

The Spirit of God guided Abel to offer an acceptable sacrifice before God. When he did, his offering received God's recognition. That was why even after his death, God still fought for him. On the other hand, Cain was not sincere before God with his offering of sacrifice and God rejected it.

You cannot keep the Word of God away from your children except you do not what them to know how to be sincere with God in their lives. Disobedience and deceit bring curses like that of Cain, who became a fugitive and vagabond on earth. Then, when we expose our children to God's Word, we spare them from trouble.

God gave His Word to us freely. Therefore, it is our duty to pass them on to our children. We are bound to transfer whatever we heard from God to our children. We must testify of the goodness of God and benefits of true obedience before our children. We are to show our children the effectiveness of God's power, His strength and His ways. God's wonderful works, as established in our testimonies, are our children's inheritance, which we must give to them.

> *"Chasten thy son while there is hope, and let not thy soul spare for his crying"* (Proverbs 19:18).

> *"6Train up a child in the way he should go: and when he is old, he will not depart from it. 15Foolishness* is *bound in the heart of a child;* but *the rod of correction shall drive it far from him. 17Bow down thine ear, and hear the words of the wise, and apply thine heart unto my knowledge"* (Proverbs 22:6, 15-17).

> *"But continue thou in the things which thou hast learned and hast been assured of, knowing of whom thou hast learned* them; *And that from a child thou hast known the holy scriptures, which are able to make thee wise unto salvation through faith which is in Christ Jesus"* (2 Timothy 3:14-15).

God permitted that children are to be chastised with love while there is hope and should not be spared no matter how much they cry. Sparing a child when he arrogantly departs from the way is giving him up to the devil. God commanded us in His Word to train our children in the way they should grow. Do not allow them to grow up in their own foolishness. They need the rod of correction. Parents must insist that their children continue in the way of God as they have learned. You must ensure this from their childhood.

> *"Furthermore we have had fathers of our flesh which corrected* us, *and we gave* them *reverence: shall we not much rather be in subjection unto the Father of spirits, and live? For they verily for a few days chastened* us *after their own pleasure; but he for*

our *profit, that* we *might be partakers of his holiness. Now no chastening for the present seemeth to be joyous, but grievous: nevertheless afterward it yieldeth the peaceable fruit of righteousness unto them which are exercised there by"* (Hebrews 12:9-11).

When you teach a child to follow the way of the Lord and how to obey parents and elders, such child would do so all through his or her lifetime. We must carry out this divine discipline in our homes. If parents could do their duties towards their children well, nations would be at peace. You may not see the immediate reward for chastising a child but with time, it brings peace.

In parent child relationship, there is no need for unreasonable harshness or severity. There is equally no need for manifestations of anger or unwarranted punishment. Parents are to show good example and train their children in a way that pleases God. Parents are not to require their children to do things God did not approve or instruct.

> *"He that begetteth a fool* doeth it *to his sorrow: and the father of a fool hath no joy"* (Proverbs 17:21).

> *"And there came a man of God unto Eli, and said unto him, Thus saith the LORD, Did I plainly appear unto the house of thy father, when they were in Egypt in Pharaoh's house? And did I choose him out of all the tribes of Israel* to be *my priest, to offer upon mine altar, to burn incense, to wear an ephod before me? and did I give unto the house of thy father all the offerings made by fire of the children of Israel? Wherefore kick ye at my sacrifice and at mine offering, which I have commanded* in my *habitation; and honorest thy sons above me, to make yourselves fat with the chiefest of all the offerings of Israel my people? Wherefore the LORD God of Israel saith, I said indeed* that *thy house, and the house of thy father, should walk before me forever: but now the LORD saith, Be it far from me; for them that honor me I will honor, and they that despise me shall be lightly esteemed. Behold, the days come, that I will cut off thine arm, and the arm of thy father's house, that there shall not be an old man in thine house. And thou shalt see an enemy* in my *habitation, in all* the wealth, *which* God *shall give Israel: and there shall not be an old man in thine house forever. And the man of thine,* whom *I shall not cut off from mine altar,* shall be *to consume thine eyes, and to grieve thine heart: and all the increase of thine house shall die in the flower of their age. And this* shall be *a sign unto thee, that shall come upon thy two sons, on Hophni and Phinehas; in one day they shall die both of them"* (1 Samuel 2:27-34).

All parents who fail to instruct and chastise their children are bound to suffer for their negligence. Children obey as far as their parents command them.

Jacob's love for Joseph and Benjamin accounted for much love and discipline he showed to them. He was more committed to them that he was to the rest of his children. That was why despite all the hatred and attempts to stop him, the love and training Joseph received from his father was instrumental for his survival. His training made him to remain faithful to God, even in hard times.

> *"And Joseph was brought down to Egypt; and Potiphar, an officer of Pharaoh, captain of the guard, an Egyptian, bought him of the hands of the Ishmeelites, which had brought him down thither. And the LORD was with Joseph, and he was a prosperous man; and he was in the house of his master the Egyptian. And his master saw that the LORD* was *with him, and that the LORD made all that he did to prosper in his hand. And Joseph found grace in his sight, and he served him: and he made him overseer over his house, and all* that *he had he put into his hand. And it came to pass from the time* that *he had made him overseer in his house, and over all that he had, that the LORD blessed the Egyptian's house for Joseph's sake; and the blessing of the LORD was upon all that he had in the house, and in the field. And he left all that he had in Joseph's hand; and he knew not ought he had, save the bread, which he did eat. And Joseph was* a *goodly* person, *and well favored"* (Genesis 39:1-6).

His faith in God gave him victory over temptations (*See* Genesis 39:7-13), and promotions (*See* Genesis 41:14-46). His godly training preserved him as a slave and a prisoner. In any environment he found himself, he sought for nothing else except the glory of God. He was tempted many times but he did not fall.

> *"Dearly beloved, I beseech* you *as strangers and pilgrims, abstain from fleshly lusts, which war against the soul; Having your conversation honest among the Gentiles: that, whereas they speak against you as evildoers, they may by* your *good works, which they shall behold, glorify God in the day of visitation"* (1 Peter 2:11-12).

People who never received any godly training always experience sudden fall when promoted. However, it was not so with Joseph. He served as a prime minister in Egypt. He was also a successful administrator, builder and protector of God's people. He had the wisdom of God, divine foresight, and was very industrious. Pharaoh rewarded him for his service and God used him to keep his people alive. His father was very happy hearing that Joseph lived. His fame, wisdom and position in Egypt gladdened his father, Jacob, until his death.

> *"And they went up out of Egypt, and came into the land of Canaan unto Jacob their father, And told him, saying, Joseph* is *yet alive, and he* is *governor over all the land*

of Egypt. And Jacob's heart fainted, for he believed them not. And they told him all the words of Joseph, which he had said unto them: and when he saw the wagons which Joseph had sent to carry him, the spirit of Jacob their father revived: And Israel said, It is *enough; Joseph my son* is *yet alive: I will go and see him before I die"* (Genesis 45:25-28).

The joy of a well-trained child and his success cannot be over emphasized. Only Jacob could tell how he felt to hear that his love and commitment upon Joseph was never a waste.

You can imagine how you would feel to hear that your child has become the president of America by the reason of good training you gave to your child. Imagine how the parents of Daniel, Shedrack, Meshack and Abednego would have felt when they heard the fame of their children in a foreign land.

"Shadrach, Meshach, and Abed–nego, answered and said to the king, O Nebuchadnezzar, we are *not careful to answer thee in this matter. If it be* so, *our God whom we serve is able to deliver us from the burning fiery furnace, and he will deliver* us *out of thine hand, O king. But if not, be it known unto thee, O king, that we will not serve thy gods, nor worship the golden image which thou hast set up"* (Daniel 3:16-18).

"Now, O king, establish the decree, and sign the writing, that it be not changed, according to the law of the Medes and Persians, which altereth not" (Daniel 6:8).

The three Hebrew children refused to bow before the idol king Nebuchadnezzar made. They disregarded the king's decree and were ready to die for their faith, whether God intervened immediately or not. Their decision infuriated the king. These Hebrew children stood their ground even in the midst of burning furnace. In the end, God delivered them.

"[23]And these three men, Shadrach, Meshach, and Abed–nego, fell down bound into the midst of the burning fiery furnace. [24]Then Nebuchadnezzar the king was astonied, and rose up in haste, and *spake, and said unto his counselors, Did not we cast three men bound into the midst of the fire? They answered and said unto the king, True, O king. [28]*Then *Nebuchadnezzar spake, and said, Blessed* be *the God of Shadrach, Meshach, and Abed–nego, who hath sent his angel, and delivered his servants that trusted in him, and have changed the king's word, and yielded their bodies, that they might not serve nor worship any god, except their own God. [29]Therefore I make a decree, That every people, nation, and language, which speak anything amiss against the God of Shadrach, Meshach, and Abed–nego, shall be cut in pieces, and their houses shall be made a dunghill: because there is no other God*

that can deliver after this sort. [30]*Then the king promoted Shadrach, Meshach, and Abed–nego, in the province of Babylon"* (Daniel 3:23-24, 28-30).

Instead of being burnt by flames, they walked in the midst of the fire. They were not hurt because Christ joined them in the fire and became their shield. Unbelievably, they walked out of the fire unhurt. Their faith in the God of Abraham, Isaac and Israel forced the king to change his wicked and self-serving decrees. And because these children trusted in their God, they got promoted in Babylon. However, one thing that stood out from the story of these children is that Jews at time trusted in God and trained their children in the way of the Lord.

"Train up a child in the way he should go: and when he is old, he will not depart from it" (Proverbs 22:6).

Greater joy and reward abound when you train your children in a godly way. Children trained by godly parents in godly homes hardly cause their parents any trouble. Rather, they are the source of joy to their parents.

CONSEQUENCE OF NOT TRAINING YOUR CHILD

Children who are not trained in the way of the Lord are likely to end their lives in regret and sorrow. Such children reject parental counsel or training and set themselves up for eternal life with devil in hell fire.

> *"And I saw a great white throne, and him that sat on it, from whose face the earth and the heaven fled away; and there was found no place for them. And I saw the dead, small and great, stand before God; and the books were opened: and another book was opened, which is* the book *of life: and the dead were judged out of those things which were written in the books, according to their works. And the sea gave up the dead which were in it; and death and hell delivered up the dead, which were in them: and they were judged every man according to their works. And death and hell were cast into the lake of fire. This is the second death. And whosoever was not found written in the book of life was cast into the lake of fire"* (Revelation 20:11-15).

It is dangerous to die without Christ. A day is coming when everyone would give account of life on earth. It is called judgment day. It is going to be a terrible and fearful day really. The present earth and the atmospheric heaven will pass away. The earth and the works therein shall be burned up; just at the same time, sinners are forever put away from the presence of God.

> *"[7]But the heavens and the earth, which are now, by the same word are kept in store, reserved unto fire against the day of judgment and perdition of ungodly men. [10]But the day of the Lord will come as a thief in the night; in the which the heavens shall pass away with a great noise, and the elements shall melt with fervent heat, the earth also and the works that are therein shall be burned up.* [11]Seeing *then* that *all these things shall be dissolved, what manner* of persons *ought ye to be in* all *holy conversation and godliness, [12]Looking for and hasting unto the coming of the day of God, wherein the heavens being on fire shall be dissolved, and the elements shall melt with fervent heat? [13]Nevertheless we, according to his promise, look for new heavens and a new earth, wherein dwelleth righteousness. [14]Wherefore, beloved, seeing that ye look for such things, be diligent that ye may be found of him in peace, without spot, and blameless"* (2 Peter 3:7, 10-14).

All sinners shall be judged according to their works. God has record of what all men in all generations have done since the world began.

> *"The wicked shall be turned into hell, and all the nations that forget God"* (Psalms 9:17).

"For Tophet is ordained of old; yea, for the king it is prepared; he hath made it deep and large: the pile thereof is fire and much wood; the breath of the LORD, like a stream of brimstone, doth kindle it" (Isaiah 30:33).

"The sinners in Zion are afraid; fearfulness hath surprised the hypocrites. Who among us shall dwell with the devouring fire? Who among us shall dwell with everlasting burnings?" (Isaiah 33:14).

On that day, all men of all ages, small and great, would appear before the LORD. The seas will surrender all the people they swallowed.

"And if thy right eye offend thee, pluck it out, and cast it *from thee: for it is profitable for thee that one of thy members should perish, and not* that *thy whole body should be cast into hell"* (Matthew 5:29).

"And I say unto you, That many shall come from the east and west, and shall sit down with Abraham, and Isaac, and Jacob, in the kingdom of heaven. [12]But the children of the kingdom shall be cast out into outer darkness: there shall be weeping and gnashing of teeth" (Matthew 8:11-12).

"[41]The Son of man shall send forth his angels, and they shall gather out of his kingdom all things that offend, and them which do iniquity; [42]And shall cast them into a furnace of fire: there shall be wailing and gnashing of teeth. [49]So shall it be at the end of the world: the angels shall come forth, and sever the wicked from among the just, [50]And shall cast them into the furnace of fire: there shall be wailing and gnashing of teeth" (Matthew 13:41-42, 49-50).

PRAYERS TO RAISE GODLY CHILDREN

Bible references: Proverbs 22:6; Ephesians 6:1-4; 2 Timothy 3:15

Begin with praise and worship

1. Father Lord, give me wisdom to raise my children, in the name of Jesus.
2. I receive power to lead my children to God, in the name of Jesus.
3. I withdraw my children from the camp of the devil, in the name of Jesus.
4. I uproot ungodly characters that my children exhibit, in the name of Jesus.
5. O Lord, arise and influence my children positively, in the name of Jesus.
6. Any satanic deposit inside my children, die, in the name of Jesus.
7. Holy Ghost fire, burn evil properties in the lives of my children, in the name of Jesus.
8. Let agents of devil that were assigned to mislead my children be disgraced, in the name of Jesus.
9. Any spirit of lust that exists inside my children, die, in the name of Jesus.
10. O Lord, arise and take my children away from satanic prisons, in the name of Jesus.
11. I command the seed of Almighty to manifest among my children, in the name of Jesus.
12. Let the Spirit of obedience to God's Word possess my children, in the name of Jesus.
13. O Lord, command Your angels to guide my children into righteousness, in the name of Jesus.
14. Any yoke of devil that was placed upon my children, break to pieces, in the name of Jesus.
15. I lead my children out of marine captivity, in the name of Jesus.
16. Any strange fire that is burning because of my children, quench, in the name of Jesus.

17. O Lord, show my children Your way, in the name of Jesus.

18. Let the power to command my children to obey God's Word possess me, in the name of Jesus.

19. I destroy every satanic nature in my children, in the name of Jesus.

20. Father Lord, impart Your divine image upon my children, in the name of Jesus.

21. I destroy demonic fears that torment my children, in the name of Jesus.

22. Let the fear of God dominate the lives of my children, in the name of Jesus.

23. Lord Jesus, plant Your divine determination to obey Your Word at all cost inside my children, in the name of Jesus.

24. Let the angels of God direct the training of my children, in the name of Jesus.

25. Any power that was assigned to attack my children in their dreams, die, in the name of Jesus.

26. Heavenly Father, develop my children's brains and their spiritual lives, in the name of Jesus.

27. I cast out rebellious demons from my children, in the name of Jesus.

28. Let the knowledge of God manifest in the lives of my children, in the name of Jesus.

29. Every arrow of confusion, death and hell that was fired at my children, backfire, in the name of Jesus.

30. Every spirit of error that is militating against my children, I cast you out, in the name of Jesus.

31. Let the promises of God begin to manifest in my children's lives, in the name of Jesus.

32. Blood of Jesus, help my children to discover their destinies and fulfill them, in the name of Jesus.

33. Let my children develop well in every area of their lives, in the name of Jesus.

34. Any mistake that was prepared for my children, die, in the name of Jesus.

35. Let the Word of God be a guide to my children, in the name of Jesus.

36. O Lord, help me to love my children and have good relationship with them, in the name of Jesus.

37. I destroy every communication gap between my children and I, in the name of Jesus.

38. I disallow evil habits that have captured my children, in the name of Jesus.

39. O Lord, help me to see my children and my grand children established in Your ways, in the name of Jesus.

40. I receive power to reap the joy of training my children well, in the name of Jesus.

41. Let the love of God and other fruits of the Spirit begin to radiate in the lives of my children, in the name of Jesus.

42. I break and loose my children from captivity of death and hell, in the name of Jesus.

43. Let unmerited favor of God manifest in my children by fire, in the name of Jesus.

21
Chapter

PRAYERS TO OVERCOME AN EVIL HABIT

CHAPTER OVERVIEW

- *Discerning evil characters*
- *The old man*
- *Putting on new apparel*

DISCERNING EVIL CHARACTERS

Character is like apparel, which every man or woman wears that cannot be hidden for too long. This is true because character is a set of qualities that make somebody or something distinctive, especially somebody's qualities of mind and feeling. No matter how well a mad person dresses, once he exhibits his or her character, you would discern at once that the fellow has mental problem.

Likewise, character distinguishes a new man from an old man. In professional careers, dresses are used to distinguish professions. A footballer, police officer, nurse, soldier and security guard would wear a uniform that suits their profession.

> *"But now ye also put off all these; anger, wrath, malice, blasphemy, filthy communication out of your mouth. Lie not one to another, seeing that ye have put off the old man with his deeds; And have put on the new* man, *which is renewed in knowledge after the image of him that created him: Where there is neither Greek nor Jew, circumcision nor uncircumcision, Barbarian, Scythian, bond* nor *free: but Christ* is *all, and in all"* (Colossians 3:8-11).

There are certain characters that when you fail to put off, no matter how glorious your destiny is, they would still ruin your life. Your character identifies you with some group of people in the world. The world is a uniformed society and once you display your character, it aligns you with a certain group of people. As you can rightly tell what people do by observing the kind of clothes they wear on daily basis, you can also classify a certain group of people by their habits.

I define an evil group as a group of people that put on similar evil characters and placed themselves under an evil leadership (*See* 2 Corinthians 4:4).

Many people in the world have consciously placed themselves under the leadership of the god of this world. For such people, their minds have been blinded not to believe the gospel of Christ that can transform their lives and characters. As a result, they remain under the control of the devil.

Be mindful also that styles of clothes believers wear and stickers they put on their cars and houses they build are not enough to distinguish true Christians. What distinguishes true Christians is the spirit that dwells in them. By the fruits of their characters, you will know them. Anyone who is not born-again is bound to be at the mercy of evil habits or characters. It is probable that such persons' understanding remains darkened, and their hearts deceitful and desperately wicked.

"Having the understanding darkened, being alienated from the life of God through the ignorance that is in them, because of the blindness of their heart" (Ephesians 4:18).

"Thus said the LORD unto me; Go and stand in the gate of the children of the people, whereby the kings of Judah come in, and by the which they go out, and in all the gates of Jerusalem" (Jeremiah 17:19).

"Unto the pure all things are *pure: but unto them that are defiled and unbelieving* is *nothing pure; but even their mind and conscience is defiled"* (Titus 1:15).

"Is any man called being circumcised? Let him not become uncircumcised. Is any called in uncircumcision? Let him not be circumcised" (1 Corinthians 7:18).

The heart and mind of an unbeliever are homes to all manner of bad characters and are desperate to do evil because his conscience is deceitful and defiled. His mind remains a boiling pot of all manner of evil that are desperately waiting for an opportunity to be displayed. The will of such a person remains enslaved because the root of sin, which is the old man, is very active. The body of sin is deeply rooted in his foundation. The body of can only be destroyed when we crucify our old man on the cross of Jesus.

"Knowing this, that our old man is crucified with him, *that the body of sin might be destroyed, that henceforth we should not serve sin"* (Romans 6:6).

"That ye put off concerning the former conversation the old man, which is corrupt according to the deceitful lusts" (Ephesians 4:22).

"Lie not one to another, seeing that ye have put off the old man with his deeds" (Colossians 3:9).

All his actions are carnal because he has carnal mind, the mind of flesh that is filled with all manner of filthiness and dominated by evil habits.

"[7]Because the carnal mind is *enmity against God: for it is not subject to the law of God, neither indeed can be. [8]So then they that are in the flesh cannot please God. [9]But ye are not in the flesh, but in the Spirit, if so is that the Spirit of God dwells in you. Now if any man has not the Spirit of Christ, he is none of his. [12]Therefore, brethren, we are debtors, not to the flesh, to live after the flesh. [13]For if ye live after the flesh, ye shall die: but if ye through the Spirit do mortify the deeds of the body, ye shall live"* (Romans 8:7-9, 12-13).

Evil habit is a dominating tyrant. A hereditary evil is an inward enemy that you need to deal with urgently. Evil habit corrupts your moral nature and is able to waste a greatly destined person and send such person to hell fire. You cannot afford to take evil characters lightly.

> *"If so be that ye have heard him, and have been taught by him, as the truth is in Jesus: That ye put off concerning the former conversation the old man, which is corrupt according to the deceitful lusts; And be renewed in the spirit of your mind; And that ye put on the new man, which after God is created in righteousness and true holiness. Wherefore putting away lying, speaks every man truth with his neighbor: for we are members one of another. Be ye angry, and sin not: let not the sun goes down upon your wrath: Neither give place to the devil. Let him that stole steal no more: but rather let him labor, working with* his *hands the thing, which is good, that he may have to give to him that needed. Let no corrupt communication proceed out of your mouth, but that, which is good to the use of edifying, that it may minister grace unto the hearers. And grieve not the holy Spirit of God, whereby ye are sealed unto the day of redemption. Let all bitterness, and wrath, and anger, and clamor, and evil speaking, be put away from you, with all malice: And be ye kind one to another, tenderhearted, forgiving one another, even as God for Christ's sake hath forgiven you"* (Ephesians 4:21-32).

THE OLD MAN

A good number of Christians attend churches regularly and assume the title "Christian" without really knowing the weight and authority a Christian possesses. A Christian is one who had an encounter with Christ and has become a new creature by His grace. Old things have passed away, and a new relationship with God and his fellow man established.

The old man is the natural self that has the resemblance of Adam. It is still under the curse of Adam's sin. The difference between the old and new man is that while the old man remains under the law of sin and death, the new man remains under the law of the Spirit and life.

> *"Therefore if any man* be *in Christ,* he is *a new creature: old things are passed away; behold, all things are become new"* (2 Corinthians 5:17).

> *"And when he had found him, he brought him unto Antioch. In addition, it happened, that a whole year they assembled themselves with the church, and taught much people. And the disciples were called Christians first in Antioch"* (Acts 11:26).

Many people fill their lives with religious activities when the deeds of the old man constantly overrun their lives. Such people do not have any place for God in the lives.

CHARACTERISTICS OF THE OLD MAN

LIES: To lie is to say something that is not true in a conscious effort to deceive somebody. The bible called devil the father of all lies. Unfortunately, lying has become a way of life for so many Christians. Lying is an evil habit that you must put off at once if you want to put on the garment of righteousness. Make it a duty to speak the truth at all times no matter the consequence.

> *"Wherefore putting away lying, speaks every man truth with his neighbor: for we are members one of another"* (Ephesians 4:25).

> *"For the rich men thereof are full of violence, and the inhabitants thereof have spoken lies, and their tongue* is *deceitful in their mouth"* (Micah 6:12).

> *"Their throat* is *an open sepulcher; with their tongues they have used deceit; the poison of asps* is *under their lips"* (Romans 3:13).

Truth is the character of true Christians all over the world. God hates lies and deceit because they are not His nature, but the nature of the devil. You cannot claim to be a

Christian and tell lies to deceive your neighbor. A tongue that tells lies is defiled and needs urgent New Testament deliverance. Some Christians give untrue testimonies to deceive themselves. Such lies are the character of the devil. You cannot tell lies to please God. It is not possible.

> *"Now the Spirit speaketh expressly, that in the latter times some shall depart from the faith, giving heed to seducing spirits, and doctrines of devils; Speaking lies in hypocrisy; having their conscience seared with a hot iron"* (1 Timothy 4:1-2).

> *"But the fearful, and unbelieving, and the abominable, and murderers, and whoremongers, and sorcerers, and idolaters, and all liars, shall have their part in the lake which burneth with fire and brimstone: which is the second death"* (Revelation 21:8).

God will judge all lies no matter who is involved. Preachers must courageously rebuke and preach against lies. It is heartbreaking for a preacher or a leader to encourage lies. God would judge these are categories of people fiercely –

- ***Unbelievers*** (*See* John 3:18-20, 36).
- ***Defilers*** (*See* Leviticus 18:21-27; Deuteronomy 22: 5; Proverbs 6:16-19).
- ***Murderers*** (*See* 1 John 3:15).
- ***Whoremongers, fornicators, adulterers*** (*See* Matthew 5:27-30).
- ***Sorcerers, witches and people using familiar spirits*** (*See* Deuteronomy 18:914; 1 Samuel 28:5-11; 1 Chronicles 10:13-14; Isaiah 8:19).
- ***Idolaters*** (*See* Exodus 20:3-5; 1 John 5:21).
- ***Liars*** (*See* Revelation 21:27, 8; 22:15).

God will banish sinners from his presence forever and from the holy city. He will forever cast them into the lake of fire. They cannot stain or desecrate heaven.

STEALING: Grabbing something that belongs to another person illegally is not the character of a child of God. The grace to work and provide for oneself has been given to all men. If you have been providing for your family through stealing, it is time for you to stop. Look for a job and work with your hands in a right way. Many lazy people complain a lot for lack of jobs, but if you are diligent and determined, you will discover your talent soon in the name of Jesus.

> *"Let him that stole steal no more: but rather let him labor, working with his hands the thing, which is good, that he may have to give to him that needed"* (Ephesians 4:28).

> *"Ye shall not steal, neither deal falsely, neither lie one to another. [13]Thou shall not defraud thy neighbor, neither rob* him: *the wages of him that is hired shall not abide with thee all night until the morning"* (Leviticus 19:11, 13).

"For I the LORD love judgment, I hate robbery for burnt offering; and I will direct their work in truth, and I will make an everlasting covenant with them" (Isaiah 61:8).

"Will ye steal, murder, and commit adultery, and swear falsely, and burn incense unto Baal, and walk after other gods whom ye know not" (Jeremiah 7:9).

God gave all men diverse talents. Every serious minded person would discover his or her talent and use it to the glory of God. The reason why people steal and defraud others is that they have failed to discover their rightful places in life. No one can be happy without discovering his place in life. If you do not get to a God's ordained place for your life, you can never fulfill your destiny, no matter how much wealth you gather.

If you feel dissatisfied in the place you are right now, you could have stolen another person's place. When you fail to position yourself rightly, you may occupy another person's position. If you are paying people that work for you less that they deserve, you are stealing from them. If you receive reward for what you did not labor for, you are also stealing. When you did no work but receive wages, you are stealing. You need to start doing something. If what you are doing does not give you joy, you may be in a wrong position. If you pray with sincere heart and determination, God will give you a suitable job. Everyone on earth has a position. God cannot create you if he has no place for you to occupy on earth.

"Verily, verily, I say unto you, He that entereth not by the door into the sheepfold, but climbeth up some other way, the same is a thief and a robber" (John 10:1).

"And it came to pass after this, that Absalom prepared him chariots and horses, and fifty men to run before him. And Absalom rose up early, and stood beside the way of the gate: and it was so, *that when any man that had a controversy came to the king for judgment, then Absalom called unto him, and said, Of what city* art *thou? In addition, he said, Thy servant* is *of one of the tribes of Israel. And Absalom said unto him, See, thy matters* are *good and right; but there is no man deputed of the king to hear thee. Absalom said moreover, Oh that I were made judge in the land, that every man which hath any suit or cause might come unto me, and I would do him justice! And it was* so, *that when any man came nigh to him to do him obeisance, he put forth his hand, and took him, and kissed him. And on this manner did Absalom to all Israel that came to the king for judgment: so Absalom stole the hearts of the men of Israel"* (2 Samuel 15:1-6).

When you live your life by robbing others, you will definitely not have rest or good success. Before God created the world, He has positioned everything on earth the way they are supposed to be. You cannot come to this earth and begin to misplace things. God has placed people in their rightful places. Therefore, no one can succeed through robbery. It is foolishness to believe that if you do wrong, God will not judge you or ask you why. Every godly person must hate what God hates and love what God loves.

It is also foolishness and deceit to imagine that you are a child of God while you steal, murder, commit adultery, swear falsely, burn incense to Baal, walk after other gods and do all manner of evil things. If you live your life by doing these things, then you are a thief before God. Absalom died because he wanted the throne of his father at all cost. You might be destined for an earthly throne, but if you want it at all cost, you will surely fail. When you deceive other people, you are a thief and you must surely pay for whatever that you steal.

EVIL SPEAKING: To speak evil about other people is evil itself. It is destructive and you must put it off from your life once you are born-again. You cannot say that you are a child of God when you continue speaking evil of other people. It is very deadly and destructive.

> *"Let no corrupt communication proceed out of your mouth, but that which is good to the use of edifying, that it may minister grace unto the hearers"* (Ephesians 4:29).

> *"The LORD shall cut off all flattering lips, and the tongue that speaketh proud things"* (Psalms 12:3).

> *"Thy tongue deviseth mischiefs; like a sharp razor, working deceitfully. Thou lovest evil more than good;* and *lying rather than to speak righteousness. Selah. Thou lovest all devouring words, O* thou *deceitful tongue"* (Psalms 52:2-4).

Corruption is the work of the devil. When your mouth is corrupt, it becomes easier to engage in evil speaking. A born-again Christian asks for grace to overcome speaking evil of people at all times. It is rather strange that many people become Christians, yet they refuse to behave like Christ. They claim to be born-again but operate on their old selves, which is the carnal self. This is strange.

Corrupt communication is of the devil and his children. A good word that edifies and ministers grace to the hearer comes from God. Through your communication, people can tell where you belong. Flattering lips in God's house are working for the devil. The tongues that speak proudly will be cut off. You need to watch your tongue to prove which kingdom you belong to. You can do it yourself and judge rightly.

> *"An ungodly man diggeth up evil: and in his lips* there is *as a burning fire. A forward man soweth strife: and a whisperer separateth chief friends"* (Proverbs 16:27-28).

> *"The words of a talebearer* are *as wounds, and they go down into the innermost parts of the belly. Burning lips and a wicked heart* are as *a potsherd covered with silver*

dross. He that hated dissembleth with his lips, and layeth up deceit within him; When he speaketh fair, believes him not: for there are *seven abominations in his heart.* Whose *hatred is covered by deceit, his wickedness shall be showed before the* whole *congregation"* (Proverbs 26:22-26).

When you use your tongue to device iniquity, you have become an evil speaker. If you do not have control over what comes out of your mouth, you are also an evil speaker. If your words are sharp like a razor and full of deceit, you are an evil speaker. If you love evil more than good, you are an evil speaker. If you are comfortable and happy when you tell lies, no matter what position you occupy in the body of Christ, you are a child of the devil. If you chose to speak lies when you know the truth, you are an agent of the devil.

What you need is deliverance that comes from Christ. You need help because God did not create you to work for the devil. A true child of God would hate lies and evil speaking. God did not create you so that you can use your tongue to devour others. However, it could not be your fault because all men are born with evil tongues. However, you would be held responsible only when you refuse to accept deliverance and salvation that Jesus gives to all men freely. Jesus wants to help you acquire a new inheritance in the spirit.

"Come unto me, all ye *that labor and are heavy laden and I will give you rest. Take my yoke upon you, and learn of me; for I am meek and lowly in heart: and ye shall find rest unto your souls. For my yoke is easy, and my burden is light"* (Matthew 11:28-30).

There are people God called ungodly. How do we know such people when we see them? The Lord said they dig up evil; they look for trouble and use their lips to spread such evil like a burning fire. They use their speeches to sow strife and separate close friends. Evil speaking is a very dangerous thing. If you do not put them away from your life, they will steal your peace and joy forever. God hates evil speaking and conspiracy.

"O generation of vipers, how can ye, being evil, speaks good things? For out of the abundance of the heart the mouth speaketh. A good man out of the good treasure of the heart bringeth forth good things: and an evil man out of the evil treasure bringeth forth evil things. But I say unto you, That every idle word that men shall speak, they shall give account thereof in the Day of Judgment. For by thy words thou shall be justified, and by thy words thou shall be condemned" (Matthew 12:34-37).

The sin of evil speaking can kills more people than guns and wars do. Miriam and Aaron, Moses elder sister and brother, spoke evil against Moses and God judged them.

Miriam became a leper. Likewise, the ten spies were not allowed to enter the land of Canaan for the second time for delivering an evil judgment.

Korah, Dothan and Abiriam perished with all their family members for speaking evil. The ground opened and swallowed them alive. God hates evil speaking. The words of an evil speaker or talebearer are like wounds that go down into the innermost parts of the stomach. An injury inside the stomach is one of the most painful and disturbing wounds one can bear. The truth is that when you reject Christ, you cannot avoid evil speaking. Evil speaking is full of idle words. Keep in mind that you must give account of every evil intent, purpose and deed and idle word, which you did not repent of.

BITTERNESS AND WRATH: Bitterness and wrath are evidences that someone lacks the character of God. When the love of God resonates in your life, no amount of indignities, gossips and opposition can cause you to hate or become bitter. You will not allow bitterness or wrath to put you off the love of Christ.

> *"Let all bitterness, and wrath, and anger, and clamor, and evil speaking, be put away from you, with all malice"* (Ephesians 4:31).

> *"Looking diligently lest any man fail of the grace of God; lest any root of bitterness springing up trouble* you, *and there by many be defiled; Lest there* be *any fornicator, or profane person, as Esau, who for one morsel of meat sold his birthright. For ye know how that afterward, when he would have inherited the blessing, he was rejected: for he found no place of repentance, though he sought it carefully with tears"* (Hebrews 12:15-17).

Believers who have dealt with bitterness in their lives ought to do everything possible not to entangle themselves in bitterness again. This is because when you fall into bitterness and wrath the second time, the bondage might become double.

> *"But if ye have bitter envying and strife in your hearts, glory not, and lie not against the truth. This wisdom descendeth not from above, but* is *earthly, sensual, and devilish. For where envying and strife* is, *there* is *confusion and every evil work"* (James 3:14-16).

God hates bitterness and no one who wishes to please God would entertain bitterness and wrath. Children of God are known for being peaceful, gentle and generous, full of mercy and bearing good fruits. Children of God are impartial and are not hypocrites.

ANGER AND CLAMOR: Anger destroys all form of kindness and peace. Anger denied Moses entry into the Promised Land. If not controlled, anger can waste a whole city. Anger incites people to react violently without considering the consequences.

Anger brings hatred, retaliation and resorts to violence. However, the Scriptures implored us to:

> *"Let all bitterness, and wrath, and anger, and clamor, and evil speaking, be put away from you, with all malice"* (Ephesians 4:31).

> *"Cease from anger, and forsake wrath: fret not thyself in any wise to do evil"* (Psalms 37:8).

> *"But whoso committed adultery with a woman lacketh understanding: he that doeth it destroyed his own soul"* (Proverbs 6:32).

> *"But I say unto you, That whosoever is angry with his brother without a cause shall be in danger of the judgment: and whosoever shall say to his brother, Racas, shall be in danger of the council: but whosoever shall say, Thou fool, shall be in danger of hell fire"* (Matthew 5:22).

You must put away these things before you can convince people that you are a Christian. God commanded all His children to cease from anger and forsake wrath. Anything less than that is demonic and unacceptable by God. Anger puts people in the danger of eternal damnation.

> *"But now ye also put off all these; anger, wrath, malice, blasphemy, filthy communication out of your mouth"* (Colossians 3:8).

> *"Wherefore laying aside all malice, and all guile, and hypocrisies, and envies, and all evil speaking"* (1 Peter 2:1).

To keep malice and claim to be a child of God is contradictory. You must lay aside all forms of evil if you really want to be a friend of God. Pray fervently against these dangerous evil habits. Christians are not to grieve the Holy Spirit.

> *"And grieve not the Holy Spirit of God, whereby ye are sealed unto the day of redemption"* (Ephesians 4:30).

> *"But they rebelled, and vexed his Holy Spirit: therefore he was turned to be their enemy,* and *he fought against them"* (Isaiah 63:10).

> *"But Peter said, Ananias, why hath Satan filled thine heart to lie to the Holy Ghost, and to keep back part of the price of the land?"* (Acts 5:3).

> *"Ye stiff-necked and uncircumcised in heart and ears, ye do always resist the Holy Ghost: as your fathers* did, *so do ye"* (Acts 7:51).

When a Christian fornicates or commits adultery, he grieves the Holy Spirit (*See* Ephesians 5:3, Acts 15:28-29; Colossians 3:5).

When a Christian does anything unclean, he grieves the Holy Spirit (*See* 1 Thessalonians 4:7, Ephesians 5:3; Romans 1:23-24; 6:21).

When a Christian becomes covetous, he grieves the Holy Spirit (*See* Ephesians 5:3; Exodus 20:17; Ezekiel 33:31; Luke 12:15).

When a Christian becomes filthy and begins to live a filthy life, he grieves the Holy Spirit (*See* Ephesians 5:4; James 1:21; 2 Peter 2:10; Psalms 53:1-4).

When a Christian indulges in foolish talking, he grieves the Holy Spirit (*See* Ephesians 5:4; James 1:26-27; Proverbs 10:19; 1 Peter 3:10).

When a Christian backslides, he grieves the Holy Spirit (*See* Proverbs 26:18-19).

Many professing Christians have deviated from the standards of the Bible. However, the Word of God still stands sure. These things should not be named among Christians. Christians are not to have fellowship with darkness but are to be filled with the Holy Spirit. The Holy Spirit makes Christianity sweet and refreshing. Any character that opposes God's righteousness is an evil character that must not be found in your life.

PUTTING ON NEW APPAREL

When you become a Christian, a miracle takes place. The old man (*flesh*) dies and gives place to a new man (*spirit*). So-called Christians who retain the old man and his deeds cannot exercise authority over the old man and his activities. You have to put off the old man and all his activities before you can reign over him.

> *"But now ye also put off all these; anger, wrath, malice, blasphemy, filthy communication out of your mouth. Lie not one to another, seeing that ye have put off the old man with his deeds"* (Colossians 3:8-9).

> *"Knowing this, that our old man is crucified with* him, *that the body of sin might be destroyed, that henceforth we should not serve sin"* (Romans 6:6).

> *"Forasmuch then as Christ hath suffered for us in the flesh, arm yourselves likewise with the same mind: for he that hath suffered in the flesh hath ceased from sin; That he no longer should live the rest of* his *time in the flesh to the lusts of men, but to the will of God. For the time past of* our *life may suffice us to have wrought the will of the Gentiles, when we walked in lasciviousness, lusts, excess of wine, revellings, banqueting, and abominable idolatries: Wherein they think it strange that ye run not with* them *to the same excess of riot, speaking evil of* you*"* (1 Peter 4:1-4).

You must put off characters of the old man, which include anger, wrath, malice, blasphemy, filthy communication, lies, etc. When you become a new creature (*born of the Spirit*), filled with the power of the spirit, you have control and authority over your old nature, where devil operates. Then you can exercise authority over the flesh and all its appearances.

If you have a father who is a drunkard, you may need to exercise your spiritual power over him sometimes. For instance, when he becomes drunk and insists that he will drive, you would discern that if he does, he might possibly have an accident and kill himself. If he disagrees with your pleas and insists on driving under the influence of alcohol, what you need to do is to get ready spiritually, put on your new apparel as a police officer and prepare for action. If he speeds more than you would permit, you raise your hand of authority and stop him.

At that point, you no longer act as his son or his daughter. You are a representative of a kingdom of God and disobedience is not acceptable in the kingdom of your Father, who is in heaven. Do you know that you are a representative of heaven and an ambassador of Christ? Do you know that you belong to a royal priesthood? As a Christian, the old man of drunkenness and evil desires can no longer push you around.

You are no longer under the control of the works of the flesh. Instead, they are under your control.

> *"That ye put off concerning the former conversation the old man, which is corrupt according to the deceitful lusts; And be renewed in the spirit of your mind; And that ye put on the new man, which after God is created in righteousness and true holiness. Wherefore putting away lying, speaks every man truth with his neighbor: for we are members one of another. Be ye angry, and sin not: let not the sun goes down upon your wrath: Neither give place to the devil. Let him that stole steal no more: but rather let him labor, working with* his *hands the thing, which is good, that he may have to give to him that needed. Let no corrupt communication proceed out of your mouth, but that, which is good to the use of edifying, that it may minister grace unto the hearers. And grieve not the holy Spirit of God, whereby ye are sealed unto the day of redemption. Let all bitterness, and wrath, and anger, and clamor, and evil speaking, be put away from you, with all malice: And be ye kind one to another, tenderhearted, forgiving one another, even as God for Christ's sake hath forgiven you"* (Ephesians 4:22-32).

> *"Now the works of the flesh are manifest, which are* these; *Adultery, fornication, uncleanness, lasciviousness, Idolatry, witchcraft, hatred, variance, emulations, wrath, strife, seditions, heresies, Envyings, murders, drunkenness, revellings, and such like: of the which I tell you before, as I have also told* you *in time past, that they which do such things shall not inherit the kingdom of God"* (Galatians 5:19-21).

When you fail to recognize and assume your rights and authority as a new man of the spirit, you would remain at the mercy of the flesh (*old man*). You continue to wear your old apparel. As a Christian, you must put off the old garments of sin and flesh. A divine miracle took place immediately you were born-again. You ceased to belong to the old man. You became a new man of the spirit. Therefore, as a new man you must not respond to the desires of the flesh such as fornication, evil desires, anger, uncleanness, covetousness, wrath, malice, inordinate affection, filthiness, blasphemes, lying, etc.

> *"And have put on the new* man, *which is renewed in knowledge after the image of him that created him"* (Colossians 3:10).

> *"For in Christ Jesus neither circumcision availed anything, nor uncircumcision, but a new creature"* (Galatians 6:15).

You must put on a new spiritual lifestyle and enter into new relationship with the people of God. There are no more barriers, whether racial, cultural or social. There is no more discrimination, of slave or freeborn, educated or illiterate. You can go to God just the same way your pastor goes to God and gets whatever he prays from God.

"Now therefore ye are no more strangers and foreigners, but fellow citizens with the saints, and of the household of God; [20]*And are built upon the foundation of the apostles and prophets, Jesus Christ himself being the chief corner* stone" (Ephesians 2:19-20).

You can get your healing, break the yokes of bad habits and enjoy a new life of righteousness and abundance in Christ. You can stop any satanic move by a wave of hand of prayer and every knee must bow as you mention the name of Christ in faith.

PRAYERS TO OVERCOME AN EVIL HABIT

Bible reference: Romans 7:14-25

Begin with praise and worship

1. I break and loose myself from every evil character, in the name of Jesus.
2. I command evil identity in my life to catch fire and burn to ashes, in the name of Jesus.
3. I destroy spiritual apparel of bad character on my life, in the name of Jesus.
4. I waste any evil uniform that was designed to waste my destiny, in the name of Jesus.
5. I withdraw my life from any evil group that I involved myself, in the name of Jesus.
6. Every yoke of bad habit in my life, break, in the name of Jesus.
7. Let every property of the god of this world in my possession catch fire and burn to ashes, in the name of Jesus.
8. O Lord, clothe me with Your spiritual apparel of righteousness, in the name of Jesus.
9. Any evil lifestyle that has arrested me, release me by force, in the name of Jesus.
10. Let darkness disappear from my understanding and reasoning, in the name of Jesus.
11. O Lord, wash my mind with the blood of Jesus, in the name of Jesus.
12. Every seed of wickedness that was planted in my life, die, in the name of Jesus.
13. Let every serpent of bad habit in my life die immediately, in the name of Jesus.
14. I break and loose myself from evil desires and thoughts, in the name of Jesus.
15. Let the seed of deceit, defilement and slavery in my life die by fire, in the name of Jesus.
16. I command the presence of sin in my life to be uprooted from its root, in the name of Jesus.

17. Fire of God, burn every carnal lust and evil domination in my life, in the name of Jesus.
18. Blood of Jesus, flow into my foundation and uproot every dominating tyrant and inherited evil, in the name of Jesus.
19. I break and loose myself from corruption and strange actions, in the name of Jesus.
20. Let my encounter with my Lord Jesus deliver me perfectly from my old nature and characters, in the name of Jesus.
21. Any evil action that has refused to let me go, die, in the name of Jesus.
22. O Lord, arise and deliver me from the captivity of the old man, in the name of Jesus.
23. Let darkness in my life scatter, in the name of Jesus.
24. I break and loose myself from evil relationship, in the name of Jesus.
25. I command the deeds of the old man in my life to die, in the name of Jesus.
26. Any bad thing that has become a way of life in my life, I reject you; die, in the name of Jesus.
27. I put off evil garments of death and corruption in my life, in the name of Jesus.
28. O Lord, help me to hate lies, deceit and evil practices with perfect hatred, in the name of Jesus.
29. Any serpent on my tongue that is defiling my utterances, come out and die, in the name of Jesus.
30. O Lord, deliver me from conscious and unconscious practice of witchcrafts, in the name of Jesus.
31. Any habit that has banished me from the divine plan and promises of God, die, in the name of Jesus.
32. I deliver myself from lying and stealing, in the name of Jesus.
33. Every spirit of laziness and complaining in me, die, in the name of Jesus.
34. Any evil power that has arrested my talent, release it by force, in the name of Jesus.
35. O Lord, help me to discover my place in life and fulfill my destiny, in the name of Jesus.
36. O Lord, take me to a place You have ordained for my life, in the name of Jesus.

37. Fire of God, enter into my mouth and burn demons that are speaking through me, in the name of Jesus.

38. Let seeds of evil speaking and evil silence be uprooted from my mouth now, in the name of Jesus.

39. Father Lord, deliver me from bitterness, wrath, and clamor forever, in the name of Jesus.

40. Every good thing that I lost through evil habit, I recover you double, in the name of Jesus.

41. I discharge evil deeds of the old man from every organ of my life, in the name of Jesus.

42. Let the backbone of evil habits in my life be broken by fire, in the name of Jesus.

43. I break and loose myself from any evil relationship that is promoting bad habits in my life, in the name of Jesus.

44. Every yoke of bad habit in my life, break, in the name of Jesus.

45. I take authority over evil habits that are wasting God's nature in my life, in the name of Jesus.

46. Let the light of God enter into every dark area of my life, in the name of Jesus.

47. Blood of Jesus, renew my mind and purge my conscience of evil, in the name of Jesus.

48. I terminate any satanic program that is running in my life, in the name of Jesus.

49. You, my heaven of righteousness, open now, in the name of Jesus.

50. I refuse to respond to the desires of the flesh from today, in the name of Jesus.

51. O Lord, clothe me with new spiritual lifestyle, in the name of Jesus.

52. I walk into a new relationship with God henceforth, in the name of Jesus.

53. Every barrier or wall of partition between God and me is removed forever, in the name of Jesus.

54. Every appearance of bad habit in my life is terminated by death, in the name of Jesus.

22
Chapter

PRAYERS FOR YOUR CHILDREN'S DELIVERANCE

CHAPTER OVERVIEW

- *The most effective deliverance for children*
- *The role of the wife as a mother*
- *The love of a good husband*
- *Evil carry-over of parents' debts*
- *Evil inheritance*

THE MOST EFFECTIVE DELIVERANCE FOR CHILDREN

The most effective way to keep children out of demonic oppression is when parents maintain impeccable peace at home. When the husband and wife keep and obey God's Word, the children would have less battle to fight. Wise parents think for the good of their children and are always willing to do things that would make their children prosperous. Therefore, the best way to deliver a child from satanic attack or oppression is to keep the covered in the covenant of love, peace and protection of God.

> *"And above all these things* put on *charity, which is the bond of perfectness. And let the peace of God rule in your hearts, to the which also ye are called in one body; and be ye thankful"* (Colossians 3:14-15).

In a family where husband, wife and the children understand their roles as stipulated in the Bible, evil spirit will not have legal grounds to stand upon to plan attacks. Families that manifest true love of God always have peace of God and enjoy divine presence.

THE ROLE OF THE WIFE AS A MOTHER

The very first duty of a wife in a home is submission to the husband as God demands. Absolute submission must be observed without any condition and in the spirit of love. As Scriptures put it:

> *"Wives, submit yourselves unto your own husbands, as it is fit in the Lord"* (Colossians 3:18).

> *"That they may teach the young women to be sober, to love their husbands, to love their children,* To be *discreet, chaste, keepers at home, good, obedient to their own husbands, that the word of God be not blasphemed"* (Titus 2:4-5).

A wife's submission to her husband guides the children, especially the young women to know how to submit and be sober. Love in the family blocks evil spirit from entering into the home. Women are the owners and keepers of homes and by so doing, the children in the home learns from their mother how to obey God.

Wives who are obedient to their husbands inspire the rest of the family members to be obedient also. Submission suggests the presence of intimacy and mutual understanding between husband and wife, having one mind and will. Through submission, a wife honors her husband as her head.

> *"Even as Sara obeyed Abraham, calling him lord: whose daughters ye are, as long as ye do well, and are not afraid with any amazement"* (1 Peter 3:6).

> *"But I would have you know, that the head of every man is Christ; and the head of the woman* is *the man; and the head of Christ* is *God"* (1 Corinthians 11:3).

God ordained that the husband should be the head and wife, the body. The Scriptures declared Sarah as an epitome of submission, who honored her husband calling him lord. The duty of the wife is to obey her husband in all domestic matters and in everything except that, which is contrary to faith and pure conscience. Where God's authority is made plain, the authority of the husband that contradicts God Word ceases. In such case, it is better to obey God that men.

> *"But Peter and John answered and said unto them, Whether it be right in the sight of God to hearken unto you more than unto God, judge ye"* (Acts 4:19).

> *"Then Peter and the* other *apostles answered and said we ought to obey God rather than men"* (Acts 5:29).

The husband has the right to direct the style of his family's life and experience. He directs or regulates the education of his family members, employment and if the wife must differ from her husband's decision, it must be with respect, good manner of approach, stating her points humbly and leaving the matter to God even after detailing her reasons. It is her duty to make her husband and her entire family happy.

> *"Wives, submit yourselves unto your own husbands, as unto the Lord. For the husband is the head of the wife, even as Christ is the head of the church: and he is the savior of the body. Therefore as the church is subject unto Christ, so* let *the wives* be *to their own husbands in everything"* (Ephesians 5:22-24).

A virtuous wife cooperates with her husband in spiritual and family matters. A husband must be respected and not to be reduced to a part-time nurse or babysitter, while the wife becomes the head mistress over her husband. Women who submit to their husbands are obeying God's command and the Lord rewards them for doing so. Even when your husband is not meeting up with his responsibilities, you, as a wife, have no reason to fail in your duties too.

You must be truthful and faithful to your husband. You must recognize and joyfully accept and respect your husband's position as the head of the family as ordained by God. You should not do so only when he is kind to you or when he merits your obedience. With time, God will touch your husband and he will do all that God expects of him.

One of the greatest problems in many homes is impatient. A husband and his wife ought to be patient people in their home. You can focus on fulfilling God's command to you as an individual instead of finding faults. No wise woman will pull down her own house because she sees another woman doing so. A wise woman builds her house.

Many women have left their husbands to suffer alone because they failed to meet up with their God-given role as the head. That is how such women give the devil a place in their lives. As a result, devil stepped in and did great damages in those families. The Scriptures warned:

> *"Neither give place to the devil"* (Ephesians 4:27).

> *"Submit yourselves therefore to God. Resist the devil, and he will flee from you"* (James 4:7).

THE LOVE OF A GOOD HUSBAND

As the head of the wife, God commanded the husband to love his wife as Christ loves the church. His love for the wife should not be as ordinary people love their wives, but as Christ loves the church. A good husband does not love himself more than he loves his wife. Because love knows no struggle, animosity or fighting, a good husband loves his wife as his own body because they are one flesh.

> "[28]*So ought men to love their wives as their own bodies. He that loveth his wife loveth himself.* [29]*For no man ever yet hated his own flesh; but nourisheth and cherisheth it, even as the Lord the church:* [30]*For we are members of his body, of his flesh, and of his bones.* [31]*For this cause shall a man leave his father and mother, and shall be joined unto his wife, and they two shall be one flesh"* (Ephesians 5:31, 28-30).

A good husband has the same care for the comfort of his wife, which he has for himself. He takes her as one with himself. He nourishes and cherishes her by providing food, raiment and things that she needs.

> *"Husbands, love* your *wives, and be not bitter against them"* (Colossians 3:19).

> *"Likewise, ye husbands, dwell with* them *according to knowledge, giving honor unto the wife, as unto the weaker vessel, and as being heirs together of the grace of life; that your prayers be not hindered"* (1 Peter 3:7).

Therefore, as you honor yourself, as a husband, honor your wife the same way. If it is not possible to be harsh on yourself, do not be harsh on your wife because she is the weaker vessel. When your body needs sleep, you honor its demand. When it needs food, you do everything possible to provide food for your body. Likewise you should defend your wife, provide for her spiritually, materially and psychologically, as you would do for yourself. You have to use your strength to protect your wife as a weaker vessel. You must study your wife, delight in her and understand when she needs your attention.

> "[1]*Though I speak with the tongues of men and of angels, and have not charity, I am become* as *sounding brass, or a tinkling cymbal.* [4]*Charity suffered long,* and *is kind; charity envied not; charity vaunted not itself, is not puffed up,* [5]*Doth not behave itself unseemly, seeketh not her own, is not easily provoked, thinketh no evil;* [6]*Rejoiceth not in iniquity, but rejoiceth in the truth;* [7]*Beareth all things, believeth all things, hopeth all things, endureth all things.* [8]*Charity never faileth: but whether* there are *prophecies, they shall fail; whether* there are *tongues, they shall cease; whether* there be *knowledge, it shall vanish away"* (1 Corinthians 13:1, 4-8).

Scriptures made it binding that husbands must love and cherish their wives, as Christ loves his church. You are to comfort and support her, and seek for her best spiritual good and shun every form of anger or bitterness.

> *"Let thy fountain is blessed: and rejoice with the wife of thy youth. Let her be as the loving hind and pleasant roe; let her breasts satisfy thee at all times; and be thou ravished always with her love"* (Proverbs 5:18-19).

Husbands should be the source of their wives' joy, peace and confidence. You cannot allow anything to separate you from your wife. You must not allow any friend or family member to come between you and your wife. To leave your family and cleave to your wife is God's commandment.

The kind of relationship that exists between a husband and his wife defines the quality of defense their children get against satanic attacks. Good relationship between children and their parents is also very important. Above all, the relationship between the whole family and God, how they receive and obey the Word of God, is the most important.

> *"Children, obey your parents in the Lord: for this is right. Honor thy father and mother; (which is the first commandment with promise;) That it may be well with thee, and thou mayest live long on the earth. And, ye fathers, provoke not your children to wrath: but bring them up in the nurture and admonition of the Lord"* (Ephesians 6:1-4).

Demons cannot gain access into the life of any child who obey his parents in the Lord and honor his father and mother. There is a promise attached with children's obedient to their parents. Children who obey their parents live long and prosper on earth. It is the duty of the parents to tell their children their responsibilities and make sure that they obey. Parents are to behave lovingly to their children and make sure that they rebuke and correct them the right way.

> *"And Tamar put ashes on her head, and rent her garment of divers colors that* was *on her, and laid her hand on her head, and went on crying"* (2 Samuel 13:19).

> *"Then Adonijah the son of Haggith exalted himself, saying, I will be king: and he prepared him chariots and horsemen, and fifty men to run before him. And his father had not displeased him at any time in saying, why hast thou done so? And he also* was a *very goodly* man; *and* his mother *bare him after Absalom"* (1 Kings 1:5-6).

Parents should be good examples to their children through the lives they live. If you do not want your children to live immoral lives, then you must not allow the devil to drag you into immorality. Sin is contagious and can spread to unborn generation. Parents are not to abuse their authorities over their children by severe treatment in both word and deed.

In the occasion of correcting a child, parents should be moderate and reasonable. Their discipline must not communicate extreme anger at their children. Otherwise, they would have wasted their time trying to correct their children. Distances between children and parents should be discouraged. Otherwise, devil would take every slight advantage.

> *"Fathers, provoke not your children* to anger, *lest they be discouraged"* (Colossians 3:21).

> *"Seeing that Abraham shall surely become a great and mighty nation and all the nations of the earth shall be blessed in him? For I know him, that he will command his children and his household after him, and they shall keep the way of the LORD, to do justice and judgment; that the LORD may bring upon Abraham that which he hath spoken of him"* (Genesis 18:18-19).

God's Word must be the central focus for making every rule and regulation in the family. Fathers should not be harsh or immoderate to their children, lest they discourage them.

EVIL CARRY-OVER OF PARENTS' DEBTS

Parents who wish their children well and want to see them enjoy lives ought to deal with the consequences of their past sins properly. They must not allow devil to transfer these consequences to their children. Sin is debt to Satan. Only Jesus could pay the debt of sin. Parents must let Jesus settle the debt of their sins in order to allow their children to prosper.

For instance, when Ahab and Jezebel killed Naboth, they entered into a debt with Satan, thereby putting their children in bondage of Satan.

> *"And it came to pass, when Ahab heard that Naboth was dead, that Ahab rose up to go down to the vineyard of Jabots the Jezreelite, to take possession of it. And the word of the LORD came to Elijah the Tishbite, saying, Arise, go down to meet Ahab king of Israel, which is in Samaria: behold,* he is *in the vineyard of Naboth, whither he is gone down to possess it"* (1 Kings 21:16-18).

King Ahab and his wife, Jezebel, conspired, killed Naboth, and sowed evil into their family. Ahab rose and went to Naboth's vineyard to possess his land. As he entered into the vineyard, God sent Elisha to curse him. Elijah met him in the vineyard and rebuked him saying, *"Hast thou killed and taken possession? In the place where dogs licked the blood of Naboth shall dogs lick thy blood."*

> *"19 And thou shalt speak unto him, saying, Thus saith the LORD, Hast thou killed, and also taken possession? In addition, thou shall speak unto him, saying, Thus saith the LORD, sin the place where dogs licked the blood of Naboth shall dogs lick thy blood, even thine. 21 Behold, I will bring evil upon thee, and will take away thy posterity, and will cut off from Ahab him that pisseth against the wall, and him that is shut up and left in Israel, 22 And will make thine house like the house of Jeroboam the son of Nebat, and like the house of Baasha the son of Ahijah, for the provocation wherewith thou hast provoked* me *to anger, and made Israel to sin. 23 And of Jezebel also spake the LORD, saying, the dogs shall eat Jezebel by the wall of Jezreel. 24 Him that dieth of Ahab in the city the dogs shall eat; and him that dieth in the field shall the fowls of the air eat. 25 But there was none like unto Ahab, which did sell himself to work wickedness in the sight of the LORD, whom Jezebel his wife stirred up. 26 And he did very abominably in following idols, according to all* things *as did the Amorites, whom the LORD cast out before the children of Israel"* (1 Kings 21:19, 21-26).

The sin of Ahab and Jezebel became evil investment that transferred to their children. As a result, evil was brought upon Ahab, his posterity was taken away, and his family cut off. While his numerous children lived, evil judgment hanged over their heads.

Ahab did not settle the debt of the consequences of his sin properly when he was alive, and all his children had to die as a result.

The only way to settle a consequence of sin is through genuine repentance and receiving Jesus, who makes restitution for each member of the family. Confession and forsaking of all sins and living a life of holiness are extremely important.

> *"Wash you, make you clean; put away the evil of your doings from before mine eyes; cease to do evil; Learn to do well; seek judgment, relieve the oppressed, judges the fatherless, and pleads for the widow. Come now, and let us reason together, saith the LORD: though your sins be as scarlet, they shall be as white as snow; though they be red like crimson, they shall be as wool"* (Isaiah 1:16-18).

However, Ahab humbled himself before God when he heard of God's judgment upon him. Because of that, God deferred His judgment and transferred it to Ahab's children.

> *"And it came to pass, when Ahab heard those words, that he rent his clothes, and put sackcloth upon his flesh, and fasted, and lay in sackcloth, and went softly. And the word of the LORD came to Elijah the Tishbite, saying, Seest thou how Ahab humbleth himself before me? Because he humbleth himself before me, I will not bring the evil in his days:* but *in his son's days will I bring the evil upon his house"* (1 Kings 21:27-29).

It is worthy to note that while Ahab rent his clothes, put sackcloth upon his flesh, went softly and fasted, none of his family members repented with him. Therefore, he was isolated and was saved from the humiliating and looming consequences. sadly, his curse was to fall upon his family. He escaped the consequences of his sin of murder and the evil was carried over to his children's days. This is sad!

> *"And when Jehu was come to Jezreel, Jezebel heard* of it; *and she painted her face, and tired her head, and looked out at a window. And as Jehu entered in at the gate, she said,* Had *Zimri peace, who slew his master? And he lifted up his face to the window, and said, who is on my side? Who? In addition, there looked out to him two* or *three eunuchs. And he said, Throw her down. Therefore, they threw her down and* some *of her blood was sprinkled on the wall, and on the horses: and he trode her under foot. And when he was come in, he did eat and drink, and said, Go, see now this cursed* woman, *and bury her: for she* is *a king's daughter. And they went to bury her: but they found no more of her than the skull, and the feet, and the palms of* her *hands. Wherefore they came again, and told him. And he said, This is the word of the LORD, which he spoke by his servant Elijah the Tishbite, saying, In the portion of Jezreel shall dogs eat the flesh of Jezebel: And the carcass of Jezebel shall be as dung upon the face of the field in the portion of Jezreel;* so *that they shall not say, This is Jezebel"* (2 Kings 9:30-37).

Consider how Ahab had peace and stayed out of war for three years because of his repentance (*See* 1 Kings 20:1-3, 29-40). Nevertheless, immediately after his death, the demon in-charge of his family's evil consequences was let loose. Demons broke the family's hedge of protection and invaded the once protected family of Ahab. Jehu was anointed to overthrow Jezebel and take over the kingdom. He threw Jezebel down from the window. Her blood splashed on the walls and on the horses, and it was trodden under the foot.

> "[1]*And Ahab had seventy sons in Samaria. And Jehu wrote letters, and sent to Samaria, unto the rulers of Jezreel, to the elders, and to them that brought up Ahab's children, saying,* [6]*Then he wrote a letter the second time to them, saying, If ye* be *mine, and* if *ye will hearken unto my voice, take ye the heads of the men your master's sons, and come to me to Jezreel by tomorrow this time. Now the king's sons, being seventy persons,* were *with the great men of the city, which brought them up.* [7]*And it came to pass, when the letter came to them, that they took the king's sons, and slew seventy persons, and put their heads in baskets, and sent him them to Jezreel.* [8]*And there came a messenger, and told him, saying, They have brought the heads of the king's sons. In addition, he said, Lay ye them in two heaps at the entering in of the gate until the morning.* [10]*Know now that there shall fall unto the earth nothing of the word of the LORD, which the LORD spoke concerning the house of Ahab: for the LORD hath done* that *which he spoke by his servant Elijah.* [11]*So Jehu slew all that remained of the house f Ahab in Jezreel, and all his great men, and his kinsfolks, and his priests, until he left him none remaining"* (2 Kings 10:1, 6-8, 10-11).

It is very important that as a father or mother, when you break the hedge of your protection through sin, you must not allow your sin to put your family in bondage of Satan. Otherwise, your children would suffer terrible consequences. Repent of all the sins you committed before and after your marriage. Confess and forsake them and invite Jesus to take away every consequence of your past sins. Then make sure that you guide your children in the way of the Lord.

> "[1]*The word of the LORD came also unto me, saying,* [2]*Thou shall not take thee a wife, neither shall thou have sons or daughters in this place.* [3]*For thus saith the LORD concerning the sons and concerning the daughters that are born in this place, and concerning their mothers that bare them, and concerning their fathers that begat them in this land;* [4]*They shall die of grievous deaths; they shall not be lamented; neither shall they be buried;* but *they shall be as dung upon the face of the earth: and they shall be consumed by the sword, and by famine; and their carcasses shall be meat for the fowls of heaven, and for the beasts of the earth.* [10]*And it shall come to pass, when thou shall show this people all these words, and they shall say unto thee, wherefore hath the LORD pronounced all this great evil against us. Alternatively,*

what is *our iniquity? Or what* is *our sin that we have committed against the LORD our God?* [11]*Then shall thou say unto them, Because your fathers have forsaken me, saith the LORD, and have walked after other gods, and have served them, and have worshipped them, and have forsaken me, and have not kept my law;* [12]*And ye have done worse than your fathers; for, behold, ye walk every one after the imagination of his evil heart, that they may not hearken unto me"* (Jeremiah 16:1-4, 10-12).

Evil transfers can cause born and unborn children unimaginable suffering. It can close doors to timely marriages of the children, and open doors to divorce, separation and all manner of marital problems. Parents that love their children should not allow evil to transfer from them to the children. Evil transfers differ from family to family according to the sins of the parents.

Sometimes, evil transfers can cause abortions, marital failures, miscarriage of good things and premature deaths. It can make greatly destined people to be useless and live at the mercy of the devil. It can yoke people with evil characters that are very disgraceful and immoral. Evil transfer can lead children to addictions and bring oppression of the devil. Evil carry-over can force people to get tired of life, wish themselves death and contemplate suicide. It can capture people's progress and limit them.

There is no sort of wickedness that evil carry-over is not capable of doing. It can yoke people from birth to the grave and from the grave to hell fire. It can bring weakness, confusion, manipulation and death. Evil carry-over can keep people out of God's plan, progress and cause them to struggle without success in their lives.

"[15]*And Joshua made peace with them, and made a league with them, to let them live: and the princes of the congregation swore unto them.* [22]*And Joshua called for them, and he spoke unto them, saying, Wherefore have ye beguiled us, saying, we* are *very far from you; when ye dwell among us.* [23]*Now therefore ye* are *cursed, and there shall none of you be freed from being bondmen, and hewers of wood and drawers of water for the house of my God.* [27]*And Joshua made them that day hewers of wood and drawers of water for the congregation, and for the altar of the LORD, even unto this day, in the place which he should choose"* (Joshua 9:15, 22-23, 27).

Evil covenant puts persons, families and nations into perpetual captivity of the devil. It brings curses and wastes people's lives after many years. Joshua entered into a covenant with the wrong people and caused the princes of Israel swore in agreement. That became a binding agreement for a whole nation, born and unborn. Many years later, Saul the first king of Israel broke that covenant. The effects destroyed his family until they were left with only seven young men and a lame man.

"Then there was a famine in the days of David three years, year after year; and David enquired of the LORD. In addition, the LORD answered, It is *for Saul, and for* his *bloody house, because he slew the Gibeonites. And the king called the Gibeonites, and said unto them; (now the Gibeonites* were *not of the children of Israel, but of the remnant of the Amorites; and the children of Israel had sworn unto them: and Saul sought to slay them in his zeal to the children of Israel and Judah.) Wherefore David said unto the Gibeonites, What should I do for you? In addition, wherewith shall I make the atonement that ye may bless the inheritance of the LORD? And the Gibeonites said unto him, we will have neither silver nor gold of Saul, nor of his house; for us shall thou kill any man in Israel. In addition, he said, what ye should say,* that *would I do for you. And they answered the king, The man that consumed us, and that devised against us* that *we should be destroyed from remaining in any of the coasts of Israel, Let seven men of his sons be delivered unto us, and we will hang them up unto the LORD in Gibeah of Saul,* whom *the LORD did choose. In addition, the king said, I will give* them. *But the king spared Mephibosheth, the son of Jonathan the son of Saul, because of the LORD'S oath that* was *between them, between David and Jonathan the son of Saul. But the king took the two sons of Rizpah the daughter of Aiah, whom she bare unto Saul, Armoni and Mephibosheth; and the five sons of Michal the daughter of Saul, whom she brought up for Adriel the son of Barzillai the Meholathite: And he delivered them into the hands of the Gibeonites, and they hanged them in the hill before the LORD: and they fell* all *seven together, and were put to death in the days of harvest, in the first* days, *in the beginning of barley harvest"* (2 Samuel 21:1-9).

After dealing with the family of Saul, the curse of evil transfer continued after his death. It brought famine for three years in Israel during the time of David. It was after three years that David was able to discover the cause of the famine through prayers. The family of Saul became bloody and it affected the whole nation of Israel. Saul broke a covenant Joshua entered into many years earlier.

One lesson you need to learn from here is that if your family is bloody or you have blood in your linage, you need to silence every blood crying against you and your family. One can enter into evil covenant through unconscious family inheritance. If there is blood crying in your foundation, you need to do something urgently or else you may continue suffering for an evil you did not commit.

EVIL INHERITANCE

The realities of evil inheritance cannot be over emphasized. Consider how Gehazi, the servant of Elisha, took a bribe and when his master confronted him, he denied. Because of that, he received a curse that extended to his unborn generation. He was so foolish and stubborn that even after he received the curse, he did not repent.

> *"But he went in, and stood before his master. In addition, Elisha said unto him, whence* comest thou, *Gehazi? And he said, Thy servant went no whither. And he said unto him, Went not mine heart* with thee, *when the man turned again from his chariot to meet thee?* Is it *a time to receive money, and to receive garments, and olive yards, and vineyards, and sheep, and oxen, and menservants, and maidservants? The leprosy therefore of Naaman shall cleave unto thee and unto thy seed forever. And he went out from his presence a leper* as white *as snow"* (2 Kings 5:25-27).

> *"But unto every one of us is given grace according to the measure of the gift of Christ"* (Ephesians 4:7).

> *"Be sober, be vigilant; because your adversary the devil, as a roaring lion, walketh about, seeking whom he may devour: Whom resist steadfast in the faith, knowing that the same afflictions are accomplished in your brethren that are in the world"* (1 Peter 5:8-9).

There are different levels involved in deliverance. For instance, when you sin and refuse to acknowledge your sin, repent, confess and forsake it, you build a house for demons to live in. These demons may dwell in about seven levels of your life. However, when you acknowledge your sin, repent and forsake it, you have only one level of demons to fight. That is why some people's deliverances are harder than others are.

Sadly, many parents invite demons to dwell in several levels in the lives of their unborn children. Some people join evil societies to make money and fame. That is when devil allows you to buy wealth on credit. However, someday, devil and his demons will rise against you and your whole family.

Evil seal is a satanic document containing his program for any individual, family, group or nation. At times, it may be one, two three or even up to seven. The document contains terrible plagues and woes, and all that Satan wants to accomplish.

Foolish and thoughtless people think that it is good to do whatever they can to get money and live big, without considering the consequences. Such people kill and enter into evil covenants thinking they are doing good investments for the future of their children. However, we know that what Gehazi stored for his children was leprosy.

One of the sons of prophets lived a holy life. He did take bribe and he died as a debtor. People could have blamed him for not taking bribe to make his family live comfortably. Nevertheless, he remained a righteous person that feared the Lord. His family suffered lack and humiliation, but God blessed them at last. Gehazi, who decided to help himself, received curse unto himself and his children.

> *"But Gehazi, the servant of Elisha the man of God, said, Behold, my master hath spared Naaman this Syrian, in not receiving at his hands that which he brought: but,* as *the LORD liveth, I will run after him, and take somewhat of him. So Gehazi followed Naaman. In addition, when Naaman saw* him *running after him, he lighted down from the chariot to meet him, and said, is* all *well? And he said, all* is *well. My master hath sent me, saying, Behold, even now there be come to me from mount Ephraim two young men of the sons of the prophets: give them, I pray thee, a talent of silver, and two changes of garments. And Naaman said, Be content, takes two talents. In addition, he urged him, bound two talents of silver in two bags, with two changes of garments, and laid* them *upon two of his servants; and they bare* them *before him. And when he came to the tower, he took* them *from their hand, and bestowed* them *in the house: and he let the men go, and they departed"* (2 Kings 5:20-24).

People that are possessed by demons know how to be clever and deceptive. They always think that God was slow to responding to their needs. That is why they always devise means to help themselves. Sadly, they would never learn that they would always receive curses upon themselves.

> *"Now there cried a certain woman of the wives of the sons of the prophets unto Elisha, saying, Thy servant my husband is dead; and thou knows that thy servant did fear the LORD: and the creditor is come to take unto him my two sons to be bondmen. And Elisha said unto her, what should I do for thee? Tell me, what hast thou in the house? In addition, she said, Thine handmaid hath not anything in the house, save a pot of oil. Then he said, Go, borrow thee vessels abroad of thy entire neighbor's,* even *empty vessels; borrow not a few. And when thou art come in, thou shall shut the door upon thee and upon thy sons, and shall pour out into all those vessels, and thou shall set aside that which is full"* (2 Kings 4:1).

The devil is so wicked. That is why God put enmity between the devil and us (*See* Genesis 3:15). No matter what he offers you, you have more to lose than you can ever gain from him. He is very wicked and a tyrant. The son of the prophet died a debtor with the fear of God in his family, but God enriched his family afterward.

"And Elisha said unto her, what shall I do for thee? Tell me, what hast thou in the house? In addition, she said, Thine handmaid hath not anything in the house, save a pot of oil. Then he said, Go, borrow thee vessels abroad of thy entire neighbor's, even *empty vessels; borrow not a few. And when thou art come in, thou shall shut the door upon thee and upon thy sons, and shall pour out into all those vessels, and thou shalt set aside that which is full. So she went from him, and shut the door upon her and upon her sons, who brought* the vessels *to her; and she poured out. And it came to pass, when the vessels were full, that she said unto her son, Bring me yet a vessel. In addition, he said unto her,* there is *not a vessel more. In addition, the oil stayed. Then she came and told the man of God. And he said, Go, sell the oil, and pay thy debt, and live thou and thy children of the rest"* (2 Kings 4:2-7).

Recall that the curse of immorality upon the tribe of Judah started with their father, Judah, when he committed fornication and laid immoral foundation for his generation.

"And it came to pass at that time that Judah went down from his brethren, and turned in to a certain Adullamite, whose name was *Hirah. And Judah saw there a daughter of a certain Canaanite, whose name* was *Shuah; and he took her, and went in unto her"* (Genesis 38:1-2).

Immorality became the lifestyle of everyone in his or her tribe. It was an evil inheritance. Sin of immorality captured and destroyed many greatly destined people in that tribe. David was also a victim.

"And it came to pass, after the year was expired, at the time when kings go forth to battle, *that David sent Joab, and his servants with him, and all Israel; and they destroyed the children of Ammon, and besieged Rabbah. However, David tarried still at Jerusalem. And it came to pass in an evening tide, that David arose from off his bed, and walked upon the roof of the king's house: and from the roof he saw a woman washing herself; and the woman* was *very beautiful to look upon. And David sent and enquired after the woman. In addition,* one *said,* Is *not this Bath–sheba, the daughter of Eliam, the wife of Uriah the Hittite? And David sent messengers, and took her; and she came in unto him, and he lay with her; for she was purified from her uncleanness: and she returned unto her house. And the woman conceived, and sent and told David, and said, I am with child"* (2 Samuel 11:1-5).

David stayed back home at the time of war. He committed immorality, killed the husband of a woman and married her. God sent a prophet to expose and rebuke him, and he repented. Though he repented, the sword he used to kill Uriah never departed from his family. His ancestor Judah invited immoral demons in his linage, but David invited the sword, premature death and war.

"Now therefore the sword shall never depart from thine house; because thou hast despised me, and hast taken the wife of Uriah the Hittite to be thy wife. Thus saith the LORD, Behold, I will raise up evil against thee out of thine own house, and I will take thy wives before thine eyes, and give them *unto thy neighbor, and he shall lie with thy wives in the sight of this sun. For thou didst it secretly: but I will do this thing before all Israel, and before the sun. And David said unto Nathan, I have sinned against the LORD. In addition, Nathan said unto David, the LORD also hath put away thy sin; thou shalt not die. Howbeit, because by this deed thou hast given great occasion to the enemies of the LORD to blaspheme, the child also* that is *born unto thee shall surely die"* (2 Samuel 12:10-14).

David repented and began to confront spirits of immorality and murder. He overcame them but his children never did. One day, the spirit of immorality invaded one of his sons, Amnon, and he forced his sister Tamar and raped her. The spirit of murder overcame one of his sons called Absalom and he took the family sword of murder that killed Uriah and killed his brother Amnon.

"14 Howbeit he would not hearken unto her voice: but, being stronger than she, forced her, and lay with her. 28 Now Absalom had commanded his servants, saying, Mark ye now when Amnon's heart is merry with wine, and when I say unto you, Smite Amnon; then kill him, fear not: have not I commanded you? Be courageous, and be valiant. 29 And the servants of Absalom did unto Amnon as Absalom had commanded. Then all the king's sons arose, and every man gat him up upon his mule, and fled. 32 And Jonadab, the son of Shimeah David's brother, answered and said, Let not my lord suppose that *they have slain all the young men the king's sons; for Amnon only is dead: for by the appointment of Absalom this hath been determined from the day that he forced his sister Tamar"* (2 Samuel 13:14, 28-29, 32).

One day, Absalom picked up the family sword of war and declared himself king while his father was still alive. He stole the hearts of Israel and declared war against David, his father. In the events that followed, twenty thousand men were killed.

"7 Where the people of Israel were slain before the servants of David, and there was there a great slaughter that day of twenty thousand men. *8 For the battle was there scattered over the face of all the country: and the wood devoured more people that day than the sword devoured. 15 And ten young men that bare Joab's armor compassed about and smote Absalom, and slew him"* (2 Samuel 18:7-8, 15).

Absalom also died in that battle and Ahithophel hanged himself. Absalom's revolt caused David and the whole nation of Israel great distress. A consequence of evil inheritance can spread from an individual to the family and to the nation if unchecked. Before Absalom died, the demon of immorality influenced him to have sex with ten women in the public.

"Thus saith the LORD, Behold, I will raise up evil against thee out of thine own house, and I will take thy wives before thine eyes, and give them unto thy neighbor, and he shall lie with thy wives in the sight of this sun. For thou didst it secretly: but I will do this thing before all Israel and before the sun" (2 Samuel 12:11-12).

"Then said Absalom to Ahithophel, Give counsel among you what we shall do. And Ahithophel said unto Absalom, Go in unto thy father's concubines, which he hath left to keep the house; and all Israel shall hear that thou art abhorred of thy father: then shall the hands of all that are *with thee be strong. So they spread Absalom a tent upon the top of the house; and Absalom went in unto his father's concubines in the sight of all Israel. And the counsel of Ahithophel, which he counseled in those days,* was *as if a man had enquired at the oracle of God: so* was *all the counsel of Ahithophel both with David and with Absalom"* (2 Samuel 16:20-23).

The best cure for sin is to avoid it from the onset. Absalom, under the influence of the evil investment of his father, committed immorality publicly with his own father's concubines. This act was done on top of an open building. Later, Adonijah, one of the sons of David, asked for Abishag, his father's wife. His tribal immoral demons overwhelmed him to ask for his father's wife.

Solomon, who was also filled with immoral demons, killed him and married his father's wife. It was unfortunate that David's children all along desired their father's wives while he lived. The demon of immorality is very wicked and a tyrant. Under the same demonic influence, Solomon started marrying until he married seven hundred wives and three hundred concubines, who influenced him against God. (*See* 1 Kings 1:5-40; 2:13-25; 11:1-9; 29-30).

David witnessed the worst events in his own family. His son became a traitor to his throne. He witnessed death and murder in his own family. His own children insulted him most (*See* 2 Samuel 16:5-14). The reason why he cried at the death of Absalom was that he realized that he invested evil that his children harvested. He knew that he was the cause of their problems. He caused some of his children to go to hell (*See* 2 Samuel 11:2-27; 12:10-19). He overcame some of the demons, but they overcame his children.

"Send thine hand from above; rid me, and deliver me out of great waters, from the hand of strange children" (Psalms 144:7).

The queen of heaven, the woman in charge of abomination from the waters captured his children and used them against David and the whole nation.

"And there came one of the seven angels which had the seven vials, and talked with me, saying unto me, Come hither; I will shew unto thee the judgment of the great whore that sitteth upon many waters: With whom the kings of the earth have

committed fornication, and the inhabitants of the earth have been made drunk with the wine of her fornication. So he carried me away in the spirit into the wilderness: and I saw a woman sit upon a scarlet colored beast, full of names of blasphemy, having seven heads and ten horns. And the woman was arrayed in purple and scarlet color, and decked with gold and precious stones and pearls, having a golden cup in her hand full of abominations and filthiness of her fornication: And upon her forehead was *a name written, MYSTERY, BABYLON THE GREAT, THE MOTHER OF HARLOTS AND ABOMINATIONS OF THE EARTH"* (Revelation 17:1-5).

The reason why Jesus came through the tribe of Judah was to frustrate the spirit of war and immorality. When you invite Jesus into your tribe, family and life, He will perfect your deliverance and break every seal of bondage in your life. The devil took away every good thing from Nazareth but Jesus restored them double.

"And Nathanael said unto him, Can there any good thing come out of Nazareth? Philip saith unto him, Come and see. Jesus saw Nathanael coming to him, and saith of him, Behold an Israelite indeed, in who is no guile" (John 1:46-47).

"And one of the elders saith unto me, Weep not: behold, the Lion of the tribe of Judah, the Root of David, hath prevailed to open the book, and to lose the seven seals thereof" (Revelation 5:5).

Take your whole family and all your children to Lion of the tribe of Judah, the Root of David and He will open your seal of bondage and set you and all your children free.

"Come unto me, all ye *that labor and are heavy laden and I will give you rest. Take my yoke upon you, and learn of me; for I am meek and lowly in heart: and ye shall find rest unto your souls. For my yoke* is *easy, and my burden is light"* (Matthew 11:28-30).

Jesus is waiting for you now, respond quickly.

PRAYERS FOR YOUR CHILDREN'S DELIVERANCE

Bible references: Ephesians 6:1-4; Proverbs 6:22-23, 23:22; Isaiah 49:24-26

Begin with praise and worship

1. Every enemy in my home that is influencing my children, die, in the name of Jesus.
2. Any evil transfer from my parents and myself into my children, die, in the name of Jesus.
3. I lose my children from the bondage of my place of birth, in the name of Jesus.
4. Every demonic mark that is upon my children, I erase you by force, in the name of Jesus
5. I reject any evil counsel that was designed to destroy destinies of my children, in the name of Jesus.
6. Every evil spirit that is living inside my children, come out by fire, in the name of Jesus.
7. Blood of Jesus, speak the word of salvation into my children, in the name of Jesus.
8. Any inherited curse and covenant that is attacking my children, break and expire, in the name of Jesus.
9. Let any curse that was issued upon my children by anyone living or dead expire by force, in the name of Jesus.
10. I cast out demons that destroy children from the lives of my children, in the name of Jesus.
11. Let any initiation that has taken place over my children expire, in the name of Jesus.
12. I terminate every demonic activity that is going on against my children, in the name of Jesus.
13. Any evil dream that was designed to enslave my children, be frustrated, in the name of Jesus.
14. Any evil sacrifice that was offered for my children, expire, in the name of Jesus.
15. O Lord, deliver my children from evil captivity and bondage, in the name of Jesus.

16. Any strange character that exists in the lives of my children, die now, in the name of Jesus.

17. I terminate evil relationships that my children have gotten into, in the name of Jesus.

18. Any strange fire that is burning my children, quench, in the name of Jesus.

19. I nullify any evil marriage that was prepared to trap my children, spiritually or physically, in the name of Jesus.

20. I lift off every satanic embargo that was placed upon my children, in the name of Jesus.

21. Any sin that was designed to attract my children, die, in the name of Jesus.

22. Any evil influence that is luring my children, I resist you by force, in the name of Jesus.

23. O Lord, empower my children to submit to Your divine authority, in the name of Jesus.

24. I cast out every spirit of waste that has captured my children, in the name of Jesus.

25. Any evil habit that is destroying my children, I destroy you, in the name of Jesus.

26. I destroy evil weapons that were prepared against my children, in the name of Jesus.

27. Every enemy of obedience and righteousness in the lives of my children, I disgrace you, in the name of Jesus.

28. I remove my children from evil groups and altars of darkness, in the name of Jesus.

29. I waste any strange spirit that has vowed to waste my children, in the name of Jesus.

30. O Lord, safeguard my children from painful mistakes and wrong choices, in the name of Jesus.

31. I disallow and deliver my children from marrying their enemies, in the name of Jesus.

32. Lord Jesus, take my children to their places in life to fulfill their destinies, in the name of Jesus.

33. Every root of sin in the lives of my children, I dismantle you, in the name of Jesus.

34. Let the angels of God take away my children from evil paths, in the name of Jesus.

35. I cast out demons that seek to possess my children, in the name of Jesus.

36. I release my children from evil prisons, spiritual and physical, in the name of Jesus.

37. Let diseases, sicknesses and premature deaths lose their holds over my children, in the name of Jesus.

38. O Lord, perfect Your plans over my children, in the name of Jesus.

23

Chapter

PRAYERS TO LIVE AN EXCELLENT LIFE

CHAPTER OVERVIEW

- *Biblical icons of excellence*
- *The price of excellence*
- *Road to a believer's excellent life*
- *Calmness and composure in chaotic situations*
- *Courage during crisis*

BIBLICAL ICONS OF EXCELLENCE

When we search through the bible, it is easy to identify many icons of excellence, who should be our role models. However, in this book, I will choose Joseph as our perfect example; one who excelled among his equals in the Old Testament despite all the hatred and attempts to stop him. His life became an embodiment of faithfulness during hard times. He was a dreamer of greatness from his childhood. Unfortunately, everyone around him either misunderstood or persecuted him. Nevertheless, he still excelled during hard times.

> *"And Joseph was brought down to Egypt; and Potiphar, an officer of Pharaoh, captain of the guard, an Egyptian, bought him of the hands of the Ishmaelite, which had brought him down thither. And the LORD was with Joseph, and he was a prosperous man; and he was in the house of his master the Egyptian. And his master saw that the LORD* was *with him, and that the LORD made all that he did to prosper in his hand. And Joseph found grace in his sight, and he served him: and he made him overseer over his house, and all* that *he had he put into his hand. And it came to pass from the time* that *he had made him overseer in his house, and over all that he had, that the LORD blessed the Egyptian's house for Joseph's sake; and the blessing of the LORD was upon all that he had in the house, and in the field. And he left all that he had in Joseph's hand; and he knew not ought he had, save the bread, which he did eat. And Joseph was* a *goodly* person, *and well favored"* (Genesis 39:1-6).

As a slave boy in the house of Potiphar, who was an officer of Pharaoh and captain of the guard, Joseph excelled. The Lord was with Joseph even in a foreign land because he maintained his relationship with God. He became a prosperous man in-charge of his masters business. He found grace enough to work in the sight of his master. His excellent spirit exposed him to leadership and his master made him the general overseer of his household.

> *"And Joseph's master took him, and put him into the prison, a place where the king's prisoners* were *bound: and he was there in the prison. But the LORD was with Joseph, showed him mercy, and gave him favor in the sight of the keeper of the prison. And the keeper of the prison committed to Joseph's hand all the prisoners that* were *in the prison; and whatsoever they did there, he was the doer* of it. *The keeper of the prison looked not to anything* that was *under his hand; because the LORD was with him, and* that *which he did, the LORD made* it *to prosper"* (Genesis 39:20-23).

From being an overseer in the house of Potiphar, Joseph was thrown into prison for refusing to commit fornication with Potiphar's wife (*See* Genesis 39:7-13). Yet, God remained with him in the prison.

While in the prison, the spirit of excellence manifested in Joseph and God showed him mercy. He found favor in the sight of the keeper of the prison. All the prisoners were committed to his care. Joseph excelled above other prisoners and prospered in the prison. He maintained his relationship with man and God everywhere he went and remained godly in times of sudden promotion and prosperity. Amazingly, it came to a point Pharaoh had to consult a prisoner.

> *"Then Pharaoh sent and called Joseph and they brought him hastily out of the dungeon: and he shaved himself, and changed his raiment, and came in unto Pharaoh. And Pharaoh said unto Joseph, I have dreamed a dream, and there is none that can interpret it: and I have heard say of thee,* that *thou canst understand a dream to interpret it. And Joseph answered Pharaoh, saying, It is not in me: God shall give Pharaoh an answer of peace. And Pharaoh said unto Joseph, In my dream, behold, I stood upon the bank of the river: And, behold, there came up out of the river seven kine, fat fleshed and well favored; and they fed in a meadow"* (Genesis 41:14-18).

While in prison, Joseph retained his excellent spirit. His excellence in the prison exposed him to pharaoh and he called him out of the prison. He came out of prison, and within a short time, his garment was changed with a clean robe because of the king's commandment. From the prison, he stood before Pharaoh.

One area he manifested his excellence was his ability to interpret dreams. You need to discover your area of excellence and prayerfully develop it to the highest capacity. You cannot be Jack-of-all-trades and master of none. When you discover your area of excellence, you can succeed anywhere you go to in life and excel above others, even where you are hated. As long as you maintain your relationship with God without compromise or negotiation with devil, you will surely excel.

> *"And it came to pass, when his master heard the words of his wife, which she spoke unto him, saying, After this manner did thy servant to me; that his wrath was kindled. And Joseph's master took him, and put him into the prison, a place where the king's prisoners* were *bound: and he was there in the prison. But the LORD was with Joseph, showed him mercy, and gave him favor in the sight of the keeper of the prison. And the keeper of the prison committed to Joseph's hand all the prisoners that* were *in the prison; and whatsoever they did there, he was the doer of it. The keeper of the prison looked not to anything* that was *under his hand; because the LORD was with him, and* that *which he did, the LORD made* it *to prosper"* (Genesis 39:19-23).

Your area of excellence puts you ahead of others to do extraordinary things that are not common. It makes you go at least one inch above others. It singles you out in a crowd and makes you the best among them. Joseph's area of excellence was his ability to interpret dreams. Joseph knew his limits, but his confidence in such times was God. Excellent people do not stop where their strength, wisdom, knowledge and ability stop.

Joseph said to pharaoh, *"It is not me, God shall give Pharaoh an answer of peace."* Pharaoh replied, *"I told of this unto the magicians, but there was none that could declare it to me."*

There is always a difference between a child of God and a magician. The spirit that rules a child of God is not the same with the spirit that rules a magician.

> *"[16]Then will we give our daughters unto you, and we will take your daughters to us, and we will dwell with you, and we will become one people. [24]And unto Hamor and unto Shechem his son hearkened all that went out of the gate of his city; and every male was circumcised, all that went out of the gate of his city"* (Genesis 34:16, 24).

> *"[8]Then came in all the king's wise* men*: but they could not read the writing, nor make known to the king the interpretation thereof. [10]*Now *the queen, by reason of the words of the king and his lords, came into the banquet house:* and *the queen spoke and said, O king, live forever: let not thy thoughts trouble thee, nor let thy countenance be changed: [11]There is a man in thy kingdom, in whom* is *the spirit of the holy gods; and in the days of thy father light and understanding and wisdom, like the wisdom of the gods, was found in him; whom the king Nebuchadnezzar thy father, the king,* I say, *thy father, made master of the magicians, astrologers, Chaldeans,* and *soothsayers; [12]For as much as an excellent spirit, and knowledge, and understanding, interpreting of dreams, and showing of hard sentences, and dissolving of doubts, were found in the same Daniel, whom the king named Belteshazzar: now let Daniel be called, and he will show the interpretation"* (Daniel 5:8, 10-12).

Natural talents and occult divination are different from gifts that God gives. An excellent and talented unbeliever cannot go as far as a true believer who is gifted could go.

> *"And in the second year of the reign of Nebuchadnezzar, Nebuchadnezzar dreamed dreams, wherewith his spirit was troubled, and his sleep brake from him. Then the king commanded to call the magicians, and the astrologers, and the sorcerer's, and the Chaldeans, for to shew the king his dreams. Therefore, they came and stood before the king. And the king said unto them, I have dreamed a dream, and my spirit was troubled to know the dream"* (Daniel 2:1-3).

It is puzzling that Nebuchadnezzar, a great genius, a warrior and king in the height of occultism and prosperity, was troubled by a dream and all his wise men failed to interpret his dream. It is startling.

Today, the world's best brains and first-class scientists in all scientific fields are battling in vain to redefine the universe and man's existence. However, God is searching for men from among His people who will stand out like Joseph, Daniel and his three companions and declare before the world leaders, '*Thus says the Lord.*' God gives His beloved sleep but sleeplessness is common among great men, who are enemies of God.

> "It is *vain for you to rise up early, to sit up late, to eat the bread of sorrows:* for *so he gives his beloved sleep*" (Psalms 127:2).
>
> *"The sleep of a laboring man* is *sweet, whether he eats little or much: but the abundance of the rich will not suffer him to sleep"* (Ecclesiastes 5:12).
>
> *"As for thee, O king, thy thoughts came into thy mind upon thy bed, what should come to pass hereafter: and he that revealed secrets makes known to thee what shall come to pass"* (Daniel 2:29).

Still on Joseph, he purposely allowed Pharaoh to go into details to explain his dreams. After listening, he simply addressed the king saying, *"The dream of pharaoh is one, God has shown you what He is about to do."*

We need men like Joseph in our generation, whom God would use to evangelize the world. It is an open challenge and an indictment to us Christians that we have failed to nurture men who are qualified for God's use.

THE PRICE OF EXCELLENCE

Often, the journey to excellence is very rough. Most times, it starts with hatred from your own people. Most people do not have interest in tracing the difficult origins of people's excellences. People do not care how the story began; they want to know how it ended. That is why most people desire to be like people with excellent spirit without desiring to pay such prices as they paid.

Like David, people did not know what he went through before he was able to serve his generation according to God's will.

> *"For David, after he had served his own generation by the will of God, fell on sleep, and was laid unto his fathers, and saw corruption"* (Acts 13:36).

Though he was the choice of God, his family members did not recognize him as king at first (*See* 1 Samuel 16:1-13). Men would always reject God's choice.

> *"And I raised up of your sons for prophets, and of your young men for Nazarites. Is it not even thus, O ye children of Israel? saith the LORD. But ye gave the Nazarites wine to drink; and commanded the prophets, saying, Prophesy not"* (Amos 2:11-12).

> *"I am come in my Father's name, and ye receive me not: if another shall come in his own name, him ye will receive"* (John 5:43).

> *"[18]And saw him saying unto me, Make haste, and get thee quickly out of Jerusalem: for they will not receive thy testimony concerning me. [22]And they gave him audience unto this word, and* then *lifted up their voices, and said, Away with such a* fellow *from the earth: for it is not fit that he should live"* (Acts 22:18, 22).

The brethren of Joseph hated him without any cause. If Joseph had fought back, he would have lost his ministry. He would have aborted the gift of God on his life. He would have enjoyed fornication for a few minutes and died as a nonentity.

People also rejected Jesus who came from God. Paul was God's choice, but people rejected him and many shouted at him to depart, and others lifted up their voices and cried, '*Away with such a fellow from the earth, for it is not fit that he should live."*

A common experience among people God chooses is always rejection by people for whom salvation was determined by God. However, the way those who have been chosen react to things determines whether they would excel or fail. Men do not always choose excellent people. God does. However, such people always face rejection at the onset. It is a great gift to be divinely appointed.

There is a price to pay as one with an excellent spirit. If you are young, God can empower you to excel. If you are old, you can still recover all your loss and still excel. God called Samuel and Jeremiah through direct communication. Yet, God called Aaron at the age of 83 through Moses, God's messenger. God called Elisha through divine revelation to Elijah and inner confirmation of the spirit within Elisha himself.

Paul was called by God through the Lord Jesus appearing to him in a dramatic but thundering event on the road to Damascus. All these men had almost similar things in common. People rejected them, hated them, conspired against them and opposed them fiercely.

That is why no matter the level of any opposition you face, God demands righteousness, commitment to Him, to the word, to His people and to the service of His ministry, even at the cost of your life. You must have a determined and a purposeful heart; a heart that fears God and is pure, with an uncompromising commitment to maintain an excellent life in the spirit.

As a young Jewish man, Paul had a very rich profile and belonged to the highly rated class of the Jews. In Jewish way of life, he was a noble scholar. He persecuted the church of God in defense of his religion, which he believed was the true religion God permitted. He was very zealous after the traditions of his father.

> *"For ye have heard of my conversation in time past in the Jews' religion, how that beyond measure I persecuted the church of God, and wasted it: And profited in the Jews' religion above many my equals in mine own nation, being more exceedingly zealous of the traditions of my father's"* (Galatians 1:13-14).

> *"Circumcised the eighth day, of the stock of Israel, of the tribe of Benjamin, an Hebrew of the Hebrews; as touching the law, a Pharisee; Concerning zeal, persecuting the church; touching the righteousness which is in the law, blameless"* (Philippians 3:5-6).

Paul was circumcised on the eighth day after his birth according to the Jewish tradition. He came from the tribe of Benjamin, a Hebrew of Hebrews. As regarding to the law, he was a Pharisees. In addition, touching his obedience to the law, he was blameless. He was a doctor of law and among the highest and the best. He excelled above his equals in everything he did during his time. Nevertheless, he saw his limitations when the excellence that was Christ Jesus confronted him. When he compared his former excellence in the world with that which was in Christ, he opted for the excellence that was in Christ Jesus. Jesus became his gain.

> *"7But what things were gain to me, those I counted loss for Christ. 8Yea doubtless, and I count all things* but *loss for the excellence of the knowledge of Christ Jesus my Lord: for whom I have suffered the loss of all things, and do count them* but *dung, that I may win Christ, 10That I may know him, and the power of his resurrection, and the fellowship of his sufferings, being made conformable unto his death"* (Philippines 3:7-8, 10).

> *"Whereupon, O king Agrippa, I was not disobedient unto the heavenly vision"* (Acts 26:19).

Paul narrated his encounter to King Agrippa on his way to Damascus. He told the king how he punished believers of Jesus Christ in every synagogue and compelled them to blaspheme. On his way to Damascus, he encountered God's power and excellence, and bowed to the heavenly vision.

Paul wrote many things before his conversion. He knew the kingdom of darkness too well. He had experienced the raw power of the occult and the priesthood of evil altars.

The day he started doubting the occult powers was the morning of resurrection. That morning, he knew that the power that overtook evil kingdoms and the occult scattered his personal altars, and raised Jesus Christ from the dead was more powerful. However, he did not know how to encounter that highest power.

> *"And Saul, yet breathing out threatening and slaughter against the disciples of the Lord, went unto the high priest, And desired of him letters to Damascus to the synagogues, that if he found any of this way, whether they were men or women, he might bring them bound unto Jerusalem. And as he journeyed, he came near Damascus: and suddenly there shined round about him a light from heaven: And he fell to the earth, and heard a voice saying unto him, Saul, Saul, why persecutes thou me? And he said, Who art thou, Lord? In addition, the Lord said, I am Jesus whom thou persecute:* it is *hard for thee to kick against the pricks. And he trembling and astonished said, Lord, what wilt thou have me to do? And the Lord* said *unto him, Arise, and go into the city, and it shall be told thee what thou must do"* (Acts 9:1-6).

> *"But if the Spirit of him that raised up Jesus from the dead dwell in you, he that raised up Christ from the dead shall also quicken your mortal bodies by his Spirit that dwelled in you"* (Romans 8:11).

After that encounter, Paul knew that the power of Christ surpassed every other power. He tested the power of the occult, traditions and customs until the day he met with Christ face to face. Every power he knew and his mental storehouse faded away at the appearance of Christ. What did Paul see? He saw the resurrected Christ and the open heaven. He saw the throne of God and all the angels surrounding Christ. He had known Christ before as the son of God, the son of man, the divine teacher, the great soul winner, the defender of the weak, the good shepherd, the servant, etc.

However, when he encountered Him on his way to Damascus, he saw encountered His glory, authority, purity, wisdom, victory and omniscience. He saw the wisdom of Jesus in its totality. Paul witnessed wisdom of Jesus and His overwhelming knowledge. Seeing all these things made Paul's acclaimed excellences to fade away.

When Paul saw Christ in His glorious triumph over all the powers of darkness that Paul worshipped, he bowed. He could not stand the great beauty, brilliance and great glory of Christ. Therefore, he fell down and became blind.

No matter how much you have excelled or how much you have achieved, if you have not had an encounter with Christ, your excellence amount to nothing and worse than filthy rags. Excellence outside the knowledge of Christ is useless and unproductive. They fade away easily and are worse than pollution and defilement.

However, the knowledge and encounter with Christ is the beginning of all excellences. Even after that encounter, Christ continued to reveal his excellences to Paul on daily basis. No matter how much you have excelled, you need more of Jesus everyday for His excellences are inexhaustible.

> *"Not as though I had already attained, either were already perfect: but I follow after, if that I may apprehend that for which also I am apprehended of Christ Jesus. Brethren, I count not myself to have apprehended but* this *one thing* I do, *forgetting those things, which are behind, and reaching forth unto those things, which are before, I press toward the mark for the prize of the high calling of God in Christ Jesus. Let us therefore, as many as be perfect, is thus minded: and if in anything ye be otherwise minded, God shall reveal even this unto you. Nevertheless, where do we have already attained, let us walk by the same rule, let us mind the same thing.* [17]*Brethren, be followers together of me, and mark them which walk so as ye have us for an ensample"* (Philippians 3:12-17).

Let us therefore pray for more excellences from God than we have received. He wants to do more for us than He had done already. Therefore, in order to excel, you must first surrender your life to Christ.

> *"Come unto me, all* ye *that labor and are heavy laden and I will give you rest. Take my yoke upon you, and learn of me; for I am meek and lowly in heart: and ye shall find rest unto your souls. For my yoke* is *easy, and my burden is light"* (Matthew 11:28-30).

> *"Jesus saith unto him, I am the way, the truth, and the life: no man cometh unto the Father, but by me"* (John 14:6).

If you are born again already, you need to press forward for an improvement that comes only from Christ. If you are sick, recall that Jesus healed the sick in their numbers and empowered His disciples to do the same. If you are poor or hungry, Jesus fed people that were hungry in their thousands and they were left with much. If you are possessed by demons, Jesus cast out demons and set captives free. He will do the same for you in the name of Jesus.

> *"*[1]*After these things the Lord appointed other seventy also, and sent them two and two before his face into every city and place, whither he himself would come.* [17]*And the seventy returned again with joy, saying, Lord, even the devils are subject unto us through thy name.* [18]*And he said unto them, I beheld Satan as lightning fall from heaven.* [19] *Behold, I give unto you power to tread on serpents and scorpions, and over all the power of the enemy: and nothing shall by any means hurt you"* (Luke 10:1, 17-19).

If you are confused or troubled, remember He calmed a great storm and commanded it to be still. If you are lying at the point of death, Jesus can give you abundant life. If you are already in the grave or witches and wizards have buried your destiny, Jesus can command you and your destiny out of the grave as He did to Lazarus.

> *"Jesus therefore again groaning in himself cometh to the grave. It was a cave, and a stone lay upon it. Jesus said, Take ye away the stone. Martha, the sister of him that was dead, saith unto him, Lord, by this time he stinketh: for the hath been* dead *four days. Jesus saith unto her, Said I not unto thee, that, if thou wouldest believe, thou shouldest see the glory of God? Then they took away the stone* from the place *where the dead were laid. In addition, Jesus lifted up* his *eyes, and said, Father, I thank thee that thou hast heard me. And I knew that thou hearest me always: but because of the people, which standby I said* it, *that they may believe that thou hast sent me. And when he thus had spoken, he cried with a loud voice, Lazarus, comes forth. And he that was dead came forth, bound hand and foot with grave clothes: and his face was bound about with a napkin. Jesus saith unto them, Loose him, and let him go"* (John 11:38-44).

If you have been toiling in your life without success, Jesus met Peter like that and made him catch great fishes in a moment of time. If you are disabled, bed-ridden or unclean, Jesus can make you whole. If you are terrible sinner, He can take you to paradise today and forgive all your sins. I know you need Christ in your life. Surrender your life for Him to come in as your savior.

CALMNESS AND COMPOSURE IN CHAOTIC SITUATIONS

Fruits of excellence: There are distinctive fruits of excellence that distinguishes people with excellent spirits. When things are going well, it is hard to spot people of excellence. Nevertheless, when things become difficult, their excellent spirit radiates like light.

> *"16Then the king commanded, and they brought Daniel, and cast* him *into the den of lions.* Now *the king spoke and said unto Daniel, Thy God whom thou serve continually, he will deliver thee. 17And a stone was brought, and laid upon the mouth of the den; and the king sealed it with his own signet, and with the signet of his lords; that the purpose might not be changed concerning Daniel. 20And when he came to the den, he cried with a lamentable voice unto Daniel:* and *the king spoke and said to Daniel, O Daniel, servant of the living God, is thy God, whom thou serve continually, able to deliver thee from the lions. 21Then said Daniel unto the king, O king, lives forever. 22My God hath sent his angel, and hath shut the lions' mouths, that they have not hurt me: forasmuch as before him innocence was found in me; and also before thee, O king, have I done no hurt"* (Daniel 6:16-17, 20-22).

Daniel knew that his colleagues were planning against him. Even after the decree was signed, he did not complain, rather he went to God in prayers. He knew how to handle difficult situations.

Calmness and composure in times of chaos is one of the evidences of the spirit of excellence in a person's life. The same thing happened to Shedrack, Meshach and Abednego. They told king Nebuchadnezzar, *"We are not careful to answer you in this matter. Go ahead and quickly do what you have decided to do against us but we will never bow down to your idol."*

When Joseph's brothers faced him finally, his first reaction was calmness. He found himself under stress and high emotional strains, yet he was calm and composed. With calmness and remarkable moral power, he refused to give way to bitterness, self-pity and despair. He overcame his difficulties with courageous sense of responsibility and high moral value. Earlier, he had rejected, with respect and high level of boldness and calmness, an immoral invitation from a strange woman. He was falsely accused but he was never bitter or vengeful.

> *"And it came to pass, when she saw that he had left his garment in her hand, and was fled forth, That she called unto the men of her house, and spoke unto them, saying, See, he hath brought in an Hebrew unto us to mock us; he came in unto me to lie with me, and I cried with a loud voice: And it came to pass, when he heard that I lifted up my voice and cried, that he left his garment with me, and fled, and got him out. And*

> *she laid up his garment by her, until his lord came home. And she spoke unto him according to these words, saying, The Hebrew servant, which thou hast brought unto us, came in unto me to mock me: And it came to pass, as I lifted up my voice and cried, that he left his garment with me, and fled out. And it came to pass, when his master heard the words of his wife, which she spoke unto him, saying, After this manner did thy servant to me; that his wrath was kindled"* (Genesis 39:13-19).

He calmly waited for God to vindicate him. He did not complain, murmur, regret or exhibit vengeance. God did not disappoint him.

> *"Then Daniel answered with counsel and wisdom to Arioch the captain of the king's guard, which was gone forth to slay the wise* men *of Babylon: He answered and said to Arioch the king's captain, why* is *the decree* so *hasty from the king? Then Arioch made the thing known to Daniel"* (Daniel 2:14-15).

Likewise, Daniel did not run away or complain but he calmly requested why the decree was made in haste.

COURAGE DURING CRISIS

When Belshazzar, the grandson of Nebuchadnezzar, recognized the handwriting on the wall, he was greatly troubled. His countenance fell and his thoughts troubled him. His joints were loosed and his knees smote against the other. None of his wise men could read the writings nor interpret them. When Daniel was invited, he was so bold and courageous.

> "16 *And I have heard of thee, that thou canst make interpretations, and dissolve doubts: now if thou canst read the writing, and make known to me the interpretation thereof, thou shall be clothed with scarlet, and* have *a chain of gold about thy neck, and shall be the third ruler in the kingdom.* 17 *Then Daniel answered and said before the king, Let thy gifts be to thyself, and give thy rewards to another; yet I will read the writing unto the king, and make known to him the interpretation.* 25 *And this* is *the writing that was written, MENE, MENE, TEKEL, UPHARSIN.* 26 *This* is *the interpretation of the thing: MENE; God hath numbered thy kingdom, and finished it.* 27 *TEKEL; Thou art weighed in the balances, and art found wanting.* 28 *PERES; Thy kingdom is divided, and given to the Medes and Persians.* 30 *In that night was Belshazzar the king of the Chaldeans slain"* (Daniel 5:16-17, 25-28, 30).

> *"Then Daniel went in, and desired of the king that he would give him time, and that he would show the king the interpretation"* (Daniel 2:16).

In times of crises, people with excellent spirit are always courageous. They are always confident and committed to God. The confidence of a person with excellent spirit is in his God. They believe that God hears their prayers even at the very last minutes. In times of trouble, fear, doubt, unbelief and discouragement have no place in them.

> "10 *Now when Daniel knew that the writing was signed, he went into his house; and his windows being open in his chamber toward Jerusalem, he kneeled upon his knees three times a day, and prayed, and gave thanks before his God, as he did aforetime.* 21 *Then said Daniel unto the king, O king, lives forever.* 22 *My God hath sent his angel, and hath shut the lions' mouths, that they have not hurt me: forasmuch as before him innocence was found in me; and also before thee, O king, have I done no hurt"* (Daniel 6:10, 21-22).

They do not allow prevailing circumstances to bring doubts, fear or discouragement to them. In Daniel's case, he simply asked more time to consult his God. This is a good model to copy. Always ask more time to consult God.

> *"Then Daniel went in, and desired of the king that he would give him time, and that he would show the king the interpretation. Then Daniel went to his house, and made*

the thing known to Hananiah, Mishael, and Azariah, his companions: That they would desire mercies of the God of heaven concerning this secret; that Daniel and his fellows should not perish with the rest of the wise men *of Babylon. Then was the secret revealed unto Daniel in a night vision. Then Daniel blessed the God of heaven"* (Daniel 2:16-19).

"The secret things belong *unto the LORD our God: but those* things which are *revealed* belong *unto us and to our children forever, that* we *may do all the words of this law"* (Deuteronomy 29:29).

He knew that God has information to every secret on earth. His only concern was that he needed time to commune with God. He believed there was an answer even before he started praying. The wise thing for him to do was to pray. There was no place for fear, doubt or discouragement. Finally, God revealed the meaning of the writings to Daniel.

What Is excellence? To excel is to rise and be distinguished among others. It also means to outshine and be the best among equals. Someone with an excellent spirit would always rule over others.

> *"It pleased Darius to set over the kingdom an hundred and twenty princes, which should be over the whole kingdom; And over these three presidents; of whom Daniel* was *first: that the princes might give accounts unto them, and the king should have no damage. Then this Daniel was preferred above the presidents and princes, because an excellent spirit* was *in him; and the king thought to set him over the whole realm. Then the presidents and princes sought to find occasion against Daniel concerning the kingdom; but they could find none occasion nor fault; forasmuch as he* was *faithful, neither was there any error or fault found in him. Then said these men, We shall not find any occasion against this Daniel, except we find* it *against him concerning the law of his God"* (Daniel 6:1-5).

In the days of king Darius, who ruled about one hundred and twenty seven provinces, he set one hundred and twenty wise princes over the provinces he ruled. Over the princes, he set three presidents. Daniel became the chief president, who ruled over the other two. The other presidents accounted to Daniel.

The reason why Daniel was preferred above the other presidents was that an excellent spirit was in him. Excellence means outstanding, first-rated, exceptional, superior or best of the best. To have an excellent spirit is to have the most valuable quality that cannot be surpassed easily.

Excellence is a state of perfection. However, looking at excellence from a scriptural dimension, it is a process. It is a commitment to the highest values, which God has given to us. It involves developing and implementing our God-given potentials to the highest capacity to the glory of God and to the goodness of man.

This cannot be possible, however, without salvation from sin, curse and death. Jesus is our only Savior who saves us and intercedes for us before His Father in heaven in order to help us fulfill our destinies on earth.

> *"How God anointed Jesus of Nazareth with the Holy Ghost and with power: who went about doing good and healing all that were oppressed of the devil; for God was with him"* (Acts 10:38).

Jesus was anointed by the Holy Ghost to do us good and to deliver us from evil. Therefore, a man's perfection and excellence starts the day he gives his life to Jesus. If you have done this, you need to press forward for the mark of a high calling, which is the state of perfection, holiness of life and daily work with Christ who only is our redeemer, sanctifier and coming king. Praise the Lord!

PRAYERS TO LIVE AN EXCELLENT LIFE

Bible references: Daniel 6:1-28; Genesis 41:37-44

Begin with praise and worship

1. I remove evil powers that stand between excellence and me by force, in the name of Jesus.
2. O Lord, empower me to excel above my equals, in the name of Jesus.
3. Any evil character that is pulling my life down, I destroy and cast you off, in the name of Jesus
4. Any Goliath that is challenging my life, die in shame, in the name of Jesus.
5. I command satanic marks in my life to disappear, in the name of Jesus.
6. O Lord, empower me to live a faithful life before my God at all cost, in the name of Jesus
7. Every yoke of limitation that was placed upon my life, disappear forever, in the name of Jesus.
8. Any person that was assigned to pull me down, I expose and disgrace you, in the name of Jesus.
9. O Lord, help me to excel everywhere I go in life, in the name of Jesus.
10. Let the power to maintain the best relationship with God and man possess me, in the name of Jesus.
11. I receive grace and divine anointing to excel beyond all human imagination, in the name of Jesus.
12. Let the mercy of God and divine favor begin to pursue and overtake me, in the name of Jesus.
13. I command the spirit of godliness to possess me, in the name of Jesus.
14. Anointing for promotion and prosperity in every situation, possess me now, in the name of Jesus.
15. Any satanic load in my life, give way to God's Spirit, in the name of Jesus.

16. O Lord, empower me to take actions that will help me to excel, in the name of Jesus.

17. Let sudden power of overwhelming excellence come upon me now, in the name of Jesus.

18. Every garment of shame, reproach and disgrace in my life, catch fire and burn to ashes, in the name of Jesus.

19. O Lord, empower me to identify my areas of excellence on time, in the name of Jesus.

20. I refuse to be distracted by the devil and his agents in my life, in the name of Jesus.

21. Anointing to pursue my area of excellence with focus, fall upon me, in the name of Jesus.

22. Any strange fire that is burning good things of my life, die, in the name of Jesus.

23. I command my life to begin to give birth to extraordinary things to the glory of God, in the name of Jesus.

24. O Lord, move me above my superiors, in the name of Jesus.

25. Any power that is standing against my advancement, die, in the name of Jesus.

26. O Lord, take me above my strength, wisdom, knowledge and ability, in the name of Jesus.

27. I bring all my enemies under me by force, in the name of Jesus.

28. Father Lord, help me to develop my talents and my divine gifts today, in the name of Jesus.

29. Lord Jesus, make me greater than the greatest genius in my field, in the name of Jesus does.

30. O hand of God, push me higher than the world's bests and first class scientists, in the name of Jesus.

31. O Lord, help me to discover new things in my field, in the name of Jesus.

32. I scatter the brains of the enemies of my excellence, in the name of Jesus.

33. I abort the dreams of the enemies of my excellence, in the name of Jesus.

34. O Lord, give me the grace to pay the price of excellence, in the name of Jesus.

35. I receive the power and ability to start divine projects and finish well, in the name of Jesus.

36. Blood of Jesus, empower me to satisfy my teachers above their requirements, in the name of Jesus.

37. Let my wisdom, knowledge and understanding supersede all that are in my field, in the name of Jesus.

38. I refuse to embark on useless and unprofitable projects, in the name of Jesus.

39. Every enemy of my excellence is destroyed, in the name of Jesus.

40. Every demonic condition for excellence, I reject you, in the name of Jesus.

41. O Lord, take me higher than the highest person in my field of profession, in the name of Jesus.

42. Let the hand of God remove every satanic roof over my profession, in the name of Jesus.

43. Let anyone that is planning to stop divine movement in my life die, in the name of Jesus.

44. Let divine excellence displace every other excellence in my life, in the name of Jesus.

45. Let divine ability take me above human abilities by force, in the name of Jesus.

46. O Lord, arise and perform a miracle of divine excellence in my life, in the name of Jesus.

47. Let the excellence of the ungodly be disgraced by my divine excellence, in the name of Jesus.

48. Father Lord, empower me to enjoy the fruit of my excellence now and in eternity, in the name of Jesus.

49. Any death that was programmed to kill my excellence, fail woefully, in the name of Jesus.

50. Father Lord, bless my me to reach to eternity, in the name of Jesus.

51. O Lord, use my excellence to better the world and to populate heaven above hell fire, in the name of Jesus.

24

Chapter

PRAYERS FOR COLLEGE AND UNIVERSITY STUDENTS

CHAPTER OVERVIEW

- *Youths and learning*
- *A call for labor before harvest*
- *Consequences of being uneducated*
- *Caution for students*

YOUTHS AND LEARNING

Most people in our colleges and universities are youths. These youths have ideas, goals, needs and desires that motivate them to pursue their futures with vigor. They aim at living a life of ideals and often they shun advices from elders concerning true realities of life.

Consequently, they usually fall into diverse problems like loneliness, rejection, failure, etc. Some of these youths are victims of broken homes and are subjects to contradictory values about life in general.

> *"And, behold, one of the children of Israel came and brought unto his brethren a Midianitish woman in the sight of Moses, and in the sight of all the congregation of the children of Israel, who* were *weeping* before *the door of the tabernacle of the congregation. And when Phinehas, the son of Eleazar, the son of Aaron the priest, saw* it, *he rose up from among the congregation, and took a javelin in his hand; And he went after the man of Israel into the tent, and thrust both of them through, the man of Israel, and the woman through her belly. Therefore, the plague was stayed from the children of Israel. And those that died in the plague were twenty and four thousand"* (Numbers 25:6-9).

Youths know how to live by the standards and values of their peers, the media, leaders, etc. This has caused so many youths to find themselves in unexpected and unpleasant situations. Whenever problems trap, they begin to look for desperate ways out. Some of them join bad gangs as a result.

Some seek solace in illicit sex for love and satisfaction, which is only permitted in marriage. Some go into drugs to find meanings to their lives and fulfillment, which are only found in Christ. Others go to defend causes and revolutions to achieve personal liberty. Some go into music for ideas and communication. Others go into fashion for identity.

Youths are a group of people that are passing through early phases of life and they are full of vigor, vitality and ideas, wanting to spend them on something worthy. Our youths need positive direction and guidance. When they are rightly guided, they will be capable to do exploits. Youths need proper mobilization. Otherwise, they may waste their treasures for other things or remain ineffective.

The world is filled with army of energetic, zealous, aggressive and gifted youths, who could be very instrumental to the betterment of our world when equipped and commissioned. It is important for every youth to discover his or her talents, gifts and leadership qualities while in college or universities. Without that, many youths will come out of school to be part of the problems in societies. They need God and without God's knowledge, their strength will be diverted against God's plan. If that happens, the world will suffer just like in the time of Noah.

> *"And it came to pass, as they journeyed from the east, that they found a plain in the land of Shinar; and they dwelt there. And they said one to another, Go to, let us make brick, and burn them thoroughly. In addition, they had brick for stone, and slime had they for mortar. And they said, Go to, let us build us a city and a tower, who is top* may reach *unto heaven; and let us make us a name, lest we be scattered abroad upon the face of the whole earth. And the LORD came down to see the city and the tower, which the children of men builded. And the LORD said, Behold, the people is one, and they have all one language; and this they begin to do: and now nothing will be restrained from them, which they have imagined to do. Go to, let us go down, and there confound their language, that they may not understand one another's speech. So the LORD scattered them abroad from thence upon the face of all the earth: and they left off to build the city. Therefore is the name of it called Babel; because the LORD did there confound the language of all the earth: and from thence did the LORD scatter them abroad upon the face of all the earth"* (Genesis 11:2-9).

The sons of Noah were young energetic, zealous and aggressive youths who were equipped but not divinely commissioned. They carried out their activities outside the will of God and He was not pleased with them.

Youths who want to successful must do everything in their power to have a close relationship with God. The herdsmen of Lot and Abraham were mostly youths but they have not knowledge about God. They started gossiping and caused separation between Abraham and Lot.

> *"[7]And there was strife between the herdsmen of Abram's cattle and the herdsmen of Lot's cattle: and the Canaanite and the Perizzite dwelled then in the land. [8]And Abram said unto Lot, Let there be no strife, I pray thee, between thee, and me and between my herdsmen and thy herdsmen; for we* be *brethren.* [9]Is *not the whole land before thee. Separate thyself, I pray thee, from me: if* thou wilt, take *the left hand, then I will go to the right; or if* thou depart *to the right hand, then I will go to the left. [11]Then Lot chose him all the plain of Jordan; and Lot journeyed east: and they separated themselves the one from the other. [12]Abram dwelled in the land of Canaan, and Lot dwelled in the cities of the plain, and pitched* his *tent toward Sodom. [13]But the men of Sodom* were *wicked and sinners before the LORD exceedingly. [14]And the LORD said unto Abram, after that Lot was separated from him, Lift up now thine*

eyes, and look from the place where thou art northward, and southward, and eastward, and westward" (Genesis 13:7-9, 11-14).

Because of strife and hardness of Lot's heart, he got attracted to worldliness in Sodom and Gomorrah. Abraham played maturity and sought for God's will. The gossips of Lot's unbelieving herdsmen Lot carried him away and he went into a city that was marked for destruction.

It is highly important for youths in colleges and other training institutions to know God. Learn how to involve God in whatever you do in life. Do not follow the crowd or walk by sight. The just shall live by faith.

Esau was a young man with an enormous zeal. However, he did not consider the consequences of his foolish decision. By so doing, he ate his future and that of his unborn generation.

"And Jacob sod pottage: and Esau came from the field and he was *faint: And Esau said to Jacob, Feed me, I pray thee, with that same red* pottage; *for I* am *faint: therefore was his name called Edom. And Jacob said, Sell me this day thy birthright. And Esau said, Behold, I am at the point to die: and what profit shall this birthright do to me? And Jacob said, Swear to me this day; and he swore unto him: and he sold his birthright unto Jacob. Then Jacob gave Esau bread and pottage of lentils; and he did eat and drink, and rose up, and went his way: thus Esau despised* his *birthright"* (Genesis 25:29-34).

The problem with many youths in places of learning is ignorance. They do not care to know God. They rush into life without consulting God, who is the owner of life. They want to enjoy the things of life at the expense of their future joy and happiness. Because of a plate of food, Esau sold his birthright and destroyed his future and that of his entire generation. Youths who do not know God will not understand the meaning of patience and waiting upon God. The desires for temporary satisfaction above spiritual blessings will continue to waste and harvest the future of many greatly destined youths.

"And Jesus said, Make the men sit down. Now there was much grass in the place. Therefore, the men sat down, in number about five thousand. And Jesus took the loaves; and when he had given thanks, he distributed to the disciples, and the disciples to them that were set down; and likewise of the fishes as much as they would. When they were filled, he said unto his disciples, Gather up the fragments that remain, that nothing be lost. Therefore, they gathered them *together, and filled twelve baskets with the fragments of the five barley loaves, which remained over and above unto them that had eaten. Then those men, when they had seen the miracle that Jesus did, said, this is of a truth that prophet that should come into the world. When*

Jesus therefore perceived that they would come and take him by force, to make him a king, he departed again into a mountain himself alone" (John 6:10-15).

Whatever you do not get from God through His son, Jesus Christ, will not give you peace or fulfillment. Youths who do not know God always embrace the joy of temporary blessings without seeing the agonies that lie therein. The devil has deceived many youths by giving them flashy things, which are only temporary in order to hijack their great destinies (*See* John 6:25-35, 60, 66).

"[6]He hath said in his heart, I shall not be moved: for I shall *never* be *in adversity. [13]Wherefore doth the wicked contemn God? He hath said in his heart, Thou wilt not require* it. *[14]Thou hast seen* it; *for thou beholdest mischief and spite, to requite* it *with thy hand: the poor committed him unto thee; thou art the helper of the fatherless. [15]Break thou the arm of the wicked and the evil man: seek out his wickedness until thou find none. [16]The LORD* is *King forever and ever: the heathen are perished out of his land"* (Psalms 10:6, 13-16).

A wise person considers the consequences of his or her actions and weighs the cost of such actions in connection to the future. When you weigh your actions through the Word of God and prayers, you will discover that some immediate pleasantries do not worth the endless sufferings they attract as consequences. The devil can solve your immediate problems to purchase your tomorrow's joy, and then leaves you in agony for the rest of eternity. Be wise!

A CALL FOR LABOR BEFORE HARVEST

It is highly regrettable that many students do not know why they are in school. Many others who would have made best of their times at schools pass through schools but do not acquire knowledge. Going to study in a place of learning is like going to labor in a garden. There would always be a time of reckoning.

> *"And he spoke many things unto them in parables, saying, Behold, a sower went forth to sow; And when he sowed, some* seeds *fell by the way side, and the fowls came and devoured them up: Some fell upon stony places, where they had not much earth: and forthwith they sprung up, because they had no deepness of earth: And when the sun was up, they were scorched; and because they had no root, they withered away. And some fell among thorns; and the thorns sprung up, and choked them: But other fell into good ground, and brought forth fruit, some a hundredfold, some sixtyfold, some thirtyfold"* (Matthew 13:3-8).

Do not allow irrelevant things to occupy your time while at school instead of facing their studies. Many students spend their times for study in pleasures, socializing and clubbing. They do not have timetables and programs for themselves, so they follow the crowd and waste their precious times doing non-essential things.

> *"And Dinah the daughter of Leah, which she bare unto Jacob, went out to see the daughters of the land. And when Shechem the son of Hamor the Hivite, prince of the country, saw her, he took her, and lay with her, and defiled her. And his soul clave unto Dinah the daughter of Jacob, and he loved the damsel, and spoke kindly unto the damsel"* (Genesis 34:1-3).

Recall how Dinah, the daughter of Jacob, engaged herself in a useless visitation and lost her virginity to an uncircumcised stranger. Because of that single careless visitation, a lot of blood was shade by her brothers, Simeon and Levi. Likewise, useless visitations can ruin your life at school.

> *"And it came to pass on the third day, when they were sore, that two of the sons of Jacob, Simeon and Levi, Dinah's brethren, took each man his sword, and came upon the city boldly, and slew all the males. And they slew Humor and Shechem his son with the edge of the sword, and took Dinah out of Shechem's house, and went out The sons of Jacob came upon the slain, and spoiled the city, because they had defiled their sister. They took their sheep, and their oxen, and their asses, and that which* was *in the city, and that which* was *in the field, And all their wealth, and all their little ones, and their wives took they captive, and spoiled even all that* was *in the house"* (Genesis 34:25-29).

Simeon and Levi, Dinah's brothers, slew all the males in Shechem. They spoiled the city and took all their wealth. Over the years, Simeon and Levi were cursed for their anger and murder, which caused their unborn generations to suffer as a result.

> "[1]*And Jacob called unto his sons, and said, Gather yourselves together, that I may tell you* that *which shall befall you in the last days.* [2]*Gather yourselves together, and hear, ye sons of Jacob; and hearken unto Israel your father.* [5]*Simeon and Levi* are *brethren; instruments of cruelty* are in *their habitations.* [6]*O my soul, come not thou into their secret; unto their assembly, mine honor, be not thou united: for in their anger they slew a man, and in their self-will they digged down a wall.* [7]*Cursed* be *their anger, for* it was *fierce; and their wrath, for it was cruel: I will divide them in Jacob, and scatter them in Israel"* (Genesis 49:1-2, 5-7).

> *"Now the name of the Israelite that was slain,* even *that was slain with the Midianitish woman,* was *Zimri, the son of Salu, a prince of a chief house among the Simeonites"* (Numbers 25:14).

Students should mind their studies and not use their precious times for pleasure and useless ventures, moving up and down or rioting. Every student should consider him or herself a lucky person because there are uncountable bright and intelligent youths all over the world who do not have the opportunity to attend schools. In the developing nations, most youths do not get the opportunity to be educated. Consider yourself fortunate as a student.

> *"But other fell into good ground, and brought forth fruit, some a hundredfold, some sixtyfold, some thirtyfold. Who hath ears to hear, let him hear"* (Matthew 13:8-9).

It is sad that students, who were born to good families, came out of schools with results less than average level. They got thirty-fold instead of a hundred-fold. They had the same opportunities with those who got hundred-fold, yet they fell short. This is so sad.

What possibly went wrong with them? They started having pleasures without labor when they began. They were not aware why they were in school or the deceiver deceived them. Whatever be the case, they failed. Some dropped out without achieving anything or the purpose why they were sent to school. Others finished but came out still unknowledgeable. They never allowed knowledge to get into them, so they came out as failures.

CONSEQUENCES OF BEING UNEDUCATED

Being uneducated in this sophisticated world can be very costly. It can limit and relegate a person to a pit. Privileged and educated people are not helping matters. They increasing seek to become more sophisticated every passing day. They despise uneducated people and do not want to be associated with them. Uneducated youths trouble societies and destroy other people's destinies. This is true but sad.

A school is an institution that provides instruction and learning. It is a place where students, college or university, are taught. Students go to school to broaden their wisdom and knowledge.

They go to school to receive extra details on specific knowledge or skill and to be disciplined. That is why students who are diligent often make the best students. Likewise, it is also possible to attend school without learning anything. Students who are not diligent and do not know the purpose of their being at school often make the worst students.

Parents or guardians are the first teachers and instructors one can get. God was the first to instruct Adam. He put Adam and Eve in the garden of Eden and provided everything they needed. God instructed them what they should or should not do. Unfortunately, they were not diligent enough to obey all instructions.

> *"And the LORD God took the man, and put him into the Garden of Eden to dress it and to keep it. And the LORD God commanded the man, saying, Of every tree of the garden thou mayest freely eat: But of the tree of the knowledge of good and evil, thou shalt not eat of it: for in the day that thou eatest thereof thou shalt surely die"* (Genesis 2:15-17).

Unschooled students easily lose their places in life and hand the control of their destinies to their enemies. It is a good thing that one is taught how to live. It is a good thing to obey instructions.

> *"Now the serpent was more subtle than any beast of the field which the LORD God had made. In addition, he said unto the woman, Yea, hath God said, ye shall not eat of every tree of the garden? And the woman said unto the serpent, we may eat of the fruit of the trees of the garden: But of the fruit of the tree, which is in the midst of the garden, God, hath said, Ye shall not eat of it, neither shall ye touch it, lest ye die. And the serpent said unto the woman, Ye shall not surely die: For God doth know that in the day ye eat thereof, then your eyes shall be opened, and ye shall be as gods, knowing good and evil. And when the woman saw that the tree was good for food,*

and that it was *pleasant to the eyes, and a tree to be desired to make* one *wise, she took of the fruit thereof, and did eat, and gave also unto her husband with her; and he did eat"* (Genesis 3:1-6).

A good student keeps instructions but unschooled student abandons instructions and obeys the devil. Ironically, many students pass their exams without learning what they were taught. A person who does not practice or put his knowledge into action demonstrates that he has not been schooled properly.

The best student is not always one who scores the highest marks in exams, but also one who puts into practice what he was taught at school and keeps the rules and regulations. The ability to pass a written test without putting them into practice was not the only purpose you went to school. Adam passed every exam but when it came to implementation, he failed woefully.

"And out of the ground the LORD God formed every beast of the field and every fowl of the air; and brought them *unto Adam to see what he would call them: and whatsoever Adam called every living creature that* was *the name thereof. And Adam gave names to all cattle, and to the fowl of the air, and to every beast of the field; but for Adam there was not found an help meet for him"* (Genesis 2:19-20).

"And when the woman saw that the tree was *good for food, and that it* was *pleasant to the eyes, and a tree to be desired to make* one *wise, she took of the fruit thereof, and did eat, and gave also unto her husband with her; and he did eat"* (Genesis 3:6).

It is sad to attend school without learning. The same parents taught Cain and Abel. However, in practice, Abel passed because he put all that he was taught into practice. Cain failed because he wanted to do a new thing that was unacceptable. It is possible to fail sometimes, but it is unacceptable to continue failing because you failed earlier. When God is involved in your learning, you cannot add or subtract from what you are taught.

"For I testify unto every man that heareth the words of the prophecy of this book, If any man shall add unto these things, God shall add unto him the plagues that are written in this book: And if any man shall take away from the words of the book of this prophecy, God shall take away his part out of the book of life, and out of the holy city, and from *the things which are written in this book"* (Revelation 22:18-19).

That was the problem with Cain and that was why he failed woefully and became the first vagabond on earth and a fugitive forever. You cannot add to God's instruction or subtract from it if you really want to be a good student in the grace of God.

"And in process of time it came to pass, that Cain brought of the fruit of the ground an offering unto the LORD. And Abel, he also brought of the firstlings of his flock and of the fat thereof. In addition, the LORD had respect unto Abel and to his offering: But unto Cain and to his offering he had not respected. In addition, Cain was very wroth, and his countenance fell. And the LORD said unto Cain, Why art thou wroth? In addition, why is thy countenance fallen? If thou doest well, shall thou not be accepted? In addition, if thou do not well, sin lieth at the door. And unto thee shall be *his desire, and thou shall rule over him"* (Genesis 4:3-7).

You can add a new knowledge, invent new things in addition to what your human teacher has taught you, or even improve on them, but you cannot add or subtract from God's formula because when you do, you will have a problem. More so, the knowledge you have acquired cannot be enough for you to succeed. If you try to put God out of your knowledge, you get more confused.

"And the whole earth was of one language, and of one speech. And it came to pass, as they journeyed from the east, that they found a plain in the land of Shinar; and they dwelt there. And they said one to another, Go to, let us make brick, and burn them thoroughly. In addition, they had brick for stone, and slime had they for mortar. And they said, Go to, let us build us a city and a tower, who is top may reach *unto heaven; and let us make us a name, lest we be scattered abroad upon the face of the whole earth. And the LORD came down to see the city and the tower, which the children of men builder. And the LORD said, Behold, the people* is *one, and they have all one language; and this they begin to do: and now nothing will be restrained from them, which they have imagined to do. Go to, let us go down, and there confound their language, that they may not understand one another's speech. So the LORD scattered them abroad from thence upon the face of all the earth: and they left off building the city. Therefore is the name of it called Babel; because the LORD did there confound the language of all the earth: and from thence did the LORD scatter them abroad upon the face of all the earth"* (Genesis 11:1-9).

God can help you to improve on what you were taught at school and become more effective than your teachers. However, you cannot be greater than God is or achieve anything good without Him. That was why Jesus said, *"For without Me, you can do nothing"* (John 15:5).

"The secret things belong *unto the LORD our God: but those* things which are *revealed* belong *unto us and to our children forever, that* we *may do all the words of this law"* (Deuteronomy 29:29).

"And such as do wickedly against the covenant shall he corrupt by flatteries: but the people that do know their God shall be strong, and do exploits" (Daniel 11:32).

"For the preaching of the cross is to them that perish foolishness; but unto us which are saved it is the power of God. For it is written, I will destroy the wisdom of the wise, and will bring to nothing the understanding of the prudent. Where is the wise? Where is *the scribe? Where* is *the disputer of this world? Hath not God made foolish the wisdom of this world? For after that in the wisdom of God the world by wisdom knew not God, it pleased God by the foolishness of preaching to save them that believe. For the Jews require a sign, and the Greeks seek after wisdom: But we preach Christ crucified, unto the Jews a stumbling block, and unto the Greeks foolishness; But unto them which are called, both Jews and Greeks, Christ the power of God, and the wisdom of God. Because the foolishness of God is wiser than men; and the weakness of God is stronger than men"* (1 Corinthian 1:18-25).

Parents are to pray for their children at school

Parents are responsible for praying for their children at school. A good parent cannot ignore this responsibility if they wish their children to prosper in their academics and become useful to themselves and others. This is the reason why parents are to be born-again so that God can hear their prayers. If you want your children to experience peace and happiness, worship God for their sakes frequently.

"And, ye fathers, provoke not your children to wrath: but bring them up in the nurture and admonition of the Lord" (Ephesians 6:4).

"Seeing that Abraham shall surely become a great and mighty nation and all the nations of the earth shall be blessed in him? For I know him, that he will command his children and his household after him, and they shall keep the way of the LORD, to do justice and judgment; that the LORD may bring upon Abraham that which he hath spoken of him" (Genesis 18:18-19).

"And that thou mayest tell in the ears of thy son, and of thy son's son, what things I have wrought in Egypt, and my signs which I have done among them; that ye may know how that I am *the LORD"* (Exodus 10:2).

"Only take heed to thyself, and keep thy soul diligently, lest thou forget the things which thine eyes have seen, and lest they depart from thy heart all the days of thy life: but teach them thy sons, and thy sons' sons; Specially the day that thou stoodest before the LORD thy God in Horeb, when the LORD said unto me, Gather me the people together, and I will make them hear my words, that they may learn to fear me all the days that they shall live upon the earth, and that *they may teach their children"* (Deuteronomy 4:9-10).

Any parents that are trusting God for a child must be ready to obey God's commandments concerning child training. No one should pray or wish to have a child he would not bring up in the way of God. God commanded fathers not to provoke their children to wrath. You have to bring them up and admonish them in the way of the Lord. It is a sin to bring a child into this world without guiding that child to God, the source of all things.

Any parents that fail to introduce their children to Jesus Christ have failed their children. The main responsibility of parents is to not only give birth or feed their children with natural food. Their main responsibility is to show them the way back to God.

God gave Abraham a child at his old age because God proved Abraham as someone who would train his household in the way of the Lord. God declared that Abraham would be great. The reason for Abraham's greatness was his ability to command his children to do justice and judgment on earth. Sadly, Adam spent 930 years on earth and his only achievement was that he begat sons and daughters who had no reference to God. The same thing happened to Seth after spending 912 years on earth.

Parents are not to forget God, and His teachings. They are to teach their children the way of the Lord so that they would live long on earth. Anything less than this is a failure on the part of parents.

> *"Therefore shall ye lay up these my words in your heart and in your soul, and bind them for a sign upon your hand, that they may be as frontlets between your eyes. And ye shall teach them your children, speaking of them when thou sittet in thine house, and when thou walkest by the way, when thou liest down, and when thou risest up. And thou shalt write them upon the door posts of thine house, and upon thy gates: That your days may be multiplied, and the days of your children, in the land which the LORD sware unto your fathers to give them, as the days of heaven upon the earth"* (Deuteronomy 11:18-21).

Parents must inculcate the Word of God in the hearts, souls and memories of their children. They are to establish their children in the way of the Lord. Fathers must influence their children to incline their ears to the Word of God. Let it be said to your children until they meditate, memorize and are able to say, '*My father and mother taught me to do this.*'

The Word of God is the best legacy you can bequeath to your children, from generation to another generation. They must see you quote God's Word, praise the Lord and proclaim His greatness and the wonderful works He has done. Children should imitate their parent's positive actions about God. Parents must chasten their children at early stages when there is still hope; when they still have ears to hear and eyes to see God's goodness.

"Chasten thy son while there is hope, and let not thy soul spare for his crying" (Proverbs 19:18).

"[6]Train up a child in the way he should go: and when he is old, he will not depart from it. [15]Foolishness is *bound in the heart of a child;* but *the rod of correction shall drive it far from him. [17]Bow down thine ear, and hear the words of the wise, and apply thine heart unto my knowledge"* (Proverbs 22:6, 15, 17).

It is good to start training, correcting and guiding your child on time before the child grows up. When you train them on time, they will not depart from what they learnt when they grow up. In the absence of the Word of God, foolish actions and decisions will continue to rule and reign in the hearts of your children. However, God's Word is able to rid your children of evil in their hearts and replace their foolishness with divine knowledge.

"And that from a child thou hast known the Holy Scriptures, which are able to make the wise unto salvation through faith which is in Christ Jesus. All scripture is *given by inspiration of God, and* is *profitable for doctrine, for reproof, for correction, for instruction in righteousness"* (2 Timothy 3:15-16).

"Furthermore we have had fathers of our flesh which corrected us, *and we gave* them *reverence: shall we not much rather be in subjection unto the Father of spirits, and live? For they verily for a few days chastened* us *after their own pleasure; but he for* our *profit, that* we *might be partakers of his holiness. Now no chastening for the present seemeth to be joyous, but grievous: nevertheless afterward it yielded the peaceable fruit of righteousness unto them which are exercised there by"* (Hebrews 12:9-11).

Paul told Timothy to continue in the things he learnt about God from his childhood. The Word of God in the hearts of children is like a guide to them in times of troubles and temptations. Any heart that is void of the Word of God would have nothing to lean on in times of trouble and temptation.

When a child is about to fall into trouble or damnation, the heart and soul spews out words in the heart in defense. It profits to accept God's instruction and reject the devil's traps. The Word of God enables children to accept divine rebuke and chastisement without grudge. It also helps them to endure hardship as good soldiers of Christ.

The Word of God empowers children to accept corrections without murmuring or regret. It enables them to accept instructions based on divine righteousness, in the hope of receiving rewards for obedience from God. The Word of God in the life of a child helps him to be calm and composed in times of chaos. It brings hope where there seems to be no hope. It can announce a child out and brings honor to him among the elders.

"But Daniel purposed in his heart that he would not defile himself with the portion of the king's meat, nor with the wine which he drank: therefore he requested of the prince of the eunuchs that he might not defile himself" (Daniel 1:8).

"Then the king promoted Shadrach, Meshach, and Abed–nego, in the province of Babylon" (Daniel 3:30).

"So this Daniel prospered in the reign of Darius, and in the reign of Cyrus the Persian" (Daniel 6:28).

CAUTION FOR STUDENTS

Students are to embrace godly guidance for it is their place of safety. Each school has laws and regulations that guide it. When students follow these laws and regulations properly, they become highly successful. Students who do not obey laws and regulations do not prosper in whatever they do in their lives.

The school management and teachers are to be as parents to their students. The successes of their students hugely depend on them. As a student, you must obey your teachers and those that look after you as there were you parents.

> *"Children, obey your parents in the Lord: for this is right"* (Ephesians 6:1).

> *"He that loved father or mother more than me is not worthy of me: and he that loved son or daughter more than me is not worthy of me"* (Matthew 10:37).

When you love your teachers, no matter how bad or poor their teachings are, you would always understand them. Students are to obey the laws of their schools, as far as they are in agreement with the Word of God. No teacher or school board have the right to demand bribe from a student. No teacher has right to demand a student to submit his or her body for sexual gratification to pass exams.

> *"But Peter and John answered and said unto them, Whether it be right in the sight of God to hearken unto you more than unto God, judge ye"* (Acts 4:19).

> *"When my father and my mother forsake me, then the LORD will take me up"* (Psalms 27:10).

When a teacher promotes you in an exam because you bribed the teacher or gave your body for sexual gratification, you have offended God. If you break God's law to get anything you want, you will not enjoy it. You need to stay with God and do everything right to get things right.

> *"[10]My son, if sinners entice thee, consent thou not. [11]If they say, Come with us, let us lay wait for blood, let us lurk privily for the innocent without cause: [12]Let us swallow them up alive as the grave; and whole, as those that go down into the pit: [13]We shall find all precious substance, we shall fill our houses with spoil: [14]Cast in thy lot among us; let us all have one purse: [15]My son, walk not thou in the way with them; refrain thy foot from their path: [16]For their feet run to evil, and make haste to shed blood. [24]Because I have called, and ye refused; I have stretched out my hand, and no man regarded; [25]But ye have set at nought all my counsel, and would none of my reproof: [26]I also will laugh at your calamity; I will mock when your fear cometh; [27]When your fear cometh as desolation, and your destruction cometh as a whirlwind;*

when distress and anguish cometh upon you. [28]Then shall they call upon me, but I will not answer; they shall seek me early, but they shall not find me" (Proverbs 1:10-16, 24-28).

Faithful students avoid pleasures at school and face their studies. They do not cheat in exams because demons would possess their certificates. Even when you get a good job with such certificate, you will share your salaries with the devil or have a boss that will always demand the same thing that you did at school. If you bribed or committed immorality, that evil spirit will always demand the same everywhere you go. Be warned! It is a good thing for students to do right always.

PRAYERS FOR COLLEGE AND UNIVERSITY STUDENTS

Bible references: Daniel 1:8, 6:1-5

Begin with praise and worship

1. Father Lord, help me to interpret my vision in this school, in the name of Jesus.
2. Any evil spirit that has followed me to this school, I cast you out, in the name of Jesus.
3. I break and loose myself from the bondage of any evil altar and its priests, in the name of Jesus.
4. Every demonic force that attacks people in this school, I am not your candidate, in the name of Jesus.
5. Blood of Jesus, single me out for academic excellence in this school, in the name of Jesus.
6. Let the thunder of God destroy every enemy of my academics in this school, in the name of Jesus.
7. I withdraw my destiny from the captivity of campus altars, in the name of Jesus.
8. I command the strongman of this institution to bow down before me, in the name of Jesus.
9. Let the spirit of God empower me for academic excellence in first-class grade, in the name of Jesus.
10. Every destroyer of knowledge in this school, I break myself from your evil control, in the name of Jesus.
11. Holy Ghost fire, burn enemies of my academic destiny, in the name of Jesus.
12. I destroy powers that want to force me to serve devil in this place, in the name of Jesus.
13. O Lord, pattern my life as a youth according to Your perfect plan, in the name of Jesus.
14. I will use my youthful strength to the glorify of God in this school, in the name of Jesus.

15. Any arrow of evil diversion that was fired at my life, backfire, in the name of Jesus.
16. Every arrow of sickness and destruction that was fired at my destiny, backfire, in the name of Jesus.
17. Blood of Jesus, preserve me from corruption and defilement, in the name of Jesus.
18. I break and loose myself from the yoke of immorality, in the name of Jesus.
19. Let seeds of evil desires and thoughts that was planted in my life die, in the name of Jesus.
20. Let any power that wants me to overstay in this school die, in the name of Jesus.
21. Father Lord, use my youthful energy for Your service, in the name of Jesus.
22. I refuse to join multitudes to do evil in this school, in the name of Jesus.
23. Let angels of the living God arise and mobilize me to do right things, in the name of Jesus.
24. I reject evil movements that are assigned to waste my time, in the name of Jesus.
25. Let my youthful heaven for divine prosperity open and bless me, in the name of Jesus.
26. O Lord, help me to discover my purpose for being in this school, in the name of Jesus.
27. Every enemy of God's plans for my youth, die, in the name of Jesus.
28. Let yokes of devil that are dragging me into error break to pieces, in the name of Jesus.
29. Any evil force that was assigned to misdirect me, scatter in shame, in the name of Jesus.
30. Father Lord, develop my brain and spiritual life to serve You in this school, in the name of Jesus.
31. Any evil companion that was assigned to lead me into problems in this school, I separate from you, in the name of Jesus.
32. Let the fire of God burn evil documents that were written against me, in the name of Jesus.
33. O Lord, help me to learn all that I am suppose to learn in this school, in the name of Jesus.
34. Father Lord, empower me to come out of this school with first-class, in the name of Jesus.

35. Let the power of God direct me to meet the right people in this school, in the name of Jesus.

36. Blood of Jesus, empower me to be favored by everyone in this school, in the name of Jesus.

37. Any strange movement going on around me, I demobilize you, in the name of Jesus.

38. Every arrow of death and hell that was fired at me in this school, backfire, in the name of Jesus.

39. Let evil blood, disease, germ, sickness and destruction that is flowing inside me dry up and die, in the name of Jesus.

40. O Lord, protect me from evil in this school, in the name of Jesus.

41. I withdraw my case file from evil places in this world, in the name of Jesus

25

Chapter

PRAYERS FOR SUCCESS IN EXAMINATION

CHAPTER OVERVIEW

- Determination to pass all your exams
- Christians can defeat witchcraft powers

DETERMINATION TO PASS ALL YOUR EXAMS

Periodic examination is one of the traditional ways to determine whether students understood what they were taught. It is also a way to encourage students to give accounts of what they have studied over a period.

However, there are forces that could let students write their examinations successfully but would not allow them to get good results. Other times, these powers would make sure you fail your favorite subjects. Evil powers work in mysterious ways. They are destiny killers and destroyers. These are works of the devil and Jesus came to destroy them.

> *"The thief cometh not, but for to steal, to kill, and to destroy: I am come that they might have life, and that they might have it more abundantly"* (John 10:10).

Evil forces work with human agents who aid them to perfect their works on earth. This is called the powers of witchcraft.

> *"And Samuel said, Hath the LORD as great delight in burnt offerings and sacrifices, as in obeying the voice of the LORD? Behold, to obey is better than sacrifice, and to hearken than the fat of rams. For rebellion is as the sin of witchcraft and stubbornness is as iniquity and idolatry. Because thou hast rejected the word of the LORD, he hath also rejected thee from being king"* (1 Samuel 15:22-23).

When they possess people with these powers, they disobey God's Word without regards. This is how people become rebellious, stubborn and very wicked all of a sudden.

They can summon evil powers to carry out evil assignments during the time of examination. If such student does not pray very well and have people praying for him, he may be under evil influence throughout the examination period.

Witches have meetings upon meetings for the sake of one victim who they want to carry out an assignment for them at school. Many students have wondered why they failed to give correct answers to the question they know very well. The reason is that they are under the influence of witchcraft. They steal information from your brain and make your brain blank when you need it most. At other times, they may not allow you to study without understanding.

Witchcraft powers labor to subdue students during examination periods. Witches and wizards can bend what is straight and make you believe they are still straight.

Doubting the existence of witchcraft and not praying against their forces can cause you more trouble. You may perceive that something is wrong but you cannot understand what it is. They use their powers to dominate, manipulate and control student minds. They work with many evil spirits that oppose the Holy Spirit. God was so angry against evil spirit that He placed a death penalty against those who practiced it in the day of Moses.

> *"A man also or woman that hath a familiar spirit, or that is a wizard, shall surely be put to death: they shall stone them with stones: their blood shall be upon them"* (Leviticus 20:27).

> *"Thou shall not suffer a witch to live"* (Exodus 22:18).

In Israel, those who practiced witchcraft were not allowed to live. However, when the children of Israel entered into Egypt, it became a common practice. Those who knew how to fight witchcraft powers could not make much impact in that generation.

Today, witches are everywhere. They are at homes, offices and in people. When Daniel saw himself in Babylon, all his colleagues were witches and wizards. The spirit that ruled them was contrary to the spirit that ruled Daniel.

> *"Then the presidents and princes sought to find occasion against Daniel concerning the kingdom; but they could find none occasion nor fault; forasmuch as he was faithful, neither was there any error or fault found in him. Then said these men, We shall not find any occasion against this Daniel, except we find it against him concerning the law of his God"* (Daniel 6:4-5).

If the only way you know to fight witches and wizard is complaining, making noise and claiming your rights, they would finish eventually. Days are gone when only illiterates and fools operate as witchcraft. Some of the most intelligent people on earth are also witches.

> *"Then these presidents and princes assembled together to the king, and said thus unto him, King Darius, live forever. All the presidents of the kingdom, the governors, and the princes, the counselors, and the captains, have consulted together to establish a royal statute, and to make a firm decree, that whosoever shall ask a petition of any God or man for thirty days, save of thee, O king, he shall be cast into the den of lions. Now, O king, establish the decree, and sign the writing, that it be not changed, according to the law of the Medes and Persians, which altered not. Wherefore king Darius signed the writing and the decree"* (Daniel 6:6-9).

Witches have powers to make research intelligently and power to confuse any leadership. At times, they use evil summons and spiritual powers to get information before acting. That is why most leaders are under their influence.

> *"Then the presidents and princes sought to find occasion against Daniel concerning the kingdom; but they could find none occasion nor fault; forasmuch as he was faithful, neither was there any error or fault found in him"* (Daniel 6:4).

> *"And when he came to him, behold, he stood by his burnt offering, and the princes of Moab with him. And Balak said unto him, what hath the LORD spoken?"* (Numbers 23:17).

Witches and wizards access wicked powers from the earth and from the heavenly bodies. They always want to remain spiritual without submitting to God or have regards to God's Word. Witchcraft is the act of causing continuous and relentless torments, oppressions, and dullness of the mind against people, especially with satanic instruments.

> *"[1]And Balaam said unto Balak, Build me here seven altars, and prepare me here seven oxen and seven rams. [2]And Balak did as Balaam had spoken; and Balak and Balaam offered on every altar a bullock and a ram. [3]And Balaam said unto Balak, Stand by thy burnt offering, and I will go: peradventure the LORD will come to meet me: and whatsoever he sheweth me I will tell thee. In addition, he went to a high place. [13]And Balak said unto him, Come, I pray thee, with me unto another place, from whence thou mayest see them: thou shalt see but the utmost part of them, and shalt not see them all: and curse me them from thence. [14]And he brought him into the field of Zophim, to the top of Pisgah, and built seven altars, and offered a bullock and a ram on every altar"* (Numbers 23:1-3; 13-14).

Witches are determined evildoers and can keep an intelligent student beyond the years required of him to spend at school. They may offer a sacrifice to manipulate your brain, dull your mind and weaken your ability in a particular subject. They can spend money, time and brainstorm to find out where your strength is to destroy them. If they see that you love pleasures and immorality very well, they will take your desires to the extreme. With that such yoke, they will keep you away from your studies. They can also hand you over to a woman or man you cannot refuse. Through that Jezebel or sugar daddy, they will ruin your destiny. No matter how strong you are, they will use an evil partner to ruin your life eventually.

> *"And she said unto him, How canst thou say, I love thee, when thine heart is not with me? Thou hast mocked me these three times, and hast not told me wherein thy great strength lieth. And it came to pass, when she pressed him daily with her words, and urged him, so that his soul was vexed unto death; That he told her all his heart,*

and said unto her, There hath not come a razor upon mine head; for I have been a Nazarite unto God from my mother's womb: if I be shaven, then my strength will go from me, and I shall become weak, and be like any other man. And when Delilah saw that he had told her all his heart, she sent and called for the lords of the Philistines, saying, Come up this once, for he hath shewed me all his heart. Then the lords of the Philistines came up unto her, and brought money in their hand. And she made him sleep upon her knees; and she called for a man, and she caused him to shave off the seven locks of his head; and she began to afflict him, and his strength went from him. And she said, The Philistines be upon thee, Samson. In addition, he awoke out of his sleep, and said, I will go out as at other times before, and shake myself. And he wist not that the LORD was departed from him" (Judges 16:15-20).

Witchcraft is very terrible and when you overcome it, half of your problems would be over. Every department of satanic kingdom masters witchcraft. Witchcraft is the coordinating centre of the operations of the devil and an intercourse with all manner of wicked evil spirits. No agent of the devil can operate without using witchcraft; it is not possible.

"Then Elisha the high priest rose up with his brethren the priests, and they builded the sheep gate; they sanctified it, and set up the doors of it; even unto the tower of Meah they sanctified it, unto the tower of Hananeel. And next unto him builded the men of Jericho. Next to them builded Zaccur the son of Imri. But the fish gate did the sons of Hassenaah build, who also laid the beams thereof, and set up the doors thereof, the locks thereof, and the bars thereof. And next unto them repaired Meremoth the son of Urijah, the son of Koz. Next unto them repaired Meshullam the son of Berechiah, the son of Meshezabeel. And next unto them repaired Zadok the son of Baana" (Nehemiah 3:1-4).

Any city that is under witchcraft attacks is always bloody, filled with lies and fraudulent. Robber's dens are common in such cities. Devil allows wicked people in such cities to use everything in the devil's armor to destroy human beings and stop them from fulfilling their divine destinies.

"And he brought me to the door of the court; and when I looked, beholds a hole in the wall. Then said he unto me, Son of man, dig now in the wall: and when I had digged in the wall, beholds a door. And he said unto me, Go in, and behold the wicked abominations that they do here. So I went in and saw; and behold every form of creeping things, and abominable beasts, and all the idols of the house of Israel, portrayed upon the wall round about. And there stood before them seventy men of the ancients of the house of Israel, and in the midst of them stood Jaazaniah the son of Shaphan, with every man his censer in his hand; and a thick cloud of incense went up. Then said he unto me, Son of man, hast thou seen what the ancients of the house

of Israel do in the dark, every man in the chambers of his imagery? For they say, The LORD seeth us not; the LORD hath forsaken the earth" (Ezekiel 8:7-12).

"Then said Saul unto his servants, Seek me a woman that hath a familiar spirit that I may go to her, and enquire of her. And his servants said to him, Behold, there is a woman that hath a familiar spirit at Endor" (1 Samuel 28:7).

Occult grandmasters and evil church elders who are in league with the devil can penetrate through the walls to attack their victims. They can press their legs on the wall or hit the wall and travel to any place according to their ranks. Some of them have private air spaces.

A late president in one African country once arrested a younger wizard in his air space and hung him there until morning. The man remained on air while crying and shouting the name of that senior late president, asking him to release him. This shows you how cruel witches and wizards can be.

God told Ezekiel that he would pour out fury upon witches and wizards to accomplish His anger. There is a judgment waiting for unrepentant witches and wizards and it will soon manifest. Witchcraft is more complicated than most people think.

The weapons of witchcraft are grounded deeply in manipulation and control of others to gain advantage over people. It started in heaven when Lucifer rebelled against God and His authority.

"Thine heart was lifted up because of thy beauty, thou hast corrupted thy wisdom by reason of thy brightness: I will cast thee to the ground, I will lay thee before kings, that they may behold thee" (Ezekiel 28:17).

"How art thou fallen from heaven, O Lucifer, son of the morning! How art thou cut down to the ground, which didst weaken the nations! For thou hast said in thine heart, I will ascend into heaven, I will exalt my throne above the stars of God: I will sit also upon the mount of the congregation, in the sides of the north: I will ascend above the heights of the clouds; I will be like the most High" (Isaiah 14:12-14).

The spirit of the devil that is working in the world works in many schools as well. The word witchcraft is a combination of two words - (i) *Witch*, which means to bend and (ii) *craft*, which means deceit. One of the best definitions of witchcraft is *deception that makes one to bend*. However, thanks to God because He has given every Christian enough weapon to destroy witchcraft powers successfully.

> *"Finally, my brethren, be strong in the Lord, and in the power of his might. Put overall armor of God that ye may be able to stand against the wiles of the devil. For we wrestle not against flesh and blood, but against principalities, against powers, against the rulers of the darkness of this world, against spiritual wickedness in high places. Wherefore take unto you the whole armor of God that ye may be able to withstand in the evil day, and having done all, to stand. Stand therefore, having your loins girt about with truth, and having on the breastplate of righteousness; And your feet shod with the preparation of the gospel of peace; Above all, taking the shield of faith, wherewith ye shall be able to quench all the fiery darts of the wicked. And take the helmet of salvation, and the sword of the Spirit, which is the word of God"* (Ephesians 6:10-17).

The power and resources of God are readily available for use by true Christians. No believer should shy away or pretend that there is no war going on against them from the witchcraft world. We have been commanded to put on the whole armor of God to be able to stand Satan in the evil days.

Many Christians have failed in life because they neglected or ignored the manifestation of witchcraft powers in their lives. They did not know how wicked and strong witchcraft manipulations in their lives are. By the time they discover that they were under manipulation, severe damages would have been done.

> *"And it came to pass, when she pressed him daily with her words, and urged him, so that his soul was vexed unto death; That he told her all his heart, and said unto her, There hath not come a razor upon mine head; for I have been a Nazarite unto God from my mother's womb: if I be shaven, then my strength will go from me, and I shall become weak, and be like any other man. And when Delilah saw that he had told her all his heart, she sent and called for the lords of the Philistines, saying, Come up this once, for he hath showed me all his heart. Then the lords of the Philistines came up unto her, and brought money in their hand. And she made him sleep upon her knees; and she called for a man, and she caused him to shave off the seven locks of his head; and she began to afflict him, and his strength went from him. And she said, The Philistines be upon thee, Samson. In addition, he awoke out of his sleep, and said, I will go out as at other times before, and shake myself. In addition, he wist not that the*

LORD was departed from him. But the Philistines took him, and put out his eyes, and brought him down to Gaza, and bound him with fetters of brass; and he did grind in the prison house" (Judges 16:16-21).

God's power was there to help and strengthen Samson but he did not use it well. We are all to resist the works of the devil and the manipulations of witchcrafts. You must put on God's armor, resist and stand against the devil and witchcraft. A Roman soldier would never go to war without putting his helmet on. It is surprising how Christians go to war without wearing the whole armor of God.

"And take the helmet of salvation, and the sword of the Spirit, which is the word of God" (Ephesians 6:17).

"But let us, who are of the day, be sober, putting on the breastplate of faith and love; and for a helmet, the hope of salvation" (1 Thessalonians 5:8).

The helmet protects the head from arrows and broadsword. Do not allow any witch or wizard to rob you of your salvation, not even for a moment. Do not give the devil a place in your life even for a split second. No affliction has enough power to destroy Christians who stand firm and do not compromise the truth. If you remain loyal, faithful and obedient to God's eternal and unchanging truth, His power will protect you and preserve you from the manipulations of witchcrafts. Our faith is a priceless treasure, which you must hold fast.

"Forasmuch as ye know that ye were not redeemed with corruptible things, as silver and gold, from your vain conversation received by tradition from your fathers; But with the precious blood of Christ, as of a lamb without blemish and without spot" (1 Peter 1:18-19).

"For ye are bought with a price: therefore glorify God in your body, and in your spirit, which are God's" (1 Corinthians 6:20).

Do not give anything in exchanged for your faith, in order to overcome witchcraft attacks and make heaven at last. Fight for your faith especially in times of trials, distress and perplexity.

"But ye, beloved, building up yourselves on your most holy faith, praying in the Holy Ghost, Keep yourselves in the love of God, looking for the mercy of our Lord Jesus Christ unto eternal life. And of some have compassion, making a difference: And others save with fear, pulling them out of the fire; hating even the garment spotted by the flesh" (Jude 20-23).

In your efforts to defend your faith, God promised to be with you always. Witchcraft weapons are more effective in the presence of the works of the flesh. The works of the flesh essentially link us to sin, defilement and evil. God demanded that Christians must live in the spirit, not in the flesh.

> *"Now the works of the flesh are manifest, which are these; Adultery, fornication, uncleanness, lasciviousness, Idolatry, witchcraft, hatred, variance, emulations, wrath, strife, seditions, heresies, envyings, murders, drunkenness, revellings, and such like: of the which I tell you before, as I have also told you in time past, that they which do such things shall not inherit the kingdom of God"* (Galatians 5:19-21).

Idolatry and witchcraft are works of the flesh that manifest themselves through illicit relationship with unseen world. It is a spiritual intercourse with the devil. When a person begins to live in the flesh, he becomes dead spiritually. It leads to loss of God's kingdom and its privileges. If you really want to overcome the works of the flesh, you must remember that God is forever present everywhere you are, even in the dark.

One funny thing about witchcraft is that one can practice it without knowing. Your close friend may be casting spells of witchcrafts on you without you knowing it. There are characters that are common with witchcraft. If you find these characters in your life or your friend's life, then you need deliverance. You need to repent and forsake your sins immediately. You do not need to operate in a coven before you realize that you are a witch or wizard. You may not even fly at night to qualify for witchcraft.

If your lifestyle is abominable and immoral, you need to pray against witchcraft because you may have been bewitched.

> *"Notwithstanding I have a few things against thee, because thou sufferest that woman Jezebel, which calleth herself a prophetess, to teach and to seduce my servants to commit fornication, and to eat things sacrificed unto idols. And I gave her space to repent of her fornication; and she repented not. Behold, I will cast her into a bed, and them that commit adultery with her into great tribulation, except they repent of their deeds. And I will kill her children with death; and all the churches shall know that I am he who searched the reins and hearts: and I will give unto every one of you according to your works"* (Revelation 2:20-23).

If your lifestyle is all about seducing men and committing fornication, you may have fallen into the hands of witchcraft. If you have slept with a seductress, you could have been initiated. Many people are dealing with iniquities they have failed to bring under control. This is how the spirit of witchcraft functions. It cannot allow people to stop committing a particular sin that defiles their bodies. That is how you know you have a witchcraft deposit in your life.

Witches are wicked. They can be using you without you knowing. Once they make a deposit in your body through sin, they start using you to do witchcraft works. That is how the desire to do iniquity overpowers many people until they commit sin. You could be a leader in the church, school or fellowship, but if you fail to deal with the seed of witchcraft in your life, it would spread in the congregation of God's people. You spread it to other people without your knowledge.

> *"And Nadab and Abihu, the sons of Aaron, took either of them his censer, and put fire therein, and put incense thereon, and offered strange fire before the LORD, which he commanded them not"* (Leviticus 10:1).

> *"And Nadab and Abihu died before the LORD, when they offered strange fire before the LORD, in the wilderness of Sinai, and they had no children: and Eleazar and Ithamar ministered in the priest's office in the sight of Aaron their father"* (Numbers 3:4).

I used to know one woman who had a seductive spirit deposited inside her. She spread demons of immorality to many ministers in the church. The ministers in turn spread them to members. Strange beings would take her to certain to have sex with her when seductive demons in her depleted. According to her, some ministers had sex with her while trying to deliver her. I know many people that became victims to her evil strange powers.

> *"[7]Wherefore the sin of the young men was very great before the LORD: for men abhorred the offering of the LORD. [22]Now Eli was very old, and heard all that his sons did unto all Israel; and how they lay with the women that assembled at the door of the tabernacle of the congregation. [23]And he said unto them, why do you such things? For I hear of your evil dealings by this entire people"* (1 Samuel 2:17, 22-23).

It is not an ordinary feeling to see a woman or a man and begin to have strange and lustful feelings towards that person. The truth is that you are under an evil influence at that point. All you need do is to flee. Witchcraft powers are sometimes subtle and can come in many ways. We are in battle and you need the power of God more because you cannot run away all the time. You need to confront some of them sometimes.

You cannot run away from witchcraft powers all the time. Sometimes, you need to confront and subdue such powers and rescue people that are perishing. This is what distinguishes senior deliverance ministers. I am not talking about age or experience but the grace of God. When you fail to recognize the grace of God in your life, you may die like a fish that suddenly finds out that it is in a dry land. Ask God for the grace to know what to do when you want to confront witchcraft powers. Be mindful of the fact that witchcraft attacks can come from respectable leaders. Do not take anything for granted.

"The word which came unto Jeremiah from the LORD in the days of Jehoiakim the son of Josiah king of Judah, saying, Go unto the house of the Rechabites, and speak unto them, and bring them into the house of the LORD, into one of the chambers, and give them wine to drink. Then I took Jaazaniah the son of Jeremiah, the son of Habaziniah, and his brethren, and all his sons, and the whole house of the Rechabites; And I brought them into the house of the LORD, into the chamber of the sons of Hanan, the son of Igdaliah, a man of God, which was by the chamber of the princes, which was above the chamber of Messiah the son of Shallum, the keeper of the door: And I set before the sons of the house of the Rechabites pots full of wine, and cups, and I said unto them, Drink ye wine. But they said, We will drink no wine: for Jonadab the son of Rechab our father commanded us, saying, Ye shall drink no wine, neither ye, nor your sons forever" (Jeremiah 35:1-6).

Sometimes, witchcraft attacks can come from your loved ones, those you cannot refuse things easily. It can come from your immediate employer, like the wife of Potiphar. It may come at your weakest moments through your own appetite.

"And Jacob sod pottage: and Esau came from the field and he was faint: And Esau said to Jacob, Feed me, I pray thee, with that same red pottage; for I am faint: therefore was his name called Edom. And Jacob said, Sell me this day thy birthright. And Esau said, Behold, I am at the point to die: and what profit shall this birthright do to me? And Jacob said, Swear to me this day; and he swore unto him: and he sold his birthright unto Jacob. Then Jacob gave Esau bread and pottage of lentiles; and he did eat and drink, and rose up, and went his way: thus Esau despised his birthright" (Genesis 25:29-34).

At times, you may fail to recognize that you are going through temptation or being attacked by witchcraft. If you pitch your tent near Sodom, very close to a tempting Delilah, you must be sober and vigilant. If Jezebels crowd your office, you must watch and pray all the time. You may need more grace than those living or working in a Christian establishment. If all your roommates are carnal, you need to be sober and vigilant. You simply cannot fight witchcraft battles with human techniques.

"Hast thou not known? Hast thou not heard that the everlasting God, the LORD, the Creator of the ends of the earth, fainteth not, neither is weary? There is no searching of his understanding. He giveth power to the faint; and to them that have no might he increase strength. Even the youths shall faint and be weary and the young men shall utterly fall: But they that wait upon the LORD shall renew their strength; they shall mount up with wings as eagles; they shall run, and not be weary; and they shall walk, and not faint" (Isaiah 40:28-31).

Without the grace of God, any of us can be weak at any time. A wise person would separate himself from every appearance of evil. Do not join in witchcraft activities.

"When thou art come into the land which the LORD thy God giveth thee, thou shalt not learn to do after the abominations of those nations. There shall not be found among you any one that maketh his son or his daughter to pass through the fire, or that useth divination, or an observer of times, or an enchanter, or a witch, Or a charmer, or a consulter with familiar spirits, or a wizard, or a necromancer. For all that do these things are an abomination unto the LORD: and because of these abominations the LORD, thy God doth drive them out from before thee. Thou shall be perfect with the LORD thy God" (Deuteronomy 18:9-13).

The reason you need to be vigilant is that witches can live in the same hostel with you. They can study in the same classroom with you also. Do not be afraid of them. You will know them by their fruits. They use domination, intimidations, evil control, fear, rebellion and stubborn attitudes in their dispositions. All you have to use to defeat them is the whole armor of God.

"Finally, my brethren, be strong in the Lord, and in the power of his might. Put armor of God that ye may be able to stand against the wiles of the devil. for we wrestle not against flesh and blood, but against principalities, against powers, against the rulers of the darkness of this world, against spiritual wickedness in high places. Wherefore take unto you the whole armor of God that ye may be able to withstand in the evil day, and having done all, to stand. Stand therefore, having your loins girt about with truth, and having on the breastplate of righteousness; And your feet shod with the preparation of the gospel of peace; Above all, taking the shield of faith, wherewith ye shall be able to quench all the fiery darts of the wicked. And take the helmet of salvation, and the sword of the Spirit, which is the word of God" (Ephesians 6:10-17).

When they apply weapons of threat, violation of rules, disobedience to authorities, faultfinding, accusations and sexual immorality, trust our God for deliverance. At other times, they may try to use confusion and memory failures. You must remain prayerful and determined to please God. They may also use weapons of judgmental attitude, evil instigation and all manner of manipulation. You must take your stand until the end.

When you fail at school, you would find life difficult in the world. Now is the time to fight your battles. You have to study to show yourself approved unto God so that they cannot put you to shame.

"Study to shew thyself approved unto God, a workman that needed not to be ashamed, rightly dividing the word of truth" (2 Timothy 2:15).

If you are not born-again, you need to be born-again to pass your exams and come out with good results. You can repent, confess and forsake all your sins, and it shall be well with you.

PRAYERS FOR SUCCESS IN EXAMINATION

Bible references: Daniel 1:8, 6:1-5

Begin with praise and worship

1. Father Lord, enhance my brain for the sake of the approaching examination, in the name of Jesus.
2. I command evil forces of darkness that dispute my academic success to scatter and die, in the name of Jesus.
3. I lift every embargo that was placed on my academics and career, in the name of Jesus.
4. I receive power to pass every exam with distinction, in the name of Jesus.
5. Let powers that would help me to make best results possess me, in the name of Jesus.
6. Every demon that kills destinies, I cast you out, die, in the name of Jesus.
7. I disgrace satanic agents that were assigned to bring failures into my life, in the name of Jesus.
8. I frustrate witchcraft attacks on my academic breakthroughs, in the name of Jesus.
9. Let any demon that was released to attack me during examination go back to its senders, in the name of Jesus.
10. Father Lord, teach me how to understand every subject and the way to answer questions well, in the name of Jesus.
11. Blessed Holy Spirit, direct me to the right topics to study at the right times, in the name of Jesus.
12. Every arrow of confusion that was fired at my brain, backfire, in the name of Jesus.
13. O Lord, send You angels to teach me everything I need to know, in the name of Jesus.
14. Father Lord, empower me to state facts that would satisfy examiners, in the name of Jesus.
15. Let my reasoning power be rightly focused, in the name of Jesus.

16. O Lord, give me the grace to read and study with understanding, in the name of Jesus.

17. Any evil power that has occupied my brain, die, in the name of Jesus.

18. Let the fire of God burn every enemy of my academic excellence, in the name of Jesus.

19. I deliver any area of my brain that is under attacks by fire, in the name of Jesus.

20. I break and loose myself from the spirit of failure at the edge of miracle, in the name of Jesus.

21. O Lord, help me to become more intelligent than my teachers, in the name of Jesus.

22. I disgrace anything that is distracting my academic pursuits, in the name of Jesus.

23. Any evil plantation that is bringing failures into my life, die, in the name of Jesus.

24. Let every yoke of academic failures in my life break to pieces, in the name of Jesus.

25. Let evil altars that are ministering failures into my life scatter, in the name of Jesus.

26. Any demonic program that is contending with my academic program, die, in the name of Jesus.

27. I command any power that intimidates me during exams to die, in the name of Jesus.

28. Blood of Jesus, wash my brain for academic success, in the name of Jesus.

29. Any worldly activity that is contending with my academic activities, I reject you, in the name of Jesus.

30. I break and loose myself from evil yoke of immorality and evil lust, in the name of Jesus.

31. I terminate evil movements for the sake of my exams and results, in the name of Jesus.

32. O Lord, grant me favor before the graders of my scripts, in the name of Jesus.

33. Let weapons of witchcraft that is fighting my academics waster their owners, in the name of Jesus.

34. O Lord, let me be composed and organized enough to write well, in the name of Jesus.

35. I frustrate any agent of devil that has vowed to manipulate my results, in the name of Jesus.

36. O Lord, let my excellent performance frustrate my enemies, in the name of Jesus.

37. I refuse to compromise my faith because of any examinations, in the name of Jesus.

38. Let my examination materials cooperate with me during examination, in the name of Jesus.

39. Let any evil plan to demote me in any exam fail woefully, in the name of Jesus.

40. Let the information that would attract the highest marks appear to me, in the name of Jesus.

26

Chapter

PRAYERS FOR AN EXCELLENT JOB

CHAPTER OVERVIEW

- *Divine assignment*
- *Personal evangelism*
- *Prayer unlocks impossible things*

DIVINE ASSIGNMENT

Millions of people all over the world today are looking for jobs. Most of them are youths, who are sick, tired, and almost confused because of idleness. Christians among them are crying, praying and almost blaming God and people for their predicaments. However, the truth is that God did not create anyone on earth without provisions for what to do. God demonstrated this when He gave Adam work to do.

> *"And the LORD God took the man, and put him into the Garden of Eden to dress it and to keep it. And the LORD God commanded the man, saying, Of every tree of the garden thou mayest freely eat: But of the tree of the knowledge of good and evil, thou shall not eat of it: for in the day that thou eatest thereof thou shall surely die"* (Genesis 2:15-17).

God has provided men with work from the beginning of time. Vast fields of the earth are enough for all men to work. However, God wants every man to accomplish a particular purpose on earth. There is always a garden to dress and a job to keep. When Jesus came to earth, He did not waste time looking for jobs or doing every other job that was advertised. He went about doing what God called Him to do. What has God called you to do on earth?

> *"And it came to pass, that after three days they found him in the temple, sitting in the midst of the doctors, both hearing them, and asking them questions. And all that heard him were astonished at his understanding and answers. And when they saw him, they were amazed: and his mother said unto him, Son, why hast thou thus dealt with us? Behold, thy father and I have sought thee sorrowing. And he said unto them how is it that ye sought me. Wist ye not that I must be about my Father's business?"* (Luke 2:46-49).

Jesus discovered His job on time. He was in the midst of the doctors, hearing and asking them questions. Though Jesus knew His calling, He submitted to His parent's care until He was old enough to start His work fully. His parents took care of Him, and taught Him how to work and live.

Unfortunately, many young ministers have abandoned schools without acquiring enough training because they discovered their calling early. That was not what Jesus did. Jesus submitted to His parents until it was right time for Him to start His ministry. He was obedient to His parents and elders. He increased in wisdom, stature and favor with God and man. Before He started His ministry, He allowed the Holy Ghost to lead Him into times of prayers for an open heaven.

> *"[21]Now when all the people were baptized, it came to pass, that Jesus also being baptized, and praying, the heaven was opened, [22]And the Holy Ghost descended in a bodily shape like a dove upon him, and a voice came from heaven, which said, Thou art my beloved Son; in thee I am well pleased. [1]And Jesus being full of the Holy Ghost returned from Jordan, and was led by the Spirit into the wilderness, [2]being forty days tempted of the devil. And in those days he did eat nothing: and when they were ended, he afterward hungered"* (Luke 3:21-22; 4:1-2).

Jesus did not launch into ministry directly from His parent's care and training even though He had all the qualifications, wisdom and training to do so. He surrendered to the Holy Spirit first, who led Him to pray. He submitted to John the Baptist to be baptized in water. His heaven opened and God spoke, the Holy Spirit descended upon Him as a dove before He was ready for His ministry and then He was tempted by devil.

> *"And the devil said unto him, If thou be the Son of God, commands this stone that it be made bread. And Jesus answered him, saying, It is written, That man shall not live by bread alone, but by every word of God"* (Luke 4:3-4).

> *"Then saith Jesus unto him, Get thee hence, Satan: for it is written, Thou shall worship the Lord thy God, and him only shall thou serve. Then the devil leave him, and, behold, angels came and ministered unto him"* (Matthew 4:10-11).

He overcame the devil and angels ministered to Him from henceforth.

PERSONAL EVANGELISM

Many countries have developed programs for their youths and young graduates who graduated from schools. For instance, in Nigeria, young university graduates go through one-year orientation program and service to their country. Without it, they cannot get any job from the Nigerian government or even political assignments.

Such periods help young people to develop their experiences. For young Christians, it is time to know what God would have you do for the rest of your life through prayers. As a Christian student, you must have been evangelizing and preaching to others. Now that you are out of school or you lost your job, you need to commit more time to personal evangelism as you pray for an excellent job.

Use your time profitably to do more work for Jesus, as you pray for an excellent job. You may not have such a wonderful time again in your lifetime. For the mean time, see yourself as a *watchman*, like Ezekiel, the prophet, in your area of expertise.

> *"Son of man, I have made thee a watchman unto the house of Israel: therefore hear the word at my mouth, and give them warning from me. When I say unto the wicked, Thou shall surely die; and thou givest him not warning, nor speaks to warn the wicked from his wicked way, to save his life; the same wicked* man *shall die in his iniquity; but his blood will I require at thine hand. Yet if thou warn the wicked, and he turn not from his wickedness, nor from his wicked way, he shall die in his iniquity; but thou hast delivered thy soul. Again, when a righteous man doth turn from his righteousness, and commit iniquity, and I lay an obstacle before him, he shall die: because thou hast not given him warning, he shall die in his sin, and his righteousness, which he hath done, shall not be remembered; but his blood will I require at thine hand. Nevertheless if thou warn the righteous man, that the righteous sin not, and he doth not sin, he shall surely live, because he is warned; also thou hast delivered thy soul"* (Ezekiel 3:17-21).

Study your Bible and attend fellowships. Go for personal evangelism while you prayerfully trust God for a good job. If you are serious with personal evangelism, you will win souls for God more. You have the opportunity to plant seeds that would germinate in years to come. You may be evangelizing to another *Paul* or future presidents of the world.

> *"And they that be wise shall shine as the brightness of the firmament; and they that turn many to righteousness as the stars forever and ever"* (Daniel 12:3).

"But when he saw the multitudes, he was moved with compassion on them, because they fainted, and were scattered abroad, as sheep having no shepherd. Then saith he unto his disciples, the harvest truly is *plenteous, but the laborers* are *few; Pray ye therefore the Lord of the harvest, that he will send forth laborers into his harvest"* (Matthew 9:36-38).

The time you have no job to do is a valuable time. Most youths use this time to socialize, attend parties, play games like *cards, ludo* and *draft*, or gossip, or read worldly novels, or visit film houses, and fornicate. However, you should use your own time to please God through evangelism and winning souls for God.

Do not throw away such valuable time or give it to the devil. You will soon shine as the brightness of the firmament because you are turning many to righteousness. The people you are preaching to may not repent immediately. They may even insult you but keep talking to people about Christ. Personal evangelism is good news from the living God to a lost person.

"For God so loved the world that he gave his only begotten Son, that whosoever believeth in him should not perish, but have everlasting life. For God sent not his Son into the world to condemn the world; but that the world through him might be saved" (John 3:16-17).

Gospel is the message of God to man and men must hear it. Preach with compassion and pray that God empowers His Word to save sinners.

Evangelism is your responsibility: Evangelism is very important to believers. Some Christians who evangelized got discouraged because they do not really understand what evangelism was all about. Evangelism is a duty for every Christian and a debt that must be paid. It is out of not only charity, but also a duty and responsibility of every Christian.

"I am debtor both to the Greeks, and to the Barbarians; both to the wise, and to the unwise. So, as much as in me is, I am ready to preach the gospel to you that are at Rome also. For I am not ashamed of the gospel of Christ: for it is the power of God unto salvation to everyone that believeth; to the Jew first, and also to the Greek" (Romans 1:14-16).

"And he said unto them, Go you into all the world, and preach the gospel to every creature" (Mark 16:15).

Bringing people to God through evangelism is what God loves most. It is a command given to all believers. Not witnessing to others about the saving power of Christ is to disobey God's command. When you look back at your past life, you would see that you were once lost. If someone did not preach to you, it would have been another story. That is why you must preach to someone else.

> *"The wicked shall be turned into hell,* and *all the nations that forget God"* (Psalm 9:17).

> *"Neither is there salvation in any other: for there is none other name under heaven given among men, whereby we must be saved"* (Acts 4:12).

Souls are very precious to God and many people are perishing and rushing into eternity without Christ. Every soul is very important to God and more precious than all the good things on earth put together.

> *"For what shall it profit a man, if he shall gain the whole world, and lose his own soul?"* (Mark 8:36).

According to research, 65 people die every minute in most developed nations. In a year, about 8,000,000 people die and most of them die without Christ.

In most cities of the world, sinners are always the majority and they need the gospel. You must have a deep burning like the compassion Christ would have whenever He met sinners or people tormented by the devil. You must be willing to suffer for the salvation of others because there is great reward for doing so.

> "And *how I kept back nothing that was profitable* unto you, *but have showed you, and have taught you publicly, and from house to house, Testifying both to the Jews, and also to the Greeks, repentance toward God, and faith toward our Lord Jesus Christ. And now, behold, I go bound in the spirit unto Jerusalem, not knowing the things that shall befall me there: Save that the Holy Ghost witnessed in every city, saying that bonds and afflictions abide me. But none of these things move me, neither count I my life dear unto myself, so that I might finish my course with joy, and the ministry, which I have received of the Lord Jesus, to testify the gospel of the grace of God"* (Acts 20:20-24).

See no trouble as too great, any humiliation as too deep, or suffering as too severe in your attempt to save a soul through personal evangelism. Our labors of love must be to save souls. Evangelism is a costly ministry that demands self-denial, discipline and diligence. It is for those who are sure of their faith in Christ and have compassion to see other souls repent. You must study the scriptures, live above sin and be a true child of God.

> *"Depart ye, depart ye, go ye out from thence, touch no unclean* thing*; go ye out of the midst of her; be ye clean, that bear the vessels of the LORD"* (Isaiah 52:11)

"Having therefore obtained help of God, I continue unto this day, witnessing both to small and great, saying none other things than those which the prophets and Moses did say should come: That Christ should suffer, and *that he should be the first that should rise from the dead, and should show light unto the people, and to the Gentiles. And as he thus speaks for himself, Festus said with a loud voice, Paul, thou art beside thyself; much learning doth make thee mad"* (Acts 26:22-24).

You must also intercede for people you preach to for their conversion. Ask God to open their eyes to see the sacrifice Christ offered on the cross of Calvary. Always try to lead each sinner to a meaningful decision. Lead him or her to a confession and prayers of repentance. Handle them personally and involve them in fellowship with other believers.

"Not forsaking the assembling of ourselves together, as the manner of some is; but exhorting one another*: and so much the more, as ye see the day approaching"* (Hebrews 10:25).

Doctors have discovered that getting patients involved in some kind of work, a technique called occupational therapy had remarkable healing effects on patients. Let doctors get involved in evangelism also.

Prayer evangelism: Prayer evangelism is a request that came directly from Christ when He went about the cities and villages teaching and preaching the gospel of the kingdom. He had compassion for the multitudes of people He encountered on each city. Most people in those cities were sinners, sick and diseased.

"And Jesus went about all the cities and villages, teaching in their synagogues, and preaching the gospel of the kingdom, and healing every sickness and every disease among the people. But when he saw the multitudes, he was moved with compassion on them, because they fainted, and were scattered abroad, as sheep having no shepherd. Then saith he unto his disciples, the harvest truly is *plenteous, but the laborers* are *few; Pray ye therefore the Lord of the harvest, that he will send forth laborers into his harvest"* (Matthew 9:35-38).

These multitudes were scattered all over the places as sheep having no shepherd. Jesus was deeply moved and He asked for prayers on their behalf. His request was, *"Pray ye therefore the Lord of the harvest that He will send forth laborers into His harvest."* From the above reference, we took the title of our discussion: prayer evangelism.

"For whosoever shall call upon the name of the Lord shall be saved. How then shall they call on him in whom they have not believed? In addition, how shall they believe in him of whom they have not heard? And how shall they hear without a preacher? And how shall they preach, except they be sent? As it is written, how beautiful are the feet

of them that preach the gospel of peace, and bring glad tidings of good things" (Romans 10:13-15).

The assurance we have is that when we obey this command, salvation would be recorded. People will call on God if they know Him and believe in His saving power. God sends prayer evangelists to pray for the salvation of sinners, heal the sick and deliver the oppressed and diseased.

"Ask, and it shall be given you; seek, and ye shall find; knock, and it shall be opened unto you: for every one that asked receiveth; and he that seeketh findeth; and to him that knocked it shall be opened" (Matthew 7:7-8).

WHAT IS PRAYER?

a. Prayer is an expression of commitment and trust we have in God

b. It is the medium to express our desires and needs by way of petition to God.

c. It is also a way of expressing our appreciation and thankfulness to God.

"Be careful for nothing; but in everything by prayer and supplication with thanksgiving let your requests be made known unto God" (Philippians 4:6).

WHAT IS EVANGELISM?

a. Evangelism is the process of telling people about Jesus Christ and what He did for humanity.

b. It is the preaching of the gospel of our Lord Jesus Christ to every creature, every tribe, and every nation of the earth.

> *"And he said unto them, Go ye into the entire world, and preach the gospel to every creature"* (Mark 16:15).

Prayer and evangelism are two inseparable weapons required by a believer who wants to obey the commandment of our Lord Jesus Christ regarding witnessing. You cannot substitute one for another. It is necessary for every believer to pray and evangelize.

> *"How then shall they call on him in whom they have not believed? In addition, how shall they believe in him of whom they have not heard? And how shall they hear without a preacher?"* (Romans 10:14).

When you evangelize or witness, the Holy Spirit works within the person to whom you witnessed to, to soften and prepare his heart for salvation. God himself now brings about circumstances and events to get the person's attention, and cause him to reevaluate his entire life and beliefs and then reach a decision to accept Jesus Christ.

> *"No man can come to me, except the Father which hath sent me draw him: and I will raise him up at the last day"* (John 6:44).

Prayer evangelism therefore is a kind of prayer that moves God to bring about some circumstances in the life of the targeted person, persons or nation, which would compel him (them) to accept Christ and be born-again.

With traditional evangelism, you usually pray for a person while you share the gospel with him afterwards. However, in prayer evangelism, you pray for a person aggressively before you witness to him. Also, in prayer evangelism, you may pray while another person witnesses. Susan Wesley, Mary Slessor, Catharine Booth, who founded salvation army, Florence Crawford (Apostolic Faith), Martin Luther's wife are all great women who won souls for Christ. Someone through prayers converted Miss Phoebe Bestleth who was mightily used.

Three things can increase people's chances of becoming born-again.

a. The written Word of God – Bible
b. Your lifestyle – our lives are like written epistles that others read on daily basis.
c. Prayer evangelism.

Benefits of prayer evangelism are many. They include

- It allows you to overcome geographical barriers.
- It allows you to overcome political barriers.
- It allows you to overcome religious barriers.
- You can pray for specific places, person, and nations at a time.
- It helps you to reach people cut off from the reach of the gospel.

HOW TO PRAY FOR UNBELIEVERS

a. You must be born-again in order to have victory over sin.

b. Identify relatives of the person you are praying for; sons, daughters, etc, and pray for them

c. Make a list of people you want to pray for and pray for them specifically and periodically.

d. Set aside at least 30 minutes in a day to pray for them.

e. Move from that level to meeting with your neighbors physically.

f. Before you part with your money, pray that the recipient would be blessed and be born-again.

g. Identify villages, cities and nations and pray for them.

h. Pray for faces you see in television sets.

WHAT PRAYERS TO PRAY

a. Pray that the Holy Ghost prepares people's hearts to accept Christ.

b. Pray that God brings circumstances that would prepare them to listen to the gospel and repent.

c. Pray for God to prepare someone they would listen to, to preach to them.

d. Pray that God removes any obstacle that would prevent their salvation.

For Example, you can pray like this -

- O Lord, let _______ become a good Christian.
- O Lord, raise a preacher that will preach to _______ to repent.
- O Lord, join _______ to a God-fearing friend that will preach to him.

There are people who prayed for others in the bible but people did not pray for them. Such people include:

1. JESUS

"Therefore will I divide him a portion *with the great, and he shall divide the spoil with the strong; because he hath poured out his soul unto death: and he was numbered with the transgressors; and he bare the sin of many, and made intercession for the transgressors"* (Isaiah 53:12).

"Wherefore he is able also to save them to the uttermost that come unto God by him, seeing he ever liveth to make intercession for them" (Hebrews 7:25).

"[15]I pray not that thou shouldest take them out of the world, but that thou shouldest keep them from the evil. [20]Neither pray I for these alone, but for them also which shall believe on me through their word; [21]That they all may be one; as thou, Father, art *in me, and I in thee, that they also may be one in us: that the world may believe that thou hast sent me"* (John 17:15, 20-21).

"Who is he that condemned? It is *Christ that died, yea rather, that is risen again, who is even at the right hand of God, who also make intercession for us"* (Romans 8:34).

The apostles and all that benefited from Christ's ministry forsook Him when he needed them most at the cross to suffer alone. He prayed to God and God heard Him.

(*See* Matthew 26:46-50, 58-59, 69-75; 27:39-46, 50)

2. MOSES

"And the LORD said unto Moses, Go, get thee down; for thy people, which thou brightest out of the land of Egypt, have corrupted themselves*: They have turned aside quickly out of the way which I commanded them: they have made them a molten calf, and have worshipped it, and have sacrificed thereunto, and said, These* be *thy gods, O Israel, which have brought thee up out of the land of Egypt. And the LORD said unto Moses, I have seen this people, and, behold, it* is *a stiff-necked people: Now therefore let me alone, that my wrath may wax hot against them, and that I may consume them: and I will make of thee a great nation. And Moses besought the LORD his God, and said, LORD, why doth thy wrath wax hot against thy people, which thou hast brought forth out of the land of Egypt with great power, and with a mighty hand? Wherefore should the Egyptians speak, and say, For mischief did he bring them out, to slay them in the mountains, and to consume them from the face of the earth? Turn from thy fierce wrath, and repent of this evil against thy people. Remember Abraham, Isaac, and Israel, thy servants, to whom thou swarest by thine own self, and saidst unto them, I will multiply your seed as the stars of heaven, and all this land that I have spoken of will I give unto your seed, and they shall inherit* it *forever. And the LORD repented of the evil which he thought to do unto his people"* (Exodus 32:7-14).

"And the LORD said unto Moses, How long will this people provoke me? In addition, how long will it be ere they believe me, for all the signs, which I have showed among them? I will smite them with the pestilence, and disinherit them, and will make of thee a greater nation and mightier than they. And Moses said unto the LORD, Then the Egyptians shall hear it, *(for thou brightest up this people in thy might from among them;) And they will tell* it *to the inhabitants of this land:* for *they have heard that thou LORD* art *among this people, that thou LORD art seen face to face, and* that *thy cloud standeth over them, and* that *thou goest before them, by day time in a pillar of a cloud, and in a pillar of fire by night. Now* if *thou shall kill all this people as one man, then the nations which have heard the fame of thee will speak, saying, Because the LORD was not able to bring this people into the land which he swore unto them, therefore he hath slain them in the wilderness. And now, I beseech thee, let the power of my Lord be great, according as thou hast spoken, saying, The LORD* is *longsuffering, and of great mercy, forgiving iniquity and transgression, and by no means clearing* the guilty, *visiting the iniquity of the fathers upon the children unto the third and fourth* generation. *Pardon, I beseech thee, the iniquity of this people according unto the greatness of thy mercy, and as thou hast forgiven this people, from Egypt even until now. And the LORD said, I have pardoned according to thy word: But* as *truly* as *I live, all the earth shall be filled with the glory of the LORD"* (Numbers 14:11-21).

a. When Pharaoh persecuted the children of Israel, Moses prayed for them (*See* Exodus 5:1-22).

b. When Pharaoh wanted to deal with them, Moses prayed for them (*See* Exodus 7:12-15, 20-29; 8:31; 9:8-11, 27-30, 33-35, 8-10; 10:18-19).

c. When the Egyptians pursued them, Moses prayed for them (*See* Exodus 14:13-15, 5-12, 19-31).

d. When they lacked water, Moses prayer for them (*See* Exodus 17:1-7).

e. When the Amalekites fought them, Moses prayed for them (*See* Exodus 17:15-16).

f. When Aaron built idol for them and God wanted to promote Moses and destroy them, Moses prayed for them (*See* Exodus 32:7-35; Numbers 14:1-4, 6-10, 22-37, 40-45).

g. When they were under a burden, Moses prayed for them (*See* Numbers 11:2, 11-30).

h. When Miriam became a leper, Moses prayed for her (*See* Numbers 12:1-16).

i. When God wanted to smite them with pestilence, Moses prayed for them (*See* Number 14:1-25).

j. When the daughters of Zelophehad lost their father's inheritance, Moses went to God on their behalf (*See* Numbers 27:1-11).

k. He went to God and received the constitution for Israel. (*See* Deuteronomy 9:9, 11, 7-20, 25).

However, when Moses entered into trouble, no one prayed for him (*See* Deuteronomy 3:23-28; Number 27:12-17; Deuteronomy 31:1-2, 14-15; 32:44-52; 34:1-7, 10-12. However, God did not abandon him. God buried him and later brought him into the Promised Land he prayed to enter.

> *"And after six days Jesus taketh Peter, James, and John his brother, and bringeth them up into a high mountain apart, And was transfigured before them: and his face did shine as the sun, and his raiment was white as the light. And, behold, there appeared unto them Moses and Elias talking with him"* (Matthew 17:1-3).

It is time to pray for people, yourself and your future. You can get the best job on earth if you so desire. As you do the works of the Lord, He will do your own work. He that watered shall be watered. If you have worked for God, you need to join us in this program. This is the time to pray for you for a good job. You need it, you deserve it and God will give it to you.

> *"Moreover the word of the LORD came unto Jeremiah the second time, while he was yet shut up in the court of the prison, saying, Thus saith the LORD the maker thereof,*

the LORD that formed it, to establish it; the LORD is *his name; Call unto me, and I will answer thee, and show thee great and mighty things, which thou knows not"* (Jeremiah 33:1-3).

Even when others cannot pray for you, start praying for yourself.

PRAYER UNLOCKS IMPOSSIBLE THINGS

Many things would be possible when we pray. Among them are salvation and peace of mind (*See* John 1:12; 3:16; Romans 10:6-13). Sanctification, victory, power in service, full redemption, healing, all manner of physical, material and spiritual needs (*See* Acts 26:18; 1 John 4:4, 5:3-5; Galatians 3:2, 14; Acts 1:8; Mark 5:34; James 5:14-15; Luke 17:11-19; Matthew 16:19, 17:20; Matthew 18:18-20; 21:21-22, 9:23, 11:20-24; Luke 17:5-6; John 14:13-14, 15:7, 16:23-24).

a. Abraham prayed for a child and God gave him Isaac. Isaac prayed for a child and God gave him Jacob and Esau.

b. Ishmael prayed for provision and God heard his voice. He received open heaven and the eyes of his mother were opened to see a well of water in the wilderness (*See* Genesis 21:17-21).

c. Jacob prayed for a change and God changed his name (*See* Genesis 32:24-30).

d. The children of Israel prayed against the Egyptian's bondage and God heard their cry and sent Moses to deliver them (*See* Exodus 2:22-25).

e. Joshua and the elders of Israel prayed and God showed them what to do to get victory from their enemies (*See* Joshua 7:1-26).

f. Joshua prayed for victory over his enemies and God stopped the sun and the moon for a whole day to give him victory (*See* Joshua 10:12-15).

g. Hannah prayed and God opened her womb to conceive and deliver Samuel after many years of reproach and barrenness (*See* 1 Samuel 1:7-28).

h. David prayed against Saul's plot to kill him and God showed him a way of escape (*See* 1 Samuel 33:9-15).

i. Elijah prayed and God closed heaven for three years and six months. He prayed again and God opened heaven for abundant rain (*See* 1 Kings 17:1-46, 18:1-29).

j. Elisha prayed for power and God gave him a double portion of Elijah's power (*See* 2 Kings 2:9-15).

k. Hezekiah prayed and God reversed the judgment of death on him and added 15 years to his years on earth (*See* 2 Kings 20:1-7)

l. Jabez prayed against poverty and God answered, blessed him and enlarged his coast (*See* 1 Chronicles 4:9-10)

m. Asa and Judah prayed and God gave them rest from war for many years (*See* 2 Chronicles 14:4, 16-8).

n. Jehoshaphat prayed and God took over the battles of his life and delivered him from his stubborn enemies (*See* 2 Chronicles 20:1-30).

o. Manasseh prayed and God forgave him of all his wickedness and cleared him from sin (*See* 2 Chronicles 33:1-19).

p. Jeremiah prayed and God delivered him, showed him great and mighty things, which he never knew before (*See* Jeremiah 33:1-3).

q. Ezekiel prayed and God commanded flesh to come upon dry bones (*See* Ezekiel 37:1).

r. Jonah prayed and marine fish vomited him.

s. Daniel prayed and lions became afraid of him and killed his enemies (*See* Daniel 6:1-30).

t. The worst thief on earth prayed at the cross and Jesus took him to heaven (*See* Luke 23:39-43).

u. Jesus prayed and heaven's gate opened for you and me (*See* John 19:28-30).

PRAYERS FOR AN EXCELLENT JOB

Bible references: Nehemiah 2:1-8, Daniel 6:1-5, Esther 6:1-14, 2:1-23

Begin with praise and worship

1. O Lord, give me a job that will provide all my needs and help me fulfill my destiny, in the name of Jesus.
2. Father Lord, raise people that will help me get an excellent job, in the name of Jesus.
3. Every curse that is placed upon my certificate, I remove you by force, in the name of Jesus.
4. Blood of Jesus, empower my curriculum vitae to be preferred above others, in the name of Jesus.
5. Father Lord, give me an job that will make me a better Christian, in the name of Jesus.
6. Any evil personality that is blocking my job is removed, in the name of Jesus.
7. O Lord, retire or sack any stubborn enemy that is blocking my employment, in the name of Jesus.
8. Blood of Jesus, cleanse any evil mark that was placed on my forehead, in the name of Jesus.
9. I disgrace evil personalities that are sitting upon my job, in the name of Jesus.
10. I command any evil personality that is sitting upon my job to be unseated, in the name of Jesus.
11. Let that person that would help me get a job be well positioned, in the name of Jesus.
12. Every yoke of unemployment in my life, break to pieces, in the name of Jesus.
13. Every satanic obstacle that is standing against my job is removed, in the name of Jesus.
14. Any power that is wasting my efforts to get an excellent job is wasted, in the name of Jesus.

15. Let any curse that is placed upon me to hinder me from getting a good job expire, in the name of Jesus.

16. Every adversary that has vowed to stop me from getting a job is disgraced, in the name of Jesus.

17. Any satanic condition that would placed upon my job is removed miraculously, in the name of Jesus.

18. O Lord, grant me favor to get an excellent job, in the name of Jesus.

19. Every Goliath that is confronting my job, die, in the name of Jesus.

20. I break the backbone of the devil that is preventing me from getting an excellent job, in the name of Jesus.

21. O Lord, link me to a job that will empower me to prosper above my equals, in the name of Jesus.

22. Every spirit of unemployment that is warring against my destiny is frustrated, in the name of Jesus.

23. Every evil grip on my employment, lose your hold over my job, in the name of Jesus.

24. Blood of Jesus, close every satanic case-file against my job, in the name of Jesus.

25. I remove the foothold of enemies against my job forever, in the name of Jesus.

26. I dismantle every demonic opposition against my employment, in the name of Jesus.

27. Let any change that will put my employment in motion manifest by force, in the name of Jesus.

28. Let the divine anointing to get an excellent job fall upon my life, in the name of Jesus.

29. I disband every host of wickedness against my employment, in the name of Jesus.

30. Any strongman that opposes my employment, die, in the name of Jesus.

31. Any witchcraft womb that has swallowed my job, vomit it by force, in the name of Jesus.

32. I command any bewitchment that is holding my employment to release it now, in the name of Jesus.

33. Any satanic mark that is preventing me from getting a good job, disappear, in the name of Jesus.

34. O Lord, arise and empower me to get a good paying job, in the name of Jesus.
35. Any evil king or queen that was enthroned to deny me of a good employment, I dethrone you now, in the name of Jesus.
36. I tear down any evil altar that is keeping me out of good jobs, in the name of Jesus.
37. I destroy every satanic weapon that is keeping me out of good jobs, in the name of Jesus.
38. Any power that is speaking impossibilities over my employment is disgraced, in the name of Jesus.
39. Every Red Sea that is standing before my employment is divided immediately, in the name of Jesus.
40. Every unrepentant opposition that is standing against my job opportunity, fall down and die, in the name of Jesus.
41. Any evil brain that is thinking against my job, scatter and bow, in the name of Jesus.
42. Let the ways of the demonic angels be dark and slippery forever, in the name of Jesus.
43. Blood of Jesus, speak an excellent job into my life, in the name of Jesus.
44. Every evil meeting that was summoned to keep me out of job, scatter to my favor, in the name of Jesus.
45. O Lord, give me a job that will transform my destiny forever, in the name of Jesus.
46. I disarm every evil power that is standing against my employment, in the name of Jesus.
47. O Lord, bless me with the best job by Your power, in the name of Jesus.
48. Let the job that will open doors for my greatness appear now, in the name of Jesus.

27

Chapter

PRAYERS FOR A JOB INTERVIEW

CHAPTER OVERVIEW

- *Walking with God in faithfulness*
- *Carrying the cross*
- *Attacks from evil tongues*
- *Persecution and opposition at a work place*
- *Preparing for an interview*
- *Crying to God*

WALKING WITH GOD IN FAITHFULNESS

Walking with God demands that you yield yourself unreservedly onto God for His use. This is the best thing a believer would do in other to experience divine favor from God and be preferred by God and man in times of great need.

> *"When a man's ways please the LORD, he maketh even his enemies to be at peace with him"* (Proverbs 16:7).

> *"I beseech you therefore, brethren, by the mercies of God, that ye present your bodies a living sacrifice, holy, acceptable unto God,* which is *your reasonable service. And be not conformed to this world: but be ye transformed by the renewing of your mind, that ye may prove what* is *that good, and acceptable, and perfect, will of God"* (Romans 12:1-2).

If your life pleases God, He makes your enemies to favor you and prefer you above others. The first battle a child of God needs to fight is the battle of total withdrawal from the devil and total surrender to God. If you want to get a job that would please God, then you have to fight to keep God's Word and obey him in all things.

> *"It pleased Darius to set over the kingdom an hundred and twenty princes, which should be over the whole kingdom; And over these three presidents; of whom Daniel* was *first: that the princes might give accounts unto them, and the king should have no damage. Then this Daniel was preferred above the presidents and princes, because an excellent spirit* was *in him; and the king thought to set him over the whole realm"* (Daniel 6:1-3).

Daniel was among the candidates interviewed by King Darius to oversee the kingdom. When his name was short-listed, he did everything possible to be preferred above others. After the first interview, one hundred and twenty princes were employed. These princes were interviewed again and Daniel emerged as number one among the best three presidents. The other two presidents were to account to Daniel. He was preferred above them because an excellent spirit was in him.

Daniel, Joseph and many godly people paid heavy prices before they got to their positions. They all carried their crosses faithfully before they were given their assignments. Therefore, you need the mercy of God to deliver you from ungodly people before you can get to certain positions in life. You need to contend with oppressors and enemies of righteousness before you could reach to your job.

> "[1]*Be merciful unto me, O God: for man would swallow me up; he fighting daily oppressed me.* [2]*Mine enemies would daily swallow* me *up: for* they be *many that* [5]*Every day they wrest my words: all their thoughts* are *against me for evil.* [6]*They gather themselves together, they hide themselves, they mark my steps, when they wait for my soul"* (Psalms 56:1-2, 5-6).

These enemies of righteousness monitor righteous people in order to use their words to put them into troubles. They place the righteous under surveillance in order to find faults. They did it to Daniel and so many others in the bible.

> "[4]*Then the presidents and princes sought to find occasion against Daniel concerning the kingdom; but they could find none occasion nor fault; forasmuch as he* was *faithful, neither was there any error or fault found in him.* [5]*Then said these men, We shall not find any occasion against this Daniel, except we find* it *against him* [13]*Then answered they and said before the king, That Daniel, which* is *of the children of the captivity of Judah, regarded not thee, O king, nor the decree that thou hast signed, but maketh his petition three times a day.* [14]*Then the king, when he heard* these *words, was sore displeased with himself, and set* his *heart on Daniel to deliver him: and he labored until the going down of the sun to deliver him.* [15]*Then these men assembled unto the king, and said unto the king, Know, O king, that the law of the Medes and Persians* is, *that neither decree nor statute, which the king established, may be changed.* [16]*Then the king commanded, and they brought Daniel, and cast* him *into the den of lions.* Now *the king spoke and said unto Daniel, Thy God whom thou Servest continually, he will deliver thee"* (Daniel 6:4-5, 13-16).

A godly person who wishes to work with unbelievers, proud and violent men must be ready to carry his cross. This is because they will rise against you no matter how best you perform in your interview or job. They recompense evil for good and speak evil against in place of truth.

The ungodly people in the days Jesus held counsels together against Him. They sought for many ways to destroy Him (*See* Psalms 86:14; Jeremiah 18:20; Matthew 12:14-19).

"And the Lord said, Simon, Simon, behold, Satan hath desired to have you, that he may sift you as wheat" (Luke 22:31).

"For we wrestle not against flesh and blood, but against principalities, against powers, against the rulers of the darkness of this world, against spiritual wickedness in high places*"* (Ephesians 6:12).

"Be sober, be vigilant; because your adversary the devil, as a roaring lion, walked about, seeking whom he may devour" (1 Peter 5:8).

Jesus told Peter that Satan had desired to have him sifted him as wheat. There are forces that are fighting to put many good people out of office. These powers are more spiritual than physical. If you do not know how to fight spiritual warfare, they will put you out of job through evil means no matter how best you performed.

When Daniel excelled in interviews, evil people monitored him to make sure they put him out of office. If Daniel was unknowledgeable about spiritual warfare, he would have not fulfilled his destiny. The devil who is the god of this world is trying his best to take over the world and place his people in the best positions. Because of this, a great struggle lies before every believer. If you do not fight, they will put you in a corner and make sure that you work while others enjoy the fruits of your labor. God's children are supposed to occupy best positions on earth but this has not been the case. That was how evil people fought Daniel until he was removed from the office as number one to the dungeon of death, the den of hungry lions

"Then the king commanded, and they brought Daniel, and cast him *into the den of lions.* Now *the king spoke and said unto Daniel, Thy God whom thou servest continually, he will deliver thee. And a stone was brought, and laid upon the mouth of the den; and the king sealed it with his own signet, and with the signet of his lords; that the purpose might not be changed concerning Daniel"* (Daniel 6:16-17).

"Then was Nebuchadnezzar full of fury, and the form of his visage was changed against Shadrach, Meshach, and Abed–nego: therefore *he spoke, and commanded that they should heat the furnace one seven times more than it was won't to be heated. And he commanded the most mighty men that* were *in his army to bind Shadrach, Meshach, and Abed–nego,* and *to cast* them *into the burning fiery furnace. Then these men were bound in their coats, their hosen, and their hats, and their* other *garments, and were cast into the midst of the burning fiery furnace. Therefore because the king's commandment was urgent, and the furnace exceeding hot, the flame of the fire slew those men that took up Shadrach, Meshach, and Abed–nego. And these three men, Shadrach, Meshach, and Abed–nego, fell down bound into the midst of the burning fiery furnace"* (Daniel 3:19-23).

Many godly and greatly destined people today have no jobs. Government policies all over the world have chased many devout Christians out of jobs and imprisoned others spiritually. Like was easy for Shedrack, Meshack and Abednego in Zion but in Babylon, they faced satanic a policy that removed them from the throne to the dungeon of death, a burning fiery furnace.

As long as you are in this world, you are bound to face people like Nebuchadnezzar. When you lift the banner of Jesus, the king of kings, descendants of Nebuchadnezzar that are committed to the god of this world would be furious, energized by the spirit of this age to attack you. I will discuss many areas of attack in this book. You have to be prayerful in order to deal with these areas to get the job that would lead you into divine rest on earth.

ATTACKS FROM EVIL TONGUES

You need to understand that people who are determined to serve God, even those who served Him in the past experienced attacks from evil tongues and authorities. People with religious spirits without Christ attack true believers and God's ministers with their tongues. Their tongues are as painful as sting of wasps. That is why you need to guard your heart with the armor of God.

Cain said horrible things to Abel. When Abel insisted on doing the right thing, Cain attacked and killed him hoping to live in the world without a rival.

> *"And the LORD said unto Cain, Why art thou wroth? And why is thy countenance fallen? If thou doest well, shall thou not be accepted? And if thou do not well, sin lieth at the door. And unto thee* shall be *his desire, and thou shall rule over him. And Cain talked with Abel his brother: and it happened, when they were in the field, that Cain rose up against Abel his brother, and slew him. And the LORD said unto Cain, Where* is *Abel thy brother? And he said I know not:* Am *I my brother's keeper?"* (Genesis 4:6-9).

There are people in offices who would do worst things than Cain did. They would expect you to fulfill evil conditions before they give you a job. They are determined to force you to sell your birthright for a job. Their demands are not good and are against God's will. It has been like that since the days of Daniel, Joseph, etc. Therefore, chose to obey God rather than yield to their foolish demands.

> *"And it came to pass after these things, that his master's wife cast her eyes upon Joseph; and she said, lie with me. But he refused, and said unto his master's wife, Behold, my master wotteth not what* is *with me in the house, and he hath committed all that he hath to my hand;* There is *none greater in this house than I; neither hath he kept back anything from me but thee, because thou* art *his wife: how then can I do this great wickedness, and sin against God?"* (Genesis 39:7-9).

> *"But Peter and John answered and said unto them, Whether it be right in the sight of God to hearken unto you more than unto God, judge ye"* (Acts 4:19).

When you attend any job interview and they require you to do things that contradict God's Word, refuse such jobs because they are not meant for you. It is better to give up such jobs than to give up on God. However, if the job were yours, no such demands would be attached to it.

Sometimes, you need to be purposeful like Daniel. Purposefulness brings blessings and promotions to the highest offices.

"But Daniel purposed in his heart that he would not defile himself with the portion of the king's meat, or with the wine which he drank: therefore he requested of the prince of the eunuchs that he might not defile himself. Now God had brought Daniel into favor and tender love with the prince of the eunuchs. And the prince of the eunuchs said unto Daniel, I fear my lord the king, who hath appointed your meat and your drink: for why should he see your faces worse liking than the children, which are *of your sort? Then shall ye make* me *endanger my head to the king. Then said Daniel to Melzar, whom the prince of the eunuchs had set over Daniel, Hananiah, Mishael, and Azariah, Prove thy servants, I beseech thee, ten days; and let them give us pulse to eat, and water to drink. Then let our countenances be looked upon before thee, and the countenance of the children that eat of the portion of the king's meat: and as thou seest, deal with thy servants. So he consented to them in this matter, and proved them ten days. And at the end of ten days their countenances appeared fairer and fatter in flesh than all the children, which did eat the portion of the king's meat. Thus Melzar took away the portion of their meat and the wine that they should drink; and gave them pulse. As for these four children, God gave them knowledge and skill in all learning and wisdom: and Daniel had understanding in all visions and dreams. Now at the end of the days that the king had said he should bring them in, then the prince of the eunuchs brought them in before Nebuchadnezzar. And the king communed with them; and among them all was found none like Daniel, Hananiah, Mishael, and Azariah: therefore stood they before the king. And in all matters of wisdom* and *understanding that the king enquired of them he found them ten times better than all the magicians* and *astrologers that* were *in his entire realm. And Daniel continued* even *unto the first year of King Cyrus"* (Daniel 1:8-21).

When you take a stand for God and contend for your faith, you will get the job God made for you. Do not comprise and think you would repent later because you may not be able to contend with the sort of demons that would come after you for being loyal to Satan and betraying God.

"And David said unto Nathan, I have sinned against the LORD. And Nathan said unto David, the LORD also hath put away thy sin; thou shalt not die. Howbeit, because by this deed thou hast given great occasion to the enemies of the LORD to blaspheme, the child also that is *born unto thee shall surely die. And Nathan departed unto his house. And the LORD struck the child that Uriah's wife bare unto David, and it was very sick. David therefore be sought God for the child; and David fasted, and went in, and lay all night upon the earth"* (2 Samuel 12:13-16).

"I have fought a good fight, I have finished my *course, I have kept the faith"* (2 Timothy 4:7).

We are living in the last days and we must contend for the faith earnestly as Paul did. Look around you and see how people have falling away from the truth. You cannot afford to fall away from truth also. You need to guard your faith for very soon, the bridegroom shall come and only those who have oil in their lamps shall go in with him to the marriage feast.

> *"Then all those virgins arose, and trimmed their lamps. And the foolish said unto the wise, Give us of your oil; for our lamps are gone out. But the wise answered, saying,* Not so; *lest there be not enough for you and us: but go ye rather to them that sell, and buy for yourselves. And while they went to buy, the bridegroom came; and they that were ready went in with him to the marriage: and the door was shut"* (Matthew 25:7-10).

Your faith is a priceless treasure, which you must guard and hold fast. Do not exchange your faith with anything in this world. There are ungodly men and enemies of faith who go from place to place to seduce people into evil jobs. Cain tried to influence Abel but he failed to convince him. If you get a job through unrighteous means, you would be expected to sustain that job through so many other unrighteousness means. It is a very perilous thing to dine with Satan because you would pay with your soul.

> *"Even so the tongue is a little member and boasted great things. Behold how great a matter a little fire kindleth! And the tongue* is *a fire, a world of iniquity: so is the tongue among our members, that it defileth the whole body, and setteth on fire the course of nature; and it is set on fire of hell"* (James 3:5-6).

> *"An ungodly man diggeth up evil: and in his lips* there is *as a burning fire. A forward man sowed strife: and a whisperer separated chief friends. A violent man enticed his neighbor, and leaded him into the way* that is *not good. He shutteth his eyes to devise forward things: moving his lips he bringeth evil to pass"* (Proverbs 16:27-30).

There are people whose bosses would not allow to rest without making one evil demand or another. When you get such jobs at all cost, how would you get fulfillment? The sting that would come from the tongues of fellow evil workers in the same office would make you uncomfortable. Undoubtedly, you have offended God by comprising to do evil in order to get such evil jobs.

Obviously, the mode of operations in such offices or organization would contradict God's Word and His plans for your life. Fellow workers would always plan evil, speak evil and sow strife to separate you from God. Do not accept any job that demands you to commit sin as a requirement because it will eventually take you to hell fire.

"As a mad man *who casted firebrands, arrows, and death, So* is *the man* that *deceived his neighbor, and saith, Am not I in sport? Where no wood is,* there *the fire goeth out: so where* there is *no talebearer, the strife ceaseth.* As *coals* are *to burning coals, and wood to fire;* so is *a contentious man to kindle strife. The words of a talebearer* are *as wounds, and they go down into the innermost parts of the belly. Burning lips and a wicked heart* are as *a potsherd covered with silver dross. He that hateth dissembled with his lips, and layeth up deceit within him; When he speaketh fair, believe him not: for* there are *seven abominations in his heart.* Whose *hatred is covered by deceit; his wickedness shall be showed before the* whole *congregation"* (Proverbs 26:18-26).

"Thou shall be hid from the scourge of the tongue: neither shall thou be afraid of destruction when it cometh" (Job 5:21).

"Thou shall hide them in the secret of thy presence from the pride of man: thou shall keep them secretly in a pavilion from the strife of tongues" (Psalms 31:20).

You do not need a well-paid job that would subject you to wickedness, deception, slander, conspiracy, strife, criticism, betrayal, and contention. You need God's grace to work in some places. If God really wants you to be in any place, He provides the grace you need to get the job without compromise. It is better to get a job where the presence of God and His grace will be enough to sustain you than to jump into the territory of devil and his hosts.

When you force yourself to compromise and sin to get a well-paid job, you dig a horrible pit for your life. God said that *he who so diggeth a pit shall fall therein, and he that rolleth a stone, it will return upon him*. Mind you, not every job you see would suit you. Watch and pray so that you do not jump into a job that belongs to someone else.

PERSECUTION AND OPPOSITION AT A WORK PLACE

Persecution is the common experience for all believers, as test and temptation come to all people in life. Tests reveal our inner strength and weakness. Temptations come to divert and destroy you. God permits temptations to come to Christians to reveal where their trust lies and to grant them opportunities to seek for more grace from Him. Tests prove your faith, loyalty and faithfulness to God. That is why we cannot rule out that these things are for our good also.

> *"The word which came unto Jeremiah from the LORD in the days of Jehoiakim the son of Josiah king of Judah, saying, Go unto the house of the Rechabites, and speak unto them, and bring them into the house of the LORD, into one of the chambers, and give them wine to drink"* (Jeremiah 35:1-2).

> *"I am come to send fire on the earth; and what will I, if it be already kindled? But I have a baptism to be baptized with; and how am I straitened till it be accomplished! Suppose ye that I am come to give peace on earth? I tell you, Nay; but rather division: For from henceforth there shall be five in one house divided, three against two, and two against three. The father shall be divided against the son, and the son against the father; the mother against the daughter, and the daughter against the mother; the mother in law against her daughter in law, and the daughter in law against her mother in law"* (Luke 12:49-53).

If you are ignorant of the scriptures, you will surely fall in time of temptation. If you compromise your faith to get a job, you will face temptations, persecutions, trials and tests that you may not overcome easily. When a Christian gets a job, he carries with him the fire of the gospel to spread in the place he works. As a result, there is bound to be persecution, but God's grace will be sufficient to protect him.

However, if you give bribe or commit immorality to get a job, you will not be able to carry the fire of God to your place of work. Strange fires from unbelievers will burn you instead because they knew how you got your job. Those fires can destroy your relationship with God and take you to hell fire. Ironically, if you would not assent to subsequent evil compromises, you may lose that job or face more strange fires as long as you remain in that job. Therefore, it is better to pray that God gives you the right job than for you to get it at all cost.

> *"Now this man purchased a field with the reward of iniquity; and falling headlong, he burst asunder in the midst, and all his bowels gushed out. And it was known unto all the dwellers at Jerusalem; insomuch as that field is called in their proper tongue, Aceldama, that is to say, the field of blood. For it is written in the book of Psalms, Let*

his habitation be desolate, and let no man dwell therein: and his bishoprick let another take" (Acts 1:18-20).

When you acquire a job through evil means, God's presence cannot be there to fight your battles for you. You can only succeed by God's grace and without that, you will certainly fail.

"But the LORD hath taken you, and brought you forth out of the iron furnace, even *out of Egypt, to be unto him a people of inheritance, as* ye are *this day* (Deuteronomy 4:20).

"Therefore they did set over them taskmasters to afflict them with their burdens. In addition, they built for Pharaoh Treasure cities, Pithom and Raamses. But the more they afflicted them, the more they multiplied and grew. In addition, they were grieved because of the children of Israel. And the Egyptians made the children of Israel to serve with rigor: And they made their lives bitter with hard bondage, in morter, and in brick, and in all manner of service in the field: all their service, wherein they made them serve, was *with rigor"* (Exodus 1:11-14).

Many Christians are under severe oppression in many offices. They blame God and quote His promises in vain. Some have backslidden and are on their way to hell fire. They have quickly forgotten the means through which they got their jobs. Some forgot how they became busy and abandoned God after getting their jobs. When they had no jobs, they were faithful to God. Now they have one, they have no time for God.

Many Christians have become slaves to their employers. Their responsibilities have increased but their salaries remained the same. The more they labored, the more their employers distressed them with all manners of hard work. How would such person have time to enjoy a quality relationship with God? This is sad.

In many countries of the world today, employers have distorted labor laws to emasculate the content of character and convictions about God as a precondition to get and retain a job. Those who consent to evil conditions become children of the devil. Their cries do not get to God because they were not God's children. A Christian who sells his birthright to get a job hoping to repent later has been deceived.

"For if we sin willfully after that we have received the knowledge of the truth, there remained no more sacrifice for sins, But a certain fearful looking for of judgment and fiery indignation, which shall devour the adversaries. He that despised Moses' law died without mercy under two or three witnesses: Of how much sorer punishment, suppose ye, shall he be thought worthy, who hath trodden underfoot the Son of God, and hath counted the blood of the covenant, where with he was sanctified, an unholy thing, and hath done despite unto the Spirit of grace?" (Hebrews 10:26-29).

"Because I have called, and ye refused; I have stretched out my hand, and no man regarded; But ye have set at nought all my counsel, and would none of my reproof: I also will laugh at your calamity; I will mock when your fear cometh; When your fear cometh as desolation, and your destruction cometh as a whirlwind; when distress and anguish cometh upon you. Then shall they call upon me, but I will not answer; they shall seek me early, but they shall not find me" (Proverbs 1:24-28)

The reason why oppression, injustice, poverty, denials of fundamental human rights, slavery, afflictions and humiliation are on the increase is that these victims have refused to embrace God. Those few that claim they are on God's side do not know how to pray the right prayers.

Pharaoh dealt with other nationalities in Egypt but when the children of Israel cried unto God, He heard them and sent Moses to deliver them from Pharaoh. Devil can oppose you as you search for jobs. You may even stay longer than necessary in the labor market. However, if you would get a job approved by God at the right time, no one can remove you or oppress you and go scot-free. Your duty is to prayerfully get a job without compromise and see how God will prosper you and defend you to the end.

PREPARING FOR AN INTERVIEW

When you are preparing for any interview, put your whole confidence in God. He can do anything for the sake of His child that trusts in Him.

> *"It is better to trust in the LORD than to put confidence in man.* It is *better to trust in the LORD than to put confidence in princes"* (Psalms 118:8-9).

> *"For the LORD shall be thy confidence, and shall keep thy foot from being taken"* (Proverbs 3:26).

Scriptures declared that it is better to trust in the LORD than to put confidence in man or in princes. Esther and Mordecai were slaves in a foreign land. However, when all the fair young virgins were to be interviewed in Shushan, Mordecai encouraged Esther to trust in God and attend. They all came into the custody of Hege the king's chamberlain, keeper of the women. As a slave, Esther was not known or recognized. Esther had no father or mother but Mordecai brought her up as his own child.

> "Now *in Shushan the palace there was a certain Jew, whose name* was *Mordecai, the son of Jar, the son of Shimei, the son of Kish, a Benjamite; Who had been carried away from Jerusalem with the captivity which had been carried away with Jeconiah king of Judah, whom Nebuchadnezzar the king of Babylon had carried away. And he brought up Hadassah, that* is, *Esther, his uncle's daughter: for she had neither father nor mother, and the maid* was *fair and beautiful; whom Mordecai, when her father and mother were dead, took for his own daughter"* (Esther 2:5-7).

Because Mordecai taught Esther about God, Esther put all her trust in God when she was taken to the King's palace. She obtained favor and kindness from people at the palace, and pleased Hegai, who speedily gave her things for purification. He provided everything she needed. Esther was not qualified because she was a slave girl but she was bold and had faith in God. Mordecai wanted Esther to succeed. So he prayed everyday for her and monitored what went on.

> *"So it came to pass, when the king's commandment and his decree was heard, and when many maidens were gathered together unto Shushan the palace, to the custody of Hegai, that Esther was brought also unto the king's house, to the custody of Hegai, keeper of the women. And the maiden pleased him, and she obtained kindness of him; and he speedily gave her things for purification, with such things as belonged to her, and seven maidens,* which were *meet to be given her, out of the king's house: and he preferred her and her house cleaners unto the best* place *of the house of the women. Esther had not showed her people or her kindred: for Mordecai had charged her that, she should not show* it. *And Mordecai walked every day before the court of the*

women's house, to know how Esther did, and what should become of her" (Esther 2:8-11).

Mordecai visited the palace every day to know what happened. He was determined to see that Esther was provided with everything she would need to meet up with all expectations. He was always around to monitor Esther, to give her advice and encouragement to be bold and refused to be intimidated.

In addition, through prayer and fasting, he made sure that Esther met up with all demands. She was there with all her credentials. When it was her time to see the king, she went in humility and simplicity, not with too much make up as many ladies would do. Esther was more natural and required nothing but what the keeper of the women appointed.

> *"Now when the turn of Esther, the daughter of Abihail the uncle of Mordecai, who had taken her for his daughter, was come to go in unto the king, she required nothing but what Hegai the king's chamberlain, the keeper of the women, appointed. In addition, Esther obtained favor in the sight of all-them that looked upon her. So Esther was taken unto king Ahasuerus into his house royal in the tenth month, which* is *the month Tebeth, in the seventh year of his reign. And the king loved Esther above all the women, and she obtained grace and favor in his sight more than all the virgins; so that he set the royal crown upon her head, and made her queen instead of Vashti. Then the king made a great feast unto all his princes and his servants,* even *Esther's feast; and he made a release to the provinces, and gave gifts, according to the state of the king"* (Esther 2:15-18).

Finally, Esther passed the rigorous test and obtained favor in the sight of the king, who loved her above all other virgins. She received the royal crown upon her head and became the queen. Likewise, when you do all that you are supposed to do and trust God through prayer and fasting, you will surely get the job that God has for you at the right time. When Mordecai did what he was supposed to do and his job was given to Haman, he did not stop trusting God. Do not stop trusting God because you have not gotten a job.

> *"In those days, while Mordecai sat in the king's gate, two of the king's chamberlains, Bigthan and Teresh, of those which kept the door, were worth, and sought to lay hand on the king Ahasuerus. And the thing was known to Mordecai, who told it unto Esther the queen; and Esther certified the king* thereof *in Mordecai's name. And when inquisition was made of the matter, it was found out; therefore they were both hanged on a tree: and it was written in the book of the chronicles before the king"* (Esther 2:21-23).

Do not use any evil means to acquire a job. The king ignored Mordecai and promoted Haman on the job that belonged to Mordecai. Haman was promoted and was made second in command above all princes that were with him.

> *"After these things did king Ahasuerus promote Haman the son of Hammedatha the Agagite, and advanced him, and set his seat above all the princes that* were *with him. And all the king's servants that* were *in the king's gate, bowed, and reverenced Haman: for the king had so commanded concerning him. However, Mordecai bowed not, nor did* him *reverence. Then the king's servants, which* were *in the king's gate, said unto Mordecai, Why transgresses thou the king's commandment? Now it came to pass, when they spoke daily unto him, and he hearkened not unto them, that they told Haman, to see whether Mordecai's matters would stand: for he had told them that, he* was *a Jew. And when Haman saw that Mordecai bowed not, nor did him reverence, then was Haman full of wrath"* (Esther 3:1-5).

Haman did Mordecai's job while Mordecai remained the gatekeeper at the king's gate. Though he was not promoted, he did not stop praying and trusting His God. However, when the man that took his job started attacking him and condemned him to death, he went into prayers of warfare.

> *"[1]When Mordecai perceived all that was done, Mordecai rent his clothes, and put on sackcloth with ashes, and went out into the midst of the city, and cried with a loud and a bitter cry; [8]Also he gave him the copy of the writing of the decree that was given at Shushan to destroy them, to show* it *unto Esther, and to declare* it *unto her, and to charge her that she should go in unto the king, to make supplication unto him, and to make request before him for her people. [15]Then Esther bade* them *return Mordecai* this answer, *[16]Go, gather together all the Jews that are present in Shushan, and fast ye for me, and neither eat nor drink three days, night or day: I also and my maidens will fast likewise; and so will I go in unto the king, which* is *not according to the law: and if I perish, I perish. [17]So Mordecai went his way, and did according to all that Esther had commanded him"* (Esther 4:1, 8, 15-17).

Haman was authorized to pass a decree to eliminate Mordecai and his people in one day. Letters were sent into all the king's provinces, to kill all Jews, both young and old, little children and women, in one day and to take the spoil of them for a prey. As people were getting ready for that day, Mordecai, Esther and all Jews went into prayers and the rest is history. Something incredible happened on the very night they started praying.

> *"[1]On that night could not the king sleep, and he commanded to bring the book of records of the chronicles; and they were read before the king. [10]Then the king said to Haman, Make haste,* and *take the apparel and the horse, as thou hast said, and do even so to Mordecai the Jew, that sitteth at the king's gate: let nothing fail of all that*

thou hast spoken. [11]Then took Haman the apparel and the horse, and arrayed Mordecai, and brought him on horseback through the street of the city, and proclaimed before him, Thus shall it be done unto the man whom the king delighted to honor" (Esther 6:1, 10-11).

"[10]So they hanged Haman on the gallows that he had prepared for Mordecai. Then was the king's wrath pacified. [1]On that day did the king Ahasuerus give the house of Haman the Jews' enemy unto Esther the queen. And Mordecai came before the king; for Esther had told what he was *unto her. [2]And the king took off his ring, which he had taken from Haman, and gave it unto Mordecai. And Esther set Mordecai over the house of Haman"* (Esther 7:10; 8:1-2).

If you are denied of a job because you are a child of God, keep praying and believing God, you will receive a better job and you recover your lost.

CRYING TO GOD

David was an example of one who had unwavering confidence in God. He cried to God many times in his troubles. Having fought and passed through several storms of life, he came to love God with a lot of trust. Nothing can overcome a person who has faith in God. Nothing but confidence in God and ceaseless prayers will deliver any believer from the storms of life. In a seemingly hopeless situation, you need to look up to God alone. To trust and have confidence in God is to cast your burden on Him when it is too heavy for your shoulder to carry.

> "[7]*Shall they escape by iniquity? In thine anger cast down the people, O God.* [8]*Thou tellest my wanderings: put thou my tears into thy bottle:* are they *not in thy book?* [9]*When I cry unto thee, then shall mine enemies turn back: this I know; for God* is *for me.* [12]*Thy vows* are *upon me, O God: I will render praises unto thee.* [13]*For thou hast delivered my soul from death:* wilt *not thou deliver my feet from falling, that I may walk before God in the light of the living?"* (Psalm 56:7-9, 12-13).

God will not ignore the cries of His children who trust in Him for deliverance. In times of David's troubles, he cried unto God and he knew that God heard all his prayers. The prayers of God's children are preserved and answers come in due time. God knows when his children are in trouble and responds at appropriate times.

> *"Be merciful unto me, O God, be merciful unto me: for my soul trusted in thee: yea, in the shadow of thy wings will I make my refuge, until* these *calamities be overpast. I will cry unto God most high; unto God that performed* all things *for me. He shall send from heaven, and save me* from *the reproach of him that would swallow me up. Selah. God shall send forth his mercy and his truth"* (Psalms 57:1-3).

> *"And it came to pass in process of time that the king of Egypt died: and the children of Israel sighed by reason of the bondage, and they cried, and their cry came up unto God by reason of the bondage. And God heard their groaning, and God remembered his covenant with Abraham, with Isaac, and with Jacob. And God looked upon the children of Israel, and God had respect unto them"* (Exodus 2:23-25).

> *"Their heart cried unto the Lord, O wall of the daughter of Zion, let tears run down like a river day and night: give you no rest; let not the apple of thine eye cease. Arise, cry out in the night: in the beginning of the watches pour out thine heart like water before the face of the Lord: lift up thy hands toward him for the life of thy young children, that faint for hunger in the top of every street"* (Lamentations 2:18-19).

To cry to God is to make earnest supplications to Him.

WHEN DO WE CRY UNTO GOD?

- When the nation needs national deliverance.
- When you need healing.
- In time of confusion, weakness or when you are expecting something from God.
- When your reasons can no longer carry you through or when you get discouraged in life.
- When you are at the crossroad of life.
- During crisis, fear and hopeless situation.
- In times of difficult problem, calamity or political problem.

Moses got tired of the complaints of the children of Israel and went to the mountain to pray. That was where God gave him guidelines, a law and divine program to guide Israel.

Esther and Mordecai did pray and the death decree against them and their people was reversed. Daniel cried unto God and lions in the den had respect and fear for him. Nehemiah did and the president gave him a national assignment. Hannah did and she conceived and gave birth to Samuel. Jehoshaphat did and God took over his battle and confused his enemies. Jabez did and he was delivered from inherited poverty, lack and destructions. Elijah did it and God preserved his life and fed him for many years. Elisha did it and God empowered him with double anointing. Joshua did it and sun stood still for many hours. You can cry for help or intercession.

> *"And he said, Let me go, for the day breaketh. And he said, I will not let thee go, except thou bless me"* (Genesis 32:26).
>
> *"And Moses returned unto the LORD, and said, Oh, this people have sinned a great sin, and have made them gods of gold. Yet now, if thou wilt forgive their sin—; and if not, blot me, I pray thee, out of thy book which thou hast written"* (Exodus 32:31-32).
>
> *"Have mercy upon me, O God, according to thy loving-kindness: according unto the multitude of thy tender mercies blot out my transgressions. Wash me thoroughly from mine iniquity, and cleanse me from my sin"* (Psalms 51:1-2).
>
> *"And he said unto Jesus, Lord, remember me when thou comest into thy kingdom"* (Luke 23:42).
>
> *"For this thing I besought the Lord thrice that it might depart from me. And he said unto me, my grace is sufficient for thee: for my strength is made perfect in weakness.*

Most gladly therefore will I rather glory in my infirmities, that the power of Christ may rest upon me" (2 Corinthians 12:8-9).

Your cry can also be for cleansing, salvation and deliverance or for employment. You can be preferred above others in any interview if you have confidence in God. Therefore, learn how to pray and trust in God and it shall be well with you.

PRAYERS FOR A JOB INTERVIEW

Bible reference: Esther 2:1-23

Begin with praise and worship

1. Father Lord, make my appearance to be acceptable to the panel, in the name of Jesus.
2. Let my presentation convince my interviewers by fire, in the name of Jesus.
3. Let the blood of Jesus remove every curse that was placed upon my credentials, in the name of Jesus
4. I lift off every embargo that was placed upon my certificate, in the name of Jesus.
5. I break every yoke of joblessness in my life, in the name of Jesus.
6. Father Lord, let my presentation be acceptable, in the name of Jesus.
7. I command unmerited favor to follow me in my job interview, in the name of Jesus.
8. Let the hearts of my interviewers favor me in this interview, in the name of Jesus.
9. O Lord, pour Your spirit of grace upon excellence and me to perform well, in the name of Jesus.
10. Let my appearance be like that of an angel, in the name of Jesus.
11. Let my wisdom and knowledge be recognized during my interview, in the name of Jesus.
12. I demobilize any evil movement that is going on against me, in the name of Jesus.
13. O Lord, crown my efforts with honor and success, in the name of Jesus.
14. Let divine fullness follow me from beginning to the end, in the name of Jesus.
15. I command the result of my interview to be extremely successful, in the name of Jesus.
16. Let every question that I would be asked be answered perfectly, in the name of Jesus.
17. Let every organ of my body receive boldness and intelligence, in the name of Jesus.

18. Let my promotion, acceptance and offer come from God, in the name of Jesus.
19. O Lord, raise me up through this interview without rivals, in the name of Jesus.
20. I command my interviewers to be by my side, in the name of Jesus.
21. I decree that my enemies will accept me above others in this interview, in the name of Jesus.
22. O Lord, arise and use this interview to advance me in life, in the name of Jesus.
23. Let the people that will decide on my case favor me, in the name of Jesus.
24. O Lord, retire, remove or sack any person that opposes my success, in the name of Jesus.
25. Any divine substitute that will move me above other competitors, take place now, in the name of Jesus.
26. Let my rivals in this interview favor me, in the name of Jesus.
27. Every yoke of failure upon my life in this interview, beak to pieces, in the name of Jesus.
28. I disarm the brains of my unrepentant competitors in this interview, in the name of Jesus.
29. I refused to be pushed to a second position, in the name of Jesus.
30. Any reason that would make my stubborn enemies to reject me in this interview, die, in the name of Jesus.
31. Any evil record that would be presented against me, die, in the name of Jesus.
32. Every stubborn enemy against my success, receive confusion and favor me, in the name of Jesus.
33. Anything that must happen for me to get this job to the glory of God, happen now, in the name of Jesus.
34. O Lord, if You must kill, kill, if You must destroy, destroy, for me to get this job, in the name of Jesus.
35. I disgrace agents of devil that have vowed to stop me from getting this job, in the name of Jesus.
36. Whatever will make me to excel above my contemporaries, I receive you now, in the name of Jesus.
37. Any strongman on my way to get this job is removed dead or alive, in the name of Jesus.

38. Let the person that would write or sign my appointment letter do it by force, in the name of Jesus.

39. Any opposition on my way to this employment is removed at all cost, in the name of Jesus.

40. I disorganize the mental storehouse of my stubborn enemies for this job to favor me, in the name of Jesus.

41. O Lord, use this job to advance me and prosper me, in the name of Jesus.

28

Chapter

PRAYERS TO PROGRESS IN YOUR CAREER

CHAPTER OVERVIEW

- *A faithful worker*
- *Obedience in the office*
- *A hard-worker who is resented*
- *Jesus Christ came to serve*

A FAITHFUL WORKER

To work and to be faithful are two different things. Not all workers are faithful. However, to be faithful at work brings progress and this is important. Joseph was worker who was faithful in his office. How he reacted to stress, strains and misfortunes are remarkable. He maintained a good relationship with the people around him wherever he found himself. He refused to in give to bitterness, self-pity or despair but rather overcame them with courage, sense of responsibilities and high moral values. He had confidence in God. He was kind and used wisdom in his dealings with others and in every work committed to his care.

> *"And Joseph was brought down to Egypt; and Potiphar, an officer of Pharaoh, captain of the guard, an Egyptian, bought him of the hands of the Ishmeelites, which had brought him down thither. And the LORD was with Joseph, and he was a prosperous man; and he was in the house of his master the Egyptian. And his master saw that the LORD* was *with him, and that the LORD made all that he did to prosper in his hand. And Joseph found grace in his sight, and he served him: and he made him overseer over his house, and all* that *he had he put into his hand. And it came to pass from the time* that *he had made him overseer in his house, and over all that he had, that the LORD blessed the Egyptian's house for Joseph's sake; and the blessing of the LORD was upon all that he had in the house, and in the field. And he left all that he had in Joseph's hand; and he knew not ought he had, save the bread which he did eat. And Joseph was* a *goodly* person, *and well favored"* (Genesis 39:1-6).

> *"If thou faint in the day of adversity, thy strength is small"* (Proverbs 24:10).

Joseph did not compromise his faith in God. He did not walk by sight or changed his character or religion. For so many people, relocation to a new place would result to a change of character but not so with Joseph. He remained faithful to God wherever he went. Joseph fought and overcame every temptation, covetousness, lust, fleshly gratification, inordinate affection and ambition. He was tempted by well-respected influential women, the first lady, in the person of the wife of Potiphar, his master, but God helped him.

Joseph understood the benefits of winning spiritual warfare. However, evil neighbors, people with demonized and unclean spirits, who were readily empowered to crush him beneath the weight of sin, surrounded him. He overcame them all by God's grace with a remarkable high moral strength.

"When the unclean spirit is gone out of a man, he walketh through dry places, seeking rest; and finding none, he saith, I will return unto my house whence I came out. And when he cometh, he findeth it *swept and garnished. Then goeth he, and taketh* to him *seven other spirits more wicked than himself; and they enter in, and dwell there: and the last* state *of that man is worse than the first"* (Luke 11:24-26).

The devil used all means available, people, things and circumstances to tempt Joseph, but Joseph used God's grace, and he came out victorious. Likewise, the devil may tempt you in the office through corruption but you can overcome him by the grace of God.

"When I saw among the spoils a goodly Babylonish garment, and two hundred shekels of silver, and a wedge of gold of fifty shekels weight, then I coveted them, and took them; and, behold, they are hid in the earth in the midst of my tent, and the silver under it" (Joshua 7:21).

"Now the serpent was more subtil than any beast of the field which the LORD God had made. And he said unto the woman, Yea, hath God said, Ye shall not eat of every tree of the garden? And the woman said unto the serpent, We may eat of the fruit of the trees of the garden: But of the fruit of the tree which is *in the midst of the garden, God hath said, Ye shall not eat of it, neither shall ye touch it, lest ye die. And the serpent said unto the woman, Ye shall not surely die: For God doth know that in the day ye eat thereof, then your eyes shall be opened, and ye shall be as gods, knowing good and evil. And when the woman saw that the tree* was *good for food, and that it* was *pleasant to the eyes, and a tree to be desired to make* one *wise, she took of the fruit thereof, and did eat, and gave also unto her husband with her; and he did eat"* (Genesis 3:1-6).

"And it came to pass in an evening tide, that David arose from off his bed, and walked upon the roof of the king's house: and from the roof he saw a woman washing herself; and the woman was *very beautiful to look upon. And David sent and enquired after the woman. And one said, Is not this Bath–sheba, the daughter of Eliam, the wife of Uriah the Hittite? And David sent messengers, and took her; and she came in unto him, and he lay with her; for she was purified from her uncleanness: and she returned unto her house. And the woman conceived, and sent and told David, and said, I am with child"* (2 Samuel 11:2-5).

Devil may entice you through the eyes of the mind as he did to Eve. At other times, he would try to overcome you and influence you through the behavior of evil companions or lead you into temptation and sin through the carelessness of others as he did to David using Bathsheba. If you are committed to pleasing God in any office you find yourself, you will be able to respect God and receive your rewards eventually. Let us have the mind to please God in our offices at all times no matter the circumstances.

"Watch and pray, that ye enter not into temptation: the spirit indeed is *willing"* (Matthew 26:41).

"My son, if sinners entice thee, consent thou not. If they say, Come with us, let us lay wait for blood, let us lurk privily for the innocent without cause: Let us swallow them up alive as the grave; and whole, as those that go down into the pit: We shall find all precious substance, we shall fill our houses with spoil: Cast in thy lot among us; let us all have one purse: My son, walk not thou in the way with them; refrain thy foot from their path" (Proverbs 1:10-15).

You must recognize every tempter wherever you find them and resist them with all your strength. Use the written Word of God to resist the devil and all his agents at all times. The reason for multitudes of problems in many offices is that many believers are under the power of the devil. You must see every tempter as God's enemy and you must fight them with spiritual weapons. God cannot leave you alone to fight the devil with your natural power.

"There hath no temptation taken you but such as is common to man: but God is *faithful, who will not suffer you to be tempted above that ye are able; but will with the temptation also make a way to escape, that ye may be able to bear* it*"* (1 Corinthians 10:13).

"Finally, brethren, whatsoever things are true, whatsoever things are *honest, whatsoever things* are *just, whatsoever things* are *pure, whatsoever things* are *lovely, whatsoever things* are *of good report; if* there be *any virtue, and if* there be *any praise, think on these things"* (Philippians 4:8).

"The Lord knoweth how to deliver the godly out of temptations, and to reserve the unjust unto the day of judgment to be punished" (2 Peter 2:9).

The saints who overcame the devil did not get themselves involved with the affairs of this world. They avoided them at all cost. They fled from youthful lusts and strove vehemently against sin, cut off every source of temptation from their offices as much as it laid in their powers, they resisted the devil to the end. They distanced themselves from things that represented corruption. You need to pray and watch in faith to succeed in our world today. Learn how to put on your complete spiritual armor. Be sober and vigilant and fight with all your strength as if your eternal destiny would be determined by the outcome of the immediate battle.

"For we wrestle not against flesh and blood, but against principalities, against powers, against the rulers of the darkness of this world, against spiritual wickedness in high places. *Wherefore take unto you the whole armor of God that ye may be able to withstand in the evil day, and having done all, to stand. Stand therefore, having*

your loins girt about with truth, and having on the breastplate of righteousness; And your feet shod with the preparation of the gospel of peace; Above all, taking the shield of faith, wherewith ye shall be able to quench all the fiery darts of the wicked. And take the helmet of salvation, and the sword of the Spirit, which is the word of God: Praying always with all prayer and supplication in the Spirit, and watching thereunto with all perseverance and supplication for all saints" (Ephesians 6:12-18).

No matter your spiritual experience and ability in the past, do not be lazy or take things for granted because many have been destroyed because of this.

Finally, remember that Christ has paid in full the price for our victory. Therefore, insist on complete victory and freedom that comes from His death without compromise, negotiation or agreement with the devil and all his agents.

OBEDIENCE IN THE OFFICE

Paul in his letter to the Colossians addressed the issue of relationship with God and our relationship with one another. Employees are to obey their employers, just as servants obey their masters. Obedience must come from the heart as unto the Lord who rewards every good service. Obedience to the masters from the servants should not be with eye service, as men pleasers do but with singleness of heart, fearing God.

> *"Servants, obey in all things* your *masters according to the flesh; not with eye service, as men pleasers; but in singleness of heart, fearing God: And what soever ye do, do* it *heartily, as to the Lord, and not unto men"* (Colossian 3:22-23).

God requires obedience from all of us in our dealings with God and man.

> *"Now therefore, if ye will obey my voice indeed, and keep my covenant, then ye shall be a peculiar treasure unto me above all people: for all the earth* is *mine: And ye shall be unto me a kingdom of priests, and an holy nation. These* are *the words which thou shalt speak unto the children of Israel"* (Exodus 19:5-6).

> *"Therefore shall ye keep all the commandments which I command you this day, that ye may be strong, and go in and possess the land, whither ye go to possess it; And that ye may prolong* your *days in the land, which the LORD swore unto your fathers to give unto them and to their seed, a land that floweth with milk and honey"* (Deuteronomy 11:8-9).

What servants and masters should have in mind in our dealings with one another is obedience to God. God regards covenant keepers as peculiar treasure unto Himself above all people, kingdom of priests, holy nation and His children. You have to obey rules and regulations to the letter with all your heart. It is a requirement from God and a right thing to do.

> *"And it shall come to pass, if thou shalt hearken diligently unto the voice of the LORD thy God, to observe* and *to do all his commandments which I command thee this day, that the LORD thy God will set thee on high above all nations of the earth: And all these blessings shall come on thee, and overtake thee, if thou shalt hearken unto the voice of the LORD thy God. Blessed* shalt *thou* be *in the city, and blessed* shalt *thou* be *in the field. Blessed* shall be *the fruit of thy body, and the fruit of thy ground, and the fruit of thy cattle, the increase of thy kine, and the flocks of thy sheep. Blessed* shall be *thy basket and thy store. Blessed* shalt *thou* be *when thou comest in, and blessed* shalt *thou* be *when thou goest out. The LORD shall cause thine enemies that rise up against thee to be smitten before thy face: they shall come out against thee*

one way, and flee before thee seven ways. The LORD shall command the blessing upon thee in thy storehouses, and in all that thou settest thine hand unto; and he shall bless thee in the land which the LORD thy God giveth thee. The LORD shall establish thee a holy people unto himself, as he hath sworn unto thee, if thou shalt keep the commandments of the LORD thy God, and walk in his ways. And all people of the earth shall see that thou art called by the name of the LORD; and they shall be afraid of thee. And the LORD shall make thee plenteous in goods, in the fruit of thy body, and in the fruit of thy cattle, and in the fruit of thy ground, in the land which the LORD sware unto thy fathers to give thee. The LORD shall open unto thee his good treasure, the heaven to give the rain unto thy land in his season, and to bless all the work of thine hand: and thou shalt lend unto many nations, and thou shalt not borrow. And the LORD shall make thee the head, and not the tail; and thou shalt be above only, and thou shalt not be beneath; if that thou hearken unto the commandments of the LORD thy God, which I command thee this day, to observe and to do them: *And thou shalt not go aside from any of the words which I command thee this day,* to *the right hand, or* to *the left, to go after other gods to serve them"* (Deuteronomy 28:1-14).

For you to get your rights, benefits and entitlements, you must obey stipulated rules and regulations at the place of work. You must do this whether your servant or master fulfilled his or not. You break God's covenant when you fail to keep your own part of covenant. When you carry out your responsibilities in the office as instructed, God will answer your prayers for progress, blessing and promotion. God expects that you hearken diligently to His voice to observe all His commandments. Many people quote the Word of God and claim His promises in vain without observing simple rules in their offices or organization.

You can only claim God's promises and see the manifestations when you hearken unto His voice and honor rules and regulations in your place of work as a master or servant.

"There shall not any man be able to stand before thee all the days of thy life: as I was with Moses, *so I will be with thee: I will not fail thee, nor forsake thee. Be strong and of a good courage: for unto this people shalt thou divide for an inheritance the land, which I sware unto their fathers to give them. Only be thou strong and very courageous, that thou mayest observe to do according to all the law, which* Moses *my servant commanded thee: turn not from it* to *the right hand or* to *the left, that thou mayest prosper whithersoever thou goest. This book of the law shall not depart out of thy mouth; but thou shalt meditate therein day and night, that thou mayest observe to do according to all that is written therein: for then thou shalt make thy way prosperous, and then thou shalt have good success"* (Joshua 1:5-8).

Some people forcefully take things that God did not give to them and then call such things blessings. Such cannot be blessings from God because while they add sorrows to you, blessings of God add no sorrow. Many discovered this truth when it was too late. True blessings of God always come through obedience to God's Word, whether at your place of work and anywhere you go. The only time you are allowed to take a stand against any rule is when it contradicts God's Word.

> *"But Peter and John answered and said unto them, Whether it be right in the sight of God to hearken unto you more than unto God, judge ye"* (Acts 4:19).

Obedience to God's Word over man's rule attracts blessings. When you choose to obey God instead of man, you receive blessings in and outside the city. Lord will fight for you when opposition rises because of your obedience. The enemy would rage but the end will bring blessings to you. Let no one be afraid of losing anything for obeying God's Word. Whatever you give up, God is able to give to you a hundred fold.

> *"Servants, be obedient to them that are* your *masters according to the flesh, with fear and trembling, in singleness of your heart, as unto Christ; Not with eye service, as men pleasers; but as the servants of Christ, doing the will of God from the heart; With good will doing service, as to the Lord, and not to men: Knowing that whatsoever good thing any man doeth, the same shall he receive of the Lord, whether* he be *bond or free"* (Ephesians 6:5-8)

> *"Exhort* servants to be obedient unto their own masters, *and* to please *them* well in all *things*; not answering again" (Titus 2:9).

There have been instances in the church where younger ministers ruled over their elders. In such circumstances, you have to obey the authority that put such young person in office. You ought to obey as though you are obeying Christ. Whenever a leader is placed over you, obey as if you are obeying Christ for God is not a respecter of persons. He demands righteousness and justice always. Employees are to carry out goals set by their employers with determination. Employees must be trustworthy, hardworking and faithful in all assignments so that God is glorified. Disciplined workers or employees are not lazy or disobedient at work.

> *"For I am a man under authority, having soldiers under me: and I say to this* man, *Go, and he goeth; and to another, Come, and he cometh; and to my servant, Do this, and he doeth* it" (Matthew 8:9).

> *"Servants,* be *subject to* your *masters with all fear; not only to the good and gentle, but also to the froward"* (1 Peter 2:18).

"[1]Let as many servants as are under the yoke count their own masters worthy of all honor, that the name of God and his *doctrine be not blasphemed"* (1 Timothy 6:1).

While your employer pays you earnings, if you are faithful, God rewards you more. You must work as a man under authority and be ready to carry out every instruction without grudges. You have no right to disobey a wicked master as long as his instruction does not contradict God's Word. This is very important.

"[13]As the cold of snow in the time of harvest, so is *a faithful messenger to them that send him: for he refresheth the soul of his masters. [18]Whoso keepeth the fig tree shall eat the fruit thereof: so he that waiteth on his master shall be honored"* (Proverbs 25:13; 27:18).

"Masters, give unto your *servants that which is just and equal; knowing that ye also have a Master in heaven"* (Colossians 4:1).

"At his day thou shalt give him his hire, neither shall the sun go down upon it; for he is poor, and setteth his heart upon it: lest he cry against thee unto the LORD, and it be sin unto thee" (Deuteronomy 24:15).

It is your responsibility to make your employer happy by carrying out his instructions with joy and singleness of purpose. The truth is that obedience brings honor. If your rights, benefits and entitlement are withheld, cry to God and He will hear from heave and fight for you. Masters or employers who sit on servants' or employees' wages would be punished especially if such servants pray. It is sin to pay your workers less than what their work deserves. We all have a Master in heaven, whether you are a master and servant.

"Knowing that of the Lord ye shall receive the reward of the inheritance: for ye serve the Lord Christ. But he that doeth wrong shall receive for the wrong which he hath done: and there is no respect of persons" (Colossians 3:24-25).

"So that a man shall say, Verily there is a reward for the righteous: verily he is a God that judgeth in the earth" (Psalms 58:11).

"The LORD rewarded me according to my righteousness: according to the cleanness of my hands hath he recompensed me. For I have kept the ways of the LORD, and have not wickedly departed from my God. For all his judgments were *before me: and* as for *his statutes, I did not depart from them. I was also upright before him, and have kept myself from mine iniquity. Therefore the LORD hath recompensed me according to my righteousness; according to my cleanness in his eye sight"* (2 Samuel 22:21-25).

The reason why you must obey is that God rewards all obedience. Even when you are paid less and overworked, continue to be obedient and faithful to God, who sees and knows all things. God rewards people according to their obedience and righteousness. If you keep God's Word in your heart and do what is right, your reward will surely come someday.

> *"I the LORD search the heart,* I *try the reins, even to give every man according to his ways,* and *according to the fruit of his doings"* (Jeremiah 17:10).

> *"And, behold, I come quickly; and my reward* is *with me, to give every man according as his work shall be"* (Revelation 22:12).

God searches the heart and He knows when you are working and when you are not. God would judge all our works. The truth of the matter is that a reward for every good work comes from God, who is not a respecter of person. Every work will pass through divine scale and God will reward every work accordingly.

Wherever you work, do it as you are working for the Lord. Do not be guided by inequality or injustice that may prevail. Serve with total commitment and do not change your behavior because the Lord gives reward at His appointed time.

> *"Not with eye service, as men pleasers; but as the servants of Christ, doing the will of God from the heart; With good will doing service, as to the Lord, and not to men: Knowing that whatsoever good thing any man doeth, the same shall he receive of the Lord, whether* he be *bond or free"* (Ephesians 6:6-8).

A HARD-WORKER WHO IS RESENTED

A diligent man receives his reward whether the devil likes it or not. Rewards may be delayed but cannot be denied. No one can mock God. Whatever a man sows, he must reap it.

> *"Be not deceived; God is not mocked: for whatsoever a man soweth, that shall he also reap. For he that soweth to his flesh shall of the flesh reap corruption; but he that soweth to the Spirit shall of the Spirit reap life everlasting. And let us not be weary in well doing: for in due season we shall reap, if we faint not"* (Galatians 6:7-9).

Joseph's brethren hated him without any cause. Jesus' kinsmen also hated Him. Potiphar's wife accused Joseph falsely. Potiphar ordered Joseph's arrest, imprisoned him without a fair trial but he remained faithful in prison. Joseph did not complain or murmured in bitterness or defended himself or fought back. He put his trust in the LORD because only God was his defense.

> *"And Joseph was brought down to Egypt; and Potiphar, an officer of Pharaoh, captain of the guard, an Egyptian, bought him of the hands of the Ishmeelites, which had brought him down thither. And the LORD was with Joseph, and he was a prosperous man; and he was in the house of his master the Egyptian. And his master saw that the LORD* was *with him, and that the LORD made all that he did to prosper in his hand. And Joseph found grace in his sight, and he served him: and he made him overseer over his house, and all* that *he had he put into his hand. And it came to pass from the time* that *he had made him overseer in his house, and over all that he had, that the LORD blessed the Egyptian's house for Joseph's sake; and the blessing of the LORD was upon all that he had in the house, and in the field. And he left all that he had in Joseph's hand; and he knew not ought he had, save the bread which he did eat. And Joseph was a goodly* person, *and well favored"* (Genesis 39:1-6).

(*See also* Genesis 37:3-11, 18-36; Luke 19:11-14; John 7:7; 15:18, 25).

Joseph trusted God and remained faithful to God as a beloved son of his father, though he was a slave and a prisoner in a foreign land. He worked hard wherever he found himself seeking nothing but the glory of God.

> *"And we know that all things work together for good to them that love God, to them who are the called according to* his *purpose"* (Romans 8:28).

> *"I know both how to be abased, and I know how to abound: everywhere and in all things I am instructed both to be full and to be hungry, both to abound and to suffer*

need. I can do all things through Christ which strengtheneth me" (Philippians 4:12-13).

"Many are *the afflictions of the righteous: but the LORD delivereth him out of them all"* (Psalms 34:19).

The people he loved sold him, yet he loved them. A highly respected person tempted him but he refused to sacrifice his relationship with God. Ironically, some people can only overcome temptations if they come from people they do not like, know or respect. Joseph was tempted but because his focus was to glorify God, he was able to overcome them all. He never allowed adverse conditions around him or the people he depended on for provisions and respected very well to make him deny God.

"There hath no temptation taken you but such as is common to man: but God is *faithful, who will not suffer you to be tempted above that ye are able; but will with the temptation also make a way to escape, that ye may be able to bear* it*"* (1 Corinthians 10:13).

Joseph believed that what God revealed to him in dreams would happen as long as he obeyed God and kept His commandments. He was a man who mastered how to live in times of plenty and lack. His reactions in difficult times are examples of true faithfulness to God.

"[37]*And the thing was good in the eyes of Pharaoh, and in the eyes of all his servants.* [38]*And Pharaoh said unto his servants, Can we find* such a one *as this* is, *a man in whom the Spirit of God* is? [39]*And Pharaoh said unto Joseph, Forasmuch as God hath shewed thee all this,* there is *none so discreet and wise as thou* art: [40]*Thou shalt be over my house, and according unto thy word shall all my people be ruled: only in the throne will I be greater than thou.* [41]*And Pharaoh said unto Joseph, See, I have set thee over all the land of Egypt.* [45]*And Pharaoh called Joseph's name Zaphnath–paaneah; and he gave him to wife Asenath the daughter of Poti–pherah priest of On. And Joseph went out over* all *the land of Egypt.* [46]*And Joseph* was *thirty years old when he stood before Pharaoh King of Egypt. And Joseph went out from the presence of Pharaoh, and went throughout all the land of Egypt.* [47]*And in the seven plenteous years the earth brought forth by handfuls.* [48]*And he gathered up all the food of the seven years, which were in the land of Egypt, and laid up the food in the cities: the food of the field, which* was *round about every city, laid he up in the same.* [49]*And Joseph gathered corn as the sand of the sea, very much, until he left numbering; for* it was *without number"*(Genesis 41:37-41, 45-49).

Joseph did not spend any useless time in his life. Even as a beloved son of his father, he was not lazy and he refused anyone to pamper him. Right from childhood, he was a great dreamer and a gifted interpreter of dreams. He went to Shechem to supply food to his brethren. He passed through the valley of Hebron to Dothan just to make sure that his brethren ate some food. They stripped off his coat of many colors, cast him into a dried pit, and ate the food without him. Later, they sold him to Ishmaelite traders for twenty pieces of silver. Anywhere Joseph found himself, he never allowed self-pity, grudges or regret to occupy his mind. He was always busy doing all things to the glory of God.

Finally, he became a leader in Pharaoh's palace in Egypt, and was second in command in the whole nation. He became a prime minister in Egypt, a good administrator, builder and a protector of God's people and nation. Joseph was an example of a hard worker, who had wisdom, foresight, good planning skills and vision.

Joseph saw himself as a servant of God and a defender of His people. He served God and humanity. He did spend his time in nightclubs, cinemas, football pitches or playing cards. He spent his entire life, money and energy in serving God and his generation.

> *"Even as the Son of man came not to be ministered unto, but to minister, and to give his life a ransom for many"* (Matthew 20:28).

> *"For whether* is *greater, he that sitteth at meat, or he that serveth?* Is *not he that sitteth at meat? But I am among you as he that serveth"* (Luke 22:27).

The love of Christ did not end in his heart. He expressed it and showed it practical.

JESUS CHRIST CAME TO SERVE

When Jesus did His ministry on earth, He only served people and gave life to people that were sick. He did not demand services. That was why He gave His life as a ransom for many. Whenever you get into any office, prepare your mind to serve others and do not expect anyone to serve you in return.

At the last supper, while His disciples were still eating, Jesus Christ His garment, took a towel, girded Himself and washed His disciples' feet and wiped them with the towel. What a humble Savior!

> *"How God anointed Jesus of Nazareth with the Holy Ghost and with power: who went about doing good, and healing all that were oppressed of the devil; for God was with him"* (Acts 10:38).

> *"[1]When he was come down from the mountain, great multitudes followed him. [2]And, behold, there came a leper and worshipped him, saying, Lord, if thou wilt, thou canst make me clean. [3]And Jesus put forth* his *hand, and touched him, saying, I will; be thou clean. And immediately his leprosy was cleansed. [4]And Jesus saith unto him, See thou tell no man; but go thy way, shew thyself to the priest, and offer the gift that Moses commanded, for a testimony unto them. [14]And when Jesus was come into Peter's house, he saw his wife's mother laid, and sick of a fever. [15]And he touched her hand, and the fever left her: and she arose, and ministered unto them"* (Matthew 8:1-4; 14-15).

Jesus Christ had both the mind and the will to serve. Though He had the right to demand for services of others, He did not but served. Determine to serve as you move into your new place of work. Offer your services to God and humanity. Jesus served with love and compassion. You can do the same.

> *"He that findeth his life shall lose it: and he that loseth his life for my sake shall find it. He that receiveth you receiveth me, and he that receiveth me receiveth him that sent me. He that receiveth a prophet in the name of a prophet shall receive a prophet's reward; and he that receiveth a righteous man in the name of a righteous man shall receive a righteous man's reward. And whosoever shall give to drink unto one of these little ones a cup of cold* water *only in the name of a disciple, verily I say unto you, he shall in no wise lose his reward"* (Matthew 10:39-47).

> *"Serving the Lord with all humility of mind, and with many tears, and temptations, which befell me by the lying in wait of the Jews"* (Acts 20:19).

> *"And when the Syrians of Damascus came to succor Hadadezer king of Zobah, David slew of the Syrians two and twenty thousand men"* (2 Samuel 8:5).

"Confess your *faults one to another, and pray one for another, that ye may be healed. The effectual fervent prayer of a righteous man availeth much"* (James 5:16).

The washing of feet was an ancient oriental custom of great importance, which was a mark of hospitality. The tenderness, the totality and nobility in Christ's case is an example for you to follow. Nevertheless, Christ is not demanding physical washing of feet but respect for one another. He demands our simplicity and sincerity, selflessness and humility. He wants us to be serious at work and sensitive whenever the need arises. Our service, respect and honor for each other must be rendered according to biblical principles (*See* Acts 4:19).

PRAYERS TO PROGRESS IN YOUR CAREER

Bible reference: Daniel 6:1-18

Begin with praise and worship

1. Father Lord, arrest and destroy any power that is sitting upon my promotion, in the name of Jesus.
2. You evil character that is harvesting my labor, I command you to die, in the name of Jesus.
3. Any disgrace that was prepared for me in my office, backfire by force, in the name of Jesus.
4. Every Red Sea and Pharaoh that has vowed to terminate my life, receive destruction, in the name of Jesus.
5. O Lord, bring me into favor with the decision makers in my office, in the name of Jesus.
6. Let unrepentant enemies of my blessings in my office receive demotion, in the name of Jesus.
7. Let my good records in this office begin to manifest, in the name of Jesus.
8. I release my rights, benefits and entitlements hidden in this office, in the name of Jesus.
9. My efforts in this office will not be in vain, in the name of Jesus.
10. Blood of Jesus, remove any evil cloud that is covering my glory in this office, in the name of Jesus.
11. I destroy evil records that were kept against me in this office, in the name of Jesus.
12. I remove any unrepentant enemy that is fighting to remove me from this office, in the name of Jesus.
13. Any witch or wizard that is attacking me in this office, make unpardonable mistake that will expose you and favor me, in the name of Jesus.
14. O Lord, promote me above my stubborn enemies in this office, in the name of Jesus.

15. Let my hidden greatness manifest in this office from henceforth, in the name of Jesus.

16. Anyone that has vowed to torment me in this office, receive angelic torments, in the name of Jesus.

17. O Lord, help me to do what is right in this office by Your power, in the name of Jesus.

18. I command all unfriendly friends in this office to be exposed and disgraced, in the name of Jesus.

19. Any power that wants me to go empty handed from this office, fail woefully and die, in the name of Jesus.

20. Any strongman that was unleashed for my sake in this office, die, in the name of Jesus.

21. O Lord, empower me to do my work with all diligence in this office, in the name of Jesus.

22. I command every place in my office to be conducive and enjoyable, in the name of Jesus.

23. Let my enemies in this office become confused, tired and resign by force, in the name of Jesus.

24. Angles of the living God, force my enemies to make heartbreaking and painful mistakes to my favor, in the name of Jesus.

25. I remove the protection and evil backbones of my unrepentant enemies, in the name of Jesus.

26. O Lord, transfer the joy of all my enemies to me by fire, in the name of Jesus.

27. Every evil plot against me in this office, fall on my enemies and vindicate me, in the name of Jesus.

28. Father Lord, avenge me of my adversaries in this office speedily, in the name of Jesus.

29. Let all hired adversaries in this office confess to death, in the name of Jesus.

30. Any arrow of death that was fired at me in this office, backfire, in the name of Jesus.

31. Let poisons prepared against me in this office be mistakenly receive by my enemies, in the name of Jesus.

32. Owners of evil load in this office, appear and carry your loads, in the name of Jesus.

33. I refuse to cooperate with the enemies of my progress in this office, in the name of Jesus.

34. I receive victory over the forces of wickedness against my life, in the name of Jesus.

35. Every weapon of failure and impossibilities against me in this office, destroy my enemies, in the name of Jesus.

36. Any agent of sin and all manner of defilement and pollution against me in this office, I overcome you, in the name of Jesus.

37. Power to live right, holy and unpolluted in this office, possess me by fire, in the name of Jesus.

38. Let agents of the devil in this office begin to fight themselves until they are sacked, in the name of Jesus.

39. Any satanic decision against me in this office, I render you invalid, in the name of Jesus.

40. Let all my helpers locate me in this office, in the name of Jesus.

41. I shall leave this office to a better place in peace, in the name of Jesus.

42. Every faultfinder against me in this office, die, in the name of Jesus.

43. Let my respect, honor and dignity be preserved forever, in the name of Jesus.

29

Chapter

PRAYERS FOR HEALTHY LIVING AND LONG LIFE

CHAPTER OVERVIEW

- *God is the source of long life*
- *Consequences of sin*
- *God's covenant of healing*
- *God is faithful in keeping covenant*
- *The acts of Jesus*

GOD IS THE SOURCE OF LONG LIFE

Long life is a gift from God. He promised to satisfy His children long life and peace. Besides God, there is no other source of long life and peace. Let no man deceive you, God is the only source of long life.

> *"That thou mayest love the LORD thy God, and that thou mayest obey his voice, and that thou mayest cleave unto him: for he is thy life, and the length of thy days: that thou mayest dwell in the land which the LORD sware unto thy fathers, to Abraham, to Isaac, and to Jacob, to give them"* (Deuteronomy 30:20).

> *"He asked life of thee, and thou gavest it him, even length of days forever and ever"* (Psalms 21:4).

> *"For length of days, and long life, and peace, shall they add to thee"* (Proverbs 3:2).

God wants His children to enjoy healthy living and long life. He does want you to wallow in sickness and disease, which are from Satan. That is why you need to enter the covenant of healing with God immediately.

Devil is the source of strange sicknesses, diseases and afflictions. Though the causes vary, the main source is Satan through his instrument of sin.

Let's consider Job for instance, Job was perfectly sound in health before the devil visited him and smote him with sores and boils from the sole of his foot to his head.

> *"7 So went Satan forth from the presence of the LORD, and smote Job with sore boils from the sole of his foot unto his crown"* (Job 2:7).

> *"14 Afterward Jesus findeth him in the temple, and said unto him, Behold, thou art made whole: sin no more, lest a worse thing come unto thee. 44 Ye are of* your *father the devil, and the lusts of your father ye will do. He was a murderer from the beginning, and abode not in the truth, because there is no truth in him. When he speaketh a lie, he speaketh of his own: for he is a liar, and the father of 10 The thief cometh not, but for to steal, and to kill, and to destroy: I am come that they might have life, and that they might have* it *more abundantly"* (John 8:44; 10:10; 5:14).

The bible described the devil as a murderer. When God created man, there was no sickness or diseases because God saw that everything that He created was good. However, when devil came, he murdered man's goodness and health. He stole man's peace and joy and began to afflict men with sickness and diseases. Devil does not visit people for nothing. His purpose is to kill people's joy and peace, or steal and destroy the good things that God created for man's happiness on earth.

Devil's principal weapon is sin, which he uses to separate us from God, our creator, before attacking our destinies with all manner of problems. However, God has not left us at the mercy of the devil. He sent Christ to destroy the works of the devil. That was why the best advice Christ gave to people was, *"Go and sin no more lest a worse thing come unto thee"* (*See* John 5:14).

If you can avoid sin and devil, you will surely live long with sound health. You need good health to fulfill your purpose on earth. However, if you are sick already, receive your healing through the Word of God, in the name of Jesus. Do whatever that is in your power to separate yourself from sin and the devil.

CONSEQUENCES OF SIN

Sin has many consequences but the worst is separation from God, which is eternal death. It is possible to be alive physically on earth while you are dead before God spiritually. Sin is extremely deadly and dangerous.

> "[1]*And you* hath he quickened, *who were dead in trespasses and sins;* [12]*That at that time ye were without Christ, being aliens from the commonwealth of Israel, and strangers from the covenants of promise, having no hope, and without God in the world"* (Ephesians 2:1, 12).

> *"And whosoever was not found written in the book of life was cast into the lake of fire"* (Revelation 20:15).

Death is a separation from life. While physical death is the separation of the soul and spirit from the body, spiritual death is a separation from God. The second death is the final, permanent and eternal separation from God. If you are a sinner, you have been separated from God spiritually. There can be no communication between you and God. That is why you need Christ urgently before it is too late. Consequences of sin are many but I will only mention a few here.

Adam and Eve were separated from God the day they ate fruits from the forbidden tree. God cursed them and they became enemies of God. Cain killed his brother Abel and received a curse. He became the first vagabond and fugitive on earth. The sons of Noah started their lives without involving God. The consequence of their rebellion was that God put confusion among them by scattering their language and scattered them upon the face of the earth and they stopped their project.

> *"And the whole earth was of one language, and of one speech. And it came to pass, as they journeyed from the east, that they found a plain in the land of Shinar; and they dwelt there. And they said one to another, Go to, let us make brick, and burn them throughly. And they had brick for stone, and slime had they for morter. And they said, Go to, let us build us a city and a tower, whose top* may reach *unto heaven; and let us make us a name, lest we be scattered abroad upon the face of the whole earth. And the LORD came down to see the city and the tower, which the children of men builded. And the LORD said, Behold, the people* is *one, and they have all one language; and this they begin to do: and now nothing will be restrained from them, which they have imagined to do. Go to, let us go down, and there confound their language, that they may not understand one another's speech. So the LORD scattered them abroad from thence upon the face of all the earth: and they left off to build the city"* (Genesis 11:1-8).

If you read the bible well, you will discover that every sin has a consequence. It is better not to sin at all. However, if you sin, you need to repent and forsake that sin immediately and ask God for forgiveness.

> *"He that covereth his sins shall not prosper: but whoso confesseth and forsaketh* them *shall have mercy"* (Proverbs 28:13).

Sarah, the wife of Abraham, because of her barrenness empowered her house cleaner to take over her position. The consequence of that sin was that her house cleaner disrespected her, grieved Abraham and gave birth to a child and that brought a polygamous war in Abraham's family.

The people of Sodom and Gomorrah became wicked and some of them became blind instantly. God later destroyed their cities and all their people with brimstone and fire (*See* Genesis 18:16, 20; 19:5-9). The wife of Lot became uncontrollably worldly and looked back in disobedience to God's instruction. She became a pillar of useless salt.

Esau was so careless to despise his birthright and he regretted it the rest of his life. There is always a consequence for every sin.

> *"And Jacob sod pottage: and Esau came from the field, and he* was *faint: And Esau said to Jacob, Feed me, I pray thee, with that same red* pottage; *for I* am *faint: therefore was his name called Edom. And Jacob said, Sell me this day thy birthright. And Esau said, Behold, I am at the point to die: and what profit shall this birthright do to me? And Jacob said, Swear to me this day; and he swore unto him: and he sold his birthright unto Jacob. Then Jacob gave Esau bread and pottage of lentiles; and he did eat and drink, and rose up, and went his way: thus Esau despised* his *birthright"* (Genesis 25:29-34).

Reuben, the first son of Jacob, committed an abomination by sleeping with Bilhab, his father's concubine. As a result, he lost his excellent spirit, position and rights of the first-born, and all the blessings attached to it. His father cursed him and it affected his unborn children.

Miriam spoke against Moses and she was locked away from her people for seven days because leprosy attacked her. Korah, Dathan, Abiriam were so popular and it entered into their heads. They ganged up against a divinely constituted body, Moses and Aaron. They envied, conspired and murmured against them, and accused them wrongly. The consequence of that sin was that the earth opened her mouth and ate them alive together with all their families (*See* Numbers 16:1-35).

Sin can destroy a person, a whole family or nation and take them to hell fire if they refuse to repent.

"The wicked shall be turned into hell, and *all the nations that forget God"* (Psalms 9:17).

"Be not deceived; God is not mocked: for whatsoever a man soweth, that shall he also reap. For he that soweth to his flesh shall of the flesh reap corruption; but he that soweth to the Spirit shall of the Spirit reap life everlasting" (Galatians 6:7-8).

Sin is an open invitation to the devil and his agents into a person's life. It can destroy a whole family, business and eat up human fleshes. Sin can cause war, death and make people to lose everything they have to the devil. Sin can bring thorns to someone's life.

More so, sin is disobedience to God's Word. It is breaking God's commandment. It can arrest a person and hand him over to devil, his worst enemy. Sin can sell a whole nation to their enemies to be tormented for seven, eight, twenty years or even to eternity.

"[12]And the children of Israel did evil again in the sight of the LORD: and the LORD strengthened Eglon the king of Moab against Israel, because they had done evil in the sight of the LORD. [13]And he gathered unto him the children of Ammon and Amalek, and went and smote Israel, and possessed the city of palm trees. [14]So the children of Israel served Eglon the king of Moab eighteen years. [1]And the children of Israel again did evil in the sight of the LORD, when Ehud was dead. [2]And the LORD sold them into the hand of Jabin king of Canaan, that reigned in Hazor; the captain of whose host was *Sisera, which dwelt in Harosheth of the Gentiles. [3]And the children of Israel cried unto the LORD: for he had nine hundred chariots of iron; and twenty years he mightily oppressed the children of Israel"* (Judges 3:12-14; 4:1-3).

The worst mistake someone can make in his life is to commit sin, and then postpone his repentance or refuse to repent of his sin. Sin can enter into any city and empower the devil to kill, cause war and cause people to be defeated in their lives. Sin brings captivity, dethrones people from their positions and terminates destinies. Sin can defeat a person, all his friends and helpers. Sin can attack victims with incurable diseases to death.

"Yet he sent prophets to them, to bring them again unto the LORD; and they testified against them: but they would not give ear. And the Spirit of God came upon Zechariah the son of Jehoiada the priest, which stood above the people, and said unto them, Thus saith God, Why transgress ye the commandments of the LORD, that ye cannot prosper? Because ye have forsaken the LORD, he hath also forsaken you. And they conspired against him, and stoned him with stones at the commandment of the king in the court of the house of the LORD. Thus Joash the king remembered not the kindness which Jehoiada his father had done to him, but slew his son. And when he died, he said, The LORD look upon it, and require it. And it came to pass at the end of the year, that *the host of Syria came up against him: and they came to Judah and*

Jerusalem, and destroyed all the princes of the people from among the people, and sent all the spoil of them unto the king of Damascus. For the army of the Syrians came with a small company of men, and the LORD delivered a very great host into their hand, because they had forsaken the LORD God of their fathers. So they executed judgment against Joash. And when they were departed from him, (for they left him in great diseases,) his own servants conspired against him for the blood of the sons of Jehoiada the priest, and slew him on his bed, and he died: and they buried him in the city of David, but they buried him not in the sepulchres of the kings. And these are they that conspired against him; Zabad the son of Shimeath an Ammonitess, and Jehozabad the son of Shimrith a Moabitess. Now concerning *his sons, and the greatness of the burdens* laid *upon him, and the repairing of the house of God, behold, they* are *written in the story of the book of the kings. And Amaziah his son reigned in his stead"* (2 Chronicles 24:19-27).

Sin can open your life for demonic possession and attacks with all manners of sickness and diseases. Sin brings fear, evil storms, lameness, dumbness, blindness and poverty.

"Afterward Jesus findeth him in the temple, and said unto him, Behold, thou art made whole: sin no more, lest a worse thing come unto thee" (John 5:14).

"Come unto me, all ye *that labor and are heavy laden, and I will give you rest. Take my yoke upon you, and learn of me; for I am meek and lowly in heart: and ye shall find rest unto your souls. For my yoke* is *easy, and my burden is light"* (Matthew 11:28-30).

The best cure for sin is true repentance and forsaking of all sins. If you would acknowledge your sins, confess and forsake them, every problem in your life would fall off eventually.

"And Samuel spake unto all the house of Israel, saying, If ye do return unto the LORD with all your hearts, then *put away the strange gods and Ashtaroth from among you, and prepare your hearts unto the LORD, and serve him only: and he will deliver you out of the hand of the Philistines. Then the children of Israel did put away Baalim and Ashtaroth, and served the LORD only"* (1 Samuel 7:3-4).

I want you to take a decision for God today. Take a decision against sin, return to God with all your heart and decide to serve God only. You need a sound health for without it, you cannot fulfill your destiny.

GOD'S COVENANT OF HEALING

People in covenant of healing with God have been freed from all manner of sickness and diseases that are common to people outside the same covenant. It is amazing how people ignore such an awesome covenant and wallow under the yoke of sicknesses and diseases.

A covenant child of God pays attention to God's voice to do what is right in the sight of God. He hears God's Word, keeps all His statues and avoids anything that would displease God.

> *"And said, If thou wilt diligently hearken to the voice of the LORD thy God, and wilt do that which is right in his sight, and wilt give ear to his commandments, and keep all his statutes, I will put none of these diseases upon thee, which I have brought upon the Egyptians: for I am the LORD that healeth thee"* (Exodus 15:26).

God blesses those who are in His covenant and keeps sickness and diseases away from their houses because they obey and serve God. The promises of God for healing bring God's healing and deliverance. People who are in God's covenant cannot die prematurely and suffer misfortune.

> *"And ye shall serve the LORD your God, and he shall bless thy bread, and thy water; and I will take sickness away from the midst of thee. There shall nothing cast their young, nor be barren, in thy land: the number of thy days I will fulfill. I will send my fear before thee, and will destroy all the people to whom thou shalt come, and I will make all thine enemies turn their backs unto thee. And I will send hornets before thee, which shall drive out the Hivite, the Canaanite, and the Hittite, from before thee. I will not drive them out from before thee in one year; lest the land become desolate, and the beast of the field multiply against thee. By little and little I will drive them out from before thee, until thou be increased, and inherit the land. And I will set thy bounds from the Red sea even unto the sea of the Philistines, and from the desert unto the river: for I will deliver the inhabitants of the land into your hand; and thou shalt drive them out before thee"* (Exodus 23:25-31).

When you come under God's covenant of healing, barrenness and strange sicknesses cannot harass because you are a child of covenant. Enemies turn away and fall before children of covenant. On their arrival anywhere, enemies are put to flight in their thousands.

> *"Wherefore it shall come to pass, if ye hearken to these judgments, and keep, and do them, that the LORD thy God shall keep unto thee the covenant and the mercy which he swore unto thy fathers: And he will love thee, and bless thee, and multiply thee: he*

will also bless the fruit of thy womb, and the fruit of thy land, thy corn, and thy wine, and thine oil, the increase of thy kine, and the flocks of thy sheep, in the land which he swore unto thy fathers to give thee. Thou shalt be blessed above all people: there shall not be male or female barren among you, or among your cattle. And the LORD will take away from thee all sickness, and will put none of the evil diseases of Egypt, which thou knowest, upon thee; but will lay them upon all them *that hate thee"* (Deuteronomy 7:12-15).

A covenant child of God obtains mercy in times of trouble and calamity. God's love manifests to them when they face difficult situations. God's covenant is blessing and multiplication. The womb of a child of covenant is fruitful. The bible said that God will bless your womb, land, corn, wine, oil and increase your kine, flocks of your sheep in the land where the Lord gave you.

Children of covenant need to be where God wants them to be. When Satan manipulates you out of your place of blessing and protection, you will have enormous battles to fight. For a covenant child to inherit all that God has provided fully, he must be located where God has destined him to be. He must not allow witches and wizards to manipulate him to make wrong choices. Even when you are at the right place, you ought to be obedient to God's Word in other to partake of His covenant of healing.

When you are at the right place and keep God's Word, God will bless you above people of the land, who do not share in the covenant of healing. Problems may come but God will take them away from you.

"Who forgiveth all thine iniquities; who healeth all thy diseases" (Psalms 103:3).

"Surely he hath borne our griefs, and carried our sorrows: yet we did esteem him stricken, smitten of God, and afflicted. But he was wounded for our transgressions, he was bruised for our iniquities: the chastisement of our peace was upon him; and with his stripes we are healed" (Isaiah 53:4-5).

When you confess your sins and determine to forsake them, God will forgive you and take all sicknesses and diseases away from your life. What Christ did on the cross is enough to secure your healing and keep you out of sicknesses and diseases.

When Jesus accepted death on the cross, He carried away our grief, sorrows and diverse problems. He suffered all that we are supposed to suffer. He was wounded for our sake. He was bruised, stricken, smitten and afflicted on our behalf. Where we were supposed to be chastised and stripped naked, he took our place in order to secure our peace forever.

"When the even was come, they brought unto him many that were possessed with devils: and he cast out the spirits with his *word, and healed all that were sick: That it might be fulfilled which was spoken by Esaias the prophet, saying, Himself took our infirmities, and bare* our *sicknesses"* (Matthew 8:16-17).

"Is any sick among you? let him call for the elders of the church; and let them pray over him, anointing him with oil in the name of the Lord: And the prayer of faith shall save the sick, and the Lord shall raise him up; and if he have committed sins, they shall be forgiven him" (James 5:14-15).

When you present all these things to the devil and refuse to be brought under his torture, he will bow and flee. Being ignorant of this truth and failing to resist the devil may keep you in bound and out of peace with God for the rest of your life.

Devil likes to attack children of God's covenant often with sickness, but this is illegal. The devil has no right to demand for the suffering of a child of God who is in covenant with God. If he does, children of God's covenant must reject devil's demands with all their strength, resist him and do everything possible to stop the devil.

You can also report the devil to God or call for the elders of the church to pray for you. You can anoint your body with oil to invite the presence of God's spirit, using the name of the Lord Jesus Christ. When you pray, believe in your prayers that God is able to bring everything under control. Even when you commit sin, do not allow the devil to afflict you with sickness. Confess those sins, turn around, and rebuke the devil.

"Who his own self bare our sins in his own body on the tree that we, being dead to sins, should live unto righteousness: by whose stripes ye were healed" (1 Peter 2:24).

"So then faith cometh *by hearing, and hearing by the word of God"* (Romans 10:17).

It is wrong for the devil to bring punishment upon an innocent person. The death and stripes of Jesus set us free from every punishment.

GOD IS FAITHFUL IN KEEPING COVENANT

God is extremely committed in keeping His own part of the covenant. Once you keep your own part of the covenant with God, He fulfills His own. Our confidence is that God has never failed in any covenant.

> *"And Moses went up unto God, and the LORD called unto him out of the mountain, saying, Thus shalt thou say to the house of Jacob, and tell the children of Israel; Ye have seen what I did unto the Egyptians, and* how *I bare you on eagles' wings, and brought you unto myself. Now therefore, if ye will obey my voice indeed, and keep my covenant, then ye shall be a peculiar treasure unto me above all people: for all the earth* is *mine: And ye shall be unto me a kingdom of priests, and an holy nation. These* are *the words, which thou shalt speak unto the children of Israel. And Moses came and called for the elders of the people, and laid before their faces all these words which the LORD commanded him. And all the people answered together, and said, All that the LORD hath spoken we will do. And Moses returned the words of the people unto the LORD"* (Exodus 19:3-8).

Covenant with God makes one special before God. It separates a person or people and distinguishes them from the crowd. Children of God's covenant are kingdom of priests, holy nation and called out people of God. God does not allow anyone or anything to harm such people. Evil powers identify covenant children and respect them. If you are a covenant child of God and you know your rights, no evil authority can harass you and go scot-free.

> *"He brought them forth also with silver and gold: and there was not one feeble person among their tribes"* (Psalms 105:37).

> *"And they journeyed from mount Hor by the way of the Red sea, to compass the land of Edom: and the soul of the people was much discouraged because of the way. And the people spake against God, and against Moses, Wherefore have ye brought us up out of Egypt to die in the wilderness? For* there is *no bread, neither* is there any *water; and our soul loatheth this light bread. And the LORD sent fiery serpents among the people, and they bit the people; and much people of Israel died. Therefore the people came to Moses, and said, We have sinned, for we have spoken against the LORD, and against thee; pray unto the LORD, that he take away the serpents from us. And Moses prayed for the people. And the LORD said unto Moses, Make thee a fiery serpent, and set it upon a pole: and it shall come to pass, that every one that is bitten, when he looketh upon it, shall live. And Moses made a serpent of brass, and put it upon a pole, and it came to pass, that if a serpent had bitten any man, when he beheld the serpent of brass, he lived"* (Numbers 21:4-9).

Where children of covenant dwell is sacred place. Poverty, problems and all manner of evil are not allowed to operate freely there. No matter how weak they appear physically, they are special before God. If you take them captive, their God will deliver them without silver or gold. If they enter into trouble, no matter how big, they will be delivered. No mountain, sea or people can stop their journey of life. They will come out from every problem because God is committed and ever faithful to keep His own part of the covenant. Even at the point of death, obedient covenant children who call upon God and look up to Him are delivered.

> *"For a multitude of the people, even many of Ephraim, and Manasseh, Issachar, and Zebulun, had not cleansed themselves, yet did they eat the Passover otherwise than it was written. But Hezekiah prayed for them, saying, The good LORD pardon every one That prepareth his heart to seek God, the LORD God of his fathers, though* he be *not* cleansed *according to the purification of the sanctuary. And the LORD hearkened to Hezekiah, and healed the people"* (2 Chronicles 30:18-20).

When a covenant child of God commits sin and becomes unclean, God can still deliver him. By acknowledging his faults, confessing them and repenting, a child of covenant receives pardon and answers to his prayers. If a covenant child of God prepares his heart to serve God, the Lord will cleanse him and purify his hearts. When such a person is sick, God heals and delivers him.

> *"Bless the LORD, O my soul: and all that is within me,* bless *his holy name. Bless the LORD, O my soul, and forget not all his benefits: Who forgiveth all thine iniquities; who healeth all thy diseases; Who redeemeth thy life from destruction; who crowneth thee with lovingkindness and tender mercies; Who satisfieth thy mouth with good* things; so that *thy youth is renewed like the eagle's"* (Psalms 103:1-5).

There are so many benefits in partaking in the covenant of healing with God. God forgives the iniquities of His children of covenant and heals all their disease. God redeems the loss among His children of covenant and saves them from destruction. It is not so with people who are not in covenant with God. He crowns the children of His covenant with His loving kindness and tender mercies. However, if you are a child of covenant, God will satisfy you with good things, so that your youth is renewed like that of an eagle.

> *"Fools because of their transgression, and because of their iniquities, are afflicted. Their soul abhorreth all manner of meat; and they draw near unto the gates of death. Then they cry unto the LORD in their trouble,* and *he saveth them out of their distresses. He sent his word, and healed them, and delivered* them *from their destructions"* (Psalms 107:17-20).

The benefits of entering into the covenant of healing are so many. If you are a sinner but you became wise enough to cry unto God, you will benefit from His covenant. If a murderer can be wise to cry to God for his sins, repent and forsake them, God will answer his prayer. Many people have transgressed because of ignorance. Their ignorance put them under the affliction of the devil.

If you are a victim of the worst sickness like HIV or other incurable diseases, or you are at the point of death, there is hope. Come and partake in this healing covenant with God today and cry unto Him for healing and mercies. If you would take this simple step today, your troubles will end and God will deliver, heal and save you from all your troubles according to His promises concerning you. God will send His word and His word will trace you to wherever you are and heal all your diseases.

> *"If my people, which are called by my name, shall humble themselves, and pray, and seek my face, and turn from their wicked ways; then will I hear from heaven, and will forgive their sin, and will heal their land"* (2 Chronicles 7:14).

> *"My son, attend to my words; incline thine ear unto my sayings. Let them not depart from thine eyes; keep them in the midst of thine heart. For they are life unto those that find them, and health to all their flesh"* (Proverbs 4: 20-22).

God's Word generates faith in the heart and gives life to dead organs of the body. Healing is the mercy of God in action. No sickness or problem can withstand the mighty Spirit of God. The bodies of the children of covenant are God's temples and God is able to cleanse sickness and all manner of satanic afflictions in His temple.

> *"And ye shall know the truth, and the truth shall make you free. If the Son therefore shall make you free, ye shall be free indeed"* (John 8:32, 36).

Jesus healed the sick by rebuking the devil and casting out evil spirits that caused sicknesses. He did it by the power of the Holy Ghost, which also dwells in you. If Jesus could rebuke and cast out evil spirits that caused sicknesses, a child of covenant with God can do the same.

> *"Verily, verily, I say unto you, He that believeth on me, the works that I do shall he do also; and greater* works *than these shall he do; because I go unto my Father. And whatsoever ye shall ask in my name, that will I do, that the Father may be glorified in the Son. [14]If ye shall ask any thing in my name, I will do* it*"* (John 14:12-14).

THE ACTS OF JESUS

"And Jesus went about all Galilee, teaching in their synagogues, and preaching the gospel of the kingdom, and healing all manner of sickness and all manner of disease among the people. And his fame went throughout all Syria: and they brought unto him all sick people that were taken with divers diseases and torments, and those which were possessed with devils, and those which were lunatick, and those that had the palsy; and he healed them. And there followed him great multitudes of people from Galilee, and from *Decapolis, and* from *Jerusalem, and* from *Judaea, and* from *beyond Jordan"* (Matthew 4:23-25).

As you read this book, I pray that all manner of sickness and diseases in your life are destroyed, in Jesus name - Amen.

Recall how Jesus met a leper who did not know his rights and cleansed him of his leprosy (*See* Matthew 8:1-4). He saw a servant who was sick of palsy and cast out the evil spirit behind the sickness (*See* Matthew 8:5-13). He visited Peter's house and touched his mother in-law and the fever that troubled her life left without negotiation (*See* Matthew 8:14-15). He came in contact with many people who were possessed by the devil and cast out the evil spirits with His Words and healed them all (*See* Matthew 8:16-17). He met two blind men who believed in Him and he opened their eyes.

"After this there was a feast of the Jews; and Jesus went up to Jerusalem. Now there is at Jerusalem by the sheep market *a pool, which is called in the Hebrew tongue Bethesda, having five porches. In these lay a great multitude of impotent folk, of blind, halt, withered, waiting for the moving of the water. For an angel went down at a certain season into the pool, and troubled the water: whosoever then first after the troubling of the water stepped in was made whole of whatsoever disease he had. And a certain man was there, which had an infirmity thirty and eight years. When Jesus saw him lie, and knew that he had been now a long time* in that case, *he saith unto him, Wilt thou be made whole? The impotent man answered him, Sir, I have no man, when the water is troubled, to put me into the pool: but while I am coming, another steppeth down before me. Jesus saith unto him, Rise, take up thy bed, and walk.* [9]*And immediately the man was made whole, and took up his bed, and walked: and on the same day was the Sabbath"* (John 5:1-9).

It does not matter how bad your situations are. Are you a child of covenant with God? If you are not, enter into the covenant of healing with God today and your situation will not be the same again.

"If my people, which are called by my name, shall humble themselves, and pray, and seek my face, and turn from their wicked ways; then will I hear from heaven, and will forgive their sin, and will heal their land" (2 Chronicles 7:14).

PRAYERS FOR HEALTHY LIVING AND LONG LIFE

Bible references: Proverbs 19:4; Deuteronomy 28:1-14

Begin with praise and worship

1. Every satanic interest in my life, I reject you, in the name of Jesus.
2. Let the power in the stripes of Jesus destroy every sickness and disease in my life, in the name of Jesus.
3. I command every door that was opened to sickness and disease in my body to close forever, in the name of Jesus.
4. Every property of the devil in my life, be roasted by fire, in the name of Jesus.
5. I uproot the root of sin in my life, in the name of Jesus.
6. Father Lord, give me sound health all the days of my life, in the name of Jesus.
7. Any invitation given to the devil into my life, I withdraw you by fire, in the name of Jesus.
8. I recover every good thing that I have ever lost in life double, in the name of Jesus.
9. I break and loose myself from the captivity of the spirit of death and hell, in the name of Jesus.
10. O Lord, deliver me from the mercy of devil and his agents, in the name of Jesus.
11. O Lord, empower me to avoid devil and sin forever, in the name of Jesus.
12. Every enemy of sound health in my body, die, in the name of Jesus.
13. Let the blood of Jesus destroy the consequences of every sin in my life, in the name of Jesus.
14. I command every part of my organ to receive immediate deliverance now, in the name of Jesus.
15. Any seed of witchcraft that is living inside me, die, in the name of Jesus.
16. Let the foundation of sin, witchcraft and evil in my life collapse by thunder, in the name of Jesus.

17. Let the earth open its mouth and swallow every demon of sickness in my life, in the name of Jesus.

18. I enter into a healing covenant with God today, in the name of Jesus.

19. I cast out of my life unclean spirits that are in-charge of premature deaths in my life, in the name of Jesus.

20. Any evil covenant that exists in my life, break, in the name of Jesus.

21. Every seed of unfruitfulness and disease in my life, die by fire, in the name of Jesus.

22. Any witch or wizard that is promoting sickness in my life, I expose and disgrace you by the blood of Jesus, in the name of Jesus.

23. Every arrow of grief, sorrow and suffering that was fired into my life, I fire you back, in the name of Jesus.

24. Let every yoke of affliction and demonic oppression in my life break, in the name of Jesus.

25. I resist every evil movement against my health, in the name of Jesus.

26. O Lord, open my eyes and show me what to do to enjoy sound health forever, in the name of Jesus.

27. Father Lord, empower me with perfect peace and divine serenity forever, in the name of Jesus.

28. Every seed of infirmity in my life, die by thunder without mercy, in the name of Jesus.

29. Any evil covenant that is promoting sickness in my life, break, in the name of Jesus.

30. Any curse that is energizing ill health in my life, expire, in the name of Jesus.

31. I reject all negative medical reports that were spoken over my health, in the name of Jesus.

32. O Lord, arise and deliver me from all manner of sicknesses, in the name of Jesus.

33. O Lord, anoint me and drive away evil presence in my life, in the name of Jesus.

34. Any sickness that is lodging in my body, come out and die, in the name of Jesus.

35. Every spirit of torment and sickness in my life, I destroy you, in the name of Jesus.

36. I cast out evil spirits that are punishing me with demonic health, in the name of Jesus.

37. Any evil leg or hand in my life, walk out and die, in the name of Jesus.
38. Any evil padlock that is locking up my health, break, in the name of Jesus.
39. Father Lord, empower me to live above sickness and disease, in the name of Jesus.
40. Any strange fire that is burning inside me, quench, in the name of Jesus.
41. Any evil river that is flowing into my life, dry up, in the name of Jesus.
42. Blood of Jesus, speak me out of every problem, in the name of Jesus.
43. I purge out satanic poisons in my body, in the name of Jesus.
44. Every enemy of my strength and health, die, in the name of Jesus.
45. Father Lord, deliver me from all evil, in the name of Jesus.
46. I revoke every satanic embargo that was placed upon my health, in the name of Jesus.
47. Let every part of my life begin to resist demons of sickness and disease, in the name of Jesus.
48. Blood of Jesus, flow into my foundation and set me free from sickness, in the name of Jesus.
49. Any evil sacrifice that was made for the sake of my health, expire, in the name of Jesus.
50. I release my health from demonic captivities forever, in the name of Jesus.
51. I attack demons that are attacking my health with the blood of Jesus, in the name of Jesus.
52. Let darkness that harbors unclean spirits in my life disappear forever, in the name of Jesus.
53. Every evil utterance that was uttered against my health by anyone, living or dead, expire, in the name of Jesus.
54. I break every yoke of unbearable health on my life to pieces, in the name of Jesus.
55. Any evil force that has invaded my health, rush out of my life and die, in the name of Jesus.
56. I walk out from the gate of sickness and death by force, in the name of Jesus.
57. I command the healing and deliverance of my body, soul and spirit to take effect immediately, in the name of Jesus.

58. Let divine surgical equipments enter my body, soul and spirit to remove every disease and sickness, in the name of Jesus.

59. By the power in the Word of God, I rebuke every sickness and disease in my life, in the name of Jesus.

60. Let spiritual and physical leprosy in my life die, in the name of Jesus.

61. Let every incurable disease and impossibility die in my life, in the name of Jesus.

62. Any evil spirit that is living in my body, I dispossess you, in the name of Jesus.

63. I command every organ of my body, soul and spirit to miscarry and abort every problem, in the name of Jesus.

64. Every stranger in my life, come out and die, in the name of Jesus.

65. Let the hiding place of sickness in my body be discovered and destroyed, in the name of Jesus.

If you repent, the blood of Jesus will speak for your deliverance and healing (*See* Matthew 26:28; 1 John 1:7; Isaiah 1:18).

30

Chapter

PRAYERS TO LIVE AND END YOUR LIFE WELL

CHAPTER OVERVIEW

- *The prodigal child*
- *All humanity is lost without Christ*
- *Preparing for challenges of life*
- *True commitments in life*

THE PRODIGAL CHILD

It is never too late to start all over again in life, in order to live and end your life well. The prodigal son began in a very bad way. He took the portion of goods that belonged to him and took his journey to a far country. He lavished the portion of his wealth on worthless living until he fell into famine.

The only good thing about the prodigal son was that he was not lazy. Instead, he did whatever was necessary for his survival, even rearing pigs. Though he made grievous mistakes in his life, he did not allow devil to destroy him. When he found out that hunger was knocking at his door, he quickly joined himself to a citizen of that country and he was offered a job in the field where he was to feed swine.

> *"And the son said unto him, Father, I have sinned against heaven, and in thy sight, and am no more worthy to be called thy son. But the father said to his servants, Bring forth the best robe, and put* it *on him; and put a ring on his hand, and shoes on* his *feet: And bring hither the fatted calf, and kill* it*; and let us eat, and be merry: For this my son was dead, and is alive again; he was lost, and is found. And they began to be merry"* (Luke 15:21-24).

He is a quick starter who never allowed his bad condition to destroy him. He left the field, resigned from where he was feeding the swine when he could not comfort himself anymore. He was not proud or ashamed of going back to his source, his father. He remembered that he had a rich father. He had a change of mind and cautioned himself. He took another quick decision and decided to return to his father even if it is to work as one of the servants.

He examined himself and accepted his faults. He took a good decision, confessed his sins and owned up to his failures. He said to himself and to the heaven and earth, *I have sinned*. He saw himself as an unworthy person. He knew that his father's servants had enough bread to spare. He started another journey back to his rich father. That journey back to his father earned him acceptance as a son and everyone rejoiced to have him back except his elder brother.

> *"Now the serpent was more subtle than any beast of the field which the LORD God had made. Moreover, he said unto the woman, Yea, hath God said, ye shall not eat of every tree of the garden? And the woman said unto the serpent, we may eat of the fruit of the trees of the garden: But of the fruit of the tree, which is in the midst of the garden, God, hath said, Ye shall not eat of it, neither shall ye touch it, lest ye die. And the serpent said unto the woman, Ye shall not surely die: For God doth know that in*

the day ye eat thereof, then your eyes shall be opened, and ye shall be as gods, knowing good and evil. And when the woman saw that the tree was *good for food, and that it* was *pleasant to the eyes, and a tree to be desired to make* one *wise, she took of the fruit thereof, and did eat, and gave also unto her husband with her; and he did eat"* (Genesis 3:1-6).

ALL HUMANITY IS LOST WITHOUT CHRIST

When Adam and Eve sinned, they hid themselves from God. In the end, God judged them and drove them out of His presence. In Adam, all men became sinners and captives to sin, judgment and death. Sin made man to rebel against God, thereby, incurring death penalty.

> *"All we like sheep have gone astray; we have turned everyone to his own way; and the LORD hath laid on him the iniquity of us all"* (Isaiah 53:6).

> *"For all have sinned, and come short of the glory of God"* (Romans 3:23).

Man being under the sentence of death could not pay the debt of his penalty to live again to fulfill his purpose on earth. This made God to initiate a redemption plan for man by sending His only begotten Son to reconcile us back to our God, our source and creator. That is why God is still calling you to return to Him.

> *"Come unto me, all* ye *that labor and are heavy laden, and I will give you rest. Take my yoke upon you, and learn of me; for I am meek and lowly in heart: and ye shall find rest unto your souls. For my yoke* is *easy, and my burden is light"* (Matthew 11:28-30).

The prodigal son returned to his earthly father on his own. He overcame the oppositions on his way. However, Jesus is inviting you to come back to God. Many people blame the prodigal son for his useless lifestyle. However, a critical look at the prodigal son's repentance shows that he is better than most us. All men have gone astray and many have done the worst thing by rejecting Jesus, who is the only way back to God.

> *"Jesus saith unto him, I am the way, the truth, and the life: no man cometh unto the Father, but by me"* (John 14:6).

Jesus Christ is a divine provision, the only way back to God. He is the only one who met the conditions demanded by the scripture to redeem man from the captivity of the devil. The atonement of Christ is the reconciliation of sinful man to God, made possible through the perfect sacrifice and death of Christ. There is no salvation outside the blood of Jesus Christ. If you reject the blood of Jesus and refuse to accept His sacrifice, you will no longer find favor with God. Christ's death is the only thing that satisfies the demands of divine justice when He died in our place.

> *"For God so loved the world, that he gave his only begotten Son, that whosoever believeth in him should not perish, but has everlasting life. For God sent not his Son*

into the world to condemn the world; but that the world through him might be saved" (John 3:16-17).

All humanity has the opportunity to repent, believe and follow Christ back to our creator.

"Look unto me, and be ye saved, all the ends of the earth: for I am *God, and* there is *none else"* (Isaiah 45:22).

"The next day John seeth Jesus coming unto him, and saith, Behold the Lamb of God, which take away the sin of the world" (John 1:29).

Anyone who rejects sacrifice of Jesus on the cross of Calvary is eternally condemned for not accepting in invitation to return to God. In addition, repentance is turning away from all sins completely. It is when a sinner turns away from sin with all his heart. No matter how corrupt, averse, spiritually blind, deaf or dead you are, if you accept Christ, He will give you abundant life and bring you back to Your Father, the creator of heaven and earth. What a great privilege!

"For by grace are ye saved through faith; and that not of yourselves: it is *the gift of God"* (Ephesians 2:8).

"For whosoever shall call upon the name of the Lord shall be saved" (Romans 10:13).

Salvation is God's grace and Christ already paid the price when He accepted to die for humanity on the cross of Calvary. Take a decision to return to God today before it is too late!

PREPARING FOR CHALLENGES OF LIFE

Life is full of challenges and we all need thorough preparation to face the challenges of life. The best time to start preparing for adulthood is from childhood. The development of physical, emotional, temperamental, social and spiritual aspects of our lives begins when we are young. These things would make up who we become in our adulthood.

Before you think of marriage, you need to become independent of your parents. You need to develop a matured life of discipline, temperance, self-denial and unselfishness.

> *"For three* things *the earth is disquieted, and for four* which *it cannot bear: For a servant when he reignite; and a fool when he is filled with meat; For an odious* woman *when she is married; and a handmaid that is heir to her mistress"* (Proverb 30:21-23).

> *"[8]And the LORD God planted a garden eastward in Eden; and there he put the man whom he had formed. [15]And the LORD God took the man, and put him into the Garden of Eden to dress it and to keep it. [18]And the LORD God said,* It is *not good that the man should be alone; I will make him a help meet for him"* (Genesis 2:8, 15, 18).

No one jumps into life without due preparation and succeeds. You must be a child before you become a man. You must serve others before others serve you. God gave Adam great responsibility in the garden to dress it and to keep it. Adam had a good job. He was doing something before the Lord gave him a wife. This is very important point for you to grasp.

Life of industry is very important if you must face the challenges of life successfully. The most important preparation is for one to have an intimate relationship with God through Jesus Christ. You must receive salvation, live a life of purity and do everything to please God.

> *"For which of you, intending to build a tower, sitteth not down first, and counteth the cost, whether he have* sufficient *to finish* it? *Lest haply, after he hath laid the foundation, and is not able to finish* it, *all that behold* it *begin to mock him, Saying, this man began to build, and was not able to finish"* (Luke 14:28-30).

As you prepare to marry and face realities of life, make sure that you are on the same path with Jesus Christ. None can succeed without Christ no matter how much that person tried. However, you have to be mindful of the fact that pressures of whom to marry, choice of buying or renting a home, etc., can creep in. Always ask God for wisdom and direction.

Do not rush into your choice of a person to marry without making sure that God is leading you. You must determine to uphold God's purpose for your life especially in marriage. In whatever you do, you must have eternity in proper perspective in your decisions. You must have determination to do the whole will of God and fulfill His whole purpose for your life.

> *"Then was Jesus led up of the Spirit into the wilderness to be tempted of the devil"* (Matthew 4:1).

> *"To reveal his Son in me, that I might preach him among the heathen; immediately I conferred not with flesh and blood: [17]Neither went I up to Jerusalem to them which were apostles before me; but I went into Arabia, and returned again unto Damascus. [7]Be not deceived; God is not mocked: for whatsoever a man sowed, that shall he also reap"* (Galatians 1:16-17; 6:7).

Without adequate preparation, you may be disappointed sooner than you could imagine. You could be planning to set up new business and buy a house, or acquire properties and get married, but Jesus is saying that you have to prepare yourself well because these things have their challenges too.

When you plan to build a godly relationship, you have to make adequate preparation. You must sit down to think, plan and prayerfully determine what God's will for your life is in everything you want to do. The world is filled with uncompleted projects. Many died without completing the good things they started. You must count the immediate and future costs of anything you want to do or that you are about to start even before you start. The truth of the matter is that any thing you do in life without considering God first is bound to fail.

> *"It came to pass after this also, that the children of Moab, and the children of Ammon, and with them other beside the Ammonites, came against Jehoshaphat to battle. Then there came some that told Jehoshaphat, saying, There cometh a great multitude against thee from beyond the sea on this side Syria; and, behold, they are in Hazazon–tamar, which is En–gedi. And Jehoshaphat feared, and set himself to seek the LORD, and proclaimed a fast throughout all Judah"* (2 Chronicle 20:1-3).

Jehoshaphat woke up one morning and saw an army scattered all over the land against him. Though he was a child of God, he became afraid. He feared because he knew that it would be suicide mission to go into battle with multitudes of enemy soldiers. What did he do? He declared a fast to seek the Lord's help.

You do not need to engage in anything without God. The best way to prepare for the challenges of life is to involve God in everything you do in life, even before you start doing them. Jesus Christ was the only person who faced the worst enemies on earth. He was victorious not only because he is God. The Spirit of God led Him into the wilderness to prepare Him for His mission. He fasted for forty days and forty nights. He came out from fasting to face His worst enemy. He had victory over Satan because He recognized the challenges ahead and prepared Himself for them.

When Christ revealed himself to Paul, he did not conferred with flesh and blood. Paul separated himself and went to Arabia to prepare for the challenges ahead of him. You will always reap what you sowed. As I said before, Jesus Christ did not jump into life in haste. He came to save humanity; to die for our sin, but he never jumped into action until He had prepared Himself well.

For nine months, millions of people were dying and going to hell, but Jesus did not jump out of His mother's womb to save them. He knew that there was an appointed time. After His birth, many evil things continued happening. Many people were dying and rushing to hell, but He remained calm until it was time for action. Can you recognize your time for action?

> *"And he went down with them, and came to Nazareth, and was subject unto them: but his mother kept all these sayings in her heart. And Jesus increased in wisdom and stature, and in favor with God and man"* (Luke 2:51-52).

Jesus subjected himself to the care, teachings and instruction of His earthly parents until He was fully prepared. He waited until He has grown enough in wisdom. He also grew up in stature and favor with God and man.

TRUE COMMITMENTS IN LIFE

There are critical types of commitments in life I want to discuss here. Without commitments in life, life is bound to be without aim and ends in disaster.

COMMITMENT TO GOD: Your first commitment in life must be to God, if you want to succeed. Nothing can take the place of God in your life.

> *"[1]Remember now thy Creator in the days of thy youth, while the evil days come not, nor the years draw nigh, when thou shalt say, I have no pleasure in them; [13]Let us hear the conclusion of the whole matter: Fear God, and keep his commandments: for this* is *the whole* duty *of man"* (Ecclesiastes 12:1, 13).

Based on his experience in life, Solomon in his counsel to humanity said, "*Remember now without postponement your creator.*" Solomon postponed many things in his life. As a young m, now is the right time to remember God because a day is coming when you would be fed up with whatever you are pursuing now.

Everything on earth would someday become useless especially when God is not part of them. Solomon is saying that it is wise for you to remember God first when choosing your marriage partner. Give God the prime position. If devil is telling you about divorce, remember God now because if you abandon Him, when problem comes, you cannot solve it without God. During courtship, remember God. Listen to God, be guided and regulate your actions by God's Word. This is what Solomon did not do and he deviated from God.

> *"But king Solomon loved many strange women, together with the daughter of Pharaoh, women of the Moabites, Ammonites, Edomites, Zidonians,* and *Hittites; Of the nations* concerning *which the LORD said unto the children of Israel, Ye shall not go in to them, neither shall they come in unto you:* for *surely they will turn away your heart after their gods: Solomon clave unto these in love. And he had seven hundred wives, princesses, and three hundred concubines: and his wives turned away his heart"* (1 Kings 11:1-3).

Solomon realized his faults when it was too late. The reason he is advising us now is that he has been in such position before. He is saying that nobody should pursue pleasure, marriage and job offer without remembering God from the onset.

Most people remembered God after getting married, which happened to be contrary to God's will. Others remembered God after committing fornication, adultery and many abortions. Others remembered God at their old age when they no longer have strength. Anyone can remember God at any age. However, Solomon said it is better for one to remember God in his youth.

Some people remember God in their sick beds, poverty and in times of trouble. That is also good but it would be better now while evil days have not come. It is good to remember God during your courtship, honeymoon, or when conceptions are delayed or when you are looking for a child. However, it is not only when you are barren that you should remember God.

The implication of what Solomon was saying is that he made great mistakes because he should have done what was doing at his old age during his youth. It is better to serve God at your youth than when you are old. He had God's fear but it was not enough. He made grievous mistakes because he refused to develop the love and fear of God that was in him. His conclusion was *to fear God and keep His commandments* (*See* Ecclesiastes 12:13).

You need to be born-again at your youth for it is the best time to make commitment to your God. Good success in life starts when you commit your ways to God at your youthful age.

> *"According to my earnest expectation and* my *hope, that in nothing I shall be ashamed, but* that *with all boldness, as always,* so *now also Christ shall be magnified in my body, whether* it be *by life, or by death. For to me to live* is *Christ, and to die* is *gain"* (Philippians 1:20-21).

We need to give the totality of our lives to God from youth. If you want to avoid shame, disgrace and reproach in life, begin to magnify God in your body at your youth. If you want to be bold in life before God and man, begin to magnify God at your youth. Use your body to honor God, magnify him and not the devil. If you want to face life with boldness and stand against the devil and death, you have to start now to magnify God in your body. Do not use your body to magnify the devil. If you die while magnifying the Lord in your body, you have made a lot of gain. If you live, you have achieved much.

COMMITMENT TO PURITY: One of the best commitments one can make in life is to commit his life to live a pure life. If you have the problem of purity, you have a great problem in your bosom.

> *"But Daniel purposed in his heart that he would not defile himself with the portion of the king's meat, nor with the wine which he drank: therefore he requested of the prince of the eunuchs that he might not defile himself"* (Daniel 1:8).

> *"Lay hands suddenly on no man, neither be partaker of other men's sins: keep thyself pure"* (1 Timothy 5:22).

"Is there anyth*ing whereof it may be said, See, this* is *new? It hath been already of old time, which was before us"* (Ecclesiastes 1:10).

Daniel, Joseph and Enoch's successes were based on their commitments to purity. Daniel was purposeful in life and he overcame defilement in his youth. He was found ten times better than all the magicians and astrologers that competed with him in all matters of wisdom and understanding in the government. He excelled above others because he was committed to purity. He prepared himself well above others because an excellent spirit was in his life because of his commitment to purity.

"And it came to pass after these things, that his master's wife cast her eyes upon Joseph; and she said, lie with me. But he refused, and said unto his master's wife, Behold, my master witted not what is *with me in the house, and he hath committed all that he hath to my hand;* There is *none greater in this house than I; neither hath he kept back anything from me but thee, because thou* art *his wife: how then can I do this great wickedness, and sin against God?"* (Genesis 39:7-9).

"And in all matters of wisdom and *understanding that the king enquired of them he found them ten times better than all the magicians* and *astrologers that* were *in his entire realm. And Daniel continued* even *unto the first year of King Cyrus"* (Daniel 1:20-21).

"It pleased Darius to set over the kingdom an hundred and twenty princes, which should be over the whole kingdom; And over these three presidents; of whom Daniel was *first: that the princes might give accounts unto them, and the king should have no damage. Then this Daniel was preferred above the presidents and princes, because an excellent spirit* was *in him; and the king thought to set him over the whole realm"* (Daniel 6:1-3).

"And Enoch lived sixty and five years, and begat Methuselah: And Enoch walked with God after he begat Methuselah three hundred years, and begat sons and daughters: And all the days of Enoch were three hundred sixty and five years: And Enoch walked with God: and he was *not; for God took him"* (Genesis 5:21-24).

If you have not committed to purity before now, it is not late yet. Do so at once. Anything worth doing is worth doing very well. If you want to be a farmer, be the best farmer, pursue excellence to beat others. Do not be a mediocre or manage life at the lowest level. Rise up, shine, for God is with you always. You need to be distinguished and outstanding in everything you do in life.

"Notwithstanding she shall be saved in childbearing, if they continue in faith and charity and holiness with sobriety" (1 Timothy 2:15).

Arise and pursue the best things with all your strength and faith in God. Strive for personal, spiritual and emotional developments. If you need to buy a house or land, and to buy them at choice places, aim high. Learn how to relate with others and respect people, especially the elders.

> *"Trust in the LORD with all thine heart; and lean not unto thine own understanding"* (Proverbs 3:5).

> *"Rebuke not an elder, but entreat* him *as a father;* and *the younger men as brethren"* (1 Timothy 5:1).

You need to have confidence in God. Detest false life and be real to self, others and to God. It is well with you in the name of Jesus – Amen.

PRAYERS TO LIVE AND END YOUR LIFE WELL

Bible references: 2 Chronicles 7:12-15; Ecclesiastes 12:14

Begin with praise and worship

1. Blood of Jesus, deliver me from every sin that exists in my life, in the name of Jesus.
2. Blood of Jesus, cleanse pollution and defilement in my body, in the name of Jesus.
3. I uproot seeds of unprofitable hard work in my life, in the name of Jesus.
4. O Lord, deliver me from powers of fruitless efforts, in the name of Jesus.
5. I break and loose myself from constant frustration and failure, in the name of Jesus.
6. Let the yoke of demons of finance in my life beak, in the name of Jesus.
7. I lift every satanic embargo that was placed on my progress, in the name of Jesus.
8. Let God arise and deliver me from the spirit of tortoise and snail, in the name of Jesus.
9. I break and loose myself from demons of sluggish progress, in the name of Jesus.
10. I uproot the tree of non-achievement in my life, in the name of Jesus.
11. Every author of failure in my life, die, in the name of Jesus.
12. I renounce everything in my life that is less than the best, in the name of Jesus.
13. Father Lord, restore me in Your own perfect image, in the name of Jesus.
14. I command my life to dominate everything under me by force, in the name of Jesus.
15. I lift every burden of poverty in my life, in the name of Jesus.
16. I command every lack in my life to die, in the name of Jesus.
17. Father Lord, command Your glory to manifest in my life, in the name of Jesus.
18. I spoil and ruin every work of the enemy in my life, in the name of Jesus.

19. I break myself loose from the grip of failure and poverty spirit, in the name of Jesus.

20. Lord Jesus, remold and reshape my destiny to reflect Your glory, in the name of Jesus.

21. O Lord, redeem me fully from every curse and evil covenants, in the name of Jesus.

22. Father Lord, anoint me to triumph over every dark power, in the name of Jesus.

23. Let my buried destinies resurrect by force, in the name of Jesus.

24. Let God of perfect beginning, start a new work in my life, in the name of Jesus.

25. Father Lord, put me on the path of Your true riches and wealth, in the name of Jesus.

26. Every mistake that was prepared for my future, die, in the name of Jesus.

27. Father Lord, help me to overcome every challenge in my life, in the name of Jesus.

28. O Lord, give me open doors of inexhaustible income, in the name of Jesus.

29. I receive power to face realities of life with grace, in the name of Jesus.

30. I command every demonic pressure upon my life to disappear, in the name of Jesus.

31. I disgrace every messenger of disappointment in my life, in the name of Jesus.

32. I beak and loose myself from unprofitable relationships, in the name of Jesus.

33. I will consider God in every action I will take in my life from henceforth, in the name of Jesus.

34. Let any bondage I inherited in my life break, in the name of Jesus.

35. Fire of God, enter into my foundation and destroy every evil plantation, in the name of Jesus.

36. Let the blood of Jesus put in my foundation things that would help me to succeed in life, in the name of Jesus.

37. I command every evil personality against my life to die in shame, in the name of Jesus.

38. O Lord, empower me to excel in every area of life, in the name of Jesus.

39. Any witchcraft power that wants to confront my life, die, in the name of Jesus.

40. Let every evil gate that was opened to destroy my life close forever, in the name of Jesus.

41. Let destructions that are waiting for me at my end of my life die, in the name of Jesus.

42. Let that Goliath that is ready to attack my old age die, in the name of Jesus.

43. Lord Jesus, walk me to the end of my life by Your power, in the name of Jesus.

44. Let my deliverance refuse to be aborted or diverted, in the name of Jesus.

45. I break and loose my life from enemy's ridicule and mockery, in the name of Jesus.

46. Let any evil power that is sponsoring evil in my die, in the name of Jesus.

47. Let the stronghold of my enemies collapse, in the name of Jesus.

48. O Lord, arise and kill the Goliath in my life, in the name of Jesus.

49. Blood of Jesus, speak peace into my life, in the name of Jesus.

50. Let God arise and repackage my old age to be glorious, in the name of Jesus.

31

Chapter

PRAYERS FOR BREAKTHROUGH IN YOUR BUSINESS

CHAPTER OVERVIEW

- *Business breakthrough is very important*
- *Attacks on businesses from evil altars*
- *Hijacked business breakthrough*

BUSINESS BREAKTHROUGH IS VERY IMPORTANT

Every good businessperson understands what it means to experience breakthrough in business. Without this experience, the business would die naturally. While God wants you to prosper in your business, your enemy, the devil, does not want you to prosper. He wants you to fail.

That is why devil has stationed the forces of darkness in diverse places to stop people's businesses from moving forward. You could have been destined to succeed in your field of business but when you fail to deal with the forces of darkness, it would be so hard for you to make it no matter how much you try.

> *"And there came an angel of the LORD, and sat under an oak which* was *in Ophrah, that* pertained *unto Josh the Abi–ezrite: and his son Gideon threshed wheat by the winepress, to hide* it *from the Midianites. And the angel of the LORD appeared unto him, and said unto him, The LORD* is *with thee, thou mighty man of valor. And Gideon said unto him, Oh my Lord, if the LORD were with us, why then is all this befallen us. In addition, where be all his miracles, which our fathers told us of, saying, did not the LORD bring us up from Egypt? Now the LORD hath forsaken us, and delivered us into the hands of the Midianites. And the LORD looked upon him, and said, Go in this thy might, and thou shalt save Israel from the hand of the Midianites: have not I sent thee? And he said unto him, Oh my Lord, wherewith shall I save Israel? Behold, my family* is *poor in Manasseh, and I* am *the least in my father's house"* (Judges 6:11-15).

Gideon was defeated in his life by these forces. In his father's farmland, these forces occupied the place to enjoy their harvests. These powers influenced the Midianites to oppress Gideon and his people. Gideon was thrashing his father's wheat in his father's farm to hide it from the Midianites.

They cultivated the ground and planted but the Midianites enjoy their harvest. While they suffered, their enemies enjoyed their increase and harvest. It was a sad situation.

There are people today who do businesses with people's destinies. People work hard but do not get rewards for their efforts. This is not right. The devil labors to contradict God's Word and to make it invalid. God said that a man would reap what he sowed, but the devil is saying that another man would reap what you sowed. Unfortunately, that is what is happening with the businesses of many people today.

"Be not deceived; God is not mocked: for whatsoever a man sowed, that shall he also reap. For he that sowed to his flesh shall of the flesh reap corruption; but he that sowed to the Spirit shall of the Spirit reap life everlasting" (Galatians 6:7-8).

"And it came to pass, as we went to prayer, a certain damsel possessed with a spirit of divination met us, which brought her masters much gain by soothsaying: The same followed Paul and us, and cried, saying, These men are the servants of the most high God, which shew unto us the way of salvation. And this did her many days. However, Paul, being grieved, turned and said to the spirit, I command thee in the name of Jesus Christ to come out of her. In addition, he came out the same hour. And when her masters saw that the hope of their gains was gone, they caught Paul and Silas, and drew them *into the marketplace unto the rulers"* (Acts 16:16-19).

The bible had a story of a young girl that went through this kind of problem. This damsel had so much strength and power to labor. She had all that it takes to succeed, make great profit and live comfortably well to help herself and others. The devil saw this and inspired some people to invoke an evil spirit to possess her.

The duty of that evil spirit was not to reduce her strength, energy and talent but to divert all her gains to the satanic kingdom for his agents to make much gain. This kind of spirit is very wicked. This is not the spirit of premature death, sickness or weakness. It is a spirit that helps you to do more work for evil men to enjoy your labor. It is a spirit that allows people to labor and suffer, and empowers satanic agents to enjoy your harvest.

This wicked spirit possessed this young girl for many years. Her talent was employed to profit wicked people while she suffered and moved about like a mad person. She was a diviner who made much gain for her masters through soothsaying. She encountered Paul's evangelistic team and said correct things about them but Paul was grieved and he cast out the spirit that possessed her. Paul delivered her and set her free while the occult grandmasters began to record losses in their evil businesses of soul trading and destiny amputation.

"And build an altar unto the LORD thy God upon the top of this rock, in the ordered place, and take the second bullock, and offer a burnt sacrifice with the wood of the grove which thou shall cut down. Then Gideon took ten men of his servants, and did as the LORD had said unto him: and so *it was, because he feared his father's household, and the men of the city, that he could not do it by day, that he did it by night"* (Judges 6:26-27).

The case of Gideon was similar to that of this young girl. He planted threshed wheat but the Midianites came and took them all. His problem was physical but the young girl's was spiritual. Most of our battles today are more spiritual than physical. A great battle is going on between God's children and Satan's agents.

> *"For we wrestle not against flesh and blood, but against principalities, against powers, against the rulers of the darkness of this world, against spiritual wickedness in high* places" (Ephesians 6:12).

> *"For though we walk in the flesh, we do not war after the flesh: (For the weapons of our warfare* are *not carnal, but mighty through God to the pulling down of strong holds;) Casting down imaginations, and every high thing that exalted itself against the knowledge of God, and bringing into captivity every thought to the obedience of Christ"* (2 Corinthians 10:3-5).

Many people are already defeated and the result is what you see everywhere. Many business people today are not making it because of devil's agents who know how to divert their gains to make much profit. You need to start praying and asking God to reveal the cause of your problems.

ATTACKS ON BUSINESSES FROM EVIL ALTARS

Many Christians are yet to come to the knowledge of the reality of evil altars. An altar is raised, typically flat-topped, structure or area where spiritual ceremonies are performed. Principally, satanic agents, including witches and wizards, erect altars where they gather to carry out their activities and evil plans.

When satanic agents want to afflict people, they use their evil altars. When they want to waste people's progress, they use evil altars. When they want to oppress people's stars, they use evil altars. When they want to capture anointing on people's lives, they use evil altars. When they want to limit people's lives, they use evil altars. When they want to frustrate plans, they use evil altars. When they want to kill people and bury them while such people still live, they use evil altars. When they want to place a curse on someone's business, they use evil altars. When they want to place yokes of limitation on people's efforts, they use evil altars.

When they want to control people against God's will, they use evil altars. When they want to impose satanic fear on people, they use evil altars. When they want to useless someone's effort, they use evil altars. When they want to send evil forces to someone's business, they use evil altars. When they want good things to abandon someone, they use evil altars. When they want people to be tired of life, they use evil altars. When they want to arrest a promising star, they use evil altars. When they want people to live wasted lives, they use evil altars. When they want to announce people's failures, they use evil altars. When they want to summon people for evil, they use evil altars. When they want to cause confusion in any life, place or thing, they use evil altars. When they want to have access to people's health, they use evil altars. When they want to remove someone from an exalted position, they use evil altars.

When they want to eat human flesh and drink people's blood, they use evil altars. When they want to do evil transfer, they use evil altars. When they want to behead important heads, they use evil altars. When satanic agents want to fellowship with the devil, they use evil altars. When they want to introduce evil on earth, they use evil altars. When they want to block people's access to favor, they use evil altars. When they want to break marriages, they use evil altars. When they want to raise enemies, they use evil altars. Do you still doubt the activities of evil agents?

> *"[1]And Balaam said unto Balak, Build me here seven altars, and prepare me here seven oxen and seven rams. [2]And Balak did as Balaam had spoken; and Balak and Balaam offered on* every *altar a bullock and a ram. [3]And Balaam said unto Balak, Stand by thy burnt offering, and I will go: peradventure the LORD will come to meet me: and whatsoever he showed me I would tell thee. In addition, he went to a high place. [13]And Balak said unto him, Come, I pray thee, with me unto another place,*

from whence thou mayest see them: thou shall see but the utmost part of them, and shall not see them all: and curse me them from thence. [14]*And he brought him into the field of Zophim, to the top of Pisgah, and built seven altars, and offered a bullock and a ram on* every *altar"* (Numbers 23:1-3, 13-14).

King Balak once invited Balaam to kill the people of God and stop their journey to the Promised Land. To achieve their aim, they decided to build altars, have fellowship with the devil and mobilize evil spirits to kill the children of Israel. When they failed in the first seven altars, they decided to build another seven altars where they would curse them.

"And Balak said unto Balaam, Come, I pray thee, I will bring thee unto another place; peradventure it will please God that thou mayest curse me them from thence. And Balak brought Balaam unto the top of Peor that looked toward Jeshimon. And Balaam said unto Balak, Build me here seven altars, and prepare me here seven bullocks and seven rams. And Balak did as Balaam had said, and offered a bullock and a ram on every *altar"* (Numbers 23:27-30).

When they built another seven altars to the children of Israel, they still failed. When they investigated, they found out that their enchantments and divinations failed because God did not see iniquity in the camp of God's children. As a result, the people of God were united and God was with them.

"[21]*He hath not beheld iniquity in Jacob neither hath he seen perverseness in Israel: the LORD his God* is *with him and the shout of a king* is *among them.* [23]*Surely* there is *no enchantment against Jacob, neither* is there *any divination against Israel: according to this time it shall be said of Jacob and of Israel, What hath God wrought"* (Numbers 23:21, 23).

With the erection of 21 evil altars, they planned to bring iniquity to their camp. They raised agents of perversion, fired arrows of immorality and disobedience to the elders and the Word of God. They raised wayward women to seduce the children of Israel.

"[1]*And Israel abode in Shittim and the people began to commit whoredom with the daughters of Moab.* [2]*And they called the people unto the sacrifices of their gods: and the people did eat, and bowed down to their gods.* [3]*And Israel joined himself unto Baal–peor: and the anger of the LORD was kindled against Israel.* [9]*And those that died in the plague were twenty and four thousand"* (Numbers 25:1-3, 9).

Evil altars are places evil agents offer sacrifices to discover the power that holds God's children. It a place they enquire for people's destinies in order to destroy them. They discover the secret plans of God for a person or place at their alter.

"[6]And he returned unto him, and, lo, he stood by his burnt sacrifice, he, and all the princes of Moab. [17]And when he came to him, behold, he stood by his burnt offering, and the princes of Moab with him. And Balak said unto him, what hath the LORD spoken?" (Numbers 23: 6, 17).

It is a place where Gideon's breakthrough, destiny and progress were arrested.

HIJACKED BUSINESS BREAKTHROUGH

Having seen how evil agents could use evil altars to inquire about people's businesses, there is no doubt that these wicked agents have captured many people's business breakthroughs. That is why many people struggle so much and cannot give accounts of their efforts.

Satan visited Adam and Eve in form of a serpent. He convinced and influenced them to eat the forbidden fruit, which God commanded them not to eat. In so doing, devil captured their destiny.

> *"Now the serpent was more subtle than any beast of the field which the LORD God had made. In addition, he said unto the woman, Yea, hath God said, ye shall not eat of every tree of the garden? And the woman said unto the serpent, we may eat of the fruit of the trees of the garden: But of the fruit of the tree, which is in the midst of the garden, God, hath said, Ye shall not eat of it, neither shall ye touch it, lest ye die. And the serpent said unto the woman, Ye shall not surely die: [5]For God doth know that in the day ye eat thereof, then your eyes shall be opened, and ye shall be as gods, knowing good and evil. And when the woman saw that the tree* was *good for food, and that it* was *pleasant to the eyes, and a tree to be desired to make* one *wise, she took of the fruit thereof, and did eat, and gave also unto her husband with her; and he did eat"* (Genesis 3:1-6).

When you disobey the written Word of God and fail to repent, restitute and forsake such sins, devil will arrest your breakthrough. When Adam disobeyed God, He cursed him and drove him out of his inheritance, which was his place of comfort. His soil, which was the place of business, was cursed and sorrow replaced his joy. Thorns and thistles entered his business and he began to sweat and till the ground to produce what to eat.

Furthermore, when Cain killed his brother, Abel, his family became bloody. The blood of Abel cried against Cain's breakthrough. God also cursed him and he became a vagabond and the first fugitive on earth.

> *"[5]But if thou wilt not send* him, *we will not go down: for the man said unto us, ye shall not see my face, except your brother* be *with you. [6]And Israel said, Wherefore dealt ye* so *ill with me, as to tell the man whether ye had yet a brother? [7]And they said, The man asked us strictly of our state, and of our kindred, saying,* Is *your father yet alive? Have ye* another *brother? In addition, we told him according to the tenor of these words: could we certainly know that he would say, bring your brother down. [8]And Judah said unto Israel his father, Send the lad with me, and we will arise and go; that we may live, and not die, both we, and thou,* and *our little ones. [9]I will be*

surety for him; of my hand shall thou require him: if I bring him not unto thee, and set him before thee, then let me bear the blame for ever: [11]*And their father Israel said unto them, If* it must be *so now, do this; take of the best fruits in the land in your vessels, and carry down the man a present, a little balm, and a little honey, spices, and myrrh, nuts, and almonds:* [12]*And take double money in your hand; and the money that was brought again in the mouth of your sacks, carry* it *again in your hand; peradventure it* was *an oversight"* (Genesis 43:5-9, 11-12).

When you commit abortion or shed innocent blood, it will affect anything you do on earth. The blood that you shed would cry against you year after year. When you come from a bloody foundation, the same thing will happen to you. Devil has arrested many businesses because of their disobedience, blood crying against them and all manner of sins.

God asked Gideon to do something before his arrested destiny was released. He told David, I do not have problems with you. Yet, David's government was affected because he inherited the throne from a bloody man.

"[1]*Then there was a famine in the days of David three years, year after year; and David enquired of the LORD. In addition, the LORD answered,* it is *for Saul, and for* his *bloody house, because he slew the Gibeonites.* [3]*Wherefore David said unto the Gibeonites, What should I do for you? And wherewith shall I make the atonement, which ye may bless, the inheritance of the LORD?"* (2 Samuel 21:1, 3).

The people that are supposed to inherit good things from the Lord were in famine because the blood that cried against them polluted their foundation. Your business may be passing through many problems now because of the root of your family. That is why you need to find out the history of your great grandparents.

The breakthrough and investment that Lot had was destroyed in Sodom because he invested in a wrong place. You need to check where your business is located. The location of your business could be the reason why your breakthrough is under arrest.

"The word of the LORD came also unto me, saying, Thou shall not take thee a wife, neither shall thou have sons or daughters in this place. For thus saith the LORD concerning the sons and concerning the daughters that are born in this place, and concerning their mothers that bare them, and concerning their fathers that begat them in this land; They shall die of grievous deaths; they shall not be lamented; neither shall they be buried; but *they shall be as dung upon the face of the earth: and they shall be consumed by the sword, and by famine; and their carcasses shall be meat for the fowls of heaven, and for the beasts of the earth"* (Jeremiah 16:1-4).

Dinah, the virgin daughter of Jacob, visited a wrong place and she lost her virginity and destiny. Reuben slept with his father's concubine, Bilhab, and his destiny and that of his children unborn were arrested.

> "[22]*And it came to pass, when Israel dwelt in that land, that Reuben went and lay with Bilhah his father's concubine: and Israel heard* it. *Now the sons of Jacob were twelve:* [3]*Reuben, thou* art *my firstborn, my might, and the beginning of my strength, the Excellency of dignity, and the excellence of power:* [4]*Unstable as water, thou shall not excel; because thou wentest up to thy father's bed; then defiledst thou* it: *he went up to my couch"* (Genesis 35:22; 49:3-4).

Do you know why your businesses have refused to move forward? Do you know what your ancestors did? Do you know what gods or evil altars your father worshipped? God told Gideon to deal with his father's idol before he could move forward. When he obeyed God, his blessings came. Do you see why it is important to deal with your family's idols?

> "[25]*And it came to pass the same night, that the LORD said unto him, Take thy father's young bullock, even the second bullock of seven years old, and throw down the altar of Baal that thy father hath, and cut down the grove that* is *by it:* [26]*And build an altar unto the LORD thy God upon the top of this rock, in the ordered place, and take the second bullock, and offer a burnt sacrifice with the wood of the grove which thou shall cut down.* [27]*Then Gideon took ten men of his servants, and did as the LORD had said unto him: and so it was, because he feared his father's household, and the men of the city, that he could not do* it *by day, that he did* it *by night.* [24]*And Gideon sent messengers throughout all mount Ephraim, saying, Come down against the Midianites, and take before them the waters unto Beth–barah and Jordan. Then all the men of Ephraim gathered themselves together, and took the waters unto Beth–barah and Jordan.* [25]*And they took two princes of the Midianites, Oreb and Zeeb; and they slew Oreb upon the rock Oreb, and Zeeb they slew at the winepress of Zeeb, and pursued Midian, and brought the heads of Oreb and Zeeb to Gideon on the other side Jordan"* (Judges 6:25-27; 7:24-25).

If you would undo evil your fathers have done, your business would be set free and released from captivity. Achan stole an accursed thing; a Babylonian garment and all the members of his family died as a result. He lost his life, household and made Israel to suffer defeat in war. Samson chose a wife, who was a harlot, by sight. He really loved Delilah but at the end, he lost his anointing, his eyes and his life.

> "[1]*Then went Samson to Gaza, and saw there a harlot, and went in unto her.* [4]*And it happened afterward, that he loved a woman in the valley of Sorek, whose name* was *Delilah.* [5]*And the lords of the Philistines came up unto her, and said unto her, Entice him, and see wherein his great strength* lieth, *and by what* means *we may prevail*

against him, that we may bind him to afflict him: and we will give thee every one of us eleven hundred pieces *of silver.* [6]*And Delilah said to Samson, Tell me, I pray thee, wherein thy great strength* lieth, *and wherewith thou mightest be bound to afflict thee.* [7]*And Samson said unto her, If they bind me with seven green withs that were never dried, then shall I be weak, and be as another man.* [20]*And she said, The Philistines* be *upon thee, Samson. In addition, he awoke out of his sleep, and said, I will go out as at other times before, and shake myself. And he wist not that the LORD was departed from him"* (Judges 16:1, 4-7, 20).

Your business cannot suffer ordinarily. Find out why your business is suffering setbacks and ask God to show you what to do about it and you will prevail over financial crisis and have business breakthrough. Many business people started very well in life. They used to be very prosperous in business, but today, they eat from hand to mouth. Some others are watching their businesses die gradually. They wonder why they are going through such problems.

Sometimes, one has to look back in retrospect to check whether he is the cause of his problem. I remember the story of the young prophet, who was doing perfectly well until he was deceived and he went back to eat at a wrong place.

"[4]*And it came to pass, when king Jeroboam heard the saying of the man of God, which had cried against the altar in Beth–el, that he put forth his hand from the altar, saying, Lay hold on him. In addition, his hand, which he put forth against him, dried up, so that he could not pull it in again to him.* [21]*And he cried unto the man of God that came from Judah, saying, Thus saith the LORD, Forasmuch as thou hast disobeyed the mouth of the LORD, and hast not kept the commandment which the LORD thy God commanded thee,* [22]*But camest back, and hast eaten bread and drunk water in the place, of the which* the LORD *did say to thee, Eat no bread, and drink no water; thy carcass shall not come unto the sepulcher of thy fathers.* [23]*And it came to pass, after he had eaten bread, and after he had drunk, that he saddled for him the ass,* to wit, *for the prophet whom he had brought back.* [24]*And when he was gone, a lion met him by the way, and slew him: and his carcass was cast in the way, and the ass stood by it, the lion also stood by the carcass"* (1 Kings 13:4, 21-24)

Naaman was a great man, a captain of the host of the Syrian army but he was a leper. His original skin was arrested and detained in a far away country. He spent money traveling from one hospital to another. He has delivered many people including his own nation many times but he could not deliver his own skin from the demon of leprosy. He needed help but he could not get it.

"Now Naaman, captain of the host of the king of Syria, was a great man with his master, and honorable, because by him the LORD had given deliverance unto Syria: he was also a mighty man in velour, but he was *a leper. And the Syrians had gone*

out by companies, and had brought away captive out of the land of Israel a little house cleaner; and she waited on Naaman's wife. And she said unto her mistress, Would God my lord were *with the prophet that* is *in Samaria! For he would recover him of his leprosy. And* one *went in, and told his lord, saying, thus and thus said the house cleaner that* is *of the land of Israel. And the king of Syria said, Go to, go, and I will send a letter unto the king of Israel. And he departed, and took with him ten talents of silver, and six thousand* pieces *of gold, and ten changes of raiment"* (2 Kings 5:1-5).

The purpose of this book is to introduce you to the greatest deliverance minister on earth. You need deliverance from poverty, lack and business failures. What you need is information and obedience to a simple instruction and you will recover all your loss.

"And Elisha sent a messenger unto him, saying, Go and wash in Jordan seven times, and thy flesh shall come again to thee, and thou shall be clean. But Naaman was worth, and went away, and said, Behold, I thought, He will surely come out to me, and stand, and call on the name of the LORD his God, and strike his hand over the place, and recover the leper. Are *not Abana and Pharpar, rivers of Damascus, better than all the waters of Israel? May I not wash in them, and be clean? Therefore, he turned and went away in a rage. And his servants came near, and spake unto him, and said, My father,* if *the prophet had bid thee* do some *great thing, wouldest thou not have done* it? *How much rather then, when he saith to thee, Wash, and be clean? Then went he down, and dipped himself seven times in Jordan, according to the saying of the man of God: and his flesh came again like unto the flesh of a little child, and he was clean"* (2 Kings 5:10-14).

It is a matter of decision. If you decide to surrender your life to God or rededicate your life to God, you will recover all your losses and become better than the best. Noah decided to live a righteous life in the midst of corrupt business people. The result was that he found favor before God and in the time of destruction, God spared his life. God will spare your business in times of economic distress. He told Jacob to leave Laban and on his way, He changed his name.

Joseph took a decision not to commit fornication and God made him second in command in the nation of Egypt. Moses decided to stay with God's people and God blessed him and made him a deliverance minister that parted the red sea.

"[24]By faith Moses, when he was come to years, refused to be called the son of Pharaoh's daughter; [25]Choosing rather to suffer affliction with the people of God, than to enjoy the pleasures of sin for a season; [32]And what shall I more say? for the time would fail me to tell of Gideon, and of Barak, and of Samson, and of Jephthae; of David also, and Samuel, and of *the prophets: [33]Who through faith subdued kingdoms, wrought righteousness, obtained promises, stopped the mouths of lions, [34]Quenched*

the violence of fire, escaped the edge of the sword, out of weakness were made strong, waxed valiant in fight, turned to flight the armies of the aliens" (Hebrews 11:24-25, 32-34).

If you believe God today, you will subdue your own kingdom. Your business would be released from all manner of captivity, in the name of Jesus - Amen.

PRAYERS FOR BREAKTHROUGH IN YOUR BUSINESS

Bible reference: Genesis 39:1-6

Begin with praise and worship

1. Father Lord, link me up to the right business You have ordained for me, in the name of Jesus.
2. Let the power of God link me to right people to do business with, in the name of Jesus.
3. Lord Jesus, develop my business ability exceedingly, in the name of Jesus.
4. I receive advancement and growth for my business now, in the name of Jesus.
5. Any strongman that is blocking my progress in business, collapse and die, in the name of Jesus.
6. Holy Ghost fire, burn every hindrance on my way to breakthrough, in the name of Jesus.
7. I use fire to dismantle evil darkness that hovers over my business, in the name of Jesus.
8. Any evil movement against my business, stop and die, in the name of Jesus.
9. I disorganize every failure in business that was organized for me, in the name of Jesus.
10. I uproot evil altars that were built to destroy my businesses with force, in the name of Jesus.
11. Any power that is occupying my business in the spiritual world, give up the ghost, in the name of Jesus.
12. Any intimidating force that withstands my business exploits is intimidated to death, in the name of Jesus.
13. You, the ground of my business, become fertile, in the name of Jesus.
14. O Lord, bring my business to the limelight, in the name of Jesus.
15. Any evil altar that has arrested my business, release it by force, in the name of Jesus.

16. Any evil tree that was planted anywhere against my business, I dismantle you from your root, in the name of Jesus.

17. Any evil power that is destroying or harvesting my business efforts, die without mercy, in the name of Jesus.

18. O Lord, arise and give me a business that will advance me greatly, in the name of Jesus.

19. Any evil hand that is reaping good things I sowed in my business, dry up, in the name of Jesus.

20. O Lord, give me divine energy, wisdom and knowledge to do great businesses, in the name of Jesus.

21. Every satanic limitation that was placed upon my business, disappear by force, in the name of Jesus.

22. I command every demonic activity that is going on against my business to die, in the name of Jesus.

23. I oppose witches or wizards that re attacking my businesses, in the name of Jesus.

24. I reject every dream that was designed to destroy my business, in the name of Jesus.

25. Enemies of my efforts in life are wasted by fire, in the name of Jesus.

26. Any oppression that is going on against my business is terminated by force, in the name of Jesus.

27. I receive the anointing to prosper exceedingly in my business, in the name of Jesus.

28. O Lord, grant me favor to experience a business breakthrough, in the name of Jesus.

29. Any frustration that is targeting my businesses is terminated by force, in the name of Jesus.

30. Let satanic money and evil seeds that were planted to destroy my business die, in the name of Jesus.

31. Every enemy of God's will in my business, die, in the name of Jesus.

32. I terminate every evil control going on in my businesses, in the name of Jesus.

33. Every instrument of business failure in my life is roasted by fire, in the name of Jesus.

34. Every good thing that has abandoned my business, come back now, in the name of Jesus.

35. I disgrace agents of devil that were planted to destroy my business, in the name of Jesus.

36. Let evil forces against my business be removed by the power of God, in the name of Jesus.

37. Any satanic door that was opened to my business, close forever, in the name of Jesus.

38. I withdraw my business from evil contacts, in the name of Jesus.

39. Let evil priests that are ministering in my business go blind, in the name of Jesus.

40. Let bad legs that have walked into my business walk out by force, in the name of Jesus.

41. Every spirit of failure that was programmed into my business, I cast you out now, in the name of Jesus.

42. Every enemy of my business breakthroughs is arrested to death, in the name of Jesus.

43. O Lord, deliver my businesses from the hands of evil people, in the name of Jesus.

44. O Lord, command financial prosperity to overtake my business, in the name of Jesus.

45. Let evil powers that have vowed to stop my breakthrough in business die immediately, in the name of Jesus.

46. O Lord, prosper my business forever, in the name of Jesus.

47. Every messenger of failure to my business, carry your message to your sender, in the name of Jesus.

48. Let any evil plan to destroy my business scatter, in the name of Jesus.

49. Let every opportunity my business has lost come back immediately, in the name of Jesus.

50. Any graveyard that has buried my business, vomit it immediately, in the name of Jesus.

51. Let evil stones that are holding my business to a halt roll away now, in the name of Jesus.

52. Let evil covenant or curse that is frustrating my business break and expire, in the name of Jesus.

53. Any pollution and defilement that exists in my business, receive cleansing now, in the name of Jesus.

54. Blood of Jesus, deliver my business from death, in the name of Jesus.

55. I arrest evil forces that are fighting my business, in the name of Jesus.

56. I convert every defeat my business has ever suffered to victory, in the name of Jesus.

57. Let any witchcraft animal that is scattering my business die immediately, in the name of Jesus.

58. Every enemy of my breakthrough in business is disgrace, in the name of Jesus.

59. O Lord, arise and take my business to the top, in the name of Jesus.

60. You, my business, wake up from sleep and prosper exceedingly, in the name of Jesus.

32

Chapter

PRAYERS AGAINST ALL MANNER OF SICKNESS AND DISEASE

CHAPTER OVERVIEW

- *A promise of divine healing*
- *Using the name of Jesus for healing*
- *Why many Christians have not received healing*

A PROMISE OF DIVINE HEALING

God has promised divine healing to all His children, who are in covenant with Him through the blood of His Son, Jesus. The blood of Jesus brought a divine covering over sickness, disease and satanic attacks. Therefore, no sickness or disease, whether curable or incurable can stand against a child of God, who knows his rights and is determined to claim them. This is because it is only in medical books that you can find incurable diseases and terminal sicknesses. The scriptures have no space for such words.

> *"And Jesus went about all Galilee, teaching in their synagogues, and preaching the gospel of the kingdom, and healing all manner of sickness and all manner of disease among the people. And his fame went throughout all Syria: and they brought unto him all sick people that were taken with divers diseases and torments, and those, which were possessed with devils, and those, which were lunatic, and those that had the palsy; and he healed them. And there followed him great multitudes of people from Galilee, and* from *Decapolis, and* from *Jerusalem, and* from *Judaea, and* from *beyond Jordan"* (Matthew 4:23-25).

When Jesus was on earth, He healed all manner of affliction. His fame went throughout Syria and people began to bring sick people that were taken with diverse diseases and torments. Even people that were possessed by devil, lunacy and palsy were there and Jesus healed them all. No matter the name that medical people gave to your sickness or disease, they are also among the ones that Jesus destroyed.

Sickness and disease can transform themselves into different shapes, names, forms and manifestations but that cannot move Jesus Christ. These alterations can only move ignorant Christians, unbelievers and medical pundits.

> *"And no marvel; for Satan himself is transformed into an angel of light. Therefore* it is *no great thing if his ministers also be transformed as the ministers of righteousness; whose end shall be according to their works"* (2 Corinthians 11:14-15).

> *"Is there* any*thing whereof it may be said, See, this is new? It hath been already of old time, which was before us.* There is *no remembrance of former* things; *neither shall there be* any *remembrance of* things *that are to come with* those *that shall come after"* (Ecclesiastes 1:10-11).

These diseases, which include HIV, Aids, fibroid, cancer, diabetes, etc, are not new. Jesus has the cure for all these sickness and diseases in the world. Teaching His Word and preaching the gospel of the kingdom lead to healing of all manner of sickness and disease that are in the world today.

> *"And Jesus went about all Galilee, teaching in their synagogues, and preaching the gospel of the kingdom, and healing all manner of sickness and all manner of disease among the people"* (Matthew 4:23).

The true Word of God is not a respecter of any manner of sicknesses and diseases.

MEDICINE FOR DIVINE HEALING

When you learn how to spend enough time in the presence of God through His Word, no sickness or diseases would tarry in your body for long.

> *"He sent his word, and healed them, and delivered* them *from their destructions"* (Psalms 107:20).

> *"My son, attend to my words; incline thine ear unto my sayings. Let them not depart from thine eyes; keep them in the midst of thine heart. For they are life unto those that find them, and health to all their flesh"* (Proverbs 4:20-22).

> *"And ye shall know the truth, and the truth shall make you free"* (John 8:32).

When God wants to heal the sick, He sends His Word. When He wants to deliver, He sends His Word. When He wants to stop devil from destruction, He sends His Word. The most and only effective medicine for healing and deliverance is God's Word. Even as a child of God, you are expected to obey God's Word to receive your healing and deliverance. Study God's Word, meditate on it and let it penetrate into your heart and healing would take place. The devil cannot endure God's Word how much more sickness and diseases. When you know this truth and believe it, your freedom and deliverance from all the works of the devil is near.

> *"3Surely he shall deliver thee from the snare of the fowler,* and *from the noisome pestilence. 4He shall cover thee with his feathers, and under his wings shall thou trust: his truth* shall be thy *shield and buckler. 5Thou shall not be afraid for the terror by night;* or *for the arrow* that *flieth by day;* 6Nor *neither for the pestilence that walketh in darkness; nor for the destruction* that *wasteth at noonday. 7A thousand shall fall at thy side, and ten thousand at thy right hand;* but *it shall not come nigh thee. 10There shall no evil befall thee; neither shall any plague come nigh thy dwelling"* (Psalms 91:3-7, 10).

"The centurion answered and said, Lord, I am not worthy that thou shouldest come under my roof: but speak the word only, and my servant shall be healed" (Matthew 8:8).

The Word of God brings healing and keeps you in health. God's Word fights pestilence, fear, terrorism, evil arrows, deaths, evil, plagues, suicides, evil spirits, grievous vexation and torments. The centurion told Christ to send his Word only and his servant would be healed. This is a powerful statement.

"And this is the confidence that we have in him, that, if we ask any thing according to his will, he heareth us: And if we know that he hear us, whatsoever we ask, we know that we have the petitions that we desired of him"(1 John 5:14-15).

"I can of mine own self do nothing: as I hear, I judge: and my judgment is just; because I seek not mine own will, but the will of the Father which hath sent me" (John 5:30).

"How God anointed Jesus of Nazareth with the Holy Ghost and with power: who went about doing good, and healing all that were oppressed of the devil; for God was with him" (Acts 10:38).

Healing of your body is God's will for your life. Praying according to God's will brings healing to your body. Therefore, this is another drug for divine healing. Jesus came to this world to do the will of His Father. His empowerment and anointing was used to do good, healing all manner of sickness and diseases and God was with Him.

"And the LORD will take away from thee all sickness, and will put none of the evil diseases of Egypt, which thou knowest, upon thee; but will lay them upon all them *that hate thee"* (Deuteronomy 7:15).

"For the truth's sake, which dwelleth in us, and shall be with us forever" (2 John 2).

"Thy kingdom come. They will be done in earth, as it is *in heaven"* (Matthew 6:10).

God promised His children through Moses that He will take away every sickness from their midst. If you have any sickness or disease in your body, pray to God based on His Word and as He promised. He will take away every sickness according as He has promised. All you need is to believe that He is able to take away every sickness when you ask Him. God promised to prosper you in health. It is His will to bring His kingdom on earth as it is in heaven. So that those who are born-again would live on earth without sickness as if they are in heaven.

"Surely he hath borne our griefs, and carried our sorrows: yet we did esteem him stricken, smitten of God, and afflicted" (Isaiah 53:4).

"The thief cometh not, but for to steal, and to kill, and to destroy: I am come that they might have life, and that they might have it *more abundantly"* (John 10:10).

One of the reasons Jesus Christ died was to take away all our grief, sorrow, and afflictions. God does not want sickness and diseases to prevail in the lives of His dear children. Christians who allow sickness and disease to reign over their bodies do not enjoy the full benefit of the stripes of Christ and His death on the cross of Calvary. Jesus died that He may destroy the works of the devil, which include sickness and diseases.

USING THE NAME OF JESUS FOR HEALING

Believers, who know how to use the name of God and His Son, Jesus Christ, cannot remain at the mercy of sickness and disease. Many promises, blessings and power accompany the name of God and His Son, Jesus Christ.

> *"And said, If thou wilt diligently hearken to the voice of the LORD thy God, and wilt do that which is right in his sight, and wilt give ear to his commandments, and keep all his statutes, I will put none of these diseases upon thee, which I have brought upon the Egyptians: for I* am *the LORD that healeth thee"* (Exodus 15:26).

> *"The name of the LORD is a strong tower: the righteous runneth into it, and is safe"* (Proverbs 18:10).

Obedience to the Word of God, which is right in the sight of God and keeping His commandments, can move the hand of God to heal all manner of disease and sickness in your life. Calling the name of the Lord in times of trouble provides security and safety. God cannot forsake those that call upon His name with faith.

> *"Wherefore God also hath highly exalted him, and given him a name which is above every name: That at the name of Jesus every knee should bow, of* things *in heaven, and* things *in earth, and* things *under the earth; And* that *every tongue should confess that Jesus Christ* is *Lord, to the glory of God the Father"* (Philippians 2:9-11).

As people's names carry power, so do some places and things. However, all these names, places and things would bow at the mention of the name of Jesus Christ. His name subdues other names. Every problem and knee would bow at the mention of the name of Jesus Christ. No name or person under heaven and earth can challenge the name of Jesus Christ. In fact, every tongue confesses that Christ is the Lord of lords and King of kings.

> *"And Jesus answered and said unto him, Blessed art thou, Simon Bar–jona: for flesh and blood hath not revealed* it *unto thee, but my Father which is in heaven. And I say also unto thee, That thou art Peter, and upon this rock I will build my church; and the gates of hell shall not prevail against it"* (Matthew 16:17-18).

> *"Now Peter and John went up together into the temple at the hour of prayer,* being *the ninth* hour. *And a certain man lame from his mother's womb was carried, whom they laid daily at the gate of the temple which is called Beautiful, to ask alms of them that entered into the temple; Who seeing Peter and John about to go into the temple asked an alms. And Peter, fastening his eyes upon him with John, said, Look on us. And he gave heed unto them, expecting to receive something of them. Then Peter*

said, Silver and gold have I none; but such as I have give I thee: In the name of Jesus Christ of Nazareth rise up and walk. And he took him by the right hand, and lifted him *up and immediately his feet and anklebones received strength. And he leaping up stood, and walked, and entered with them into the temple, walking, and leaping, and praising God"* (Acts 3:1-8).

Whenever it is time for prayers, the powers of darkness tremble and fear because of the mentioning of the name of Christ. There was a man who was lame from his mother's womb. They carried him to the gate of the temple on daily basis to beg. The devil limited him greatly. The day he saw Peter and John entering the temple, he asked for arms. He was so fortunately to meet people who had something better than money. That day, when the name of Christ was mentioned, his lame legs that have lasted for forty years healed at that instant. Glory be to God for the name of Jesus Christ!

When you understand the efficacy and power in the name of Jesus Christ, you will discover that the name of Jesus is better than silver and gold. The power in the name of Jesus entered into the joints of the lame man and lifted him up. He started using his legs immediately because his feet and ankles received strength and he started walking and entered into the temple he had not entered since he was crippled. He entered into the temple and saw God and His Son face to face like other worshippers. He could not enter the temple because he was not fit until Christ intervened and produced the miracle of healing and deliverance that pushed him into the temple.

With the name of Jesus Christ, you can walk into any office or nation. You can walk your health out of captivity of the devil and you can walk yourself out of hospital bed with the name of Jesus.

"And his name through faith in his name hath made this man strong, whom ye see and know: yea, the faith which is by him hath given him this perfect soundness in the presence of you all" (Acts 3:16).

"Be it known unto you all, and to all the people of Israel, that by the name of Jesus Christ of Nazareth, whom ye crucified, whom God raised from the dead, even *by him doth this man stand here before you whole"* (Acts 4:10).

"Because he hath set his love upon me, therefore will I deliver him: I will set him on high, because he hath known my name. He shall call upon me, and I will answer him: I will be with him in trouble; I will deliver him, and honor him. With long life will I satisfy him and show him my salvation" (Psalms 91:14-16).

If you know how to mention the name of Christ in faith, you can command sickness, diseases and infirmities out of your life. You can walk your family, business into the international community and every good place on earth. You can command cancer, ulcer, poverty, failures and all manner of sickness and diseases and they will obey. The name of Christ can heal, save, sanctify, deliver, baptize and take you to heaven to enjoy your eternity with God and all His saints.

However, there are categories of people that do not experience the power in the name of Jesus. They include people who love God, but do not know how to call upon His name. God wants to heal them and deliver them from sicknesses and troubles but they feel too big to call upon the name of Jesus Christ. There are people who use the name of Jesus but do not have faith in Him. Therefore, they do not experience the power in name of Jesus. There are also people who use the name of Jesus while they live in sin. You cannot live in sin for grace to abound.

> *"And the evil spirit answered and said, Jesus I know, and Paul I know; but who are ye? And the man in whom the evil spirit was leaped on them, and overcame them, and prevailed against them, so that they fled out of that house naked and wounded. And this was known to all the Jews and Greeks also dwelling at Ephesus; and fear fell on them all and the name of the Lord Jesus was magnified. And many that believed came, and confessed, and shewed their deeds. Many of them also which used curious arts brought their books together, and burned them before all* men*: and they counted the price of them, and found* it *fifty thousand* pieces *of silver"* (Acts 19:15-19).

It is very painful to die in sickness or remain in trouble while the name of Jesus is waiting for you to invoke it to bring healing and deliverance. God promised to answer those that call upon Him, and to be with them until all their enemies come under their feet. He also promised us long life. Therefore, do not allow sickness and disease to cut your life short. You need His salvation.

> *"Verily, verily, I say unto you, He that believeth on me, the works that I do shall he do also; and greater* works *than these shall he do; because I go unto my Father. And whatsoever ye shall ask in my name, that will I do, that the Father may be glorified in the Son"* (John 14:12-13).

No sickness or disease can stand before the mighty name of Jesus. Your body does not deserve a wicked and merciless disease that is feeding on your flesh. Your flesh and blood is not meant to be food for evil spirits. You can resist them today with the name of Jesus and they will surely bow. Your body is the temple of God, not a satanic dining table for launch, breakfast and supper. Invite Christ into your life at once. Let Him chase sickness and disease away and keep His temple clean and free of sin, sickness, diseases and satanic attacks. You can do the works that Jesus did through His name.

> *"And ye shall serve the LORD your God, and he shall bless thy bread, and thy water; and I will take sickness away from the midst of thee. There shall nothing cast their young, nor be barren, in thy land: the number of thy days I will fulfill. I will send my*

fear before thee, and will destroy all the people to whom thou shall come, and I will make all thine enemies turn their backs unto thee. And I will send hornets before thee, which shall drive out the Hivite, the Canaanite, and the Hittite, from before thee. I will not drive them out from before thee in one year; lest the land become desolate and the beast of the field multiply against thee. By little and little I will drive them out from before thee, until thou be increased, and inherit the land. And I will set thy bounds from the Red sea even unto the sea of the Philistines, and from the desert unto the river: for I will deliver the inhabitants of the land into your hand; and thou shall drive them out before thee" (Exodus 23:25-31).

I have searched the Scriptures and discovered that God is not happy that His children remain in sickness. He promised to bless our bread, our water and take sickness away from us. No part of your body is permitted to be barren or lack anything that promotes sound health, abundant life and peace. Your body would receive healing and deliverance when you start using the name of Jesus Christ in prayer.

"[18]And Jesus came and spake unto them, saying, all power is given unto me in heaven and in earth. [20]Teaching them to observe all things whatsoever I have commanded you: and, lo, I am with you always, even *unto the end of the world. Amen"* (Matthew 28:18, 20).

"For by him were all things created, that are in heaven, and that are in earth, visible and invisible, whether they be *thrones, or dominions, or principalities, or powers: all things were created by him, and for him: And he is before all things, and by him all things consist"* (Colossian 1:16-17).

"Then he called his twelve disciples together, and gave them power and authority over all devils, and to cure diseases" (Luke 9:1).

Our God has enough power to destroy the enemies of our sound health and keep us out of pain and sorrow throughout our stay on earth. Healing is the mercy of God in action for His people. The power in the name of Jesus is waiting to be invited into your body to deal with sicknesses and diseases that exist in your life.

Do not be afraid to ask God to heal you because He is waiting for you to ask. Jesus, who has all powers, wants to heal you completely. If you have received Christ into your life, then you have received the source and possessor of all powers. Jesus is the source of the power to heal you and keep your health forever and ever.

"But Jesus beheld them, *and said unto them, With men this is impossible; but with God all things are possible"* (Matthew 19:26).

"Behold, I give unto you power to tread on serpents and scorpions, and over all the power of the enemy: and nothing shall by any means hurt you" (Luke 10:19).

"For the eyes of the LORD run to and fro throughout the whole earth, to show him strong in the behalf of them whose heart is perfect toward him. Herein thou hast done foolishly: therefore from henceforth thou shall have wars" (2 Chronicles 16:9).

God has given all powers in heaven and earth to Jesus Christ. All things were created for Him and by Him, both things that are on earth and in heaven, visible and invisible. Every throne, dominion, principalities and powers are under His control, including sickness and disease. As a Christian, you have the power to destroy every sickness and problem.

WHY MANY CHRISTIANS HAVE NOT RECEIVED HEALING

The bible is filled with great promises of assurance for answers to our prayers when we pray for healing. Believers have many reasons they pray for healing. We pray for healing because we need to serve God in good health and fulfill our destinies on earth. When God answers our prayers, we have joy, but when He delays, we worry and doubt. Whenever we do not receive answers to our prayers, God cannot be faulted. The fault remains with us believers. You need to know things that make God not to answer your prayers sometimes.

NOT IN COVENANT WITH GOD

When a believer backslides, he breaks his covenant relationship with God. He is no longer in covenant with God. It would be difficult for God to reach that believer for healing. His prayers cannot be answered until he repents and returns to God.

> *"Behold, ye trust in lying words that cannot profit. Will ye steal, murder, and commit adultery, and swear falsely, and burn incense unto Baal, and walk after other gods whom ye know not; And come and stand before me in this house, which is called by my name, and say, we are delivered to do all these abominations. Is this house, which is called by my name, becomes a den of robbers in your eyes? Behold, even I have seen* it, *saith the LORD"* (Jeremiah 7:8-11).

Many backsliders are deceived to believe that their prayers can be answered without true repentance and restitution. Millions of people are praying all over the world but only few receive answers. It is strange to believe that thieves, murderers and adulterers would continue in sin and insist that God answers their prayers. God demands repentance before praying for blessings or healing.

> *"Then came the word of the LORD of hosts unto me, saying, Speak unto all the people of the land, and to the priests, saying, When ye fasted and mourned in the fifth and seventh* month, *even those seventy years, did ye at all fast unto me,* even to *me? And when ye did eat, and when ye did drink, did not yet eat* for you, *and drink* for yourselves? Should ye *not* hear *the words, which the LORD hath cried by the former prophets, when Jerusalem was inhabited and in prosperity, and the cities thereof round about her, when* men *inhabited the south and the plain? And the word of the LORD came unto Zechariah, saying, Thus speaketh the LORD of hosts, saying, Execute true judgment, and shew mercy and compassions every man to his brother: oppress not the widow, nor the fatherless, the stranger, nor the poor; and let none of you imagine evil against his brother in your heart"* (Zechariah 7:4-10).

Some people believe that the number of times they pray determines how God would answer their prayers. This is not true. Others are deceived to believe that when they hire a prayer contractor, God will answer them immediately and heal them. However, God made it clear that if you are an oppressor, liar, or you are living in sin, you need to repent first and then pray. God will answer and show mercy and compassion to repented sinners. More so, when you continue praying without repentance, the devil may answer your prayers and deceive you forever. Another group of people is unrelenting sinners who have refused to repent and yet they pray and expect God to hear them.

"But as many as received him, to them gave the power to become the sons of God, even *to them that believe on his name: Which were born, not of blood, nor of the will of the flesh, nor of the will of man, but of God. And the Word was made flesh, and dwelt among us, (and we beheld his glory, the glory as of the only begotten of the Father,) full of grace and truth. John bare witness of him, and cried, saying, This was he of whom I spoke, He that cometh after me is preferred before me: for he was before me"* (John 1:12-15).

"And this gospel of the kingdom shall be preached in the entire world for a witness unto all nations; and then shall the end come" (Matthew 24:14).

You have to take the first step, which is to receive Christ and He empowers you to become part of His kingdom. Then you would benefit from His covenant of healing. You have to become a son before you can benefit from a father's will. Sadly, many people do not consider this important step.

"And this is the confidence that we have in him, that, if we ask any thing according to his will, he heareth us: And if we know that he hear us, whatsoever we ask, we know that we have the petitions that we desired of him" (1 John 5:14-15).

Without entering into covenant with God through Christ, God may not answer your prayers for healing and any other answer for your healing has no godly foundation. Any healing, deliverance or freedom that lacks absolute commitment to Christ as Savior is useless and temporal. If you have sin in your heart and refuse to repent, and yet pray for healing, the Lord will not answer you no matter how long you pray or who prays for you. The bible was clear on this:

"If I regard iniquity in my heart, the Lord will not hear me*"* (Psalms 66:18).

"Cry aloud, spare not, lift up thy voice like a trumpet, and shew my people their transgression, and the house of Jacob their sins. Yet they seek me daily, and delight to know my ways, as a nation that did righteousness, and forsook not the ordinance of their God: they ask of me the ordinances of justice; they take delight in approaching to

God. Wherefore have we fasted, say they, *and thou sees not?* Wherefore *have we afflicted our soul, and thou takes' no knowledge? Behold, in the day of your fast ye find pleasure, and exact all your labors. Behold, ye fast for strife and debate, and to smite with the fist of wickedness: ye shall not fast,* as ye do this *day, to make your voice to be heard on high. Is it such a fast that I have chosen? A day for a man to afflict his soul?* Is it *to bow down his head as a bulrush, and to spread sackcloth and ashes* under him*? Wilt thou call this a fast, and an acceptable day to the LORD?"* (Isaiah 58:1-5).

Sin separates one from God's plans. Many people spend so much time to pray, fast and do everything possible to get their healing when they have refused to end their wickedness. It would be hard for God to answer such people.

"Acquaint now thyself with him, and be at peace: thereby good shall come unto thee. Receive, I pray thee, the law from his mouth, and lay up his words in thine heart. [23]*If thou return to the Almighty, thou shalt be built up, thou shall put away iniquity far from thy tabernacles. Then shall thou layup gold as dust and the* gold *of Ophir as the stones of the brooks. Yea, the Almighty shall be thy defense, and thou shall have plenty of silver. For then shall thou have thy delight in the Almighty, and shall lift up thy face unto God. Thou shall make thy prayer unto him, and he shall hear thee, and thou shall pay thy vows.* [28]*Thou shall also decree a thing, and it shall be established unto thee: and the light shall shine upon thy ways"* (Job 22:21-28).

"For if our heart condemns us, God is greater than our heart, and knoweth all things. Beloved, if our heart condemns us not, then *has we confidence toward God. And whatsoever we ask, we receive of him, because we keep his commandments, and do those things that are pleasing in his sight"* (1 John 3:20-22).

God demands holiness, victory over sin and Christian life that is consistent with His Word before one could pray for healing and deliverance. Make peace with God and fellow humans before praying for your healing. If you do what you are supposed to do before God and man, God will surely answer your prayers. When you pray for good health that you would use to serve the devil, God knows. You must convince God that you will use your health to honor and serve Him as your God.

"From whence come *wars and fightings among you?* Come they *not hence,* even *of your lusts that war in your members? Ye lust, and have not: ye kill, and desire to have, and cannot obtain: ye fight and war, yet ye have not, because ye ask not. Ye ask, and receive not, because ye ask amiss, that ye may consume* it *upon your lusts"* (James 4:1-3).

"And when Jesus was come into Peter's house, he saw his wife's mother laid, and sick of a fever. [15]And he touched her hand, and the fever left her: and she arose, and ministered unto them" (Matthew 8:14-15).

Fever used to be a very deadly sickness. It is still deadly but medical science has discovered drugs for it. In the days of Peter, it was terminal without drugs. Jesus had visited Peter's business, his fish industry, without visited his home. Later, He visited Peter's home when his mother in-law made up her mind to serve Christ and minister to others. The case was not that Peter did not pray for the healing of his mother in-law. Maybe the woman had not made up her mind to minister unto the people of God before her sickness.

Likewise, you could have been praying for healing, deliverance or a ministerial position. But if you have not made up your mind to serve God with your health, money, position, God knows and that may delay your healing and deliverance.

"The secret things belong *unto the LORD our God: but those* things which are *revealed* belong *unto us and to our children for ever, that* we *may do all the words of this law"* (Deuteronomy 29:29).

God knows what you want to use your health, money and position to do. No one can hide his thoughts, desires and intentions from God. He is omniscience. He knows all things.

"Save thy people, and bless thine inheritance: feed them also, and lift them up forever" (Psalms 28:9).

"If ye abide in me, and my words abide in you, ye shall ask what ye will, and it shall be done unto you" (John 15:7).

When you ignore the Word of God concerning a matter and then you go ahead to fast and pray for your deliverance, God will not heal you. If you hide iniquity in your heart or evil intentions, God cannot visit your home. He only visited Peter's house when his mother in-law was ready to minister to the people of God. That is why when you turn away your ears from hearing the Word of God, it is an abomination and God will not regard your prayers.

If God would deliver you from poverty and sickness this day, will you spend the rest of your life to minister for Him in thanksgiving? If Jesus would visit your marriage now, supply all your needs and make you rich, will you use your health and wealth to minister to others for His sake? If God would invite you today to bless you with wealth and put you in a high position, will you use all that you have to minister to others for Him? He came to Peter's house, touched the hand of his mother in-law and she rose from her sick bed and ministered to Him. Therefore, do not ignore God's Word in your life again.

> *"A son honorest* his *father, and a servant his master: if then I* be *a father, where* is *mine honor? In addition, if I* were *a master, where* is *my fear? Saith the LORD of hosts unto you, O priests that despise my name. In addition, ye say, wherein have we despised thy name? Ye offer polluted bread upon mine altar; and ye say, wherein have we polluted thee? In that ye say, the table of the LORD* is *contemptible. And if ye offer the blind for sacrifice,* is it *not evil? In addition, if ye offer the lame and sick,* is it *not evil? Offer it now unto thy governor; will he be pleased with thee, or accept thy person? Saith the LORD of hosts. And now, I pray you, beseeches God that he will be gracious unto us: this hath been by your means: will he regard your persons? saith the LORD of hosts"* (Malachi 1:6-9).

Abide in Word of God and He will deliver you, heal and bless you. If you are a child of God, then you ought to honor His Word. If God is your Father, how do you honor Him in your life? The woman of Shunammite honored the servant of God and she had a son at her old age. What is the proof that you have God as your Father? Do you sow seeds to promote His work? Are you ministering to others for Him? Do you still fornicate, covet evil things, live unclean life, etc, and still claim to be God's child? You are living in deceit. You do not have the seed of God in you. If you say that God is your Father, then you need to live as Christ lived.

> *"But ye have not so learned Christ; If so be that ye have heard him, and have been taught by him, as the truth is in Jesus"* (Ephesians 4:20-21).

You must possess Him holiness, speak the truth, give no place to the devil, give liberally and speak words to edify and minister grace to your hearers. If God is your Father, you must stop lying.

> *"Let him that stole steal no more: but rather let him labor, working with* his *hands the thing which is good, that he may have to give to him that needed"* (Ephesians 4:28).

> *"Ye shall not steal, neither deal falsely, neither laid one to another. Thou shall not defraud thy neighbor, neither rob* him: *the wages of him that is hired shall not abide with thee all night until the morning"* (Leviticus 19:11, 13).

You must overcome bitterness and wrath (*See* Ephesians 4:31; Hebrews 12:15-17). You must also overcome anger, clamor, malice and grieving of the Holy Spirit. These things come from Satan.

"Cease from anger, and forsake wrath: fret not thyself in any wise to do evil" (Psalm 37:8).

"Wherefore laying aside all malice, and all guile, and hypocrisies, and envies, and all evil speaking" (1 Peter 2:1).

"But Peter said, Ananias, why hath Satan filled thine heart to lie to the Holy Ghost, and to keep back part *of the price of the land?"* (Acts 5:3).

Those who have God as their Father forgive themselves, pray for themselves, comfort themselves, minister to themselves, submit and bear each other's burdens. Once you meet up with divine demands, your healing will appear.

"And said, If thou wilt diligently hearken to the voice of the LORD thy God, and wilt do that which is right in his sight, and wilt give ear to his commandments, and keep all his statutes, I will put none of these diseases upon thee, which I have brought upon the Egyptians: for I am *the LORD that health thee"* (Exodus 15:26).

"If my people, which are called by my name, shall humble themselves, and pray, and seek my face, and turn from their wicked ways; then will I hear from heaven, and will forgive their sin, and will heal their land" (2 Chronicles 7:14).

Healing and deliverance is God's will for you, so pray, believe and claim them.

PRAYERS AGAINST ALL MANNER OF SICKNESS AND DISEASE

Bible reference: Matthew 4:23-25

Begin with praise and worship

1. Father Lord, walk me along the path of divine healing, in the name of Jesus.
2. Let the backbone of all incurable sicknesses in my life be broken, in the name of Jesus.
3. I reject every negative medical report for my life with all my heart, in the name of Jesus.
4. Lord Jesus, gather every sickness and disease in my life and destroy them, in the name of Jesus.
5. Any hardship, suffering and torment that devil has brought into my life, be terminated to death, in the name of Jesus.
6. Every enemy of my health, wherever you are, die, in the name of Jesus.
7. Any problem in my life caused by ignorance, die, in the name of Jesus.
8. O Lord, show me how to come out of every problem, in the name of Jesus.
9. I transform the blood of Jesus into drugs to heal my body, soul and spirit, in the name of Jesus.
10. I hit the head of my stubborn problems with the power in God's Word, in the name of Jesus.
11. Any evil program that is going on against my health is terminated in shame, in the name of Jesus.
12. Let the healing power in the Word of God heal my sick body, soul and spirit, in the name of Jesus.
13. I command every enemy of divine health in my life to die, in the name of Jesus.
14. Any power that is defiling the Word of God for my healing is disgraced forever, in the name of Jesus.
15. I receive the anointing in the Word of God for my healing and deliverance, in the name of Jesus.

16. Every sickness and disease in my family is taken away now, in the name of Jesus.

17. Let my faith in the Word of God increase now, in the name of Jesus.

18. O Lord, empower me to live on this earth without sickness, in the name of Jesus.

19. I break and loose myself from every sickness and disease, in the name of Jesus.

20. Let the stripes of Jesus confront and conquer every sickness and disease in my life, in the name of Jesus.

21. I put my head on the cross of Calvary to drink and bath with the blood of Jesus for my healing, in the name of Jesus.

22. I attack every problem in my life with the precious blood of Jesus, in the name of Jesus.

23. Let promises of God for my sound health begin to manifest, in the name of Jesus.

24. Holy Ghost fire, burn the forces of evil against my deliverance, in the name of Jesus.

25. Let the Word of God and the name of Jesus protect me against sickness, in the name of Jesus.

26. O Lord, give my body, soul and spirit true divine health and freedom today, in the name of Jesus.

27. Let my body carry the power that is in the name of Jesus for my healing today, in the name of Jesus.

28. Every other name that is contending against my healing, bow and surrender to Christ's name, in the name of Jesus.

29. Every witchcraft embargo that was placed upon my healing is lifted by force, in the name of Jesus.

30. Any evil leg that is standing against my healing and health, break to pieces, in the name of Jesus.

31. Let evil darkness that is surrounding my divine health die immediately, in the name of Jesus.

32. Every curse that was placed upon my health, expire, in the name of Jesus.

33. O Lord, empower my body to discharge every sickness and disease, in the name of Jesus.

34. I command every area of my life to miscarry every manner of problem in it, in the name of Jesus.

35. Let any power that is making my life bitter die, in the name of Jesus.

36. I present the name of Jesus to impossibilities in my life, in the name of Jesus.

37. Every inherited sickness and disease in my life, die, in the name of Jesus.

38. Let the yoke of incurable sickness and disease in my life break now, in the name of Jesus.

39. Every trouble in my life is troubled unto death, in the name of Jesus.

40. I fire back arrows of sickness and disease fired into my life, in the name of Jesus.

41. Let the powers that are promoting sickness and disease in my life die, in the name of Jesus.

42. Father Lord, command Your healing power to fall upon me now, in the name of Jesus.

43. I refuse to die under the influence of sickness and disease, in the name of Jesus.

44. Uproot any tree of sickness and disease that my ancestors or I planted, in the name of Jesus.

45. Arrows of sickness and disease that were fired at my life by enemies, I fire you back, in the name of Jesus.

46. Every dream of sickness that was designed to keep me under sickness and disease, I reject you, in the name of Jesus.

47. O Lord, help me to live in sound health all the days of my life, in the name of Jesus.

48. Blood of Jesus wash every part of my life and free them from problems, in the name of Jesus.

49. Any agent of premature death that is following me around, fail woefully, in the name of Jesus.

50. Any pain that was designed to torment my life, die, in the name of Jesus.

51. Let the backbone of destructive sickness and disease in my life break, in the name of Jesus.

52. I break and loose myself from inherited family sicknesses and diseases, in the name of Jesus.

53. I receive power to resist problems in my life until they bow, in the name of Jesus.

54. I block every door opened to problems in my life forever, in the name of Jesus.

55. Father Lord, bless and empower my bread and water as from today, in the name of Jesus.

56. Let the enemies of my health be wasted now, in the name of Jesus.

57. By the mercy of God, I command my body to receive the grace to be free from sickness, in the name of Jesus.

58. Let every manner of fear that was delegated to destroy my health die, in the name of Jesus.

59. Let the Word of God enter in every area of my life and command my healing and health, in the name of Jesus.

60. Every prison yard that has locked up my health, unlock them by force, in the name of Jesus.

61. I receive the blessings that I have lost to ill health, in the name of Jesus.

62. Every satanic reason for holding my health captive is destroyed by the blood and stripes of Jesus, in the name of Jesus.

63. Let the blood and stripes of Jesus enter into the land of the living and dead to deliver me, in the name of Jesus.

64. Let divine healing, health and good things of life visit me and abide with me forever, in the name of Jesus.

33

Chapter

PRAYERS FOR A HAPPY MARRIED LIFE

CHAPTER OVERVIEW

- *The covenant of marriage*
- *How marriages come under attack*
- *Trust God to lead you to marry*
- *How God guides His children*

THE COVENANT OF MARRIAGE

While everyone desires to marry (or be married), few people really take their time to study and understand the true meaning of the covenant of marriage. It is highly important to understand the covenant of marriage before going into it so that you could be successful.

In this book, you will learn what it entails to make a good decision and how to know it is the will of God or not. Armed with this knowledge, you will get married and remain happy to the end. Many people rush into marriage without planning what they want to get out of it. Others know what they are supposed to get but do not know how to get them. Some depend on their partners and are ready to take anything from them. Because of this, many people have married whomever it was that came to marry them. Failing to find out what God has said or His plans for your marriage would make you to accept even what the devil or his agents offer you. The marriage institution started from the beginning, so no one has any excuse to fail.

> "[18]*And the LORD God said,* it is *not good that the man should be alone; I will make him a help meet for him.* [19]*And out of the ground the LORD God formed every beast of the field and every fowl of the air; and brought* them *unto Adam to see what he would call them: and whatsoever Adam called every living creature that* was *the name thereof.* [22]*And the rib, which the LORD God had taken from man, made he a woman, and brought her unto the man"* (Genesis 2:18-19, 22).

Marriage covenant is a lifetime covenant. In this particular covenant, God does not expect it to be broken. Once this covenant is broken, every other covenant with God concerning your life is affected.

> *"Yet ye say, wherefore? Because the LORD hath been witness between thee and the wife of thy youth, against whom thou hast dealt treacherously: yet is she thy companion, and the wife of thy covenant. And did not he make one? Yet had he the residue of the spirit. In addition, wherefore one? That he might seek a godly seed. Therefore, take heed to your spirit, and let none deal treacherously against the wife of his youth. For the LORD, the God of Israel, saith that he hateth putting away: for* one *covereth violence with his garment, saith the LORD of hosts: therefore take heed to your spirit that ye deal not treacherously"* (Malachi 2:14-16).

God is a witness between any man and woman that enter into this covenant of marriage. God monitors every detail of the man's actions or the woman's actions towards each other. You cannot dissolve marriage once it is contracted and confirmed.

God hates treacherous dealings in marriage. God commanded that a married couple should stay together the rest of their lives. Therefore, it is wrong to rush into marriage or be careless over the choice of your partner. Covenant is a very serious issue because if you break it ignorantly, you will definitely suffer for it.

> *"[1]Then there was a famine in the days of David three years, year after year; and David enquired of the LORD. In addition, the LORD answered,* it is *for Saul, and for* his *bloody house, because he slew the Gibeonites. [2]And the king called the Gibeonites, and said unto them; (now the Gibeonites* were *not of the children of Israel, but of the remnant of the Amorites; and the children of Israel had sworn unto them: and Saul sought to slay them in his zeal to the children of Israel and Judah.) [3]Wherefore David said unto the Gibeonites, What should I do for you? In addition, wherewith shall I make the atonement that ye may bless the inheritance of the LORD? [6]Let seven men of his sons be delivered unto us, and we will hang them up unto the LORD in Gibeah of Saul,* whom *the LORD did choose. In addition, the king said, I will give* them. *[9]And he delivered them into the hands of the Gibeonites, and they hanged them in the hill before the LORD: and they fell* all *seven together, and were put to death in the days of harvest, in the first* days, *in the beginning of barley harvest"* (2 Samuel 21:1-3, 6, 9).

The reason many people are suffering today is because they broke a covenant or they are one with people that broke a covenant. A broken covenant affects children, born and those yet to be born.

> *"Remember, O LORD, what is come upon us: consider, and behold our reproach. Our inheritance is turned to strangers, our houses to aliens. We are orphans and fatherless, our mothers* are *as widows. We have drunken our water for money; our wood is sold unto us. [5]Our necks* are *under persecution: we labor,* and *have no rest. We have given the hand* to *the Egyptians,* and to *the Assyrians, to be satisfied with bread"* (Lamentations 5:1-6).

It brings reproach and seizure of inheritance. It causes its victims to lose their blessings to strangers and aliens. It increases the number of orphans, widowers and widows in a place. Broken covenant is very destructive and leads people into bondage and captivity. The terrible part of it is that many victims of broken covenants are not aware of it. They suffer because of evil inheritance. It can reduce a greatly destined prince to a slave boy or house cleaner. Can you imagine someone who was destined to become a president cleaning the streets and begging for handouts? This is disaster.

> *"Our fathers have sinned,* and are *not; and we have borne their iniquities. Servants have ruled over us: there is none that doth deliver* us out *of their hand. We gat our bread with* the peril *of our lives because of the sword of the wilderness"* (Lamentations 5:7-9).

What you are going through now could be because of a broken covenant. If your father is a polygamous man, then you could be a victim of inherited evil covenant. That may be the reason why family or circumstances are pushing you to make a wrong choice of your partner. You need to study your foundation very well before you make a choice of whom to marry.

> *"The word of the LORD came also unto me, saying, Thou shall not take thee a wife, neither shall thou have sons or daughters in this place. For thus saith the LORD concerning the sons and concerning the daughters that are born in this place, and concerning their mothers that bare them, and concerning their fathers that begat them in this land; They shall die of grievous deaths; they shall not be lamented; neither shall they be buried;* but *they shall be as dung upon the face of the earth: and they shall be consumed by the sword, and by famine; and their carcasses shall be meat for the fowls of heaven, and for the beasts of the earth"* (Jeremiah 16:1-4).

You can correct other mistakes in other areas of life or put them away but not in the covenant of marriage. If you do so, it affects your relationship with God for God hates putting away of legal partners. Covenant is a legal contract that binds you and your partner for life on earth.

> *"But if ye bite and devour one another, take heed that ye be not consumed one of another"* (Galatians 5:15).

As soon as marriage is ordained, it becomes an unalterable and an irrevocable commitment. Breaking the covenant of marriage is not a mere thing because it can ruin a generation yet to be born. If you decide to separate from your partner and live apart, you would be tempted to sin. If you divorced and remarried, then you are living on earth committing adultery. It is contrary to the Word God.

> *"Without understanding, covenant breakers, without natural affection, implacable, unmerciful: Who knowing the judgment of God, that they which commit such things are worthy of death, not only do the same, but have pleasure in them that do them"* (Romans 1:31-32).

When you have limited understanding about marriage, you are likely to break this covenant. Once you break the covenant of marriage, it destroys your affection and your character. The emergence of hatred at home signals the failure of marriage. Other things that could break any marriage include having unforgiving spirit and being inconsiderate and unmerciful. At that point, if you do nothing, you will no longer regard the consequence of your actions that would attract God's judgment.

Soon you would begin to question certain principles that guide marriage, which you believed in earlier. You may even write, teach and preach to others to deviate from faith. But if you are keeper of a marriage covenant, you will always show mercy and forgiveness to your partner.

HOW MARRIAGES COME UNDER ATTACK

When couples begin to find faults among themselves, divorce spirit enters into their marriage. Whether your wife knows how to cook or not, you have no right to divorce her. You have been bound to remain with your husband even when he does not know how to dress his bed, dress very well or speak good grammar. He may not know how to make you happy or tell you he loves you but he is your lawful husband.

It is better not to marry at all than to marry and discover that your wife or husband is not the right person God has ordained for you. That is why you need to take time to confirm God's will before taking the marriage vow. God will not give you two women that are alive to marry or allow you to divorce and re-marry. It cannot be His will.

> *"The Pharisees also came unto him, tempting him, and saying unto him, is it lawful for a man to put away his wife for every cause? And he answered and said unto them, Have ye not read, that he which made* them *at the beginning made them male and female, And said, For this cause shall a man leave father and mother, and shall cleave to his wife: and they twain shall be one flesh? Wherefore they are no more twain, but one flesh. What therefore God hath joined, let not man put asunder. They say unto him, why did Moses then command to give a writing of divorcement, and to put her away? He saith unto them, Moses because of the hardness of your hearts suffered you to put away your wives: but from the beginning, it was not so. And I say unto you, whosoever shall put away his wife, except* it be *for fornication, and shall marry another, committed adultery: and whoso married her who is put away doth commit adultery"* (Matthew 19:3-9).

You are not permitted to kill your wife or husband in order to marry again because when you do, you become a murderer. I am talking to the single men and women, bachelors and unmarried women who have never married. Think very well, look very well, and pray very well before you make your final decision because the woman you are going to marry will remain with you for life. If she gives you the forbidden fruit, you still do not have the right to poison her or divorce her.

The reason why you should wait enough and make sure that God directs you is that many people are now suffering because they made wrong choices of marriage partner. There are husbands and wives that are living together but they do not discuss or plan together. They eat from the same plate but they are not one indeed. They are like two traders in the same shop that do not think alike.

A couple whose marriage is suffering attacks from devil must have failed to consider each other, comfort and admonish each other. They must have failed to submit to each other, prefer each other, forgive and bear each other's burden. They are not praying for themselves or greeting each other. Yet God has commanded them to do so, as a debt they owe each other (*See* 1 Thessalonians 4:18; Hebrews 10:24; Colossians 3:13; 1 Peter 5:5; Romans 12:10). When you love your partner truly, you would practice the above things daily with joy and gladness.

> *"Confess* your *faults one to another, and pray one for another, that ye may be healed. The effectual fervent prayer of a righteous man availed much"* (James 5:16).

> *"Not forsaking the assembling of ourselves together, as the manner of some* is; *but exhorting* one another: *and so much the more, as ye see the day approaching"* (Hebrews 10:25).

> *"Forbearing one another, and forgiving one another, if any man have a quarrel against any: even as Christ forgave you, so also* do *ye"* (Colossians 3:13).

A husband and his wife should pray for each other and fellowship together because they are one before God. If you are not married yet, I want to believe that you will allow God to lead you to your angel. I pray your marriage would be likened to heaven on earth. When you trust God enough, you would notice that the best thing that could take place on earth after your salvation is a good marriage. Do not worry. Christian marriage is different from societal marriage or the marriage of backslidden believers. Trust God and He will crown your life with a godly spouse.

TRUST GOD TO LEAD YOU TO MARRY

Right from the beginning of time, God made the woman for the man. God's purpose for marriage is partnership, procreation, pleasure, protection, preservation of purity and provision. None of these things can be obtain elsewhere other than marriage.

> "[28]*And God blessed them, and God said unto them, Be fruitful, and multiply, and replenish the earth, and subdue it: and have dominion over the fish of the sea, and over the fowl of the air, and over every living thing that moved upon the earth.* [18]*And the LORD God said,* It is *not good that the man should be alone; I will make him a help meet for him"* (Genesis 2:18; 1:28).

> *"Drink waters out of thine own cistern and running waters out of thine own well. Let thy fountains be dispersed abroad,* and *rivers of waters in the streets. Let them be only thine own, and not strangers' with thee. Let thy fountain be blessed: and rejoice with the wife of thy youth"* (Proverbs 5:15-18).

> *"Likewise, ye husbands, dwell with* them *according to knowledge, giving honor unto the wife, as unto the weaker vessel, and as being heirs together of the grace of life; that your prayers be not hindered"* (1 Peter 3:7).

> *"Nevertheless,* to avoid *fornication, let every man have his own wife, and let every woman have her own husband"* (1 Corinthians 7:2).

> *"But if any provide not for his own, and especially for those of his own house, he hath denied the faith, and is worse than an infidel"* (1 Timothy 5:8).

Trust God and lean on Him for provisions so that He fulfills His purpose for your marriage in your lifetime. You need God's leading in this area no matter how wise you are because God is the only one capable of connecting you to the best partner. An unsaved person is blind to the future and ignorant of the consequences of today's decision about the future. The Scriptures puts it this way:

> *"There is a way that seemed right unto a man, but the end thereof* are *the ways of death"* (Proverbs 16:25).

> *"O LORD, I know that the way of man* is *not in himself:* it is *not in man that walked to direct his steps"* (Jeremiah 10:23).

> *"And it came to pass, when they were come, that he looked on Eliab, and said, Surely the LORD'S anointed* is *before him. But the LORD said unto Samuel, Look not on his countenance, or on the height of his stature; because I have refused him: for* the

LORD seeth *not as man seeth; for man looked on the outward appearance, but the LORD looked on the heart"* (1 Samuel 16:6-7).

You may have succeeded in making good choices in other areas of your life but when it comes to marriage, you need to consult God from the beginning. Even a true child of God should not rush into any decision without God leading him.

Samuel would have made a terrible mistake in his choice of the first king of Israel. Everyone needs God at the point of making a choice of whom to marry or else there are bound to be mistakes as many couples are regretting today and wishing they never got married. Only God has the eyes to see what is good for you especially in the area of marriage. That is why you cannot do without God in the issue of marriage.

> *"[16]And I will bring the blind by a way* that *they knew not; I will lead them in paths* that *they have not known: I will make darkness light before them, and crooked things straight. These things will I do unto them, and not forsake them. [19]Who* is *blind, but my servant? Or deaf, as my messenger* that *I sent? Who is blind as* he that is *perfect, and blind as the LORD'S servant? [20]Seeing many things, but thou observes not; opening the ears, but he heareth not. [8]Then shall thy light break forth as the morning, and thine health shall spring forth speedily: and thy righteousness shall go before thee; the glory of the LORD shall be thy rewarded"* (Isaiah 42:16, 19-20; 58:8).

When you ignore God while making a choice and then invite Him to see and approve your choice, you may not get His approval. No matter what you see and know about a person, your knowledge is limited (*See* Acts 10:9-20; 16:6-10; 2 Corinthians 3:5).

> *"For we are but of yesterday, and know nothing, because our days upon earth are a shadow"* (Job 8:9).

> *"Likewise the Spirit also helped our infirmities: for we know not what we should pray for as we ought: but the Spirit itself makes intercession for us with groaning which cannot be uttered. And he that searched the hearts knoweth what* is *the mind of the Spirit, because he makes intercession for the saints according to* the will of *God. And we know that all things work together for good to them that love God, to them who are the called according to* his *purpose"* (Romans 8:26-28).

Do not desert God now that you are thinking of whom to marry. Otherwise, you may suffer terrible mistakes. Every believer needs God's guidance especially when making a choice of a marriage partner. God will be happy when you tell Him to help you choose a life partner. In this way, you would have involved Him. God is able to follow you all the way to make sure that you succeed.

The truth is that man cannot direct his ways or steps. However, many wise men have followed the paths they discovered for themselves without God only to find out that they have made great mistakes when it was too late. God does not want you to be a victim of such terrible mistakes. Therefore, commit your ways to Him and He shall cause you to prosper. To understand the will of God for your life, you must commit your ways unto God and follow Him patiently with prayers.

No man can boast of knowing tomorrow because only God knows tomorrow. Your decision of whom you married would be weighed in the future. Therefore, do not boast of limited things you see now. God knows everything about yesterday, today and tomorrow, even eternity. The money, cars and material things you are see now may no longer be available tomorrow. It would be a terrible mistake to put your trust in them.

Beauty is still available because slayers of beauty may be waiting for you to exhaust all your strength. On the other hand, do certificate and credentials provide all the confidence you need? Remember they are only ordinary papers. More so, there is the possibility of the brain malfunctioning tomorrow and all the papers and credentials would be useless and unprofitable. You do not have the capability to tell much about yourself, how much more another person. It is better to put your trust in the Lord and hope for the best.

There are credible information about you, which only God knows. God knows the woman or man that can stay with you at all cost and ones that will abandon you when you need them most. Do not choose your partner by sight because you may regret it later.

> *"For they that are after the flesh do mind the things of the flesh; but they that are after the Spirit the things of the Spirit. For to be carnally minded* is *death; but to be spiritually minded* is *life and peace. Because the carnal mind* is *enmity against God: for it is not subject to the law of God, neither indeed can be"* (Romans 8:5-7).

> *"[11]For what man knoweth the things of a man, save the spirit of man which is in him? Even so, the things of God knoweth no man, but the Spirit of God. [14]But the natural man receiveth not the things of the Spirit of God: for they are foolishness unto him: neither can he know* them, *because they are spiritually discerned"* (1 Corinthians 2:11, 14).

Only God can know the content of the human heart. Therefore, allow God to be your matchmaker, if you want to succeed in marriage. As you pray, close your eyes to receive and open it to see whom God has given to you. He promised to lead us even when we are blind. You need to say, "O Lord, is it Your will. Let Your will be done." Great people of God who failed to do allow the will of God for their marriages are regretting now.

"[16]*And I will bring the blind by a way* that *they knew not; I will lead them in paths* that *they have not known: I will make darkness light before them, and crooked things straight. These things will I do unto them, and not forsake them.* [19]*Who* is *blind, but my servant? Alternatively, deaf, as my messenger* that *I sent? Who* is *blind as* he that is *perfect, and blind as the LORD'S servant?* [20]*Seeing many things, but thou observes not; opening the ears, but he heareth not"* (Isaiah 42:16, 19-20).

It is better to allow God to show you your partner than to show God whom you have chosen to marry. God may not argue with you but if you come back to complain, He might as well not listen.

"[22]Whoso *findeth a wife findeth a good* thing, *and obtained favor of the LORD.* [14]*House and riches* are *the inheritance of fathers: and a prudent wife* is *from the LORD"* (Proverbs 18:22; 19:14).

"For I know the thoughts that I think toward you, saith the LORD, thoughts of peace, and not of evil, to give you an expected end. Then shall ye call upon me, and ye shall go and pray unto me, and I will hearken unto you. And ye shall seek me, and find me, *when ye shall search for me with all your heart"* (Jeremiah 29:11-13).

God is omniscience, perfect and has never made any mistake. Therefore, you need to trust Him. The best testimony about marriage is to say, "The Lord gave my partner to me, and it is a great favor."

You can get houses and riches or inherit them from your earthly father, but only God gives a wife or husband. If you want a virtuous and prudent wife, go to the Lord. Even before you were born, God had ordained your spouse. So, do not rush out to do it on your own way. Ask God to lead you. His thoughts towards you are of peace and not of evil, to give you an expected end. He will be happy and well pleased if you cast your problems unto Him. If you ask and you do not find, seek Him with all your heart and He will grant you your heart desires.

"[3]*Trust in the LORD, and do good;* so *shall thou dwell in the land, and verily thou shall be fed.* [4]*Delight thyself also in the LORD; and he shall give thee the desires of thine heart.* [5]*Commit thy way unto the LORD; trust also in him; and he shall bring* it *to pass.* [25]*I have been young, and* now *am old; yet have I not seen the righteous forsaken, nor his seed begging bread.* [11]*For the LORD God* is *a sun and shield: the LORD will give grace and glory: no good* thing *will he withhold from them that walk uprightly"* (Psalms 37:3-5, 25; 84:11).

God is eternal, all knowing and cannot be deceived. While physical appearances and empty promises can deceive you, they cannot deceive God. In fact, He has promised to guide us. So why would you not trust Him and get the best from Him? Trust in the

Lord and remain faithful and committed to His Word. Commit all your ways unto Him now and depend on Him fully. His plans for you would make you happy today, tomorrow and forever. He will be a sun that would rise to lead your marriage and a shield to protect your marriage. Your marriage will never lack God's grace and glory when you allow God to lead you. Likewise, no good thing will lack in your marriage according to His Word.

> *"But Zion said, the LORD hath forsaken me, and my Lord have forgotten me. Can a woman forget her sucking child, that she should not have compassion on the son of her womb? Yea, they may forget, yet will I not forget thee"* (Isaiah 49:14-15).

> *"[22]The light of the body is the eye: if therefore thine eye be single, thy whole body shall be full of light. [23]But if thine eye were evil, thy whole body shall be full of darkness. If therefore the light that is in thee be darkness, how great* is *that darkness! [24]No man can serve two masters: for either he will hate the one, and love the other; or else he will hold to the one, and despise the other. Ye cannot serve God and mammon. [25]Therefore I say unto you, Take no thought for your life, what ye shall eat, or what ye shall drink; nor yet for your body, what ye shall put on. Is not the life more than meat, and the body than raiment? [26]Behold the fowls of the air: for they sow not, neither do they reap, nor gather into barns; yet your heavenly Father feedeth them. Are ye not much better than they? [27]Which of you by taking thought can add one cubit unto his stature. [28]And why take ye thought for raiment? Consider the lilies of the field, how they grow; they toil not, neither do they spin: [29]And yet I say unto you, That even Solomon in all his glory was not arrayed like one of these. [30]Wherefore, if God so clothe the grass of the field, which today is, and tomorrow is cast into the oven,* shall he *not much more* clothe *you, O ye of little faith? [31]Therefore take no thought, saying, what shall we eat? Alternatively, what shall we drink? Alternatively, Wherewithal shall we be clothed? [32](For after all these things do the Gentiles seek :) for your heavenly Father knoweth that ye have need of all these things. [11]And when the Pharisees saw* it, *they said unto his disciples, Why eateth your Master with publicans and sinners?"* (Matthew 6:22-32; 9:11).

Learn how to lean on Him and look out for pressures from yourself and people around you. Do not do anything without the leading and support of God. Avoid any custom or tradition that opposes God's Word. Do not accept to marry anyone you do not like or love based on someone else's dreams, visions, prophecy or description. Insist on spiritual compatibility not only intellectual, monetary or physical compatibility. Be convinced that God is leading you before going to the altar for marriage vow and holy covenant. Seek God's kingdom first and you will get all that you would need in your marriage.

HOW GOD GUIDES HIS CHILDREN

Major decisions in life like marriage require divine guidance. Marital decision determines the direction one would follow in his life and may suggest how he may end his life both on earth and in eternity.

> *"Consider mine enemies; for they are many; and they hate me with cruel hatred"* (Psalms 25:19).

> *"And thine ears shall hear a word behind thee, saying, This* is *the way, walk ye in it, when ye turn to the right hand, and when ye turn to the left"* (Isaiah 30:21).

It is important therefore that believers surrender to God humbly for divine guidance. One who is guided by God will not experience sorrow or regret on earth. Wisdom guides believers to submit to God in order to enjoy His promise of guidance.

> *"Now it came to pass, as David sat in his house, that David said to Nathan the prophet, Lo, I dwell in an house of cedars, but the ark of the covenant of the LORD* remained *under curtains. Then Nathan said unto David, Do all that* is *in thine heart; for God* is *with thee. And it came to pass the same night, that the word of God came to Nathan, saying, Go and tell David my servant, Thus saith the LORD, Thou shall not build me an house to dwell in"* (1 Chronicles 17:1-4).

When you desire to hear from men instead of God, you would likely believe man rather than the Lord. God may not even bother talking to you if you have set your mind to get approval from men. You are to hear from God and confirm it through other means like men, not hear from man and force God to approve your marriage.

Likewise, you have to scrutinize your dreams and prove it repeatedly to know if God is involved how much more another person's dreams. This is because some dreams emanate from daily activities, thoughts, desires, intentions, imaginations and plans. However, few dreams come from God but you must be sure. It is wrong to seek advice from unserious ministers or backslidden prophets when you know that they no longer hear from God. When you are sure of your relationship with God, He would guide you and when He does, you will know.

> *"I will instruct thee and teach thee in the way which thou shall go: I will guide thee with mine eye"* (Psalms 32:8).

> *"The lines are fallen unto me in pleasant* places; *yea, I have a goodly heritage. I will bless the LORD, who hath given me counsel,: my reins also instruct me in the night seasons. I have set the LORD always before me: because* he is *at my right hand, I shall not be moved. Therefore, my heart is glad and my glory rejoices: my flesh shall*

rest in hope. For thou wilt not leave my soul in hell; neither wilt thou suffer thine Holy One to see corruption. Thou wilt shew me the path of life: in thy presence is *fullness of joy; at thy right hand* there are *pleasures for evermore"* (Psalms 16:6-11).

God's guidance is a promise God would fulfill. Many believers believe in God's guidance and God guides such people. If you believe that God will guide you, He would and you will not regret it. God knows when you make Him number one in your life. When He proves that, He is happy to see you do His will to the end. When God is the one that leads you, His presence will never leave you as long as you stay with Him. It brings joy and peace to hand over the mantle of your marriage to God from the beginning until the end.

"To he the porter opened; and the sheep hear his voice: and he calleth his own sheep by name, and leaded them out. And when he putteth forth his own sheep, he goeth before them, and the sheep follow him: for they know his voice. And a stranger will they not follow, but will flee from him: for they know not the voice of strangers" (John 10:3-5).

"I have yet many things to say unto you, but ye cannot bear them now. Howbeit when he, the Spirit of truth, is come, he will guide you into all truth: for he shall not speak of himself; but whatsoever he shall hear, that *shall he speak: and he will shew you things to come"* (John 16:12-13).

"And I will pray the Father, and he shall give you another Comforter, that he may abide with you forever" (John 14:16).

God sees our efforts to come to Him and He rewards them. He is able to open your ears to hear His voice. If He is the one leading you, He would carry you along. You cannot doubt God's presence if you are truly a child of God. He will reveal all things to you by His spirit.

"And he said, Go forth, and stand upon the mount before the LORD. And, behold, the LORD passed by, and a great and strong wind rent the mountains, and brake in pieces the rocks before the LORD; but *the LORD* was *not in the wind: and after the wind an earthquake;* but *the LORD* was *not in the earthquake: And after the earthquake a fire;* but *the LORD* was *not in the fire: and after the fire a still small voice"* (1 Kings 19:11-12).

"And the cherubim's were lifted up. This is *the living creature that I saw by the river of Chebar"* (Ezekiel 10:15).

> *"Father, glorify thy name. Then came there a voice from heaven,* saying, *I have both glorified* it, *and will glorify* it *again. The people therefore, that stood by, and heard* it, *said that it thundered: others said, an angel spake to him. Jesus answered and said, This voice came not because of me, but for your sakes"* (John 12:28-30).

When you listen quietly, God will speak to you through His Spirit. This voice is of the indwelling Spirit of God. You can recognize voices of family members even when you are inside your room or bathroom. Likewise, if you belong to God's family, you would discern when your father or a stranger is speaking. This is true and natural. When a thief enters into your house, your little child can discern it is a stranger's voice even when he tries to pretend.

Everyone at home recognizes the voice of each member of the family. The only thing you need to do is to make sure you become a member of the family of God and learn the voices of each member. Until you can easily say, 'This is the one talking.' Jesus did not find it difficult to discern the voice of devil speaking through Peter and to know when God spoke through him also. Believe it; you would hear God when He speaks unless you are not His child.

> *"And* though *the Lord give you the bread of adversity, and the water of affliction, yet shall not thy teachers be removed into a corner any more, but thine eyes shall see thy teachers: And thine ears shall hear a word behind thee, saying, This* is *the way, walk ye in it, when ye turn to the right hand, and when ye turn to the left"* (Isaiah 30:20-21).

Learn how to hear when God speaks henceforth. In that way, God can penetrate your heart and produce a deep conviction that cannot break easily. Do not wait until you are about to marry to start hearing from God. Sometimes, answers to your prayers could flash through your mind like a light or knowledge that comes suddenly and refuses to go even when you try to throw it off or forget it. At other times, thought or conviction can come slowly or gradually until they consume you.

> *"That the LORD called Samuel: and he answered, here* am *I. And he ran unto Eli, and said, Here* am *I; for thou calledst me. In addition, he said, I called not; lie down again. In addition, he went and lay down. And the LORD called yet again, Samuel. And Samuel arose and went to Eli, and said, Here* is *I; for thou didst call me. In addition, he answered, I called not, my son; lie down again. Now Samuel did not yet know the LORD neither was the word of the LORD yet revealed unto him. And the LORD called Samuel again the third time. And he arose and went to Eli, and said, Here* is *I; for thou didst call me. And Eli perceived that the LORD had called the child"* (1 Samuel 3:4-8).

"Afterward I came unto the house of Shemaiah the son of Delaiah the son of Mehetabeel, who was *shut up; and he said, Let us meet together in the house of God, within the temple, and let us shut the doors of the temple: for they will come to slay thee; yea, in the night will they come to slay thee. And I said, Should such a man as I flee? In addition, who* is there, *that, being as I* am, *would go into the temple to save his life? I will not go in. And, lo, I perceived that God had not sent him; but that he pronounced this prophecy against me: for Tobiah and Sanballat had hired him"* (Nehemiah 6:10-12).

God has not changed the way He communicates with His people. He is still speaking today but the only thing is that many Christians are like Samuel at his youth, who could not discern the voice of God instantly. When God called him, he ran to Eli until he learnt how to hear and recognize God's voice. Eli knew it was God but Samuel did not know.

Nehemiah did not see God face to face, but the Word of God came to him. He perceived it was the Word of God and avoided evil and satanic traps. Such perception can come suddenly or gradually also but when it settles, you will know that this is the will of God. The Spirit of Christ helped him to know God's will.

"And immediately when Jesus perceived in his spirit that they so reasoned within themselves, he said unto them, why reason you these things in your hearts?" (Mark 2:8).

"But he perceived their craftiness, and said unto them, why tempt you me?" (Luke 20:23).

"And Jeremiah said, the word of the LORD came unto me, saying, Behold, Hanameel the son of Shallum thine uncle shall come unto thee, saying, Buy thee my field that is *in Anathoth: for the right of redemption* is *thine to buy* it. *So Hanameel mine uncle's son came to me in the court of the prison according to the word of the LORD, and said unto me, Buy my field, I pray thee, that is in Anathoth, which* is *in the country of Benjamin: for the right of inheritance* is *thine, and the redemption* is *thine; buy* it *for thyself. Then I knew that this* was *the word of the LORD"* (Jeremiah 32:6-8).

Likewise, Jeremiah did not see God face to face but the Word of God came to him. Whenever the inspiration came, he spoke them out as he received them. The will of God may come to you as a strong impression and when it does, you will know.

"[9]Now when much time was spent, and when sailing was now dangerous, because the fast was now already past, Paul admonished them, *[10]And said unto them, Sirs; I perceive that this voyage will be with hurt and much damage, not only of the lading and ship, but also of our lives. [11] Nevertheless the centurion believed the master and*

[21]But after long abstinence Paul stood forth in the midst of them, and said, Sirs, ye should have hearkened unto me, and not have loosed from Crete, and to have gained this harm and loss" (Acts 27:9-11; 21).

As you start watching and listening to the voice of the Holy Ghost, you will be able to discover God's will for your marriage and other areas in your life.

"[19]While Peter thought on the vision, the Spirit said unto him, Behold, three men seek thee. [21]Then Peter went down to the men which were sent unto him from Cornelius; and said, Behold, I am he whom ye seek: what is the cause wherefore ye are come?" (Acts 10:19; 21).

Sometimes you would ponder or doubt what the Lord has put in your heart or the vision you have received. That is when God sends another person to confirm it.

"Now there were in the church that was at Antioch certain prophets and teachers; as Barnabas, and Simeon that was called Niger, and Lucius of Cyrene, and Manaen, which had been brought up with Herod the tetrarch, and Saul. As they ministered to the Lord, and fasted, the Holy Ghost said, Separate me Barnabas and Saul for the work whereunto I have called them. And when they had fasted and prayed, and laid their *hands on them, they sent* them *away"* (Acts 13:1-3).

"Now when they had gone throughout Phrygia and the region of Galatia, and were forbidden of the Holy Ghost to preach the word in Asia, After they were come to Mysia, they assayed to go into Bithynia: but the Spirit suffered them not. And they passing by Mysia came down to Troas. And a vision appeared to Paul in the night; There stood a man of Macedonia, and prayed him, saying, Come over into Macedonia, and help us. And after he had seen the vision, immediately we endeavored to go into Macedonia, assuredly gathering that the Lord had called us for to preach the gospel unto them" (Acts 16:6-10).

God is able to send someone else to confirm what He has shown you in a vision or dream. God is not limited to lead in only one or two ways. The spirit of God can restrain you or caution you against carrying out a certain action or decision and then you find out that you are no longer willing or zealous to put that particular decision into action.

Sometimes, you may find yourself in confusion, sorrow, doubt, darkness or disturbance in your spirit because of a particular decision. At that point, you must wait and confirm God's will repeatedly before going further.

"[14]For God speaketh once, yea twice, yet man *perceived it not. [15]In a dream, in a vision of the night, when deep sleep falleth upon men, in slumbering upon the bed;*

[16]Then he opened the ears of men, and sealed their instruction, [17]That he may withdraw man from his *purpose, and hide pride from man. [23]If there be a messenger with him, an interpreter, one among a thousand, to shew unto man his uprightness: [24]Then he is gracious unto him, and saith, Deliver him from going down to the pit: I have found a ransom"* (Job 33:14-17; 23-24).

"Set me as a seal upon thine heart, as a seal upon thine arm: for love is *strong as death; jealousy* is *cruel as the grave: the coals thereof* are *coals of fire,* which hath a *most vehement flame. Many waters cannot quench love, neither can the floods drown it: if* a *man would give all the substance of his house for love, it would utterly be contemned"* (Songs of Solomon 8:6-7).

God is able to lead you also through direct revelation or divinely imparted love towards a particular person. However, His revelation cannot contradict His will in any way. Likewise, God cannot tell or inspire you to marry a Delilah or Jezebel. If your love grows for Jezebel or Delilah, it cannot be the will of God. You cannot marry someone that worships idol and hope to convert her later. It is better to convert him or her first before thinking of marriage.

"Behold, I and the children whom the LORD hath given me are *for signs and for wonders in Israel from the LORD of hosts, which dwelled in mount Zion. And when they shall say unto you, Seek unto them that have familiar spirits, and unto wizards that peep, and that mutter: should not a people seek unto their God? For the living to the dead?"* (Isaiah 8:18-19).

Your convictions about God must not differ. God cannot instruct you to marry an unbeliever who hates God and His children. We all know that God can lead someone through powerful divinely imparted love. This type of love can be bestowed upon the hearts of both couple supernaturally for each other and not one-sided. It is wrong for you to marry someone that does not love you. The love we are talking about is not temporal attraction, familiarity or self-induced love. We are talking about the supernatural love from God.

Do not marry someone because of beauty, material possession or position if you do not love him or her enough to live with him for better or worse. If you are about getting married and suddenly you lose your peace, spiritual joy and love, you have to stop for a rethink. You may need to seek God again. The troubling of spirit, sense of sorrow or lack of peace as if you have lost something valuable because of your decision may be a check and an indication that you are about to enter into bondage. Do not marry anyone because you pity him or her. This is so dangerous and always counterproductive.

PRAYERS FOR A HAPPY MARRIED LIFE

Bible references: Deuteronomy 7:1-4; Joshua 21:43-45

Begin with praise and worship

1. Any covenant that is fighting against God's will for my life, break, in the name of Jesus.
2. Father Lord, lead me into Your perfect will for my marriage and keep me in it, in the name of Jesus.
3. Let any power that is pushing me into satanic plans against God's plans be frustrated, in the name of Jesus.
4. Blood of Jesus, speak me into Your perfect will for my marriage, in the name of Jesus.
5. O Lord, lay the foundation of my marriage by Yourself, in the name of Jesus.
6. I refuse to be manipulated into making a wrong choice, in the name of Jesus.
7. I break and loose myself from any evil contact that was designed to take me away from God's will for my life, in the name of Jesus.
8. Lord Jesus, deliver me from any evil relationship that is leading me into a wrong marriage, in the name of Jesus.
9. O Lord, deliver me from the consequences of any covenant that I have ever broken, in the name of Jesus.
10. Let the curse and covenant of late marriage in my life break and expire, in the name of Jesus.
11. Every inherited evil covenant and curse in my life, I reject you, in the name of Jesus.
12. Anyone that is about to entice me into a wrong choice, I break away from you, in the name of Jesus.
13. I reject manipulation, bewitchment and spells that would lead me away from God's will for my life, in the name of Jesus.
14. Any wrong marriage that was arranged for me anywhere, I reject you, in the name of Jesus.

15. I break and loose myself from arrows of confusion in my choice of marriage partner, in the name of Jesus.

16. Any witch or wizard that has vowed to divert me from the will of God in marriage, fail, in the name of Jesus.

17. O Lord, anoint me to enter into a marriage that would strengthen faith, in the name of Jesus.

18. I command a perfect life partner to manifest and appear before me, in the name of Jesus.

19. I remove any power, thing or person that is blocking me from getting married to the right person, in the name of Jesus.

20. Let everything devil has put in place to deny me of God's perfect will in marriage be removed, in the name of Jesus.

21. Let the power of darkness that has vowed that I will not get married happily die, in the name of Jesus.

22. Father Lord, convince the perfect life partner to accept me fully and forever, in the name of Jesus.

23. O Lord, give me best partner that would help me to fulfill Your purpose, in the name of Jesus.

24. Let the marriage that would give me God's best in partnership, pleasures and fulfillment appear, in the name of Jesus.

25. Let that person that was ordained by God to fulfill my purpose of procreation, protection and provision appear, in the name of Jesus.

26. O Lord, use my life partner, whom I pray to meet, to preserve my purity, in the name of Jesus.

27. Father, lead me to a place where I can find the bone of my bone and the flesh of my flesh, in the name of Jesus.

28. Power that will bring my partner where I am, manifest and do so by force, in the name of Jesus.

29. O Lord, command my partner to accept me above any other, in the name of Jesus.

30. Lord Jesus, give me a life partner that would never expire or fade before my eyes, in the name of Jesus.

31. Let my life partner accept me above the way I do, in the name of Jesus.

32. O Lord, You know the best partner that is fit for me. Let him/her appear now, in the name of Jesus.

33. Powers that mislead others in the choices of marriage and are now fighting against me, die, in the name of Jesus.

34. Any power that is pulling my partner or me away, die, in the name of Jesus.

35. I disgrace any evil personality that wants to force me into a marriage that is against the will of God, in the name of Jesus.

36. O Lord, help me to succeed in every area of my life, in the name of Jesus.

37. Let intimidating power of God fall upon my partner and me to surrender to God's will, in the name of Jesus.

38. Let fake life partners that are coming my way fade away by force, in the name of Jesus.

39. Any evil garment that is covering my life partner or me, catch fire, burn to ashes, in the name of Jesus.

40. O Lord, I need You to lead me into the right marriage, in the name of Jesus.

41. Any marriage that was designed to ruin my destiny, I reject you, in the name of Jesus.

42. O Lord, replace my eyes with Yours that I may see Your will for my marriage, in the name of Jesus.

43. Father Lord, empower me to ignore and reject anything that was designed to mislead me, in the name of Jesus.

44. O Lord, be in-charge of my marriage from the beginning to the end, in the name of Jesus.

45. You, my will, plan and purpose, give way to God to rule and reign forever, in the name of Jesus.

46. O Lord, You are the best matchmaker, have Your way and link me to the best partner, in the name of Jesus.

47. I reject every marriage that was arranged by hell and I accept the one that was arranged by heaven, in the name of Jesus.

48. I reject demonic dreams, visions and prophecies from the devil, in the name of Jesus.

49. O Lord, give me a partner that will never cause me to regret my marriage, in the name of Jesus.

50. Blood of Jesus, speak my marriage out from the arrest of evil spirits, in the name of Jesus.

51. Let the marriage that will give me peace, rest and every good thing in life appear, in the name of Jesus.

52. Let the partner that will take me to divinely expected end manifest, in the name of Jesus.

53. Father Lord, let everything You have created do Your will, in the name of Jesus.

54. Father Lord, use every creature to confirm that You are leading me into this marriage, in the name of Jesus.

55. Let evil messengers in my marriage carry their messages to their senders, in the name of Jesus.

56. O Lord, make Your ways plain before my eyes, in the name of Jesus.

57. Let the light that would lead me to my life partner appear, in the name of Jesus.

58. Holy Spirit, minister to every enemy of my marriage to surrender and support me, in the name of Jesus.

59. Let the glory of my marriage appear, in the name of Jesus.

60. Let my choice of marriage partner be used to bless the world, in the name of Jesus.

34
Chapter

PRAYERS TO BUY A HOME AND SETTLE DOWN

CHAPTER OVERVIEW

- *A godly home: A place of rest*
- *Buying a Christian home*
- *Qualities of a good wife*
- *From earthly home to eternal home*

A GODLY HOME: A PLACE OF REST

Most Christians do not consider praying to buy their own homes. While other prayers are also important, you cannot ignore this aspect. When thinking of getting married, you should also think of building your own house or buying a home where you will live with your family. If you do not have enough finance now, start making provisions for it because it is very necessary to have a roof over your head.

> *"When they had made an end of dividing the land for inheritance by their coasts, the children of Israel gave an inheritance to Joshua the son of Nun among them: According to the word of the LORD they gave him the city which he asked, even Timnath–serah in mount Ephraim: and he built the city, and dwelt therein. These are the inheritances, which Eleazar the priest, and Joshua the son of Nun, and the heads of the fathers of the tribes of the children of Israel, divided for an inheritance by lot in Shiloh before the LORD, at the door of the tabernacle of the congregation. So they made an end of dividing the country"* (Joshua 19:49-51).

When we speak of a home of your own, we mean a personal property. You need a place where your children can call home. This is also the family house and a place of origin.

LEAVING YOUR PARENTS

When you get married, heaven opens a new chapter for your family and God commissions His angels to take you to your personal home. This is the confidence we have as Christians.

> *"18 And the LORD God said, it is not good that the man should be alone; I will make him a help meet for him. 21 And the LORD God caused a deep sleep to fall upon Adam, and he slept: and he took one of his ribs, and closed up the flesh instead thereof; 22 And the rib, which the LORD God had taken from man, made he a woman, and brought her unto the man. 23 And Adam said, this is now bone of my bones, and flesh of my flesh: she shall be called Woman, because she was taken out of Man. 24 Therefore shall a man leave his father and his mother, and shall cleave unto his wife: and they shall be one flesh"* (Genesis 2:18, 21-24).

Nevertheless, you need to have a source of income before getting married. That is when you are qualified to think of your personal house instead of rented apartment. God has made provisions for that already. Recall that when God created Adam and Eve, He provided a home for them as well.

"And the LORD God planted a garden eastward in Eden; and there he put the man whom he had formed. And out of the ground made the LORD God to grow every tree that is pleasant to the sight, and good for food; the tree of life also in the midst of the garden, and the tree of knowledge of good and evil. And a river went out of Eden to water the garden; and from thence it was parted, and became into four heads. The name of the first is Pison: that is it, which compasseth the whole land of Havilah, where there is gold, And the gold of that land is good: there is bdellium and the onyx stone. And the name of the second river is Gihon: the same is it that compasseth the whole land of Ethiopia. And the name of the third river is Hiddekel: that is it, which goeth toward the east of Assyria. In addition, the fourth river is Euphrates. And the LORD God took the man, and put him into the Garden of Eden to dress it and to keep it" (Genesis 2:8-15).

As you progress in your career or business, save all the money you can and make plans to buy your own personal home. Always remember that God blessed you to be fruitful and multiply, replenish the earth and subdue it until you have dominion over other creatures.

"And God blessed them, and God said unto them, Be fruitful, and multiply, and replenish the earth, and subdue it: and have dominion over the fish of the sea, and over the fowl of the air, and over every living thing that moveth upon the earth" (Genesis 1:28).

"And he answered and said unto them, Have ye not read, that he which made them at the beginning made them male and female, And said, For this cause shall a man leave father and mother, and shall cleave to his wife: and they twain shall be one flesh? Wherefore they are no more twain, but one flesh. What therefore God hath joined together, let not man put asunder" (Matthew 19:4-6).

Most men do not struggle to fulfill God's destiny. They understand that God is there to provide help. Leaving your parents does not mean that you are no longer under their care. Rather, it lunches you into life of productivity and being a man that you are expected to be. A husband and wife should fight together and form a family.

LEAVING TO SETTLE DOWN

Leaving your parents, guardians or anybody that takes care of you, spiritually and physically, is one of the greatest battles you must fight in your life. The forces of evil that are responsible to keep people in their parents' houses are too many and would do everything in their power to keep you in bondage. When Abel decided to serve his God and established a holy family, his elder brother Cain killed him.

"[3]And in process of time it came to pass, that Cain brought of the fruit of the ground an offering unto the LORD. [5]But unto Cain and to his offering he had not respected. In addition, Cain was very wroth, and his countenance fell. [6]And the LORD said unto Cain, Why art thou wroth? In addition, why is thy countenance fallen? [7]If thou doest well, shalt thou not be accepted? In addition, if thou does not well, sin lieth at the door. In addition, unto thee shall be his desire, and thou shalt rule over him. [8]And Cain talked with Abel his brother: and it happened, when they were in the field, that Cain raised up against Abel his brother, and slew him. [9]And the LORD said unto Cain, Where is Abel thy brother? And he said I know not: Am I my brother's keeper?" (Genesis 4:3, 5-9).

Either Satan wants you to depend on people in his kingdom or he wants you to serve him before you are permitted to settle down in life. Abel's enemies, including Cain, his elder brother, vowed that Abel would not have freedom of worship or be a man of his own. The anger of Cain against Abel was demonically motivated. His talks and demands were demonic also. The death of Abel was more spiritual than physical.

"And it came to pass, as they journeyed from the east, that they found a plain in the land of Shinar; and they dwelt there. And they said one to another, Go to, let us make brick, and burn them thoroughly. In addition, they had brick for stone, and slime had they for mortar. And they said, Go to, let us build us a city and a tower, whose top may reach unto heaven; and let us make us a name, lest we be scattered abroad upon the face of the whole earth" (Genesis 11:2-4).

Evil forces that prevent people from leaving their parents and settling down according to God's will would only allow you to settle down if you would accept to remain under their bondage. They want your independence according to their terms. Before they allow someone to settle down, they want that person to abandon God and serve devil. They want to ensure that more people build houses and settle down without God in their lives.

If you are under the curse of devil, he cannot permit you to involve God when searching for the right person. When you want to build or buy a house, he wants you to do it without involving God. However, when you insist in marrying the right wife, get children and get a good job, you are in for his troubles. The solution is to come out of the curse of devil and come under the covenant of Jesus and His blood.

Devil does not want you to settle down the right way. He would always attack with all manner of problems. He wants to attack your marriage, job, health and finances or even manipulate you to buy a wrong house where he is in-charge. In such houses, you would experience incessant attacks from witches and diverse problems. You see yourself face to face with divorce and separation.

Devil does not want Christians to settle down the right way. Millions of people that have left their parents are not settled in peace yet. It is not good to buy a home and have no peace. A home is made up of a husband, wife, children and other members of the family. However, a home cannot be what God wants it to be if there is no love in that home.

> *"Husbands, love your wives, even as Christ also loved the church, and gave himself for it; That he might sanctify and cleanse it with the washing of water by the word, That he might present it to himself a glorious church, not having spot, or wrinkle, or any such thing; but that it should be holy and without blemish. So ought men to love their wives as their own bodies. He that loved his wife loved himself. For no man ever yet hated his own flesh; but nourished and cherished it, even as the Lord the church: For we are members of his body, of his flesh, and of his bones. For this cause shall a man leave his father and mother, and shall be joined unto his wife, and they two shall be one flesh. This is a great mystery: but I speak concerning Christ and the church. Nevertheless let every one of you in particular so love his wife even as himself; and the wife see that she reverence her husband"* (Ephesians 5:25-33).

A husband must love his wife as God commanded. He must die to self. He must be a sacrificial and holy husband, a sharing father and an understanding leader of the family. He must share his love equal to the members of his family so that there is no room for animosity, struggle and fight. Marriage should be nothing but a perfect and glorious union.

> *"That they may teach the young women to be sober, to love their husbands, to love their children"* (Titus 2:4).

> *"[8]Owe no man anything, but to love one another: for he that loved another hath fulfilled the law. [10] Love worked no ill to his neighbor: therefore love is the fulfilling of the law"* (Romans 13:8, 10).

For any family to achieve its glorious destiny, love must be at the center. You can do everything to buy a home, get good furniture and other comfortable things but if there is no love, you do not have a home. When we speak of a Christian home, we mean a home where the husband has modeled the love Christ has for the church, and shepherded for the sheep. A good husband sees no danger in losing his wife provided he does not love his wife more than he loves God.

> *"Now there is at Jerusalem by the sheep market a pool, which is called in the Hebrew tongue Bethesda, having five porches"* (John 5:2).

> *"Now there is at Jerusalem by the sheep market a pool, which is called in the Hebrew tongue Bethesda, having five porches"* (John 13:1).

"We know that we have passed from death unto life, because we love the brethren. He that loved not his brother abideth in death. Whosoever hated his brother is a murderer: and ye know that no murderer hath eternal life abiding in him. Hereby perceive we the love of God, because he laid down his life for us: and we ought to lay down our lives for the brethren. But whoso hath this world's good, and seeth his brother have need, and shutteth up his bowels of compassion from him, how dwelled the love of God in him? My little children, let us not love in word, neither in tongue; but in deed nor in truth" (1 John 3:14-18).

God is searching for a husband that is willing to deny himself, bear toil and trial to provide and care for his wife, defend her and protect his household. When we speak of buying a home, it is more than buying your house physically. We mean securing your home spiritually before purchasing it. A physical home filled with good things without love is just a house and a place where enemies live together.

BUYING A CHRISTIAN HOME

From the beginning of time, God determined it was good for His people to have a good place to live. That was why He created the Garden of Eden and put Adam and his wife in it. God wanted a place where He would rest each time He wished. He planned it, purposed it and provided it from the beginning.

> *"[18]And the LORD God said, it is not good that the man should be alone; I will make him a help meet for him. [20]And Adam gave names to all cattle and to the fowl of the air, and to every beast of the field; but for Adam there was not found a helpmeet for him. [22]And the rib, which the LORD God had taken from man, made him a woman, and brought her unto the man. [24]Therefore shall a man leave his father and his mother, and shall cleave unto his wife: and they shall be one flesh"* (Genesis 2:18, 20, 22, 24).

> *"For this cause shall a man leave his father and mother, and shall be joined unto his wife, and they two shall be one flesh"* (Ephesians 5:31).

God said it was not good to have a home without a wife. What He pronounced as *not good* in the days of Adam is still not good today. You can have all that you desired for in your life like cattle, birds, land, servants, etc. However, if you do not have a wife, your home is not complete.

Most young and unmarried men think that what they need most is money in order to get married but that is not true. You need God first, who then would give you a wife, the flesh of your flesh and bone of your bone, and wealth. In addition, some men would do everything to get money and build a house before thinking of getting a wife. That may be good but the best thing is for a man to know God. When you know God, He provides you a home and a wife to make you complete.

When you strive to get a home without God in it, the devil may give you his daughter to marry. But when you have God without a home, He is able to give you a wife and a home. Therefore, the most important thing is that everything you have comes from the Lord. Some men have killed and done many evil things in order to get whatever they wanted. Eventually, they got it but do not have peace.

Buying a home or building a house without God is regrettable and useless. Wife, home, money or material things without God in them would constitute a big problem. Only God can give you a good home. The sons of Noah had all they needed to own physical homes, yet they failed.

> *"And the LORD came down to see the city and the tower, which the children of men builder. And the LORD said, Behold, the people is one, and they have all one*

language; and this they begin to do: and now nothing will be restrained from them, which they have imagined to do. Go to, let us go down, and there confound their language, that they may not understand one another's speech. So the LORD scattered them abroad from thence upon the face of all the earth: and they left off to build the city" (Genesis 11:5-8).

Anything you are doing without God in it will fail eventually. Many people have closed their ears and eyes to the gospel. They struggle to get money, job and build houses here and there without God. That was what the sons of Noah did but they failed. You may have defrauded people, killed and did all manner of evil things to get whatever you wanted but you will not have peace. Others, after doing all manner of evil things, would invite God to bless their evil wealth. They look for the most beautiful, educated and intelligent women to marry. Things may be working for you now but someday, problem would set in because you have refused to involve God from the beginning.

"Send thine hand from above; rid me, and deliver me out of great waters, from the hand of strange children" (Psalms 144:7).

As a woman, you may be searching for a man with wealth. You may find such man eventually. However, if he does not know God, you may live a miserable life on earth. Some men are often kind to other women but wicked to their wives. In such homes, no matter what you have in it, it cannot be a home. Some peoples' homes are like wrestling field, drinking spot or graveyard. A husband that does not have time for his wife has no home. A husband that does not love his wife has no home. A husband that does not protect his wife has no home. A husband that beats his wife has no home. He may have the best business, best house in the city and the largest bank account but he has no home.

A husband that cannot provide for his family and control his children has no home. A husband that cannot guide, protect, provide and teach his children has no home. He may be seen as the head but he is only a figurehead. Such husband, even when he is fully involved in the church but is not in-charge of affairs in his house, he has no home. A head that does not stay with the body is no longer the head. A committed head of the family stays with the body until death. That is how a good husband should be to his wife and the members of the family.

"For the husband is the head of the wife, even as Christ is the head of the church: and he is the savior of the body" (Ephesians 5:23).

"But I would have you know, that the head of every man is Christ; and the head of the woman is the man; and the head of Christ is God" (1 Corinthians 11:3).

"One that ruleth well his own house, having his children in subjection with all gravity; (For if a man know not how to rule his own house, how shall he take care of the church of God?)" (1 Timothy 3:4-5).

Naturally, a man feeds, protects, cleanses and cares for his body. He takes care of any part of his organ that is sick and allows his legs and hands to rest when they are tired. He cares for his body, grants them rest, and sympathizes with his body when it is weak. He allows his eyes to close for sleep when he is tired. It is stupidity for someone to use his hands to beat himself, or someone to pluck out his eyes. Such hand is not normal and such a person is not normal.

A man that beats his wife or exposes her weaknesses to his parents and outsiders is not a good head. No normal husband can abuse his wife and remain normal. Many beautiful houses are not homes because the inhabitants are not with God who is the head of the universe and the creator of heaven and earth.

QUALITIES OF A GOOD WIFE

A good wife accepts the divinely ordained headship of her husband not because the husband is good and merits it but because God ordained it. She submits to her husband as unto the Lord in all things.

> *"Wives, submit yourselves unto your own husbands, as unto the Lord. For the husband is the head of the wife, even as Christ is the head of the church: and he is the savior of the body. Therefore as the church is subject unto Christ, so let the wives be to their own husbands in everything"* (Ephesians 5:22-24).

> *"Likewise, ye wives, be in subjection to your own husbands; that, if any obey not the word, they also may without the word be won by the conversation of the wives; While they behold your chaste conversation coupled with fear"* (1 Peter 3:1-2).

> *"Wives, submit yourselves unto your own husbands, as it is fit in the Lord"* (Colossians 3:18).

A Christian wife is supposed to be tender, lovely, gentle and meek at home and everywhere. It is her duty to obey and submit herself to her husband except in what is contrary to faith and pure conscience.

> *"But Peter and John answered and said unto them, Whether it be right in the sight of God to hearken unto you more than unto God, judge ye"* (Acts 4:19).

> *"Then Peter and the other apostles answered and said we ought to obey God rather than men"* (Acts 5: 29).

She submits in domestic matters, family rules and in everything that is godly. The husband has the right to direct things while the wife submits. In submitting, it has to be as unto the Lord and not in a grudge as if she is doing favor to her husband.

> *"But let it be the hidden man of the heart, in that which is not corruptible, even the ornament of a meek and quiet spirit, which is in the sight of God of great price. For after this manner in the old time the holy women also, who trusted in God, adorned themselves, being in subjection unto their own husbands: Even as Sara obeyed Abraham, calling him lord: whose daughters ye are, as long as ye do well, and are not afraid with any amazement"* (1 Peter 3:4-6).

A good wife lives with meek and quiet spirit in the sight of God and all men. Esther learnt how to be obedient and submissive from her uncle, Mordecai, after she lost her father. She obeyed her uncle and submitted to all his charges. When the king saw her quality and meek spirit, he preferred Esther above other virgins. She obtained grace and favor in the sight of the king, and was crowned the Queen. With obedience, meek and humble spirit, Esther found favor before the king who granted all her request.

> *"And it fell on a day, that Elisha passed to Shunem, where was a great woman; and she constrained him to eat bread. Therefore, it was that as soft as he passed by, he turned in thither to eat bread. And she said unto her husband, Behold now, I perceive that this is an holy man of God, which passed by us continually. Let us make a little chamber, I pray thee, on the wall; and let us set for him there a bed, and a table, and a stool, and a candlestick: and it shall be, when he cometh to us that he shall turn in thither"* (2 Kings 4:8-10).

Likewise, the woman of Shunem is worthy of emulation. She could have been providing for her family and built their house. Yet, she did not contend for her husband's position. She was the one who saw the need to accommodate Elisha in their home, but she sought for her husband's approval first. She demonstrated a life of a submissive woman.

Another submissive woman worthy of emulation is Elizabeth. Her character radiated the character of God. She was a righteous woman who walked in the commandments of God without blame. Though she had no child, there was peace and divine presence in her home even at her old age.

> *"[5]There was in the days of Herod, the king of Judea, a certain priest named Zacharias, of the course of Abia: and his wife was of the daughters of Aaron, and her name was Elisabeth. [6]And they were both righteous before God, walking in all the commandments and ordinances of the Lord blameless. [7]And they had no child, because that Elisabeth was barren, and they both were now well stricken in years. [23]And it came to pass, that, as soon as the days of his ministration were accomplished, he departed to his own house. [24]And after those days his wife Elisabeth conceived, and hid herself five months, saying, [25]Thus hath the Lord dealt with me in the days wherein he looked on me, to take away my reproach among men. [57]Now Elisabeth's full time came that she should be delivered; and she brought forth a son. [58]And her neighbors and her cousins heard how the Lord had showed great mercy upon her; and they rejoiced with her. [59]And it came to pass, that on the eighth day they came to circumcise the child; and they called him Zacharias, after the name of his father. [60]And his mother answered and said, Not so; but he shall be called John. [61]And they said unto her, there is none of thy kindred that is called by this name. [62]And they made signs to his father, how he would have him called. [63]And he asked for a writing table, and wrote, saying, His name is John. In addition, they marveled all. [64]And his mouth was opened immediately, and his tongue loosed, and he spake, and praised God"* (Luke 1:5-7; 23-25, 57-64).

At old age, Elizabeth was still humble, meek and submissive to her husband and God. God visited her at her old age and she conceived. Her joy was complete at the birth of their son, John. There are other women of noble character in the Bible like Mary the mother of Christ (*See* Luke 2:19; Matthew 2:13-14, 19-22; Luke 2:41-48).

Some of the qualities of a good wife include reverence for God and her husband, humility, meekness, quietness, loving, diligence, dependable, prayerful and hospitality. When you have a loving and submissive wife, and obedient children, your home would be heaven on earth.

As a wife, you may not have all these qualities but believe that things will change for the best as you pray through selected prayer points at the end of this book. With the grace of God, you can bring these qualities into your home today. If you do not have the finance you need, begin to pray and God would provide finances for you to buy a home. If you have finances already, may God give you the wisdom to buy a home in a place where you will never lack God's presence forever.

FROM EARTHLY HOME TO ETERNAL HOME

The earthly home is a shadow or model of our heavenly home. Therefore, if your earthly home lacks the presence of God, how can you partake in the heavenly home? Ask God to come into your home today as we wait for the return of our Lord Jesus Christ.

> *"Let not your heart be troubled: ye believe in God, believe also in me. In my Father's house are many mansions: if it were not so, I would have told you. I go to prepare a place for you. And if I go and prepare a place for you, I will come again, and receive you unto myself; that where I am, there ye may be also. And whither I go ye know, and the way ye know"* (John 14:1-4).

Saints who maintained their faith on earth would be home with Christ eternally. In heaven, believers will enjoy fellowship, rest, holiness, service and glory with God forever. Even true believers who did not acquire a physical home on earth will reign with other believers of all ages as citizens of the new heaven. No matter how comfortable, peaceable, restful or enjoyable your home here on earth is, you have a better home in heaven. We are only ambassadors on earth.

> *"For our conversation is in heaven; from whence also we look for the Savior, the Lord Jesus Christ: Who shall change our vile body, that it may be fashioned like unto his glorious body, according to the working whereby he is able even to subdue all things unto himself"* (Philippians 3:20-21).

> *"Now then we are ambassadors for Christ, as though God did beseech you by us: we pray you in Christ's stead, be ye reconciled to God"* (2 Corinthians 5:20).

It is good to own a home here on earth. It is your right because the earth and its fullness belong to our Father in heaven. However, your focus should be the heavenly home. We are just strangers here on earth. Our home is in heaven. Our Father is in heaven. Our Savior is there. Our homes, names, lives, treasures, affections, hearts, inheritance and citizenship are all there. Jesus is the only way to paradise, our heavenly home.

> *"Thomas saith unto him, Lord, we know not whither thou goest; and how can we know the way? Jesus saith unto him, I am the way, the truth, and the life: no man cometh unto the Father, but by me"* (John 14:5-6).

If you are not born-again yet, then you are not at peace with God through Jesus Christ. Therefore, you will not come to heaven. Those that will live in the heavenly home are those born of the Spirit here on earth and lead a good spiritual homes where Christ reigns.

"And I heard a great voice out of heaven saying, Behold, the tabernacle of God is with men, and he will dwell with them, and they shall be his people, and God himself shall be with them, and be their God. And God shall wipe away all tears from their eyes; and there shall be no more death, neither sorrow, nor crying, neither shall there be any more pain: for the former things are passed away" (Revelation 21:3-4).

"And there shall be no more curse: but the throne of God and of the Lamb shall be in it; and his servants shall serve him: And they shall see his face; and his name shall be in their foreheads" (Revelation 22:3-4).

Your name must be written in the book of life here on earth with a testimony of a spiritual home on earth before you can be admitted into the heavenly home. The fearful, unbelieving, abominable, murderers, whoremongers, fornicators, adulterers, sorcerers, witches and wizards, occultists and all those that use familiar spirits, idolaters and all liars will not be allowed to enter into the home in heaven.

"[8]But the fearful, and unbelieving, and the abominable, and murderers, and whoremongers, and sorcerers, and idolaters, and all liars, shall have their part in the lake which burnet with fire and brimstone: which is the second death. [27]And there shall in no wise enter into it anything that defiled, neither whatsoever worked abomination, or maketh a lie: but they which are written in the Lamb's book of life" (Revelation 21:8, 27).

"And whosoever was not found written in the book of life was cast into the lake of fire" (Revelation 20:15).

"For without are dogs, and sorcerers, and whoremongers, and murderers, and idolaters, and whosoever loved and maketh a lie" (Revelation 22:15).

Other references: *(John 9:18-22; Matthew 10:33-36; John 3:18-20, 36; Leviticus 18:21-27; Deuteronomy 22:5; Proverbs 6:16-19; 1 John 3:15; Matthew 5:27-30; Deuteronomy 18:9-14; 1 Samuel 28:5-11; 1 Chronicles 10:13-14; Isaiah 8:19; Exodus 20:3-5; 1 John 5:21).*

It is not possible, no matter how clever you are, to enter into heaven and desecrate the eternal home of the Lord's children. No sinner would be allowed in to stain or desecrate the holy home of the bride and the lamb. All sinners shall be banished from the presence of God and from the eternal home of the saints forever. They shall be cast into the lake of fire forever. In the new heaven, we shall hunger or thirst no more.

"There is a river, the streams whereof shall make glad the city of God, the holy place of the tabernacles of the most High" (Psalms 46:4).

"And he showed me a pure river of water of life, clear as crystal, proceeding out of the throne of God and of the Lamb. In the midst of the street of it, and on either side of the

river, was there the tree of life, which bare twelve manner of fruits, and yielded her fruit every month: and the leaves of the tree were for the healing of the nations. And there shall be no more curse: but the throne of God and of the Lamb shall be in it; and his servants shall serve him: And they shall see his face; and his name shall be in their foreheads. And there shall be no night there; and they need no candle, neither light of the sun; for the Lord God gives them light: and they shall reign forever and ever" (Revelation 22:1-5).

We shall fast or cry no more. We shall have access to the water of life in our eternal home as a continuous reminder that Christ truly gives the water of life. In our eternal home, the tree of life yields a different type of fruit. It would be a great disappointment for you to know this and yet not experience it. Are you going to allow the devil or the little enjoyment on earth to deny you of your eternal rest in the eternal home? It would be a great and eternal loss. It will not be your portion in Jesus name.

"Jesus saith unto them, Bring of the fish which ye have now caught. Simon Peter went up, and drew the net to land full of great fishes, an hundred and fifty and three: and for all there were so many, yet was not the net broken. Jesus saith unto them, Come and dine. In addition, none of the disciples durst ask him, who art thou? Knowing that it was the Lord. Jesus then cometh, and taketh bread, and giveth them, and fish likewise. This is now the third time that Jesus showed himself to his disciples, after that he was risen from the dead" (John 21:10-14).

"15 And he said unto them, With desire I have desired to eat this Passover with you before I suffer: 16 For I say unto you, I will not any more eat thereof, until it be fulfilled in the kingdom of God. 17 And he took the cup, and gave thanks, and said, Take this, and divide it among yourselves: 18 For I say unto you, I will not drink of the fruit of the vine, until the kingdom of God shall come. 29 And I appoint unto you a kingdom, as my Father hath appointed unto me; 30 That ye may eat and drink at my table in my kingdom, and sit on thrones judging the twelve tribes of Israel" (Luke 22:15-18, 29-30).

The leaves of the tree of life will heal all that would come into the heavenly home. There shall be no curse, no more death or pains.

"In the midst of the street of it, and on either side of the river, was there the tree of life, which bare twelve manner of fruits, and yielded her fruit every month: and the leaves of the tree were for the healing of the nations. And there shall be no more curses: but the throne of God and of the Lamb shall be in it; and his servants shall serve him" (Revelation 22:2-3).

"And God shall wipe away all tears from their eyes; and there shall be no more death, neither sorrow, nor crying, neither shall there be any more pain: for the former things are passed away" (Revelation 21:4).

The tree of life will ensure joy and health to all that would enter into the eternal home. Our Lord Jesus is the designer of this city and He promised to build it with His Father and afterwards returns to take us home. The city is full of blazing and brilliance glory of God. Everything in that city is clear as crystal with good design and perfect symmetry. It will be able to contain billions of people with billions of empty spaces left. You cannot afford to miss this eternal home.

"In my Father's house are many mansions: if it were not so, I would have told you. I go to prepare a place for you" (John 14:2).

"Because strait is the gate, and narrow is the way, which leaded unto life, and few there be that find it" (Matthew 7:14).

Unfortunately, many will not be there. Where will you be and where will you spend your eternity?

"[11]He that is unjust, let him be unjust still: and he which is filthy, let him be filthy still: and he that is righteous, let him be righteous still: and he that is holy, let him be holy still. [15]For without are dogs, and sorcerers, and whoremongers, and murderers, and idolaters, and whosoever loved and maketh a lie. [18] For I testify unto every man that hearten the words of the prophecy of this book, If any man shall add unto these things, God shall add unto him the plagues that are written in this book: [19] And if any man shall take away from the words of the book of this prophecy, God shall take away his part out of the book of life, and out of the holy city, and from the things which are written in this book" (Revelation 22:11, 15, 18-19).

"The wicked shall be turned into hell, and all the nations that forget God" (Psalms 9:17).

Unrepentant sinners will separate from God forever. They will be thrown into the lake of fire forever. However, the redeemed, those who are made righteous through the blood of Jesus Christ will remain righteous forever while all unrepentant sinners will retain their evil and sinful nature forever.

"And he stewed me a pure river of water of life, clear as crystal, proceeding out of the throne of God and of the Lamb" (Revelation 22:1).

"Come unto me, all ye that labor and are heavy laden and I will give you rest. Take my yoke upon you, and learn of me; for I am meek and lowly in heart: and ye shall

find rest unto your souls. For my yoke is easy, and my burden is light" (Matthew 11:28-30).

This may be your last chance and final invitation to accept Jesus into your life. Therefore, I beg you to respond now. Give your life to Christ, repent, confess all your sins and forsake them. Life is too short. Your end on earth is much closer than you think. You need to live a spiritual life on earth in a godly home. Start building your home today.

"But seek ye first the kingdom of God, and his righteousness; and all these things shall be added unto you" (Matthew 6:33).

PRAYERS TO BUY A HOME AND SETTLE DOWN

Bible reference: Joshua 21:43-45

Begin with praise and worship

1. Father Lord, help me to locate a home, get money and buy it to Your glory, in the name of Jesus.
2. Any strongman that lives in my land of promise, die, in the name of Jesus.
3. Lord Jesus, provide money for me to buy a home this year, in the name of Jesus.
4. I receive the ability to start saving money to purchase a house, in the name of Jesus.
5. Any power that is militating against my savings for buying a house, die, in the name of Jesus.
6. I command every demon that is attacking my savings to die, in the name of Jesus.
7. O Lord, give me wisdom and divine ability to save enough money to buy a good house, in the name of Jesus.
8. I destroy problems that were designed to swallow my finances for the new house, in the name of Jesus.
9. O Lord, arise and increase my income this year, in the name of Jesus.
10. I refuse to enter into any trouble that would stop me from buying a house, in the name of Jesus.
11. Let any evil tongue that is rising against my plans to buy a house receive fire, in the name of Jesus.
12. Father Lord, give me financial explosion this year by fire, in the name of Jesus.
13. Let the handwriting of my enemies be erased that I may buy my house, in the name of Jesus.
14. Let any spiritual house in my land of promise, collapse in the name of Jesus.
15. Let spiritual owners of my new house release it and die, in the name of Jesus.

16. Every evil sacrifice that was done in my house for my sake, expire, in the name of Jesus.

17. Any evil personality that is living inside my new house, die, in the name of Jesus.

18. I paralyze evil powers that have vowed to keep me as a tenant forever, in the name of Jesus.

19. O Lord, empower me financially to buy a new house of Your choice without debts, in the name of Jesus.

20. I break and loose myself from the power of financial and material poverty, in the name of Jesus.

21. I trample upon every problem that is preventing me from buying a family house this year, in the name of Jesus.

22. I lift every satanic embargo that was placed upon my new house, in the name of Jesus.

23. Any evil activity that is preventing me from buying a new house this year is frustrated, in the name of Jesus.

24. O Lord, arise and finance my new house at the right time, in the name of Jesus.

25. O Lord, help me to buy a house in a right place where Your peace reigns, in the name of Jesus.

26. I chase away evil spirits that are residing at the location of my new house, in the name of Jesus.

27. O Lord, lead me to a place where I would live and call my own, in the name of Jesus.

28. Let every opposition that is standing against my new house disappear, in the name of Jesus.

29. O Lord, empower me to buy a house at a place and city of choice, in the name of Jesus.

30. Let the angels of God walk me into the right place to buy a house, in the name of Jesus.

31. Let spiritual residents of my divinely new house vacate by fire, in the name of Jesus.

32. Every satanic soldier that is militating against my plans to buy a house at the right place, die, in the name of Jesus.

33. Father Lord, sponsor me financially to purchase a house at the right place, in the name of Jesus.

34. Any power that is forcing me to buy a house at a wrong place, die, in the name of Jesus.

35. Let my God arise and create an opportunity for me to buy the right house, in the name of Jesus.

36. Any power that has vowed to confine me to my parent's house, die, in the name of Jesus.

37. I receive power to leave my parents and buy a personal house, in the name of Jesus.

38. Any attack that is going on against my business or work, be frustrated, in the name of Jesus.

39. Let household witchcraft powers that have vowed that I will not own a house be disgraced, in the name of Jesus.

40. Any evil altar that has arrested my house spiritually, release it now, in the name of Jesus.

41. I disgrace evil personalities that have vowed that I will never own a house, in the name of Jesus.

42. I discard satanic pressures to buy a house at a wrong place, in the name of Jesus.

43. I break every yoke or bondage upon my life not to buy a personal house, in the name of Jesus.

44. I refuse to do evil in order to prosper before I buy a house, in the name of Jesus.

45. I receive power not to do evil before I buy a house, in the name of Jesus.

46. I refuse to buy a house without involving God fully, in the name of Jesus.

47. I refuse to pack into a house where evil spirits are living, in the name of Jesus.

48. Every enemy of God in the new house I want to buy, vacate by force, in the name of Jesus.

49. Let the hosts of heaven provide and lead me to buy a Christian home, in the name of Jesus.

50. I refuse to get a house on earth that will cause me to miss heaven, in the name of Jesus.

51. Father Lord, help me to buy a house where only You will reign, in the name of Jesus.

52. Father Lord, empower my wife/husband to beautify our new home, in the name of Jesus.

53. Let my home be the habitation of God and His saints on earth, in the name of Jesus.

54. Let my wife, husband and children attract divine presence at home, in the name of Jesus.

55. Let everything that would perfect my home according to God's Word appear by force, in the name of Jesus.

56. Let every enemy of my home be expose and disgraced, in the name of Jesus.

57. I hand over the keys of my new home to God, in the name of Jesus.

58. Any invitation that was given to devil and his agents, I withdraw you, in the name of Jesus.

59. I disgrace any stubborn demon that has vowed not to leave my home to death, in the name of Jesus.

60. Let the beauty of the Lord possess my new home, in the name of Jesus.

61. Any good thing my home is lacking even before I buy it, appear, in the name of Jesus.

62. I bring God, the host of heaven and every good thing into my home before I buy it, in the name of Jesus.

63. Let evil messengers that were assigned to my new home be frustrated, in the name of Jesus.

64. Any satanic giant in my home, die before I buy the house, in the name of Jesus.

65. Let warriors from heaven march into my home before I come in to settle, in the name of Jesus.

66. Let any Cain in my new home die, in the name of Jesus.

67. I destroy every bad thing in my new home, in the name of Jesus.

68. Let any evil in my home face divine defeats, in the name of Jesus.

69. Let the angels of God invade my home before I buy it, in the name of Jesus.

70. Let any Amorite, Canaanite and other Hittites in my home be destroyed, in the name of Jesus.

71. Thou death from God, kill every enemy of my family before I move in with my family, in the name of Jesus.

72. Father Lord, take me into my home without defilement or pollution, in the name of Jesus.

73. Owners of evil load in my home, appear and carry your loads, in the name of Jesus.

74. Let soldiers from heaven conduct a search in my home and chase evil away before my arrival, in the name of Jesus.

75. I refuse to enter into covenant with devil and his agents in my new home, in the name of Jesus.

35 Chapter

PRAYERS TO RECEIVE FINANCIAL MIRACLES

CHAPTER OVERVIEW

- *The purpose of God's blessing*
- *Preparing for financial miracles*
- *Need for spiritual resurrection*

THE PURPOSE OF GOD'S BLESSING

God has established a purpose for blessing His people. The main purpose God blesses His children is to establish His covenant. As it is written, "...*For it is He that giveth thee power to get wealth, that He may establish His covenant which He sware unto thy fathers, as it is this day*" (Deuteronomy 8:18).

Whatever God does, have a purpose attached to it. Sadly, many people that are praying for financial breakthrough, help, miracles and blessings have no idea of the purpose of God's blessings. That is why some people are not receiving answers to their prayers.

I have come across believers that were praying for financial miracles without having plans of what to do when finances come. Human beings would also ensure that their financial help is worthwhile and well accounted for. You may be a good Christian but if you do not have a good plan on how to invest your money, God may not answer your prayers no matter how much fasting and prayers you observe.

> "*Likewise, I say unto you, there is joy in the presence of the angels of God over one sinner that repented. And he said, a certain man had two sons: and the younger of them said to his father, Father, gives me the portion of goods that falleth to me. In addition, he divided unto them his living. And not many days after the younger son gathered all together, and took his journey into a far country, and there wasted his substance with riotous living. And when he had spent all, there arose a mighty famine in that land; and he began to be in want. And he went and joined himself to a citizen of that country; and he sent him into his fields to feed swine. And he would fain have filled his belly with the husks that the swine did eat: and no man gave unto him*" (Luke 15:10-16).

God cannot give you what you cannot use very well no matter how much pressure you put on Him. The prodigal son had no experience and plans on how to use his portion of wealth. Yet, he insisted for it until his father divided his wealth and gave him his portion. He traveled to a far country and wasted his substance through riotous living. If it were not for God's grace, he would have died in his suffering and poverty.

God is ready to bless you and answer all your prayers but you must be experienced and have plans on how to invest. He could be delaying your prayers purposely to see if you would come up with a plan or trust Him for a plan. Many people who are praying for financial help or miracles must convince God that they are ready to invest. Then after your prayers, you have to wait for God's time for the manifestation of the answers to your prayers.

The prodigal son acquired a huge experience after wrecking his life. A wise man learns from the mistakes of others. Otherwise, he repeats the same mistakes. Make plans on how to invest your finances and when you convince God, He releases your heart desire and bless you financially.

> *"And when he came to himself, he said, How many hired servants of my father's have bread enough and to spare, and I perish with hunger! I will arise and go to my father, and will say unto him, Father, I have sinned against heaven, and before thee, And is no more worthy to be called thy son: make me as one of thy hired servants. And he arose, and came to his father. However, when he was yet a great way off, his father saw him, had compassion, ran, fell on his neck, and kissed him. And the son said unto him, Father, I have sinned against heaven, and in thy sight, and am no more worthy to be called thy son"* (Luke 15:17-21).

Without adequate preparations, answers to your prayers may not be released until you have a good plan on how to use God's blessings.

> *"For which of you, intending to build a tower, sitteth not down first, and counteth the cost, whether he has sufficient to finish it? Lest haply, after he hath laid the foundation, and is not able to finish it, all that behold it begin to mock him, Saying, This man began to build, and was not able to finish"* (Luke 14:28-30).

Jesus taught His disciples the need for diligent preparation. He taught them how needful it was to sit down and count the cost of everything they wanted to do before doing them. God knows that devil is still fighting believers in the world. When you look at the majority of people around you, you will sense that most people are under the control and influence of the devil.

Devil can give someone wealth as long as he would use it to serve him. Do not lust after people that throw money around. When you see someone who got his wealth from God, you will know. Likewise, you will know someone who got his wealth from devil. Where they spend their money and how they spend it and the company they keep would hint the source of their wealth.

> *"Behold, the heaven and the heaven of heavens is the LORD'S thy God, the earth also, with all that therein is"* (Deuteronomy 10:14).

> *"The land shall not be sold forever: for the land is mine; for ye are strangers and sojourners with me"* (Leviticus 25:23).

> *"But who am I, and what is my people, that we should be able to offer so willingly after this sort? For all things come of thee and of thine own have we given thee"* (1 Chronicles 29:14).

God is the owner of the universe. He has planned how the universe would be. Because the devil's chief work is to oppose God, he steals wealth and gives to his agents to use them contrary to God's wish. Nevertheless, if you want to get blessings from God, you must be prepared to use God's blessing to His glory alone. That is why you cannot conform to the standards of the world.

You must be willing at all times to offer whatever you received from God back to Him the way He wants, not how you want. That was the problem that God had with Cain. He sacrificed to God on his own terms and God rejected his sacrifice.

> *"But unto Cain and to his offering he had not respected. In addition, Cain was very wroth, and his countenance fell. And the LORD said unto Cain, Why art thou wroth? In addition, why is thy countenance fallen? If thou doest well, shalt thou not be accepted? In addition, if thou do not well, sin lieth at the door. In addition, unto thee shall be his desire, and thou shalt rule over him. And Cain talked with Abel his brother: and it came to pass, when they were in the field, that Cain rose up against Abel his brother, and slew him"* (Genesis 4:5-8).

Whatever you receive from God belongs to God. Therefore, you must be willing at all times to listen to Him and discover how to offer those things back to His glory.

> *"The earth is the LORD'S, and the fullness thereof; the world, and they that dwell therein"* (Psalms 24:1).

> *"For every beast of the forest is mine, and the cattle upon a thousand hills"* (Psalms 50:10).

> *"According to the word that I covenanted with you when ye came out of Egypt, so my spirit remained among you: fear ye not"* (Haggai 2:5).

> *"For the earth is the Lord's, and the fullness thereof"* (1 Corinthians 10:26).

The earth and all the people living on it belong to God. Naturally, no one has any right to use anything on earth without God's permission. He owns the universe. Nevertheless, God is willing to bless His children and prosper them above others. It is also important to understand that none of God's blessings or prosperity should be used to glorify self or the devil. When you get this right and are willing to obey, God will give you financial miracles to prosper you.

People are continuously performing evil sacrifices all over the world using animals that should glorify God.

> *"1And Balaam said unto Balak, Build me here seven altars, and prepare me here seven oxen and seven rams. 2And Balak did as Balaam had spoken; and Balak and*

Balaam offered on every altar a bullock and a ram. [3]And Balaam said unto Balak, Stand by thy burnt offering, and I will go: peradventure the LORD will come to meet me: and whatsoever he sheweth me I will tell thee. In addition, he went to a high place. [13]And Balak said unto him, Come, I pray thee, with me unto another place, from whence thou mayest see them: thou shalt see but the utmost part of them, and shalt not see them all: and curse me them from thence. [14]And he brought him into the field of Zophim, to the top of Pisgah, built seven altars, and offered a bullock and a ram on every altar. [27]And Balak said unto Balaam, Come, I pray thee, I will bring thee unto another place; peradventure it will please God that thou mayest curse me them from thence. [28]And Balak brought Balaam unto the top of Poor that looked toward Jeshimon. [29]And Balaam said unto Balak, Build me here seven altars, and prepare me here seven bullocks and seven rams. [30]And Balak did as Balaam had said, and offered a bullock and a ram on every altar" (Numbers 23:1-3, 13-14, 27-30).

Ignorantly, such people offer sacrifices to devil, who takes over their lives and empowers them to do more evil. This is sad. The worst is that people have departed so much from God that they offer their souls that God created in His image to devil in exchange for wealth. How sad!

"Do ye thus requite the LORD, O foolish people and unwise? Is not he thy father that hath bought thee? Hath he not made thee, and established thee?" (Deuteronomy 32:6).

"And he caused his children to pass through the fire in the valley of the son of Hinnom: also he observed times, and used enchantments, and used witchcraft, and dealt with a familiar spirit, and with wizards: he wrought much evil in the sight of the LORD, to provoke him to anger" (2 Chronicles 33:6).

I do not think God would bless you when He knows that you will not use your blessings to glorify Him. Positions, wealth and the good things of life are the inheritance of all believers. Sadly, most believers are not ready or prepared to use their blessings well.

God may decide to shut the doors of financial blessings if He knows that such blessing would make His children lose their souls. That is the reason why many believers suffer today. God is searching for true and sincere believers who will serve Him and use His blessings to bless others and win lost souls back to Him.

"But know that the LORD hath set apart him that is godly for himself: the LORD will hear when I call unto him" (Psalms 4:3).

"My beloved is *mine, and I* am *his: he feuded among the lilies"* (Songs of Solomon 2:16).

"[7]Even every one that is called by my name: for I have created him for my glory, I have formed him; yea, I have made him. [21]This people have I formed for myself; they shall shew forth my praise" (Isaiah 43:7, 21).

"For whether we live, we live unto the Lord; and whether we die, we die unto the Lord: whether we live therefore, or die, we are the Lord's" (Romans 14:8).

God has prepared all blessings His children would need. So, if you are not ready to compromise your faith, He can go to any extent to bless you. Every believer belongs to God by creation and by redemption. We also belong to God because He watches over our lives and preserves us all.

"And the word of the LORD came unto him, saying, Arise, get thee to Zarephath, which belonged to Zion, and dwell there: behold, I have commanded a widow woman there to sustain thee. So he arose and went to Zarephath. And when he came to the gate of the city, behold, the widow woman was there gathering of sticks: and he called to her, and said, Fetch me, I pray thee, a little water in a vessel that I may drink. And as she was going to fetch it, he called to her, and said, Bring me, I pray thee, a morsel of bread in thine hand. And she said, As the LORD thy God liveth, I have not a cake, but an handful of meal in a barrel, and a little oil in a cruise: and, behold, I am gathering two sticks, that I may go in and dress it for me and my son, that we may eat it, and die. And Elijah said unto her, Fear not; go and do as thou hast said: but make me thereof a little cake first, and bring it unto me, and after make for thee and for thy son. For thus saith the LORD God of Israel, the barrel of meal shall not waste, neither shall the cruse of oil fail, until the day that the LORD sendeth rain upon the earth. And she went and did according to the saying of Elijah: and she, and he, and her house, did eat many days. And the barrel of meal wasted not, neither did the curse of oil fail, according to the word of the LORD, which he spake by Elijah" (1 Kings 17:8-16).

"But seek ye first the kingdom his righteousness; and all these things shall be added unto you" (Matthew 6:33).

"But ye are a chosen generation, a royal priesthood, an holy nation, a peculiar people; that ye should show forth the praises of him who hath called you out of darkness into his marvelous light" (1 Peter 2:9).

God rules over everything in heaven and on earth because He created all things. He rules our lives because He created and redeemed us. That is why while unbelievers spend their time serving the devil, believers must spend their time to serve God alone. You must dedicate your time, money, talent, gift and life to God.

PREPARING FOR FINANCIAL MIRACLES

Diligent Christians understand the principle and benefits of preparation. Every good cause demands adequate preparation and planning. Trusting God for financial miracles and prosperity are not left out. They also require some preparation. The best way to start is to return to your original estate, which is in Christ Jesus. That is the surest way to attain a godly financial breakthrough.

> *"If ye then be risen with Christ, seek those things which are above, where Christ sitteth on the right hand of God. Set your affection on things above, not on things on the earth. For ye are dead and your life is hid with Christ in God. When Christ, who is our life, shall appear, and then shall ye also appear with him in glory"* (Colossians 3:1-4).

God made man from the dust of the earth and breathed life into him, which was the Spirit of God. Sadly, man fell from grace when he disobeyed God and since that time, man's natural tendency is to seek after earthly things without God who created him. That is why things keep getting worse.

> *"The wicked, through the pride of his countenance, will not seek after God: God is not in all his thoughts"* (Psalms 10:4).

> *"For all seek their own, not the things which are Jesus Christ's"* (Philippians 2:21).

> *"And he hath brought thee near to him and all thy brethren the sons of Levi with thee: and seek ye the priesthood also?"* (Numbers 16:10).

> *"And it came to pass, when he heard that I lifted up my voice and cried, that he left his garment with me, and fled, and got him out"* (Genesis 39:15).

Christ is the one who has the power to regenerate man and renew his affection and ambition that would be acceptable in the sight of God. Otherwise, man would remain under devil's structure, seeking fame, financial prosperity, fashion and pleasure without God.

NEED FOR SPIRITUAL RESURRECTION

If there is no spiritual resurrection, your affection, ambition and quest for fame, money and pleasures remain corrupt. You must be crucified with Christ and die with Him before your ambition for financial miracles, fame and quest for anything on earth would be meaningful.

> *"I am crucified with Christ: nevertheless I live; yet not I, but Christ lived in me: and the life which I now live in the flesh I live by the faith of the Son of God, who loved me, and gave himself for me"* (Galatians 2:20).

> *"For if we have been planted together in the likeness of his death, we shall be also in the likeness of his resurrection: Knowing this, that our old man is crucified with him, that the body of sin might be destroyed, that henceforth we should not serve sin. For he that is dead is freed from sin. Now if we be dead with Christ, we believe that we shall also live with him"* (Romans 6:5-8).

When you repent and give your life to Christ, you are raised with Jesus in resurrection. Your desires would be heaven-bound because you see yourself as a citizen of heaven. This will differentiate your desires from those who are not born-again. You will be motivated to seek God first before seeking other things. You will realize that God is in control.

A genuine Christian will happily cast off earthly ambitions and desires and reject any evil condition attached to anything such person wants. That is when you are able to enjoy wealth when it comes because there is no sorrow attached to it. God is involved fully and is ready to defend, protect and preserve all blessings you receive from Him.

> *"I would seek unto God, and unto God would I commit my cause"* (Job 5:8).

> *"But seek ye first the kingdom of God, and his righteousness; and all these things shall be added unto you"* (Matthew 6:33).

> *"For they that say such things declare plainly that they seek a country. And truly, if they had been mindful of that country from whence they came out, they might have had opportunity to return. But now they desire a better country, that is, a heavenly: wherefore God is not ashamed to be called their God: for the hath prepared for them a city"* (Hebrews 11:14-16).

> *"For here have we no continuing city, but we seek one to come"* (Hebrews 13:14).

Believers who received financial blessing and other blessings from God always seek for the welfare of God's people. They are always preoccupied with Christ and heaven.

They are not wasteful because they return whatever they have to God and render their accounts faithfully.

> *"Let us walk honestly, as in the day; not in rioting and drunkenness, not in chambering and wantonness, not in strife and envying. But put ye on the Lord Jesus Christ, and make not provision for the flesh, to fulfill the lusts thereof"* (Romans 13:13-14).

> *"Whether therefore ye eat, or drink, or whatsoever ye do, do all to the glory of God"* (1 Corinthians 10:31).

> *"See then that ye walk circumspectly, not as fools, but as wise, Redeeming the time, because the days are evil"* (Ephesians 5:15-16).

They walk with God having eternity in view. Such people do not riot or engage in envy, strife and drunkenness. They do not give room for flesh to manifest its fruits in their lives to fulfill its lusts. They do everything to the glory of God.

They avoid doing foolish things. Instead, they redeem the time knowing that the days are evil. They commit their ways unto the Lord and wait patiently for God's time while seeking for His kingdom. Regarding not their personal challenges, they seek the welfare of God's people everywhere they go.

Children of God who are determined to experience financial miracles yield their lives to the Lord without reservation and keep themselves from profane things. They know how to trust the Lord at all times and keep receiving blessing from the Him always.

> *"I beseech you therefore, brethren, by the mercies of God, that ye present your bodies a living sacrifice, holy, acceptable unto God, which is your reasonable service. And be not conformed to this world: but be ye transformed by the renewing of your mind, that ye may prove what is that good, and acceptable, and perfect, will of God"* (Romans 12:1-2).

> *"And then shall many be offended, and shall betray one another, and shall hate one another. And many false prophets shall rise, and shall deceive many. And because iniquity shall abound, the love of many shall wax cold. But he that shall endure unto the end, the same shall be saved"* (Matthew 24:10-13).

Circumstances that surround believers' lives do not affect their love for God. They do not consider immediate benefit to render service to God. They yield their lives to doing God's will in times of difficulties, trials, joy and prosperity. They took up their crosses and followed Christ.

"Then said Jesus unto his disciples, If any man will come after me, let him deny himself, and take up his cross, and follow me. For whosoever will save his life shall lose it: and whosoever will lose his life for my sake shall find it" (Matthew 16:24-25).

"And he that taketh not his cross, and followed after me, is not worthy of me" (Matthew 10:38).

It is a good thing to surrender your plans and vision to God at all times, no matter the circumstance. Do not seek to please the flesh or allow things of this world to control you. Give up anything that stands against the glory of God in your life. Learn to take a stand for God even when you are under pressure and enduring persecution.

"And he said unto his sons, Saddle me the ass. Therefore, they saddled him the ass: and he rode thereon, And went after the man of God, and found him sitting under an oak and he said unto him, Art thou the man of God that camest from Judah? In addition, he said, I am. Then he said unto him, Come home with me, and eat bread. And he said, I may not return with thee, nor go in with thee: neither will I eat bread nor drink water with thee in this place: For it was said to me by the word of the LORD, Thou shalt eat no bread nor drink water there, nor turn again to go by the way that thou camest. He said unto him, I am a prophet also as thou art; and an angel spake unto me by the word of the LORD, saying, Bring him back with thee into thine house, that he may eat bread and drink water. However, he lied unto him. So he went back with him, and did eat bread in his house, and drank water" (1 Kings 13:13-19).

"Then said his wife unto him; dost thou still retain thine integrity? Curse God, and die. But he said unto her, Thou speakest as one of the foolish women speaketh. What? Shall we receive well at the hand of God, and shall we not receive evil? In all this did not Job sin with his lips" (Job 2:9-10).

Problems or chastisements do not make true believers to modify or remodel their trust for God. They pursue victory over sin, sickness and poverty daily as if those battles determine their destiny. Even while fighting, they are conscious of God's presence.

"And she said, Behold, thy sister in law is gone back unto her people, and unto her gods: return thou after thy sister in law. And Ruth said, Entreat me not to leave thee, or to return from following after thee: for whither thou goest, I will go; and where thou lodgest, I will lodge: thy people shall be my people, and thy God my God: Where thou diest, will I die, and there will I be buried: the LORD do so to me, and more also, if ought but death part thee and me. When she saw that she was steadfastly minded to go with her, then she left speaking unto her" (Ruth 1:15-18).

"That I may know him, and the power of his resurrection, and the fellowship of his sufferings, being made conformable unto his death; If by any means I might attain

unto the resurrection of the dead. Not as though I had already attained, either were already perfect: but I follow after, if that I may apprehend that for which also I am apprehended of Christ Jesus. Brethren, I count not myself to have apprehended: but this one thing I do, forgetting those things which are behind, and reaching forth unto those things which are before, I press toward the mark for the prize of the high calling of God in Christ Jesus" (Philippians 3:10-14).

Problems that force ordinary to change their minds and convictions about God do not have any influence on genuine believers. They are determined to offer their lives to please God. Regardless of what is persuading them to return to *Egypt*, they cannot succumb to pressures. Their conviction about God is firmly rooted.

Genuine Christians take the people of God as brethren because salvation brought them into God's family. They die and resurrect with Christ and abide in Him forever and ever. They pursue God's knowledge every day, experiencing the suffering of Jesus, and are willing to carry the mandate of His suffering to all the corners of the earth. No matter how perfect and holy they are, they are never satisfied because they want to attain God's perfection. They pursue to reach the high level with holiness and press forward for the best in everything they do.

"And every man that striveth for the mastery is temperate in all things. Now they do it to obtain a corruptible crown; but we can incorruptible. I therefore so run, not as uncertainly; so fight I, not as one that beateth the air: But I keep under my body, and bring it into subjection: lest that by any means, when I have preached to others, I myself should be a castaway" (1 Corinthians 9:25-27).

"Are they Hebrews? So am I. Are they Israelites? So am I. Are they the seed of Abraham? So am I. Are they ministers of Christ. (I speak as a fool) I am more; in labors more abundant, in stripes above measure, in prisons more frequent, in deaths oft. Of the Jews five times received I forty stripes save one. Thrice was I beaten with rods, once was I stoned, thrice I suffered shipwreck, a night and a day I have been in the deep; In journeying often, in perils of waters, in perils of robbers, in perils by mine own countrymen, in perils by the heathen, in perils in the city, in perils in the wilderness, in perils in the sea, in perils among false brethren; In weariness and painfulness, in watchings often, in hunger and thirst, in fastings often, in cold and nakedness. Beside those things that are without, that which cometh upon me daily, the care of all the churches. Who is weak, and I am not weak? Who is offended, and I burn not?" (2 Corinthians 11:22-29).

"Wherefore seeing we also are compassed about with so great a cloud of witnesses, let us lay aside every weight, and the sin which doth so easily beset us, and let us run with patience the race that is set before us, Looking unto Jesus the author and finisher

of our faith; who for the joy that was set before him endured the cross, despising the shame, and is set down at the right hand of the throne of God" (Hebrews 12:1-2).

They fight with weapons of prayer and righteousness, striving for God's best, to obtain an incorruptible crown. They do not move until they see God move ahead of them and not even the confrontations from the devil and death can compel them to take action against God and His Word. They bring every fleshly or physical desire under subjugation to obey the leading of the Holy Ghost.

God does not delay in blessing such people with financial miracles and prosperity that will glorify His name. Such Christians are constant in their purpose to serve God, and are disciplined to reach their divine destination. They work so hard as well. They can move into the snow to harvest what they have sowed that is about to be wasted.

Such Christians can give up position or respect and take up any journey or pay any price to glorify the name of the Lord, if what they are expected to do would please God and glorify His name. They despise class distinctions, racial restrictions, and confront all limitations to obey God's instructions. They have deep desire for the type of compassion Christ had that compelled Jesus to sacrifice all that was necessary for the salvation of humanity. They embark on fervent praying, tireless journeys, shed tears, undergo hardships and endure pains to do God's will. Their crowns are secured in heaven.

Let consider Joseph. His brothers heated him without any reasonable cause. Yet, his dreams of greatness came true despite all horrible attempts to stop him. His life is a model of faithfulness and total surrender to God, even in hard times.

"1And Joseph was brought down to Egypt; and Potiphar, an officer of Pharaoh, captain of the guard, an Egyptian, bought him of the hands of the Ishmeelites, which had brought him down thither. 2And the LORD was with Joseph, and he was a prosperous man; and he was in the house of his master the Egyptian. 3And his master saw that the LORD was with him, and that the LORD made all that he did to prosper in his hand. 4And Joseph found grace in his sight, and he served him: and he made him overseer over his house, and all that he had he put into his hand. 5And it came to pass from the time that he had made him overseer in his house, and over all that he had, that the LORD blessed the Egyptian's house for Joseph's sake; and the blessing of the LORD was upon all that he had in the house, and in the field. 6And he left all that he had in Joseph's hand; and he knew not ought he had, save the bread, which he did eat. In addition, Joseph was a goodly person, and well favored. 20And Joseph's master took him, and put him into the prison, a place where the king's prisoners were bound: and he was there in the prison. 21But the LORD was with Joseph, and shewed him mercy, and gave him favor in the sight of the keeper of the prison. 22And the keeper of the prison committed to Joseph's hand all the prisoners

that were in the prison; and whatsoever they did there, he was the doer of it. [23]*The keeper of the prison looked not to anything that was under his hand; because the LORD was with him, and that which he did, the LORD made it to prosper"* (Genesis 39:1-6; 20-23).

Joseph was victorious through temptations, godly in times of sudden promotion and prosperity. His exalted promotion never made him to refocus or to remodel his life. He remained faithful and obedient to God. He was a hard working believer everywhere he went. He served God, pleased Him and stood for the truth in the midst of hatred, rejection, temptation and imprisonment without fair trials. As a prisoner, he never denied God. He believed in God, remained faithful, worked hard in every environment, seeking nothing but the glory of God. He never allowed adverse conditions around him to make him question or forget God.

"Flee fornication. Every sin that a man doeth is without the body; but he that committed fornication sinneth against his own body" (1 Corinthians 6:18).

"Dearly beloved, I beseech you as strangers and pilgrims, abstain from fleshly lusts, which war against the soul; Having your conversation honest among the Gentiles: that, whereas they speak against you as evildoers, they may by your good works, which they shall behold, glorify God in the day of visitation" (1 Peter 2:11-12).

He was tempted but was not overcome. God is looking for people like Joseph in our generation to prosper them not only financially but in every aspect of life. He is looking for people who will flee fornication, and all manner of sexual perversions in this generation. God is looking for people whose hearts are after righteousness at all cost. He wants to prosper such people in our generation. He is searching for people who are consistent in serving Him, to empower them with the nine gifts of the Holy Ghost to overturn human failures globally.

God is searching for men who are holy with excellent spirit. He is looking for people He would empower and send to the world. God is searching for men who will represent Him before the heathen and overthrow their god's and dragons. He is looking for a man whose heart is perfect towards Him; who will conduct notable meetings to deliver the oppressed from every kind of bondage. He needs renewed men, who are clothed with humility, wise as serpents, harmless as doves, simple as children, compassionate as the Savior, strong in faith and not staggering at the promises of God.

"[37]*And the thing was good in the eyes of Pharaoh, and in the eyes of all his servants.* [38]*And Pharaoh said unto his servants, Can we find such a one as this is, a man in whom the Spirit of God is?* [39]*And Pharaoh said unto Joseph, Forasmuch as God hath shewed thee all this, there is none so discreet and wise as thou art:* [40]*Thou shalt be over my house, and according unto thy word shall all my people be ruled: only in the*

throne will I be greater than thou. [41]And Pharaoh said unto Joseph, See, I have set thee over all the land of Egypt. [45]And Pharaoh called Joseph's name Zaphnath–paaneah; and he gave him to wife Asenath the daughter of Poti–pherah priest of on. In addition, Joseph went out over all the land of Egypt. [46]And Joseph was thirty years old when he stood before Pharaoh King of Egypt. Moreover, Joseph went out from the presence of Pharaoh, and went throughout all the land of Egypt. [47]And in the seven plenteous years the earth brought forth by handfuls. [48]And he gathered up all the food of the seven years, which were in the land of Egypt, and laid up the food in the cities: the food of the field, which was round about every city, laid him up in the same. [49]And Joseph gathered corn as the sand of the sea, very much, until he left numbering; for it was without number" (Genesis 41:37-41, 45-49).

When God found Joseph, He did not hesitate to use him. He brought him out of the prison and gave him an exalted promotion. Knowing that sudden promotions often resulted in sudden falls, God knew Joseph and yet trusted him. Joseph became a man of honor and a prosperous prince in a foreign land. Joseph succeeded in every aspect of life and pleased God in all aspects.

As a prince in Egypt, he was a good planner, an organizer, an industrialist and a great leader. God is looking for men with that kind of spirit who will not waste His blessings with riotous people in strange lands. He wants men who are really approved unto Him, workers that will not be disgraced by strange Delilah's and Jezebels of our generation, or be put to shame by corruptions; men clothed with divine authority and faith in God. Such men have faith in prayers to lock and unlock, to bind and loose.

"This is the generation of them that seek him that seek thy face, O Jacob. Selah. Lift up your heads, O ye gates; and be ye lift up, ye everlasting doors; and the King of glory shall come in. Who is this King of glory. The LORD strong and mighty, the LORD mighty in battle. Lift up your heads, O ye gates; even lift them up, ye everlasting doors; and the King of glory shall come in. Who is this King of glory. The LORD of hosts, he is the King of glory. Selah" (Psalms 24:6-10).

God is challenging our generation to present to Him men He would use to bless the rest of the world. He wants a man whose soul is strongly longing for Him, whose eyes are focused on God. He wants faithful people that would be presidents, governors, industrialists, and people He would place as managers all over the world to manage the earth to His glory. God is after your heart.

"[26]If any man come to me, and hate not his father, and mother, and wife, and children, and brethren, and sisters, yea, and his own life also, he cannot be my disciple. [29]Lest haply, after he hath laid the foundation, and is not able to finish it, all that behold it begin to mock him, [30]Saying, This man began to build, and was not able to finish. [31]Or what king, going to make war against another king, sitteth not

down first, and consulteth whether he is able with ten thousand to meet him that cometh against him with twenty thousand? [32]*Or else, while the other is yet a great way off, he sendeth an ambassage, and desireth conditions of peace.* [33]*So likewise, whosoever he be of you that forsaketh not all that he hath, he cannot be my disciple"* (Luke 14:26, 29-33).

"Likewise, ye younger, submit you unto the elder. Yea, all of you be subject one to another, and be clothed with humility: for God resisteth the proud, and giveth grace to the humble" (1 Peter 5:5).

"And Elijah went to shew himself unto Ahab. In addition, there was a sore famine in Samaria. And Ahab called Obadiah, which was the governor of his house. (Now Obadiah feared the LORD greatly: For it was so, when Jezebel cut off the prophets of the LORD, that Obadiah took an hundred prophets, and hid them by fifty in a cave, and fed them with bread and water" (1 Kings 18:2-4).

The blessed Holy Trinity and all the angels in heaven are looking for righteous men. They are looking for people who will shun corruption and lust of the flesh, and focus on how to set the captives free. Are you willing to be empowered so that you can be busy always to do God's business? Are you ready to be purged, cleansed, inflamed, renewed, sanctified and anointed to be the richest man on earth and use your wealth to God's glory?

Are you ready to pray in secret, search for purity and preach the truth? Are you ready to be sound in divine principles and carry this holy fire to the end? If you prepare yourself today and pray, God will answer you. Determine the area of your life that you want God to prosper in and you will be prosperous. God is waiting for you. Be sure of your salvation and true relationship with God.

PRAYERS TO RECEIVE FINANCIAL MIRACLES

Bible references: Haggai 2:8; Deuteronomy 10:14; Psalms 24:1, 50:10

Begin with praise and worship

1. Father Lord, deliver me from enemies of my financial breakthrough, in the name of Jesus.
2. Blood of Jesus, speak financial miracles into my life, in the name of Jesus.
3. Let yoke of financial predicaments in my life break forever, in the name of Jesus.
4. Any strange fire that is consuming my financial breakthrough, quench, in the name of Jesus.
5. O Lord, direct me to a project that would bring financial success, in the name of Jesus.
6. Lord Jesus, prepare me for financial miracles, in the name of Jesus.
7. I bind and cast out the spirit of waste and evil diversion from my life, in the name of Jesus.
8. Father Lord, help me to use the much You have given me already well, in the name of Jesus.
9. I receive power to manage wealth and prosper exceedingly, in the name of Jesus.
10. Let evil sacrifices and curses that want to destroy my life expire, in the name of Jesus.
11. I destroy any evil power that wants to influence me, in the name of Jesus.
12. I disgrace every enemy of my financial breakthrough, in the name of Jesus.
13. Let God guide my affections, in the name of Jesus.
14. O Lord, help me to spend my money with eternity in view, in the name of Jesus.
15. Let worldly desires that were assigned to waste my money be frustrated, in the name of Jesus.
16. O Lord, help me to know Your plan for my finances, in the name of Jesus.

17. O Lord, help me to use my finances to run my Christian race and obtain an incorruptible crown, in the name of Jesus.

18. Father Lord, give me dumbfounding financial miracles this year, in the name of Jesus.

19. Every demon of embarrassment and lack in my life, I cast you out, in the name of Jesus.

20. Let the yoke of financial bondage in my life beak, in the name of Jesus.

21. Every satanic embargo on my finance is lifted, in the name of Jesus.

22. I arrest and destroy every demon of financial poverty in my life, in the name of Jesus.

23. Any evil power that wants to paralyze my potentials with plaques of financial handicap, die, in the name of Jesus.

24. O Lord, send money into my account from the bank of heaven, in the name of Jesus.

25. Open the storehouse of heaven for my financial breakthrough, in the name of Jesus.

26. I command the windows of heaven to open for my sake today, in the name of Jesus.

27. Father Lord, pour Your financial blessings in my life by fire, in the name of Jesus.

28. I receive power to give to God and others the way God demands, in the name of Jesus.

29. Every devourer that is attacking my finance, die, in the name of Jesus.

30. Lord Jesus, command men to rise and bless me, in the name of Jesus.

31. Every demonic hindrance on my financial prosperity is removed by force, in the name of Jesus.

32. Angels of the living God, break into every demonic bank and release my money, in the name of Jesus.

33. Any strongman that has confiscated my money, release it and die, in the name of Jesus.

34. Let my financial possession in captivity be release to me today, in the name of Jesus.

35. I gather my finances that are scattered all over the places, in the name of Jesus.

36. O Lord, favor me exceedingly by Your mercy with financial miracles, in the name of Jesus.

37. I dismantle evil roadblocks that are mounted for my financial breakthrough, in the name of Jesus.

38. Lord Jesus, remove strange finances that are in my possession, in the name of Jesus.

39. Father Lord, bless me with a multimillion-business idea, in the name of Jesus.

40. Any evil personality that is sitting upon my finances, die, in the name of Jesus.

41. Any satanic department that is holding my finances, release them by force, in the name of Jesus.

42. Let my finances be too hot for devil to touch, in the name of Jesus.

43. Let money begin to come into my life from multiple sources, in the name of Jesus.

44. I open multiple doors for my financial miracles, in the name of Jesus.

45. Let any demon that opposes my financial miracle die, in the name of Jesus.

46. I reject evil and financial failures to prevail in my life, in the name of Jesus.

47. Every ungodly delay to my financial miracles is terminated, in the name of Jesus.

48. Let the angels of God roll away stones that are holding my financial breakthrough, in the name of Jesus.

49. Enemies of my financial miracles, I cut your heads off, in the name of Jesus.

50. Any demon of poverty on suicide mission in my life, die alone, in the name of Jesus.

51. Let financial demons that are dragging me towards failure die, in the name of Jesus.

52. Every evil force that is gathering against my financial miracles, scatter in disgrace, in the name of Jesus.

53. Any arrow of financial death that was fired at my finance, backfire, in the name of Jesus.

54. Let the path to my financial miracles clear now, in the name of Jesus.

55. Any strange fire that is burning my finances, quench, in the name of Jesus.

56. I command every instrument of financial lack in my life to catch fire and burn to ashes, in the name of Jesus.

57. O Lord, help me to experience financial miracles in my life every day, in the name of Jesus.

58. Lord, empower me to prosper financially by Your grace, in the name of Jesus.

59. Father Lord, bulldoze my way to financial breakthrough by force, in the name of Jesus.

60. Let demon of financial destruction bow before me, in the name of Jesus.

61. I tear down financial obstacles in my life, in the name of Jesus.

62. Let witchcraft animals vomit my finances, in the name of Jesus.

63. Lord Jesus, empower me to excel above others financially, in the name of Jesus.

36

Chapter

PRAYERS FOR CHRISTMAS

CHAPTER OVERVIEW

- *Another Christmas is approaching*
- *The origin of Christmas*
- *Rejection and acceptance*
- *The spirit of Christmas*
- *Christian lifestyle during Christmas*

ANOTHER CHRISTMAS IS APPROACHING

Whether you like it or not, Christmas has come to stay in our spiritual consciousness. It has become paramount to discuss the issue of Christmas because most people are misinformed and do not understand the true meaning of Christmas. It is very unfortunate that people who observe Christmas do not know the true meaning of Christmas or its purpose.

Christmas has become an international and interdenominational feast that virtually everybody in the world observes. Many people bow down to the devil during the time of Christmas without knowing it.

> *"Nebuchadnezzar the king made an image of gold, whose height was threescore cubits, and the breadth thereof six cubits: he set it up in the plain of Dura, in the province of Babylon. Then Nebuchadnezzar the king sent to gather together the princes, the governors, and the captains, the judges, the treasurers, the counselors, the sheriffs, and all the rulers of the provinces, to come to the dedication of the image which Nebuchadnezzar the king had set up. Then the princes, the governors, and captains, the judges, the treasurers, the counselors, the sheriffs, and all the rulers of the provinces, were gathered together unto the dedication of the image that Nebuchadnezzar the king had set up; and they stood before the image that Nebuchadnezzar had set up"* (Daniel 3:1-3).

During the time of Nebuchadnezzar, the king of Babylon, he made an image of gold and gave a commandment that everyone in the world must worship his idol. All the people in authority, princes, governors, captains, judges, etc. consented and began to bow down to Nebuchadnezzar's idol and it became a universal worship.

Have you ever asked yourself why it is during the period of Christmas that crimes and all manner of unimaginable atrocities are committed? Have you asked why Christmas is always a period of mass deaths or why it is a period of increased sexual immoralities all over the world? It has been observed that cultism increase to its highest levels at Christmas. It has become a time for excessive speeding by land, air and sea travelers all over the world. Many people and things are forced to move during Christmas periods. It is also an opportunity for price hiking of goods and services, cheating and gambling.

> *"And Lot went up out of Zoar, and dwelt in the mountain, and his two daughters with him; for he feared to dwell in Zoar: and he dwelt in a cave, he and his two daughters. And the firstborn said unto the younger, Our father is old, and there is not a man in the earth to come in unto us after the manner of all the earth: Come, let*

us make our father drink wine, and we will lie with him, that we may preserve seed of our father. And they made their father drink wine that night: and the firstborn went in, and lay with her father; and he perceived not when she lay down, nor when she arose. And it came to pass on the morrow, that the firstborn said unto the younger, Behold, I lay yester night with my father: let us make him drink wine this night also; and go thou in, and lie with him, that we may preserve seed of our father. And they made their father drink wine that night also: and the younger arose, and lay with him; and he perceived not when she lay down, nor when she arose. Thus were both the daughters of Lot with child by their father. And the firstborn bare a son, and called his name Moab: the same is the father of the Moabites unto this day. And the younger, she also bare a son, and called his name Ben–ammi: the same is the father of the children of Ammon unto this day" (Genesis 19:30-38).

Christmas periods are times when people force their parents, friends and enemies to drink to stupor. It is a time of drunkenness, misdeeds and reckless sexual perversions. It is a time to spread venereal diseases. The spirit behind Christmas is evil and very destructive.

THE ORIGIN OF CHRISTMAS

The new Lexicon Webster's encyclopedia described Christmas as the annual festival observed by Christians on December 25, commemorating the birth of Jesus Christ. It is also described as the period before and after December 25, the birthday of Jesus Christ. Jesus Christ was not actually born December 25.

Why then are Christians celebrating it as His birthday? One will conclude that Christmas is possibly a mixture of paganism and Christianity because Christmas is made up of two words, *Christ* and *mass*.

Paul warned Christians in Colossian to beware of backslidden philosophizers who would manipulate the faith in Christ with vain or unnecessary deceits, which are after the tradition of men or the way the worldly people do things.

> *"Beware lest any man spoil you through philosophy and vain deceit, after the tradition of men, after the rudiments of the world, and not after Christ. For in him dwelled all the fullness of the Godhead bodily. And ye are complete in him, which is the head of all principality and power"* (Colossians 2:8-10).

He told them not to shift from Christ's teachings or allow deceivers to add or subtract because those who are in Christ are complete. He taught that they do not need any tradition, worldliness or observation of any law or feast to be complete as Christians.

> *"16Let no man therefore judge you in meat, or in drink, or in respect of an holyday, or of the new moon, or of the Sabbath days: 18Let no man beguile you of your reward in a voluntary humility and worshipping of angels, intruding into those things which he hath not seen, vainly puffed up by his fleshly mind, 20Wherefore if ye be dead with Christ from the rudiments of the world, why, as though living in the world, are ye subject to ordinances, 21Touch not; taste not; handle not"* (Colossians 2:16; 18; 20-21).

Therefore, any feast that does not encourage people to repent and live a holy life must not be allowed to continue to destroy Christians. The problem has been the inclusion of *Christ* in the pagan *mass*.

WHAT IS A MASS?

Considering critically the purpose of Christmas and the elaborate rituals that include prayers for the dead that are associated with the mass celebrated during Christmas, it is difficult to see how our historical Jesus of Nazareth can be linked with the mass. The question is – can Jesus Christ attend the type of Christmas that we celebrate today?

In one of the Jewish feasts that Jesus attended in Jerusalem, He left the drinking and sinful crowd to identify with impotent folks and blind people.

> *"After this there was a feast of the Jews; and Jesus went up to Jerusalem. Now there is at Jerusalem by the sheep market a pool, which is called in the Hebrew tongue Bethesda, having five porches. In these lay a great multitude of impotent folk, of blind, halt, withered, waiting for the moving of the water. For an angel went down at a certain season into the pool, and troubled the water: whosoever then first after the troubling of the water stepped in was made whole of whatsoever disease he had. And a certain man was there, which had an infirmity thirty and eight years. When Jesus saw him lie, and knew that he had been now a long time in that case, he saith unto him, Wilt thou be made whole? The impotent man answered him, Sir, I have no man, when the water is troubled, to put me into the pool: but while I am coming, another stepped down before me. Jesus saith unto him, Rise, take up thy bed, and walk. And immediately the man was made whole, and took up his bed, and walked: and on the same day was the Sabbath"* (John 5:1-9).

I doubt if Christ would attend 99% of programs that take place during Christmas. Most people in the world today practice religion without Christ and righteousness. Religion is people's way of trying to reach God while Christianity is God's way of reach out to humankind. Christianity is a way of life not religion.

THE BIRTHDAY OF OUR LORD JESUS CHRIST

History has proved that December 25 was not actually the day Jesus Christ was born. The celebration of December 25 as the birthday of Jesus Christmas started in the western churches 40 years after the death of the Lord (*Cambridge Encyclopedia, 4th Ed. 200*). It was a Christian substitute for the pagan festival held on the same date to celebrate the *unconquered sun*. However, the Eastern Orthodox Churches chose to celebrate theirs in early January.

The word *Christmas* is derived from the old English Cristes maese (Christ's Mass). In Germany, the world is *'whinchat'* (Holy night) similar to the version being used in some Slavic languages. The French Noel probably comes also from the Latin Natalie.

Although its ultimate origin is disputed, the word *Yule* comes into modern English from Anglo-Saxon (a geol ca feast, particularly, 'the feast of the winter solstice'). It is not possible to determine the exact date of the birth of Jesus Christ, either from the evidence of the gospels or from Jewish tradition.

> *"And this taxing was first made when Cyrenius was governor of Syria. And all went to be taxed, every one into his own city. And Joseph also went up from Galilee, out of the city of Nazareth, into Judæa, unto the city of David, which is called Bethlehem; (because he was of the house and lineage of David: To be taxed with Mary his espoused wife, being great with child. And so it was, that, while they were there, the days were accomplished that she should be delivered. And she brought forth her firstborn son, wrapped him in swaddling clothes, and laid him in a manger; because there was no room for them in the inn. [11]For unto you is born this day in the city of David a Savior, which is Christ the Lord"* (Luke 2:2-7; 11).

During the first three century of the Christian era, there was considerable opposition in the church to the pagan custom of celebrating birthdays, although there is some indication that a purely religious commemoration of the birth of Christ was included in the feast of the epiphany.

Clement Alexandria mentioned the existence of the feast in Egypt about the year AD 2000 and we have some evidence that it was observed on various dates in many areas. After the triumph of Constantine, the church at Rome assigned December 25 as the date for the celebrations of the birth of Jesus Christ, possibly about AD 320 or 353 (Colliers Encyclopedia, 1990). By the end of the 4th century, the Christian world was completely celebrating Christmas on that date with the exception of the eastern churches where it was celebrated on January 6.

REJECTION AND ACCEPTANCE

The choice of December 25 was probably influenced by the fact that on this day the Romans celebrated the maturate feast of the sun god (Natalis solis invincti) and that the Saturnalia came at this time. The indication is that the church in this way grasped the opportunity to turn the people from a pagan observance of the winter solstice to a day of adoration of Christ.

In northern Europe, the Teutonic tribes celebrated the winter solstice, when they were converted to Christianity and developed many customs and traditions that became part of the feast of Christmas. Thus during the middle ages, the festival became the most popular one at the year, celebrated in church and at home with a blend of pagan activities and Christian devotion that is even alien to it today. The suppression of the mass during the Reformation led to a sharp change in the observance of Christmas in some countries.

For instance, in England, the puritan condemned the celebration and from 1612 to 1652 issued a series of ordinances forbidding all church services and festivities. The pilgrims carried over this feeling to America and it was not until the nineteenth century wave of Irish and Germany immigration that enthusiasm for the feast began to spread throughout the country. Objections were swept aside and the old tradition revived among Protestants as well as Catholics. We can therefore see that if the argument is that Christ was born on December 25, it is unexplainable. When Christ was born, there were shepherds abiding in the field keeping watch over their flock by night.

> *"And there were in the same country shepherds abiding in the field, keeping watch over their flock by night. And, lo, the angel of the Lord came upon them, and the glory of the Lord shone round about them: and they were sore afraid. And the angel said unto them, Fear not: for, behold, I bring you good tidings of great joy, which shall be to all people. For unto you is born this day in the city of David a Savior, which is Christ the Lord"* (Luke 2:8-11).

Shepherds in Palestine do not abide in the field by night during the middle of winter. According to Adam Clark, "As these shepherds had not yet brought home their flock, it is a presumptive argument that October had not yet commenced, and consequently, our Lord could not have been born on December 25th when no flocks were out in the field"

According to this fact of Adam Clark, the nativity in December 25 should be given up. The bible does not expressly tell us the date of the birth of Jesus Christ but there are indications that it was probably in the autumn of the year. We knew that Jesus was crucified in the spring at the time of Passover. Figuring His ministry in the last three and half years, this would place the beginning of the ministry in the autumn. At that time, He was about thirty years old.

> *"And Jesus himself began to be about thirty years of age, being (as was supposed) the son of Joseph, which was the son of Heli"* (Luke 3:23).

> *"From thirty years old and upward even until fifty years old, all that enter into the host, to do the work in the tabernacle of the congregation"* (Numbers 4:3).

That age was the official age for a man to become a minister in the ancient Hebrew setting. Jesus turned thirty in the autumn, which proved his birthday was in the autumn, thirty years before. At the time of His birth, Joseph and Mary had gone to Bethlehem to be taxed. Joseph traveled from Galilee, out of the city of Nazareth, to Judea, the city of David, which is called Bethlehem.

Some ancient records indicated that the middle of winter was usually the time for taxing. A more logical time of the year would have being during the autumn, at the end of the harvest. If this were the case, it would be the season for the feast of Tabernacles at Jerusalem, which would explain why Mary went with Joseph.

> *"[7] And she brought forth her firstborn son, and wrapped him in swaddling clothes, and laid him in a manger; because there was no room for them in the inn. [41] Now his parents went to Jerusalem every year at the feast of the Passover"* (Luke 2:7; 41).

This assertion also explained why there were no rooms at the inn in Bethlehem. According to Josephus, Jerusalem was a city of about 120,000 inhabitants, but during the feasts, there were as many as 2,000,000 people in Jerusalem. Such vast crowds not only filled Jerusalem but also the surrounding towns including Bethlehem, which was only five miles to the south. If the journey of Mary and Joseph were indeed to attend the feast, as well as to be taxed, then this would place the birth of Jesus in the autumn of the year.

It is not crucial that we must know the exact date on which Christ was born. Nevertheless, the important thing is that He was born and He redeemed humankind from perdition, opening the gate of heaven for us. It is this important fact of history that should be emphasized instead of being blurred for mere celebration. Early believers commemorated the death of Jesus Christ, not his birth.

> *"For as often as ye eat this bread, and drink this cup, ye do shew the Lord's death till he come"* (1 Corinthians 11:26).

The Catholic Encyclopedia says, "Christmas was not among the earliest festivals of the church. Irenacus and Tertullian omitted it from their list of feasts". Later when churches at various places began to celebrate the birthday of Christ, there were diverse opinions as to the accurate day. It was not until the later part of the 4th century before the Roman church began observing December 25 as the birthday of Jesus Christ.

Yet, by the 5th century AD, the Roman church ordered that the birth of Jesus Christ be forever observed on this date even though that date was the day of old Roman feast of the birth of Sol (sun), the Roman sun god. Frazer said, "The largest pagan religious cult, which fostered the celebration of December 25 as a holy day throughout the Roman and Greek world was the pagan *sun worship* – Mithraism. This winter festival was also called the Nativity, that is, the '*nativity of the sun god.*'

The confusing question today is whether this pagan festival was responsible for the fixing of December 25 by the Roman church at the birth of Jesus Christ. The Catholic Encyclopedia answered that, "The well known solar feast of *Natalis invinci* (the nativity of the unconquered sun) celebration on 25 December has a strong claim on the responsibility for our December date"

As pagan solar customs were being Christianized at Rome, it is understood that confusion would naturally result. Some began to take Jesus for sol, the sun – God. It took the boldness of Tertullian to correct the theological error and to assert that sol was not even a Christian. Augustine denounced the heretical identification of Christ with sol. Pope Leo bitterly reproved pro-sol Christians at the very door step of the Apostle's basilica who were turning to adore the rising sun.

The winter festival was very popular in the ancient times. For instance, in the days of the Teutonic barbarians in the ancient Egyptian civilization, the period of winter solstice was always a period of rejoicing and festivity. The popularity of the season brought about its adoption as the time of the birth of Christ by the Roman church. Today, the Roman Saturnalia has influenced most of our present Christian customs. It is a common knowledge that much of what is associated with Christians (the holidays, exchange of gifts and general feeling of geniality) is a carryover from the Roman winter feast of Saturnalia. They are all appearances of ancient paganism.

Tertullian mentioned that the practice of exchange of gifts was part of the Saturnalia. There is nothing wrong with giving of gifts, but the spirit associated with it is the problem and those involved in the exchange of gifts are caught in the web of the Saturnalia worship. The wise men also presented gifts to Christ, not to worship Saturnalia as done during Christmas.

> *"And they came with haste, and found Mary, and Joseph, and the babe lying in a manger"* (Luke 2:16).
>
> *"When they had heard the king, they departed; and, lo, the star, which they saw in the east, went before them, till it came and stood over where the young child was.*

When they saw the star, they rejoiced with exceeding great joy. And when they were come into the house, they saw the young child with Mary his mother, and fell down, and worshipped him: and when they had opened their treasures, they presented unto him gifts; gold, and frankincense, and myrrh" (Matthew 2:9-11).

THE SPIRIT OF CHRISTMAS

Clearly, the spirit that manifests during Christmas cannot be the spirit of Christ. There have been people in the scriptures that celebrated religious feasts without the Spirit of God guiding them. They preferred to offer sacrifices and made feasts unto God without allowing God into their lives or surrendering their lives to God. They offered burnt offerings, peace offerings and all sort of offerings to the Lord in their hearts. They ate, drank, danced and committed immorality, yet they called upon the name of the Lord. Similarly, today people fornicate, steal, kill, and yet celebrate Christmas. This is very sad.

> *"And all the people brake off the golden earrings which were in their ears, and brought them unto Aaron. And he received them at their hand, and fashioned it with a graving tool, after he had made it a molten calf: and they said, These be thy gods, O Israel, which brought thee up out of the land of Egypt. And when Aaron saw it, he built an altar before it; and Aaron made proclamation, and said, tomorrow is a feast to the LORD. And they rose up early on the morrow, and offered burnt offerings, and brought peace offerings; and the people sat down to eat and to drink, and rose up to play. And the LORD said unto Moses, Go, get thee down; for thy people, which thou brightest out of the land of Egypt, have corrupted themselves: They have turned aside quickly out of the way which I commanded them: they have made them a molten calf, and have worshipped it, and have sacrificed thereunto, and said, These be thy gods, O Israel, which have brought thee up out of the land of Egypt"* (Exodus 32:3-8).

Some sinners, who masquerade as Christians are prepared to die defending their churches or their small groups. They believe that they are fighting for God when they defend their false doctrine not minding whether their doctrines are right or wrong, biblical or heretical. Such people will end up in hell fire if they die without repentance.

> *"For laying aside the commandment of God, ye hold the tradition of men, as the washing of pots and cups: and many other such like things ye do. And he said unto them, Full well ye reject the commandment of God, that ye may keep your own tradition"* (Mark 7:8-9).

The big question is – how much Christmas is Christianity? None at all. None of it is biblical. The Lord commanded none of it. None of it is apostolic and the early born-again Christians observed none of it as we have seen above. Only backslidden people make much noise about Christmas. For the backsliding church, Christmas is a time of bewitchment, sin and confusion. Most celebrants are worse off after Christmas celebration because they are debilitated, empty, siphoned, bewitched, depleted financially and spiritually empty. To some people, Christmas is a time of family crisis.

"[11]Israel hath sinned, and they have also transgressed my covenant which I commanded them: for they have even taken of the accursed thing, and have also stolen, and dissembled also, and they have put it even among their own stuff. [12]Therefore the children of Israel could not stand before their enemies, but turned their backs before their enemies, because they were accursed: neither will I be with you any more, except ye destroy the accursed from among you. [25]And Joshua said, why hast thou troubled us? The LORD shall trouble thee this day. Moreover, all Israel stoned him with stones, and burned them with fire, after they had stoned them with stones. [26]And they raised over him a great heap of stones unto this day. Therefore, the LORD turned from the fierceness of his anger. Wherefore the name of that place was called, The valley of Achor, unto this day" (Joshua 7:11-12, 25-26).

It is one of the notorious times that people commit unimaginable atrocities to satisfy their coveted needs. It is a time people take evil decisions, evil and wicked deeds are committed, many girls lose their virginity, armed robbers operate, people are poisoned, kidnapped and child trafficking increases. Christmas is a horrible period in the world today.

"Woe to the bloody city! It is all full of lies and robbery; the prey departed not; The noise of a whip, and the noise of the rattling of the wheels, and of the prancing horses, and of the jumping chariots. The horseman lifted up both the bright sword and the glittering spear: and there is a multitude of slain, and a great number of carcasses; and there is none end of their corpses; they stumble upon their corpses: Because of the multitude of the whoredoms of the well-favored harlot, the mistress of witchcrafts, that selleth nations through her whoredoms, and families through her witchcrafts" (Nahum 3:1-4).

During Christmas, unprecedented among of lives are lost in road accidents. People tell lies to get money for Christmas and parties. It is a time many enter into evil groups and evil noises multiply. Many people make contacts with evil spirits, diseases and evil sacrifices. Others embark on absurd projects at all cost at the expense of joy and peace of others. Christmas is also a time of heightened burial ceremonies, evil harvests and all manner of sexual shows of immoral perversion. It is a time of spiritual war and demonic demonstrations. There is hardly anything good spiritually about Christmas.

"Now Absalom had commanded his servants, saying, Mark ye now when Amnon's heart is merry with wine, and when I say unto you, Smite Amnon; then kill him, fear not: have not I commanded you? Be courageous, and be valiant. And the servants of Absalom did unto Amnon as Absalom had commanded. Then all the king's sons arose, and every man gat him up upon his mule, and fled" (2 Samuel 13:28-29).

Christmas ought to be a day of evangelism if you must remember the birthday of Christ. It must be a day to pray for people, reflect soberly and show true love to everyone. Christmas period should not be a time to promote carnal lusts or enthrone fleshly desires.

> *"Wherefore putting away lying, speaks every man truth with his neighbor: for we are members one of another. Be ye angry, and sin not: let not the sun goes down upon your wrath: Neither give place to the devil. Let him that stole steal no more: but rather let him labor, working with his hands the thing, which is good, that he may have to give to him that needed. Let no corrupt communication proceed out of your mouth, but that, which is good to the use of edifying, that it may minister grace unto the hearers. And grieve not the holy Spirit of God, whereby ye are sealed unto the day of redemption. Let all bitterness, and wrath, and anger, and clamor, and evil speaking, be put away from you, with all malice"* (Ephesians 4:25-31).

If you truly want to remember the birth of your Lord and Savior, you would be sober. If the majority of the world decided to remember the birth of Christ in December, that period would have been dedicated to Jesus Christ in honor of what He did for humanity. It must be a period to give ourselves to Christ and examine our faith. It must not be a period of lying, anger and honor to devil, corruption or grieving of the Holy Spirit. Put away bitterness, wrath, clamor, evil speaking, malice and all evil.

CHRISTIAN LIFESTYLE DURING CHRISTMAS

A Christian is expected to live a consistent Christian life every day. The uniform teaching of the Scriptures is that believers should lead lives that are pleasing to God at all times, once they come into His kingdom. As a born-again Christian, God wished that you developed a life that would conform totally to the very image of Christ. There are things believers are not supposed to do once they are born-again. If you want to remember the birthday of your Lord, Savior and king, you must put away all evil characters before, during and after Christmas.

> *"Endeavoring to keep the unity of the Spirit in the bond of peace. [4]There is one body, and one Spirit, even as ye are called in one hope of your calling"* (Ephesians 4:3-4).

If you truly want to give Christ a befitting birthday gift, do away with sin in your life. You need to repent from the sins you have already committed and forsake them once and forever. Always remember that:

> *"He that covereth his sins shall not prosper: but whoso confesseth and forsakes them shall have mercy"* (Proverbs 28:13).

> *"If we confess our sins, he is faithful and just to forgive us our sins, and to cleanse us from all unrighteousness"* (1 John 1:9).

> *"He that committed sin is of the devil; for the devil sinneth from the beginning. For this purpose, the Son of God was manifested, that he might destroy the works of the devil. Whosoever is born of God doth not commit sin; for his seed remained in him: and he cannot sin, because he is born of God"* (1 John 3:8-9).

Some people would increase wickedness and all manner of evil before and during Christmas, hoping to repent after Christmas. It is very strange to give to your Savior wickedness as a gift with the hope of repentance after insulting Him. If you would confess your sins now that Christmas has not come or even at Christmas and forsake them forever, Christ will forgive you and cleanse you of all unrighteousness. However, if you keep committing sin, it is evident that you are a child of devil.

Here are things you need to stop doing if you really want to celebrate Christmas with Christ.

d. **Fornication** (*See* Ephesians 5:3; Acts 15:28-29; Colossians 3:5).

e. **Uncleanness** (*See* Ephesians 5:3; Romans 1:23-24; 6:21; 1 Thessalonians 4:7).

f. **Covetousness** (*See* Ephesians 5:3; Colossians 3:5; Exodus 20:17; Ezekiel 33:21; Luke 12:15).

g. **Filthiness** (*See* Ephesians 5:4; James 1:21; 2 Peter 2:10; Psalms 53:1-4).

h. **Foolishness or foolish talking** (*See* Ephesians 5:4; James 1:26-27; Proverbs 10:19; 1 Peter 3:10).

i. **Jesting** (*See* Ephesians 5:4; Proverbs 26:18-19).

j. **Lying** (*See* Ephesians 4:25; Micah 6:12; Romans 3:13; 2 Corinthians 11:13; 1 Timothy 4:1-2; Revelation 21:8).

k. **Stealing** (*See* Ephesians 4:28; Leviticus 19:11, 13; Isaiah 61:8; Jeremiah 7:9; John 10:1; 2 Samuel 15:1-6).

l. **Bitterness and wrath** (*See* Ephesians 4:31; Hebrews 12:15-17; James 3:14-16).

m. **Malice** (*See* Ephesians 4:31; Colossians 3:8; 1 Peter 2:21).

n. **Grieving the Holy Spirit** (*See* Ephesians 4:30; Isaiah 63:10; Acts 5:3; 7:51).

You must use the period of Christmas to please God and not desire to get quick success, achievement or fulfill man-made goal against God's will. It must not be a time to be proud or crave for popularity and praises of men. Though many people are deviating from true faith, but take a stand to please God at all cost.

> *"And Jesus came and spake unto them, saying, all power is given unto me in heaven and in earth. Go ye therefore, and teach all nations, baptizing them in the name of the Father, and of the Son, and of the Holy Ghost: Teaching them to observe all things whatsoever I have commanded you: and, lo, I am with you always, even unto the end of the world. Amen"* (Matthew 28:18-20).

True love always translates into action. The sound and biblical teaching of true religion is visiting and caring for those who need attention and help.

> *"Pure religion and undefiled before God and the Father is this, To visit the fatherless and widows in their affliction, and to keep himself unspotted from the world"* (James 1:27).

The goal of any Christian should be to touch lost souls with the gospel and bring sinners to Christ. Our labor will not be in vain.

> *"Therefore, my beloved brethren, be ye steadfast, unmovable, always abounding in the work of the Lord, forasmuch as ye know that your labor is not in vain in the Lord"* (1 Corinthians 15:58).

PRAYERS FOR CHRISTMAS

Bible reference: Mark 2:1-52

Begin with praise and worship

1. O Lord, empower me to get the true blessing of salvation and genuine sanctification, in the name of Jesus.
2. Every enemy of my trust in God is frustrated, in the name of Jesus.
3. Blood of Jesus, flow into my life and perfect Your work of reconciliation, in the name of Jesus.
4. O Lord, help me to understand and benefit from true meaning and purpose of Christmas, in the name of Jesus.
5. Father Lord, empower me to feast with Christ in this Christmas, in the name of Jesus.
6. I repent for the years I celebrated Christmas without Christ, in the name of Jesus.
7. Let my heaven open for blessings as I celebrate this year's Christmas with Christ, in the name of Jesus.
8. I withdraw myself from evils associated with the feast of Christmas, in the name of Jesus.
9. I separate myself from sins and atrocities attached to the remaining Christmas in my lifetime, in the name of Jesus.
10. Every good thing that past Christmas has stolen from my life, I recover you double, in the name of Jesus.
11. I break the yoke of demons that operate during Christmas, in the name of Jesus.
12. I recover all blessings that Christmas has stolen from my life, in the name of Jesus.
13. I separate myself from evil trend of excessive spending and worldliness, in the name of Jesus.
14. Any evil that is prepared for me during this Christmas, die, in the name of Jesus.
15. I command demons that operate at Christmas to be arrested to death, in the name of Jesus.

16. I neutralize demonic attacks that were assigned to waste my life, in the name of Jesus.

17. Any negative report that was prepared against me during this Christmas, I reject you, in the name of Jesus.

18. Let the birth of our Lord Jesus manifest fully in my life this season, in the name of Jesus.

19. Let people repent en masse through me during this Christmas, in the name of Jesus.

20. I destroy any spirit that would separate me from Christ through Christmas, in the name of Jesus.

21. I cast out every demonic ritual that is attached to my Christ, in the name of Jesus.

22. Any evil prayer that is going on for my sake during this Christmas, die in the name of Jesus.

23. Lord Jesus, appear and identify with me during this Christmas, in the name of Jesus.

24. Father Lord, help me to conduct a decent birthday party for Jesus Christ during this Christmas, in the name of Jesus.

25. I cast out the pagan spirit that wants to enter into my Christmas, in the name of Jesus.

26. Lord Jesus, appear in the Christmas of this year and bless me greatly, in the name of Jesus.

27. I refuse to follow the multitudes to do evil, in the name of Jesus.

28. Lord, empower me to honor You before, during and after Christmas, in the name of Jesus.

29. Father, help me to involve Jesus fully through the remaining Christmas in my life, in the name of Jesus.

30. May Jesus accept and reward my offering during this Christmas, in the name of Jesus.

31. I destroy evil celebrations that are attached to my Christianity by fire, in the name of Jesus.

32. I refuse to observe any tradition that is not consistent with scriptures, in the name of Jesus.

33. The spirit of Christmas cannot weaken, empty, or siphon my life this year, in the name of Jesus.

34. I break and loose myself from the spirit that inspires people to do evil during Christmas, in the name of Jesus.

35. Any demon that spreads evil during Christmas, I cast you out, in the name of Jesus.

36. I deliver myself from evil contacts that follow Christmas, in the name of Jesus.

37. Let my lifestyle during this Christmas conform to the life of Christ, in the name of Jesus.

38. Blood of Jesus, wash me from sin now, during and after Christmas, in the name of Jesus.

39. Lord Jesus, I surrender my life to You as Your birthday gift, in the name of Jesus.

40. O Lord, use me as an instrument to diminish wickedness on earth, in the name of Jesus.

41. Let Christ in me save sinners en masse this season and thereafter, in the name of Jesus.

42. Father Lord, bless me this Christmas as never before, in the name of Jesus.

43. I disband and dismiss every obstacle to my blessing this season, in the name of Jesus.

44. Let the forces against my blessing scatter in shame, in the name of Jesus.

45. Father Lord, take me away from the spirit of the tail forever, in the name of Jesus.

46. I command enemies that are holding my blessing to release them, in the name of Jesus.

47. Father Lord, release money into my account from the heavenly bank, in the name of Jesus.

48. I enter into the stronghold of the strongman that has stolen my blessings and I release my blessings by force, in the name of Jesus.

49. Every agent of poverty on assignment in my life, die, in the name of Jesus.

50. I break and loose myself from debt and lack, in the name of Jesus.

51. O Lord, increase my helpers and command them to bless me without stopping, in the name of Jesus.

52. Every agent of delay for my financial and material blessings, die, in the name of Jesus.

53. I walk out from the tail region to the frontline of divine blessings, in the name of Jesus.

54. Every instrument of failure in my life, catch fire, in the name of Jesus.

55. Father Lord, baptize my life with all manner of blessings, in the name of Jesus.

37

Chapter

PRAYERS FOR WIDOWS AND ORPHANS

CHAPTER OVERVIEW

- *A widow's commitment to God*
- *Characteristics of a virtuous widow*
- *Universal call for backslidden widows to return to God*
- *God loves widows and orphans*
- *When widows and orphans pray*

A WIDOW'S COMMITMENT TO GOD

While no one can question God for calling any of us to glory, it is very important that a widow or widower commit his or her life in the hands of God. God truly comforts the heart and provides relief. Therefore, it cannot be better elsewhere.

It is not possible for one to be committed to God without being born-again. To be a born-again is the beginning of every success and the beginning of a true Christian or spiritual life. Human successes on earth depend on seeds we planted. This is a godly principle.

> *"And Jesus sat over against the treasury, and beheld how the people cast money into the treasury: and many that were rich cast in much. And there came a certain poor widow, and she threw in two mites, which make a farthing. And he called unto him his disciples, and saith unto them, Verily I say unto you, That this poor widow hath cast more in, than all they which have cast into the treasury: For all they did cast in of their abundance; but she of her want did cast in all that she had, even all her living"* (Mark 12:41-44).

> *"Be not deceived; God is not mocked: for whatsoever a man soweth, that shall he also reap. For he that soweth to his flesh shall of the flesh reap corruption; but he that soweth to the Spirit shall of the Spirit reap life everlasting. And let us not be weary in well doing: for in due season we shall reap, if we faint not"* (Galatians 6:7-9).

The eyes of the Lord see every human activity on earth. God expects every human to sow good seeds according to what he or she has received. Jesus monitors every activity on earth to see how committed you are. Poor and rich widows are expected alike to contribute to the propagation of the gospel. No matter how poor you are, Jesus expects a little from what you have. Widows who are not born-again yet are expected to be born-again just like every other true believer on earth.

> *"And there was one Anna, a prophetess, the daughter of Phanuel, of the tribe of Aser: she was of a great age, and had lived with an husband seven years from her virginity; And she was a widow of about fourscore and four years, which departed not from the temple, but served God with fastings and prayers night and day. And she coming in that instant gave thanks likewise unto the Lord, and spake of him to all them that looked for redemption in Jerusalem"* (Luke 2:36-38).

> *"There was a man of the Pharisees, named Nicodemus, a ruler of the Jews: The same came to Jesus by night, and said unto him, Rabbi, we know that thou art a teacher*

come from God: for no man can do these miracles that thou doest, except God be with him. Jesus answered and said unto him, Verily, verily, I say unto thee, Except a man be born again, he cannot see the kingdom of God" (John 3:1-3).

Anna was a widow who kept herself pure and holy and God empowered her with gifts of a prophet. She was only married for seven years before her husband died. Though she married as a virgin, she remained a widow for about 84 years as a prophet. She worked for God in the temple, fasting and praying night and day. Eventually, she lived to see Christ whom she prayed for his coming for many years.

Susannah Wesley was a poor woman who invested in her children through prayers and gave the world John and Charles Wesley as fruit of her labor. Dwight L. Moody in his Chicago meeting of October, 1876, told a story to encourage Christian women to pray for the salvation of their loved ones. At one of the meetings at Nashville, during the war, a young man came to him, trembling from head to toe. 'What is the trouble,' he asked. "There was a letter I got from my sister and she told me that every night, as the sun goes down, she goes on her knees and prays for me".

This man was brave and had fought many battles. He could stand in front of the canon, yet a simple letter completely distressed him.

"I have been trembling ever since I received it," he said. Six hundred miles away and the faith of the girl were at work and the brother felt its influence. Previously, he did not believe in prayer, he did not believe in Christianity, he did not believe in his mother's bible. His mother was a prayerful woman, and when she died, she left a prayerful daughter. When God saw her faith and heard her prayer, He answered her prayers. That young man eventually gave his life to Jesus. Praise God!

At Meurfessbore, a similar incident took place. A young man received a letter from his mother that read, "My dear boy, you do not know how I am burdened for your salvation. Every morning and evening, I go into my closet and pray for you, that you may be led to the cross of Christ. You may die in battle or in the hospitals and O, my son, I want you to become a Christian. I do not know but this might be my last letter to you".

Later, this lieutenant came to Dwight L. Mood and said, "I have just heard of my mother's death and I have prayed for forgiveness of my sins." He gained conversion through his mother's faith. Although she has gone to glory, her voice was still heard.

Anna was a praying widow and a prophetess of God for 84 years. Her major prayer point was that God would send a redeemer to the world. God honors women that obey His Word.

"[1]Rebuke not an elder, but entreat him as a father; and the younger men as brethren; [2]The elder women as mothers; the younger as sisters, with all purity. [3]Honor widows that are widows indeed. [4]But if any widow has children or nephews let them learn first to show piety at home, and to requite their parents: for that is good and acceptable before God. [5]Now she that is a widow indeed, and desolate, trusted in God, and continueth in supplications and prayers night and day. [6]But she that liveth in pleasure is dead while she liveth. [9]Let not a widow be taken into the number under threescore years old, having been the wife of one man" (1 Timothy 5:1-6, 9).

The Lord cares for widows. He honors also. A widow who sleeps around is not a Christian. Widows who break other people's marriage, commits adultery and they are not virtuous women. A widow that lives in pleasure is spiritually dead.

In his first letter to Timothy, Paul instructed Timothy that widows ought to have report of good works before God.

"[1]Well reported of for good works; if she have brought up children, if she have lodged strangers, if she have washed the saints' feet, if she have relieved the afflicted, if she have diligently followed every good work" (1 Timothy 5:10).

Widows should commit to every good work. God knows how to use righteous widows to accomplish good works. Recall how God used a widow to take care of Elijah in Zarephath.

"[8]And the word of the LORD came unto him, saying, [9]Arise, get thee to Zarephath, which belonged to Zidon, and dwell there: behold, I have commanded a widow woman there to sustain thee. [10]So he arose and went to Zarephath. And when he came to the gate of the city, behold, the widow woman was there gathering of sticks: and he called to her, and said, Fetch me, I pray thee, a little water in a vessel that I may drink. [11]And as she was going to fetch it, he called to her, and said, Bring me, I pray thee, a morsel of bread in thine hand. [12]And she said, As the LORD thy God liveth, I have not a cake, but an handful of meal in a barrel, and a little oil in a cruse: and, behold, I am gathering two sticks, that I may go in and dress it for me and my son, that we may eat it, and die. [15]And she went and did according to the slaying of Elijah: and she, and he, and her house, did eat many days" (1 Kings 17:8-12, 15).

"But I tell you of a truth, many widows were in Israel in the days of Elias, when the heaven was shut up three years and six months, when great famine was throughout all the land; But unto none of them was Elias sent, save unto Sarepta, a city of Sidon, unto a woman that was a widow" (Luke 4:25-26).

CHARACTERISTICS OF A VIRTUOUS WIDOW

A widow who prepares herself and lives in righteousness, indeed will receive God's blessings. God will send her help in time of trouble. God commanded Elijah to go to Zarephath, which belonged to Zidon and dwell there with a widow. A true widow receives God's commandments. She sustains the life of the saints. She does not use her body to destroy the people of God. She does not seduce men of God or waste people's lives. The widow of Zarephath sustained took care of the saints of God and God rewarded her accordingly.

Virtuous widows are women of faith. They trust God and His prophets. They obey God's Word and love God.

WIDOWS FACE DIVERSE TEMPTATIONS

All widows face tests and temptations, though they may vary. Tests come to reveal our inner strength and meekness. Temptations come divert or destroy you. God permits Christians to experience temptations to reveal the depth of their faith and to grant them opportunities to seek more grace from Him. In addition, tests come to prove our faith, loyalty and faithfulness.

God may have allowed other false prophets; men of God who were weak morally to tempt the widow of Zarephath but she overcame them. She proved she was ready to die after eating her last food instead of committing immorality to get more food from backslidden prophets.

> *"[14]And went after the man of God, and found him sitting under an oak: and he said unto him, Art thou the man of God that camest from Judah? In addition, he said, I am. [15]Then he said unto him, Come home with me, and eat bread. [18]He said unto him, I am a prophet also as thou art; and an angel spoke unto me by the word of the LORD, saying, Bring him back with thee into thine house, that he may eat bread and drink water. However, he lied unto him. [19]So he went back with him, did eat bread in his house, and drank water. [23]And it came to pass, after he had eaten bread, and after he had drunk, that he saddled for him the ass, to wit, for the prophet whom he had brought back. [24]And when he was gone, a lion met him by the way, and slew him: and his carcass was cast in the way, and the ass stood by it, the lion also stood by the carcass"* (1 Kings 13:14-15, 18-19, 23-24).

Today, many backslidden men and women of God are hunting for widows and widowers to sleep with them. Many widows have compromised and found themselves in trouble. Now they are crying for help with no one answering them.

"Having damnation, because they have cast off their first faith. And withal they learn to be idle, wandering about from house to house; and not only idle, but tattlers also and busybodies, speaking things, which they ought not. I will therefore that the younger women marry, bear children, guide the house, give none occasion to the adversary to speak reproachfully" (1 Timothy 5:12-14).

"And Abigail hasted, and arose, and rode upon an ass, with five damsels of hers that went after her; and she went after the messengers of David, and became his wife" (1 Samuel 25:42).

It is better for a widow to pray and marry again than to stay single and defile her body and those of other people. Even the so-called men of God and old prophets try to tempt or seduce you, take your stand firmly and refuse to backslide. Learn from Anna, who dedicated herself to the service of God and remained pure for 84 years. The grace that God gave to her is still available today.

The widow of Zarephath overcame all advances from men and great promises and provisions that were attached to sin of compromise. She waited until God sent a true man of God to help her out of her situation.

The wife of one of the sons of the prophets would have presented her body to the creditors as an option to spare her two sons but she preferred to keep her body for the Lord.

"Now there cried a certain woman of the wives of the sons of the prophets unto Elisha, saying, Thy servant my husband is dead; and thou knows that thy servant did fear the LORD: and the creditor is come to take unto him my two sons to be bondmen" (2 Kings 4:1).

"3Then I took Jaazaniah the son of Jeremiah, the son of Habaziniah, and his brethren, and all his sons, and the whole house of the Rechabites; 4And I brought them into the house of the LORD, into the chamber of the sons of Hanan, the son of Igdaliah, a man of God, which was by the chamber of the princes, which was above the chamber of Messiah the son of Shalom, the keeper of the door: 5And I set before the sons of the house of the Rechabites pots full of wine, and cups, and I said unto them, Drink ye wine. 6But they said, We will drink no wine: for Jonadab the son of Rechab our father commanded us, saying, Ye shall drink no wine, neither ye, nor your sons for ever: 8Thus have we obeyed the voice of Jonadab the son of Rechab our father in all that he hath charged us, to drink no wine all our days, we, our wives, our sons, nor our daughters" (Jeremiah 35:3-6, 8).

Many widows have defiled their bodies because of weak backslidden prophets. The first temptation in history came from Satan in the form of a subtle creature, snake. Thus,

Adam was seduced through his wife, Eve, who was the closest person next to him. That is why you want to remain watchful because your own temptation may come through a person you are so familiar with or a person in position with wealth and influence.

At times, it is difficult to say *no* to ministers of God or someone you respect very well and hold at a very high esteem. Many people have been deceived and destroyed because they assumed that any idea or suggestion that comes from men in high position must be accurate. Temptations may not have much effect on you when they come from people you hate or do not respect. The truth is that you must be careful because the more you honor or respect certain persons, the more likely temptations would come through them.

> *"[2]And the LORD was with Joseph, and he was a prosperous man; and he was in the house of his master the Egyptian. [6]And he left all that he had in Joseph's hand; and he knew not ought he had, save the bread, which he did eat. In addition, Joseph was a goodly person, and well favored. [7]And it came to pass after these things, that his master's wife cast her eyes upon Joseph; and she said, lie with me. [8]But he refused, and said unto his master's wife, Behold, my master wotteth not what is with me in the house, and he hath committed all that he hath to my hand; [9]There is none greater in this house than I; neither hath he kept back anything from me but thee, because thou art his wife: how then can I do this great wickedness, and sin against God? [10]And it came to pass, as she spoke to Joseph day by day, that he hearkened not unto her, to lie by her, or to be with her. [11]And it came to pass about this time that Joseph went into the house to do his business; and there was none of the men of the house there within. [12]And she caught him by his garment, saying, Lie with me: and he left his garment in her hand, and fled, and got him out"* (Genesis 39:2, 6-12).

> *"Then said his wife unto him; dost thou still retain thine integrity? Curse God, and die. But he said unto her, Thou speakest as one of the foolish women speaketh. What? Shall we receive well at the hand of God, and shall we not receive evil? In all this did not Job sin with his lips"* (Job 2:9-10).

Many widows find it hard to deny themselves and follow Jesus, who said that if any man or woman, of whatever rank or class in any nation of the world, would follow Him, let that person deny him or herself, then take up his or her cross and follow Him."

Anna followed Him and she was not disappointed. The wife of one of the sons of the prophets followed God and she was not disappointed. If you follow Jesus, He will not disappoint you.

> *"The blessing of him that was ready to perish came upon me: and I caused the widow's heart to sing for joy"* (Job 29:13).

"A father of the fatherless, and a judge of the widows, is God in his holy habitation" (Psalms 68:5).

God is calling on all widows to be steadfast in their faith in God and trust in Him for all their needs.

UNIVERSAL CALL FOR BACKSLIDDEN WIDOWS TO RETURN TO GOD

The only cure for sin is repentance. God cannot be happy with the way widows are being treated all over the world. Governments and the church must wrestle the rights, benefits and entitlements of widows out of the hands of their oppressors. However, God is calling them into repentance.

This is a wonderful opportunity to repent of your sins as a widow and make friends with God. This may be the last time to do so, therefore, you do not have plenty of time.

> *"Seek ye the LORD while he may be found, call ye upon him while he is near: Let the wicked forsake his way, and the unrighteous man his thoughts: and let him return unto the LORD, and he will have mercy upon him; and to our God, for he will abundantly pardon"* (Isaiah 55:6-7).

> *"Wash you, make you clean; put away the evil of your doings from before mine eyes; cease to do evil; Learn to do well; seek judgment, relieves the oppressed, judge the fatherless, and plead for the widow. Come now, and let us reason together, saith the LORD: though your sins be as scarlet, they shall be as white as snow; though they be red like crimson, they shall be as wool. If ye be willing and obedient, ye shall eat the good of the land: But if ye refuse and rebel, ye shall be devoured with the sword: for the mouth of the LORD hath spoken it"* (Isaiah 1:16-20).

Repentance means the turning away from all known sins or changing of one's mind, purpose and action from evil to good. After repentance, a sinner abhors sin and turns all his heart away from sin. When a sinner repents, consecrates his life to God and remains faithful to God's Word, God will turn his life around and fight his battles.

> *"For this is a heinous crime; yea, it is an iniquity to be punished by the judges"* (Job 31:11).

> *"Jesus said unto him, If thou canst believe, all things are possible to him that believeth"* (Mark 9:23).

> *"For this is my blood of the new testament, which is shed for many for the remission of sins"* (Matthew 26:28).

GOD LOVES WIDOWS AND ORPHANS

God established His love for widows and orphans through the Scriptures. He did so because God cares for their safety and provision. That is why widows and orphans should have no reason to suffer in silence or lack.

> *"Ye shall not afflict any widow, or fatherless child"* (Exodus 22:22).

> *"He doth execute the judgment of the fatherless and widow, and loveth the stranger, in giving him food and raiment"* (Deuteronomy 10:18).

> 9*And the Levite, (because he hath no part nor inheritance with thee,) and the stranger, and the fatherless, and the widow, which are within thy gates, shall come, and shall eat and be satisfied; that the LORD thy God may bless thee in all the work of thine hand which thou doest"* (Deuteronomy 14:29).

> *"And thou shalt rejoice before the LORD thy God, thou, and thy son, and thy daughter, and thy manservant, and thy maidservant, and the Levite that is within thy gates, and the stranger, and the fatherless, and the widow, that are among you, in the place which the LORD thy God hath chosen to place his name there"* (Deuteronomy 16:11).

To afflict or maltreat any widow or orphan is breaking of God's commandment. Widows and their children are sacred before God. His judgment will fall on those who oppress widows or their children. While blessings follow people who bless widows and their family, curses follow those that oppress them.

A wise person does not afflict widows and their families. During harvests, God commanded farmers also to remember widows and orphans and bless them. Business people and civil servants should also remember to bless widows and orphans. It is a good thing to do so. Those that obey God's Word concerning widows and orphans cannot lack God's help when they need it. The church and other organizations are mandated to help widows and orphans too.

> *"When thou hast made an end of tithing all the tithes of thine increase the third year, which is the year of tithing, and hast given it unto the Levite, the stranger, the fatherless, and the widow, that they may eat within thy gates, and be filled; Then thou shalt say before the LORD thy God, I have brought away the hallowed things out of mine house, and also have given them unto the Levite, and unto the stranger, to the fatherless, and to the widow, according to all thy commandments which thou hast commanded me: I have not transgressed thy commandments, neither have I forgotten them"* (Deuteronomy 26:12-13).

The reason why many businesses succeed and others fail is because of the way they treat widows and orphans in their midst. When you maltreat widows and the fatherless, you will not prosper and your own children stand the risk of becoming fatherless (*See* Deuteronomy 24:19-10, 26:12-13; Job 24:21, 31:16; Psalms 94:6).

To withhold blessings from widows and orphans is a very big mistake. You cannot allow expectations of widows and orphans to fail. One of the reasons for violent and untimely deaths and multiplication of widows and orphans in the cities today is because of maltreatment of widows and their children.

If you sit on the right of your friend's children who is dead, you will soon die and your own children will face the same treatment you made other children to face. If you refuse to execute judgment or equally distribute your brother's will because you want to make gains out of it, it will soon be your turn. If you kill your brother to befriend or marry his wife, you will soon die and your children will become fatherless. You are digging your own grave by rejoicing over the death of a brother. It is an evil investment for your whole family if you maltreat widows or orphans.

> *"Let his children be fatherless, and his wife a widow"* (Psalms 109:9).

> *"Learn to do well; seek judgment relieves the oppressed, judge the fatherless, plead for the widow.* 23*Thy princes are rebellious, and companions of thieves: every one loveth gifts, and followed after rewards: they judge not the fatherless, neither doth the cause of the widow come unto them"* (Isaiah 1:17, 23).

> *"Therefore hear now this, thou that art given to pleasures, that dwellest carelessly, that sayest in thine heart, I am, and none else beside me; I shall not sit as a widow, neither shall I know the loss of children"* (Isaiah 47:8).

A wise person stands for God and widows to execute right judgment, stands by the truth, and defends widows and their children. Do not join others to oppress widows but plead for their course. Do not take bribes from widows and orphans. To oppress widows and orphans is unwise. To do them wrong, violence or shed their blood is like touching the apple of God's eyes.

A city that maltreats widows and the fatherless will be desolate with time. If you sit upon the right of widows or delay the judgment of the fatherless, you will pay for it. You may succeed in oppressing widows for a while but your judgment will surely come in a more destructive way.

> *"How much she hath glorified herself, and lived deliciously, so much torment and sorrow give her: for she saith in her heart, I sit a queen, and am no widow, and shall see no sorrow"* (Revelation 18:7).

"They drive away the ass of the fatherless, they take the widow's ox for a pledge" (Job 24:3).

"Thou hast sent widows away empty, and the arms of the fatherless have been broken" (Job 22:9).

"Those that remain of him shall be buried in death: and his widows shall not weep" (Job 27:15).

You must be very careful when dealing with widows or orphans (*See* Jeremiah 7:6, 22:3; Lamentations 1:1, Ezekiel 22:7; Zechariah 7:9-10; Malachi 3:5). People that oppress widows do not die in peace and their children cannot go free. To send a widow away empty and break the arms of the fatherless, or deny their rights, benefits and entitlements is a big risk. Robbing the fatherless and making their mothers preys is the worst thing to do. It pains God to see widows maltreated.

"Therefore deliver up their children to the famine, and pour out their blood by the force of the sword; and let their wives be bereaved of their children, and be widows; and let their men be put to death; let their young men be slain by the sword in battle" (Jeremiah 18:21).

"And I will give thee into the hand of them that seek thy life, and into the hand of them whose face thou fearest, even into the hand of Nebuchadnezzar king of Babylon, and into the hand of the Chaldeans" (Jeremiah 22:25).

"Woe unto you, scribes and Pharisees, hypocrites! For ye devour widows' houses, and for a pretence make long prayer: therefore ye shall receive the greater damnation" (Matthew 23:14).

The children of people who oppress widows and their children will be delivered to famine. Jesus rebuked the Pharisees for devouring widow's houses and yet assumed that their long prayers would save them. If you oppress widows and orphans, repent now or your reward comes upon you suddenly (*See* Isaiah 10:2; Jeremiah 15:8).

"Be ye therefore ready also: for the Son of man cometh at an hour when ye think not" (Luke 12:40).

Oppressors of widows and orphans and witches and wizards are always convening to prevent widows from praying against them. They use evil powers to manipulate them from praying. These wicked powers defile the few widows who try to pray through dreams. They use weapons of sin, fear, doubts, and discouragements to attack widows and their prayers. They also use manipulations, intimidations and violation of God's Word, authority, money, confusions and sexual perversion as weapons to separate these widows from God. When they achieve this, widow's prayers will be effective.

> *"If I regard iniquity in my heart, the Lord will not hear me: But verily God hath heard me; he hath attended to the voice of my prayer. Blessed be God, which hath not turned away my prayer or his mercy from me"* (Psalms 66:18-20).

> *"Then ye answered and said unto me, We have sinned against the LORD, we will go up and fight, according to all that the LORD our God commanded us. In addition, when ye had girded on every man his weapons of war, ye were ready to go up into the hill. And the LORD said unto me, Say unto them, Go not up, neither fights; for I am not among you; lest ye be smitten before your enemies. So I spake unto you; and ye would not hear, but rebelled against the commandment of the LORD, and went presumptuously up into the hill. And the Amorites, which dwelt in that mountain, came out against you, and chased you, as bees do, and destroyed you in Seir, even unto Hormah. And ye returned and wept before the LORD; but the LORD would not hearken to your voice, nor give ear unto you"* (Deuteronomy 1:41-45).

If widows can do away with committing sin and obey God's Word, they will have power over their oppressors and the devil.

> *"Ye shall not afflict any widow or fatherless child. If thou afflict them in any wise, and they cry at all unto me, I will surely hear their cry; And my wrath shall wax hot, and I will kill you with the sword; and your wives shall be widows, and your children fatherless"* (Exodus 22:22-24).

> *"Cursed be he that perverted the judgment of the stranger, fatherless, and widow. And all the people shall say, Amen"* (Deuteronomy 27:19).

> *"The LORD will destroy the house of the proud: but he will establish the border of the widow"* (Proverbs 15:25).

God's concern for the widows and the fatherless is evident through the Scriptures. The Word of God assures widows and orphans of God's immediate answers to their prayers. Some oppressors of widows still live in prosperity because those widows' prayers are abomination before the Holy God. No oppressor can oppress a widow or the fatherless and be free from a curse. God is waiting for widows and the fatherless to pray and their borders will be established.

> *"And there was one Anna, a prophetess, the daughter of Phanuel, of the tribe of Aser: she was of a great age, and had lived with an husband seven years from her virginity; And she was a widow of about fourscore and four years, which departed not from the temple, but served God with fasting and prayers night and day"* (Luke 2:36-37).

> *"But unto none of them was Elias sent, save unto Sarepta, a city of Sidon, unto a woman that was a widow"* (Luke 4:26).

> *"And he spake a parable unto them to this end, that men ought always to pray, and not to faint; Saying, There was in a city a judge, which feared not God, neither regarded man: And there was a widow in that city; and she came unto him, saying, Avenge me of mine adversary. And he would not for a while: but afterward he said within himself, Though I fear not God, nor regard man; Yet because this widow troubleth me, I will avenge her, lest by her continual coming she weary me"* (Luke 18:1-5).

Prophet Anna lost her husband at a youthful age. She must have had many rich men, young and old, making advances at her but she turned their evil requests down. The Lord kept her alive for 84 years as a true prophet through her prayers. Devil, death and oppressors could not deny her prayers. The same happened to the widow of Zarephath and her children. They lived and survived in the time of famine until the day of prosperity in Israel. Majority of her oppressors must have died before God visited the land. Right from the day she obeyed the Word of God by taking care of prophet Elijah, she never lacked any good thing until the day she died.

> *"For the LORD God is a sun and shield: the LORD will give grace and glory: no good thing will he withhold from them that walk uprightly"* (Psalms 84:11).

Not even a wicked king can deny an upright and prayerful widow of her right or oppress her and go scot-free.

> *"Leave thy fatherless children, I will preserve them alive; and let thy widows trust in me"* (Jeremiah 49:11).

> *"[16]And the barrel of meal wasted not, neither did the curse of oil fail, according to the word of the LORD, which he spoke by Elijah. [23]And Elijah took the child, and brought him down out of the chamber into the house, and delivered him unto his mother: and Elijah said, See, thy son liveth"* (1 Kings 17:16, 23).

God does not ignore the prayers of innocent widows and orphans. When widows live right before God, He answers their prayers with ease. God is ready to defend and perform miracles for righteous widows more than they are willing to ask. If you want God to answer your prayers, obey His Word and keep His commandments.

God does not leave widows to fight oppressors with their natural strength. He promised to answer the widows and the fatherless whenever they call on Him. In times of oppression, persevere in prayers and keep your faith no matter the pressures. Do not allow threats of the oppressor to sweep off your faith in God. God cannot disappoint you. Believe God and trust Him in the darkest hours. He will surely come to your rescue.

PRAYERS FOR WIDOWS AND ORPHANS

Bible references: Exodus 22:22-23; 1 Kings 17:8-24, 2 Kings 8:1-6, 4:1-7

Begin with praise and worship

1. O Lord, write my name in the book of life, in the name of Jesus.
2. Lord Jesus, destroy any sin that is standing between You and me, in the name of Jesus.
3. I unseat any evil personality that is sitting upon my rights by force, in the name of Jesus.
4. Any agent of poverty, suffering and hardship in my life, be disgraced, in the name of Jesus.
5. O Lord, avenge me of my adversaries, in the name of Jesus.
6. Father Lord, help me to discover my purpose in life as a widow/orphan, in the name of Jesus.
7. I receive the burden to intercede for the body of Christ one earth, in the name of Jesus.
8. O Lord, empower me to remain righteous as a widow/orphan, in the name of Jesus.
9. Almighty God, send me help from above and deliver me from my enemies, in the name of Jesus.
10. Any spirit of seduction in my life is wasted, in the name of Jesus.
11. Any temptation that is compelling me to break God's law, I overcome you, in the name of Jesus.
12. Any evil personality that was assigned to seduce me to become God's enemy, be frustrated, in the name of Jesus.
13. I disgrace agents of devil that were anointed to deceive me, in the name of Jesus.
14. O Lord, arise and vindicate me by fire, in the name of Jesus.
15. Every serpent of immorality that was delegated to waste my life, die, in the name of Jesus.

16. O Lord, wash and keep me pure from all manner of sin, in the name of Jesus.
17. I destroy any problem that has vowed to overthrow my faith in Christ, in the name of Jesus.
18. Let every intimidating Goliath against me be destroyed in shame, in the name of Jesus.
19. Every enemy of my prosperity is frustrated, in the name of Jesus.
20. Blood of Jesus, flow into my life and quench every evil fire that is burning within me, in the name of Jesus.
21. Every enemy of righteousness in my life, die, in the name of Jesus.
22. Any evil dream sent to pollute my life, die, in the name of Jesus.
23. O Lord, arise and keep me safe from devourers of widows/orphans, in the name of Jesus.
24. O Lord, expose the murderers of my husband, in the name of Jesus.
25. Holy Ghost fire, chases away any man or woman that is sitting on my husband's property, in the name of Jesus.
26. O Lord, expose all unfriendly friends of my husband, in the name of Jesus.
27. Let every insult and disgrace released against me backfire, in the name of Jesus.
28. Let all unfriendly friends of my family be disgraced, in the name of Jesus.
29. O Lord, empower me to take my stand for God, in the name of Jesus.
30. Let evil arrows that were fired at my family return back to senders, in the name of Jesus.
31. I reject evil conditions my helpers demand before helping me, in the name of Jesus.
32. I refuse to enter into any evil covenant because of suffering, in the name of Jesus.
33. Let any man or woman that is delaying my miracle be frustrated, in the name of Jesus.
34. Any curse that was placed upon my life because I am a widow, go back to your sender, in the name of Jesus.
35. I reject every evil visitor that was invoked against me from the grave, in the name of Jesus.
36. O Lord, protect my family from my husband's enemies, in the name of Jesus.

37. Blood of Jesus, enter into the grave and resurrect all my buried blessings, in the name of Jesus.

38. Any satanic padlock on my life, break to pieces, in the name of Jesus.

39. Let the angels of the living God fight for my rights, benefits and entitlement, in the name of Jesus.

40. Every arrow of death that was fired at my family, I fire you back, in the name of Jesus.

41. Any evil altar that was raised against my family, be roasted by fire, in the name of Jesus.

42. Every evil spirit that was sent to torment me, go back to your sender now, in the name of Jesus.

43. Any evil sacrifice that was offered for my sake, expire, in the name of Jesus.

44. Any place they call my name for evil, blood of Jesus, answer for me, in the name of Jesus.

45. Anyone that wants to kill me because of property, die immediately, in the name of Jesus.

46. Let every evil meeting being conveyed for my life end to my favor, in the name of Jesus.

47. Every enemy of my life, receive confusion, in the name of Jesus.

48. Any Goliath in my husband's family that has risen up against me is disgraced, in the name of Jesus.

49. Let every good thing that God has said about me begin to manifest, in the name of Jesus.

50. O Lord, keep me alive and healthy in time of my harvest, in the name of Jesus.

51. Let all evil utterances ever said against me expire to my favor, in the name of Jesus.

52. Let every plan against my life be exposed and be disgraced, in the name of Jesus.

53. Angels of the living God, defend my life, in the name of Jesus.

54. Let my mockers begin to mock themselves, in the name of Jesus.

55. Let any will written concerning my family and me be rightly executed, in the name of Jesus.

56. O Lord, arise and oppress my oppressors, in the name of Jesus.

57. Let angels that protect widows and orphans fight for me, in the name of Jesus.
58. O Lord, provide for me and take care of all my troubles, in the name of Jesus.
59. Let my prayers enter into the ears of God now, in the name of Jesus.
60. Any satanic trap that was set for my family and me, catch your owners, in the name of Jesus.

38

Chapter

PRAYERS AGAINST PREMATURE DEATH

CHAPTER OVERVIEW

- *Your life is not for sale*
- *Satan tempts believers*
- *Different forms of premature death*
- *Grievous death*
- *Long life without reverence to God*
- *Victims of premature death*

YOUR LIFE IS NOT FOR SALE

God is the creator of all things in heaven and on earth. He created life and He is the source of all spiritual and physical things. The devil has no right to claim anything as his in the universe that God made. The worst devil could do was to go around deceiving people to believe that the earth belongs to him. However, the truth is that the earth, the fullness thereof, and all the people therein belong to God.

"Behold, the heaven and the heaven of heavens is the LORD'S thy God, the earth also, with all that therein is" (Deuteronomy 10:14).

"The land shall not be sold forever: for the land is mine; for ye are strangers and sojourners with me" (Leviticus 25:23).

"But who am I, and what is my people, that we should be able to offer so willingly after this sort? For all things come of thee and of thine own have we given thee" (1 Chronicles 29:14).

God has the right of ownership to your life, time and possessions. In order to fulfill your destiny, live long and enjoy God's provision and presence, you must allow God to rule over your life without any rival. Except God controls your time, money and talent, devil will wrestle control over them in your life.

"Do ye thus requite the LORD, O foolish people and unwise? Is not He thy father that hath bought thee? Hath he not made thee, and established thee?" (Deuteronomy 32:6).

"The earth is the LORD'S, and the fullness thereof; the world, and they that dwell therein" (Psalms 24:1).

"Behold, all souls are mine; as the soul of the father, so also the soul of the son is mine: the soul that sinned, it shall die" (Ezekiel 18:4).

"For in him we live, and move, and have our being; as certain also of your own poets have said, For we are also his offspring" (Acts 17:28).

You have to understand that you are God's property and that you do not belong to yourself, anyone else or the devil. You are expected to give yourself, your whole life, time, possession and talent to God. This is the wisest thing to do as a Christian.

When God created man, He created him in His image and likeness. Man walked in innocence, holiness and purity. He was good, righteous and holy, the crown of creation and a little lower than the angels.

> *"And God said, Let us make man in our image, after our likeness: and let them have dominion over the fish of the sea, and over the fowl of the air, and over the cattle, and over all the earth, and over every creeping thing that creepeth upon the earth. So God created man in his own image, in the image of God created he him; male and female created he them"* (Genesis 1:26-27).

> *"And have put on the new man, which is renewed in knowledge after the image of him that created him"* (Colossians 3:10).

From the beginning, there was nothing like sickness, pain, poverty, suffering or lack. God created all that man needed to make him live happily forever without suffering or pain. There was no need for healing or deliverance. These things came into existence immediately Adam and Eve sinned.

> *"And the LORD God took the man, and put him into the Garden of Eden to dress it and to keep it. [16]And the LORD God commanded the man, saying, Of every tree of the garden thou mayest freely eat: [17]But of the tree of the knowledge of good and evil, thou shall not eat of it: for in the day that thou eatest thereof thou shall surely die"* (Genesis 2:15-17).

Adam and Eve disobeyed God's commandment and surrendered their lives and leadership position to the devil. Thus, man lost his position and provisions from God.

> *"Now the serpent was more subtle than any beast of the field which the LORD God had made. In addition, he said unto the woman, Yea, hath God said, ye shall not eat of every tree of the garden? And the woman said unto the serpent, We may eat of the fruit of the trees of the garden: But of the fruit of the tree which is in the midst of the garden, God hath said, Ye shall not eat of it, neither shall ye touch it, lest ye die. And the serpent said unto the woman, Ye shall not surely die: For God doth know that in the day ye eat thereof, then your eyes shall be opened, and ye shall be as gods, knowing good and evil. And when the woman saw that the tree was good for food, and that it was pleasant to the eyes, and a tree to be desired to make one wise, she took of the fruit thereof, and did eat, and gave also unto her husband with her; and he did eat"* (Genesis 3:1-6).

> *"And one cried unto another, and said, Holy, holy, holy, is the LORD of hosts: the whole earth is full of his glory"* (Isaiah 6:3).

"He is the Rock, his work is perfect: for all his ways are judgment: a God of truth and without iniquity, just and right is he" (Deuteronomy 32:4).

Sin came into the world because of the wrong choice made by free mortal agents. Adam's sin brought all humanity under a curse. All men in Adam became sinners and captives to sin and death. Man became a rebel before God having broken His law and incurred His wrath that led to his premature death. Since then, man has been under the curse of death. He could not overturn his death penalty to live, enjoy freedom of worship and carry out the divine purpose for which God created him originally.

Eve listened to the lies of Satan, looked thoughtfully at the forbidden fruit, doubted God and desired what God had forbidden. She ate the forbidden fruit and later gave to Adam to eat. They were separated from God because of their sin of disobedience. The consequence of their fall was disaster. Premature death originated from here. All men by birth inherit a sinful nature and needs to repent of sin to live long to fulfill their destiny on earth.

Unless you return to God, you remain spiritually dead, separated from God and will never fulfill your purpose on earth or spend eternity with God after death. Jesus Christ came for this purpose.

"For the Son of man is come to seek and to save that which was lost" (Luke 19: 10).

"And saying, The time is fulfilled, and the kingdom of God is at hand: repent ye, and believe the gospel" (Mark 1:15).

"Come unto me, all ye that labor and are heavy laden and I will give you rest. Take my yoke upon you, and learn of me; for I am meek and lowly in heart: and ye shall find rest unto your souls. For my yoke is easy, and my burden is light" (Matthew 11:28-30).

Man's redemption required one who was worthy to suffer and die in man's place because of his sin. When redemption takes place, a guilty person becomes free to enjoy life as if he never committed any sin in his life. He becomes righteous and free of the consequences of sins he committed because Jesus has suffered for his sake and paid the full price for his redemption. He is free and no longer under the condemnation of sin and death.

"Surely he hath borne our grief's, and carried our sorrows: yet we did esteem him stricken, smitten of God, and afflicted. But he was wounded for our transgressions, he was bruised for our iniquities: the chastisement of our peace was upon him; and with his stripes we are healed" (Isaiah 53: 4-5).

A saved person is redeemed and he is no longer under the bondage of the devil. He owes his life to Christ and is supposed to live for Christ to please Him. He is supposed to repent of all his sins and accept Christ as his Lord and Savior. He should ask Christ to forgive him and empower him to go and sin no more.

> *"Come unto me, all ye that labor and are heavy laden and I will give you rest. Take my yoke upon you, and learn of me; for I am meek and lowly in heart: and ye shall find rest unto your souls. [30]For my yoke is easy, and my burden is light"* (Matthew 11:28-30).

Repentance is turning away from sin, Satan and returning to God. It leads to a sincere change of mind, purpose and action. A repented person does not live his life in disobedience to God's Word. Instead, he abhors sin and commits to righteousness.

> *"He that committed sin is of the devil; for the devil sinned from the beginning. For this purpose, the Son of God was manifested, that he might destroy the works of the devil. Whosoever is born of God doth not commit sin; for his seed remained in him: and he cannot sin, because he is born of God. In this the children of God are manifest, and the children of the devil: whosoever doeth not righteousness is not of God, neither he that loveth not his brother"* (1 John 3:8-10).

After your repentance, you are to resist Satan and his works, or anything that opposes righteousness of God. Obey God's Word and live by it. You will fulfill your purpose in this world because you are created for a purpose. In addition, remember that devil is also in this world until God judges him finally and throws him in the lake of fire forever. The devil moves about trying to gain new converts to his kingdom.

> *"Now there was a day when the sons of God came to present themselves before the LORD and Satan came also among them. And the LORD said unto Satan, Whence comest thou? Then Satan answered the LORD, and said, From going to and fro in the earth, and from walking up and down in it"* (Job 1:6-7).

> *"Hereafter I will not talk much with you: for the prince of this world cometh, and hath nothing in me"* (John 14:30).

Resist the devil and do not listen or obey him. Otherwise, he causes a separation between you and God and you become a slave to Satan again. At that point, he can kill you untimely. However, if you remain faithful to Jesus, you cannot die prematurely.

> *"The thief cometh not, but for to steal, and to kill, and to destroy: I am come that they might have life, and that they might have* it *more abundantly"* (John 10:10).

> *"If ye abide in me, and my words abide in you, ye shall ask what ye will, and it shall be done unto you"* (John 15:7).

Therefore, you have a choice as to whom you want to follow and God cannot force you. If you want the devil to mess your life up, it is your choice but if you would decide to receive Christ, you will not die young without fulfilling your destiny. God did not promise that devil would not tempt you and I. God even permitted Satan to tempt Jesus but he did not find any evil thing in him.

SATAN TEMPTS BELIEVERS

When you become a believer, devil and his agents cannot stop tempting you. They will entice you with things you love most and when you yield, you become their slave and a potential candidate of premature death.

> *"[3]Neither yield ye your members as instruments of unrighteousness unto sin: but yield yourselves unto God, as those that are alive from the dead, and your members as instruments of righteousness unto God. [14]For sin shall not have dominion over you: for ye are not under the law, but under grace. [16]Know ye not, that to whom ye yield yourselves servants to obey, his servants ye are to whom ye obey; whether of sin unto death, or of obedience unto righteousness?"* (Romans 6:16, 13-14).

Temptation in itself is not sin but yielding to temptation is sin. When sin comes into someone's life, it comes with bondage of premature death. God allows us to be tested or tempted to reveal our inner strength or weakness. Through temptation, you learn and prove your faith, loyalty and faithfulness to God. If you overcome temptation, God would protect you but when you fall, devil gains control of your life and you are exposed to his attacks any time.

One who yields to the devil and falls into temptations has rejected God's protection. He becomes a traitor and outcast before God; a captive to the devil. He risks his name being removed from the book of life and written in the book of premature death. Everything would be against him. God forsakes him and the devil attacks him at will. (*See* Exodus 32:33; Ezra 8:22; 1 Samuel 15:22; 1 Timothy 5:14-16, 16:14; Deuteronomy 8:58-63).

The worst that could happen to a believer is to yield to temptations and backslide.

> *"For some are already turned aside after Satan"* (1 Timothy 5:15).

> *"Now the Spirit speaketh expressly, that in the latter times some shall depart from the faith, giving heed to seducing spirits, and doctrines of devils; Speaking lies in hypocrisy; having their conscience seared with a hot iron"* (1 Timothy 4:1-2).

> *"For if after they have escaped the pollutions of the world through the knowledge of the Lord and Savior Jesus Christ, they are again entangled therein, and overcome, the latter end is worse with them than the beginning. For it had been better for them not to have known the way of righteousness, then, after they have known it, to turn from the holy commandment delivered unto them. But it is happened unto them according to the true proverb, The dog is turned to his own vomit again; and the sow that was washed to her wallowing in the mire"* (2 Peter 2:20-22).

A backslidden believer is slave of the devil, who sears his conscience with hot iron. Sorrow and affliction will be his portion. As he lives on earth, the wrath of God would follow him. He is spiritually dead and the shadow of sickness, terror, shame, incurable disease and death hang upon his head. The only way out for such a backslidden believer is not prayer, fighting or deliverance. Repentance, restitution and consecration are the immediate step you must take. This can turn the wrath of God away and restore you back to God's favor.

> *"The thief cometh not, but for to steal, and to kill, and to destroy: I am come that they might have life, and that they might have it more abundantly"* (John 10:10).

> *"[32]And ye shall know the truth and the truth shall make you free. [36]If the Son therefore shall make you free, ye shall be free indeed"* (John 8:32, 36).

I read the story of Robert Robinson, author of the Hymn "*Come, thou fount of every blessing*". Robert wandered into sin. Because of this, he became deeply troubled in his spirit. Hoping to relieve his mind, he decided to travel. During his journeys, he became acquainted with a young woman who asked him what he thought of a hymn she had just been reading. To his greatest surprise, he found out it was no other but his own composition. He tried to avoid the woman's question, but she insisted and continued to press on him for an answer.

In a moment, he began to weep bitterly. With tears streaming down his cheeks, he said, "I am the one who wrote that hymn many years ago, I would give anything to experience again the joy I knew then." Although greatly surprised, she reassured him that the "streams of mercy" mentioned in his song still flowed. Robinson was deeply touched. Turning his "wondering heart" to the Lord, he was restored to full fellowship.

If you are a backslider, you do not need to remain under the power of darkness. Return to God, your rock of safety.

> *"If I shut up heaven that there be no rain, or if I command the locusts to devour the land, or if I send pestilence among my people; If my people, which are called by my name, shall humble themselves, and pray, and seek my face, and turn from their wicked ways; then will I hear from heaven, and will forgive their sin, and will heal their land"* (2 Chronicles 7:13-14).

Consequences of living outside the grace of God are many. It includes withdrawal of God's presence, sufferings, sickness and mysterious deaths. Minor problems would pursue and conquer those who live their lives without God. The blessings will be turned into a curse for them. Cry to God for His mercy, forgiveness and grace to live right before Him again. Seek for fellowship with God again through fervent prayers. As you return to God in repentance, repair your altar and lay your life before God. He will prolong your life so you would fulfill your destiny.

DIFFERENT FORMS OF PREMATURE DEATH

Many people are not aware that this world is filled with evil agents that cause premature deaths. Others do not believe it. Do you know that the earth is filled with more dead people than people alive are? Billions of dead people move around on earth without hindrance. Most people you see walking around are nothing but walking corpse. Before men, they are alive but before God, they are dead.

> *"And you hath he quickened, who were dead in trespasses and sins; Wherein in time past ye walked according to the course of this world, according to the prince of the power of the air, the spirit that now worked in the children of disobedience"* (Ephesians 2:1-2).

> *"And whosoever was not found written in the book of life was cast into the lake of fire"* (Revelation 20:15).

Spiritual death is separation from God while the second death is permanent or eternal separation from God Almighty. God knows people the spirit of premature death possesses. He warned His children not to enter into covenant with such people. Agreement with such people can cause a transfer of such demons into them. I am talking about people who are alive and are walking in the streets but they are condemned criminals before God that can die at anytime because they are under the bondage of the devil. This people may be okay physically looking beautiful and prosperous, but their lives hang in a balance.

> *"The word of the LORD came also unto me, saying, Thou shalt not take thee a wife, neither shalt thou have sons or daughters in this place. For thus saith the LORD concerning the sons and concerning the daughters that are born in this place, and concerning their mothers that bare them, and concerning their fathers that begat them in this land; They shall die of grievous deaths; they shall not be lamented; neither shall they be buried; but they shall be as dung upon the face of the earth: and they shall be consumed by the sword, and by famine; and their carcasses shall be meat for the fowls of heaven, and for the beasts of the earth"* (Jeremiah 16:1-4).

When you marry such person, you stand the danger of losing your life and good things that God had prepared for you. At times, demons of premature deaths reside in a family, place or thing. It can also take over an environment or a city.

GRIEVOUS DEATH

Grievous death is a wicked spirit that pursues people until it destroys them. Spirits of dead people, visitors from graveyards and heavy yokes burden its victims. It subjects such people to severe pain, suffering and sorrow. It inflicts injuries upon them with powers from the tombs. It is unimaginable that many people in this world are under the oppression of grievous death, which brings heartbreaking and painful occurrences upon them. Everything they touch dies young.

Grievous death does not always kill the principal person involved. Instead, it kills every good thing around the person and leaves the person alive to suffer without help. This kind of death is always ready to kill every good thing the victim initiates. This means that any project or activity the victim would initiate on earth would die a grievous death. None of the victim's projects would be allowed to reach the completion stage. The victim suffers alone and bears the cost of his losses alone without people's concern or care. It means that whenever the person enters into trouble or is in need of help, nobody would have pity for him.

Death would encircle the person's life. Though he remains alive physically, every good thing will desert his life. This is the kind of persons that people forget or avoid while they still live, as if they are dung upon the face of the earth. Their presence irritates people as rejection and hatred characterize their lives on earth. Every good thing avoids such people. Devil fights, pursues and keeps them in famine and destitute of every good thing. People would use their services to make much gain and later dump them.

> *"And it came to pass, as we went to prayer, a certain damsel possessed with a spirit of divination met us, which brought her masters much gain by soothsaying: The same followed Paul and us, and cried, saying, These men are the servants of the most high God, which show unto us the way of salvation. And this did her many days. However, Paul, being grieved, turned and said to the spirit, I command thee in the name of Jesus Christ to come out of her. In addition, he came out the same hour. And when her masters saw that the hope of their gains was gone, they caught Paul and Silas, and drew them into the marketplace unto the rulers"* (Acts 16:16-19).

> *"Because of the multitude of the whoredoms of the well-favored harlot, the mistress of witchcrafts, that selleth nations through her whoredoms, and families through her witchcrafts"* (Nahum 3:4).

There are people who are in covenant with the devil. They receive power to attack people with premature death. Some people believe they are useless to themselves, their parents and the society when they are useful to wicked occult grandmasters and they are making much gain through them. They make sure that such people live a long life as long as they are helping them make gains on other people's lives.

All the voices that come from mad people as they walk up and down the cities have lots of meaning. Some things you do that people consider useless is usually useful elsewhere to some people. The losses and failures you record in your life are gains elsewhere to some people. Your mistakes, worries and wasted efforts may bring pains to you but they generate much gain you cannot imagine for some people.

Some of the worst witchcrafts on earth are witchcrafts of manipulation, ignorance and evil transfer of human efforts. Often, the person that causes your pains, barrenness and marital failures to make gain is very close to you. The rich man used his occult powers to manipulate Lazarus through his desires. Of a truth, he fed Lazarus all the days of his life with crumbs but his wealth that made him to fare luxuriously came from the manipulated destiny of the poor beggar, Lazarus. That is the mystery of premature death. They can offer you as a sacrifice in an evil altar but physically you will be alive to cause others to make gains. That is another form of premature death.

> *"There was a certain rich man, which was clothed in purple and fine linen, and fared sumptuously every day: And there was a certain beggar named Lazarus, which was laid at his gate, full of sores, And desiring to be fed with the crumbs which fell from the rich man's table: moreover the dogs came and licked his sores. And it came to pass, that the beggar died, and was carried by the angels into Abraham's bosom: the rich man also died, and was buried"* (Luke 16:19-22).

Lazarus was not born a beggar. He was a greatly destined person. But the rich man manipulated him, offered him as a sacrifice and dumped him in his gate to attract riches for him. The demons of incurable sores ate up his destiny to enrich the rich man to cloth himself in purple fine linen and to fare extravagantly every day. This is an evil transfer from one of the worst soul traders on earth. You may not understand this but what I am talking about is a spiritual matter.

> *"[6]And he returned unto him, and, lo, he stood by his burnt sacrifice, he, and all the princes of Moab. [17]And when he came to him, behold, he stood by his burnt offering, and the princes of Moab with him. And Balak said unto him, what hath the LORD spoken?"* (Numbers 23:6, 17).

> *"And the merchants of the earth shall weep and mourn over her; for no man buyeth their merchandise any more: The merchandise of gold, and silver, and precious stones, and of pearls, and fine linen, and purple, and silk, and scarlet, and all thyine wood, and all manner vessels of ivory, and all manner vessels of most precious wood, and of brass, and iron, and marble, And cinnamon, and odors, and ointments, and*

frankincense, and wine, and oil, and fine flour, and wheat, and beasts, and sheep, and horses, and chariots, and slaves, and souls of men" (Revelation 18:11-13).

"Tarshish was thy merchant by reason of the multitude of all kind of riches; with silver, iron, tin, and lead, they traded in thy fairs. [13]Javan, Tubal, and Meshach, they were thy merchants: they traded the persons of men and vessels of brass in thy market" (Ezekiel 27:12-13).

There are people who are busy everyday offering sacrifices to discover people that are born with great talents. They want to know what God has said concerning such people. Once they discover them, they use them to make much gain. Such persons' deaths or deliverance affects their businesses on earth. They can allow you to live long on earth like Methuselah without reverence to God. The bible calls them the merchants of souls of men. They are destiny killers. Ezekiel said they traded the persons of men. They can bewitch a whole city and deceive even the wisest.

"But there was a certain man, called Simon, which beforetime in the same city used sorcery, and bewitched the people of Samaria, giving out that himself was some great one: To whom they all gave heed, from the least to the greatest, saying, This man is the great power of God. And to him they had regard, because that of long time he had bewitched them with sorceries" (Acts 8:9-11).

Premature death comes in various forms. You can die prematurely and yet live as the oldest in your village. In another way, some people die physically when they are about to be celebrated in life. Others die after they have finished their trainings and are about to assist their aged parents.

"And the woman conceived, and bares a son at that season that Elisha had said unto her, according to the time of life. And when the child was grown, it fell on a day that he went out to his father to the reapers. And he said unto his father, My head, my head. In addition, he said to a lad, carry him to his mother. And when he had taken him, and brought him to his mother, he sat on her knees till noon, and then died" (2 Kings 4:17-20).

LONG LIFE WITHOUT REVERENCE TO GOD

Some people need to embark on a radical prayer mission to discover their destiny. It is of no use to live long and be unhappy while you make much gain for others, who rejoice and enjoy their lives at your own expense. The greatest mistake that Abel made that sent him to early grave was seeing his worst enemy as a good brother. He trusted him and allowed him to take him to an evil field where he killed him. Do not follow people anyhow. No matter how close the person is to you, if your faith contradicts his, be careful otherwise, he lures you outside of God's presence or at occult altars where if you refuse to offer sacrifice, you will be killed.

> *"And Cain talked with Abel his brother: and it came to pass, when they were in the field, that Cain rose up against Abel his brother, and slew him"* (Genesis 4:8).

When you place yourself where God wants you to stay, it would be hard to die prematurely. You will live long to fulfill your destiny on earth. I believe Cain took Abel to his evil altar, a place to commune with the devil; an evil field.

> *"And Balak said unto him, Come, I pray thee, with me unto another place, from whence thou mayest see them: thou shalt see but the utmost part of them, and shall not see them all: and curse me them from thence. And he brought him into the field of Zophim, to the top of Pisgah, and built seven altars, and offered a bullock and a ram on every altar"* (Numbers 23:13-14).

There are people who are not in the occult. They are not unbelievers or sinners, yet they are walking corps. Nothing such people do can prosper. They go to church, pray very well but they are not available for good things. What is the problem? I think the problem is that they must have allowed someone they trusted to take them to an evil field; an evil altar or they inherited evil altars from their place of birth. You cannot enter into an evil altar and come back without an evil load or burden. You cannot be summoned into an evil altar without receiving a burden, a yoke or problems. That is why you need to pray very well all the times. As the bible puts it:

> *"Pray without ceasing"* (1 Thessalonians 5:17).

Abel went to an evil field because he was honoring an invitation from his only brother. He never came back alive. Some people may actually come back alive with an evil load. Others may never come back complete themselves any more. Balak and Balaam could not kill the children of Israel but they gave them the yoke of iniquity and perversion to commit immorality and thousands of them died in the wilderness prematurely.

> *"[21]He hath not beheld iniquity in Jacob, neither hath he seen perverseness in Israel: the LORD his God is with him, and the shout of a king are among them. [23]Surely*

there is no enchantment against Jacob, neither is there any divination against Israel: according to this time it shall be said of Jacob and of Israel, What hath God wrought" (Numbers 23:21, 23).

"[1]And Israel abode in Shittim and the people began to commit whoredom with the daughters of Moab. [2]And they called the people unto the sacrifices of their gods: and the people did eat, and bowed down to their gods. [3]And Israel joined himself unto Baal–peor: and the anger of the LORD was kindled against Israel. [9]And those that died in the plague were twenty and four thousand" (Numbers 25:1-3, 9).

You need to pray the prayers in this book because many people are carrying the yoke of premature deaths. You may be dead without knowing it.

Seth lived 912 years on earth without reverence to God. The only achievement mentioned about him was that he was a baby-making machine. He begets sons and daughters who had no reference to God. His son lived 905 years giving birth to children that are not godly. His son Caiman lived 910 years producing sons and daughters. His son, Mahalaleel, followed suit by living 895 unproductive years. His son Jared lived 962. Methuselah, his grandson, lived 969 to become the man that spent the longest time on earth without reverence to God. His life was very unfruitful as compared with others because he abandoned the good examples his father, Enoch, lived out.

"And Enoch lived sixty and five years, and begat Methuselah: And Enoch walked with God after he begat Methuselah three hundred years, and begat sons and daughters: And all the days of Enoch were three hundred sixty and five years: And Enoch walked with God: and he was not; for God took him. And Methuselah lived an hundred eighty and seven years, and begat Lamech: And Methuselah lived after he begat Lamech seven hundred eighty and two years, and begat sons and daughters: And all the days of Methuselah were nine hundred sixty and nine years: and he died" (Genesis 5:21-27).

a. Some victims wed with water spirit personalities who come at times to have sex with them in the dreams or feed them in the dreams. In addition, once this takes place, they either abort any good thing or miscarry already conceived blessings. The victims face disappointment or bad luck.

b. Some victims do not marry at all and if they marry, they marry late or marry a wrong person who will never make them happy at all.

c. Some victims experience marital crisis, separation, divorce or terrible marriage instability.

d. Some victims do not conceive, others conceive but miscarry while those who give birth give birth to polluted children who will not give them joy in life.

"Send thine hand from above; rid me, and deliver me out of great waters, from the hand of strange children" (Psalms 144:7).

e. They frustrate every effort of uncompromising victims, keep them in touch with only their enemies and send true helpers away from their reach.

f. Efforts they put in life do not produce results, things that happen to them do not always have natural causes or explanations, and trials that come into their lives come in sequence without giving them rest.

g. They are marked with marks of hatred, rejection, reproach, shame and disgrace.

h. They are not allowed to enjoy their lives because not every good thing they start reaches completion in peace or on time. They take last positions regardless of their outstanding intelligence. Their ends are never successful or peaceful.

i. They experience multiple difficulties in every venture and get angry and irritated at their helpers.

j. They record multiple or avoidable heartbreaking mistakes

k. They face all manner of attacks in their dreams. Manipulations and things that normally happen to them are unusual and abnormal.

l. They dream of their places of birth often, where they lived before, old schools with old schools uniforms, rewriting exams they wrote many years ago.

m. They experience blockages at the age of breakthroughs, miracles and inability to complete any project in peace.

n. They are always being oppressed and identified for errors.

o. Their enemies discover their destinies and arrest their stars, influence them to do wrong things, capture their progresses and bury their promising stars and greatness.

As I mentioned earlier, some people may need to embark on a radical prayer mission in order to recover what they have lost so that they can fulfill their destinies.

> *"Then Esther bade them return Mordecai this answer, Go, gather together all the Jews that are present in Shushan, and fast ye for me, and neither eat nor drink three days, night or day: I also and my maidens will fast likewise; and so will I go in unto the king, which is not according to the law: and if I perish, I perish"* (Esther 4:15-16).

> *"On that night could not the king sleep, and he commanded to bring the book of records of the chronicles; and they were read before the king"* (Esther 6:1).

Joshua did it and the sun and the moon stood still for a whole day. Hannah did it and her barren womb opened. Jehoshaphat did it and all his enemies bowed. Jacob did it and God changed his name. Mary and Martha did it and their brother, Lazarus, came back to life.

> *"And when he thus had spoken, he cried with a loud voice, Lazarus, comes forth. 44And he that was dead came forth, bound hand and foot with grave clothes: and his face was bound about with a napkin. Jesus saith unto them, Loose him, and let him go"* (John 11:43-44).

> *"With long life will I satisfy him, and show him my salvation"* (Psalms 91:16).

You have the backing of God's Word to live a long life and fulfill your destiny on earth. You have no reason to fail in this life.

> *"For David, after he had served his own generation by the will of God, fell on sleep, and was laid unto his fathers, and saw corruption"* (Acts 13:36).

Daniel refused to allow lions in the den to eat him. Therefore, do not allow evil powers to waste your life. You are more than a conqueror in Christ Jesus.

PRAYERS AGAINST PREMATURE DEATH

Bible references: Isaiah 38:1-9; John 11:1-3, 14, 38-44; Luke 7:11-17

Begin with praise and worship

1. Every invitation I gave to premature death to my life, I withdraw you by force, in the name of Jesus.
2. Let inherited bondage of premature death in my life break, in the name of Jesus.
3. I cast out every evil spirit that was assigned to kill me, in the name of Jesus.
4. Blood of Jesus, repurchase my life from the captivity of death, in the name of Jesus.
5. Every demon of death that is following me about is discharge by fire, in the name of Jesus.
6. Let attacks on my life from the grave end by force, in the name of Jesus.
7. Every messenger of premature death in my life, carry your message to your sender, in the name of Jesus.
8. Any evil spirit that is following me from the grave, return back immediately, in the name of Jesus.
9. Any strange fire from the tomb that is burning in my life, quench now, in the name of Jesus.
10. O Lord, arise and withdraw my life from the salve market of death, in the name of Jesus.
11. Let invisible property of death in my life catch fire and burn to ashes, in the name of Jesus.
12. Fire of God, burn to ashes every enemy of abundant life in my life, in the name of Jesus.
13. I command my life to escape from the captivity of death, in the name of Jesus.
14. O Lord, resurrect every dead thing that will make me happy in life, in the name of Jesus.
15. I revoke any evil burial that has taken place against my life, in the name of Jesus.

16. Any demon of sickness that is attacking my life, die, in the name of Jesus.

17. I cast out every sickness and disease that was programmed into my life, in the name of Jesus.

18. Any evil spirit on suicide mission in my life is cast out, in the name of Jesus.

19. I remove my life from the spirit of death that kills en masse, in the name of Jesus.

20. I terminate every program of premature death against my life, in the name of Jesus.

21. Every good thing I have lost to the spirit of death and hell, I recover you double, in the name of Jesus.

22. Let the covenant of premature death over my life break to pieces, in the name of Jesus.

23. Let blood of Jesus cleanse any sin that would attract premature death, in the name of Jesus.

24. Every yoke of death upon my life, break, in the name of Jesus.

25. Let the redemption power in the blood of Jesus redeem me from premature death, in the name of Jesus.

26. I break and loose myself from the pain that comes with death, in the name of Jesus.

27. Let my body, soul and spirit reject and overcome death, in the name of Jesus.

28. I break and loose myself from death spell from hell that is common in my place of birth, in the name of Jesus.

29. Any area of my life that was captured by timely death, receive full deliverance, in the name of Jesus.

30. Let every yoke of sin in my life that has vowed to drag me to premature death and hell break, in the name of Jesus.

31. Let suffering and hardship that come from premature deaths leave my life, in the name of Jesus.

32. Blood of Jesus, speak me out from premature deaths, in the name of Jesus.

33. Let redeeming power in Christ Jesus redeem me fully from every sin, in the name of Jesus.

34. I receive the power to sin no more, in the name of Jesus.

35. Any manipulation that is going on against my life from hell, die, in the name of Jesus.

36. I break and loose myself from evil judgments of the devil, in the name of Jesus.
37. Any condemnation on my life from the department of death, expire in the name of Jesus.
38. Let demons that escort people to death avoid me forever, in the name of Jesus.
39. I receive grace to overcome temptations that were designed to hand me over to death, in the name of Jesus.
40. Blood and stripes of Jesus, terminate every problem in my life, in the name of Jesus.

39

Chapter

PRAYERS TO ENJOY YOUR WEALTH AND RICHES

CHAPTER OVERVIEW

- *Definition of true success*
- *The end of occult wealth*
- *The reward of occultism*

DEFINITION OF TRUE SUCCESS

Many people have tried to define *success* and all its implications. However, success of God is not the same as the success of the world. The two are far apart in meaning and implication. One thing that is differentiates the two is, while godly success is permanent, world success is temporal.

Anyone who has decided to pursue true wealth and riches regards failure as the worst enemy. The worse failure is not the failure that usually occurs at the beginning or the middle of a journey. The worst failure is that one that strikes at the end of a journey, when success is expected.

Aristotle Onassis was a shipping tycoon who was worth one billion dollars. He owned houses, villas and apartments in various cities, the luxurious Lonian Island, priceless art collections, and the world's most expensive yacht – the 325 ft *Christiana* complete with luxurious bathrooms outfitted in sienna marbles and gold-plated faucets. He started his life with only $60 in his pocket to become one of the world's wealthiest men.

Onassis was rarely without beautiful and famous women around him. He once proclaimed. "*It is the people with money who are the royalty now*." In his quest for riches, he built his entire life around a foundation that was not godly or solid. Time magazine reported that he began to feel the heat in 1973.

Onassis life changed dramatically when his son, Alexander, was killed in a plane crash. He aged overnight. As his health failed, his business acumen failed. Concurrently, the Arab oil prices hit his shipping industry hard. Death claimed him on March 1975, after his assets dropped from an estimated one billion to $200 million during his last years on earth.

Most rich men in the world fail miserably because they fail to build their lives and businesses around God.

> *"There was a man of the Pharisees, named Nicodemus, a ruler of the Jews: The same came to Jesus by night, and said unto him, Rabbi, we know that thou art a teacher come from God: for no man can do these miracles that thou doest, except God be with him. Jesus answered and said unto him, Verily, verily, I say unto thee, Except a man be born again, he cannot see the kingdom of God"* (John 3:1-3).

> *"Behold, thou hast made my days as a handbreadth; and mine age is as nothing before thee: verily every man at his best state is altogether vanity. Selah. Surely every man*

walked in a vain shew: surely they are disquieted in vain: he heaped up riches, and knoweth not who shall gather them" (Psalms 39:5-6).

Your wealth includes your children and all the people under your care. No matter how much money you made or how much reputation you got, when you fail to help your children and people under your care grow in the right direction, you are a failure. It is not the so much of you in the pages of newspapers or massive properties all over the world or the money in the bank. What matters is how much of your godly characters you used to lead people to God.

To be remarkably successful, other people must succeed through you. You must help them find God. Unless more people come to maturity and have testimony of good relationship with God, no one should count him or herself a successful person.

"And the men rose up from thence, and looked toward Sodom: and Abraham went with them to bring them on the way. And the LORD said, Shall I hide from Abraham that thing which I do; Seeing that Abraham shall surely become a great and mighty nation, and all the nations of the earth shall be blessed in him. For I know him, that he will command his children and his household after him, and they shall keep the way of the LORD, to do justice and judgment; that the LORD may bring upon Abraham that which he hath spoken of him" (Genesis 18:16-19).

The success of Abraham was based on his ability to communicate God to his children and his household. The generation of Sodom and Gomorrah failed because they could not communicate with God. J. R. Miller once said, *"The only thing that walks back from the tomb and refuses to be buried is the character of a man."* This is true. The character of a man outlives him. It cannot be buried.

John C. Maxwell once said, "The bottom line in leadership is not how far we advance ourselves but how far we advance others."

A rich man's success is not measured with how much money he has in the bank but how much of his money is invested on others. A rich man's success is measured with how many people he made rich and not how much rich he was. If you want to keep your wealth, keep it inside human beings not in the bank or on perishable things.

"When thou cutest down thine harvest in thy field, and hast forgot a sheaf in the field, thou shalt not go again to fetch it: it shall be for the stranger, for the fatherless, and for the widow: that the LORD thy God may bless thee in all the work of thine hands. When thou beatest thine olive tree, thou shalt not go over the boughs again: it shall be for the stranger, for the fatherless, and for the widow" (Deuteronomy 24:19-20).

When you use your riches to help others, God remembers you in times of troubles. Wealth and riches are from God and are entrusted into your hands so that all humanity can benefit from it. If you do not have this mind, God may not entrust true riches into your hands.

"Both riches and honor come of thee, and thou reigns over all; and in thine hand is power and might; and in thine hand it is to make great, and to give strength unto all. And he died in a good old age, full of days, riches, and honor: and Solomon his son reigned in his stead" (1 Chronicles 29:12, 28).

"Let no man seek his own, but every man another's wealth" (1 Corinthians 10:24).

"A little that a righteous man hath is better than the riches of many wicked" (Psalms 37:16).

Riches, wealth and honor come from God. You must use them to glorify God. When you position yourself to use God's provision very well, God will make you great. David was very meek. He was a man after God's own heart and God made sure he lacked nothing. He used God's gift to glorify God and he died in a good old age, full of days, in riches and honor. That is the will of God for all His children.

David was brave, courageous and bold to lead the children of Israel to subdue God's enemies. His major secret in his victories in life was that he regarded and fought Israel enemies as God's enemies. In addition, he dedicated his spoils of war to the Lord.

"Them also king David dedicated unto the LORD, with the silver and the gold that he brought from all these nations; from Edom, and from Moab, and from the children of Ammon, and from the Philistines, and from Amalek" (1 Chronicles 18:11).

"Every man also to whom God hath given riches and wealth, and hath given him power to eat thereof, and to take his portion, and to rejoice in his labor; this is the gift of God" (Ecclesiastes 5:19).

"Then answered all the wicked men and men of Belial, of those that went with David, and said, Because they went not with us, we will not give them ought of the spoil that we have recovered, save to every man his wife and his children, that they may lead them away, and depart. Then said David, Ye shall not do so, my brethren, with that which the LORD hath given us, who hath preserved us, and delivered the company that came against us into our hand. For who will hearken unto you in this matter? But as his part is that goeth down to the battle, so shall his part be that tarrieth by the stuff: they shall part alike" (1 Samuel 30:22-24).

David did not seek for his welfare or build empires to himself. He sought for the welfare of God's people and determined to satisfy both the weak and strong. A wicked man can accumulate the whole world and yet would not be satisfied. However, a godly person shares the little he has. No one should be rich for himself alone. It is a gift from God to be satisfied and contented with what the Lord has given to you. If you do not distribute your wealth the way God who provided them wants, He will send enemies into your house with a curse upon your wealth.

> *"And thou shall see an enemy in my habitation, in all the wealth which God shall give Israel: and there shall not be an old man in thine house forever"* (1 Samuel 2:32).

> *"Trust not in oppression, and become not vain in robbery: if riches increase, set not your heart upon them"* (Psalms 62:10).

Do not set your heart upon riches because enemies can intrude at the peak of your riches and wealth or at an old age. Enemies can operate externally or internally. One of your children could be used to destroy all that you have gathered and your life and family would be ruined prematurely. Because the heart of the wicked is in his wealth, he will die in sorrow as the enemy wastes his riches. The enemy in the house of the wicked will waste all that he invested in his children and grandchildren. His wealth and good things in his house will go into captivity because he refused to use them to honor the Lord by helping others.

> *"And all their wealth, and all their little ones, and their wives took they captive, and spoiled even all that was in the house"* (Genesis 34:29).

> *"For Mordecai the Jew was next unto king Ahasuerus, and great among the Jews, and accepted of the multitude of his brethren, seeking the wealth of his people, and speaking peace to all his seed"* (Esther 10:3).

That is how God transfers the wealth of the wicked to godly people, who would use them for the welfare of God's people.

Occult wealth and riches are not genuine blessings. They are fictitious. Cain killed his brother because he wanted to possess his property. Likewise, if you are a murderer or you poison someone in order to get wealth, your wealth and riches is defiled, polluted and contaminated.

> *"And Cain talked with Abel his brother: and it came to pass, when they were in the field, that Cain rose up against Abel his brother, and slew him"* (Genesis 4:8).

If you practice sorcery or commit adultery, swear falsely and oppress other people to make gain, you are an enemy of God. Your wealth is defiled. When you deride God's law and influence people to stumble because you want to make gain, your wealth is corrupt. When you oppress laborers, widows and rob God in tithes and offerings, your wealth is stinking. When you practice wickedness to make gain, or deal treacherously with people, your wealth is an abomination before God.

If you shed innocent blood to make gain or forsake God to pursue the things of this world, your wealth will not profit you. When you commit whoredom, swear falsely, lie, steal and become a snare to others for the sake of making profit, your wealth is abomination before God. If you transgress God's commandments and take or give bribe to gain favor, your wealth will not profit you. If you became ungrateful to God, worship idol and rebel against God, your wealth cannot be a blessing to you. (*See* Hosea 2:1-13; 4:19; 9:1-17; 12:1-14). If you do human sacrifice and enlarge your coast through evil practices, your wealth stinks.

> *"Thus saith the LORD; For three transgressions of the children of Ammon, and for four, I will not turn away the punishment thereof; because they have ripped up the women with child of Gilead, that they might enlarge their border"* (Amos 1:13).

> *"2Pass ye unto Calneh, and see; and from thence go ye to Hamath the great: then go down to Gath of the Philistines: be they better than these kingdoms? Alternatively, their border greater than your border? 6That drink wine in bowls, and anoint themselves with the chief ointments: but they are not grieved for the affliction of Joseph. 12Shall horses run upon the rock. Will one plow there with oxen? For ye have turned judgment into gall and the fruit of righteousness into hemlock"* (Amos 6:2, 12, 6).

If you tread upon poor people, afflict the just, pervert justice, contend with God, make a city bloody, and cover up evil to make money, you are corrupt (*See* Amos 8:1-13; 2:1-11; 3:1; 6:1-16; Nahum 1:1-5; 2:8-13; Habakkuk 1:1-4). When you hunt for your brother's life, rejoice in evil and refuse to repent and forsake your sins, you risk spending your eternity in hell. Anything you do without God to make gains is evil and surely all the riches and wealth of the occult and wicked people will end.

THE REWARD OF OCCULTISM

Satan is the god of occultism. In the occult, they kill, destroy and steal people's destinies to make money. Occult men and women may live to enjoy their lives but at the peak of their enjoyment, they die. Most of them die when life appears meaningful and enjoyable.

> *"They spend their days in wealth, and in a moment go down to the grave"* (Job 21:13).

> *"Thou sellest thy people for nought, and dost not increase thy wealth by their price"* (Psalms 44:12).

You may sacrifice the destiny of other people to get wealth, but you will not enjoy your wealth, no matter how long you live on earth. Occult people do not enjoy their lives on earth because the devil they serve is not faithful. He has never been good to anyone because it is not his nature to be good.

> *"[6]They that trust in their wealth, and boast themselves in the multitude of their riches; [10]For he seeth that wise men die, likewise the fool and the brutish person perish, and leave their wealth to others"* (Psalms 49:6, 10).

> *"Lest strangers be filled with thy wealth; and thy labors be in the house of a stranger"* (Proverbs 5:10).

> *"A man to whom God hath given riches, wealth, and honor, so that he wanted nothing for his soul of all that he desired, yet God gives him not power to eat thereof, but a stranger eateth it: this is vanity, and it is an evil disease"* (Ecclesiastes 6:2).

The devil can deceive you to kill and get money. He can compel you to trust him as you do evil but he would turn around later to torment you. Devil knows how to deceive rich men to do evil but cannot allow them to enjoy their wealth. They die shameful deaths.

> *"Let mount Zion rejoice, let the daughters of Judah be glad, because of thy judgments. Walk about Zion, and go round about her: tell the towers thereof"* (Psalms 48:11-12).

Some of them leave their wealth behind, which also destroys their children. Others would live and witness helplessly how their wealth slips out of their hands to other people. At their old age, their careless and foolish children would waste all their investments. Demons that own their wealth cannot allow their children to be useful in life.

"Lest strangers be filled with thy wealth; and thy labors be in the house of a stranger; And thou mourn at the last, when thy flesh and thy body are consumed, And say, How have I hated instruction, and my heart despised reproof; And have not obeyed the voice of my teachers, nor inclined mine ear to them that instructed me! I was almost in all evil in the midst of the congregation and assembly" (Proverbs 5:10-14).

Most rich people die in regrets, shame and reproach. They would soon realize their mistakes when it is too late. Sickness, disease and the demons that owned their riches will consume their bodies. They will be taken from one hospital to another and demons will torment them until they die. The devil can lead them to visit all evil places in search of healing. By the time devil has finished using them, he will eat up their bodies. That is how God exposes them always.

There are people in this world that have every good thing they needed. They struggle all the days of their lives to accumulate wealth. However, by the time they will settle down to enjoy their success, sorrowful events begin to unfold all around them. Others would eat and drink all the things they have gotten but one sickness will end their journey on earth and take them to hell fire. I want you to take some time to study and meditate on this passage:

"He hath swallowed down riches and he shall vomit them up again: God shall cast them out of his belly. He shall suck the poison of asps: the viper's tongue shall slay him. He shall not see the rivers, the floods, the brooks of honey and butter. That which he labored for shall he restore, and shall not swallow it down: according to his substance shall the restitution be, and he shall not rejoice therein. Because he hath oppressed and hath forsaken the poor; because he hath violently taken away a house which he builded not; Surely, he shall not feel quietness in his belly, he shall not save of that which he desired. There shall none of his meat be left; therefore shall no man look for his goods. In the fullness of his sufficiency he shall be in straits: every hand of the wicked shall come upon him. When he is about to fill his belly, God shall cast the fury of his wrath upon him, and shall rain it upon him while he is eating. He shall flee from the iron weapon and the bow of steel shall strike him through. It is drawn, and cometh out of the body; yea, the glittering sword cometh out of his gall: terrors are upon him. All darkness shall be hid in his secret places: a fire not blown shall consume him; it shall go ill with him that is left in his tabernacle. The heaven shall reveal his iniquity; and the earth shall rise up against him. The increase of his house shall depart and his goods shall flow away in the day of his wrath. This is the portion of a wicked man from God, and the heritage appointed unto him by God" (Job 20:15-29).

I hope you read the above passage gently and diligently. You will agree that it is foolishness to come into this world and pursue riches and wealth without true blessings from the creator. The devil can make you to spend your youth pursuing all manner of evil things. You may offer human sacrifice and oppress people at will. The devil can empower you to overpower people that are stronger than you are. You can even join occult groups and become popular without any rival. Devil knows how to set you up.

However, the truth is that every sin you commit opens doors of your body for legion of demons to enter and possess your body. Imagine all the sins of your youth and old age amounting to uncountable demons. Wicked demons normally make wicked people to feel very comfortable in their evil ways. Sadly, there will come a time the same demons will unleash terror upon you and your children. You cannot have peace.

> *"His bones are full of the sin of his youth, which shall lie down with him in the dust. Though wickedness be sweet in his mouth, though he hide it under his tongue; Though he spare it, and forsake it not; but keep it still within his mouth: Yet his meat in his bowels is turned, it is the gall of asps within him"* (Job 20:11-14).

Devil influences people to withdraw their trust in God. That is when you become weak in your faith in God. Ironically, that is when you grow stronger in witchcraft activities. The only thing on earth that would keep you satisfied is to do more wicked things. At that point, your prosperity will increase as you do more things that are unimaginable. You will store up riches waiting for a time you need them most. Unfortunately, demons will haunt you instead.

> *"[7]Lo, this is the man that made not God his strength; but trusted in the abundance of his riches, and strengthened himself in his wickedness. [12]Behold, these are the ungodly, which prosper in the world; they increase in riches"* (Psalms 52:7; 73:12).

> *"There is a sore evil which I have seen under the sun, namely, riches kept for the owners thereof to their hurt. But those riches perish by evil travail: and he begetteth a son, and there is nothing in his hand"* (Ecclesiastes 5:13-14).

I have taken some time to observe some wicked people. I also observed some righteous people until I concluded that godly wealth and riches could not be achieved through struggle. The race of life is not to the swift, nor the battle to the strong. To enter into this world and jump into success and wealth without reverence or gratefulness to God as the source is the worst thing that can happen to someone.

> *"I returned, and saw under the sun, that the race is not to the swift, nor the battle to the strong, neither yet bread to the wise, nor yet riches to men of understanding, nor yet favor to men of skill; but time and chance happened to them all. For man also*

knoweth not his time: as the fishes that are taken in an evil net, and as the birds that are caught in the snare; so are the sons of men snared in an evil time, when it falleth suddenly upon them" (Ecclesiastes 9:11-12).

"[11]As the partridge sitteth on eggs, and hatchet them not; so he that getteth riches, and not by right, shall leave them in the midst of his days, and at his end shall be a fool. [36]Therefore mine heart shall sound for Moab like pipes, and mine heart shall sound like pipes for the men of Kir–heres: because the riches that he hath gotten are perished" (Jeremiah 17:11; 48:36).

"And they shall make a spoil of thy riches, and make a prey of thy merchandise: and they shall break down thy walls, and destroy thy pleasant houses: and they shall lay thy stones and thy timber and thy dust in the midst of the water" (Ezekiel 26:12).

Anyone who wants to make true riches and enjoy life ought to study the Scriptures very well. You will also find this book very valuable and note all scriptural references here. It is good to struggle and work hard but you have to acknowledge God first. You must be born-again and be reconciled to God, your creator.

"For all have sinned, and come short of the glory of God" (Romans 3:23).

Even when you have all the wisdom, skill and ability to run around and accumulate riches, you need God certainly. The race is not to the swift, nor the battle to the strong neither bread to the wise nor yet riches to men of understanding (*See* Ecclesiastes 9:11).

It is good to get rich, but it must be gotten in a right way. It is better to be a fool and be wise later than to be wise at first and a fool later. God loves those who come to Him seeking for His wisdom. Any wisdom outside God and Christ, His Son, is worst than foolishness and is as empty as nothing. All wise, wicked and rich sinners would discover their folly when it is late. What is the wisdom in struggling, fighting and laboring for what would spoil or fall to prey?

"Thy riches, and thy fairs, thy merchandise, thy mariners, and thy pilots, thy calkers, and the occupiers of thy merchandise, and all thy men of war, that are in thee, and in all thy company which is in the midst of thee, shall fall into the midst of the seas in the day of thy ruin"(Ezekiel 27:27).

"And Jesus looked round about, and saith unto his disciples, how hardly shall they that have riches enter into the kingdom of God! And the disciples were astonished at his words. But Jesus answered again, and saith unto them, Children, how hard is it for them that trust in riches to enter into the kingdom of God!" (Mark 10:23-24).

"Charge them that are rich in this world, that they be not high-minded, nor trust in uncertain riches, but in the living God, who giveth us richly all things to enjoy" (1 Timothy 6:17).

"Your riches are corrupted, and your garments are motheaten" (James 5:2).

The power that controls the riches and wealth of sinners is from the waters. Powers from the sea use satanic agents and wicked and wealthy people to commit unimaginable atrocities. The reason why Jesus said that it is hard for a rich man to enter the kingdom of God is because they have sold themselves to the devil. Their eyes are blinded to the gospel of Christ. The devil has made them to hate God and blind them from seeing God's power. They trust in their riches so much that they prefer it above God's kingdom. God's power is readily available to deliver rich sinners but they love money more than the salvation of their souls. They have made devil their god and master. They have been deceived to see only the power of the devil without seeing God's power.

"In whom the god of this world hath blinded the minds of them which believe not, lest the light of the glorious gospel of Christ, who is the image of God, should shine unto them" (2 Corinthians 4:4).

"Your riches are corrupted and your garments are moth-eaten" (James 5:2).

When a sinner's heart seeks for the salvation of Jesus Christ and confesses Jesus as His Lord and Savior, Jesus Christ will save him, no matter how sinful he was. All humanity has this amazing opportunity to be saved through repentance, faith and grace of God. It is by grace that we all are saved, but you must repent first.

The devil cannot stop a determined sinner who is ready to return to God's kingdom. When you turn away from your sins, have a change of mind and purpose, Christ will pardon you of all your sins and empower you to be a child of God.

"[12]But as many as received him, to them gave the power to become the sons of God, even to them that believe on his name: [32]And ye shall know the truth, and the truth shall make you free. [36]If the Son therefore shall make you free, ye shall be free indeed" (John 1:12, 8:32, 36).

"And Zacchæus stood, and said unto the Lord; Behold, Lord, the half of my goods I give to the poor; and if I have taken anything from any man by false accusation, I restore him fourfold" (Luke 19:8).

It will not take you anything to make this decision. You do not have to pay any price or consult anyone to be born-again. Take a decision to cease from every sin, hate sin and abhor every manner of sinful life and you are sure to receive pardon and salvation from Jesus Christ.

PRAYERS TO ENJOY YOUR WEALTH AND RICHES

Bible references: Genesis 30:30; Job 42:10-12

Begin with praise and worship

1. Every inherited sinful lifestyle that destroys riches and wealth in my family, I reject you, die, in the name of Jesus.
2. I cast out every spirit of failure in my life forever, in the name of Jesus.
3. Let foundational failures in my life collapse by thunder, in the name of Jesus.
4. I walk out from satanic failures and defeats, in the name of Jesus.
5. I command every failure that was programmed into my life from start to finish to be destroyed, in the name of Jesus.
6. Any witchcraft mouth that was opened to swallow my riches and wealth, close forever, in the name of Jesus.
7. I destroy any power that is assigned to destroy my godly character, in the name of Jesus.
8. Let the fire of God burn every evil investment in my possession, in the name of Jesus.
9. I break and loose myself from evil relationship that is working against my wealth, in the name of Jesus.
10. O Lord, deliver me from getting the wealth of sorrow, in the name of Jesus.
11. O Lord, help me to restore things I have acquired wrongly in my life, in the name of Jesus.
12. I refuse to keep back the riches that I acquired against God's will, in the name of Jesus.
13. I receive power, wisdom and knowledge to advance people's lives with my wealth, in the name of Jesus.
14. Father Lord, appear and influence me to invest my wealth rightly, in the name of Jesus.

15. I cast out any demon that was assigned to divest my investments, in the name of Jesus.

16. I command my riches and wealth to glorify God alone at all times, in the name of Jesus.

17. O Lord, give me courage to invest my wealth according to Your directives, in the name of Jesus.

18. Father Lord, help me to seek for the welfare of the children of God, in the name of Jesus.

19. O Lord, deliver me from being rich to myself alone, in the name of Jesus.

20. I command my wealth to be distributed in the way God wants, in the name of Jesus.

21. Let my riches and wealth take billions of people to heaven, in the name of Jesus.

22. I destroy every occult influence over my riches and wealth, in the name of Jesus.

23. Let the enemies of my riches and wealth be exposed and disgraced, in the name of Jesus.

24. Any arrow of death that was fired at me to take over my wealth, backfire, in the name of Jesus.

25. Every evil conspiracy against me because of my wealth, fail woefully, in the name of Jesus.

26. Blood of Jesus, flow into my wealth and riches and purify it, in the name of Jesus.

27. Let the Holy Ghost fire surround my wealth forever, in the name of Jesus.

28. Any wicked personality that wants to destroy my wealth and family, die, in the name of Jesus.

29. Let all the unfriendly friends of my wealth and riches be disgraced, in the name of Jesus.

30. I lift every satanic embargo that was placed upon my wealth, in the name of Jesus.

31. Any battle that is going on against my riches and wealth is terminated, in the name of Jesus.

32. Any evil leg that has walked into my wealth, riches and family, walk out now, in the name of Jesus.

33. Let the oppressors of my destiny because of my wealth be oppressed, in the name of Jesus.

34. O Lord, empower me to use my wealth to help the needy, in the name of Jesus.

35. I receive power to create wealth, in the name of Jesus.

36. Let evil forces that have vowed to abort my wealth die, in the name of Jesus.

37. O Lord, empower me to manage and control my wealth rightly, in the name of Jesus.

38. I break and loose my wealth from the captivity of water spirits, in the name of Jesus.

39. Father Lord, use my wealth and riches to raise billionaires for your kingdom, in the name of Jesus.

40. Every enemy of my wealth, die, in the name of Jesus.

41. Any strange fire that was programmed into my life, wealth and family, quench forever, in the name of Jesus.

40

Chapter

PRAYERS FOR SOUND SLEEP AND REST

CHAPTER OVERVIEW

- *Yokes of the devil*
- *Yokes of Satan identified*
- *God breaks yokes for believers*
- *Fear: agent of sleepless nights*
- *When sleeps departs*
- *Benefits of sound sleep*

YOKES OF THE DEVIL

When God created the universe, He looked at the universe and attested that the universe He made was good. The world is still good today. However, the problem is that Satan has filled the world God created with all manner of evil. He has filled the world with his yoke and burdens.

In fact, devil's presence on earth converted the whole world into a battleground. A great struggle lies before every man or woman on earth. It is clear from the look of things that there is war going on between God's children and Satan's agents. The Bible affirmed this truth. That is what Paul saw and experienced that he likened believer's life on earth to wrestling, warfare and fight.

> *"For we wrestle not against flesh and blood, but against principalities, against powers, against the rulers of the darkness of this world, against spiritual wickedness in high* places" (Ephesians 6:12).

> *"For though we walk in the flesh, we do not war after the flesh: (For the weapons of our warfare* are *not carnal, but mighty through God to the pulling down of strong holds;) Casting down imaginations, and every high thing that exalted itself against the knowledge of God, and bringing into captivity every thought to the obedience of Christ"* (2 Corinthians 10:3-5).

Many Christian are under the yoke of devil already. It is sad that believers who possess power of Christ can become captives of Satan. Evil forces are fighting to make sure that people are limited in their capacities to stop them from achieving God's purpose for their lives on earth. You ought to strive in order to overcome evil forces and to do this, you must be temperate in all things.

There is always a price to pay and a crown to receive at the end. These evil powers are invisible, spiritual and at times, they manifest physically using their human agents. These human agents are not the targets of our prayers. The target of our prayers is evil spirits that possess these evil agents. That is why our prayers are not against flesh and blood or human begins. When we pray *'die die,* we target evil spirits behind evil actions in order to separate the human agents from those spirits.

Through our prayers, we cast down their imaginations and force them to submit to Christ.

> *"The LORD of hosts hath sworn, saying, Surely as I have thought,* so *shall it come to pass; and as I have purposed,* so *shall it stand: That I will break the Assyrian in*

my land, and upon my mountains tread him under foot: then shall his yoke depart from off them, and his burden depart from off their shoulders. This is the purpose that is purposed upon the whole earth: and this is the hand that is stretched out upon all the nations. For the LORD of hosts hath purposed, and who shall disannul it? And his hand is stretched out, and who shall turn it back?" (Isaiah 14:24-27).

God's thought towards you is to disable the devil, break his yokes upon you and set you free. However, you must understand what yokes really are. Evil yoke comes in different ways. Some come in the form of troubles, sickness, unseen enemies, chronic diseases, mysterious loss of money, collapsing of business or sudden disappearance of good things of life, etc.

Someone with devil's yoke cannot think well. When he goes to bed at night, he cannot be able to sleep. If he slept at all, he would be distracted by useless dreams. Such person is always sick and or he feels deep heat inside his body even when he appears very healthy on the outside. When doctors examine him, they confirm they are perfectly okay when they are not. They would die slowly until it becomes apparent their bodies have been consumed by sickness.

Another category of people under devil's yoke is people that have good plans on what to do when they get money. However, as soon as the money comes, unseen forces influence them to squander the money. Before they could realize they had plans, they have spent all the money. This is devil's yoke. Such people cannot enjoy sound sleep and rest.

Many rich people have useless and wayward children. They have every good thing around them, yet they cannot get sound sleep. Others think excessively and turn around many times on their beds at nights. They cannot sleep and have peace of mind. This is satanic yoke and God has promised to break it.

YOKES OF SATAN IDENTIFIED

A yoke is anything that does not allow you to enjoy your life in Christ. Yokes of Satan keep many people under burden and suffering. These insoluble problems defeat people, arrest vital parts of their lives, and take them captives. Yokes counter people's peace and their rest or sleep. It keeps people in bondage and kills them. That is why you need to do everything in your power to set yourself free from satanic yokes.

> *"Israel hath sinned, and they have also transgressed my covenant which I commanded them: for they have even taken of the accursed thing, and have also stolen, and dissembled also, and they have put* it *even among their own stuff. Therefore the children of Israel could not stand before their enemies, but turned* their *backs before their enemies, because they were accursed: neither will I be with you any more, except ye destroy the accursed from among you"* (Joshua 7:11-12).

God had previously delivered the children of Israel from bondage in Egypt but sin brought them into bondage again. When the yoke of sin is upon you, it separates you from God and His divine help. The consequence is that every little problem would defeat you and minor enemies would drive you away from your inheritance.

Yoke of sin brings people under curse. When someone is under a curse, he cannot have sound sleep, peace of mind or rest. It was the thought of Hagar's disobedience and her presence that gave Sarah many sleepless nights. Likewise, Pharaoh made the lives of children of Israel unbearable. They passed through years of restlessness and suffering.

It is the yoke of the devil to pass through years of restlessness and suffering and you must deal with it so that you can worship God. When you look around prayerfully, you will discover a *Pharaoh* that needs to be dealt with before you can have your rest and sound sleep.

Many in Israel hoped in vain that someday Pharaoh would somehow release them. If you really want to break loose from Pharaoh's captivity, you must prepare for a battle. Pharaoh would not set his captives free casually. Sleepless nights and days come because of the presence of *Pharaoh* in people's lives.

However, Satan's chief yoke that can deny someone a sound sleep is sin. When you remain under the yoke of sin, God cannot fight your battles or deliver you from crisis. God may plan to deliver you but when He beholds iniquity in your life, He turns away His face. No matter how much you suffer or weep and pray for so many nights, if there are iniquities in your life, your sufferings will only increase.

Iniquities empowers devil to take you away from where God has originally placed you and God cannot do anything about it. Every sin you commit has a cord that links you to a particular problem. These problems ensure that you do not have sound sleep and rest at nights.

Many people are running up and down searching for solutions to their problems, while the conditions get worse. Why is it so? The cord of sin that links them to such problems needs to be broken before they can be totally free. They get many instructions, counsels and doctors' reports, yet deliverance has not come.

Every problem in this life has scriptural prescription from God and once God's prescriptions are obtained and obeyed, deliverance and freedom take place. However, many people get so many prescriptions yet they die because what they got was not from God. It is a tragedy for you to die in your sins.

Peace, rest, joy and sound sleep without freedom from sin is deceitful and temporal. You cannot disobey God, commit murder, go to bed to enjoy sound sleep and rest. You cannot defraud people or commit immorality and hope to have peace of mind. Whatever peace you have as a sinner is deceitful because you cannot cheat or deceive God. You must reap the evil you are sowing.

> *"No man that warreth entangleth himself with the affairs of* this *life; that he may please him who hath chosen him to be a soldier"* (2 Timothy 2:4).

> *"And they came over unto the other side of the sea, into the country of the Gadarenes. And when he was come out of the ship, immediately there met him out of the tombs a man with an unclean spirit, Who had* his *dwelling among the tombs; and no man could bind him, no, not with chains: Because that he had been often bound with fetters and chains, and the chains had been plucked asunder by him, and the fetters broken in pieces: neither could any* man *tame him. And always, night and day, he was in the mountains, and in the tombs, crying, and cutting himself with stones. But when he saw Jesus afar off, he ran and worshipped him, And cried with a loud voice, and said, What have I to do with thee, Jesus,* thou *Son of the most high God? I adjure thee by God, that thou torment me not. For he said unto him, Come out of the man,* thou *unclean spirit. And he asked him, What* is *thy name? And he answered, saying, My name* is *Legion: for we are many"* (Mark 5:1-9).

No one can serve God and Satan at the same time. Do you really desire for sound sleep and peaceful rest? Then repent of all your sins and avoid them forever. You cannot entangle yourself with the affairs of this life and yet be a good soldier of Christ. If you want peace and sound sleep, you have to please God. You have to hate sin, turn away from them, and have a change of mind, purpose and action.

GOD BREAKS YOKES FOR BELIEVERS

Satan tried to place yokes upon Abraham, Sarah and Elizabeth but God intervened and broke them all. The wife of Potiphar and Delilah were yokes for Joseph and Samson respectively. Joseph trusted God's Word and God broke his yoke, while Samson failed.

Anyone you cannot conveniently say 'No' to when his or her demands contradicts God's Word is a yoke. Haman was a yoke in the life of Esther, Mordecai and all the children of Israel. Sickness, diseases, deaths and all kinds of problem are satanic yokes.

Satanic yokes give their victims no rest or peace but sleepless nights and days. This is not something to live with or mange for any reason. You must allow God to break them off your neck immediately.

Hunger, famine, poverty and lack of good things of life are different forms of satanic yoke. When an evil spirit possesses you, you are under a yoke. When you are addicted to some particular sin or under a spell or curse, you are under an evil yoke.

Here is a perfect example of a believer that was under satanic yoke.

> *"And He was teaching in one of the synagogues on the Sabbath. And, behold, there was a woman, which had a spirit of infirmity eighteen years, and was bowed together, and could in no wise lift up* herself. *And when Jesus saw her, he called* her to him, *and said unto her, Woman, thou art loosed from thine infirmity. And he laid* his *hands on her: and immediately she was made straight, and glorified God"* (Luke 13:10-13).

Jesus found this woman in a place of worship and not in witchcraft altar. That meant she was a true child of God and a believer. Nevertheless, an evil spirit of infirmity possessed her for eighteen years. She was a true child of God but she did not know it was her right to resist the devil until he flees. Christ called her a daughter of Abraham yet an evil spirit arrested and bound her for eighteen years in bondage and suffering. The same applies to so many Christians today.

> *"He spake also this parable; A certain* man *had a fig tree planted in his vineyard; and he came and sought fruit thereon, and found none"* (Luke 13:6).

> *"Submit yourselves therefore to God. Resist the devil, and he will flee from you"* (James 4:7).

If your star or destiny is under satanic oppression, then you need deliverance. If your business or your handiwork is under attacks, you need deliverance. If you are always under the influence of evil forces and they make you to take wrong decisions, you need deliverance. If your progress in business has been captured, you need deliverance. If you are greatly destined but you cannot move forward, you are under a yoke. If you are always physically weak, rejected and hated by others without cogent reasons, you are under an evil yoke. Your joy, rest and peace cannot be complete when you are under satanic yoke.

> "*Another parable put the forth unto them, saying, The kingdom of heaven is likened unto a man which sowed good seed in his field: But while men slept, his enemy came and sowed tares among the wheat, and went his way*" (Matthew 13:24-25).

If you always feel hot inside your body, you may need some prayer of deliverance. When you feel some strange movements in your body, you may be under evil yoke. If you have reoccurring nightmares that you cannot enjoy your sleep, you need deliverance. If you eat or drink in your dream, you may be under the attack of strange spirits. If evil dreams distract your sleep or you sleep and wake up in fear, you are under an evil yoke. When you are afflicted, deceived, confused or defeated in your dreams, you will never have sound sleep until you resist evil forces that are militating against your life. Some people labor in their dreams, and when they wake up, they feel terribly tired. Such people need urgent deliverance.

> "6*And the angels which kept not their first estate, but left their own habitation, he hath reserved in everlasting chains under darkness unto the judgment of the great day.* 8*Likewise also these* filthy *dreamers defile the flesh, despise dominion, and speak evil of dignities*" (Jude 1:6, 8).

If strange people or things do visit you in your dreams, you need urgent prayers. If after your dreams you experience problems or setback, you may be under an evil yoke. When you dream and feel weak spiritually that you cannot pray, you are under attack. If you experience constant failures and financial problems after your dream, you need urgent prayers.

If your health is attacked in your dreams, you need deliverance. If you experience depression and frustration after dreams, you need to break some evil yokes. If you cannot go back to sleep after a terrible dream, you need serious prayers. If you are deprived of your rights or you experience a withdrawal of favor after a dream, your happiness will not be complete. If you witness a sudden disaster, great loss or sudden death of good things after your dream, you need urgent deliverance.

If you come under pressure or fall into unexplainable poverty or oppression after your dream, your sleep will never be sound until you break the satanic yokes. Attacks of the occult in the dream can cause sleepless nights. If you feel bitter, depressed, angry and jealousy before, during or after dreams, it is a sign you could be under a yoke. If you are always worrying over a matter, you will never have a sound sleep. When you cannot have sound sleep, you are under a yoke.

> *"I am the LORD your God, which brought you forth out of the land of Egypt, that ye should not be their bondmen; and I have broken the bands of your yoke, and made you go upright"* (Leviticus 26:13).

> *"For thou hast broken the yoke of his burden and the staff of his shoulder, the rod of his oppressor, as in the day of Midian"* (Isaiah 9:4).

God did not deliver you from sin so that you would become a slave to some evil powers. You are not supposed to allow evil powers to deny you of your sleep. Oppression in the dreams denies people of sound sleep. When your mind is filled with unclean and sexual thoughts or you have sex in your dream, you will not have a sound sleep. Any kind of addiction, evil thoughts, and great loss will not allow you to have a sound sleep.

If you do not deal with evil powers that steal sleep from people's eyes, they will deal with you. Demon in-charge of sleepless nights can discover your destiny and destroy it. They can afflict people from birth to death. They can influence people to take terrible decisions. They can put a halt to good projects. They can lead victims to seek help outside the presence of God. They can close good doors and refuse to open new ones. These demons are terribly wicked.

FEAR: AGENT OF SLEEPLESS NIGHTS

Fear is an unpleasant feeling of apprehension or anxiety by the presence or anticipation of danger. Fear is a spiritual condition that is capable of overwhelming the physical. Only a strongman could arrest a person, his rest, peace and sound sleep. Fear is one of the tools devil uses to control humanity and keep them out of God's plans. Believers must not allow fear to prosper in their lives.

Fear and doubt are closely related and you must not allow them to rule over your days or nights. When a person allows fear to rule over his day or night, that person is in trouble. You are a winner in life when you conquer fear.

Interestingly, there are 365 instances of 'fear-nots' as recorded in the Bible, just as we have 365 days in a year. It then becomes a shameful thing for a Christian to fail because of fear.

> *"[10]Fear thou not; for I* am *with thee: be not dismayed; for I* am *thy God: I will strengthen thee; yea, I will help thee; yea, I will uphold thee with the right hand of my righteousness. [14]Fear not, thou worm Jacob,* and *ye men of Israel; I will help thee, saith the LORD, and thy redeemer, the Holy One of Israel. [5]Fear not: for I* am *with thee: I will bring thy seed from the east, and gather thee from the west"* (Isaiah 41:10, 14; 43:5).

> *"He shall call upon me, and I will answer him: I* will be *with him in trouble; I will deliver him, and honor him"* (Psalms 91:15).

When you are not sure of God and do not have a good relationship with Him, the devil can easily put fear in your heart. When you are not aware of God's strength, the devil will show you his strength easily to cause you to fear. When you are not sure of God's help, you would fear the devil when he appears to help you. When you are not sure of your salvation, God's righteousness and infinite mercies, you will definitely be afraid when devil roars like a lion. Believers, who know their God, cannot to fear the devil.

> *"But as one was felling a beam, the axe head fell into the water: and he cried, and said, Alas, master! For it was borrowed. And the man of God said, where fell it? In addition, he shewed him the place. And he cut down a stick, and cast* it *in thither; and the iron did swim. Therefore said he, Take* it *up to thee. And he put out his hand, and took it. Then the king of Syria warred against Israel, and took counsel with his servants, saying, in such and such a place* shall be *my camp. And the man of God sent unto the king of Israel, saying, Beware that thou pass not such a place; for thither the Syrians are come down. And the king of Israel sent to the place, which the man of God told him and warned him of, and saved himself there, not once nor*

twice. Therefore, the heart of the king of Syria was sore troubled for this thing; and he called his servants, and said unto them, Will ye not show me which of us is *for the king of Israel? And one of his servants said, None, my lord, O king: but Elisha, the prophet that* is *in Israel, telleth the king of Israel the words that thou speakest in thy bedchamber. And he said, Go and spy where he* is, *that I may send and fetch him. And it was told him, saying, Behold,* he is *in Dothan. Therefore sent he thither horses, and chariots, and a great host: and they came by night, and compassed the city about. And when the servant of the man of God was risen early, and gone forth, behold, and host compassed the city with both horses and chariots. And his servant said unto him, Alas, my master! How shall we do? And he answered, Fear not: for they that* be *with us* are *more than they that* be *with them. And Elisha prayed, and said, LORD, I pray thee, open his eyes that he may see. And the LORD opened the eyes of the young man; and he saw: and, behold, the mountain* was *full of horses and chariots of fire round about Elisha"* (2 Kings 6:5-17).

"And such as do wickedly against the covenant shall he corrupt by flatteries: but the people that do know their God shall be strong, and do exploits" (Daniel 11:32).

If you observer all things through your physical eyes only, you would be afraid of the devil and his agents. No matter how weak you are, when you are born again, God's strength will be your strength. God will remain your helper and redeemer for He is the Holy One of Israel. Do not be afraid of the news of the financial markets or stocks collapsing. God promised to help you and bring your children out of troubles. The devil may come to frightening you in the night but fear him not. God was and is still with you and will forever be with you as long as you abide in Him. True Christians do not fear.

"Fear not, little flock; for it is your Father's good pleasure to give you the kingdom" (Luke 12:32).

"And the LORD, he it is *that doth go before thee; he will be with thee, he will not fail thee, neither forsake thee: fear not, neither be dismayed"* (Deuteronomy 31:8).

Sometimes, devil may come to you in the company of millions of his demons, problems and calamities, but God has commanded you not to be afraid of him. God has never failed anyone who trusts in Him and He will never do so. He will not allow the devil to ruin your life.

As a believer that knows all the promises of God for His children, you must reject the spirit of fear. Take authority over the spirit of fear. Decide to be a winner and reject sin and compromise. Fear can destroy someone's nights, days, weeks, months and years. It is a sin to be on the side of God and be afraid of the devil at the same time. It pains God and makes Him unhappy. God expects His children to be courageous all the time.

"It is vain for you to rise up early, to sit up late, to eat the bread of sorrows: for so He giveth his beloved sleep" (Psalms 127:2).

God gives His beloved sound sleep as a blessing. That is why anything that is against your sleep is an enemy you cannot condone. Sleep is natural suspension of consciousness during which the powers of the body are restored. It is a time every organ of the body rests. Over sleeping or sleeping sickness is also very bad. Some people overwork themselves and do not find time to sleep. Jobs that take 100% of your time cannot be from God.

"Thus *I was; in the day the drought consumed me, and the frost by night; and my sleep departed from mine eyes"* (Genesis 31:40).

"On that night could not the king sleep, and he commanded to bring the book of records of the chronicles; and they were read before the king" (Esther 6:1).

"The sleep of a laboring man is *sweet, whether he eat little or much: but the abundance of the rich will not suffer him to sleep"* (Ecclesiastes 5:12).

Sleeplessness signifies that something is wrong. do not take such signals lightly. When you labor with God, your sleep must be sweet whether you eat little or much. If your riches, wealth or business does not give you peace or allow you to have a good sleep, you need serious prayers.

"For the LORD hath poured out upon you he spirit of deep sleep, and hath closed your eyes: the prophets and your rulers, the seers hath he covered" (Isaiah 29:10).

"[39]In their heat I will make their feasts, and I will make them drunken, that they may rejoice, and sleep a perpetual sleep, and not wake, saith the LORD. [57]And I will make drunk her princes, and her wise men, *her captains, and her rulers, and her mighty men: and they shall sleep a perpetual sleep, and not wake, saith the King, whose name* is *the LORD of hosts"* (Jeremiah 51:39, 57).

"And in the second year of the reign of Nebuchadnezzar Nebuchadnezzar dreamed dreams, wherewith his spirit was troubled, and his sleep brake from him" (Daniel 2:1).

God uses sleep to give His children rests and reveal hidden things to them through dreams. However, if the reverse is your case, then you have a big trouble. Demonic sleep can also be used to send the wicked out of this world. At times, a person can be attacked in his dream and his sleep will break.

BENEFITS OF SOUND SLEEP

At times God can use deep sleep to do His children good. When God wants to reveal Himself to His children, He causes deep sleep to come upon them. In the believer's dreams, there is a divine control. When devil frequents your dream, something is wrong. Believers often see God and His heavens in their dreams and visions.

> "[21]*And the LORD God caused a deep sleep to fall upon Adam, and he slept: and he took one of his ribs, and closed up the flesh instead thereof;* [12]*And when the sun was going down, a deep sleep fell upon Abram; and, lo, an horror of great darkness fell upon him.* [11]*And he lighted upon a certain place, and tarried there all night, because the sun was set; and he took of the stones of that place, and put* them *for his pillows, and lay down in that place to sleep.* [16]*And Jacob awaked out of his sleep, and he said, Surely the LORD is in this place; and I knew* it *not"* (Genesis 2:21; 15:12; 28:11, 16).

God's intervention or presence in dreams is welcomed. Dreams must be scrutinized carefully so that a believer can follow God's command. Samuel received his call when he was sleeping. God caused Saul to sleep deeply so that David could prove his innocence before Saul. Vision comes when deep sleep has fallen upon men. It is God's will for His children to sleep in safety.

> "It is *vain for you to rise up early, to sit up late, to eat the bread of sorrows:* for so *he liveth his beloved sleep"* (Psalms 127:2).

> *"Upon this I awaked, and beheld; and my sleep were sweet unto me"* (Jeremiah 31:26).

> *"Then Joseph being raised from sleep did as the angel of the Lord had bidden him, and took unto him his wife"* (Matthew 1:24).

Children of God should not be denied of their sleep because it is a gift of God to his beloved (*See* 1 Samuel 3:3; 26:12; Job 4:13; 33:15; Psalms 4:8).

If you have lost your sleep, it could be that God wants you to settle something important through prayers. Apart from that, God gives His beloved sleep and we must sleep soundly.

Joseph woke up from sleep and did as angel of the Lord had commanded him. Jesus told the disciples to sleep on and take their rest to prepare for the next day's battle. God took away sleep from king Darius so that he would remain awake and fast for the deliverance of Daniel. That was why his sleep departed.

The king in the days of Esther could not sleep because he had to check the book of records to reward God's servant. When God takes away your sleep, it must be for a reason. Apart from that, you need sound sleep to fulfill your destiny on earth. Finally, it is a sin to sleep because of laziness or to sleep on duty, when you are supposed to be working hard. If God has taken away your sleep, ask Him what you must do through prayers. Pray for a sound sleep and God would give you the grace to sleep well.

PRAYERS FOR SOUND SLEEP AND REST

BIBLE REFERENCES: Genesis 2:21; Psalms 127:2

Begin with praise and worship

1. Let the backbone of sleepless nights in my life break, in the name of Jesus.
2. I disgrace every problem that is behind my lack of peace of mind, in the name of Jesus.
3. Father Lord, give me sound sleep and rest, in the name of Jesus.
4. Every evil presence in my life, disappear, in the name of Jesus.
5. Blood of Jesus, flow into my foundation and cleanse evil pollution, in the name of Jesus.
6. Any spirit of death and hell that is tormenting my life is cast out, in the name of Jesus.
7. Let diseases and germs in any area of my body die by fire, in the name of Jesus.
8. I receive anointing for sound sleep and peace of mind, in the name of Jesus.
9. I dislodge evil forces that have invaded my life, in the name of Jesus.
10. Any organ of my body that devil has captured is released, in the name of Jesus.
11. Let any battle that is going on against my life end to my favor, in the name of Jesus.
12. I remove any evil power that is obstructing my divine peace, in the name of Jesus.
13. Let every evil visitor in my life die, in the name of Jesus.
14. Any strange fire that is burning in my life, quench, in the name of Jesus.
15. Let every serpent of darkness in the garden of my life die, in the name of Jesus.
16. Any evil power that has captured my eyes, come out and die, in the name of Jesus.
17. Enemies of my health are disgraced, in the name of Jesus.
18. Any power that attacks my sleeps, die, in the name of Jesus.
19. I dislodge every monitoring spirit that is distracting my sleep, in the name of Jesus.

20. Every arrow of sleepless night that was fired into my life, backfire, in the name of Jesus.

21. Blood of Jesus, flow into my eyes and give me sound sleep and rest, in the name of Jesus.

22. Every enemy of my brain, you are wicked, die, in the name of Jesus.

23. Let my mental storehouse receive peace and rest from God, in the name of Jesus.

24. Any evil yoke in my life that is supporting my enemy, break, in the name of Jesus.

25. I terminate the visitation of spiritual armed robbers to my life, in the name of Jesus.

26. Any evil covenant that is linking me up with demons at nights, break, in the name of Jesus.

27. Any curse of sleeplessness in my life, expire, in the name of Jesus.

28. I kill demonic angels that are on assignment against my destiny, in the name of Jesus.

29. Any invitation that my ancestors or I have given to devil, I withdraw you immediately, in the name of Jesus.

30. I command every demon that has stolen my sleep to release it by force, in the name of Jesus.

31. Any satanic worm in my life, die, in the name of Jesus.

32. Blood of Jesus, speak deliverance into my life by fire, in the name of Jesus.

33. Blood of Jesus, destroy any sin in my life that is robbing me of my sleep, in the name of Jesus.

34. Let the redeeming power of God deliver my eyes from sleeplessness, in the name of Jesus.

35. Fire of God, burn every enemy of my sleep, in the name of Jesus.

36. Every enemy of my sound sleep, receive double destruction, in the name of Jesus.

37. Let the raging fire of God burn every serpent of the night that is distracting my sleep, in the name of Jesus.

38. Any evil priest that is ministering against my sleep, receive brain disorder, in the name of Jesus.

39. Let any witch or wizard that has vowed to destroy my peace drink bitter destruction, in the name of Jesus.

40. Let the thinking faculty and reasoning power of the enemies of my sleep receive shock, in the name of Jesus.

41. Every unbearable heat on my head and other parts of my body, go back to your sender, in the name of Jesus.

42. Owners of evil loads in my life, carry your loads, in the name of Jesus.

43. I close every gate that was opened to trouble my life forever, in the name of Jesus.

44. O Lord, arise and give me sound sleep, in the name of Jesus.

Thank You So Much!

Beloved, I hope you enjoyed this book as much as I believe God has touched your heart today. I cannot thank you enough for your continued support for this prayer ministry.

I appreciate you so much for taking out time to read this wonderful prayer book, and if you have an extra second, I would love to hear what you think about this book.

Please, do share your testimonies with me by sending emails to pastor@prayermadueke.com, or through social media: www.facebook.com/prayer.madueke. I invite you also to www.prayermadueke.com to view other books I have written on various issues of life, especially on marriage, family, sexual problems and money.

I will be delighted to partner with you in organized crusades, ceremonies, marriages and Marriage seminars, special events, church ministration and fellowship for the advancement of God's Kingdom here on earth.

Thank you again, and I wish you success in your life.

God bless you.

In Christ,

Prayer M. Madueke

OTHER BOOKS BY PRAYER M. MADUEKE

- *21/40 Nights Of Decrees And Your Enemies Will Surrender*
- *Confront And Conquer*
- *35 Special Dangerous Decrees*
- *Tears in Prison*
- *The Reality of Spirit Marriage*
- *Queen of Heaven*
- *Leviathan the Beast*
- *100 Days Prayer To Wake Up Your Lazarus*
- *Dangerous Decrees To Destroy Your Destroyers*
- *The spirit of Christmas*
- *More Kingdoms To Conquer*
- *Your Dream Directory*
- *The Sword Of New Testament Deliverance*
- *Alphabetic Battle For Unmerited Favors*
- *Alphabetic Character Deliverance*
- *Holiness*
- *The Witchcraft Of The Woman That Sits Upon Many Waters*
- *The Operations Of The Woman That Sits Upon Many Waters*
- *Powers To Pray Once And Receive Answers*
- *Prayer Riots To Overthrow Divorce*
- *Prayers To Get Married Happily*
- *Prayers To Keep Your Marriage Out of Troubles*
- *Prayers For Conception And Power To Retain*
- *Prayer Retreat – Prayers to Possess Your Year*
- *Prayers for Nation Building (Vol. 1, 2 & 3)*
- *Organized student in a disorganized school*
- *Welcome to Campus*
- *Alone with God (10 series)*

CONTACTS

AFRICA

#1 Babatunde close,
Off Olaitan Street, Surulere
Lagos, Nigeria
+234 803 353 0599
pastor@prayermadueke.com,

#Plot 1791, No. 3 Ijero Close,
Flat 2, Area 1,
Garki 1 - FCT, Abuja
+234 807 065 4159

IRELAND

Ps Emmanuel Oko
#84 Thornfield Square
Cloudalkin D22
Ireland
Tel: +353 872 820 909, +353 872 977 422
aghaoko2003@yahoo.com

EUROPE/SCHENGEN

Collins Kwame
#46 Felton Road
Barking
Essex IG11 7XZ GB
Tel: +44 208 507 8083, +44 787 703 2386, +44 780 703 6916
aghaoko2003@yahoo.com

Printed in Great Britain
by Amazon

40388675R00441